Chevrolet Camaro V8 Owners Workshop Manual

Scott Mauck
and J H Haynes Member of the Guild of Motoring Writers

Models covered:

Chevrolet Camaro, Z28, Type LT,
Rally Sport and Berlinetta

ISBN 0 85696 881 1

ABCDE
FGHIJ

Printed in England   (554–2J1)

HAYNES PUBLISHING GROUP
SPARKFORD YEOVIL SOMERSET BA22 7JJ ENGLAND
distributed in the USA by
HAYNES PUBLICATIONS INC
861 LAWRENCE DRIVE
NEWBURY PARK
CALIFORNIA 91320
USA

Acknowledgements

Thanks are due to the Chevrolet Motor division of the General Motors Corporation for their assistance with technical information and supply of certain illustrations.

The Champion Spark Plug Company supplied the illustrations showing the various spark plug conditions. The bodywork repair photographs used in the manual were provided by Lloyd's Industries Limited who supply 'Turtle Wax', 'Dupli-color Holts', and other Holts range products.

Lastly we are grateful to all those people at Newbury Park, California and Sparkford, England who helped in the production of this manual. Particularly 'Spook' Caspers and Tom Schauwecker who carried out the mechanical work, Annette Cutler who designed the layout of each page and John Rose for his editorial work.

About this manual

Its aim

The aim of this manual is to help you get the best value from your car. It can do so in several ways. It can help you decide what work must be done (even should you choose to get it done by a garage), provide information on routine maintenance and servicing, and give a logical course of action and diagnosis when random faults occur. However, it is hoped that you will use the Manual by tackling the work yourself. On simpler jobs it may be quicker than booking the car into a garage, and going there twice, to leave and collect it. Perhaps most important, a lot of money can be saved by avoiding the costs the garage must charge to cover its labor and overheads.

The manual has drawings and descriptions to show the function of the various components so that their layout can be understood. Then the tasks are described and photographed in a step-by-step sequence so that even a novice can do the work.

Its arrangement

The manual is divided into thirteen Chapters, each covering a logical sub-division of the vehicle. The Chapters are each divided into Sections, numbered with single figures, eg 5; and the Sections into paragraphs (or sub-sections), with decimal numbers following on from the Section they are in, eg 5.1, 5.2, 5.3 etc.

It is freely illustrated, especially in those parts where there is a detailed sequence of operations to be carried out. There are two forms of illustration: figures and photographs. The figures are numbered in sequence with decimal numbers, according to their position in the Chapter: eg Fig. 6.4 is the 4th drawing/illustration in Chapter 6. Photographs are numbered (either individually or in related groups) the same as the Section or sub-section of the text where the operation they show is described.

There is an alphabetical index at the back of the manual as well as a contents list at the front.

References to the left or right of the vehicle are in the sense of a person in a seat facing forwards.

While every care is taken to ensure that the information in this manual is correct, no liability can be accepted by the authors or publishers for loss, damage or injury caused by any errors in, or omissions from, the information given.

Introduction to the Chevrolet Camaro

The 11-year model range which this manual covers gives an indication of the success that this American 'sports' car has enjoyed.

During this 11-year reign, the Camaro has remained basically the same, undergoing only slight body and engine changes. Due to this, the majority of the strip-down procedures included in this manual will be applicable to all models 1970 – 1981. Where differences appear they will be duly noted in the text to prevent confusion.

Contents

1970 Camaro with Rally Sport equipment

1980 Camaro Z28

General dimensions, capacities and weights

Dimensions

1970:

Overall length	188.0 in
Overall width	74.4 in
Height	50.1 in
Wheelbase	108.0 in

1971 – 1972:

As 1970 models except:

Height	50.5 in

1973:

As 1970 models except:

Overall length	188.5 in
Height	49.1 in

1974 – 1978:

As 1970 models except:

Overall length	195.4 in
Height	49.1 in

1979 – 1980:

Overall length	197.6 in
Overall width	74.5 in
Height	49.2 in
Wheelbase	108.0 in

Capacities

Engine oil:

	US quarts
All V-8 engines	4 *

* Add 1 quart extra if filter is replaced

Cooling system:

1970, 307, 350 cu in engine	16 *
402 cu in engine	24 **
1971 – 1974, 307, 350 cu in engine	15.5 *
402 cu in engine	24 **
1975 (all V-8)	17 *
1976 – 1978 (all V-8)	17.5 *
1979 (all V-8)	17 *
1980, 267, 305 cu in engine	15
350 cu in engine	16

* With A/C add 1 quart
** With A/C add 2 quarts

Fuel tank (approx):

	US gallons
1970	19.0
With evaporative control system	18.0
1971	17.0
1972 – 1973	18.0
1974 – 1978	21.0
1979 – 1980	20.8

Manual transmission:

1970 – 1980 (all) .... 3.0 pints *

* Approx to fill after draining

Automatic transmission:

	US quarts
Powerglide	
Routine change	3
Fill from dry	9.0
Turbo Hydramatic 350	
Routine change	3.0
Fill from dry	10.0
Turbo Hydramatic 400	
Routine change	3.5
Fill from dry	11.0

Curb weights *

1970	3313 lbs
1971	3313 lbs
1972	3310 lbs
1973	3354 lbs
1974	3627 lbs
1975	3733 lbs
1976	3679 lbs
1977	3663 lbs
1978	3612 lbs
1979	3610 lbs
1980	3545 lbs

* With base V-8 engine and standard accessories

Buying spare parts
and vehicle identification numbers
Refer to Chapter 13 for information related to 1981 models

Buying spare parts

Spare parts are available from many sources although they generally fall in two categories – those items which are supplied by a Chevrolet dealer and those which are supplied by auto accessory stores. In some cases the two facilities may be combined with an over-the-counter service and pre-pack display area. In some cases it may be possible to obtain parts on a service-exchange basis but, where this can be done, always make sure that the parts returned are clean and intact. Our advice regarding spare parts purchase is as follows:

Chevrolet dealers: This is the best source of supply for major items such as transmissions, engines, body panels, etc. It is also the only place to obtain parts if your vehicle is still under warranty, since the warranty may be invalidated if non-Chevrolet parts are used.

Auto accessory stores: Auto accessory stores are able to supply practically all of the items needed for repair, maitenance, tune-up and customizing. This is not only true for the vehicle but also for tools and test equipment.

Whichever source of spare parts is used it will be essential to provide information concerning the model and year of manufacture of your vehicle.

Vehicle identification numbers

Modifications are a continuing and unpublicized process in vehicle manufacture. Spare parts manuals and lists are compiled on a numerical basis, the individual vehicle numbers being essential to identify correctly the component required.

Vehicle identification number (VIN): This very important identification number can be found on a plate attached to the left top of the dashboard and can be easily seen while looking through the windshield from the outside of the car. The VIN also appears on the Vehicle Certificates of Title and Registration. It gives such valuable information as where and when the vehicle was manufactured, the model year of manufacture and the body style.

Body identification plate: This metal plate is located on the upper surface of the shroud. Like the VIN it contains valuable information about the manufacture of the car, as well as information about the way in which the vehicle is equipped. This plate is especially useful for matching the color and type of paint for repair work.

Engine identification number: The engine identification number for all Chevrolet V-8 engines can be found on a pad at the front, right-hand side of the cylinder block. It will sometimes be necessary to move the metal fuel line which is routed on top of this pad to read the stamped numbers.

Manual transmission number:

3-Speed Saginaw – lower right-hand side of the case, adjacent to the cover.

4-speed Borg Warner – rear vertical surface of the extension housing.

4-speed Muncie – rear right-hand side of the case flange.

4-speed Saginaw – lower right-hand side of case adjacent to the cover.

Automatic transmission number:

Powerglide – right rear surface of the oil pan.

Type 350 – right-hand vertical surface of the oil pan.

Type 400 – on blue tag right-hand side of the transmission.

Rear axle number: On right or left axle tube adjacent to the carrier (see Chapter 8 for example).

Generator: On top drive end frame.

Starter: Stamped on outer case, toward the rear.

Tune-up decal: Located in varying positions inside the engine compartment (see Chapter 1 for example).

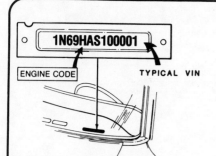

Typical VIN plate as seen from outside of the car, looking through the windshield

Manufacturer Identity [1]	Body Style [2]	Model Year [3]	Assembly Plant [4]	Unit Number [5]
1	5645	O	F	100025

[1] Manufacturers identity number assigned to all Chevrolet built vehicles.
[2] Model Identification.
[3] Last number of model year (1970).
[4] F – Flint
[5] Unit numbering will start at 000,001 or 100,001 depending on the vehicle.

Typical VIN number used during model years 1970 and 1971

Typical body identification plate attached to the engine compartment firewall

Manufacturer Identity (1)	Series Code Letter (2)	Body Style (3)	Engine Code (4)	Model Year (5)	Assembly Plant (6)	Unit Number (7)
1	M	57	H	2	F	100025

1. Manufacturer's identity number assigned to all Chevrolet built vehicles.
2. Series
3. Body Style
4. Engine
5. Last number of model year (1972)
6. F – Flint
7. Unit numbering will start at 000001 or 100001 depending on the vehicle.

Typical VIN number used during model years 1972 through 1980

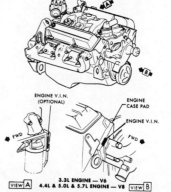

Location of engine identification number stamped to cylinder block

Tools and working facilities

Introduction

A selection of good tools is a fundamental requirement for anyone contemplating the maintenance and repair of a motor vehicle. For the owner who does not possess any, their purchase will prove a considerable expense, offsetting some of the savings made by doing-it-yourself. However, provided that the tools purchased are of good quality, they will last for many years and prove an extremely worthwhile investment.

To help the average owner to decide which tools are needed to carry out the various tasks detailed in this manual, we have compiled three lists of tools under the following headings: *Maintenance and minor repair*, *Repair and overhaul*, and *Special*. The newcomer to practical mechanics should start off with the *Maintenance and minor repair* tool kit and confine himself to the simpler jobs around the vehicle. Then, as his confidence and experience grows, he can undertake more difficult tasks, buying extra tools as, and when, they are needed. In this way, a *Maintenance and minor repair* tool kit can be built up into a *Repair and overhaul* tool kit over a considerable period of time without any major cash outlays. The experienced do-it-yourselfer will have a tool kit good enough for most repair and overhaul procedures and will add tools from the *Special* category when he feels the expense is justified by the amount of use these tools will be put to.

It is obviously not possible to cover the subject of tools fully here. For those who wish to learn more about tools and their use there is a book entitled *How to Choose and Use Car Tools* available from the publishers of this manual.

Maintenance and minor repair tool kit

The tools given in this list should be considered as a minimum requirement if routine maintenance, servicing and minor repair operations are to be undertaken. We recommend the purchase of combination wrenches (ring one end, open-ended the other); although more expensive than open-ended ones, they do give the advantages of both types of wrench.

Combination wrenches - $\frac{3}{16}$ inch through $\frac{3}{4}$ in AF
Adjustable wrench - 9 inch
Engine sump/gearbox/rear axle drain plug key (where applicable)
Spark plug wrench (with rubber insert)
Spark plug gap adjustment tool
Set of feeler gauges
Brake adjuster wrench (where applicable)
Brake bleed nipple wrench
Screwdriver - 4 in long x $\frac{1}{4}$ in dia (flat blade)
Screwdriver - 4 in long x $\frac{1}{4}$ in dia (cross blade)
Combination pliers - 6 inch
Hacksaw, junior
Tire pump
Tire pressure gauge

Grease gun (where applicable)
Oil can
Fine emery cloth (1 sheet)
Wire brush (small)
Funnel (medium size)

Repair and overhaul tool kit

These tools are virtually essential for anyone undertaking any major repairs to a motor vehicle, and are additional to those given in the *Maintenance and minor repair* list. Included in this list is a comprehensive set of sockets. Although these are expensive they will be found invaluable as they are so versatile - particularly if various drives are included in the set. We recommend the $\frac{1}{2}$ in square-drive type, as this can be used with most proprietary torque wrenches. If you cannot afford a socket set, even bought piecemeal, then inexpensive tubular box wrenches are a useful alternative.

The tools in this list will occasionally need to be supplemented by tools from the *Special* list.

Sockets (or box wrenches) to cover range in previous list
Reversible ratchet drive (for use with sockets)
Extension piece, 10 inch (for use with sockets)
Universal joint (for use with sockets)
Torque wrench (for use with sockets)
Vise grips — 8 inch
Ball pein hammer
Soft-faced hammer, plastic or rubber
Screwdriver - 6 in long x $\frac{5}{16}$ in dia (flat blade)
Screwdriver - 2 in long x $\frac{5}{16}$ in square (flat blade)
Screwdriver - 1$\frac{1}{2}$ in long x $\frac{1}{4}$ in dia (cross blade)
Screwdriver - 3 in long x $\frac{1}{8}$ in dia (electricians)
Pliers - electricians side cutters
Pliers - needle nosed
Pliers - circlip (internal and external)
Cold chisel - $\frac{1}{2}$ inch
Scriber (this can be made by grinding the end of a broken hacksaw blade)
Scraper (this can be made by flattening and sharpening one end of a piece of copper pipe)
Center punch
Pin punch
Hacksaw
Valve grinding tool (where applicable)
Steel rule/straight edge
Allen keys
Selection of files
Wire brush (large)
Jack stands
Jack (strong scissor or hydraulic type)

Special tools

The tools in this list are those which are not used regularly, are expensive to buy, or which need to be used in accordance with their manufacturers' instructions. Unless relatively difficult mechanical jobs are undertaken frequently, it will not be economic to buy many of these tools. Where this is the case, you could consider clubbing together with friends (or a motorists' club) to make a joint purchase, or borrowing the tools against a deposit from a local garage or tool hire specialist.

The following list contains only those tools and instruments freely available to the public, and not those special tools produced by the vehicle manufacturer specifically for its dealer network. You will find occasional references to these manufacturers' special tools in the text of this manual. Generally, an alternative method of doing the job without the vehicle manufacturers' special tool is given. However, sometimes, there is no alternative to using them. Where this is the case and the relevant tool cannot be bought or borrowed you will have to entrust the work to a franchised garage.

Valve spring compressor (where applicable)
Piston ring compressor (where applicable)
Balljoint separator
Universal hub/bearing puller
Impact screwdriver
Micrometer and/or vernier gauge
Dial gauge
Stroboscopic timing light
Dwell angle meter/tachometer
Universal electrical multi-meter
Cylinder compression gauge
Lifting tackle (photo)
Floor jack
Light with extension lead

Buying tools

For practically all tools, a tool dealer is the best source since he will have a very comprehensive range compared with the average garage or accessory shop. Having said that, accessory shops often offer excellent quality tools at discount prices, so it pays to shop around.

Remember, you don't have to buy the most expensive items on the shelf, but it is always advisable to steer clear of the very cheap tools. There are plenty of good tools around at reasonable prices, so ask the proprietor or manager of the shop for advice before making a purchase.

Care and maintenance of tools

Having purchased a reasonable tool kit, it is necessary to keep the tools in a clean serviceable condition. After use, always wipe off any dirt, grease and metal particles using a clean, dry cloth, before putting the tools away. Never leave them lying around after they have been used. A simple tool rack on the garage or workshop wall, for items such as screwdrivers and pliers is a good idea. Store all normal wrenches and sockets in a metal box. Any measuring instruments, gauges, meters, etc, must be carefully stored where they cannot be damaged or become rusty.

Take a little care when tools are used. Hammer heads inevitably become marked and screwdrivers lose the keen edge on their blades from time to time. A little timely attention with emery cloth or a file will soon restore items like this to a good serviceable finish.

Working facilities

Not to be forgotten when discussing tools, is the workshop itself. If anything more than routine maintenance is to be carried out, some form of suitable working area becomes essential.

It is appreciated that many an owner mechanic is forced by circumstances to remove an engine or similar item, without the benefit of a garage or workshop. Having done this, any repairs should always be done under the cover of a roof.

Wherever possible, any dismantling should be done on a clean flat workbench or table at a suitable working height.

Any workbench needs a vise: one with a jaw opening of 4 in (100 mm) is suitable for most jobs. As mentioned previously, some clean dry storage space is also required for tools, as well as the lubricants, cleaning fluids, touch-up paints and so on which become necessary.

Another item which may be required, and which has a much more general usage, is an electric drill with a chuck capacity of at least $\frac{5}{16}$ in (8 mm). This, together with a good range of twist drills, is virtually essential for fitting accessories such as wing mirrors and reversing lights.

Last, but not least, always keep a supply of old newspapers and clean, lint-free rags available, and try to keep any working area as clean as possible.

Jaw gap (in)	Wrench size
0.250	$\frac{1}{4}$ in AF
0.276	7 mm
0.313	$\frac{5}{16}$ in AF
0.315	8 mm
0.344	$\frac{11}{32}$ in AF; $\frac{1}{8}$ in Whitworth
0.354	9 mm
0.375	$\frac{3}{8}$ in AF
0.394	10 mm
0.433	11 mm
0.438	$\frac{7}{16}$ in AF
0.445	$\frac{3}{16}$ in Whitworth; $\frac{1}{4}$ in BSF
0.472	12 mm
0.500	$\frac{1}{2}$ in AF
0.512	13 mm
0.525	$\frac{1}{4}$ in Whitworth; $\frac{5}{16}$ in BSF
0.551	14 mm
0.563	$\frac{9}{16}$ in AF
0.591	15 mm
0.600	$\frac{5}{16}$ in Whitworth; $\frac{3}{8}$ in BSF
0.625	$\frac{5}{8}$ in AF
0.630	16 mm
0.669	17 mm
0.686	$\frac{11}{16}$ in AF
0.709	18 mm
0.710	$\frac{3}{8}$ in Whitworth, $\frac{7}{16}$ in BSF
0.748	19 mm
0.750	$\frac{3}{4}$ in AF
0.813	$\frac{13}{16}$ in AF
0.820	$\frac{7}{16}$ in Whitworth; $\frac{1}{2}$ in BSF
0.866	22 mm
0.875	$\frac{7}{8}$ in AF
0.920	$\frac{1}{2}$ in Whitworth; $\frac{9}{16}$ in BSF
0.938	$\frac{15}{16}$ in AF
0.945	24 mm
1.000	1 in AF
1.010	$\frac{9}{16}$ in Whitworth; $\frac{5}{8}$ in BSF
1.024	26 mm
1.063	$1\frac{1}{16}$ in AF, 27 mm
1.100	$\frac{5}{8}$ in Whitworth; $\frac{11}{16}$ in BSF
1.125	$1\frac{1}{8}$ in AF
1.181	30 mm
1.200	$\frac{11}{16}$ in Whitworth; $\frac{3}{4}$ in BSF
1.250	$1\frac{1}{4}$ in AF
1.260	32 mm
1.300	$\frac{3}{4}$ in Whitworth; $\frac{7}{8}$ in BSF
1.313	$1\frac{5}{16}$ in AF
1.390	$\frac{13}{16}$ in Whitworth; $\frac{15}{16}$ in BSF
1.417	36 mm
1.438	$1\frac{7}{16}$ in AF
1.480	$\frac{7}{8}$ in Whitworth; 1 in BSF
1.500	$1\frac{1}{2}$ in AF
1.575	40 mm; $\frac{15}{16}$ in Whitworth
1.614	41 mm
1.625	$1\frac{5}{8}$ in AF
1.670	1 in Whitworth; $1\frac{1}{8}$ in BSF
1.688	$1\frac{11}{16}$ in AF
1.811	46 mm
1.813	$1\frac{13}{16}$ in AF
1.860	$1\frac{1}{8}$ in Whitworth; $1\frac{1}{4}$ in BSF
1.875	$1\frac{7}{8}$ in AF
1.969	50 mm
2.000	2 in AF
2.050	$1\frac{1}{4}$ in Whitworth; $1\frac{3}{8}$ in BSF
2.165	55 mm
2.362	60 mm

Jacking and towing

Jacking

The jack supplied with the car should be used only for changing a wheel due to a roadside flat or for raising the car enough to allow jack stands to support the weight. Under no circumstances should repair work be done under the car while it is supported by this jack, nor should the engine be started or run while this jack is being used.

All Camaros have come equipped with a ratchet type bumper jack designed to lift one corner of the car from either the front or rear bumper. All types are used in basically the same fashion, the difference being that earlier models have a load rest bracket and a notch in the bumper as opposed to the hook which fits into a slot in the bumper for later types.

The car should be on level ground with the transmission in 'Park' (automatic) or 'Reverse' (manual transmissions). The parking brake should be firmly set. Blocking the front and rear of the wheel on the same side as the one being changed will further prevent the car from rolling.

With the lever on the jack in the 'Up' position, locate the load rest bracket or hook (depending on model) to the bumper. Before the load is taken up, remove the hubcap using the flat end of the lug wrench and slightly loosen each of the lug nuts on the wheel to be changed. Using the lug wrench as a handle, raise the car enough to remove the wheel.

Before installing the spare, remove any built-up corrosion or dirt from the drum or hub and the rear side of the spare.

Place the spare into position and slightly tighten the lug nuts, with the cone-shaped end of the nuts towards the wheel. The wheel must be seated on the hub. Change the jack lever to the 'Down' position and slowly lower the car. Once it is completely on the ground tighten all lug nuts in a diagonal fashion until tight. The hubcap can be installed now or later by placing it into position and using the heel of your hand or a rubber mallet to fully seat it.

Towing

The vehicle can be towed on all four wheels providing that speeds do not exceed 35 mph and the distance is not over 50 miles. Towing equipment specifically designed for this purpose should be used and should be attached to the main structural members of the car and not the bumper or brackets.

Safety is a major consideration when towing, and all applicable state and local laws should be obeyed. A safety chain system must be used for all towing.

While towing, the parking brake should be fully released and the transmission should be in 'Neutral'. The steering must be unlocked (ignition switch in the 'off' position). Remember that power steering and power brakes will not work with the engine off.

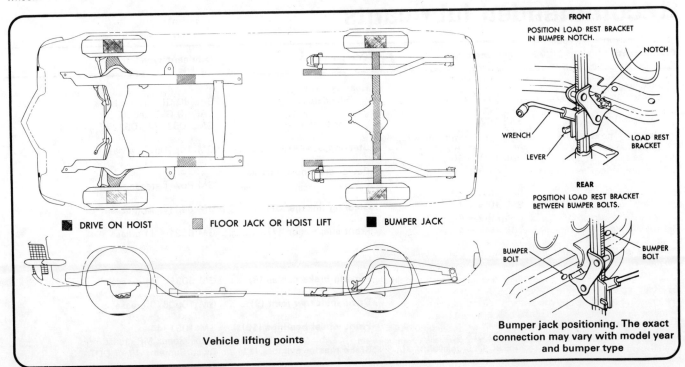

DRIVE ON HOIST   FLOOR JACK OR HOIST LIFT   BUMPER JACK

Vehicle lifting points

FRONT
POSITION LOAD REST BRACKET IN BUMPER NOTCH.

NOTCH

WRENCH

LEVER

LOAD REST BRACKET

REAR
POSITION LOAD REST BRACKET BETWEEN BUMPER BOLTS.

BUMPER BOLT

BUMPER BOLT

Bumper jack positioning. The exact connection may vary with model year and bumper type

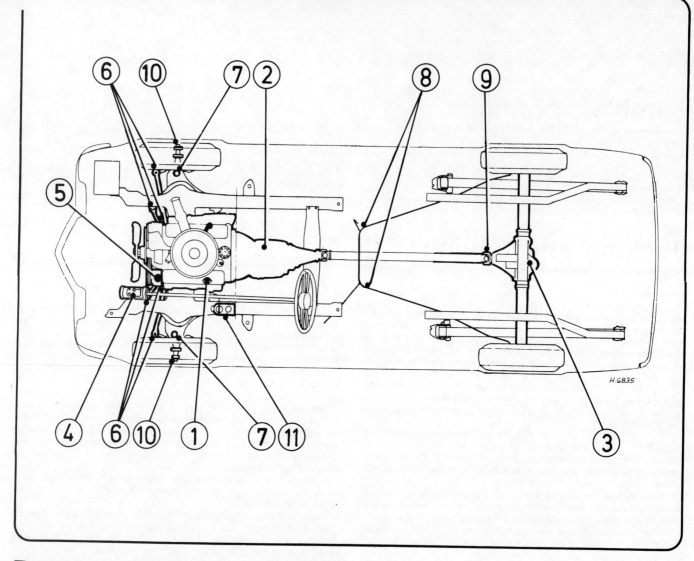

H.6835

Recommended lubricants

Component	Lubricant type
Engine (1) *	
– 30 ° to 20 ° F	SAE 5W – 20
	SAE 5W – 30
0° to 60°F	SAE 10W
	SAE 5W – 30
	SAE 10W – 30
	SAE 10W – 40
20° to 100° F	SAE 20W – 20
	SAE 10W – 30
	SAE 10W – 40
	SAE 20W – 40
	SAE 20W – 50

* Engine lubricants should be labelled SE, SF or SE/CC

Component	Lubricant type
Transmission (2)	
Manual	SAE 80 GL5 gear oil
	SAE 90 GL5 gear oil
Automatic	Dexron II fluid

Component	Lubricant type
Rear axle (3)	
Standard	SAE 80 GL5 gear oil
	SAE 90 GL5 gear oil
Positraction	GM 1052271/1052272 gear oil
Steering box (4)	GM 1051052 grease
Power steering reservoir (5)	GM Power steering fluid
Steering linkage (6)	GM 6031 – M grease
Front suspension (7)	GM 6031 – M grease
Parking brake cables (8)	GM 6031 – M grease
Drive shaft rear joint (9)	GM 1050679 grease
Front wheel bearings (10)	GM 1051344 Exxon Ronex MP grease
Brake master cylinder (11)	Delco Supreme 11 or DOT – 3 fluid

Troubleshooting

Contents

Engine

1 Engine will not rotate when attempting to start

1   Battery terminal connections loose or corroded. Check the cable terminals at the battery; tighten or clean corrosion as necessary.
2   Battery discharged or faulty. If the cable connectors are clean and tight on the battery posts, turn the key to the 'On' position and switch on the headlights and/or windshield wipers. If these fail to function, the battery is discharged.
3   Automatic transmission not fully engaged in 'Park' or manual transmission clutch not fully depressed.
4   Broken, loose or disconnected wiring in the starting circuit. Inspect all wiring and connectors at the battery, starter solenoid (at lower right side of engine) and ignition switch (on steering column).

5   Starter motor pinion jammed on flywheel ring gear. If manual transmission, place gearshift in gear and rock the car to manually turn the engine. Remove starter (Chapter 5) and inspect pinion and flywheel (Chapter 2) at earliest convenience.
6   Starter solenoid faulty (Chapter 5).
7   Starter motor faulty (Chapter 5).
8   Ignition switch faulty (Chapter 10).

2 Engine rotates but will not start

1   Fuel tank empty.
2   Battery discharged (engine rotates slowly). Check the operation of electrical components as described in previous Section (see Chapter

1).

3   Battery terminal connections loose or corroded. See previous Section.

4   Carburetor flooded and/or fuel level in carburetor incorrect. This will usually be accompanied by a strong fuel odor from under the hood. Wait a few minutes, depress the accelerator pedal all the way to the floor and attempt to start the engine.

5   Choke control inoperative (Chapters 1 and 4).

6   Fuel not reaching carburetor. With ignition switch in 'Off' position, open hood, remove the top plate of air cleaner assembly and observe the top of the carburetor (manually move choke plate back if necessary). Have an assistant depress accelerator pedal fully and check that fuel spurts into carburetor. If not, check fuel filter (Chapters 1 and 4), fuel lines and fuel pump (Chapter 4).

7   Excessive moisture on, or damage to, ignition components (Chapter 1).

8   Worn, faulty or incorrectly adjusted spark plugs (Chapter 1).

9   Broken, loose or disconnected wiring in the starting circuit (see previous Section).

10   Distributor loose, thus changing ignition timing. Turn the distributor body as necessary to start the engine, then set ignition timing as soon as possible (Chapter 1).

11   Ignition condenser faulty (Chapter 5).

12   Broken, loose or disconnected wires at the ignition coil, or faulty coil (Chapter 5).

3   Starter motor operates without rotating engine

1   Starter pinion sticking. Remove the starter (Chapter 5) and inspect.

2   Starter pinion or engine flywheel teeth worn or broken. Remove the inspection cover at the rear of the engine and inspect.

4   Engine hard to start when cold

1   Battery discharged or low. Check as described in Section 1.

2   Choke control inoperative or out of adjustment (Chapters 1 and 4).

3   Carburetor flooded (see Section 2).

4   Fuel supply not reaching the carburetor (see Section 2).

5   Carburetor worn and in need of overhauling (Chapter 4).

5   Engine hard to start when hot

1   Choke sticking in the closed position (Chapter 1).

2   Carburetor flooded (see Section 2).

3   Air filter in need of replacement (Chapter 1).

4   Fuel not reaching the carburetor (see Section 2).

5   Thermac air cleaner faulty (Chapter 1).

6   EFE (heat riser) sticking in the closed position (Chapter 1).

6   Starter motor noisy or excessively rough in engagement

1   Pinion or flywheel gear teeth worn or broken. Remove the inspection cover at the rear of the engine and inspect.

2   Starter motor retaining bolts loose or missing.

7   Engine starts but stops immediately

1   Loose or faulty electrical connections at distributor, coil or alternator.

2   Insufficient fuel reaching the carburetor. Disconnect the fuel line at the carburetor and remove the filter (Chapter 1). Place a container under the disconnected fuel line. If equipped with HEI system (1975 – 1980), disconnect wiring connector marked 'BAT' from distributor cap. If conventional system (1970 – 1974), disconnect the coil wire from the center of the distributor cap. These steps will prevent the engine from starting. Have an assistant crank the engine several revolutions by turning the ignition key. Observe the flow of fuel from the line. If little or none at all, check for blockage in the lines and/or replace the fuel pump (Chapter 4).

3   Vacuum leak at the gasket surfaces or the intake manifold and/or

carburetor. Check that all mounting bolts (nuts) are tightened to specifications and all vacuum hoses connected to the carburetor and manifold are positioned properly and are in good condition.

8   Engine 'lopes' while idling or idles erratically

1   Vacuum leakage. Check mounting bolts (nuts) at the carburetor and intake manifold for tightness. Check that all vacuum hoses are connected and are in good condition. Use a doctor's stethoscope or a length of fuel line hose held against your ear to listen for vacuum leaks while the engine is runnng. A hissing sound will be heard. A soapy water solution will also detect leaks. Check the carburetor and intake manifold gasket surfaces.

2   Leaking EGR valve or plugged PCV valve (see Chapter 6).

3   Air cleaner clogged and in need of replacement (Chapter 1).

4   Fuel pump not delivering sufficient fuel to the carburetor (see Section 7).

5   Carburetor out of adjustment (Chapter 4).

6   Leaking head gasket. If this is suspected, take the car to a repair shop or GM dealer where this can be pressure checked without the need to remove the heads.

7   Timing chain or gears worn and in need of replacement (Chapter 2).

8   Camshaft lobes worn, necessitating the removal of the camshaft for inspection (Chapter 2).

9   Engine misses at idle speed

1   Spark plugs faulty or not gapped properly (Chapter 1).

2   Faulty spark plug wires (Chapter 1).

3   Faulty or incorrectly set contact breaker points (1970 – 1974 models only). Also check for excessive moisture on distributor components and/or damage (Chapter 1).

4   Carburetor choke not operating properly (Chapter 1).

5   Sticking or faulty emissions systems (see Troubleshooting in Chapter 6).

6   Clogged fuel filter and/or foreign matter in fuel. Remove the fuel filter (Chapter 1) and inspect.

7   Vacuum leaks at carburetor, intake manifold or at hose connections. Check as described in Section 8.

8   Incorrect idle speed (Chapter 1) or idle mixture (Chapter 4).

9   Incorrect ignition timing (Chapter 1).

10   Uneven or low cylinder compression. Remove plugs and use compression tester as per manufacturer's instructions.

10   Engine misses throughout driving speed range

1   Carburetor fuel filter clogged and/or impurities in the fuel system (Chapter 1). Also check fuel output at the carburetor (see Section 7).

2   Faulty or incorrectly gapped spark plugs (Chapter 1).

3   Incorrectly set ignition timing (Chapter 1).

4   Contact points faulty or incorrectly set (1970 – 1974 models only). At the same time check for a cracked distributor cap, disconnected distributor wires, or damage to the distributor components (Chapter 1).

5   Leaking spark plug wires (Chapter 1).

6   Emissions system components faulty (see Troubleshooting section, Chapter 6).

7   Low or uneven cylinder compression pressures. Remove spark plugs and test compression with gauge.

8   Weak or faulty ignition coil or condenser (1970 – 1974 models, see Chapter 5).

9   Weak or faulty HEI ignition system (1975 – 1980 models, see Chapter 5).

10   Vacuum leaks at carburetor, intake manifold or vacuum hoses (see Section 8).

11   Engine stalls

1   Carburetor idle speed incorrectly set (Chapter 1).

2   Carburetor fuel filter clogged and/or water and impurities in the

fuel system (Chapter 1).
3   Choke improperly adjusted or sticking (Chapter 1).
4   Distributor components damp, points out of adjustment or damage to distributor cap, rotor, etc. (Chapter 1).
5   Emission system components faulty (Troubleshooting section, Chapter 6.
6   Faulty or incorrectly gapped spark plugs. (Chapter 1). Also check spark plug wires (Chapter 1).
7   Vacuum leak at the carburetor, intake manifold or vacuum hoses. Check as described in Section 8.
8   Valve lash incorrectly set (Chapter 2).

12 Engine lacks power

1   Incorrect ignition timing (Chapter 1).
2   Excessive play in distributor shaft. At the same time check for worn or maladjusted contact points, faulty distributor cap, wires, etc. (Chapter 1).
3   Faulty or incorrectly gapped spark plugs (Chapter 1).
4   Carburetor not adjusted properly or excessively worn (Chapter 4).
5   Weak coil or condensor (Chapter 5).
6   Faulty HEI system coil (Chapter 5).
7   Brakes binding (Chapters 1 and 9).
8   Automatic transmission fluid level incorrect, causing slippage (Chapter 1).
9   Manual transmission clutch slipping (Chapter 1).
10 Fuel filter clogged and/or impurities in the fuel system (Chapter 1).
11 Emission control systems not functioning properly (see Troubleshooting, Chapter 6).
12 Use of sub-standard fuel. Fill tank with proper octane fuel.
13 Low or uneven cylinder compression pressures. Test with compression tester, which will also detect leaking valves and/or blown head gasket.

13 Engine backfires

1   Emissions systems not functioning properly (see Troubleshooting, Chapter 6).
2   Ignition timing incorrect (Section 1).
3   Carburetor in need of adjustment or worn excessively (Chapter 4).
4   Vacuum leak at carburetor, intake manifold or vacuum hoses. Check as described in Section 8.
5   Valve lash incorrectly set, and/or valves sticking (Chapter 2).

14 Pinging or knocking engine sounds on hard acceleration or uphill

1   Incorrect grade of fuel. Fill tank with fuel of the proper octane rating.
2   Ignition timing incorrect (Chapter 1).
3   Carburetor in need of adjustment (Chapter 4).
4   Improper spark plugs. Check plug type with that specified on tune-up decal located inside engine compartment. Also check plugs and wires for damage (Chapter 1).
5   Worn or damaged distributor components (Chapter 1).
6   Faulty emission systems (see Troubleshooting, Chapter 6).
7   Vacuum leak. (Check as described in Section 8).

15 Engine 'diesels' (continues to run) after switching off

1   Idle speed too fast (Chapter 1).
2   Electrical solenoid at side of carburetor not functioning properly (not all models, see Chapter 4).
3   Ignition timing incorrectly adjusted (Chapter 1).
4   Thermac air cleaner valve not operating properly (see Troubleshooting, Chapter 6).
5   Excessive engine operating temperatures. Probable causes of this are: malfunctioning thermostat, clogged radiator, faulty water pump. (See Chapter 3).

Engine electric

16 Battery will not hold a charge

1   Alternator drive belt defective or not adjusted properly (Chapter 1).
2   Electrolyte level too low or too weak (Chapter 1).
3   Battery terminals loose or corroded (Chapter 1).
4   Alternator not charging properly (Chapter 5).
5   Loose, broken or faulty wiring in the charging circuit (Chapter 5).
6   Short in vehicle circuitry causing a continual drain on battery.
7   Battery defective internally.

17 Ignition light fails to go out

1   Fault in alternator or charging circuit (Chapter 5).
2   Alternator drive belt defective or not properly adjusted (Chapter 1).

18 Ignition light fails to come on when key is turned

1   Ignition light bulb faulty (Chapter 10).
2   Alternator faulty (Chapter 5).
3   Fault in the printed circuit, dash wiring or bulb holder (Chapter 10).

Engine fuel system

19 Excessive fuel consumption

1   Dirty or choked air filter element (Chapter 1).
2   Incorrectly set ignition timing (Chapter 1).
3   Choke sticking or improperly adjusted (Chapter 1).
4   TCS emission system not functioning properly (not all cars, see Chapter 6).
5   Carburetor idle speed and/or mixture not adjusted properly (Chapters 1 and 4).
6   Carburetor internal parts excessively worn or damaged (Chapter 4).
7   Low tire pressure or incorrect tire size (Chapter 1).

20 Fuel leakage and/or fuel odor

1   Leak in a fuel feed or vent line (Chapter 6).
2   Tank overfilled. Fill only to automatic shut-off.
3   ECS emission system filter in need of replacement (Chapter 6).
4   Vapor leaks from ECS system lines (Chapter 6).
5   Carburetor internal parts excessively worn or out of adjustment (Chapter 4).

Engine cooling system

21 Overheating

1   Insufficient coolant in system (Chapter 1).
2   Fan belt defective or not adjusted properly (Chapter 1).
3   Radiator core blocked or radiator grille dirty and restricted (Chapter 3).
4   Thermostat faulty (Chapter 3).
5   Freewheeling clutch fan not functioning properly. Check for oil leakage at the rear of the cooling fan, indicating the need for replacement (Chapter 3).
6   Radiator cap not maintaining proper pressure. Have cap pressure tested by gas station or repair shop.
7   Ignition timing incorrect (Chapter 1).

22 Overcooling

1   Thermostat faulty (Chapter 3).

2 Inaccurate temperature gauge (Chapter 10).

23 External water leakage

1 Deteriorated or damaged hoses. Loose clamps at hose connections (Chapter 1).
2 Water pump seals defective. If this is the case, water will drip from the 'weep' hole in the water pump body (Chapter 3).
3 Leakage from radiator core or header tank. This will require the radiator to be professionally repaired (see Chapter 3 for removal procedures).
4 Engine drain plugs or water jacket freeze plugs leaking (see Chapters 2 and 3).

24 Internal water leakage

Note: *Internal coolant leaks can usually be detected by examining the oil. Check the dipstick and inside of valve cover for water deposits and an oil consistency like that of a milkshake.*
1 Faulty cylinder head gasket. Have the system pressure-tested professionally or remove the cylinder heads (Chapter 2) and inspect.
2 Cracked cylinder bore or cylinder head. Dismantle engine and inspect (Chapter 2).

25 Water loss

1 Overfilling system (Chapter 1).
2 Coolant boiling away due to overheating (see causes in Section 15).
3 Internal or external leakage (see Sections 22 and 23).
4 Faulty radiator cap. Have the cap pressure tested.

26 Poor coolant circulation

1 Inoperative water pump. A quick test is to pinch the top radiator hose closed with your hand while the engine is idling, then let loose. You should feel a surge of water if the pump is working properly (Chapter 3).
2 Restriction in cooling system. Drain, flush and refill the system (Chapter 1). If it appears necessary, remove the radiator (Chapter 3) and have it reverse-flushed or professionally cleaned.
3 Fan drive belt defective or not adjusted properly (Chapter 1).
4 Thermostat sticking (Chapter 3).

Clutch

27 Fails to release (pedal pressed to the floor – shift lever does not move freely in and out of reverse

1 Improper linkage adjustment (Chapter 8).
2 Clutch fork off ball stud. Look under the car, on the left side of transmission.
3 Clutch disc warped, bent or excessively damaged (Chapter 8).

28 Clutch slips (engine speed increases with no increase in road speed)

1 Linkage in need of adjustment (Chapter 8).
2 Clutch disc oil soaked or facing worn. Remove disc (Chapter 8) and inspect.
3 Clutch disc not seated in. It may take 30 or 40 normal starts for a new disc to seat.

29 Grabbing (juddering) on take-up

1 Oil on clutch disc facings. Remove disc (Chapter 8) and inspect. Correct any leakage source.
2 Worn or loose engine or transmission mounts. These units may

move slightly when clutch is released. Inspect mounts and bolts.
3 Worn splines on clutch gear. Remove clutch components (Chapter 8) and inspect.
4 Warped pressure plate or flywheel. Remove clutch components and inspect.

30 Squeal or rumble with clutch fully engaged (pedal released)

1 Improper adjustment; no lash (Chapter 8).
2 Release bearing binding on transmission bearing retainer. Remove clutch components (Chapter 8) and check bearing. Remove any burrs or nicks, clean and relubricate before reinstallation.
3 Weak linkage return spring. Replace the spring.

31 Squeal or rumble with clutch fully disengaged (pedal depressed)

1 Worn, faulty or broken release bearing (Chapter 8).
2 Worn or broken pressure plate springs (or diaphragm fingers) (Chapter 8).

32 Clutch pedal stays on floor when disengaged

1 Bind in linkage or release bearing. Inspect linkage or remove clutch components as necessary.
2 Linkage springs being over-traveled. Adjust linkage for proper lash. Make sure proper pedal stop (bumper) is installed.

Manual transmission

Note: *All the following Section references contained within Chapter 7.*

33 Noisy in neutral with engine running

1 Input shaft bearing worn (Sections 11 – 14).
2 Damaged main drive gear bearing (Sections 11 – 14).
3 Worn countergear bearings (Sections 11 – 14).
4 Worn or damaged countergear anti-lash plate (Sections 11 – 14).

34 Noisy in all gears

1 Any of the above causes, and/or:
2 Insufficient lubricant (see checking procedures in Chapter 1).

35 Noisy in one particular gear

1 Worn, damaged or chipped gear teeth for that particular gear (Sections 11 – 14).
2 Worn or damaged synchronizer for that particular gear (Sections 11 – 14).

36 Slips out of high gear

1 Transmission loose on clutch housing (Section 3).
2 Shift rods interfering with engine mounts or clutch lever (Section 2).
3 Shift rods not working freely (Section 2).
4 Damaged mainshaft pilot bearing (Section 10).
5 Dirt between transmission case and clutch housing, or misalignment of transmission (Section 10).
6 Worn or improperly adjusted linkage (Section 2).

37 Difficulty in engaging gears

1 Clutch not releasing fully (see clutch adjustment, Chapter 8).

2 Loose, damaged or maladjusted shift linkage. Make a thorough inspection, replacing parts as necessary. Adjust as described in Section 2.

38 Fluid leakage

1 Excessive amount of lubricant in transmission (see Chapter 1 for correct checking procedures. Drain lubricant as required).
2 Side cover loose or gasket damaged (Sections 7 – 9).
3 Rear oil seal or speedometer oil seal in need of replacement (Section 6).

Automatic transmission

Note: *Due to the complexity of the automatic transmission, it is difficult for the home mechanic to properly diagnose and service this component. For problems other than the following, the vehicle should be taken to a reputable mechanic.*

39 Fluid leakage

1 Automatic transmission fluid is a deep red color, and fluid leaks should not be confused with engine oil which can easily be blown by air flow to the transmission.
2 To pinpoint a leak, first remove all built-up dirt and grime from around the transmission. Degreasing agents and/or steam cleaning will achieve this. With the underside clean, drive the car at low speeds so the air flow will not blow the leak far from its source. Raise the car and determine where the leak is coming from. Common areas of leakage are:
  a) Fluid pan: tighten mounting bolts and/or replace pan gasket as necessary (see Chapter 1).
  b) Rear extension: tighten bolts and/or replace oil seal as necessary (Chapter 8).
  c) Filler pipe: replace the rubber oil seal where pipe enters transmission case.
  d) Transmission oil lines: tighten connectors where lines enter transmission case and/or replace lines.
  e) Vent pipe: transmission over-filled and/or water in fluid (see checking procedures, Chapter 1).
  f) Speedometer connector: replace the O-ring where speedometer cable enters transmission case.

40 General shift mechanism problems

1 Sections 4 and 5 in Chapter 7 deal with checking and adjusting the shift linkage on automatic transmissions. Common problems which may be attributed to maladjusted linkage are:
  a) Engine starting in gears other than 'P' (Park) or 'N' (Neutral).
  b) Indicator on quadrant pointing to a gear other than the one actually being used.
  c) Vehicle will not hold firm when in 'P' (Park) position.
  Refer to Sections 4 or 5 in Chapter 7 to adjust the manual linkage.

41 Transmission will not downshift with accelerator pedal pressed to the floor

1 Sections 6 and 7 in Chapter 7 deal with adjusting the downshift cable or downshift switch to enable the transmission to downshift properly.

42 Engine will start in gears other than 'P' (Park) or 'N' (Neutral)

1 Sections 8 and 9 in Chapter 7 deal with adjusting the neutral start switches used with automatic transmissions.

43 Transmission slips, shifts rough, is noisy or has no drive in forward or reverse gears

1 There are many probable causes for the above problems, but the home mechanic should concern himself only with one possibility; fluid level.
2 Before taking the vehicle to a specialist, check the level of the fluid and condition of the fluid as described in Chapter 1. Correct fluid level as necessary or change the fluid and filter if needed. If problem persists, have a professional diagnose the probable cause.

Drive shaft

44 Leakage of fluid at front of drive shaft

1 Defective transmission rear oil seal. See Chapter 7 for replacing procedures. While this is done, check the splined yoke for burrs or a rough condition which may be damaging the seal. If found, these can be dressed with crocus cloth or a fine dressing stone.

45 Knock or clunk when transmission is under initial load (just after transmission is put into gear)

1 Loose or disconnected rear suspension components. Check all mounting bolts and bushings (Chapter 1).
2 Loose drive shaft bolts. Inspect all bolts and nuts and tighten to torque specifications (Chapter 8).
3 Worn or damaged universal joint bearings. Test for wear (Chapter 8).

46 Metallic grating sound consistent with road speed

1 Pronounced wear in the universal joint bearings. Test for wear (Chapter 8).

47 Vibration

Note: *Before it can be assumed that the drive shaft is at fault, make sure the tires are perfectly balanced and perform the following test.*
1 Install a tachometer inside the car to monitor engine speed as the car is driven. Drive the car and note the engine speed at which the vibration (roughness) is most pronounced. Now shift the transmission to a different gear and bring the engine speed to the same point.
2 If the vibration occurs at the same engine speed (rpm) regardless of which gear the transmission is in, the drive shaft is NOT at fault since the drive shaft speed varies.
3 If the vibration decreases or is eliminated when the transmission is in a different gear at the same engine speed, refer to the following probable causes.
4 Bent or dented drive shaft. Inspect and replace as necessary (Chapter 8).
5 Undercoating or built-up dirt, etc. on the drive shaft. Clean the shaft thoroughly and test.
6 Worn universal joint bearings. Remove and inspect (Chapter 8).
7 Drive shaft and/or companion flange out of balance. Check for missing weights on the shaft. Remove drive shaft (Chapter 8) and reinstall 180° from original position. Retest. Have drive shaft professionally balanced if problem persists.

Rear axle

48 Noise – same when in drive as when vehicle is coasting

1 Road noise. No corrective procedures available.
2 Tire noise. Inspect tires and tire pressures (Chapter 1).
3 Front wheel bearings loose, worn or damaged (Chapter 1).

49 Vibration

1 See probable causes under 'Drive shaft'. Proceed under the

guidelines listed for the drive shaft. If the problem persists, check the rear wheel bearings by raising the rear of the car and spinning the wheels by hand. Listen for evidence of rough (noisy) bearings. Remove and inspect (Chapter 8).

50 Oil leakage

1   Pinion oil seal damaged (Chapter 8).
2   Axle shaft oil seals damaged (Chapter 8).
3   Differential inspection cover leaking. Tighten mounting bolts or replace the gasket as required (Chapter 1).

Brakes

Note: *Before assuming a brake problem exists, check: that the tires are in good condition and are inflated properly (see Chapter 1); the front end alignment is correct; and that the vehicle is not loaded with weight in an unequal manner.*

51 Vehicle pulls to one side under braking

1   Defective, damaged or oil contaminated disc pad on one side. Inspect as described in Chapter 1. Refer to Chapter 9 if replacement is required.
2   Excessive wear of brake pad material or disc on one side. Inspect and correct as necessary.
3   Loose or disconnected front suspension components. Inspect and tighten all bolts to specifications (Chapter 1).
4   Defective caliper assembly. Remove caliper and inspect for stuck piston or damage (Chapter 9).

52 Noise (high pitched squeak without brake applied)

1   Front brake pads worn out. This noise comes from the wear sensor rubbing against the disc. Replace pads with new ones immediately (Chapter 9).

53 Excessive brake pad travel

1   Partial brake system failure. Inspect entire system (Chapter 1) and correct as required.
2   Insufficient fluid in master cylinder. Check (Chapter 1) and add fluid and bleed system if necessary.
3   Rear brakes not adjusting properly. Make a series of starts and stops while the vehicle is in 'R' (Reverse). If this does not correct the situation remove drums and inspect self-adjusters (Chapter 1).

54 Brake pedal appears spongy when depressed

1   Air in hydraulic lines. Bleed the brake system (Chapter 9).
2   Faulty flexible hoses. Inspect all system hoses and lines. Replace parts as necessary.
3   Master cylinder mountings insecure. Inspect master cylinder bolts (nuts) and torque-tighten to specifications.
4   Master cylinder faulty (Chapter 9).

55 Excessive effort required to stop vehicle

1   Power brake servo not operating properly (Chapter 9).
2   Excessively worn linings or pads. Inspect and replace if necessary (Chapter 1).
3   One or more caliper pistons (front wheels) or wheel cylinders (rear wheels) seized or sticking. Inspect and rebuild as required (Chapter 9).
4   Brake linings or pads contaminated with oil or grease. Inspect and replace as required (Chapter 1).
5   New pads or linings fitted and not yet 'bedded in'. It will take a while for the new material to seat against the drum (or rotor).

56 Pedal travels to floor with little resistance

1   Little or no fluid in the master cylinder reservoir caused by: leaking wheel cylinder(s); leaking caliper piston(s); loose, damaged or disconnected brake lines. Inspect entire system and correct as necessary.

57 Brake pedal pulsates during brake application

1   Wheel bearings not adjusted properly or in need of replacement (Chapter 1).
2   Caliper not sliding properly due to improper installation or obstructions. Remove and inspect (Chapter 9).
3   Rotor not within specifications. Remove the rotor (Chapter 9) and check for excessive lateral run-out and parellelism. Have the rotor professionally machined or replace it with a new one.

Suspension and steering

58 Car pulls to one side

1   Tire pressures uneven (Chapter 1).
2   Defective tire (Chapter 1).
3   Excessive wear in suspension or steering components (Chapter 1).
4   Front end in need of alignment. Take car to a qualified specialist.
5   Front brakes dragging. Inspect braking system as described in Chapter 1.

59 Shimmy, shake or vibration

1   Tire or wheel out of balance or out of round. Have professionally balanced.
2   Loose, worn or out of adjustment wheel bearings (Chapter 1).
3   Shock absorbers and/or suspension components worn or damaged (Chapter 11).

60 Excessive pitching and/or rolling around corners or during braking

1   Defective shock absorbers. Replace as a set (Chapter 11).
2   Broken or weak coil springs and/or suspension components. Inspect as described in Chapter 11.

61 Excessively stiff steering

1   Lack of lubricant in steering box (manual) or power steering fluid reservoir (Chapter 1).
2   Incorrect tire pressures (Chapter 1).
3   Lack of lubrication at steering joints (Chapter 1).
4   Front end out of alignment.
5   See also Section 63 'Lack of power assistance'.

62 Excessive play in steering

1   Loose wheel bearings (Chapter 1).
2   Excessive wear in suspension or steering components (Chapter 1).
3   Steering gear out of adjustment (Chapter 11).

63 Lack of power assistance

1   Steering pump drive belt faulty or not adjusted properly (Chapter 1).
2   Fluid level low (Chapter 1).
3   Hoses or pipes restricting the flow. Inspect and replace parts as necessary.
4   Air in power steering system. Bleed system (Chapter 11).

64 Excessive tire wear (not specific to one area)

1   Incorrect tire pressures (Chapter 1).
2   Tires out of balance. Have professionally balanced.
3   Wheels damaged. Inspect and replace as necessary.
4   Suspension or steering components excessively worn (Chapter 1).

65 Excessive tire wear on outside edge

1   Inflation pressures not correct (Chapter 1).
2   Excessive speed on turns.
3   Front end alignment incorrect (excessive toe-in). Have professionally aligned.

4   Suspension arm bent or twisted.

66 Excessive tire wear on inside edge

1   Inflation pressures incorrect (Chapter 1).
2   Front end alignment incorrect (toe-out). Have professionally aligned.
3   Loose or damaged steering components (Chapter 1).

67 Tire tread worn in one place

1   Tires out of balance. Balance tires professionally.
2   Damaged or buckled wheel. Inspect and replace if necessary.
3   Defective tire.

Safety first!

Regardless of how enthusiastic you may be about getting on with the job at hand, take the time to ensure that your safety is not jeopardized. A moment's lack of attention can result in an accident, as can failure to observe certain simple safety precautions. The possibility of an accident will always exist, and the following points should not be considered a comprehensive list of all dangers. Rather, they are intended to make you aware of the risks and to encourage a safety conscious approach to all work you carry out on your vehicle.

Essential DOs and DON'Ts

DON'T rely on a jack when working under the vehicle. Always use approved jackstands to support the weight of the vehicle and place them under the recommended lift or support points.

DON'T attempt to loosen extremely tight fasteners (i.e. wheel lug nuts) while the vehicle is on a jack — it may fall.

DON'T start the engine without first making sure that the transmission is in Neutral (or Park where applicable) and the parking brake is set.

DON'T remove the radiator cap from a hot cooling system — let it cool or cover it with a cloth and release the pressure gradually.

DON'T attempt to drain the engine oil until you are sure it has cooled to the point that it will not burn you.

DON'T touch any part of the engine or exhaust system until it has cooled sufficiently to avoid burns.

DON'T siphon toxic liquids such as gasoline, antifreeze and brake fluid by mouth, or allow them to remain on your skin.

DON'T inhale brake lining dust — it is potentially hazardous (see *Asbestos* below)

DON'T allow spilled oil or grease to remain on the floor — wipe it up before someone slips on it.

DON'T use loose fitting wrenches or other tools which may slip and cause injury.

DON'T push on wrenches when loosening or tightening nuts or bolts. Always try to pull the wrench toward you. If the situation calls for pushing the wrench away, push with an open hand to avoid scraped knuckles if the wrench should slip.

DON'T attempt to lift a heavy component alone — get someone to help you.

DON'T rush or take unsafe shortcuts to finish a job.

DON'T allow children or animals in or around the vehicle while you are working on it.

DO wear eye protection when using power tools such as a drill, sander, bench grinder, etc. and when working under a vehicle.

DO keep loose clothing and long hair well out of the way of moving parts.

DO make sure that any hoist used has a safe working load rating adequate for the job.

DO get someone to check on you periodically when working alone on a vehicle.

DO carry out work in a logical sequence and make sure that everything is correctly assembled and tightened.

DO keep chemicals and fluids tightly capped and out of the reach of children and pets.

DO remember that your vehicle's safety affects that of yourself and others. If in doubt on any point, get professional advice.

Asbestos

Certain friction, insulating, sealing, and other products — such as brake linings, brake bands, clutch linings, torque converters, gaskets, etc. — contain asbestos. *Extreme care must be taken to avoid inhalation of dust from such products since it is hazardous to health.* If in doubt, assume that they *do* contain asbestos.

Fire

Remember at all times that gasoline is highly flammable. Never smoke or have any kind of open flame around when working on a vehicle. But the risk does not end there. A spark caused by an electrical short circuit, by two metal surfaces contacting each other, or even by static electricity built up in your body under certain conditions, can ignite gasoline vapors, which in a confined space are highly explosive. Do not, under any circumstances, use gasoline for cleaning parts. Use an approved safety solvent.

Always disconnect the battery ground (–) cable *at the battery* before working on any part of the fuel system or electrical system. Never risk spilling fuel on a hot engine or exhaust component.

It is strongly recommended that a fire extinguisher suitable for use on fuel and electrical fires be kept handy in the garage or workshop at all times. Never try to extinguish a fuel or electrical fire with water.

Fumes

Certain fumes are highly toxic and can quickly cause unconsciousness and even death if inhaled to any extent. Gasoline vapor falls into this category, as do the vapors from some cleaning solvents. Any draining or pouring of such volatile fluids should be done in a well ventilated area.

When using cleaning fluids and solvents, read the instructions on the container carefully. Never use materials from unmarked containers.

Never run the engine in an enclosed space, such as a garage. Exhaust fumes contain carbon monoxide, which is extremely poisonous. If you need to run the engine, always do so in the open air, or at least have the rear of the vehicle outside the work area.

If you are fortunate enough to have the use of an inspection pit, never drain or pour gasoline and never run the engine while the vehicle is over the pit. The fumes, being heavier than air, will concentrate in the pit with possibly lethal results.

The battery

Never create a spark or allow a bare light bulb near the battery. The battery normally gives off a certain amount of hydrogen gas, which is highly explosive.

Always disconnect the battery ground (–) cable *at the battery* before working on the fuel or electrical systems.

If possible, loosen the filler caps or cover when charging the battery from an external source. Do not charge at an excessive rate or the battery may burst.

Take care when adding water and when carrying a battery. The electrolyte, even when diluted, is very corrosive and should not be allowed to contact clothing or skin.

Always wear eye protection when cleaning the battery to prevent the caustic deposits from entering your eyes.

Household current

When using an electric power tool, inspection light, etc., which operates on household current, always make sure that the tool is correctly connected to its plug and that, where necessary, it is properly grounded. Do not use such items in damp conditions and, again, do not create a spark or apply excessive heat in the vicinity of fuel or fuel vapor.

Secondary ignition system voltage

A severe electric shock can result from touching certain parts of the ignition system (such as the spark plug wires) when the engine is running or being cranked, particularly if components are damp or the insulation is defective. In the case of an electronic ignition system, the secondary system voltage is much higher and could prove fatal.

Chapter 1 Tune-up and routine maintenance

Refer to Chapter 13 for specifications and information related to 1981 models

Contents

Specifications

Note: Additional specifications and torque settings can be found in each individual chapter.

Oil filter type .... disposable cartridge type AC PF25

Engine crankcase oil capacity .... 4 US qts; 5 US qts with new (dry) filter

Crankcase vent filter type .... AC FB59

Crankcase PCV valve type .... AC CV 774C

Radiator pressure cap rating .... 15 lbf/in^2

Thermostat type and rating .... wax pellet, 195° (180° for 402 cu in, 375 HP)

Coolant system capacity .... see Chapter 3

Distributor type:
1970 – 1974 .... mechanical breaker point type
1975 – 1980 .... breakerless. Designated HEI.

Distributor direction of rotation .... clockwise

Breaker point gap .... 0.019 in

Firing order 1–8–4–3–6–5–7–2

Spark plug type and gap .... see Tune-up decal in engine compartment or Specifications Section in Chapter 5

Ignition timing .... see Tune-up decal in engine compartment or Specifications Section in Chapter 5

Clutch pedal free-play (measured at center of pad) .... 1 to 1$\frac{1}{4}$ in

Torque specifications

	lb-ft
Oil pan drain plug	20
Spark plugs	15
Carburetor mounting nuts	12
Fuel inlet nut (fuel filter)	18
Manual transmission fill plug:	
All except Muncie 4-speed	18
Muncie 4-speed	30
Automatic transmission pan bolts	12
Rear axle filler/inspection plug	22
Rear axle cover bolts	27
Brake caliper mounting bolts	35
Wheel nuts:	
1970 models	65
1971 – 1975	70
1976 – 1980	80

1 Introduction

This Chapter was designed to help the home mechanic maintain his (or her) car for peak performance, economy, safety and longevity.

On the following pages you will find a maintenance schedule along with sections which deal specifically with each item on the schedule. Included are visual checks, adjustments and item replacements.

Servicing your car using the time/mileage maintenance schedule and the sequenced sections will give you a planned program of maintenance. Keep in mind that it is a full plan, and maintaining only a few items at the specified intervals will not give you the same results.

You will find as you service your car that many of the procedures can, and should, be grouped together, due to the nature of the job at hand. Examples of this are as follows:

If the car is fully raised for a chassis lubrication, for example, this is the ideal time for the following checks: manual transmission fluid, rear axle fluid, exhaust system, suspension, steering and the fuel system.

If the tires and wheels are removed, as during a routine tire rotation, go ahead and check the brakes and wheel bearings at the same time.

If you must borrow or rent a torque wrench, you will do best to service the spark plugs, repack (or replace) the wheel bearings and check the carburetor mounting torque all in the same day to save time and money.

The first step of this or any maintenance plan is to prepare yourself before the actual work begins. Read through the appropriate sections for all work that is to be performed before you begin. Gather together all necessary parts and tools. If it appears you could have a problem during a particular job, don't hesitate to ask advice from your local parts man or dealer service department.

Routine maintenance intervals

Every 250 miles or weekly – whichever comes first

Check the engine oil level (Section 2).
Check the engine coolant level (Section 2).
Check the windshield washer fluid level (Section 2).
Check the battery water level (if equipped with removable vent caps) (Sec 2).
Check the tires and tire pressures (Section 3).
Check the automatic transmission fluid level (Section 2).
Check the power steering fluid level (Section 2).

Every 3750 miles or 6 months – whichever comes first

Change engine oil and filter (Section 4).
Lubricate the chassis components (Section 5).

Check the cooling system (Section 6).
Check the exhaust system (Section 7).
Check the suspension and steering components (Section 8).
Check and adjust (if necessary) the engine drive belts (Section 9).
Check the fuel system components (Section 10).
Check the brake master cylinder fluid level (Section 2).
Check the manual transmission fluid level (Section 2).
Check the rear axle fluid level (Section 2).
Replace the PCV valve (Section 11).
Replace the air filter and PCV filter (Section 12).

Every 7500 miles or 12 months – whichever comes first

Check the clutch pedal free-play (manual transmission only (Section 13).
Rotate the tires (Section 14).
Check the Thermo Controlled air cleaner for proper operation (Section 15).
Check and adjust (if necessary) the engine idle speed (Section 16).
Check the EFE system (Section 17).
Replace the fuel filter (Section 18).
Check and adjust (if necessary) the engine ignition timing (Section 19).
Check the operation of the choke (Section 20).
Check the operation of the EGR valve (Section 21).
Change rear axle fluid (if car is used to pull a trailer) (Section 22).

Every 15 000 miles or 12 months – whichever comes first

Replace the spark plugs (Section 23).
Check and repack the front wheel bearings (perform this procedure whenever brakes are relined, regardless of maintenance interval) (Section 24).
Change the automatic transmission fluid and filter (if mainly driven under following conditions: heavy city traffic in hot-climate regions; in hill or mountain areas; frequent trailer pulling (Section 25).
Check the braking system (Section 26).
Check the mounting torque of the carburetor (Section 27).
Check the spark plug wires (Section 28).
Drain, flush and refill the cooling system (Section 29).
Replace the contact points, adjust dwell angle and check the distributor (1970 – 1974 models only) (Section 30).

Every 30 000 miles or 24 months – whichever comes first

Change the rear axle fluid (if car is used to pull a trailer, change at 7500 miles) (Section 2).
Change the automatic transmission fluid and filter (if driven under abnormal conditions, see 15 000 miles servicing) (Section 25).
Check the ECS emissions system and replace the charcoal canister filter (Section 31).

2 Fluid levels check

1 There are a number of components on a vehicle which rely on the use of fluids to perform their job. Through the normal operation of the car, these fluids are used up and must be replenished before damage occurs. See the Recommended Lubricants Section for the specific fluid to be used when adding is required. When checking fluid levels it is important that the car is on a level surface.

Engine oil

2 The engine oil level is checked with a dipstick which is located at the side of the engine block. This dipstick travels through a tube and into the oil pan to the bottom of the engine.

3 The oil level should be checked preferably before the car has been driven, or about 15 minutes after the engine has been shut off. If the oil is checked immediately after driving the car, some of the oil will remain in the upper engine components, thus giving an inaccurate reading on the dipstick.

4 Pull the dipstick from its tube and wipe all the oil from the end with a clean rag. Insert the clean dipstick all the way back into the oil pan and pull it out again. Observe the oil at the end of the dipstick (photo). At its highest point, the level should be between the 'Add' and 'Full' marks.

5 It takes approximately 1 quart of oil to raise the level from the 'Add' mark to the 'Full' mark on the dipstick. Do not allow the level to drop below the 'Add' mark as this may cause engine damage due to oil starvation. On the other hand, do not overfill the engine by adding oil above the 'Full' mark as this may result in oil-fouled spark plugs, oil leaks or oil seal failures.

6 Oil is added to the engine after removing a twist-off cap located either on the rocker arm cover or through a raised tube near the front of the engine. The cap should be duly marked 'Engine oil' or similar wording. An oil can spout or funnel will reduce spills as the oil is poured in.

7 Checking the oil level can also be a step towards preventative maintenance. If you find the oil level dropping abnormally, this is an indication of oil leakage or internal engine wear which should be corrected. If there are water droplets in the oil, or it is milky looking, this also indicates component failure and the engine should be checked immediately. The condition of the oil can also be checked along with the level. With the dipstick removed from the engine, take your thumb and index finger and wipe the oil up the dipstick, looking for small dirt particles or engine filings which will cling to the dipstick (photo). This is an indication that the oil should be drained and fresh oil added (Section 4).

Engine coolant

8 Most vehicles are equipped with a pressurized coolant recovery system which makes coolant level checks very easy. A clear or white coolant reservoir attached to the inner fender panel is connected by a hose to the radiator cap. As the engine heats up during operation, coolant is forced from the radiator, through the connecting tube and into the reservoir. As the engine cools, this coolant is automatically drawn back into the radiator to keep the correct level.

9 The coolant level should be checked when the engine is cold. Merely observe the level of fluid in the reservoir, which should be at or near the 'Full cold' mark on the side of the reservoir. If the system is completely cooled, also check the level in the radiator by removing the cap. Some systems also have a 'Full hot' mark to check the level when the engine is hot.

10 If your particular vehicle is not equipped with a coolant recovery system, the level should be checked by removing the radiator cap. However, the cap should not under any circumstances be removed while the system is hot, as escaping steam could cause serious injury. Wait until the engine has completely cooled, then wrap a thick cloth around the cap and turn it to its first stop. If any steam escapes from the cap, allow the engine to cool further. Then remove the cap and check the level in the radiator. It should be about 2 to 3 inches below the bottom of the filler neck.

11 If only a small amount of coolant is required to bring the system up to the proper level, regular water can be used. However, to maintain the proper antifreeze/water mixture in the system, both should be mixed together to replenish a low level. High-quality antifreeze offering protection to -20° should be mixed with water in the

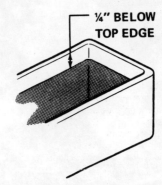

Fig. 1.1 Checking brake fluid in the master cylinder (Sec 2)

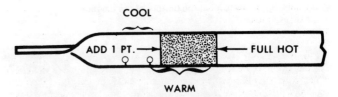

Fig. 1.2 The automatic transmission dipstick and typical markings (Sec 2)

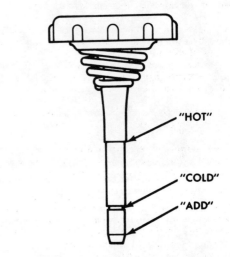

Fig. 1.3 The cap with built-in dipstick for the power steering pump (Sec 2)

proportion specified on the container. Do not allow antifreeze to come in contact with your skin or painted surfaces of the car. Flush contacted areas immediately with plenty of water.

12 On systems with a recovery tank, coolant should be added to the reservoir after removing the cap at the top of the reservoir. Coolant should be added directly into the radiator on systems without a coolant recovery tank.

13 As the coolant level is checked, observe the condition of the coolant. It should be relatively clear. If the fluid is brown or a rust color, this is an indication that the system should be drained, flushed and refilled (Section 29).

14 If the cooling system requires repeated additions to keep the proper level, have the pressure radiator cap checked for proper sealing ability. Also check for leaks in the system (cracked hoses, loose hose connections, leaking gaskets, etc.).

Windshield washer

15 The fluid for the windshield washer system is located in a plastic

2.4 Checking the oil level at the bottom of the dipstick

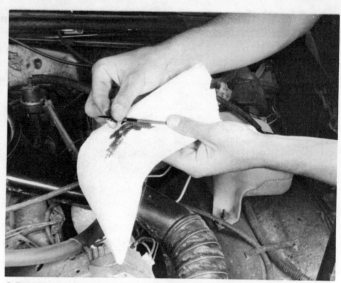

2.7 Wiping the oil on the dipstick to check for contamination

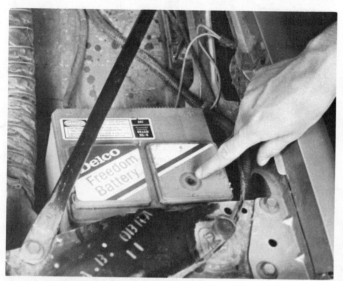

2.17 Many GM maintenance-free batteries have an 'eye' which indicates the battery condition by changing color

2.18 Removing the vent caps to check the water level in maintenance-type batteries

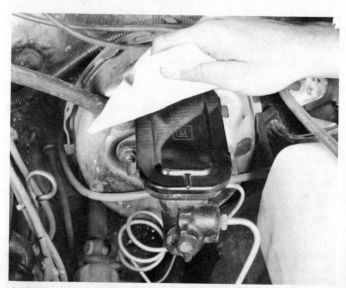

2.22 Before removing the master cylinder cap, use a clean cloth to remove dirt, grease, etc.

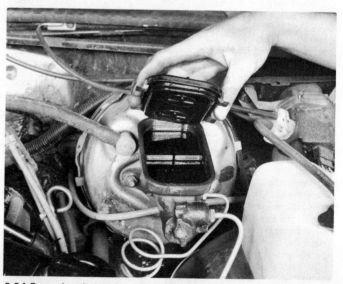

2.24 Removing the master cylinder cap to check the brake fluid level

2.37 Checking the automatic transmission fluid level with the dipstick

2.41 A clue to the fluid quality can be obtained by inspecting the fluid on the dipstick

reservoir. The level inside the reservoir should be maintained at the 'Full' mark.

16 General Motors 'Optikleen' washer solvent or its equivalent should be added through the plastic cap whenever replenishing is required. Do not use plain water alone in this system, especially in cold climates where the water could freeze.

Battery

Note: There are certain precautions to be taken when working on or near the battery: a) Never expose a battery to open flame or sparks which could ignite the hydrogen gas given off by the battery; b) Wear protective clothing and eye protection to reduce the possibility of the corrosive sulfuric acid solution inside the battery harming you (if the fluid is splashed or spilled, flush the contacted area immediately with plenty of water); c) Remove all metal jewelry which could contact the positive terminal and another grounded metal source, thus causing a short circuit; d) Always keep batteries and battery acid out of the reach of children.

17 Vehicles equipped with 'Freedom' or maintenance-free batteries require no maintenance as the battery case is sealed and has no removal caps for adding water (photo).

18 If a maintenance-type battery is installed, the caps on the top of the battery should be removed periodically to check for a low water level (photo). This check will be more critical during the warm summer months.

19 Remove each of the caps and add distilled water to bring the level of each cell to the split ring in the filler opening.

20 At the same time the battery water level is checked, the overall condition of the battery and its related components should be inspected. If corrosion is found on the cable ends or battery terminals, remove the cables and clean away all corrosion using a baking soda/water solution or a wire brush cleaning tool designed for this purpose. See Chapter 5 for complete battery care and servicing.

Brake master cylinder

21 The brake master cylinder is located on the left side of the engine compartment firewall and has a cap which must be removed to check the fluid level.

22 Before removing the cap, use a rag to clean all dirt, grease, etc. from around the cap area (photo). If any foreign matter enters the master cylinder with the cap removed, blockage in the brake system lines can occur. Also make sure all painted surfaces around the master cylinder are covered, as brake fluid will ruin paintwork.

23 Release the clip(s) securing the cap to the top of the master cylinder. In most cases, a screwdriver can be used to pry the wire clip(s) free.

24 Carefully lift the cap off the cylinder and observe the fluid level (photo). It should be approximately $\frac{1}{4}$-inch below the top edge of each reservoir.

25 If additional fluid is necessary to bring the level up to the proper height, carefully pour the specified brake fluid into the master cylinder. Be careful not to spill the fluid on painted surfaces. Be sure the specified fluid is used, as mixing different types of brake fluid can cause damage to the system. See Recommended Lubricants or your owner's manual.

26 At this time the fluid and master cylinder can be inspected for contamination. Normally, the braking system will not need periodic draining and refilling, but if rust deposits, dirt particles or water droplets are seen in the fluid, the system should be dismantled, drained and refilled with fresh fluid.

27 Reinstall the master cylinder cap and secure it with the clip(s). Make sure the lid is properly seated to prevent fluid leakage and/or system pressure loss.

28 The brake fluid in the master cylinder will drop slightly as the brake shoes or pads at each wheel wear down during normal operation. If the master cylinder requires repeated replenishing to keep it at the proper level, this is an indication of leakage in the brake system which should be corrected immediately. Check all brake lines and their connections, along with the wheel cylinders and booster (see Chapter 9 for more information).

29 If upon checking the master cylinder fluid level you discover one or both reservoirs empty or nearly empty, the braking system should be bled (Chapter 9). When the fluid level gets low, air can enter the system and should be removed by bleeding the brakes.

Manual transmission

30 Manual shift transmissions do not have a dipstick. The fluid level is checked by removing a plug in the side of the transmission case. Locate this plug and use a rag to clean the plug and the area around it.

31 With the vehicle components cold, remove the plug. If fluid immediately starts leaking out, thread the plug back into the transmission because the fluid level is alright. If there is no fluid leakage, completely remove the plug and place your little finger inside the hole. The fluid level should be just at the bottom of the plug hole.

32 If the transmission needs more fluid, use a syringe to squeeze the appropriate lubricant into the plug hole to bring the fluid up to the proper level.

33 Thread the plug back into the transmission and tighten it securely. Drive the car and check for leaks around the plug.

Automatic transmission

34 The fluid inside the transmission must be at normal operating temperature to get an accurate reading on the dipstick. This is done by driving the car for several miles, making frequent starts and stops to allow the transmission to shift through all gears.

35 Park the car on a level surface, place the selector lever in 'Park' and leave the engine running at an idle.

36 Remove the transmission dipstick (located on the right side, near the rear of the engine) and wipe all the fluid from the end of the dipstick with a clean rag.

37 Push the dipstick back into the transmission until the cap seats firmly on the dipstick tube. Now remove the dipstick again and observe the fluid on the end (photo). The highest point of fluid should be between the 'Full' mark and $\frac{1}{4}$ inch below the 'Full' mark.

38 If the fluid level is at or below the 'Add' mark on the distick, add sufficient fluid to raise the level to the 'Full' mark. One pint of fluid will raise the level from 'Add' to 'Full'. Fluid should be added directly into the dipstick guide tube, using a funnel to prevent spills.

39 It is important that the transmission not be overfilled. Under no circumstances should the fluid level be above the 'Full' mark on the disptick, as this could cause internal damage to the transmission. The best way to prevent overfilling is to add fluid a little at a time, driving the car and checking the level between additions.

40 Use only transmission fluid specified by GM. This information can be found in the Recommended Lubricants Section.

41 The condition of the fluid should also be checked along with the level (photo). If the fluid at the end of the dipstick is a dark reddish-brown color, or if the fluid has a 'burnt' smell, the transmission fluid should be changed with fresh. If you are in doubt about the condition of the fluid, purchase some new fluid and compare the two for color and smell.

Rear axle

42 Like the manual transmission, the rear axle has an inspection and fill plug which must be removed to check the fluid level.

43 Remove the plug which is located either in the removable cover plate or on the side of the differential carrier. Use your little finger to reach inside the rear axle housing to feel the level of the fluid. It should be at the bottom of the plug hole.

44 If this is not the case, add the proper lubricant into the rear axle carrier through the plug hole. A syringe or a small funnel can be used for this.

45 Make certain the correct lubricant is used, as regular and Positraction rear axles require different lubricants. You can ascertain which type of axle you have by reading the stamped number on the axle tube (See Vehicle Identification Numbers at the front of this manual).

46 Tighten the plug securely and check for leaks after the first few miles of driving..

Power steering

47 Unlike manual steering, the power steering system relies on fluid which may, over a period of time, require replenishing.

48 The reservoir for the power steering pump will be located near the front of the engine, and can be mounted on either the left or right side.

49 The power steering fluid level should be checked only after the car has been driven, with the fluid at operating temperature. The front wheels should be pointed straight ahead.

50 With the engine shut off, use a rag to clean the reservoir cap and the areas around the cap. This will help to prevent foreign material from falling into the reservoir when the cap is removed.

51 Twist off the reservoir cap which has a built-in dipstick attached to it. Pull off the cap and clean the fluid at the bottom of the dipstick with a clean rag. Now reinstall the dipstick/cap assembly to get a fluid level reading. Remove the dipstick/cap and observe the fluid level. It should be at the 'Full hot' mark on the dipstick.

52 If additional fluid is required, pour the specified lubricant directly into the reservoir using a funnel to prevent spills.

53 If the reservoir requires frequent fluid additions, all power steering hoses, hose connections, the power steering pump and the steering box should be carefully checked for leaks.

3   Tire and tire pressure checks

1   Periodically inspecting the tires can not only prevent you from being stranded with a flat tire, but can also give you clues as to possible problems with the steering and suspension systems before major damage occurs.

2   Proper tire inflation adds miles to the lifespan of the tires, allows the car to achieve maximum miles per gallon figures, and helps the overall riding comfort of the car.

3   When inspecting the tire, first check the wear on the tread. Irregularities in the tread pattern (cupping, flat spots, more wear on one side than the other) are indications of front end alignment and/or balance problems. If any of these conditions are found you would do best to take the car to a competent repair shop which can correct the problem.

4   Also check the tread area for cuts or punctures. Many times a nail or tack will imbed itself into the tire tread and yet the tire will hold its air pressure for a short time. In most cases, a repair shop or gas station can repair the punctured tire.

5   It is also important to check the sidewalls of the tire, both inside and outside. Check for the rubber being deteriorated, cut or punctured. Also inspect the inboard side of the tire for signs of brake fluid leakage, indicating a thorough brake inspection is needed immediately (Section 26).

6   Incorrect tire pressure cannot be determined merely by looking at the tire. This is especially true for radial tires. A tire pressure gauge must be used. If you do not already have a reliable gauge, it is a good idea to purchase one and keep it in the glove box. Built-in pressure gauges at gas stations are often unreliable. If you are in doubt as to the accuracy of your gauge, many repair shops have 'master' pressure gauges which you can use for comparison purposes.

7   Always check tire inflation when the tires are cold. Cold, in this case, means the car has not been driven more than one mile after sitting for three hours or more. It is normal for the pressure to increase 4 to 8 pounds or more when the tires are hot.

8   Unscrew the valve cap protruding from the wheel or hubcap and firmly press the gauge onto the valve stem. Observe the reading on the gauge and check this figure against the recommended tire pressure listed on the tire placard. This tire placard is usually found attached to the rear portion of the driver's door.

9   Check all tires and add air as necessary to bring all tires up to the recommended pressure levels. Do not forget the spare tire. Be sure to reinstall the valve caps which will keep dirt and moisture out of the valve stem mechanism.

4   Engine oil and filter change

1   Frequent oil changes may be the best form of preventative maintenance available for the home mechanic. When engine oil ages, it gets diluted and contaminated which ultimately leads to premature parts wear.

2   Although some sources recommend oil filter changes every other oil change, we feel that the minimal cost of an oil filter and the relative ease with which it is installed dictates that a new filter be used whenever the oil is changed.

3   The tools necessary for a normal oil and filter change are: a

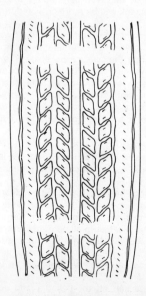

Fig. 1.4 Tire wear indicators which run across the tread when tire is in need of replacement (Sec 3)

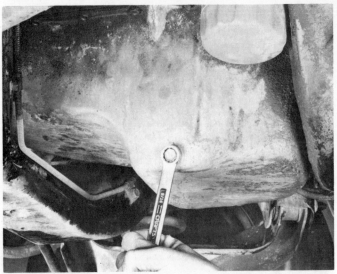

4.9A Some engines have the oil drain plug on the side of the oil pan

4.9B Removing an oil drain plug which is located on the bottom of the oil pan

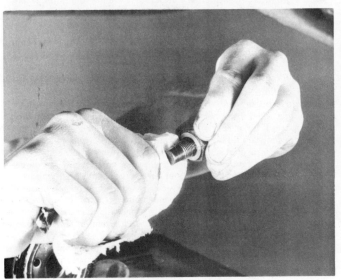

4.11 Before reinstalling, thoroughly clean the oil drain plug

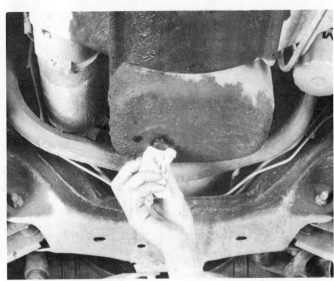

4.12 Once tightened securely, clean the area around the drain plug. This will help to readily identify any leakage

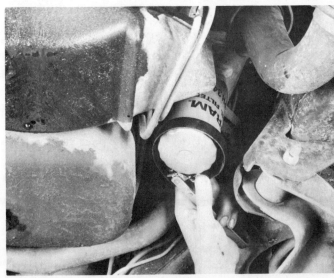

4.14 Using an oil filter wrench to loosen the filter. The canister is less likely to collapse if grasped near the bottom

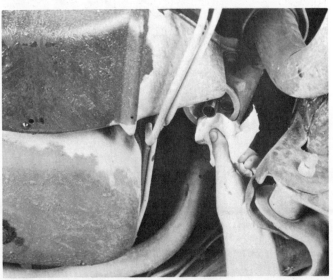

4.18 Thoroughly clean the filter mounting pedestal and check that the old rubber gasket is not stuck to the filter mount

4.19 A thin coat of clean engine oil on the new filter gasket will ensure a good seal

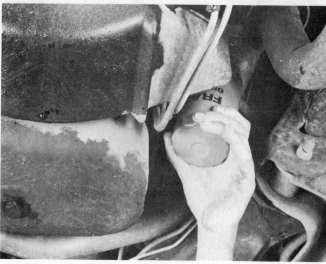

4.20 Tighten the new filter as instructed by the manufacturer. Most are tightened hand-tight, $\frac{1}{2}$ turn after the filter contacts the pedestal

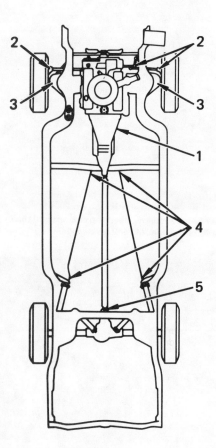

Fig. 1.5 Lubrication points during a normal chassis lubrication (Sec 5)

1	Transmission	4	Parking brake cables
2	Steering	5	Drive shaft U-joint
3	Front suspension		

wrench to fit the drain plug at the bottom of the oil pan; an oil filter wrench to remove the old filter; a container with at least a six-quart capacity to drain the old oil into; and a funnel or oil can spout to help pour fresh oil into the engine.

4   In addition, you should have plenty of clean rags and newspapers handy to mop up any spills. Access to the underside of the car is greatly improved if the car can be lifted on a hoist, driven onto ramps or supported by jack stands. Do not work under a car which is supported only by a bumper, hydraulic or scissors-type jack.

5   If this is your first oil change on the car, it is a good idea to crawl underneath and familiarize yourself with the locations of the oil drain plug and the oil filter. Since the engine and exhaust components will be warm during the actual work, it is best to figure out any potential problems before the car and its accessories are hot.

6   Allow the car to warm up to normal operating temperature. If the new oil or any tools are needed, use this warm-up time to gather everything necessary for the job. The correct type of oil to buy for your application can be found in *Recommended Lubricants* near the front of this manual.

7   With the engine oil warm (warm engine oil will drain better and more built-up sludge will be removed with the oil), raise the vehicle for access beneath. Make sure the car is firmly supported. If jack stands are used they should be placed towards the front of the frame rails which run the length of the car.

8   Move all necessary tools, rags and newspaper under the car. Position the drain pan under the drain plug. Keep in mind that the oil will initially flow from the pan with some force, so place the pan accordingly.

9   Being careful not to touch any of the hot exhaust pipe components, use the wrench to remove the drain plug near the bottom of the oil pan (photos). Depending on how hot the oil has become, you may want to wear gloves while unscrewing the plug the final few turns.

10   Allow the old oil to drain into the pan. It may be necessary to move the pan further under the engine as the oil flow reduces to a trickle.

11   After all the oil has drained, clean the drain plug thoroughly with a clean rag (photo). Small metal filings may cling to this plug which could immediately contaminate your new oil.

12   Clean the area around the drain plug opening and reinstall the drain plug (photo). Tighten the plug securely with your wrench. If a torque wrench is available, the torque setting is 20 ft-lb.

13   Move the drain pan in position under the oil filter.

14   Now use the filter wrench to loosen the oil filter (photo). Chain or metal band-type filter wrenches may distort the filter canister, but don't worry too much about this as the filter will be discarded anyway.

15   Sometimes the oil filter is on so tight it cannot be loosened, or it is positioned in an area which is inaccessible with a filter wrench. As a last resort, you can punch a metal bar or long screwdriver directly through the bottom of the canister and use this as a T-bar to turn the filter. If this must be done, be prepared for oil to spurt out of the canister as it is punctured.

16 Completely unscrew the old filter. Be careful, it is full of oil. Empty the old oil inside the filter into the dran pan.

17 Compare the old filter with the new one to make sure they are of the same type.

18 Use a clean rag to remove all oil, dirt and sludge from the area where the oil filter mounts to the engine (photo). Check the old filter to make sure the rubber gasket is not stuck to the engine mounting surface. If this gasket is stuck to the engine (use a flashlight if necessary), remove it.

19 Open one of the cans of new oil and fill the new filter with fresh oil. Also smear a light coat of this fresh oil onto the rubber gasket of the new oil filter (photo).

20 Screw the new filter to the engine following the tightening directions printed on the filter canister or packing box (photo). Most filter manufacturers recommend against using a filter wrench due to possible overtightening or damage to the canister.

21 Remove all tools, rags, etc. from under the car, being careful not to spill the oil in the drain pan. Lower the car off its support devices.

22 Move to the engine compartment and locate the oil filler cap on the engine. In most cases there will be a screw-off cap on the rocker arm cover (at the side of the engine) or a cap at the end of a fill tube at the front of the engine. In any case, the cap will most likely be labeled 'Engine Oil' or something similar.

23 If an oil can spout is used, push the spout into the top of the oil can and pour the fresh oil through the filler opening. A funnel placed into the opening may also be used.

24 Pour about 3 qts. of fresh oil into the engine. Wait a few minutes to allow the oil to drain to the pan, then check the level on the oil dipstick (see Section 2 if necessary). If the oil level is at or near the lower 'Add' mark, start the engine and allow the new oil to circulate.

25 Run the engine for only about a minute and then shut it off. Immediately look under the car and check for leaks at the oil pan drain plug and around the oil filter. If either is leaking, tighten with a bit more force.

26 With the new oil circulated and the filter now completely full, recheck the level on the dipstick and add enough oil to bring the level to the 'Full' mark on the dipstick.

27 During the first few trips after an oil change, make a point to check for leaks and also the oil level.

28 The old oil drained from the engine cannot be reused in its present state and should be disposed of. Oil reclamation centers, auto repair shops and gas stations will normally accept the oil which can be refined and used again. After the oil has cooled, it can be drained into a suitable container (capped plastic jugs, topped bottles, milk cartons, etc.) for transport to one of these disposal sites.

5 Chassis lubrication

1 A grease gun and a cartridge filled with the proper grease (see Recommended Lubricants) are usually the only equipment necessary to lubricate the chassis components. Occasionally on later model vehicles, plugs will be installed rather than grease fittings, in which case grease fittings will have to be purchased and installed.

2 Carefully look over Fig. 1.5 which shows where the various grease fittings are located. Look under the car to find these components and ascertain if grease fittings or solid plugs are installed. If there are plugs, remove them with the correct wrench and buy grease fittings which will thread into the component. A GM dealer or auto parts store will be able to find replacement fittings. Straight, as well as angled, fittings are available for easy greasing.

3 For easier access under the car, raise the vehicle with a jack and place jack stands under the frame. Make sure the car is firmly supported by the stands.

4 Before you do any greasing, force a little of the grease out the nozzle to remove any dirt from the end of the gun. Wipe the nozzle clean with a rag.

5 With the grease gun, plenty of clean rags and the location diagram, go under the car to begin lubricating the components.

6 Wipe the grease fitting nipple clean and push the nozzle firmly over the fitting nipple. Squeeze the trigger on the grease gun to force grease into the component (photo).

Note: The balljoints (one upper and one lower for each wheel) should be lubricated until the rubber reservoir is firm to the touch (photo). Do not pump too much grease into these fittings as this could rupture the

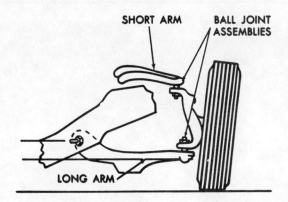

Fig. 1.6 Location of suspension balljoints (Sec 5)

reservoir. For all other suspension and steering fittings, continue pumping grease into the nipple until grease seeps out of the joint between the two components. If the grease seeps out around the grease gun nozzle, the nipple is clogged or the nozzle is not fully seated around the fitting nipple. Re-secure the gun nozzle to the fitting and try again. If necessary, replace the fitting.

7 Wipe the excess grease from the components and the grease fitting. Follow these procedures for the remaining fittings.

8 Check the universal joints on the driveshaft; some have fittings, some are factory sealed. About two pumps is all that is required for grease type universal joints. While you are under the car, clean and lubricate the parking brake cable along with its cable guides and levers. This can be done by smearing some of the chassis grease onto the cable and its related parts with your fingers. Place a few drops of light engine oil on the transmission shifting linkage rods and swivels.

9 Lower the car to the ground for the remaining body lubrication process.

10 Open the hood and smear a little chassis grease on the hood latch mechanism. If the hood has an inside release, have an assistant pull the release knob from inside the car as you lubricate the cable at the latch.

11 Lubricate all the hinges (door, hood, trunk) with a few drops of light engine oil to keep them in proper working order.

12 Finally, the key lock cylinders can be lubricated with spray-on graphite which is available at auto parts stores.

6 Cooling system check

1 Many major engine failures can be attributed to a faulty cooling system. If equipped with an automatic transmission, the cooling system also plays an integral role in transmission longevity.

2 The cooling system should be checked with the engine cold. Do this before the car is driven for the day or after it has been shut off for one or two hours.

3 Remove the radiator cap and thoroughly clean the cap (inside and out) with clean water (photo). Also clean the filler neck on the radiator. All traces of corrosion should be removed.

4 Carefully check the upper and lower radiator hoses along with the smaller diameter heater hoses. Inspect their entire length, replacing any hose which is cracked, swollen or shows signs of deterioration. Cracks may become more apparent if the hose is squeezed (photos).

5 Also check that all hose connections are tight. A leak in the cooling system will usually show up as white or rust colored deposits on the areas adjoining the leak.

6 Use compressed air or a soft brush to remove bugs, leaves, etc. from the front of the radiator or air conditioning condensor. Be careful not to damage the delicate cooling fins, or cut yourself on the sharp fins.

7 Finally, have the cap and system tested for proper pressure. If you do not have a pressure tester, most gas stations and repair shops wil do this for a minimal charge.

5.6A Pumping grease into one of the steering system grease fittings

5.6B The balljoints (upper balljoint shown) should not be over-greased

6.3 Inspecting the radiator pressure cap

6.4A Checking the upper radiator hose for cracks by squeezing it

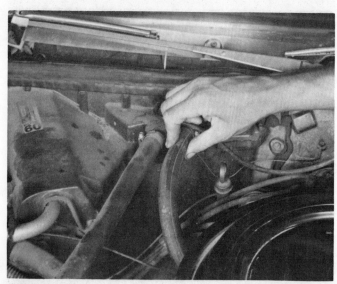

6.4B The heater hoses should also be inspected

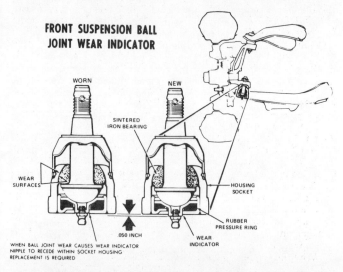

Fig. 1.7 Ball joint wear indicators used on 1974 – 1980 models
(Sec 8)

7 Exhaust system check

1 With the exhaust system cold (at least three hours after being driven), check the complete exhaust system from its starting point at the engine to the end of the tailpipe. This is best done on a hoist where full access is available.

2 Check the pipes and their connections for signs of leakage and/or corrosion indicating a potential failure. Check that all brackets and hangers are in good condition and are tight (photo).

3 At the same time, inspect the underside of the body for holes, corrosion, open seams, etc. which may allow exhaust gases to enter the trunk or passenger compartment. Seal all body openings with silicone or body putty.

4 Rattles and other driving noises can often be traced to the exhaust system, especially the mounts and hangers. Try to move the pipes, muffler and catalytic converter (if equipped). If the components can come into contact with the body or driveline parts, secure the exhaust system with new mountings.

5 This is also an ideal time to check the running condition of the engine by inspecting the very end of the tailpipe. The exhaust deposits here are an indication of engine tune. If the pipe is black and sooty (photo), or bright white deposits are found here, the engine is in need of a tune-up including a thorough carburetor inspection and adjustment.

8 Suspension and steering check

1 Whenever the front of the car is raised for service it is a good idea to visually check the suspension and steering components for wear.

2 Indications of a fault in these systems are: excessive play in the steering wheel before the front wheels react; excessive sway around corners or body movement over rough roads; binding at some point as the steering wheel is turned.

3 Before the car is raised for inspection, test the shock absorbers by pushing downward to rock the car at each corner. If you push the car down and it does not come back to a level position within one or two bounces, the shocks are worn and need to be replaced. As this is done, check for squeaks and strange noises from the suspension components. Information on shock absorber and suspension components can be found in Chapter 11.

4 Now raise the front end of the car and support firmly by jack stands placed under the frame rails. Because of the work to be done, make sure the car cannot fall from the stands.

5 Grab the top and bottom of the front tire with your hands and rock the tire/wheel on its spindle. If there is movement of more than 0.005 in, the wheel bearings should be serviced (see Section 24).

6 Crawl under the car and check for loose bolts, broken or disconnected parts and deteriorated rubber bushings (photo) on all suspension and steering components. Look for grease or fluid leaking from around the steering box. Check the power steering hoses and their connections for leaks. Check the balljoints for wear.

7 Have an assistant turn the steering wheel from side to side and check the steering components for free movement, chafing or binding. If the steering does not react with the movement of the steering wheel, try to determine where the slack is located.

9 Engine drive belt check and adjustment

1 The drive belts, or V-belts as they are sometimes called, at the front of the engine play an important role in the overall operation of the car and its components. Due to their function and material make-up, the belts are prone to failure after a period of time and should be inspected and adjusted periodically to prevent major engine damage.

2 The number of belts used on a particular car depends on the accessories installed. Drive belts are used to turn: the generator (alternator); A.I.R. smog pump; power steering pump; water pump; fan; and air conditioning compressor. Depending on the pulley arrangement, a single belt may be used for more than one of these ancillary components.

3 With the engine off, open the hood and locate the various belts at the front of the engine. Using your fingers (and a flashlight if necessary), move along the belts checking for cracks or separation. Also check for fraying and for glazing which gives the belt a shiny

appearance. Both sides of the belts should be inspected, which means you will have to twist the belt to check the underside.

4 The tension of each belt is checked by pushing on the belt at a distance halfway between the pulleys. Push firmly with your thumb and see how much the belt moves downward (deflects) (photo). A rule of thumb, so to speak, is that if the distance (pulley center to pulley center) is between 7 inches and 11 inches the belt should deflect $\frac{1}{4}$ inch. If the belt is longer and travels between pulleys spaced 12 inches to 16 inches apart, the belt should deflect $\frac{1}{2}$ inch.

5 If it is found necessary to adjust the belt tension, either to make the belt tighter or looser, this is done by moving the belt-driven accessory on its bracket.

6 For each component there will be an adjustment or strap bolt and a pivot bolt. Both bolts must be loosened slightly to enable you to move the component (photo).

7 After the two bolts have been loosened, move the component away from the engine (to tighten the belt) or toward the engine (to loosen the belt) (photo). Hold the accessory in this position and check the belt tension. If it is correct, tighten the two bolts until snug, then recheck the tension. If it is alright, fully tighten the two bolts.

8 It will often be necessary to use some sort of pry bar to move the accessory while the belt is adjusted. If this must be done to gain the proper leverage, be very careful not to damage the component being moved, or the part being pried against.

10 Fuel system check

1 There are certain precautions to take when inspecting or servicing the fuel system components. Work in a well ventilated area and do not allow open flames (cigarettes, appliance pilot lights, etc.) to get near the work area. Mop up spills immediately and do not store fuel-soaked rags where they could ignite.

2 The fuel system is under some amount of pressure, so if any fuel lines are disconnected for servicing, be prepared to catch the fuel as it spurts out. Plug all disconnected fuel lines immediately after disconnection to prevent the tank from emptying itself.

3 The fuel system is most easily checked with the car raised on a hoist where the components under the car are readily visible and accessible.

4 If the smell of gasoline is noticed while driving, or after the car has sat in the sun, the system should be thoroughly inspected immediately.

5 Remove the gas filler cap and check for damage, corrosion and a proper sealing imprint on the gasket. Replace the cap with a new one if necessary.

6 With the car raised, inspect the gas tank and filler neck for punctures, cracks or any damage. The connection between the filler neck and the tank is especially critical. Sometimes a rubber filler neck will leak due to loose clamps or deteriorated rubber; problems a home mechanic can usually rectify.

7 Do not under any circumstances try to repair a fuel tank yourself (except rubber components) unless you have considerable experience. A welding torch or any open flame can easily cause the fuel vapors to explode if the proper precautions are not taken.

8 Carefully check all rubber hoses and metal lines leading away from the fuel tank. Check for loose connections, deteriorated hose, crimped lines or damage of any kind. Follow these lines up to the front of the car, carefully inspecting them all the way. Repair or replace damaged sections as necessary.

9 If a fuel odor is still evident after the inspection, refer to Section 31 on the evaporative emissions system and Section 16 for carburetor adjustment.

11 Positive Crankcase Ventilation (PCV) valve replacement

1 The PCV valve can usually be found pushed into one of the rocker arm covers at the side of the engine. There will be a hose connected to the valve which runs to either the carburetor or the intake manifold.

2 When purchasing a replacement PCV valve, make sure it is for your particular vehicle, model year and engine size.

3 Pull the valve (with the hose attached) from its rubber grommet in the rocker arm cover (photo).

4 Using pliers or a screwdriver, depending on the type of clamp, loosen the clamp at the end of the hose and move the clamp upwards on the PCV hose (photo).

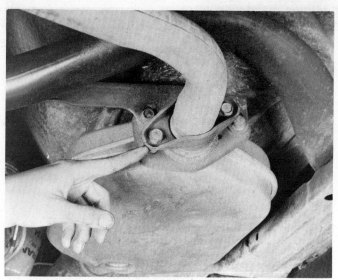

7.2 All exhaust system flanges and their connections should be inspected for signs of leakage

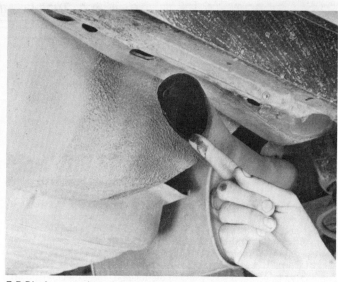

7.5 Black, sooty deposits at the end of the exhaust pipe may be an indcation that the carburetor needs adjustment or the engine is in need of a tune-up

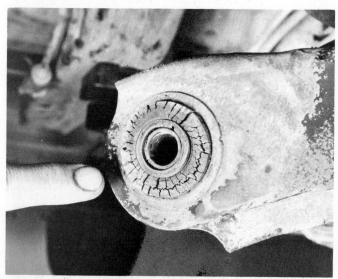

8.6 Rubber bushings in the steering and suspension systems will deteriorate and crack after a time, indicating replacement Is necessary

9.4 Testing the deflection of a drivebelt by pushing at the center with a finger

9.6 Nearly all belt-driven components have a pivot bolt (top) and a strap or adjusting bolt (near bottom of alternator shown)

9.7 Adjusting the belt tension by gently prying on the component as the adjustment bolt is tightened

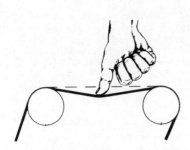

Fig. 1.8 Checking engine drivebelt tension (Sec 9)

7 in (178 mm) to 11 in (280 mm) ¼ in (64 mm) deflection
12 in (305 mm) to 16 in (406 mm) ½ in (12.7 mm) deflection

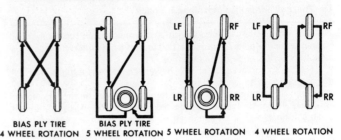

Fig. 1.9 Tire rotation diagram depending on tire type and number of tires being rotated (Sec 14)

5 Now pull the PCV valve from the end of the hose, noting its installed position and direction (photo).
6 Compare the old valve with the new one to make sure they are the same.
7 Push the new valve into the end of the hose until it is fully seated.
8 Move the hose clamp down the hose and tighten the clamp securely around the end of the hose.
9 Inspect the rubber grommet in the cover for damage and replace it with a new one if faulty.
10 Push the PCV valve and hose securely into the rocker arm cover.
11 More information on the PCV system can be found in Chapter 6.

12 Air filter and PCV filter replacement

1 At the specified intervals, the air filter and PCV filter should be replaced with new ones. A thorough program of preventative maintenance would call for the two filters to be inspected periodically between changes.
2 The air filter is located inside the air cleaner housing on the top of the engine. To remove the filter, unscrew the wing nut at the top of the air cleaner and lift off the top plate (photo). If there are vacuum hoses connected to this plate, note their positions and disconnect them.
3 While the top plate is off, be careful not to drop anything down into the carburetor.
4 Lift the air filter out of the housing (photo).
5 To check the filter, hold it up to strong sunlight, or place a flashlight or droplight on the inside of the ring-shaped filter (photo). If you can see light coming through the paper element, the filter is alright. Check all the way around the filter.
6 Wipe the inside of the air cleaner clean with a rag (photo).
7 Place the old filter (if in good condition) or the new filter (if specified interval has elapsed) back into the air cleaner housing. Make sure it seats properly in the bottom of the housing.
8 Connect any disconnected vacuum hoses to the top plate and reinstall the top plate with the wing nut.
9 On nearly all cars the PCV filter is also located inside the air cleaner housing. Remove the top plate as described previously and locate the filter on the side of the housing.
10 Loosen the hose clamp at the end of the PCV hose leading to the filter. Disconnect the hose from the filter.
11 Remove the metal locking clip which secures the filter holder to the air cleaner housing. Pliers can be used for this.
12 Remove the filter and plastic holder from the inside of the air cleaner (photo).
13 Compare the new filter with the old one to make sure they are the same.
14 Place the new filter assembly into position and install the metal locking clip on the outside of the air cleaner.
15 Connect the PCV hose and tighten the clamp around the end of the hose.
16 Reinstall the air cleaner top plate and any vacuum hoses which were disconnected.
17 A few engines will not have the PCV filter at the air cleaner, but rather the filter will be in the PCV hose at some point. To locate the

filter, find the hose leading into the side of the air cleaner housing and follow this hose to the filter.
18 Replacing 'in-line' PCV filters is usually a simple matter of disconnecting the hose from the filter and then pushing a replacement filter into the hose.
19 For more information on these filters and the systems they are a part of, see Chapter 4 and Chapter 6.

13 Clutch pedal free travel check

1 If equipped with a manual shift transmission, it is important to have the clutch free play at the proper point. Basically, free play at the clutch pedal is the point at which time the clutch components engage and the car starts moving. When the pedal is pushed all the way to the floor, the clutch parts are disengaged and the car doesn't travel. As the pedal travels away from the floor, the parts engage and the vehicle is set into motion. It is the measured distance which the pedal moves between these two points which indicates free travel.
2 With the car on a level surface, turn on the engine and allow it to idle. Apply the parking brake to prevent the car from moving.
3 Depress the clutch pedal until it is approximately ½ inch from the floor mat or carpeting.
4 Hold the pedal in this position and move the shift lever between first and reverse gears several times. If this can be done smoothly, the clutch is fully releasing and no adjustment is necessary. If the shift is not smooth, the clutch pedal free play should be adjusted.
5 If adjustment is necessary, refer to Chapter 8 for the step-by-step sequence to follow.

14 Tire rotation

1 The tires should be rotated at the specified intervals and whenever uneven wear is noticed. Since the car will be raised and the tires removed anyway, this is a good time to check the brakes (Section 26) and/or repack the wheel bearings (Section 24). Read over these sections if this is to be done at the same time.
2 The location for each tire in the rotation sequence depends on the type of tire used on your car. Tire type can be determined by reading the raised printing on the sidewall of the tire. Fig. 1.9 shows the rotation sequence for each type of tire.
3 See the information in *Jacking and Towing* at the front of this manual for the proper procedures to follow in raising the car and changing a tire; however, if the brakes are to be checked do not apply the parking brake as stated. Make sure the tires are blocked to prevent the car from rolling.
4 Preferably, the entire car should be raised at the same time. This can be done on a hoist or by jacking up each corner of the car and then lowering the car onto jack stands placed under the frame rails. Always use four jack stands and make sure the car is firmly supported all around.
5 After rotation, check and adjust the tire pressures as necessary and be sure to check wheel nut tightness.

15 Thermo controlled air cleaner check

1　All models are equipped with a thermostatically controlled air cleaner which draws air to the carburetor from different locations depending upon engine temperature.
2　This is a simple visual check; however, if access is tight, a small mirror may have to be used.
3　Open the hood and find the vacuum flapper door on the air cleaner assembly. It wil be located inside the long 'snorkel' of the metal air cleaner. Check that the flexible air hose(s) are securely attached and are not damaged.
4　If there is a flexible air duct attached to the end of the snorkel, leading to an area behind the grille, disconnect it at the snorkel. This will enable you to look through the end of the snorkel and see the flapper door inside (photo).
5　The testing should preferably be done when the engine and outside air are cold. Start the engine and look through the snorkel at the flapper door which should move to a closed position. With the door closed, air cannot enter through the end of the snorkel, but rather air enters the air cleaner through the flexible duct attached to the exhaust manifold.
6　As the engine warms up to operating temperature, the door should open to allow air through the snorkel end. Depending on ambient temperature, this may take 10 to 15 minutes. To speed up this check you can reconnect the snorkel air duct, drive the car and then check that the door is fully open.
7　If the thermo controlled air cleaner is not operating properly, see Chapter 6 for more information.

16 Engine idle speed adjustment

1　Engine idle speed is the speed at which the engine operates when no accelerator pedal pressure is applied. This speed is critical to the performance of the engine itself, as well as many engine sub-systems.
2　A hand-held tachometer must be used when adjusting idle speed to get an accurate reading (photo). The exact hook-up for these meters varies with the manufacturer, so follow the particular directions included.
3　Since GM used many different carburetors for their vehicles in the time period covered by this book, and each has its own peculiarities when setting idle speed, it would be impractical to cover all types in this Section. Chapter 4 contains information on each individual carburetor used. The carburetor used on your particular engine can be found in the Specifications Section of Chapter 4. However, all vehicles covered in this manual should have a tune-up decal in the engine compartment, usually placed near the top of the radiator (photo). The printed instructions for setting idle speed can be found on this decal, and should be followed since they are for your particular engine.
4　Basically, for most applications, the idle speed is set by turning an adjustment screw located at the side of the carburetor (photo). This screw changes the linkage, in essence, depressing or letting up on your accelerator pedal. This screw may be on the linkage itself or may be part of the idle stop solenoid. Refer to the tune-up decal or Chapter 4.
5　Once you have found the idle screw, experiment with different length screwdrivers until the adjustments can be easily made, without coming into contact with hot or moving engine components.
6　Follow the instructions on the tune-up decal or in Chapter 4, which will probably include disconnecting certain vacuum or electrical connections. To plug a vacuum hose after disconnecting it, insert a properly-sized metal rod into the opening, or thoroughly wrap the open end with tape to prevent any vacuum loss through the hose.
7　If the air cleaner is removed, the vacuum hose to the snorkel should be plugged.
8　Make sure the parking brake is firmly set and the wheels blocked to prevent the car from rolling. This is especially true if the transmission is to be in 'Drive'. An assistant inside the car pushing on the brake pedal is the safest method.
9　For all applications, the engine must be completely warmed-up to operating temperature, which will automatically render the choke fast idle inoperative.

17 EFE system (heat riser) check

1　The heat riser (used until around 1975) and the Early Fuel Evaporation (EFE) system both perform the same job, but function in

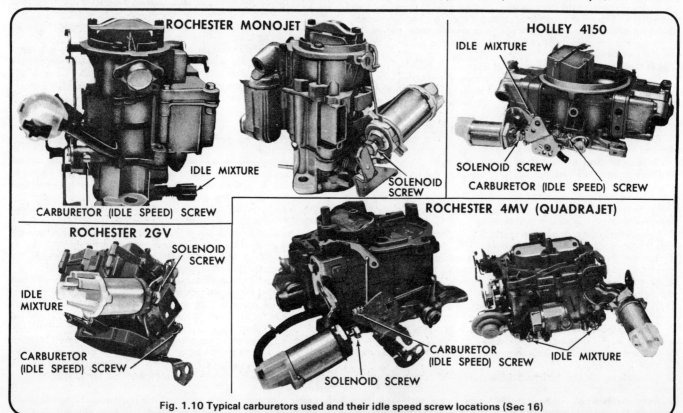

Fig. 1.10 Typical carburetors used and their idle speed screw locations (Sec 16)

11.3 Pulling the PCV valve and hose from the rocker arm cover

11.4 Pliers are used to release the hose clamp and slide it away from the valve

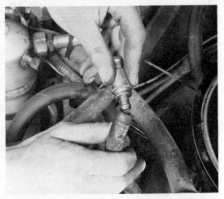

11.5 Pulling the PCV valve out of the end of the hose. Note its direction as this is done

12.2 Removing the wing nut at the top of the air cleaner assembly

12.4 With the top plate set aside, the air filter can be lifted out of the housing

12.5 If light can be easily seen through the filter element, the filter can be reused. If in doubt, replace the filter with a new one.

12.6 Before installing the filter, thoroughly clean the interior of the housing

12.12 The PCV filter on most vehicles is located inside the air cleaner housing

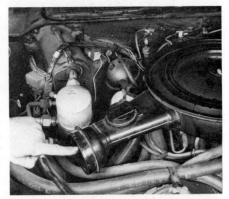

15.4 The operation of the damper door can be seen through the end of the air cleaner snorkel tube

16.2 A reliable hand-held tachometer is necessary for idle speed adjustment

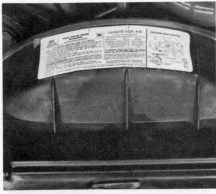

16.3 A typical tune-up decal giving valuable information specific to your engine

16.4 The carburetor idle speed screw located on the left side of the carburetor. Arrow points to electrically-operated idle solenoid

a slightly different manner.

2   The heat riser is a valve located inside the right side exhaust pipe, near the junction bewteen exhaust manifold and pipe. It can be identified by an external weight and spring.

3   With the engine and exhaust pipe cold, try moving the weight by hand. It should move freely.

4   Again with the engine cold, start the engine and observe the heat riser. Upon starting, the weight should move to the closed position. As the engine warms to normal operating temperature, the weight should move the valve to the open position, allowing a free flow of exhaust through the tailpipe. Since it could take several minutes for the system to heat up, you could mark the 'cold' weight position, drive the car, and then recheck the weight.

5   The EFE system also blocks off exhaust flow when the engine is cold. However, this system uses more precise temperature sensors and vacuum to open and close the exhaust pipe valve.

6   Locate the EFE actuator which is bolted to a bracket on the right side of the engine (photo). It will have an actuating rod attached to it which will lead down to the valve inside the pipe. In some cases the entire mechanism, including actuator, will be located at the exhaust pipe-to-manifold junction.

7   With the engine cold, have an assistant start the engine as you observe the actuating rod. It should immediately move to close off the valve. Continue observing the rod, which should slowly open the valve as the engine warms. This process may take some time, so you might want to mark the position of the rod when the valve is closed, drive the car to reach normal operating temperature, then open the hood and check that the rod has moved to the open position.

8   Further information and testing procedures can be found in Chapter 6.

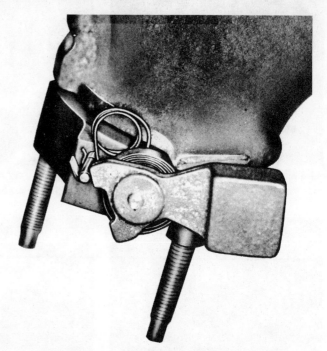

Fig. 1.11 The heat riser valve located at the connection between the exhaust manifold and the exhaust pipe (Sec 17)

18 Fuel filter replacement

1   On all GM cars, the fuel filter is located inside the fuel inlet to the carburetor (photo). It is made of pleated paper (later models) or bronze (early models). Neither type can be cleaned and reused.

2   This job should be done with the engine cold (after sitting at least three hours). The necessary tools are open end wrenches to fit the fuel line nuts. Flare nut wrenches which wrap around the nut should be used if available. In addition you will need to gather together the replacement filter (make sure it is for your specific vehicle and engine), and clean rags.

3   Remove the air cleaner assembly. If vacuum hoses must be disconnected, make sure you note their positions and/or tag them to help during the reassembly process (photo).

4   Now follow the fuel hose from the fuel pump to the point where it enters the carburetor. The fuel pump is located low on the engine, at the right front. In most cases the fuel line will be metal all the way from the pump to the carburetor.

5   Place some rags under the fuel inlet fittings to catch any fuel as the fittings are disconnected.

6   With the proper size wrench, hold the nut immediately next to the carburetor body. Now loosen the nut-fitting and the end of the metal fuel line (photo). A flare nut wrench on this fitting will help prevent slipping and possible damage. However, an open-end wrench should do the job. Make sure the larger nut next to the carburetor is held firmly while the fuel line is disconnected.

7   With the fuel line disconnected, move it slightly for better access to the inlet filter nut. Do not crimp the fuel line.

8   Now unscrew the fuel inlet filter nut which was previously held steady. As this fitting is drawn away from the carburetor body, be careful not to lose the thin washer-type gasket or the spring located behind the fuel filter. Also, pay close attention to how the filter was installed (photos).

9   Compare the old filter with the new one to make sure they are of the same length and design.

10   Reinstall the spring into the carburetor body, after inspecting it for damage or defects.

11   Place the new filter into position behind the spring. If a bronze, cone-shaped filter is used, the smaller end of the cone points away from the carburetor. The later model paper filters will have a rubber gasket and check valve at one end which should point away from the carburetor (photo).

12   Install a new washer-type gasket on the fuel inlet filter nut (a gasket is usually supplied with the new filter) and tighten the nut into

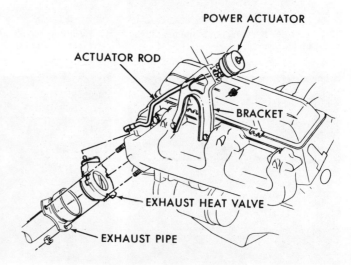

Fig. 1.12 The EFE system used to replace the heat riser for 1975 – 1980 vehicles (Sec 17)

the carburetor. Make sure it is not cross-threaded. Tighten securely, and if a torque wrench is available, tighten the nut to 18 ft-lbs. Do not over-tighten, as this area can strip easily, causing fuel leaks.

13   Hold the fuel inlet nut securely with a wrench while the fuel line is connected. Again, be careful not to cross-thread the connector. Tighten securely.

14   Plug the vacuum hose which leads to the air cleaner snorkel motor so the engine can be run.

15   Start the engine and check carefully for leaks. If the fuel line connector leaks, disconnect it using the above procedures and check for stripped or damaged threads. If the fuel line connector has stripped threads, remove the entire line and have a repair shop install a new fitting. If the threads look alright, purchase some thread sealing tape and tightly wrap the connector threads with the tape. Now reinstall and tighten securely. Inlet repair kits are available at most auto parts stores to overcome leaking at the fuel inlet filter nut.

16   Reinstall the air cleaner assembly, connecting all hoses to their original positions.

17.6 The EFE actuator located on the right side of the engine

18.1 The fuel filter is located inside the fuel inlet

18.3 Whenever the air cleaner is removed make sure the positions of all vacuum hoses are noted for easy reassembly

18.6 Two wrenches are required to loosen the fuel inlet connectors

18.8A Withdrawing the fuel inlet fitting and filter assembly

18.8B Make sure the filter spring is properly positioned

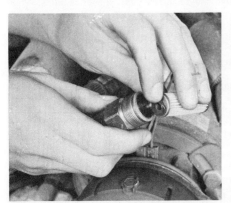

18.11 Most paper element fuel filters have a rubber gasket which should be installed away from the carburetor

19.6 A typical timing tag attached to the engine front cover. As shown here, the timing is set to 4° advanced

19.10 Pointing the timing light at the marks at the front of the engine

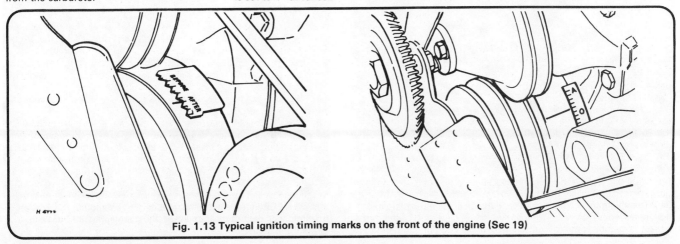

Fig. 1.13 Typical ignition timing marks on the front of the engine (Sec 19)

19 Ignition timing – adjustment

1   All vehicles are equipped with a tune-up decal inside the engine compartment. This decal gives important ignition timing settings and procedures to be followed specific to that vehicle. If information on the tune-up decal supercedes the information given in this Section, the decal should be followed.

2   At the specified intervals, whenever the contact points have been replaced, the distributor removed or a change made in the fuel type, the ignition timing must be checked and adjusted if necessary.

3   Before attempting to check the timing, make sure the contact point dwell angle is correct (Section 30 1970–1974 models only), and the idle speed is as specified (Section 16).

4   Disconnect the vacuum hose from the distributor and plug the now-open end of the hose with a rubber plug, rod or bolt of the proper size. Make sure the idle speed remains correct; adjust as necessary.

5   Connect a timing light in accordance with the manufacturer's instructions. Generally, the light will be connected to power and ground sources and to the number 1 spark plug in some fashion. The number 1 spark plug is the first one on the right as you are facing the engine from the front.

6   Locate the numbered timing tag on the front cover of the engine (photo). It is just behind the lower crankshaft pulley. Clean it off with solvent if necessary to read the printing and small grooves.

7   Locate the notched groove across the crankshaft pulley. It may be necessary to have an assistant temporarily turn the ignition off and on in short bursts without starting the engine to bring this groove into a position where it can easily be cleaned and marked. Stay clear of all moving engine components if the engine is turned over in this manner.

8   Use white soap-stone, chalk or paint to mark the groove on the crankshaft pulley. Also put a mark on the timing tab in accordance with the number of degrees called for in the Specifications (Chapter 5) or on the tune-up decal inside the engine compartment. Each peak or notch on the timing tab represents 2°. The word 'Before' or the letter 'A' indicates advance and the letter 'O' indicates Top Dead Center (TDC). Thus if your vehicle specifications call for 8° BTDC (Before Top Dead Center), you will make a mark on the timing tab 4 notches 'before' the 'O'.

9   Check that the wiring for the timing light is clear of all moving engine components, then start the engine.

10   Point the flashing timing light at the timing marks, again being careful not to come in contact with moving parts (photo). The marks you made should appear stationary. If the marks are in alignment, the timing is correct. If the marks are not aligned, turn off the engine.

11   Loosen the locknut at the base of the distributor. On GM cars this task is made much easier with a special curved distributor wrench. Loosen the locknut only slightly, just enough to turn the distributor. (See Chapter 5 for further details, if necessary).

12   Now restart the engine and turn the distributor until the timing marks coincide.

13   Shut off the engine and tighten the distributor locknut, being careful not to move the distributor.

14   Start the engine and recheck the timing to make sure the marks are still in alignment.

15   Disconnect the timing light, unplug the distributor vacuum hose and connect the hose to the distributor.

16   Drive the car and listen for 'pinging' noises. These will be most noticable when the engine is hot and under load (climbing a hill, accelerating from a stop). If you hear engine pinging, the ignition timing is too far advanced (Before Top Dead Center). Reconnect the timing light and turn the distributor to move the mark 1° or 2° in the retard direction. Road test the car again for proper operation.

17   To keep 'pinging' at a minimum, yet still allow you to operate the car at the specified timing setting, it is advisable to use gasoline of the same octane at all times. Switching fuel brands and octane levels can decrease performance and economy, and possibly damage the engine.

20 Carburetor choke check

1   The choke only operates when the engine is cold, and thus this check can only be performed before the car has been started for the day.

2   Open the hood and remove the top plate of the air cleaner assembly. It is held in place by a wing-nut at the center. If any vacuum hoses must be disconnected, make sure you tag the hoses for reinstallation to their original positions. Place the top plate and wing nut aside, out of the way of moving engine components.

3   Look at the top of the carburetor at the center of the air cleaner housing. You will notice a flat plate at the carburetor opening (photo).

4   Have an assistant press the accelerator pedal to the floor. The plate should close fully. Start the engine while you observe the plate at the carburetor. Do not position your face directly over the carburetor, as the engine could backfire, causing serious burns. When the engine starts, the choke plate should open slightly.

5   Allow the engine to continue running at an idle speed. As the engine warms up to operating temperature, the plate should slowly open, allowing more cold air to enter through the top of the carburetor.

6   After a few minutes, the choke plate should be fully open to the vertical position.

7   You will notice that the engine speed corresponds with the plate opening. With the plate fully closed, the engine should run at a fast idle speed. As the plate opens, the engine speed will decrease.

8   If during the above checks a fault is detected, refer to Chapter 4 for specific information on adjusting and servicing the choke components.

20.3 The choke plate can be seen once the air cleaner top plate has been removed

21.2 The EGR valve is a disc-shaped device mounted to the intake manifold, adjacent to the carburetor. Most are open underneath to check the diaphragm

21 Exhaust Gas Recirculation (EGR) valve check

1   On GM vehicles the EGR valve is located on the intake manifold, adjacent to the carburetor. The majority of the time, when a fault develops in this emissions system it is due to a stuck or corroded EGR valve.

2   With the engine cold to prevent burns, reach under the EGR valve and manually push on the diaphragm (photo). Using moderate pressure, you should be able to press the diaphragm up and down within the housing.

3   If the diaphragm does not move or moves only with much effort, replace the EGR valve with a new one. If you are in doubt about the quality of the valve, go to your local parts store and compare the free movement of your EGR valve with a new valve.

4   Further testing of the EGR system and component replacement procedures can be found in Chapter 6.

22 Rear axle fluid change

1   To change the fluid in the rear axle it is necessary to remove the cover plate on the differential housing. Because of this, purchase a new gasket at the same time the gear lubricant is bought.

2   Move a drain pan (at least 5 pint capacity), rags, newspapers and your wrenches under the rear of the car. With the drain pan under the differential cover, loosen each of the inspection plate bolts.

3   Remove the bolts on the lower half of the plate, but use the upper bolts to keep the cover loosely attached to the differential. Allow the fluid to drain into the drain pan, then completely remove the cover.

4   Using a lint-free rag, clean the inside of the cover and the accessible areas of the differential housing. As this is done, check for chipped gears or metal filings in the fluid indicating the differential should be thoroughly inspected and repaired (see Chapter 8 for more information).

5   Thoroughly clean the gasket mating surface on the cover and the differential housing. Use a gasket scraper or putty knife to remove all traces of the old gasket.

6   Smear a thin film of gasket sealant on the cover flange and then press a new gasket into position on the cover. Make sure the bolt holes align properly.

7   Place the cover on the differential housing and install the securing bolts. Tighten the bolts a little at a time, working across the cover in a diagonal fashion until all bolts are tight. If a torque wrench is available, the bolt torque is 25 to 30 ft-lbs.

8   Remove the inspection plug on the side of the differential housing (or inspection cover) and fill the housing with the proper lubricant until the level is at the bottom of the plug hole.

9   Securely install the plug.

23 Spark plug replacement

1   The spark plugs are located on each side of the engine on a V8 and may or may not be easily accessible for removal. If the car is equipped with air conditioning or power steering, some of the plugs may be tricky to service in which case special extension or swivel tools will be necessary. Make a survey under the hood to ascertain if special tools will be needed.

2   In most cases the tools necessary for a spark plug replacement job are: a plug wrench or spark plug socket which fits onto a ratchet wrench (this special socket will be insulated inside to protect the porcelain insulator) and a feeler gauge to check and adjust the spark plug gap. If the car is equipped with HEI ignition (1975–1980), a special spark plug wire removal tool is available for separating the wire boot from the spark plug.

3   The best policy to follow when replacing the spark plugs is to purchase the new spark plugs beforehand, adjust them to the proper gap and then replace each plug one at a time. When buying the new spark plugs it is important that the correct plug is purchased for your specific engine. This information can be found in the Specifications Section of Chapter 5, but should be checked against the information found on the tune-up decal located under the hood of your car or in the factory owner's manual. If differences exist between these sources, purchase the spark plug type specified on the tune-up decal as this information was printed for your specific engine.

4   With the new spark plugs at hand, allow the engine to thoroughly cool before attempting the removal. During this cooling time, each of the new spark plugs can be inspected for defects and the gap can be checked.

5   The gap is checked by inserting the proper thickness gauge between the electrodes at the tip of the plug. The gap between these electrodes should be the same as that given in the Specifications or on the tune-up decal. The wire should just touch each of the eletrodes. If the gap is incorrect, use the notched adjuster on the feeler gauge body to bend the curved side electrode slightly until the proper gap is achieved. Also at this time check for cracks in the spark plug body, indicating the spark plug should be replaced with a new one. If the side electrode is not exactly over the center one, use the notched adjuster to align the two.

6   Cover the fenders of the car to prevent damage to exterior paint.

7   With the engine cool, remove the spark plug wire from one spark plug. Do this by grabbing the boot at the end of the wire, not the wire itself. Sometimes it is necessary to use a twisting motion while the boot and plug wire is pulled free (photo). Using a plug wire removal tool is the easiest and safest method.

8   If compressed air is available, use this to blow any dirt or foreign material away from the spark plug area. A common bicycle pump will also work. The idea here is to eliminate the possibility of material

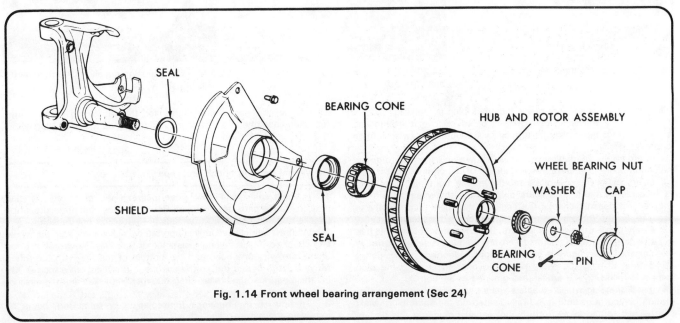

Fig. 1.14 Front wheel bearing arrangement (Sec 24)

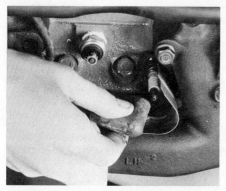

23.7 Removing a spark plug wire by grabbing at the boot rather than the wire itself

23.9A Using an insulated spark plug socket to remove a spark plug

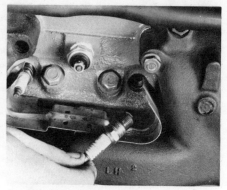

23.9B Use your fingers to loosen and tighten the spark plugs as much as possible to help prevent stripping the threads

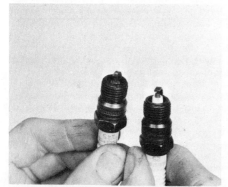

23.10 A worn and deteriorated spark plug on the left and a new one on the right

24.9 The outer wheel bearing and washer removed from the hub

24.11 A screwdriver is used to pry out the grease seal for the inner bearing

24.12 Removing the inner wheel bearing

24.20 Installing a grease-packed wheel bearing inside the hub

24.21 The adjusting nut should be tightened only initially with a wrench

falling into the engine cylinder as the spark plug is replaced.

9   Now place the spark plug wrench or socket over the plug and remove it from the engine by turning in a counter-clockwise motion (photos).

10 Compare the spark plug with those shown on page 147 to get an indication of the overall running condition of the engine (photo).

11 Insert one of the new plugs into the engine, tightening it as much as possible by hand. The spark plug should screw easily into the engine. If it doesn't, change the angle of the spark plug slightly, as chances are the threads are not matched (cross-threaded).

12 Firmly tighten the spark plug with the wrench or socket. It is best to use a torque wrench for this to ensure the plug is seated correctly. The correct torque figure is shown in Specifications.

13 Before pushing the spark plug wire onto the end of the plug, inspect it following the procedures outlined in Section 28.

14 Install the plug wire to the new spark plug, again using a twisting motion on the boot until it is firmly seated on the spark plug. Make sure wire is routed away from the hot exhaust manifold.

15 Follow the above procedures for the remaining spark plugs, replacing each one at a time to prevent mixing up the spark plug wires.

24 Wheel bearing check and repack

1   In most cases, the front wheel bearings will not need servicing until the brake pads are changed. However, these bearings should be checked whenever the front wheels are raised for any reason.

2   With the vehicle securely supported on jack stands, spin the wheel and check for noise, rolling resistance or free play. Now grab the top of the tire with one hand and the bottom of the tire with the other. Move the tire in and out on the spindle. If it moves more than 0.005 in, the bearings should be checked, then repacked with grease or replaced if necessary.

3   To remove the bearings for replacing or repacking, begin by removing the hub cap and wheel.

4   Using an Allen wrench of the proper size, remove the two bolts which secure the disc brake caliper to its support (see Chapter 9).

5   Fabricate a wood block ($1\frac{1}{16}$ inch by $1\frac{1}{16}$ inch by 2 inches in length) which will be slid between the brake pads to keep them separated. Carefully slide the caliper off the disc and insert the wood block between the pads. Use wire to hang the caliper assembly out of the way. Be careful not to kink or damage the brake hose.

6   Pry the hub grease cap off the hub using a screwdriver. This cap is located at the center of the hub.

7   Use needle-nose pliers to straighten the bent ends of the cotter pin and then pull the cotter pin out of the locking nut. Discard the cotter pin, as a new one should be used on reassembly.

8   Remove the spindle nut and its washer from the end of the spindle.

9   Pull the hub assembly outward slightly and then push it back into its original position. This should force the outer bearing off the spindle enough so that it can be removed with your fingers (photo). Remove the outer bearing, noting how it is installed on the end of the spindle.

10   Now the hub assembly can be pulled off the spindle.

11   On the rear side of the hub, use a screwdriver to pry out the inner bearing lip seal (photo). As this is done, note the direction in which the seal is installed.

12   The inner bearing can now be removed from the hub, again noting how it is installed (photo).

13   Use clean parts solvent to remove all traces of the old grease from the bearings, hub and spindle. A small brush may prove useful; however, make sure no bristles from the brush embed themselves inside the bearing rollers. Allow the parts to air dry.

14   Carefully inspect the bearings for cracks, heat discoloration, bent rollers, etc. Check the bearing races inside the hub for cracks, scoring or uneven surfaces. If the bearing races are in need of replacement, this job is best left to a repair shop which can press the new races into position.

15   Use an approved high temperature front wheel bearing grease to pack the bearings. Work the grease fully into the bearings, forcing the grease between the rollers, cone and cage.

16   Apply a thin coat of grease to the spindle at the outer bearing seat, inner bearing seat, shoulder and seal seat.

17   Put a small quantity of grease inboard of each bearing race inside the hub. Using your finger, form a dam at these points to provide extra grease availability and to keep thinned grease from flowing out of the bearing.

18   Place the grease-packed inner bearing into the rear of the hub and put a little more grease outboard of the bearing.

19   Place a new seal over the inner bearing and tap the seal with a flat plate and a hammer until it is flush with the hub.

20   Carefully place the hub assembly onto the spindle and push the grease-packed outer bearing into position (photo).

21   Install the washer and spindle nut. Tighten the nut only slightly (12 ft-lbs of torque) (photo).

22   In a forward direction, spin the hub to seat the bearings and remove any grease or burrs which could cause excessive bearing play later.

23   Put a little grease outboard of the outer bearing to provide extra grease availability.

24   Now check that the spindle nut is still tight (12 ft-lbs).

25   Loosen the spindle nut until it is just loose, no more.

26   Using your hand (not a wrench of any kind), tighten the nut until it is snug. Install a new cotter pin through the hole in the spindle and spindle nut. If the nut slits do not line up, loosen the nut slightly until they do. From the hand-tight position the nut should not be loosened any more than one-half flat to install the cotter pin.

27   Bend the ends of the new cotter pin until they are flat against the nut. Cut off any extra length which could interfere with the dust cap.

28   Install the dust cap, tapping it into place with a rubber mallet.

29   Place the brake caliper near the rotor and carefully remove the wood block spacers. Slide the caliper over the rotor. Tighten the caliper mounting bolts to 35 ft-lbs. Chapter 9 will give full details on the disc brake caliper assembly.

30   Install the tire/wheel assembly to the hub and tighten the mounting nuts.

31   Grab the top and bottom of the tire and check the bearings in the same manner as described at the beginning of this Section.

32   Lower the vehicle to the ground and fully tighten the wheel nuts. Install the hub cap, using a rubber mallet to fully seat it.

25 Automatic transmission fluid change

1   At the specified time intervals, the transmission fluid should be changed and the filter replaced with a new one. Since there is no drain plug, the transmission oil pan must be removed from the bottom of the transmission to drain the fluid.

2   Before any draining, purchase the specified transmission fluid (see *Recommended Lubricants* and a new filter. The necessary gaskets should be included with the filter; if not, purchase an oil pan gasket and a strainer-to-valve body gasket.

3   Other tools necessary for this job include: jack stands to support the vehicle in a raised position; wrench to remove the oil pan bolts; standard screwdriver; drain pan capable of holding at least 8 pints; newspapers and clean rags.

4   The fluid should be drained immediately after the car has been driven. This will remove any built-up sediment better than if the fluid were cold. Because of this, it may be wise to wear protective gloves (fluid temperature can exceed 350° in a hot transmission).

5   After the car has been driven to warm up the fluid, raise the vehicle and place it on jack stands for access underneath. Make sure it is firmly supported by the four stands placed on the frame rails.

6   Move the necessary equipment under the car, being careful not to touch any of the hot exhaust components.

7   Place the drain pan under the transmission oil pan and remove the oil pan bolts along the rear and sides of the pan. Loosen, but do not remove, the bolts at the front of the pan.

8   Carefully pry the pan downward at the rear, allowing the hot fluid to drain into the drain pan (photo). If necessary, use a screwdriver to break the gasket seal at the rear of the pan; however, do not damage the pan or transmission in the process.

9   Support the pan and remove the remaining bolts at the front of the pan. Lower the pan and drain the remaining fluid into the drain receptacle. As this is done, check the fluid for metal filings which may be an indication of internal failure.

10   Now visible on the bottom of the transmission is the filter/strainer held in place by two screws.

11   Remove the two screws, the filter and its gasket (photo).

12   Thoroughly clean the transmission oil pan with solvent. Inspect for metal filings or foreign matter (photo). Dry with compressed air if available. It is important that all remaining gasket material be removed from the oil pan mounting flange. Use a gasket scraper or putty knife for this.

13   Clean the filter mounting surface on the valve body. Again, this surface should be smooth and free of any leftover gasket material.

14   Place the new filter into position, with a new gasket between it and the transmission valve body. Install the two mounting screws and tighten securely (photo).

15   Apply a bead of gasket sealant around the oil pan mounting surface, with the sealant to the inside of the bolt holes. Press the new gasket into place on the pan, making sure all bolt holes line up.

16   Lift the pan up to the bottom of the transmission and install the mounting bolts (photo). Tighten the bolts in a diagonal fashion, working around the pan. Using a torque wrench, tighten the bolts to about 12 ft-lbs.

17   Lower the car off its jack stands.

18   Open the hood and remove the transmission fluid dipstick from its guide tube.

19   Since fluid capacities vary between the various transmission types, it is best to add a little fluid at a time, continually checking the level with the dipstick. Allow the fluid time to drain into the pan. Add fluid until the level just registers on the end of the dipstick. In most cases, a good starting point will be 4 to 5 pints added to the transmission through the filler tube (use a funnel to prevent spills).

20   With the selector lever in 'Park', apply the parking brake and start the engine without depressing the accelerator pedal (if possible). Do not race the engine at a high speed; run at slow idle only.

21   Depress the brake pedal and shift the transmission through each gear. Place the selector back into 'Park' and check the level on the dipstick (with the engine still idling). Look under the car for leaks around the transmission oil pan mating surface.

22   Add more fluid through the dipstick tube until the level on the dipstick is $\frac{1}{4}$ inch below the 'Add' mark on the dipstick. Do not allow the fluid level to go above this point, as the transmission would then be overfull, necessitating the removal of the pan to drain the excess fluid.

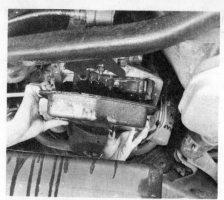
25.8 Dropping the rear end of the transmission oil pan to drain the fluid

25.11 Removing the old filter from the inside of the transmission

25.12 The inside of the fluid pan should be inspected for contamination and metal filings

25.14 Tightening a new filter into position

25.16 The fluid pan with a new gasket in place being lifted into position

26.6 Disc brake calipers have an inspection cutout to observe the disc pads

26/12A Drawing a brake drum off the wheel studs and center axle hub

26.12B Using a hammer and chisel to remove the lanced knock-out plug on the face of the drum

26.12C With the knock-out plug removed, use a small screwdriver or hook to lift the lever, then turn the sprocket with another screwdriver

26.14 Inspecting the lining thickness of the forward brake shoe

26.15 Check that all springs are in good condition

26.16 Leakage often occurs from the wheel cylinder located at the top of the brake shoes

23 Push the dipstick firmly back into its tube and drive the car to reach normal operating temperature (15 miles of highway driving or its equivalent in the city). Park the car on a level surface and check the fluid level on the dipstick with the engine idling and the transmission in 'Park'. The level should now be at the 'Full Hot' mark on the dipstick. If not, add more fluid as necessary to bring the level up to this point. Again, do not overfill.

26 Brakes check

1 The brakes should be inspected every time the wheels are removed or whenever a fault is suspected. Indications of a potential braking system fault are: the car pulls to one side when brake pedal is depressed; noises coming from the brakes when they are applied; excessive brake pedal travel; pulsating pedal; and leakage of fluid, usually seen on the inside of the tire or wheel.

Disc brakes

2 Disc brakes can be visually checked without the need to remove any parts except the wheels.

3 Raise the vehicle and place securely on jack stands. Remove the front wheels (See *Jacking and Towing* at the front of this manual if necessary).

4 Now visible is the disc brake caliper which contains the pads. There is an outer brake pad and an inner pad. Both should be inspected.

5 Most later model vehicles come equipped with a 'wear sensor' attached to the inner pad. This is a small, bent piece of metal which is visible from the inboard side of the brake caliper. When the pads wear to a danger limit, the metal sensor rubs against the disc and makes a screeching sound.

6 Inspect the pad thickness by looking at each end of the caliper and through the cut-out inspection hole in the caliper body (photo). If the wear sensor clip is very close to the rotor, or the lining material is $\frac{1}{32}$ in or less in thickness, the pads should be replaced. Keep in mind that the

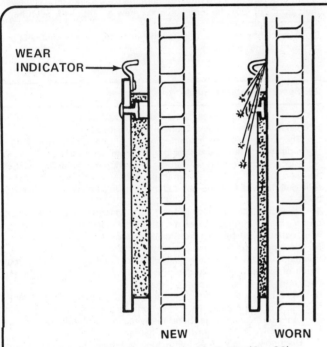

Fig. 1.15 Front disc brake wear indicator (Sec 26)

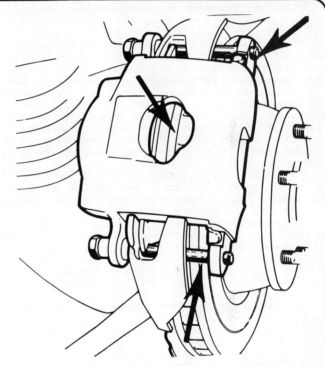

Fig. 1.16 Disc pad wear inspection points (Sec 26)

26.17 The inside surface of the brake drum should be carefully inspected for cracks, scoring, 'hot-spots' etc

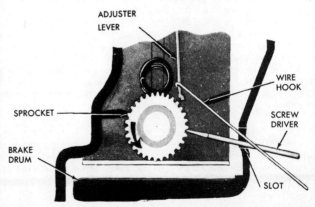

Fig. 1.17 Using a screwdriver and wire hook through the access hole to contract the brake shoes (Sec 26)

lining material is riveted or bonded to a metal backing shoe and the metal portion is not included in this measuring.

7   Since it will be difficult, if not impossible, to measure the exact thickness of the remaining lining material, if you are in doubt as to the pad quality, remove the pads for further inspection or replacement. See Chapter 9 for disc brake pad replacement.

8   Before installing the wheels, check for any leakage around the brake hose connections leading to the caliper or damage (cracking, splitting, etc.) to the brake hose. Replace the hose or fittings as necessary, referring to Chapter 9.

9   Also check the condition of the disc for scoring, gouging or burnt spots. If these conditions exist, the hub/rotor assembly should be removed for servicing (Chapter 9).

Drum brakes (rear)

10   Raise the vehicle and support firmly on jack stands. Block the front tires to prevent the car from rolling; however, do not apply the parking brake as this will lock the drums into place.

11   Remove the wheels, referring to *Jacking and Towing* at the front of this manual if necessary.

12   Mark the hub so it can be reinstalled in the same place. Use a scribe, chalk, etc. on drum and center hub and backing plate.

13   Pull the brake drum off the axle and brake assembly (photo). If this proves difficult, make sure the parking brake is released, then squirt some penetrating oil around the center hub area. Allow the oil to soak in and try again to pull the drum off. Then, if the drum cannot be pulled off, the brake shoes will have to be adjusted inward. This is done by first removing the lanced cutout in the drum or backing plate with a hammer and chisel (photo). With this lanced area punched in, rotate the drum until the opening lines up with the adjuster wheel. Pull the lever off the sprocket and then use a small screwdriver to turn the sprocket wheel which will move the linings away from the drums (photo).

14   With the drum removed, carefully brush away any accumulations of dirt and dust. Do not blow this out with compressed air or in any similar fashion. Make an effort not to inhale this dust as it contains asbestos and is harmful to your health.

15   Observe the thickness of the lining material on both the front and rear brake shoes (photo). If the material has worn away to within $\frac{1}{32}$ in of the recessed rivets or metal backing, the shoes should be replaced. If the linings look worn, but you are unable to determine their exact thickness, compare them with a new set at the auto parts store. The shoes should also be replaced if they are cracked, glazed (shiny surface), or wet with brake fluid.

16   Check that all the brake assembly springs are connected and in good condition (photo).

17   Check the brake components for any signs of fluid leakage. With your finger, carefully pry back the rubber cups on the wheel cylinder located at the top of the brake shoes (photo). Any leakage is an indication that the wheel cylinders should be overhauled immediately (Chapter 9). Also check fluid hoses and connections for signs of leakage.

18   Wipe the inside of the drum with a clean rag, and denatured alcohol. Again, be careful not to breathe the dangerous asbestos dust.

19   Check the inside of the drum for cracks, scores, deep scratches or 'hard spots' which will appear as small discolorations (photo). If these imperfections cannot be removed with fine emery cloth, the drum must be taken to a machine shop equipped to turn the drums.

20   If after the inspection process all parts are in good working condition, reinstall the brake drum (using a metal plug if the lanced knock-out was removed). Install the wheel and lower the car to the ground.

Parking brake

21   The easiest way to check the operation of the parking brake is to park the car on a steep hill, with the parking brake set and the transmission in 'Neutral'. If the parking brake cannot prevent the car from rolling, it is in need of adjustment (see Chapter 9).

27 Carburetor mounting torque

1   The carburetor is attached to the top of the intake manifold by two or four nuts. These fasteners can sometimes work loose through normal engine operation and cause a vacuum leak.

2   To properly tighten the carburetor mounting nuts, a torque wrench is necessary. If you do not own one, they can usually be rented on a daily basis.

3   Remove the air cleaner assembly, tagging each hose to be disconnected with a piece of numbered tape to make reassembly easier.

4   Locate the mounting nuts at the base of the carburetor. Decide what special tools or adapters will be necessary, if any, to tighten the nuts with a properly sized socket and the torque wrench.

5   Tighten the nuts to a torque of about 12 ft-lbs. Do not overtighten the nuts, as this may cause the threads to strip.

6   If you suspect a vacuum leak exists at the bottom of the carburetor, get a length of spare hose about the diameter of fuel hose. Start the engine and place one end of the hose next to your ear as you probe around the base of the carburetor with the other end. You will be able to hear a hissing sound if a leak exists. A soapy water solution brushed around the suspect area can also be used to pinpoint pressure leaks.

7   If, after the nuts are properly tightened, a vacuum leak still exists, the carburetor must be removed and a new gasket used. See Chapter 4 for more information.

8   After tightening nuts, reinstall the air cleaner, connecting all hoses to their original positions.

28 Spark plug wires check

1   The spark plug wires should be checked at the recommended intervals or whenever new spark plugs are installed.

2   The wires should be inspected one at a time to prevent mixing up the order which is essential for proper engine operation.

3   Disconnect the plug wire from the spark plug. A removal tool can be used for this, or you can grab the rubber boot, twist slightly and then pull the wire free. Do not pull on the wire itself, only on the rubber boot.

4   Inspect inside the boot for corrosion which will look like a white, crusty powder (photo). Later models use a conductive white grease which should not be mistaken for corrosion.

5   Now push the wire and boot back onto the end of the spark plug. It should be a tight fit on the plug end. If not, remove the wire and use a pair of pliers to carefully crimp the metal connector inside the wire boot until the fit is secure.

6   Now using a clean rag, clean the wire its entire length. Remove all built-up dirt and grease. As this is done, inspect for burns, cracks or any other form of damage. Bend the wires in several places to ensure the conductive inside wire has not hardened.

7   Disconnect the wire at the distributor (again, pulling and twisting only on the rubber boot). Check for corrosion and a tight fit in the same manner as the spark plug end. If equipped with HEI ignition (1975 and later), the distributor boots are connected to a circular retaining ring. Release the locking tabs, turn the ring upside-down and check all wire boots at the same time.

8   Reinstall the wire boot (or retaining ring) onto the top of the distributor.

9   Check the remaining spark plug wires in the same way, making sure they are securely fastened at the distributor and spark plug.

10   A visual check of the spark plug wires can also be made. In a darkened garage (make sure there is ventilation), start the engine and observe each plug wire. Be careful not to come into contact with any moving engine parts. If there is a break or fault in the wire, you will be able to see arcing or a small spark at the damaged area.

11   If it is decided the spark plug wires are in need of replacement, purchase a new set for your specific engine model. Wire sets can be purchased which are pre-cut to the proper size and with the rubber boots already installed. HEI ignition systems (1975–1980) use a different type of plug wire from conventional systems. Remove and replace each wire individually to prevent mix-ups in the firing sequence.

29 Cooling system servicing (draining, flushing and refilling)

1   Periodically, the cooling system should be drained, flushed and refilled. This is to replenish the antifreeze mixture and prevent rust and corrosion which can impair the performance of the cooling system and

28.4 Inspecting the inside of a spark plug boot

29.7 Engine drain plugs are located on each side of the engine block

29.14 Using a funnel to add coolant to the reservoir

ultimately cause engine damage.

2   At the same time the cooling system is serviced, all hoses and the fill cap should be inspected and replaced if faulty (see Section 6).

3   As antifreeze is a poisonous solution, take care not to spill any of the cooling mixture on the vehicle's paint or your own skin. If this happens, rinse immediately with plenty of clear water. Also, it is advisable to consult your local authorities about the dumping of antifreeze before draining the cooling system. In many areas reclamation centers have been set up to collect automobile oil and drained antifreeze/water mixtures rather than allowing these liquids to be added to the sewage and water facilities.

4   With the engine cold, remove the radiator pressure fill cap.

5   Move a large container under the radiator to catch the water/antifreeze mixture as it is drained.

6   Drain the radiator. Most models are equipped with a drain plug at the bottom of the radiator which can be opened using a wrench to hold the fitting while the petcock is turned to the open position. If this drain has excessive corrosion and cannot be turned easily, or the radiator is not equipped with a drain, disconnect the lower radiator hose to allow the coolant to drain. Be careful that none of the solution is splashed on your skin or in your eyes.

7   If accessible, remove the two engine drain plugs (photo). There is one plug on each side of the engine, about halfway back and on the lower edge near the oil pan rail. These will allow the coolant to drain from the engine itself.

8   On systems with an expansion reservoir, disconnect the overflow pipe and remove the reservoir. Flush it out with clean water.

9   Place a cold water hose (a common garden hose is fine) in the radiator filler neck at the top of the radiator and flush the system until the water runs clean at all drain points.

10 In severe cases of contamination or clogging of the radiator, remove it (see Chapter 3) and reverse flush it. This involves simply inserting the cold pressure hose in the bottom radiator outlet to allow the clear water to run against the normal flow, draining through the top. A radiator repair shop should be consulted if further cleaning or repair is necessary.

11 Where the coolant is regularly drained and the system refilled with the correct antifreeze/inhibitor mixture there should be no need to employ chemical cleaners or descalers.

12 To refill the system, reconnect the radiator hoses and install the drain plugs securely in the engine. Special thread sealing tape (available at auto parts stores) should be used on the drain plugs going into the engine block. Install the expansion reservoir and the overflow hose where applicable.

13 On vehicles without an expansion reservoir, refill the system through the radiator filler cap until the water level is about three inches below the filler neck.

14 On vehicles with an expansion reservoir, fill the radiator to the base of the filler neck and then add more coolant to the expansion reservoir so that it reaches the 'FULL COLD' mark (photo).

15 Run the engine until normal operating temperature is reached and with the engine idling, add coolant up to the correct level (see Section 2), then fit the radiator cap so that the arrows are in alignment with the overflow pipe. Install the reservoir cap.

16 Always refill the system with a mixture of high quality antifreeze and water in the proportion called for on the antifreeze container or in your owner's manual. Chapter 3 also contains information on anti-

freeze mixtures.

17 Keep a close watch on the coolant level and the various cooling hoses during the first few miles of driving. Tighten the hose clamps and/or add more coolant mixture as necessary.

30 Point replacement, dwell angle adjustment and distributor check (1970–1974 models only)

1   Although the contact points can be cleaned and dressed with a fine-cut contact file, it may be a false economy for the home mechanic to attempt this (photo). Due to the inaccessibility of the distributor components, it is more practical to merely replace the contact points during tune-ups.

2   The contact point set and condenser are replaced as one complete assembly. Point alignment and spring tension are factory set and require no further adjustment.

3   Whenever distributor servicing is required, as in contact point replacement, it is a good idea to use magnetized tools to prevent screws or nuts from falling down into the distributor body, requiring distributor disassembly to retrieve.

Contact point replacement

4   Remove the distributor cap by placing a screwdriver on the slotted head of the latch. Press down on the latch and give a $\frac{1}{4}$ turn to release the curved section at the bottom of the latch (photo).

5   With both latches disengaged from the distributor body, place the cap (with the spark plug wires still attached) out of the way. Use a length of wire or tape if necessary.

6   Remove the rotor, which is now visible at the top of the distributor shaft. In most cases the rotor is held in place with two screws. On some models, the rotor is merely pushed onto the shaft and can simply be lifted away. Place the rotor in a safe place where it cannot be damaged (photos).

7   If equipped with a radio frequency interference shield (RFI), remove the attaching screws and the two-piece shield to gain access to the contact points.

8   Loosen the two screws which secure the contact point set assembly to the breaker plate (photo). Do not completely remove these screws, as most point sets have slots at these locations. Slide the point set off the breaker plate.

9   Disconnect the primary and condenser wire leads at the point set (photo). These wires may be attached with a small nut (which should be loosened, but not removed) a small standard screw, or by a quick-disconnect terminal which rquires the tangs to be pressed together to un-lock.

10 The contact breaker point assembly can now be removed completely from the engine compartment.

11 The condenser can now be removed from the breaker plate. Loosen the mounting strap screw and slide the condenser out of the bracket, or completely remove the condenser and strap depending on the exact attachment (photo).

12 Before installing the new points and condenser, clean all lubricant, dirt, etc. from the breaker plate and the rotating cam surface of the distributor shaft.

13 Fully lubricate the center cam with the grease supplied with the

30.1 A set of used contact points showing the deterioration which comes after a time

30.4 Removing the distributor cap from the top of the distributor

30.6A The rotor is attached to the counter-weights

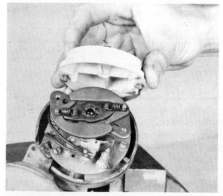

30.6B Removing the rotor which is attached with two screws

30.8 Loosening the two screws which secure the contact point assembly to the mounting plate

30.9 Disconnecting the primary wires from the points

30.11 The condenser is also attached to the breaker plate and is held by a single screw

30.18 Before adjusting the point gap, the rubbing block must be resting on one of the center cam high points (which will open the points)

30.19 With the points separated, insert a feeler gauge of the proper thickness and turn the adjusting socket with an Allen wrench

30.21 The rotor contacts should be inspected for damage or excessive burning

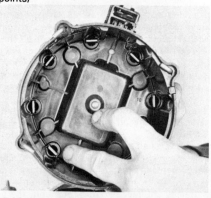

30.23 Inspecting the inside of the distributor cap

30.31 With the 'window' open, an Allen wrench can be inserted into the adjustment socket for adjusting the point dwell

new points.

14 Check the cam lubricator wick mounted on the breaker plate. The wick can be rotated to provide lubrication if it is still in good condition, but if in doubt replace the wick with a new one to provide adequate lubrication to the cam surface. It is removed by squeezing the base of the retainer together with long-nosed pliers and then lifting the unit out of the breaker plate. It is important that the cam lubricator wick be adjusted so the end of the wick just touches the cam lobes.

15 Place the new condenser into position and tighten its retaining screw.

16 Slide the new contact point set onto the breaker plate and tighten the two attaching screws.

17 Connect the primary and condenser electrical leads to the new point assembly. Make sure the leads are postioned the same as they were on removal.

18 Although the final gap between the contact points will be adjusted later (dwell angle), it is best to get an initial gap to start the engine. With the points in position and tightened to the breaker plate, see that the points rubbing block is resting on one of the high points of the center cam (photo). To move the center cam, have an assistant just click the ignition key in short bursts. If equipped with a manual transmission, place the shifter in gear and rock the car back and forth.

19 With the rubbing block on a cam high point (points fully open), place a blade-type feeler gauge between the contacts. The gap should be 0.019 in. If not correct, use an Allen wrench to turn the points set socket which wil open and close the gap (photo).

20 Install the RFI shield, if applicable.

21 Before installing the rotor, inspect it for cracks or damage. Carefully check the condition of the metal contact at the top of the rotor for excessive burning or pitting (photo). If in doubt as to its quality, replace it with a new one.

22 Install the rotor. Both types are keyed to go onto the shaft only one way. Rotors having attaching screws will have raised pegs on the bottom. Make sure the rotor is firmly seated.

23 Before installing the distributor cap, inspect it for cracks or damage. Closely examine the contacts on the inside of the cap for excessive corrosion or damage (photo). Slight scoring is normal. If in doubt as to the quality of the cap, replace it with a new one as described in Chapter 5.

24 Install the distributor cap, locking the two latches under the distributor body.

25 Start the engine and check the dwell angle and the ignition timing (Section 19).

Point dwell angle adjustment

26 Whenever new contact points are installed or original points are cleaned, the dwell angle should be checked and adjusted to proper specifications.

27 Setting the dwell angle on GM cars is actually very easy; however, a dwell meter must be used for precise adjustment. Combination tach/dwell meters are common tune-up instruments which can be purchased at a reasonable cost. An approximate setting can be achieved without a meter.

28 Connect the dwell meter following the manufacturer's instructions.

29 Start the engine and allow to run at idle until it has reached normal operating temperature. The engine must be fully warmed to achieve an accurate reading. Turn off the engine.

30 Raise the metal 'window' on the outside of the distributor cap. Prop it in the up position, using tape if necessary.

31.4 The charcoal canister is located near the front of the engine compartment and can be identified by the hoses attached to the top

31.5 Removing the filter from the bottom of the charcoal canister

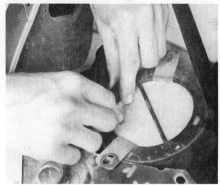
31.6 Make sure the new filter is fully seated all the way around the bottom of the canister

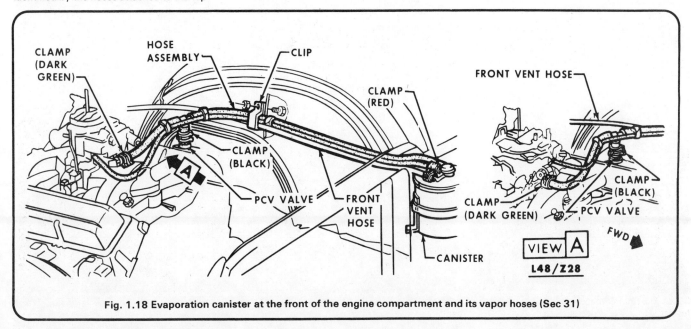
Fig. 1.18 Evaporation canister at the front of the engine compartment and its vapor hoses (Sec 31)

31 Just inside this window is the adjustment screw for the contact points. Insert an Allen wrench of the proper size into the adjustment screw socket (photo).

32 Start the engine and turn the adjusting screw as required to obtain the specified dwell reading on the meter. Dwell angle specifications are given at the beginning of Chapter 5 as well as on the tune-up decal located inside your engine compartment. If there is a discrepancy between the sources, assume the tune-up decal is correct. Remove your hand from the Allen wrench and recheck the reading.

33 Remove the Allen wrench and close the window fully. Turn off the engine and disconnect the dwell meter.

34 If you simply cannot buy, borrow or rent a dwell meter, you can get an approximate dwell setting without using a meter by the following method.

35 Start the engine and allow to idle until it has reached normal operating temperature.

36 Raise the metal window on the side of the distributor cap and insert the proper size Allen wrench into the point adjustment screw socket.

37 Turn the Allen wrench clockwise until the engine begins to misfire. Then turn the screw one half turn counter-clockwise.

38 Remove the Allen wrench and fully close the window. As soon as possible have the dwell angle checked and/or adjusted with a dwell meter. This will ensure optimum performance.

31 Evaporative Control System (ECS) filter replacement

1   The function of the ECS emissions system is to draw fuel vapors from the tank and carburetor, store them in a charcoal canister, and then burn these fumes during normal engine operation.

2   The filter at the bottom of the charcoal canister should be replaced at the specified intervals. If, however, a fuel odor is detected, the canister, filter and system hoses should immediately be inspected for fault.

3   To replace the filter, locate the canister at the front of the engine compartment. It will have between 3 and 6 hoses running out the top of it.

4   Remove the two bolts which secure the bottom of the canister to the body sheet metal (photo).

5   Turn the canister upside-down and pull the old filter from the bottom of the canister (photo). If you cannot turn the canister enough for this due to the short length of the hoses, the hoses must be duly marked with pieces of tape and then disconnected from the top.

6 Push the new filter into the bottom of the canister, making sure it is seated all the way around (photo).

7 Place the canister back into position and tighten the two mounting bolts. Connect the various hoses if disconnected.

8 The ECS system is explained in more detail in Chapter 6.

Chapter 2 Engine

Refer to Chapter 13 for specifications and information related to 1981 models

Contents

Specifications

Engine – general

Type .... V8 water-cooled, overhead valve
Firing order 1-8-4-3-6-5-7-2

Engine availability and performance

1970 models

Displacement (cu in)	Carburetor type	Horsepower @ rpm	Torque lbf ft @ rpm	Compression ratio
307	2GV	200 @ 4600	300 @ 2400	9.0:1
350	2GV	250 @ 4800	345 @ 2800	9.0:1
350	4MV	300 @ 4800	380 @ 3200	10.25:1
350	Holley 4150	360 @ 6000	380 @ 4000	11.0:1
402 (396)	4MV	350 @ 5200	415 @ 3400	10.25:1
402 (396)	Holley 4150	375 @ 5600	415 @ 3600	11.0:1

1971 models

Displacement (cu in)	Carburetor type	Horsepower @ rpm	Torque lbf ft @ rpm	Compression ratio
307	2GV	200 @ 4600	300 @ 2400	8.5:1
350	2GV	245 @ 4800	350 @ 2800	8.5:1
350	4MV (4QJ)	270 @ 4800	360 @ 3200	8.5:1
350	Holley 4150	330 @ 5600	360 @ 4000	9.0:1
402	4MV (4QJ)	300 @ 4800	400 @ 3200	8.5:1

1972 models

Displacement (cu in)	Carburetor type	Horsepower @ rpm	Torque lbf ft @ rpm	Compression ratio
307	2GV	200 @ 4600	230 @ 2400	8.5:1
350	2GV	165 @ 4000	280 @ 2400	8.5:1
350	4MV (4QJ)	200 @ 4400	300 @ 2800	8.5:1
350	4MV (4QJ)	255 @ 5600	280 @ 4000	9.0:1
402	4MV (4QJ)	240 @ 4400	345 @ 3200	8.5:1

1973 models

Displacement (cu in)	Carburetor type	Horsepower @ rpm	Torque lbf ft @ rpm	Compression ratio
307	2GV	115 @ 4000	205 @ 2000	8.5:1
350	2GV	145 @ 4000	255 @ 2400	8.5:1
350	4MV (4QJ)	175 @ 4000	270 @ 2400	8.5:1
350	4MV (4QJ)	250 @ 5200	285 @ 4000	9.0:1

1974 models

Displacement (cu in)	Carburetor type	Horsepower @ rpm	Torque lbf ft @ rpm	Compression ratio
350	2GV	145 @ 3600	250 @ 2200	8.5:1
350	4MV (4QJ)	160 @ 3800	245 @ 2400	8.5:1
350	4MV (4QJ)	185 @ 4000	270 @ 2600	8.5:1
350	4MV (4QJ)	245 @ 5200	280 @ 4000	9.0:1

1975 models

Displacement (cu in)	Carburetor type	Horsepower @ rpm	Torque lbf ft @ rpm	Compression ratio
350	2GC	145 @ 3600	250 @ 2200	8.5:1
350	M4MCA, M4MC	155 @ 3800	250 @ 2400	8.5:1

1976 models

Displacement (cu in)	Carburetor type	Horsepower @ rpm	Torque lbf ft @ rpm	Compression ratio
305	2GC	140 @ 3800	245 @ 2000	8.5:1
350	2GC	145 @ 3800	250 @ 2200	8.5:1
350	M4MC	165 @ 3800	260 @ 2400	8.5:1

1977 models

Displacement (cu in)	Carburetor type	Horsepower @ rpm	Torque lbf ft @ rpm	Compression ratio
305	2GC	145 @ 3800	245 @ 2400	8.5:1
350	M4MC	165 @ 3800	260 @ 2400	8.5:1

1978 models

Displacement (cu in)	Carburetor type	Horsepower @ rpm	Torque lbf ft @ rpm	Compression ratio
305	2 GC	140 @ 3800	2400 @ 2000	8.5:1
350	M4MC	170 @ 3800	270 @ 2400	8.5:1

1979 models

Displacement (cu in)	Carburetor type	Horsepower @ rpm	Torque lbf ft @ rpm	Compression ratio
305	M2ME	130 @ 3200	245 @ 2000	8.4:1
350	M4MC	170 @ 3800	270 @ 2400	8.2:1

1980 models

Displacement (cu in)	Carburetor type	Horsepower @ rpm	Torque lbf ft @ rpm	Compression ratio
267	M2ME	125 @ 3800	215 @ 2400	8.3:1
305	M4ME	155 @ 3800	260 @ 2800	8.6:1
350	M4ME	170 @ 3800	270 @ 2400	8.2:1

General engine dimensions

Engine Displacement	267 cu in	305 cu in	307 cu in	350 cu in	402 cu in
Bore (in)	3.50	3.736	3.875	4.00	4.126
Stroke (in)	3.48	3.48	3.25	3.48	3.76
*Cylinder bore (diameter) (in)	N/A	3.7350-3.7385	3.8745-3.8775	3.9995-4.0025	4.1246-4.1274
Out of round (max) (in)	0.002	0.002	0.002	0.002	0.002
Taper (max) (in)	0.001	0.005	0.005	0.005	0.005

*Piston oversizes available 0.001 and 0.030 in

Engine specifications – 1970 models
All dimensions given in inches

Pistons and piston rings
Piston clearance in bore
    307 and 350 (250, 300hp) engines .... 0.0027 max
    402 (350 hp) .... 0.0038 max
    402 (375 hp) .... 0.0065 max
    350 (360 hp) .... 0.0061 max
Piston ring clearance in groove
    307 engine
        Top 0.0012–0.0027
        2nd 0.0012–0.0032
        Oil control 0.000–0.005
    350 engine
        Top 0.0012–0.0032
        2nd 0.0012–0.0027
        Oil control 0.000–0.005
    402 engine
        Top 0.0017–0.0032
        2nd 0.0017–0.0032
        Oil control 0.0005–0.0065
Piston ring end gap
    307 and 350 engines
        Top 0.010–0.020
        2nd 0.013–0.025
        Oil control 0.015–0.055
    402 engine
        Top 0.010–0.020
        2nd 0.010–0.020
        Oil control 0.010–0.030
Piston pin diameter
    307, 350 engines 0.9270–0.9273
    402 engine 0.9895–0.9898
Clearance in piston .... 0.001 max
Interference fit in rod 0.0008–0.0016

Crankshaft
Main journal diameters
    307, 350 engines
        Journals 1-2-3-4 .... 2.4484–2.4493
        Journal 5 .... 2.4479–2.4488
    402 (350 hp) engine
        Journals 1-2 .... 2.7487–2.7496
        Journals 3-4 .... 2.7481–2.7490
        Journal 5 .... 2.7478–2.7488
    402 (375 hp) engine
        Journals 1-2-3-4 .... 2.7481–2.7490
        Journal 5 .... 2.7473–2.7483
Journal taper .... 0.001 max
Journal out of round .... 0.001 max
Main bearing running clearance
    No 1 .... 0.002 max
    No 2 .... 0.0035 max
Crankshaft endplay
    307, 350 engines 0.002–0.006
    402 engine 0.006–0.010
Crankpin diameter
    307, 350 engines 2.099–2.100
    402 (350 hp) engine 2.199–2.200
    402 (375 hp) engine 2.1985–2.1995
Crankpin taper .... 0.001 max
Crankpin out of round .... 0.001 max
Rod bearing running clearance .... 0.0035 max
Rod side clearance
    307, 350 engines 0.008–0.014
    402 (350 hp) engine 0.015–0.021
    402 (375 hp) engine 0.019–0.025

Camshaft
Lobe lift (intake)
    307, 350 engines 0.2600
    402 (350 hp) engine 0.2714

402 (375 hp) and 350 (360 hp) engines	0.3057
Lobe lift (exhaust)	
307, 350 engines	0.2733
402 (350 hp) engine	0.2824
402 (375 hp) engine	0.3057
350 (360 hp) engine	0.3234
Camshaft journal diameter	
307, 350 engines	1.8682–1.8692
402 engine	1.9487–1.9497
Camshaft runout	0.0015 max

Valve system

Lifter	Hydraulic except 402 (375 hp), and 350 (360 hp) which have mechanical lifters
Rocker arm ratio	
307, 350 engines	1.50 : 1
402 engine	1.70 : 1
Valve lash	
Hydraulic	One turn down from zero
Mechanical	
350 engine	
Intake	0.024 ⎫
Exhaust	0.030 ⎬ HOT
402 and 454 engine	
Intake	0.024 ⎬
Exhaust	0.028 ⎭
Valve face angle	45°
Valve seat angle	46°
Valve seat width	
(Intake)	1/32 – 1/16
(Exhaust)	1/16 – 3/32
Valve stem clearance	
(Intake)	0.0010–0.0027
(Exhaust)	0.0012–0.0029
Valve spring free length	
307, 350, 402 (375 hp) engines	2.03
402 (350 hp) engine	2.12
Valve spring installed height	
307, 350	1 23/32
402	1 7/8
Damper free length	
All engines	1.94

Engine specifications – 1971 models
All dimensions in inches
Pistons and piston rings

Piston clearance in bore	
307 engine	0.0025
350 engine	0.0027
350 (330 hp) engine	0.0061
402 engine	0.0035
Piston ring clearance in groove	
307 engine	
Top	0.0012–0.0027
2nd	0.0012–0.0032
Oil control	0.005
350 (245 hp) engine	
Top	0.0012–0.0032
2nd	0.0012–0.0032
Oil control	0.002–0.007
350 (270 hp) engine	
Top	0.0012–0.0032
2nd	0.0012–0.0027
Oil control	0.005
402 engine	
Top	0.0017–0.0032
2nd	0.0017–0.0032
Oil control	0.0005–0.0065
Piston ring end gap	
All engines Top	0.010–0.020
350 engine 2nd	0.013–0.025
307, 402 2nd	0.010–0.020
All engines Oil control	0.015–0.055
Piston pin diameter	
307, 350 engines	0.9270–0.9273
400, 402 engines	0.9895–0.9898

Clearance in piston .... 0.001 max
Interference fit in rod 0.0008–0.0016

Crankshaft

Main journal diameters
   307, 350 engines
      Journals 1-2-3-4 .... 2.4484–2.4493
      Journal 5 .... 2.4479–2.4488
   402 engine
      Journals 1-2 .... 2.7487–2.7496
      Journals 3-4 .... 2.7481–2.7490
      Journal 5 .... 2.7473–2.7483
Journal taper .... 0.001 max
Journal out of round .... 0.001 max
Main bearing running clearance
   No 1 .... 0.002 max
   No 2-3-4-5 .... 0.0035 max
Crankshaft end play
   307, 350, engines 0.002–0.006
   402 engine 0.006–0.010
Crankpin diameter
   307, 350, engines 2.099–2.100
   402 engine 2.199–2.200
Crankpin taper .... 0.001 max
Crankpin out of round .... 0.001 max
Rod bearing running clearance .... 0.0035 max
Rod side clearance
   307, 350, engines 0.008–0.014
   402 engine 0.013–0.023

Camshaft

Lobe lift (intake)
   307, 350 engines 0.2600
   350 (330 hp) engine 0.3057
   402 engine 0.2343
Lobe lift (exhaust)
   307, 350 engines 0.2733
   350 (330 hp) engine 0.3234
   402 engine 0.2343
Camshaft journal diameter
   307, 350 engines 1.8682–1.8692
   402 engine 1.9482–1.9492
Camshaft runout 0.0015

Valve system

Lifter .... Hydraulic except 350 (330 hp) which has mechanical lifter
Rocker arm ratio
   307, 350 engines .... 1.50 : 1
   402 engine .... 1.70 : 1
Valve lash
   Hydraulic .... One turn down from zero
   Mechanical (hot)
      Intake 0.024
      Exhaust 0.030
Valve face angle .... 45°
Valve seat angle .... 46°
Valve seat width
   (Intake) .... 1/32 – 1/16
   (Exhaust) .... 1/16 – 3/32
Stem clearance
   (Intake) 0.0010–0.0027
   (Exhaust) 0.0012–0.0027
Valve spring (outer) free length
   307, 350 engines 2.03
   402 engine 2.12
Valve spring (outer) installed height
   307, 350 engines 1 23/32
   402 engine 1 7/8
Valve spring (inner) free length
   402 engines only 2.06
Valve spring (inner) installed height
   402 engine only 1 25/32
Damper free length
   307, 350, engines only 1.94

Engine specifications – 1972 models
All dimensions given in inches

Pistons and piston rings

Piston clearance in bore
    307 engine 0.0025
    350 (165, 175 hp) engine 0.0027
    350 (255 hp) engine 0.0061
    402 engine 0.0035

Piston ring clearance in groove
    307 engine
        Top 0.0012–0.0027
        2nd 0.0012–0.0032
        Oil control .... 0.005 max
    350 (165 hp engine)
        Top 0.0012–0.0032
        2nd 0.0012–0.0032
        Oil control 0.002–0.007
    350 (175, 255 hp engines)
        Top 0.0012–0.0032
        2nd 0.0012–0.0027
        Oil control .... 0.005 max
    402 engine
        Top 0.0017–0.0032
        2nd 0.0017–0.0032
        Oil control 0.0005–0.0065

Piston ring end gap
    307, 402 engines
        Top 0.010–0.020
        2nd 0.010–0.020
        Oil control 0.015–0.055
    350 engine
        Top 0.010–0.020
        2nd 0.013–0.025
        Oil control 0.015–0.035

Piston pin diameter
    307, 350 (175, 255 hp) engines 0.9270–0.9273
    402 engine 0.9895–0.9898
Clearance in piston .... 0.001 max
Interference fit in rod 0.0008–0.0016

Crankshaft

Main journal diameters
    307, 350 engines
        Journal 1 .... 2.4484–2.4493
        Journal 2-3-4 .... 2.4481–2.4490
        Journal 5 .... 2.4479–2.4488
    402 engine
        Journals 1-2 .... 2.7487–2.7496
        Journals 3-4 .... 2.7481–2.7490
        Journal 5 .... 2.7473–2.7483
Crankshaft journal taper .... 0.001 max
Crankshaft journal out of round .... 0.001 max
Main bearing running clearance
    No 1 .... 0.002 max
    No 2-5 .... 0.0035 max
Crankshaft end play
    307, 350, engines 0.002–0.006
    402 engine 0.006–0.010
Crankpin diameters
    307, 350, engines 2.099–2.100
    402 engine 2.199–2.200
Crankpin taper .... 0.001 max
Crankpin out of round .... 0.001 max
Rod bearing running clearance .... 0.0035 max
Rod side clearance
    307, 350, engines 0.008–0.014
    402 engine 0.013–0.023

Camshaft

Lobe lift (Intake)
    307, 350 (165, 175 hp) engines 0.2600
    350 (255 hp) engine 0.3057
    402 engine 0.2343

Lobe lift (Exhaust)
    307, 350 (165, 175 hp) engines 0.2733
    350 (255 hp) engine 0.3234
    402 engine 0.2343
Camshaft journal diameter
    307, 350 .... 1.8682–1.8692
    402 .... 1.9482–1.9492
Camshaft runout .... 0.0015 max

Valve system

Lifter .... Hydraulic except on 350 (255 hp) mechanical
Rocker arm ratio
    307, 350 .... 1.50 : 1
    402 .... 1.70 : 1
Valve lash
    Hydraulic .... One turn down from zero
    Mechanical (hot)
        Intake 0.024
        Exhaust 0.030
Valve face angle .... 45°
Valve seat angle .... 46°
Valve seat width (Intake) .... 1/32 – 1/16
Valve seat width (Exhaust) .... 1/16 – 3/32
Valve stem clearance
    Intake 0.0010–0.0027
    Exhaust
        307, 350 engines 0.0012–0.0029
        402 engine 0.0012–0.0027
Valve spring (outer) free length
    307, 350 engines 2.03
    402 engine 2.12
Valve spring installed height
    307, 350 engines 1 23/32
    402 engine 1 7/8
Valve spring (inner) free length
    402 engine only 2.06
Valve spring (inner) installed height
    402 engine only 1 25/32

Engine specifications – 1973 models
All dimensions in inches

Pistons and piston rings

Piston clearance in bore (max)
    307 engine 0.0025
    350 engine 0.0027
    350 (245 hp) engine 0.0061
Piston ring clearance in groove
    307 engine
        Top 0.0012–0.0027
        2nd 0.0012–0.0032
        Oil control .... 0.005 max
    350 (145 hp) engine
        Top 0.0012–0.0032
        2nd 0.0012–0.0032
        Oil control 0.002–0.007
    350 (175, 245 hp)
        Top 0.0012–0.0032
        2nd 0.0012–0.0027
        Oil control .... 0.005 max
Piston ring end gap
    307 engine
        Top 0.010–0.020
        2nd 0.010–0.020
        Oil control 0.015–0.055
    350 engine
        Top 0.010–0.020
        2nd 0.013–0.025
        Oil control 0.015–0.055
Piston pin diameter
    All engines 0.9270–0.9273
Clearance in piston .... 0.001 max
Interference fit in rod 0.0008–0.0016

Crankshaft

Main journal diameters
  307, 350 engines
    Journal 1 .... 2.4484–2.4493
    Journals 2-3-4 .... 2.4481–2.4490
    Journal 5 .... 2.4479–2.4488
Journal taper .... 0.001 max
Journal out of round .... 0.001 max
Main bearing running clearance
  Journal 1 .... 0.002 max
  Journals 2-3-4-5 .... 0.0035 max
Crankshaft end play
  307, 350 engines 0.002–0.006
Crankpin diameter
  All engines 2.099–2.100
Crankpin taper .... 0.001 max
Crankpin out of round .... 0.001 max
Rod bearing running clearance
  All engines 0.0013–0.0035
Rod side clearance
  All engines 0.008–0.014

Camshaft

Lobe lift (Intake)
  307, 350 engines 0.2600
  350 (245 hp) engine 0.3000
Lobe lift (Exhaust)
  307, 350 engines 0.2733
  350 (245 hp) engine 0.3070
Camshaft journal diameter
  307, 350 engines 1.8682–1.8692
Camshaft runout .... 0.0015 max

Valve system

Lifter .... Hydraulic
Rocker arm ratio
  307, 350 engines .... 1.50 : 1
Valve lash .... One turn down from zero
Valve face angle .... 45°
Valve seat angle .... 46°
Valve seat width (Intake) .... 1/32 – 1/16
Valve seat width (Exhaust) .... 1/16 – 3/32
Valve stem clearance
  All engines (Intake) 0.0010–0.0027
  All engines (Exhaust) 0.0012–0.0029
Valve spring free length
  307, 350 engines 1.90
  350 (245 hp) engine 2.03
Valve spring installed height
  307, 350 engines 1 5/8
  350, (245 hp) engine 1 23/32
Damper free length
  All engines 1.94

Engine specifications – 1974 models
All dimensions in inches

Pistons and piston rings

Piston clearance in bore (max)
  350 (145 hp) engine 0.0025
  350 (160, 185 hp) engines 0.0027
  350 (245 hp) engine 0.0061
Piston ring clearance in groove
  350 (145 hp) engine
    Top 0.0012–0.0027
    2nd 0.0012–0.0032
    Oil control .... 0.005 max
  350 (160 hp) engine
    Top 0.0012–0.0032
    2nd 0.0012–0.0032
    Oil control 0.002–0.007
  350 (185, 245 hp)
    Top 0.0012–0.0032
    2nd 0.0012–0.0027
    Oil control .... 0.005 max

Piston ring end gap
    All engines Top 0.010–0.020
    350 (145 hp) engine 2nd 0.010–0.020
    350 (160, 185 hp) engine 2nd 0.013–0.025
    350 (245 hp) engine 2nd 0.010–0.023
    All engines Oil control 0.015–0.055
Piston pin diameter
    All engines 0.9270–0.9273
Clearance in piston .... 0.001 max
Interference fit in rod 0.0008–0.0016

Crankshaft

Main journal diameters
    350 engine
        Journal 1 .... 2.4484–2.4493
        Journals 2-3-4 .... 2.4481–2.4490
        Journal 5 .... 2.4479–2.4488
Journal taper .... 0.001 max
Journal out of round .... 0.001 max
Main bearing running clearance
    Journal 1 .... 0.002 max
    All others .... 0.0035 max
Crankshaft end play
    All engines 0.002–0.006
Crankpin diameter
    All engines 2.099–2.100
Crankpin taper .... 0.001 max
Crankpin out of round .... 0.001 max
Rod bearing running clearance
    All engines 0.0013–0.0035
Rod side clearance
    All engines 0.0008–0.014

Camshaft

Lobe lift (Intake)
    350 (145, 160, 185 hp) engines 0.2600
    350 (245 hp) engine 0.3000
Lobe lift (Exhaust)
    350 (145, 160, 185 hp) engines 0.2733
    350 (245 hp) engine 0.3070
Camshaft journal diameter
    350 engine 1.8682–1.8692
Camshaft runout .... 0.0015 max

Valve system

Lifter .... Hydraulic
Rocker arm ratio
    350 engine .... 1.50 : 1
Valve lash .... One turn down from zero
Valve face angle .... 45°
Valve seat angle .... 46°
Valve seat width
    (Intake) .... 1/32 – 1/16
    (Exhaust) .... 1/16 – 3/32
Valve stem clearance
    (Intake) 0.0010–0.0027
    (Exhaust)
        350 engine 0.0012–0.0029
Valve spring free length
    350 (145, 160, 185 hp) engine
        (Intake) 2.03
        (Exhaust) 1.91
    350 (245 hp) engine 2.03
Valve spring installed height
    350 (145, 160, 185 hp) engines 1 5/8
    350, (245 hp) engine 1 23/32
Damper free length
    All engines except 454 .... 1.94

Engine specifications – 1975 models
All dimensions in inches
Pistons and piston rings

Piston clearance in bore
    350 (2 barrel carburetor) engine .... 0.0025 max
    350 (4 barrel carburetor) engine .... 0.0027 max

Piston ring clearance in groove
   350 (2 barrel carburetor)
      Top 0.0012–0.0027
      2nd 0.0012–0.0032
      Oil control .... 0.005 max
   350 (4 barrel carburetor) engine
      Top 0.0012–0.0032
      2nd 0.0012–0.0032
      Oil control .... 0.005 max
Piston ring end gap
   All engines Top 0.010–0.020
   350 (2 barrel carburetor) 2nd 0.010–0.020
   350 (4 barrel carburetor) 2nd 0.013–0.025
   All engines   Oil control 0.015–0.055
Piston pin diameter
   All engines 0.9270–0.9273
Clearance in piston .... 0.001 max
Interference fit in rod 0.0008–0.0016

Crankshaft
Main journal diameters
   350 engine
      Journal 1 .... 2.4484–2.4493
      Journals 2-3-4 .... 2.4481–2.4490
      Journal 5 .... 2.4479–2.4488
Journal taper .... 0.001 max
Journal out of round .... 0.001 max
Main bearing running clearance
   No 1 Journal .... 0.002 max
   All others .... 0.0035 max
Crankshaft end play
   350 (2 barrel carburetor) engine 0.002–0.006
Crankpin diameter
   All engines 2.099–2.100
Crankpin taper .... 0.001 max
Crankpin out of round .... 0.001 max
Rod bearing running clearance
   350 engine 0.0013–0.0035
Rod side clearance
   350 engine 0.0008–0.014

Camshaft
Lobe lift (Intake)
   350 engine 0.3000
Lobe lift (Exhaust)
   350 engine 0.3070
Camshaft journal diameter
   350 engine 1.8682–1.8692
Camshaft runout .... 0.0015 max

Valve system
Lifter .... Hydraulic
Rocker arm ratio
   350 engine .... 1.50 : 1
Valve lash .... One turn down from zero
Valve face angle .... 45°
Valve seat angle .... 46°
Valve seat width
   (Intake) .... 1/32 – 1/16
   (Exhaust) .... 1/16 – 3/32
Valve stem clearance
   All engines (Intake) 0.0010–0.0027
   350 engine (Exhaust) 0.0012–0.0029
Valve spring free length
   350 engine 2.03
Valve spring installed height
   350 engine 1 23/32
Damper free length
   350 engine 1.94

Engine specifications – 1976 models
All dimensions in inches

Pistons and piston rings
Piston clearance in bore
   305, 350 engines .... 0.0027 max

Piston ring clearance in groove
    305, 350 engines Top 0.0012–0.0032
    305 and 350 engines 2nd 0.0012–0.0027
    All engines Oil control .... 0.005 max
Piston ring end gap
    All engines Top 0.010–0.020
    305 engine 2nd 0.010–0.025
    350 (4 barrel carburetor engine) 0.013–0.025
    All engines Oil control 0.015–0.055
Piston pin diameter
    All engines 0.9270–0.9273
Clearance in piston .... 0.001 max
Interference fit in rod 0.0008–0.0016

Crankshaft

Main journal diameters
    305, 350 engines
        Journal 1 .... 2.4484–2.4493
        Journals 2-3-4 .... 2.4481–2.4490
        Journal 5 .... 2.4479–2.4488
Journal taper .... 0.001 max
Journal out of round .... 0.001 max
Main bearing running clearance
    No 1 Journal .... 0.002 max
    All others .... 0.0035 max
Crankshaft end play
    All engines 0.002–0.006
Crankpin diameter
    305, 350 engines 2.099–2.100
Crankpin taper .... 0.001 max
Crankpin out of round .... 0.001 max
Rod bearing running clearance.. 0.0035 max
Rod side clearance
    All engines 0.008–0.014

Camshaft

Lobe lift (Intake)
    305 engine 0.2485
    350 engine 0.2600
Lobe lift (Exhaust)
    All engines 0.2733
Camshaft journal diameter
    305, 350 engines 1.8682–1.8692
Camshaft runout .... 0.0015 max

Valve system

Lifter .... Hydraulic
Rocker arm ratio
    305, 350 engines .... 1.50 : 1
Valve lash .... 3/4 turn down from zero
Valve face angle .... 45°
Valve seat angle .... 46°
Valve seat width
    (Intake) .... 1/32 – 1/16
    (Exhaust) .... 1/16 – 3/32
Valve stem clearance
    (Intake) 0.0010–0.0027
    (Exhaust) 0.0010–0.0027
Valve spring free length
    All engines 2.03
Valve spring installed height
    305, 350 engines 1 23/32
Damper free length
    All engines 1.94

Engine specifications – 1977 models
All dimensions in inches
Pistons and piston rings

Piston clearance in bore
    305, 350 engines .... 0.0027 max
Piston ring clearance in groove
    305, 350 engines Top 0.0012–0.0032
    305 and 350 engines 2nd 0.0012–0.0027
    All engines Oil control .... 0.005 max

Piston ring end gap
    All engines Top 0.010–0.020
    305 engine 2nd 0.010–0.025
    350 (4 barrel carburetor engine) 0.013–0.025
    All engines   Oil control 0.015–0.055
Piston pin diameter
    All engines 0.9270–0.9273
Clearance in piston 0.001
Interference fit in rod 0.0008–0.0016

Crankshaft

Main journal diameters
    305, 350 engines
        Journal 1 .... 2.4484–2.4493
        Journals 2-3-4 .... 2.4481–2.4490
        Journal 5 .... 2.4479–2.4488
Journal taper .... 0.001 max
Journal out of round .... 0.001 max
Main bearing running clearance
    No 1 Journal 0.002
    All others .... 0.0035 max
Crankshaft end play
    All engines 0.002–0.006
Crankpin diameter
    305, 350 engines 2.099–2.100
Crankpin taper .... 0.001 max
Crankpin out of round .... 0.001 max
Rod bearing running clearance .... 0.0035 max
Rod side clearance
    All engines 0.008–0.014

Camshaft

Lobe lift (Intake)
    305 engine 0.2485
    350 engine 0.2600
Lobe lift (Exhaust)
    All engines 0.2733
Camshaft journal diameter
    305, 350 engines 1.8682–1.8692
Camshaft runout .... 0.0015 max

Valve system

Lifter .... Hydraulic
Rocker arm ratio
    305, 350 engine .... 1.50 : 1
Valve lash .... 3/4 turn down from zero
Valve face angle .... 45°
Valve seat angle .... 46°
Valve seat width
    (Intake) .... 1/32 – 1/16
    (Exhaust) .... 1/16 – 3/32
Valve stem clearance
    (Intake) 0.0010–0.0027
    (Exhaust) 0.0010–0.0027
Valve spring free length
    All engines 2.03
Valve spring installed height
    305, 350 engines 1 23/32
Damper free length
    All engines 1.86

Engine specifications – 1978 models
All dimensions in inches

Pistons and piston rings

Piston clearance in bore
    305, 350 engines .... 0.0027 max
Piston ring clearance in groove
    305, 350 engines Top 0.0012–0.0032
    305 and 350 engines 2nd 0.0012–0.0032
    All engines Oil control .... 0.001 max
Piston ring end gap
    All engines
        Top 0.010–0.020
        2nd 0.010–0.025
    All engines   Oil control 0.015–0.055

Piston pin diameter
    All engines 0.9270–0.9273
Clearance in piston 0.001
Interference fit in rod 0.0008–0.0016

Crankshaft

Main journal diameters
    305, 350 engines
        Journal 1 .... 2.4484–2.4493
        Journals 2-3-4 .... 2.4481–2.4490
        Journal 5 .... 2.4479–2.4488
Journal taper .... 0.001 max
Journal out of round .... 0.001 max
Main bearing running clearance
    No 1 Journal 0.002
    All others .... 0.0035 max
Crankshaft end play
    All engines 0.002–0.006
Crankpin diameter
    305, 350 engines 2.099–2.100
Crankpin taper .... 0.001 max
Crankpin out of round .... 0.001 max
Rod bearing running clearance .... 0.0035 max
Rod side clearance
    All engines 0.008–0.014

Camshaft

Lobe lift (Intake)
    305 engine 0.2484
    350 engine 0.2600
Lobe lift (Exhaust)
    305 engine 0.2667
    350 engine 0.2733
Camshaft journal diameter
    305, 350 engines 1.8682–1.8692
Camshaft runout .... 0.0015 max

Valve system

Lifter .... Hydraulic
Rocker arm ratio
    305, 350 engine .... 1.50 : 1
Valve lash .... 1 turn down from zero
Valve face angle .... 45°
Valve seat angle .... 46°
Valve seat width
    (Intake) .... 1/32 – 1/16
    (Exhaust) .... 1/16 – 3/32
Valve stem clearance
    (Intake) 0.0010–0.0027
    (Exhaust) 0.0010–0.0027
Valve spring free length
    All engines 2.03
Valve spring installed height
    305, 350 engines 1 23/32
Damper free length
    All engines 1.86

Engine specifications – 1979 models
All dimensions in inches
Pistons and piston rings

Piston clearance in bore
    305, 350 engines .... 0.0027 max
Piston ring clearance in groove
    305, 350 engines Top 0.0012–0.0032
    305 and 350 engines 2nd 0.0012–0.0032
    All engines Oil control .... 0.005 max
Piston ring end gap
    All engines
        Top 0.010–0.020
        2nd 0.010–0.025
    All engines   Oil control 0.015–0.055
Piston pin diameter
    All engines 0.9270–0.9273
Clearance in piston 0.001
Interference fit in rod 0.0008–0.0016

Crankshaft

Main journal diameters
  305, 350 engines
    Journal 1 .... 2.4484–2.4493
    Journals 2-3-4 .... 2.4481–2.4490
    Journal 5 .... 2.4479–2.4488
Journal taper .... 0.001 max
Journal out of round .... 0.001 max
Main bearing running clearance
  No 1 Journal 0.002
  All others .... 0.0035 max
Crankshaft end play
  All engines 0.002–0.006
Crankpin diameter
  305, 350 engines 2.099–2.100
Crankpin taper .... 0.001 max
Crankpin out of round .... 0.001 max
Rod bearing running clearance.. 0.0035 max
Rod side clearance
  All engines 0.008–0.014

Camshaft

Lobe lift (Intake)
  305 engine 0.2484
  350 engine 0.2600
Lobe lift (Exhaust)
  305 engine 0.2667
  350 engine 0.2733
Camshaft journal diameter
  305, 350 engines 1.8682–1.8692
Camshaft runout .... 0.0015 max

Valve system

Lifter .... Hydraulic
Rocker arm ratio
  305, 350 engine .... 1.50 : 1
Valve lash .... 1 turn down from zero
Valve face angle .... 45°
Valve seat angle .... 46°
Valve seat width
  (Intake) .... 1/32 – 1/16
  (Exhaust) .... 1/16 – 3/32
Valve stem clearance
  (Intake) 0.0010–0.0027
  (Exhaust) 0.0010–0.0027
Valve spring free length
  All engines 2.03
Valve spring installed height
  305, 350 engines 1 23/32
Damper free length
  All engines 1.86

Engine specifications – 1980 models
All dimensions in inches
Pistons and piston rings

Piston clearance in bore
  All engines .... 0.0027 max
Piston ring clearance in groove
  All engines Top 0.0012–0.0032
  All engines 2nd 0.0012–0.0032
  All engines Oil control .... 0.005 max
Piston ring end gap
  All engines
    Top 0.010–0.020
    2nd 0.010–0.025
  All engines Oil control .... 0.015 to 0.055
Piston pin diameter
  All engines 0.9270–0.9273
Clearance in piston 0.001
Interference fit in rod 0.0008–0.0016

Crankshaft

Main journal diameters
    All engines
        Journal 1 .... 2.4484–2.4493
        Journals 2-3-4 .... 2.4481–2.4490
        Journal 5 .... 2.4479–2.4488
Journal taper .... 0.001 max
Journal out of round .... 0.001 max
Main bearing running clearance
    No 1 Journal 0.002
    All others .... 0.0035 max
Crankshaft end play
    All engines 0.002–0.006
Crankpin diameter
    All engines 2.099–2.100
Crankpin taper .... 0.001 max
Crankpin out of round .... 0.001 max
Rod bearing running clearance.................................... 0.0035 max
Rod side clearance
    All engines 0.008–0.014

Camshaft

Lobe lift (Intake)
    267 engine 0.357
    305 engine 0.2484
    350 engine 0.2600
Lobe lift (Exhaust)
    267 engine 0.390
    305 engine 0.2667
    350 engine 0.2733
Camshaft journal diameter
    All engines 1.8682–1.8692
Camshaft runout .... 0.0015 max

Valve system

Lifter .... Hydraulic
Rocker arm ratio
    305, 350 engine .... 1.50 : 1
Valve lash .... 1 turn down from zero
Valve face angle .... 45°
Valve seat angle .... 46°
Valve seat width
    (Intake) .... 1/32 – 1/16
    (Exhaust) .... 1/16 – 3/32
Valve stem clearance
    (Intake) 0.0010–0.0027
    (Exhaust) 0.0010–0.0027
Valve spring free length
    All engines 2.03
Valve spring installed height
    305, 350 engines 1 23/32
Damper free length
    All engines 1.86

Engine lubrication – all models

Pump .... Gear type driven from distributor shaft meshed to camshaft helical gear

Oil filter element .... Disposable cartridge type AC PF25

Crankcase oil capacity

Without oil filter change .... 4 US qts
With oil filter change .... 5 US qts

Crankcase vent filter   AC FB59

Crankcase (PCV) valve   AC CV 774C

Torque specifications (lb-ft)

	Small V8	Mk IV V8
Crankcase front cover	10	10
Flywheel housing cover	10	10
Oil filter by-pass valve	10	10

Oil pan screws		
small	10	10
large	30	18
Oil pan to front cover screws		7
Oil pump cover screws	10	10
Rocker arm cover screws	4	6
Camshaft sprocket bolt	20	20
Clutch pressure plate bolts	35	35
Distributor clamp bolts	20	20
Flywheel housing bolts	30	30
Exhaust manifold bolts	20	20
Inner bolts 350 engine	30	
Intake manifold bolts	30	30
Water outlet bolts	30	30
Water pump bolts	30	30
Connecting rod cap bolts	45	50
Cylinder head bolts	65	80
Main bearing cap bolts*	70	110
Oil pump bolts	65	65
Rocker arm stud	50	50
Flywheel bolts	60	65
Torsional damper bolt	60	85
Temperature sender unit	20	20
Oil pan drain plug	20	20
Spark plug	15	15

*Outer bolts on 4 bolt caps 65

1 General description

Starting in the model year 1970, Chevrolet incorporated a wide variety of V8 engines in the Camaro line. The cubic inch capacity of these engines varies from year to year, meeting everchanging gas mileage and emission requirements.

The workhorse in the Camaro engine lineup is the 350 cubic inch engine. This popular engine has been available in all Camaros, 1970 – 1980. Although horsepower ratings show a marked difference through the years, the basic engine design remains unchanged.

The 307 cubic inch engine, available through model year 1973, was the forerunner of today's economy-engineered powerplants. For the Camaro, the 307 was available with only the two-barrel carburetor.

The 305 cubic inch V8, introduced in 1976, and the 267 cubic inch engine (1980) are proof that the small-block Chevrolet V8 can endure in a changing automotive world.

Somewhat different in design and utility is the big-block, or Mark IV engine. This high horsepower and torque engine was available in Camaro models through 1972. Of the four big-block variations built by Chevrolet, only the 396 cubic inch engine was incorporated into the Camaro body. And while all body and engine markings indicate that the engine is a 396, it is in fact a 402 cubic-inch block. In late 1969 Chevrolet stopped using the 396 engine block, instead opting for the 402 cubic-inch basic engine block which was commonly used in the Chevrolet and GMC truck line. Most of the peripheral engine equipment remained 396. It should be noted that in this manual the big-block engine is referenced as a 402 cubic-inch.

The operations described in each Section of this Chapter apply to all engines unless specifically noted to the contrary.

2 Engine repair operations – general notes

The following engine removal operations can be performed with the engine installed and still bolted to its mounts:

1   *Removal of the intake and exhaust manifolds*
2   *Removal of the valve mechanism*
3   *Removal of the cylinder heads*
4   *Removal of the torsional damper, crankcase front cover (timing cover), front oil seal, timing chain and timing chain sprockets*
5   *Removal of the flywheel (with the transmission previously removed)*
6   *Removal of the camshaft*

The following engine removal operations can be performed with the engine installed but raised slightly off its mounts:

1   *Removal of the oil pan*
2   *Removal of the oil pump*
3   *Removal of the rear main oil seal*
4   *Removal of the pistons, connecting rods and associated bearings*
5   *Removal of the engine mounts*

The following engine removal operations can be performed only after the engine has been completely removed from the vehicle:

1   *Removal of the crankshaft*
2   *Removal of the main and camshaft bearings*

Whenever engine work is required there are some basic steps which the home mechanic should perform before any work is begun. These preliminary steps will help prevent delays during the operation. They are as follows:

a)   *Read through the appropriate Sections in this manual to get an understanding of the processes involved, tools necessary and replacement parts which will be needed.*
b)   *Contact your local GM dealer or automotive parts store to check on replacement parts availability and cost. In many cases, a decision must be made beforehand whether to simply remove the faulty component and replace it with a new or rebuilt unit or to overhaul the existing part.*
c)   *If the vehicle is equipped with air conditioning, it is imperative that a qualified specialist de-pressurize the system if this is required to perform the necessary engine repair work. The home mechanic should never disconnect any of the air conditioning system while it is still pressurized, as this can cause serious personal injury as well as possibly damage the air conditioning system. Ascertain if de-pressurization is necessary while the vehicle is still operational.*

3 Engine – removal and installation methods and precautions

1 The engine can be removed complete with transmission or independently, leaving the transmission in the vehicle. Unless heavy duty lifting equipment is available, the removal of the engine on its own is to be recommended particularly if an automatic transmission is installed as the combined weight of both units will be certainly more than one person can handle.

2 During the removal operations, make sure that any jacks used are

supplemented with axle-stands before attempting to work under the vehicle.

3   Do not smoke if fuel has been spilled and mop up fuel and oil spillages as quickly as possible.

4   If the vehicle is equipped with air conditioning, *never disconnect any of the system lines.* If the belt-driven compressor can be unbolted and moved to one side of the engine compartment to provide room to service components, this is permissible. If sufficient clearance is not obtainable then the system must be discharged by your dealer or a competent refrigeration engineer and subsequently recharged once the engine work is complete.

5   If air conditioning is fitted, avoid damage to the condenser which is mounted just ahead of the radiator.

4   Engine – removal (without transmission)

1   If the vehicle is equipped with air conditioning, the car should be driven to a GM dealer or refrigeration specialist to have the system depressurized. The air conditioning system cannot be simply unbolted and laid aside for engine removal. Do not attempt to disconnect any of the air conditioning system while it is under pressure as serious damage to the system, as well as to yourself, can occur.

2   Remove the hood. Refer to Chapter 12 for the correct procedure to follow for this job. Set the hood in a safe place where it will not be damaged.

3   Disconnect the battery cables at the battery.

4   Remove the air cleaner assembly and set aside. Make sure to identify all hoses with pieces of tape to make reassembly easier.

5   Drain the radiator and engine block, referring to Chapter 1, if necessary.

6   Disconnect the radiator hoses and transmission fluid cooler lines (if equipped) and remove the radiator and shroud (see Chapter 3).

7   Remove the fan and fan pulley at the front of the water pump.

8   Disconnect the wiring at the alternator. Mark the wires with coded pieces of tape to help identify them upon reassembly.

9   Disconnect the wires at the temperature switch. This is located between the number 1 and number 3 exhaust ports on the right cyinder head (facing the engine).

10   Disconnect the wires at the oil pressure switch or the fluid fitting if a mechanical oil pressure gauge is fitted. The oil pressure port is at the extreme rear of the engine.

11   Disconnect the wiring at the ignition coil. 1970 – 1974 models have the coil mounted at the rear, adjacent to the distributor. 1975 and later models have the coil inside the distributor cap, in which case the electrical coupler at the distributor will be disconnected. In either case, identify the disconnected wires with coded strips of tape.

12   Disconnect the accelerator linkage where it is supported at the intake manifold.

13   Disconnect the fuel line (from the gas tank) where it attaches to the fuel pump. Have an empty can and some rags handy to catch excess fuel in the system. Plug the hose to keep dirt out of the system and to prevent later fuel drainage.

14   Disconnect the fuel vapor hoses which run from the emission system charcoal canister to the engine. This canister, in most cases, is located in the engine compartment just behind the left front headlight.

15   Disconnect the vacuum hose for the power brake booster (if equipped with power brakes). This vacuum hose runs to the intake manifold, where it should be disconnected.

16   Remove the bolts which attach the power steering bracket to the engine (if equipped with power steering). Leave the hoses connected and use a length of stiff wire (a coat hanger will work well) to tie the pump assembly against the inner fender panel. Make sure it is clear of the engine and will not be damaged.

17   Remove the air conditioner compressor and its related components (if equipped).

18   The removal of the distributor and carburetor at this time is optional. Many people remove these components before engine removal due to the fact that they can be damaged as the engine assembly is lifted free of the vehicle. If it is decided that they be removed, refer to the appropriate Chapters (Chapter 5 and Chapter 4, for the removal sequence. Be sure to cover the openings in the intake manifold to prevent articles from dropping into the recesses.

19   Raise the vehicle and support firmly on jack stands.

20   Drain the oil from the oil pan (Chapter 1).

21   Disconnect the exhaust pipes at the flanges on each exhaust manifold. Penetrating oil may have to be used to loosen frozen nuts.

22   Disconnect the wires at the starter solenoid, marking each with a piece of tape to identify each for reassembly.

23   Remove the starter/solenoid assembly.

24   Remove the flywheel splash shield (manual transmission) or converter housing cover (automatic transmission) as applicable (photo).

25   On vehicles equipped with an automatic transmission remove the converter-to-flywheel bolts. This is done by working through the opening gained by the removal of the cover previously removed. It will be necessary to turn the engine by the bolt at the center of the torsional damper to bring each of the bolts into view. Mark the relative position of the converter to the flywheel with a scribe so it can be reinstalled in the same position. Use a long screwdriver in the teeth of the flywheel to prevent movement as the bolts are loosened (photo).

26   Lower the vehicle.

27   Move back into the engine compartment and make a last check that all wires and hoses are disconnected from the engine assembly and that all peripheral accessories have enough clearance.

28   Attach the hoist lifting chains to the lifting 'eyes' mounted to the engine. There is one bracket at the front of the engine and one at the rear, diagonally opposite. Make sure the chain is looped properly through the engine brackets and secured with strong nuts and bolts through the chain loops. The hook on the hoist should be over the center of the engine with the lengths of chain at equal distances so as to lift the engine straight up.

29   Raise the engine hoist until all slack is out of the chains. Do not lift any further at this time.

30   Remove the through bolt at each engine mount.

31   Remove the bolts which attach the rear of the engine to the transmission bellhousing (photo).

32   Support the transmission using a jack with wood blocks as cushioners. While under the vehicle, check that all components are clear of the engine assembly.

33   Raise the engine slightly and then pull forward to clear the clutch shaft (manual transmission). Where an automatic transmission is installed, keep the torque converter pushed well to the rear to ensure retaining the engagement of the converter tangs with the oil pump inside the transmission.

34   Carefully lift the engine straight up and out of the engine compartment, continually checking clearances around the engine. Be particularly careful that the engine does not hit the brake master cylinder, firewall, power steering pump (which is wired to the fender well) or the body nosepiece as it is rolled free of the vehicle (photos).

35   The transmission should remain supported by the floor jack or wood blocks while the engine is out of place.

5   Engine – removal (with transmission)

1   If the transmission is in need of repairs at the same time as the engine, it is wise to remove both units together. The body and frame construction of the Camaro does allow these components to be removed as a single unit, however, be forewarned that extra weight will be involved. Make sure the lifting hoist is capable of handling the extra weight and if at all possible have at least one assistant on hand to help in the procedure.

2   Initially follow the sequence outlined in Section 4, paragraphs 1 through 18.

Manual transmission

3   If equipped with a floor shift, remove the shift lever knob, and on 4-speed models the spring and T-handle.

4   Working under the car, disconnect the speedometer cable by loosening the collar with pliers, then pulling the collar and inner cable out of the transmission. Tie or tape the end of the cable out of the way.

5   Disconnect the electrical wiring at the back-up lamp switch and the TCS switch (1970 – 1974 models only). Identify these wires with coded pieces of tape to help during reassembly.

6   Disconnect the shift rods from the transmission side cover. Note the position of each and duly mark with tape to help during the reassembly process.

7   On floorshift models, remove the backdrive rod at the bellcrank and the shift control assembly from its support. The shifter assembly can then be carefully lowered and removed from under the vehicle.

4.24 Removing the flywheel cover

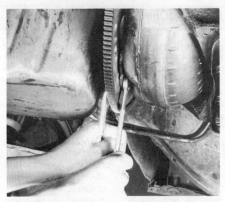

4.25 Removing the bolts which secure the torque converter to the engine drive plate (flywheel)

4.31 One of the transmission-to-engine bolts located just above the oil filter

4.34A Without the transmission, the engine should be lifted in a level position

4.34B When moving the engine out of the engine compartment be careful that the oil pan does not hit the body

5.18A Removing the transmission mounting bolts at the rear crossmember

5.18B The bolts which mount the crossmember to the frame are accessible through holes in the frame rails

5.20A When the transmission is removed with the engine, position the lifting chains so the assembly hangs at a steep angle

5.20B Use channel lock pliers or a nut and bolt through the chain links to prevent the chain from slipping through the lifting hook

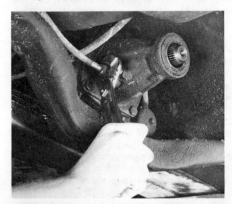

5.22 Disconnecting the speedometer from the transmission

5.26 Removing the shift linkage from the side of the transmission

6.8 Removing the converter (clutch) splash shield

8 On some later models it will be necessary to remove the catalytic converter which is supported at the transmission. (Refer to Chapter 6).

9 Disconnect the clutch linkage at the cross-shaft then remove the cross-shaft at the frame bracket.

10 Drain the oil from the engine (Chapter 1).

11 Disconnect the exhaust pipes at the manifold flanges on either side of the engine.

12 On some models equipped with a cross-over exhaust pipe, it will be necessary to remove this cross-over pipe.

13 Disconnect the wiring at the starter solenoid, marking each wire with a coded strip of tape. Remove the starter motor/solenoid.

14 Make a final check under the vehicle that all wiring and peripheral components are disconnected from the transmission and that all accessories are clear of the transmission. Move to the engine compartment and do the same.

15 Position a movable jack (floor jack or transmission jack) under the transmission oil pan using a block of wood as an insulator. Take the weight of the transmission on the jack.

16 Attach the hoist lifting chains to the lifting 'eyes' of the engine. There is one bracket at the front of the engine and one at the rear, diagonally opposite. Make sure the chain is looped properly through the engine brackets and secured with strong bolts and nuts through the chain loops. The hook on the lifting hoist should be at the center of the engine. Position the chains so the engine/transmission unit will be at a steep angle, the front being higher than the rear.

17 Raise the hoist until all slack is removed from the chains. Do not lift any further at this time.

18 Under the car, remove the transmission-to-crossmember bolts and the crossmember-to-frame bolts. Raise the transmission slightly and slide the crossmember to the rear until it can be removed (photos).

19 Remove the through-bolt at each engine mount.

20 Carefully raise the engine and lower the transmission at the same time. Do this a little at a time, checking clearances as you go. If the lifting chains are positioned properly, the engine/transmission unit will hang at a very steep angle. If it is necessary to re-position the lifting chains, carefully lower the engine back onto its mounts, with the floor jack still supporting the transmission (photos).

21 As the assembly is rolled out of the engine compartment, it may be necessary to lift the transmission slightly to clear the front body nosepiece.

Automatic transmission

22 Working under the car, disconnect the speedometer cable. Do this by loosening the collar with pliers, then pulling the inner cable and collar out of the transmission (photo).

23 Disconnect the oil cooler lines at the transmission and then completely remove these lines. Plug the ends to prevent dirt from entering the system.

24 Disconnect the vacuum line at the vacuum modulator.

25 Disconnect the electrical wiring at the transmission, depending on the model year.

26 Disconnect the shift control linkage at the transmission (photo).

6.11 Pulling the transmission away from the engine

27 Remove the drive shaft (see Chapter 8).

28 Insert a plug into the rear of the transmission to prevent fluid loss as the engine/transmission assembly is tilted upon removal. A plastic bag secured with wire or tape will generally suffice.

29 On some later models it will be necessary to remove the catalytic converter (see Chapter 6).

30 Drain the oil from the engine (Chapter 1).

31 Disconnect the exhaust pipes at the manifold flanges on either side of the engine. If equipped with an exhaust cross-over pipe, remove it.

32 Disconnect the wiring at the starter solenoid, marking each wire with a coded strip of tape. Remove the starter/solenoid from the engine.

33 Make a final check that all wiring and peripheral components are disconnected and clear of the transmission. Move to the engine compartment and do the same.

Note: *The remainder of the removal process is the same as for the manual transmission. Follow previously described steps 15 through 21.*

6 Engine/transmission removed – separation and reconnection

Manual transmission

1 Extract the screws and remove the cover plate from the lower front face of the clutch bellhousing.

2 Unscrew and remove the bolts which hold the bellhousing to the engine.

3 Support the weight of the transmission and withdraw it in a straight line so that the clutch disc is not damaged while the main drive gear is still engaged in its splined hub.

4 Refer to Chapter 8 for the following clutch component processes.

5 Unscrew each of the clutch cover bolts a turn at a time until all spring pressure is relieved.

6 Withdraw the clutch assembly from the face of the flywheel taking care not to let the clutch disc drop.

7 Reconnecting the transmission to the engine is the reverse of the separation procedure but if the clutch has been removed, the disc must be centralized.

Automatic transmission

8 Remove the cover plate from the lower front face of the converter housing (photo).

9 Unscrew each of the driveplate to torque converter bolts. The crankshaft will have to be turned to bring the bolts into view. Mark the relative position of the driveplate to the torque converter. The driveplate can be held still for bolt removal by jamming the teeth of the starter ring gear with a large screwdriver.

10 Support the transmission on blocks and then remove the converter bellhousing to engine bolts.

11 Using either a hoist or a floor jack, withdraw the engine from the transmission. While carrying out this operation, keep the torque converter pressed rearwards in full engagement with the oil pump of the transmission (photo).

12 Reconnection is a reversal of separation but align the mating marks on the torque converter and driveplate and tighten all the bolts to the specified torque.

7 Engine – installation (without transmission)

1 Lift the engine with a hoist off the engine stand. The chains should be positioned as on removal, with the engine sitting level.

2 Lower the engine into place inside the engine compartment, closely watching clearances. On manual transmissions, carefully guide the engine onto the transmission input shaft. The two components should be at the same angle, with the shaft sliding easily into the engine.

3 Install the engine mount through-bolts and the bellhousing bolts. Torque-tighten to specifications.

4 Install the remaining engine components in the reverse order of removal, referring to Section 4 as necessary.

5 Fill the cooling system with the proper coolant and water mixture (Chapter 3).

6 Fill the engine with the correct grade of engine oil (Chapter 1).

7　Check the transmission fluid level, adding fluid as necessary.

8　Connect the positive battery cable, followed by the negative cable. If sparks or arcing occurs as the negative cable is connected to the battery, check that all electrical accessories are turned off (check dome light first). If arcing still occurs, check that all electrical wiring is connected properly to the engine and transmission.

9　See Section 48 for the starting up sequence.

8 Engine – installation (with transmission)

1　With the transmission connected to the engine as described in Section 6, attach the lifting chains to the engine in the same fashion as on removal.

2　Tilt and lower the engine/transmission unit into the engine compartment, guiding the engine mounts correctly onto the frame mounts, and at the same time raising the transmission into the correct position.

3　Install the engine mount through-bolts and the rear transmission crossmember. Tighten all bolts to specification.

4　Install the remaining components in the reverse order of removal. See Section 5.

5　Adjust the clutch as described in Chapter 8.

6　Fill the cooling system with the proper coolant and water mixture (Chapter 3).

7　Fill the engine with correct grade of engine oil (Chapter 1).

8　Check the fluid level in the transmission and add fluid as necessary.

9　Connect the positive battery cable, followed by the negative cable. If sparks or arcing occurs as the negative cable is connected to the battery, check that all electrical accessories are turned off (check interior dome lights first). If arcing still occurs, check that all electrical wiring is connected properly to the engine and transmission.

10　See Section 48 for the starting-up sequence.

9 Engine mounts – replacement with engine in vehicle

1　If on inspection, the flexible mounts have become hard or are split or separated from their metal backing, they must be replaced. This operation may be carried out with the engine/transmission still in the vehicle. See Section 23 for the proper way to raise the engine while it is still in place.

Front mounts

2　Remove the through-bolt and nut.

3　Raise the engine slightly using a hoist or jack with wood block under the oil pan, then remove the mount and frame bracket assembly from the crossmember.

4　Install the new mount, install the through-bolt and nut, then tighten all the bolts to the specified torque.

Rear mount

5　Remove the crossmember to mount bolts then raise the transmission slightly using a jack.

6　Remove the mount to transmission bolts, followed by the mount.

7　Install the new mount, lower the transmission and align the crossmember to mount bolts.

8　Tighten all the bolts to the specified torque.

10 Engine – dismantling (general)

1　It is best to mount the engine on a dismantling stand but if one is not available, then stand the engine on a strong bench so as to be at a comfortable working height.

2　During the dismantling process the greatest care should be taken to keep the exposed parts free from dirt. As an aid to achieving this, it is a sound scheme to thoroughly clean down the outside of the engine, removing all traces of oil and dirt.

3　Use a water soluble grease solvent. The latter compound will make the job easier, as, after the solvent has been applied and allowed to stand for a time, a vigorous jet of water will wash off the solvent and all the grease and filth. If the dirt is thick and deeply embedded, work the solvent into it with a wire brush.

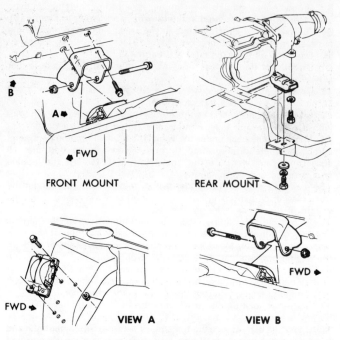

FRONT MOUNT　　　　REAR MOUNT

VIEW A　　　　VIEW B

Fig. 2.1 Engine mounts at side of engine and at transmission (Sec 9)

4　Finally wipe down the exterior of the engine with a rag and only then, when it is quite clean should the dismantling process begin. As the engine is stripped, clean each part in a bath of parts cleaner.

5　Never immerse parts which have internal oilways in solvent (such as the crankshaft) but wipe them carefully with a solvent soaked rag. Probe the oilways with a length of wire and if an air line is available, blow the oilways through to clean them.

6　Be extremely careful using combustible cleaning agents near an open flame or inside an enclosed work area. Fumes can ignite from a lighted cigarette or a hot water heater pilot light. Wipe up any fuel or cleaner spills immediately, and do not store greasy or solvent-soaked rags where they can ignite.

7　Re-use of old engine gaskets is false economy and can give rise to oil and water leaks, if nothing worse. To avoid the possibility of trouble after the engine has been reassembled, *always* use new gaskets throughout.

8　Do not throw the old gaskets away as it sometimes happens that an immediate replacement cannot be found and the old gasket is then very useful as a template. Hang up the old gaskets as they are removed on a suitable hook or nail.

9　Wherever possible, replace nuts, bolts and washers finger-tight from wherever they were removed. This helps avoid later loss and mix-ups. If they cannot be replaced then lay them out in such a fashion that it is clear from where they came.

11 Engine – major overhaul dismantling sequence

1　The Sections in this Chapter deal with removal, installation, overhaul and inspection of the various engine components. Reference should be made to appropriate Chapters for removing and servicing the ancillary engine accessories. These parts include the alternator, air pump, carburetor, etc.

2　If the engine is removed from the vehicle for a major overhaul, the entire engine should be stripped of its components. The exact order in which the engine parts are removed is to some degree a matter of personal preference, however, the following sequence can be used as a guide.

3　*Air Injection Reactor System complete with brackets (Refer to Chapter 6).*

4　*Alternator (Chapter 5).*

5　*Accessory drive belts and pulleys (if not previously removed during engine removal).*

6　*Water pump and related hoses (Chapter 3).*

11.9 Disconnecting the fuel feed line from the fuel pump

11.10 Removing the oil filter from the engine

11.12 Pulling the oil dipstick tube from the engine block

7   Fuel pump and fuel pump push rod (Chapter 4).
8   Distributor with cap and spark plug wires (Chapter 5).
9   Carburetor and fuel lines (Chapter 4) (photo).
10   Oil filter (Chapter 1) (photo).
11   Clutch pressure plate and disc (Chapter 8).
12   Oil dipstick and dipstick tube (photo).
13   Spark plugs (Chapter 1).

14 With these components removed, the general engine sub-assemblies can be removed, serviced and installed using the following Sections in this Chapter.
15 At the appropriate times, refer to Section 37 which deals with general inspection procedures and Section 42 describing the engine reassembly steps.
16 If at any time during the dismantling procedure damage is found to any of the major engine components (cylinder heads, cylinder block, crankshaft, etc.), consider the possibility of purchasing new or rebuilt assemblies as described in Section 38. This decision will in most cases alter your particular rebuilding sequence as dismantling, inspection and assembly will not be required.

12 Intake manifold – removal and installation

1   If the engine has been removed from the car, disregard the following steps which do not apply.
2   If the vehicle is equipped with air conditioning, carefully examine the routing of the A/C hoses and the mounting of the compressor. Depending on the exact system used, you may be able to remove the intake manifold without disconnecting the A/C system. If you are in doubt, take the car to a certified dealer or refrigeration specialist to have the system de-pressurized. Do not under any circumstances disconnect the A/C hoses while the system is under pressure.
3   Disconnect the negative battery cable.
4   Drain the coolant from the radiator (Chapter 1).
5   Remove the air cleaner assembly (Chapter 4).
6   Disconnect the upper radiator hose and the heater hose from the intake manifold.
7   Disconnect the accelerator linkage at the carburetor. If the cable is supported by a bracket on the manifold, this must also be removed.
8   With a container handy to catch any spillage, disconnect the fuel inlet hose at the carburetor. Plug the end of this hose to prevent dirt

from entering the system and excessive fuel seepage.
9   Disconnect all other hoses connected to the carburetor. The exact number of hoses will vary with model year. Make sure each hose is identified as to its location with strips of numbered tape. This will prevent confusion upon reassembly.
10 Remove the distributor following closely the instructions given in Chapter 5. The distributor cap with the spark plug wires attached should be taped or wired against the firewall, out of the way.
11 If equipped with an external coil (1970 – 1974), disconnect the wiring at the top of the coil. Mark each wire for reassembly.
12 Disconnect the vacuum hose leading to the power brake booster (if equipped with power brakes).
13 Remove the upper bracket for the alternator (Chapter 5).
14 Remove the air conditioning compressor bracket at the intake manifold.
15 Remove the intake manifold-to-cylinder head attaching bolts. Count the bolts to make sure all have been removed. There are 12 bolts used on small-block engines, 16 on the large-block Mark IV engines (photo).
16 Lift the manifold, complete with carburetor, free from the engine. Do not pry on the mating surfaces to break the seal as this may cause damage. On some engines it may be necessary to remove the rocker arm covers (valve covers).
17 If the intake manifold is to be replaced with another, transfer the following applicable accessories:

a)   Carburetor and carburetor attaching bolts or studs (see Chapter 4 for procedures).
b)   Temperature and/or oil pressure sending unit.
c)   Water outlet and thermostat (use new gasket).
d)   Heater hose and water pump hose adapter fittings.
e)   EGR valve (use new gasket, see Chapter 6).
f)   Emission system TVS switches (Chapter 6).
g)   Carburetor choke assembly.
h)   Ignition coil and bracket (1970 – 1974).

18 Before installing the manifold, place clean lint-free rags in the engine cavity and scrupulously clean the engine block, cylinder heads and manifold gasket surfaces. All extra gasket material and sealing compound must be removed prior to installation. Remove all dirt and gasket remnants from the engine cavity.
19 Install new front and rear seals to the engine block using RTV or

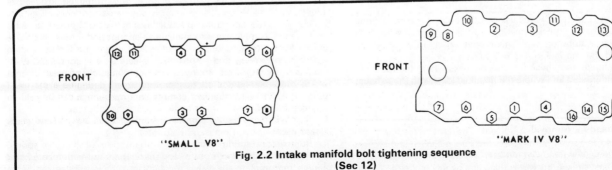

Fig. 2.2 Intake manifold bolt tightening sequence
(Sec 12)

an equivalent sealant. Extend the bead of sealant about $\frac{1}{2}$ inch up the sides of each cylinder head to seal and retain the side gaskets.

20 Place new manifold side gaskets into position on each cylinder head, again using the sealant around the water passages. Make sure the side gaskets are properly mated with the front and rear seals.

21 Lower the intake manifold into position, being careful not to disturb the gaskets. Torque the attaching bolts to specifications and in the order shown in Fig. 2.2.

22 Install the remaining components in the reverse order of removal. Reference should be made to Chapter 5 for distributor installation.

23 Fill the radiator with coolant, start the engine and check for leaks. Adjust the ignition timing and carburetor idle speed as necessary.

13 Exhaust manifold – removal and installation

1   *If the engine has been removed from the car, disregard the following steps which do not apply.*

2   If the vehicle is equipped with air conditioning, carefully examine the routing of the A/C hoses and the mounting of the compressor. Depending on the exact system used, you may be able to remove the exhaust manifolds without disconnecting the A/C system. If you are in doubt, take the car to a certified dealer or refrigeration specialist to have the system de-pressurized. Do not under any circumstances disconnect the A/C hoses while the system is under pressure.

3   Disconnect the negative battery cable.

4   Disconnect the carburetor hot-air pipe routed from the right exhaust manifold to the air cleaner.

5   Mark each spark plug wire with a strip of coded tape (numbered 1–8) and then remove each plug wire from its spark plug. Remember to pull on the rubber boot and not the wire itself. It is important that the order of these wires should not be mixed-up.

6   Remove the spark plug wiring heatshields. These four shields are held in place with a bolt into the engine block (photo).

7   Disconnect the rubber AIR hoses where they meet the manifold check valves. The single metal pipes and the AIR manifold can be removed with the exhaust manifold.

8   If equipped with power steering and/or air conditioning, remove the brackets attached to the left side manifold.

9   Disconnect the exhaust pipes from the manifold flanges. The exhaust pipes can be hung from the frame using wire.

10 If equipped with bolt locking strips, use a screwdriver to pry the metal locking strips away from the exhaust manifold bolt heads. This will enable you to put a standard wrench on the bolts (photo).

11 Remove the exhaust manifold end bolts first, followed by the center bolts. Lift the manifold with its AIR injection tubes away from the engine (photo).

12 If replacing the exhaust manifolds with new ones, the carburetor hot-air stove and the AIR injection tube system must be transfered (see Chapter 6).

13 Before installing the exhaust manifolds, clean the mating surfaces on the cylinder heads and exhaust manifolds. All leftover gasket material should be removed.

14 Place new gaskets into position on the cylinder head, using a thin film of sealer to hold them in place (photo).

15 Install the manifold and torque-tighten the center bolts first, followed by the end bolts (photo). On some models it is best to install the left rear spark plug heatshield first due to inaccessibility after the exhaust manifold is in place.

16 Install the remaining components in the reverse order of removal. Use a new gasket or packing at the exhaust manifold-to-exhaust pipe flange.

17 Connect the spark plug wires using your coding for correct firing order. This order can be quickly checked by following each wire to its location on the distributor cap. The proper order, in a clockwise rotation around the cap is 1-8-4-3-6-5-7-2.

18 Start the engine and check for exhaust leaks where the manifold meets the cylinder head and where the manifold joins with the exhaust pipes.

14 Cylinder heads – removal

1   **Note:** *If the engine has been removed from the car, disregard the following steps which do not apply.*

2   If equipped with air conditioning, the vehicle should be taken to a certified dealer or refrigeration specialist for de-pressurization. Under no circumstances should you disconnect any of the hoses while the system is under pressure.

3   Remove the intake manifold referring to Section 12.

4   Remove the exhaust manifolds referring to Section 13.

5   Remove the lower mounting bolt for the alternator and lay the alternator aside while the lower bracket is removed.

6   If equipped with air conditioning, remove the A/C compressor and forward mounting bracket. Make sure all hoses and fittings are plugged to prevent dirt from entering the system.

7   If equipped with power steering, remove the pump from its bracket and use wire to keep the pump out of the way. Do not disconnect the hoses.

8   If not done previously, drain the engine block of its coolant. Drain plugs are located on each side of the block for this.

9   Remove the rocker arm cover (valve cover) attaching bolts. Lift the cover off the cylinder head. To break the gasket seal it may be necessary to strike the front of the cover with your hand or a rubber mallet. Do not pry on the sealing surfaces.

10 It is important that each of the valve mechanism components be kept separate once removed so they can be reinstalled in their original positions. A cardboard box or rack, numbered according to engine cylinders, can be used for this.

11 Remove each of the rocker arm nuts. Place them at their correct location on the cardboard box or rack.

12 Lift each of the rocker arms, with their rocker balls, off the mounting studs. Place each component correctly on your numbered box or rack (photo).

13 Punch holes in the cardboard box or rack, then lift each of the push rods from the cylinder heads. Place each push rod in its appropriate punched hole (photos).

14 Loosen each of the cylinder head attaching bolts one turn at a time until they can be removed. Note the length of each bolt as it is removed for reinstallation (photo).

15 Count the number of bolts removed. Small-block engines have 17 bolts, big-block engines use 16.

16 With the help of an assistant, lift the heads free of the engine. Be careful, they are heavy. If the head is stuck to the engine block, do not attempt to pry it free as this may ruin the sealing surfaces. Instead, use a hammer and a block of wood, tapping upwards at each end.

17 Place the heads on wood blocks to prevent damage. Refer to the following Sections covering overhaul, inspection and installation procedures.

15 Cylinder head – dismantling

1   **Note:** *New and rebuilt cylinder heads are commonly available for GM engines at dealerships and auto parts stores. Due to the fact that some specialized tools are necessary for the dismantling and inspection of the heads, and replacement parts may not be readily available, it may be more practical and economical for the home mechanic to purchase replacement heads and install them referring to Section 21.*

2   Another alternative at this point is to take the cylinder heads complete to a competent automotive machine shop or GM dealership for the overhaul process.

3   If the complete engine is being overhauled at the same time, it may be wise to refer to Section 38 before a decision is made.

4   If it is decided to overhaul the cylinder heads, read through the following Sections first to gain an understanding of the steps involved and the tools and replacement parts necessary for the job. Proceed as follows.

5   Using a valve spring compressor (available at GM dealers or auto parts stores), compress each of the valve springs and remove the valve locking keys. Work on one valve at a time, removing the keys, then releasing the spring and removing the spring cap, spring shield (if equipped), spring and spring damper. Place these components together on the numbered box or rack used during cylinder head removal. All valve mechanism components must be kept separate so they can be returned to their original positions (photos).

6   Remove the oil seals from the stem of each valve. New seals should be used upon reassembly (photo).

7   Remove any spring shims used at the bottom of the valve spring.

8   Remove each valve, in turn, and place them in the numbered box or rack to complete the valve mechanism removal. Place the valve components in an area where they will not be mixed up.

12.15 Lifting the intake manifold off the engine and cylinder heads

13.6 The spark plug heat shields are held in place by bolts under the exhaust manifold

13.10 Thin metal locking plates are used to prevent the manifold bolts from loosening

13.11 Lifting the exhaust manifold away from the engine. The corroded tubes are part of the AIR emissions system (Chapter 6)

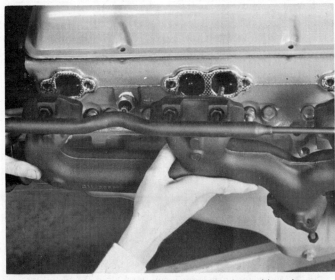

13.14 The exhaust manifold gaskets are held in place with sealant as the manifold is installed

13.15 Tightening the exhaust manifold bolts to specifications

14.12 Removing a rocker arm from its mounting stud

14.13A Pulling a push rod out of its lifter and cylinder head bore

14.13B A cardboard box with holes can be used to keep each push rod in its original position

14.14 Loosening the cylinder head mounting bolts. Before attempting to remove the head, double-check that all bolts are removed

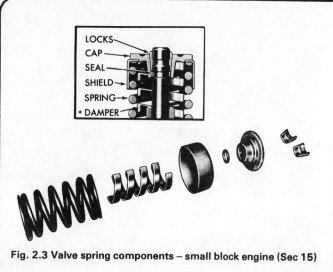

Fig. 2.3 Valve spring components – small block engine (Sec 15)

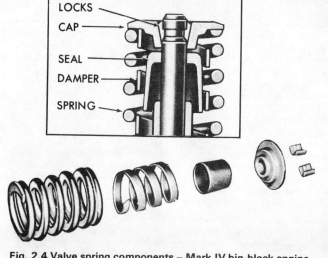

Fig. 2.4 Valve spring components – Mark IV big-block engine (Sec 15)

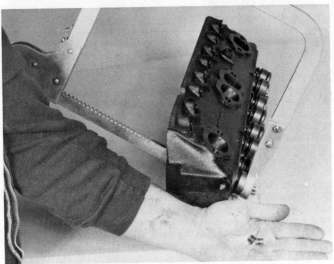

15.5A A valve spring compressor is necessary to remove the valve locks from the stem of the valve

15.5B A valve lock being drawn away from the valve stem

15.5C Following the valve locks off the valve stem will be the spring, spring shield and cap

15.6 Removing a seal from the stem of the valve

16 Cylinder head – cleaning

1   Clean all carbon from the combustion chambers and valve ports. GM tool J-8089 is designed for this purpose, however most auto parts stores will carry this cleaning attachment which is connected to a common hand drill motor.
2   Thoroughly clean the valve guides. GM tool J-8101 is available for this, as are many similar devices found at auto parts stores.
3   Use parts cleaner to remove all sludge and dirt from the rocker arms, rocker balls, push rods and valve springs. Work on one set of components at a time, returning each set to its numbered location on your box or rack.
4   A buffing wheel should be used to remove all carbon deposits from the valves. Do not mix up the order of the valves while cleaning them.
5   Clean all carbon deposits from the head gasket mating surface. Be careful not to stratch this sealing surface.
6   Clean the threads on all cylinder head attaching bolts thoroughly.

17 Cylinder head – inspection

1   Carefully inspect the head for cracks around and inside the exhaust ports, combustion chambers or external cracks into the water chamber.

2   Check the valve stem-to-bore clearance using a dial indicator. One at a time, place a valve in its installed position, with the valve head slightly (about $\frac{1}{16}$ in.) off its seat. Now attach a dial indicator to the head with the indicator point just touching the valve stem where it exits the cylinder head. Grab the top of the valve and move it from side to side, noting the movement on the dial indicator. If valve stem clearance exceeds the specifications, an oversize valve must be used, after reaming the valve guide. This is a job for your dealer or machine shop. Excessive clearance will cause excessive oil consumption; insufficient clearance will result in noisy operation and may cause the valve to stick, resulting in harsh engine operation.
3   Inspect each of the valve springs and its damper. Replace any spring which is deformed, cracked or broken.
4   Check the valve spring tension using GM tool J-8056. The springs are compressed to a specified height and then the tension required for this is measured. This is done without the dampers. If not within 10 lbs of the specified load, the spring should be replaced with a new one.
5   Inspect the rocker arm studs for wear or damage. On Mark IV V8 and some high performance small V8 heads the pushrod guides are retained by nuts on the rocker arm studs. These studs can be unscrewed for replacement of the guides. When assembling, coat the new stud with a gasket sealant and torque tighten. On small V8 engines the studs are pressed in, but replacement is considered a specialist operation involving the reaming of the stud holes 0.003 or

0.013 inch oversize, the new studs being lubricated with hypoid axle oil and pressed in to their original depth.

6   Check the push rods for warping by rolling each on a clean, flat piece of glass. Any push rod which is not perfectly straight and free from damage should be replaced with a new one.

7   Check the cylinder head for warpage. Do this by placing a straightedge across the length of the head and measuring any gaps between the straightedge and the head surface with a feeler gauge. This should be done at three points across the head gasket surface, and also in a diagonal fashion across this surface.

8   If warpage exceeds 0.006 in at any point when a straightedge which spans the entire head is used, the cylinder head should be resurfaced. Using a straightedge with a span of 6 inches, the warpage should not exceed 0.003 in. Cylinder head resurfacing is a job for a professional automotive machine shop. Also note that if a cylinder head is resurfaced, the intake manifold position will be slightly altered, requiring the manifold to be resurfaced a proportionate amount.

18 Valves and valve seats – inspection and valve grinding

1   Examine the heads of the valves for pitting and burning, especially the heads of the exhaust valves. The valves' seatings should be examined at the same time. If the pitting on valve and seat is very slight the marks can be removed by grinding the seats and valves together with coarse, and then fine, valve grinding paste.

2   Valve grinding is carried out as follows: smear a trace of coarse carborundum paste on the seat face and apply a suction grinder tool to the valve head. With a semi-rotary motion, grind the valve head to its seat, lifting the valve occasionally to redistribute the grinding paste. When a dull matt even surface finish is produced on both the valve seat and the valve, wipe off the paste and repeat the process with fine carborundum paste, lifting and turning the valve to redistribute the paste as before. A light spring placed under the valve head will greatly ease this operation. When a smooth unbroken ring of light grey matt finish is produced, on both valve and valve seat faces, the grinding operation is completed.

3   Where the valve or seat shows signs of bad pitting or burning, then the valve should be refaced by your dealer and the seat recut. If the refacing of the valve will reduce the edge of the valve head (seat width) to less than that given in the Specifications, replace the valve (photo).

4   Scrape away all carbon from the valve head and the valve stem. Carefully clean away every trace of grinding compound, taking great care to leave none in the ports or in the valve guides. Clean the valves and valve seats with a solvent soaked rag then with a clean rag, and finally, if an air line is available, blow the valves, valve guides and valve ports clean.

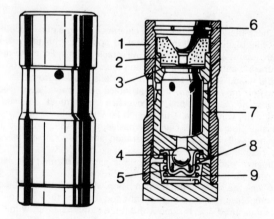

Fig. 2.5 Sectional view of a hydraulic lifter (Sec 20)

1	*Body*	6	*Pushrod seat retainer*
2	*Pushrod*	7	*Plunger*
3	*Metering valve*	8	*Check ball spring*
4	*Check ball*	9	*Plunger spring*
5	*Check ball retainer*		

19 Cylinder head – assembly

1   Make sure all valve mechanism components are perfectly clean and free from carbon and dirt. The bare cylinder head should also be clean and free from abrasive agents which may have been used for valve grinding, reaming, etc.

2   Insert a valve in the proper port.

3   Assemble the valve spring assembly for that cylinder. This will include the spring and damper, shield and cap.

4   Using the valve spring compressor, compress the assembly over the valve stem and hold in this position.

5   Install a new oil seal in the lower groove of the valve stem. Make sure it is flat and not twisted.

6   Install the valve locks and release the compressor. Make sure the lock seats properly in the upper groove of the valve stem.

7   Check the installed height of the valve springs using a narrow thin scale. Measure from the top of the shim (if present) or the spring seat to the top of the valve spring or spring shield (if used). If necessary, $\frac{1}{16}$ in shims can be used under the valve spring to bring the unit to the proper specifications. Shims are used to correct springs which are too high, as the shims will act to compress the springs slightly. At no time should the spring be shimmed to give an installed height under the minimum specified length. If the spring is too short, it should be replaced with a new one.

20 Valve lifter – removal, inspection, installation

Checking

1   Hydraulic valve lifters are normally very reliable in operation and do not require repeated adjustment.

2   A noisy valve lifter is best traced when the engine is idling. Place a length of hose or tubing near the position of each intake and exhaust valve while listening at the other end of the tube. Another method is to remove the rocker cover (valve cover) and with the engine idling, place a finger on each of the valve spring retainers in turn. If a valve lifter is faulty in operation, it will be evident from the shock felt from the retainer as the valve seats.

3   Provided adjustment is correct, the most likely cause of a noisy lifter is due to a piece of dirt being trapped between the plunger and lifter body.

Removal

4   Remove the intake manifold (Section 12).

5   Remove the push rod cover (Pontiac engines only).

6   Remove the valve cover and lift each push rod out of the cylinder bloc (see Section 14 for details).

7   To pull the lifters out of their bores a special tool can be purchased or a sharp scribe can be positioned at the top of the lifter and used to force the lifter upwards. Do not use pliers or other tools on the outside of the lifter body. Stuck lifter can sometimes be worked free by squirting carburetor cleaner around the body and then working the lifter up and down (photos).

8   Be sure to kep all lifters separated and identified so they can be installed in the same locations.

Inspection

9   After cleaning the lifters (one at a time to prevent mixing up the order), inspect for nicks, gauges, etc. Any damage at all is cause for replacement.

10 Check the bottom of the lifter (the end which rides against the camshaft) for scratches or nicks. The lifters should be replaced if the bottom shows a concave condition, with the lifter body collapsing due to wear (photos).

Installation

11 When installing the lifter, make sure they are liberally coated with 'Molykote' or its equivalent.

12 If the original lifters are reused, they must be installed into their appropriate bores.

13 Install the valve components, valve cover and intake manifold referring to the appropriate Sections

21 Cylinder heads – installation

1   If not already done, thoroughly clean the gasket surfaces on both the cylinder heads and the engine block.

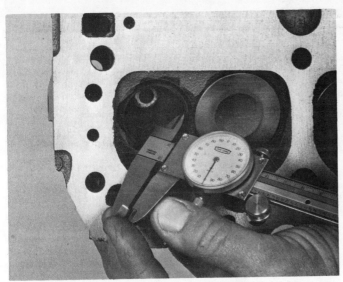

18.3 Measuring the valve seat inside the cylinder head

20.4 Using a lifter removal tool to pull a lifter from its engine bore

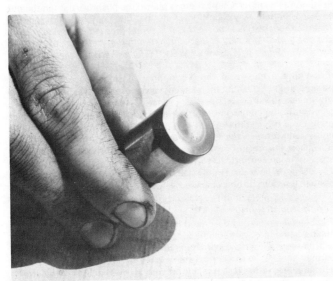

20.9 If the bottom of the lifter is collapsed or has scratches or nicks, it should be replaced with a new one

21.4 Check the new head gasket for markings which would indicate which side should be installed towards the cylinder head

21.11A Place some lubricant on the top of each valve

21.11B The lubricant should also be used on the rocker balls before installation

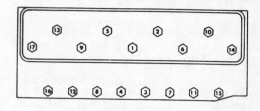
"SMALL V8"

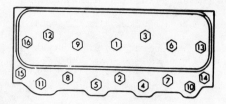
"MARK IV V8"

Fig. 2.6 Cylinder head bolt tightening sequence (Sec 21)

2   To get the proper torque readings, the threads of the attaching bolts must be free of dirt. This also goes for the threaded holes in the engine block. Run a tap through these threaded holes to ensure they are clean.

3   Ascertain which type of head gasket you are using. Engines using steel head gaskets require a thin, even coat of sealer on both sides. No sealer of any kind should be used with composition steel/asbestos gaskets.

4   Place the gasket in place over the engine block dowel pins with the bead up (some gaskets will be marked 'This side up') (photo).

5   Carefully lower the cylinder head onto the engine, over the dowel pins and the gaskets. Be careful not to move the gasket while doing this.

6   Coat the threads of the cylinder head attaching bolts with a sealing compound and install each finger-tight. Do not tighten any of the bolts at this time.

7   Tighten each of the bolts, a little at a time, in the sequence shown in Fig. 2.6. Continue tightening in this sequence until the proper torque reading is obtained. As a final check, work around the head in a logical front-to-rear sequence to make sure none of the bolts have been left out of the sequence.

8   Install the exhaust manifolds as described in Section 13.

9   Install each of the valve lifters (if removed) into its proper bore. 'Molykote' or its equivalent should be used as a coating on each lifter.

10   Place a small amount of 'Molykote' or its equivalent on each end of the push rods and install each in its original position. Make sure the push rods are seated properly in the lifter cavity.

11   Place each of the rocker arms and corresponding rocker balls onto its original stud. The rocker balls and valve stem end of the rocker arms should receive a small amount of 'Molykote' or its equivalent (photos).

12   Adjust the valves as described in Section 22.

13   Install the rocker arm covers (valve covers). Early models use a gasket to seal, while newer models use RTV sealant instead of a gasket. If, when removed, the cover has a gasket, purchase a new gasket and place it into position on the cleaned cylinder head. Tighten the attaching bolts to specifications. If no gasket was used, apply a bead of RTV sealer (or its equivalent) around the entire sealing surface of the cylinder head. This bead should be $\frac{1}{8}$ inch wide. When going around bolt holes always go round the inboard side of the holes. Install the cover while the sealer is still wet and torque the bolts to specifications.

14   Install the intake manifold with new gaskets as described in Section 12.

15   Install the remaining engine components as described in Section 14. Fill the radiator with coolant, start the engine and check for leaks. Adjust the ignition timing and valves as required. Be sure to recheck the coolant level once the engine has warmed up to operating temperature.

22 Valve lash – adjustment

Hydraulic type

1   If the work is being carried out with the engine in the vehicle, the following preliminary operations must be performed:

   a)   Remove the air cleaner
   b)   Disconnect the rocker cover vent hoses and wiring
   c)   Remove the rocker covers

Note: Viewed from the radiator end of the engine, cylinders on the right are numbered 1-3-5-7 and on the left 2-4-6-8, from front to rear.

2   Rotate the crankshaft until the mark on the torsional damper aligns with the center or O-marking on the timing indicator. If No.1 cylinder valves are moving, the engine is in No. 6 cylinder firing position and the crankshaft must be rotated 360°. If No. 1 cylinder valves are not moving, the piston is at top-dead-center (TDC) which is correct.

3   Back-off the rocker arm stud adjusting nut on No. 1 intake and exhaust valves in turn, until there is play in the pushrod; tighten the nut to just eliminate play then tighten the nut one complete turn (photo).

Note: Experience has shown that it is sometimes difficult to determine the position where play is just eliminated during lash adjustment. This can be simplified by the use of a 0.0015 feeler between the rocker and valve stem.

4   With the engine in the No. 1 firing position, as determined in paragraph 2, also adjust the exhaust valves of cylinders 3, 4 and 8 and the intake valves of cylinders 2, 5 and 7.

5   Rotate the crankshaft through 360° to align the torsional damper mark once more, then repeat paragraph 1 for exhaust valves 2, 5, 6 and 7, and intake valves 3, 4, 6 and 8.

6   Clean the gasket surfaces of the cylinder head and rocker arm cover with solvent and wipe dry with a lint-free cloth.

7   Using a new gasket, install the rocker arm cover and torque tighten the bolts to the specified value.

Mechanical type

8   Set the engine as described in paragraph 2 of this Section. If the engine has been overhauled and is being reassembled, the valve lash will have to be set cold. If the adjustment is being carried out at a normal service interval, run the engine to normal operating temperature. Adjust the lash again (hot) with an overhauled engine after it has been operated for a few miles.

9   Using a feeler blade of the appropriate thickness (see Specifications Section) adjust the lash of each valve according to the following method.

   No 1. piston at TDC. Valves to adjust:
   Intake valves of cylinder 2 and 7
   Exhaust valve of cylinders 4 and 8

Note: Viewed from the radiator end of the engine, cylinders on the right bank are numbered 1-3-5-7 and on the left 2-4-6-8, from front to rear.

Rotate the crankshaft through 180° (half turn). Valves to adjust:
   Intake valves of cylinders 1 and 8
   Exhaust valves of cylinders 3 and 6
   Rotate the crankshaft through 180° (half turn). Valves to adjust:
   Intake valves of cylinders 3 and 4
   Exhaust valves of cylinders 5 and 7
   Rotate the crankshaft through 180° (half turn). Valves to adjust:
   Intake valves of cylinders 5 and 6
   Exhaust valves of cylinders 1 and 2

23 Oil pan – removal and installation

With engine installed in vehicle

1   Disconnect the negative battery cable.

2   Remove the air cleaner assembly and set aside.

3   Remove the distributor cap to prevent breakage as the engine is raised.

4   Unbolt the radiator shroud from the radiator support and hang the shroud over the cooling fan.
5   If equipped with a big-block Mark IV engine, remove the oil dipstick and dipstick tube.
6   Raise the car and support firmly on jack stands.
7   Drain the engine oil into a suitable container.
8   Disconnect the exhaust crossover pipe at the exhaust manifold flanges. Lower the exhaust pipes and suspend them from the frame with wire.
9   If equipped with an automatic transmission, remove the converter underpan.
10 If equipped with a manual transmission, remove the starter (Chapter 5) and the flywheel cover.
11 Use a bolt at the center of the torsional damper to rotate the engine until the timing mark is straight down, at the 6 o'clock position. This will move the forward crankshaft throw upward, providing clearance at the front of the oil pan (photo).
12 Remove the through bolt at each engine mount (photo).
13 At this time the engine must be raised slightly to enable the oil pan to slide clear of the crossmember. The preferred method is to use an engine hoist or 'cherry picker'. Hook up the lifting chains as described in Section 4.
14 An alternative method can be used if extreme care is exercised. Use a floor jack and a block of wood placed under the oil pan. The wood block should spread the load across the oil pan, preventing damage or collapse of the oil pan metal. The oil pump pickup and screen is very close to the oil pan bottom, so any collapsing of the pan may damage the pickup or prevent the oil pump from drawing oil properly.
15 With either method, raise the engine slowly until wood blocks can be placed between the frame front crossmember and the engine block. The blocks should be approximately 3 inches thick. Check clearances all around the engine as it is raised. Pay particular attention to the distributor and the cooling fan (photo).
16 Lower the engine onto the wood blocks. Make sure it is firmly supported. If a hoist is being used, keep the lifting chains secured to the engine.
17 Remove the oil pan bolts. Note the different sizes used and their locations (photo).
18 Remove the oil pan by tilting it downwards at the rear and then working the front clear of the crossmember (photo). It may be necessary to use a rubber mallet to break the seal.
19 Before installing, thoroughly clean the gasket sealing surfaces on the engine block and on the oil pan. All sealer and gasket material must be removed.
20 Apply a thin film of sealer to the new side gaskets and fit them to the engine block. All bolt holes should line up properly.
21 Again using sealer, install the front and rear seals to the engine. Make sure the ends butt with the ends of the side gaskets (photos).
22 Lift the pan into position and install all bolts finger-tight. There is no specific order for torquing the bolts; however it is a good policy to tighten the end bolts first.
23 Lower the engine onto its mounts and install the through bolts. Torque-tighten these to specifications.
24 Follow the removal steps in a reverse order. Fill the engine with the correct grade and quantity of oil, start the engine and check for leaks.

With engine removed from vehicle

25 Most of the above steps will not be required if the engine has been removed from the car.
26 The pan can be simply unbolted and removed from the engine block as described in paragraphs 17 and 18.
27 Follow paragraphs 19 through 22 for installing the oil pan to the engine block.

24 Oil pump – removal and installation

1   Remove the oil pan as described in Section 23.
2   Remove the bolts securing the oil pump assembly to the rear main bearing cap. Remove the oil pump with its pickup tube and screen as an assembly from the engine block (photo).

3   To install, move the pump assembly into position and align the slot on top end of extension shaft with the drive tang on the lower end of the distributor (photo). The distributor drives the oil pump so it is essential that these two components mate properly.
4   Install the securing bolts and torque-tighten to specifications.
5   Make sure the oil pump screen is parallel with the oil pan rails. The screen must be in this position to fit into the oil pan properly.
6   Install the oil pan as described in Section 23. Pay close attention to the oil pressure gauge or warning light during the initial engine start-up period.

25 Oil pump – dismantling, examination and reassembly

1   In most cases it will be more practical and economical to replace a faulty oil pump with a new or rebuilt unit. If it is decided to overhaul the oil pump, check on internal parts availability before beginning.
2   Remove the pump cover retaining screws and the pump cover. Index mark the gear teeth to permit reassembly in the same position.
3   Remove the idler gear, drivegear and shaft from the body.
4   Remove the pressure regulator valve retaining pin, the regulator valve and the related parts.
5   If necessary, the pick-up screen and pipe assembly can be extracted from the pump body.
6   Wash all the parts in solvent and thoroughly dry them. Inspect the body for cracks, wear or other damage. Similarly inspect the gears.
7   Check the drive gear shaft for looseness in the pump body, and the inside of the pump cover for wear that would permit oil leakage past the ends of the gears.
8   Inspect the pick-up screen and pipe assembly for damage to the screen, pipe or relief grommet.
9   Apply a gasket sealant to the end of the pipe (pick-up screen and pipe assembly) and tap it into the pump body taking care that no damage occurs. If the original press-fit cannot be obtained a rear assembly must be used to prevent air leaks and loss of pressure.
10 Install the pressure regulator valve and related parts.
11 Install the drive gear and shaft in the pump body, followed by the idler gear with the smooth side towards the pump cover opening. Lubricate the parts with engine oil (photo).
12 Install the cover and torque tighten the screws.
13 Turn the driveshaft to ensure that the pump operates freely.

26 Torsional damper – removal and installation

1   **Note**: *If the engine has been removed from the car, disregard the following steps which do not apply.*
2   Loosen the alternator, power steering pump and air conditioning compressor (as required) to relieve tension on the drive belts.
3   Remove the cooling fan and the radiator shroud.
4   Remove the drive belts, noting the installed positions of each.
5   Remove the fan pulley from the water pump shaft.
6   Remove the accessory drive pulley from the torsional damper. Then remove the torsional damper retaining bolt at the center (photo).
7   Install a special torsional damper (harmonic balancer) remover to the damper. Draw the damper off the crankshaft, being careful not to drop it as it breaks free. **A common gear puller should not be used to draw the bumper as this may separate the outer portion of the damper from the inner hub. Only a puller which bolts to the inner hub should be used.**
8   Before installing the torsional damper, coat the front cover seal area (on damper) with engine oil.
9   Place the damper in position over the key on the crankshaft. Make sure the damper keyway lines up with the key.
10 Using a torsional damper installer (GM tool J-23523 or equivalent), draw the damper onto the crankshaft. This tool distributes the draw evenly around the inner hub.
11 Remove the installation tool and install the torsional damper center retaining bolt. Torque to specifications.
12 Follow the removal procedure in the reverse order for the remaining components.
13 Adjust the tension of the various belts by referring to Chapter 1.

22.3 Tightening the rocker arm while at the same time checking for movement of the pushrod (lash)

23.11 By turning the torsional damper bolt until the timing mark is at the bottom, the front crankshaft throw will be in an 'up' position

23.12 Removing the engine mount through bolt

23.15 A wood block placed between the engine mount sections

23.17 Removing the oil pan mounting bolts

23.18 Tilting the oil pan down at the rear to clear the front crossmember

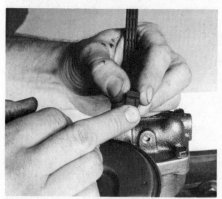

23.21A The front oil pan seal has an indentation which fits into the side gasket

23.21B Sealant is applied at the area where the front gasket meets the side gasket

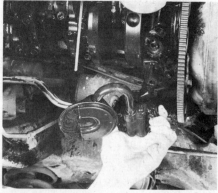

24.2 Lowering the oil pump away from the rear main bearing cap (engine installed in vehicle)

24.3 When reinstalling the oil pump make sure the shaft mates with the distributor shaft

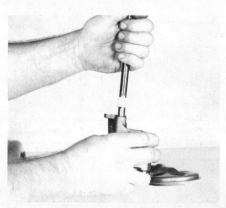

25.11 Pushing the oil pump drive shaft into the pump body

26.6 Removing the accessory drive pulley from the torsional damper

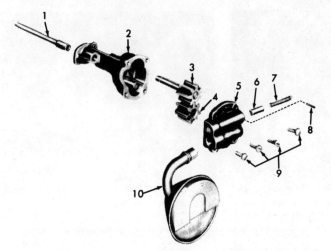

Fig. 2.7 Exploded view of small-block engine oil pump (Sec 25)

1	Driveshaft	6	Pressure regulator valve
2	Body	7	Spring
3	Gears	8	Pin
4	Idler gear	9	Cover screws
5	Pump cover	10	Pick-up screen and pipe

Fig. 2.8 Exploded view of big-block engine oil pump (Sec 25)

1	Driveshaft	7	Cover
2	Coupling	8	Pressure regulator valve
3	Body	9	Spring
4	Drive gear	10	Washer
5	Idler gear	11	Pin
6	Pick-up screen and pipe	12	Cover screws

27 Oil seal (front cover) – replacement

With front cover installed on engine

1   With the torsional damper removed (Section 26), pry the old seal out of the crankcase front cover with a large screwdriver. Be careful not to damage the front surface of the crankshaft.
2   Place the new seal into position with the open end of the seal (seal 'lip') toward the inside of the cover (photo).
3   Drive the seal into the cover until it is fully seated. GM tool J-23042 for small-block engines or J-22102 for big-block engines is available for this purpose. These tools are designed to exert even pressure around the circumference of the seal as it is hammered into place. A section of large diameter pipe or a large socket could also be used.
4   Take care not to distort the front cover.

With front cover removed from engine

5   This method is preferred, as the cover can be supported as the new seal is driven into place, preventing the possibility of cover distortion.
6   Remove the crankcase front cover as described in Section 28.
7   Pry the old seal out of its bore with a large screwdriver.
8   Support the inside of the cover, around the seal area and install the new seal in the same fashion as described above.

28 Crankcase front cover – removal and installation

1   **Note** If the engine has been removed from the car, disregard the following steps which do not apply.
2   Remove the torsional damper as described in Section 26.
3   Remove the water pump as described in Chapter 3.
4   Remove the crankcase front cover attaching bolts and remove the front cover from the engine (photo). On big-block Mark IV engines, remove the attaching bolts and then draw the cover slightly away from the engine. Cut the oil pan gasket flush with the engine block and then remove the cover.
5   Upon installation, proceed as follows:

Small V8

6   Ensure that the block and crankcase front cover are clean.
7   Use a sharp knife to remove any oil pan gasket material protruding at the oil pan to engine block junction.

8   Apply a $\frac{1}{8}$ inch bead of silicone rubber sealer (Chevrolet part No. 1051435 – or equivalent) to the joint formed at the oil pan and block, as well as the front lip of the oil pan.
9   Coat the cover gasket with a non-setting sealant, position it on the cover then loosely install the cover. First install the top four bolts loosely then install two $\frac{1}{4}$ inch – 20 x $\frac{1}{2}$ inch screws at the lower cover holes. Apply a bead of silicone sealer on the bottom of the cover then install the cover, tightening the screws alternately and evenly and at the same time aligning the dowel pins (photo).
10   Remove the two $\frac{1}{4}$ inch – 20 x $\frac{1}{2}$ inch screws and install the remaining cover screws.
11   Follow removal steps in the reverse order for the remaining components.

Mark IV V8

12   Ensure that the block and crankcase front cover are clean.
13   Cut the tabs from the new oil pan front seal, using a sharp knife. This is not applicable if oil pan removed and a new gasket set is being used.
14   Install the seal to the front cover, pressing the tips into the holes provided in the cover.
15   Coat the gasket with a non-setting sealant and position it on the cover.
16   Apply a $\frac{1}{8}$ inch bead of silicone rubber sealer (Chevrolet part No. 1051435 – or equivalent) to the joint formed at the oil pan and block.
17   Install the cover attaching screws and torque tighten to the specified value.
18   Coat the front cover seal area of the torsional damper with engine oil, place the damper in position, then use a suitable bolt and spacers to draw the damper into position. Install and torque tighten the damper retaining bolt. Take care that the damper is not damaged during this operation.
19   Install the accessory drive pulley.
20   Install remaining components in the reverse order.

29 Timing chain and sprockets – removal and installation

1   **Note**: If the engine has been removed from the car, disregard the following steps which do not apply.
2   Remove the torsional damper and crankcase cover as described in Sections 26 and 28 respectively.
3   Turn the engine until the marks on the camshaft and crankshaft sprockets are in alignment. Do not attempt to remove either sprocket or the chain until this is done (photo).

27.2 Placing a new front seal into its bore on the crankshaft front cover

28.4 Removing one of the bolts which secure the crankshaft front cover (timing cover) to the engine

28.9 Installing the front cover

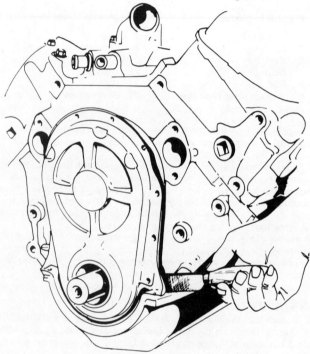

Fig. 2.9 Cutting oil pan front seal – Mark IV big-block engines only (Sec 28)

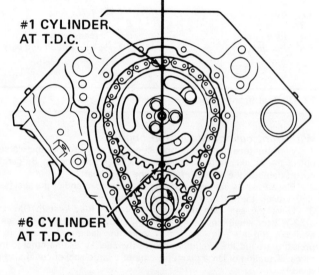

#1 CYLINDER AT T.D.C.

#6 CYLINDER AT T.D.C.

Fig. 2.11 Aligning timing marks (Sec 29)

CUT THIS PORTION FROM NEW SEAL

Fig. 2.10 Modifying oil pan seal – Mark IV big-block engines only

4   Remove the three camshaft sprocket retaining bolts and lift the camshaft sprocket and timing chain together off the front of the engine. In some cases it may be necessary to tap the sprocket with a soft-faced mallet.
5   If it is found necessary to remove the crankcase sprocket, it can be pulled from the crankshaft using a puller designed for this purpose (photo).
6   Install the crankshaft sprocket to the crankshaft by using a bolt and washer from the puller set.
7   Install the timing chain over the camshaft sprocket with slack in the chain hanging down over the crankshaft sprocket.

8   With the timing marks aligned, slip the chain over the crankshaft sprocket and then draw the camshaft sprocket into place with the three retaining bolts. Do not hammer or in any way attempt to drive the camshaft sprocket into place as this would dislodge the welsh plug at the rear of the engine.
9   With the chain and both sprockets in place, check again that the timing marks on the two sprockets are perfectly in line with each other. If not, remove the camshaft sprocket and move until the marks align.
10   Lubricate the chain with engine oil and install the remaining components in the reverse order of removal.

30 Camshaft – removal and installation

1   **Note:** *If the engine has been removed from the car, disregard the following steps which do not apply.*
2   Remove the intake manifold as described in Section 12.
3   Remove the push rods from the lifters. In order to do this, the rocker covers must be removed, and the rocker arm nuts loosened. Further information on this can be found in Section 14.
4   Remove the valve lifters, keeping each separate so they can be replaced in their original positions. Refer to Section 20 for removal information.
5   Remove the front grille (Chapter 12).
6   Remove the radiator, shroud, air conditioning condenser and hood catch support as necessary to provide clearance for the camshaft as it is drawn from the engine.

29.3 Small timing marks are located on each gear. They must be in perfect alignment

29.5 Drawing the crankshaft pulley off the crankshaft with a puller. Be careful not to damage the threads in the end of the crankshaft

29.6 A new crankshaft gear being installed

30.9 When pulling a camshaft from an engine, support it near the engine block and go slowly so the bearings are not damaged

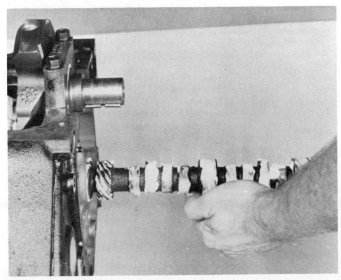

30.11 The camshaft being re-installed with plenty of lubricant on the lobes

31.4 The front camshaft bearing is easily checked for damage. The others are not so readily accessible

7   Remove the fuel pump and fuel pump push rod (Chapter 4).

8   Remove the torsional damper (Section 26), the crankcase front cover (Section 28) and the camshaft sprocket/timing chain (Section 29). Install two $\frac{5}{16}$ in – 18x4 in bolts into the camshaft bolt holes to be used as grips to pull on the camshaft.

9   Carefully draw the camshaft out of the engine block. Do this very slowly to avoid damage to the camshaft bearings as the journals pass through the bearing surfaces. Always support the camshaft with one hand near the engine block (photo).

10   Before installing the camshaft, coat each of the lobes and journals liberally with 'Molykote' or its equivalent.

11   Slide the camshaft into the engine block, again taking extra care not to damage the bearings (photo).

12   Install the remaining components in the reverse order of removal, referring to the appropriate Sections where necessary.

13   Adjust the valve lash as described in Section 22.

31   Camshaft and bearings – inspection and servicing

1   Examine the bearing surfaces and the surfaces of the cam lobes. Surface scratches, if very shallow, can be removed by rubbing with a fine emery cloth or an oilstone. Any deep scoring will necessitate a new camshaft.

2   Mount the camshaft on V-blocks and use a dial gauge to measure lobe lift and run-out. Reject a camshaft which does not meet the specified limits.

3   Measure the journal diameters using a micrometer. Reject a camshaft which does not meet the specified limits.

4   If the bearings are worn, they can be extracted using a suitable tool (Chevrolet tool set No. J-6098 is designed for this purpose) (photo). **Note**: *It will be necessary to drive out the camshaft rear plug from the block.*

5   New bearings are installed using the same tool set, but it is necessary to align the cam bearing oil holes as follows:
Small V8: No.1 bearing hole so that the oil holes are equidistant from the 6 o'clock position; No. 2 through No. 4 bearing oil holes positioned at 5 o'clock (towards left side of engine and at a position even with the bottom of the bore); No. 5 bearing oil hole at the 12 o'clock position.
Mark IV V8: No.1 through No. 4 oil hole must be aligned with the oil holes in the cam bearing bore. No. 5 bearing bore is annulus and the cam bearing must be at or near the 6 o'clock position.

6   After installing new bearings, install a new camshaft rear plug flush 1/32 inch below and parallel to the rear surface of the block.

32   Pistons, connecting rods and bearings – removal

1   Remove the oil pan, oil pump and cylinder heads as described previously in this Chapter.

2   Before the piston assemblies can be forced up through the top of the engine block, a ridge reamer should be used to remove the ridge and/or carbon deposits at the top of each cylinder (photo). Working on one cylinder at a time, turn the engine so the piston is at the bottom of its stroke. Then place a rag on top of the piston to catch the cuttings. After the ridge is removd, crank the engine until the piston is at the top of the cylinder and remove the cloth and cuttings. Failure to remove this ridge may cause damage to the piston rings, pistons or cylinder walls.

3   Inspect the connecting rods and connecting rod caps for cylinder identification. If these components are not plainly marked, identify each using a small punch to make the appropriate number of indentations (left bank – 1, 3, 5, 7, right bank – 2, 4, 6, 8).

4   Working in sequence, remove the nuts on the connecting rod stud and lift the cap (with bearing inside) off the crankshaft (photo). Place the connecting rod cap and bearing on a clean work surface marked cylinder ‡1, ‡2, ‡3, etc.

5   Push a piece of rubber or plastic tubing over the connecting rod studs to completely cover the studs. This is important as these studs could easily damage the crankshaft or cylinder wall when the piston assembly is removed (photo).

6   Push the piston/connecting rod assembly out through the top of the cylinder (photo). Place the piston with its connecting rod next to its rod cap on the sequenced work area.

7   Repeat these procedures for the remaining seven cylinders turning the crankshaft as necessary to gain access to the connecting rod nuts. Reuse the rubber or plastic tubing for each assembly.

8   Remove the bearings from the connecting rods and the connecting rod caps. This is easily done with a small screwdriver. If the engine has many miles, it is false economy to reuse the bearings, but if they are to be reinstalled place them in a numbered rack.

9   If a piston ring expanding tool is available, use this to remove each of the rings from the piston. An alternative method is to expand the ring just enough to clear the lands of the piston body. Then place strips of tin (about $\frac{1}{4}$ in. wide) under the ring at equal distances around the piston. Using a slight twisting motion, 'walk' the ring up the piston and off the top.

10   Place the rings, in their 'installed' order adjacent to the piston/connecting rod on your numbered work area.

11   Separating the connecting rod from the piston requires the removal of the piston pin. This job is best left to a dealer or automotive machine shop equipped with the proper support tools and an arbor press.

12   Do not take the time to clean and inspect the piston/rod assemblies at this time as they may have to be replaced with new units depending on the condition of the cylinder block and/or crankshaft.

33   Flywheel – removal and installation

1   The flywheel may be unbolted from the crankshaft rear flange after the removal of the transmission and in the case of a manual transmission, unbolting the clutch housing and clutch (refer to Chapters 7 and 8).

2   To prevent the crankshaft from turning as the bolts are loosened, place a block of wood between one of the crankshaft throws and the side of the engine block. An alignment tool pushed through the flywheel and against the engine block will also work (photo).

3   Before installing the flywheel, clean the mating surfaces of the flywheel and the crankshaft.

4   With manual transmissions, install the flywheel by aligning the dowel hole in the crankshaft with the dowel hole in the flywheel.

5   With automatic transmissions, install the flywheel with the torque converter attaching pads toward the transmission.

6   Tighten the bolts a little at a time until the proper torque specification is attained. It is a good idea to use a thread sealing agent (like Locktite) on the bolt threads (photo). Again, use a block of wood or a centerpunch tool against the block to prevent the flywheel from turning as the bolts are tightened.

34   Flywheel and starter ring gear – inspection

1   Examine the starter ring gear for broken or chipped teeth. If evident, the flywheel must be replaced with a new one (photo).

2   On manual transmission versions, examine for scoring on the

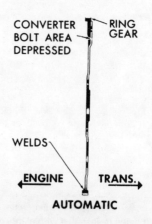

CONVERTER BOLT AREA DEPRESSED

RING GEAR

WELDS

ENGINE   TRANS.

AUTOMATIC

Fig. 2.12 Drive plate (automatic transmission) installed position (Sec 33)

32.2 With the piston at the bottom of its travel, a ridge reamer is used to remove the built-up carbon from the top of the cylinder wall

32.4 Lifting a connecting rod bearing cap off the crankshaft

32.5 Pieces of rubber hose pushed over the rod bolts will protect the crankshaft and cylinders

32.6 A piston/connecting rod assembly being pushed out of the engine block

33.2 A centerpunch tool is used here to hold the flywheel in place while the bolts are loosened

33.6 A thread sealer, like Loctite, should be used on the threads of the flywheel bolts

clutch friction face. Light scoring may be dressed out using emery cloth, but where there is deep scoring the flywheel must be replaced with a new one or clutch damage will soon occur.

3   On automatic transmission models, examine the converter securing bolt holes for elongation.

4   Replace the driveplate complete if either the starter ring gear is worn or the mounting bolt holes are elongated.

35 Crankshaft, main bearings and oil seals – removal

1   The crankshaft and main bearings should only be removed with the engine removed from the car.

2   The engine should be completely stripped of its components as described in the previous Sections of this Chapter.

3   Check that each of the 5 main bearing caps is marked in respect to its location in the engine block. If not, use a punch to make small indentations in the same fashion as for the connecting rods and caps (photo). The main bearing caps must be reinstalled in their original positions.

4   Unbolt the main bearing caps, and lift each cap and its corresponding bearing off the crankshaft (photo). Place all main bearing caps and bearings on a workspace numbered to correspond with the position of the caps in the engine block.

5   Lift the crankshaft from the engine block. Be careful not to damage it in any way (photo).

6   Remove the two halves of the rear main bearing oil seal.

7   Remove the main bearings from the cylinder block and the main bearing caps, keeping them separated as to their positions (photo).

8   The crankshaft gear at the front of the crank can be removed by using a special puller designed for this purpose.

36 Rear main oil seal – replacement (engine in car)

1   *Always replace both halves of the rear main oil seal as a unit. While the replacement of this seal is much easier with the engine removed from the car, as in a total engine rebuild, the job can be done with the engine in place.*

2   Remove the oil pan and oil pump as described prevously in this Chapter.

3   Remove the rear main bearing cap from the engine (photo).

4   Using a screwdriver, pry the lower half of the oil seal from the bearing cap (photo).

5   To remove the upper half of the seal, use a small hammer and a brass pin punch to roll the seal around the crankshaft journal. Tap one end of the seal with the hammer and punch (be careful not to strike the crankshaft) until the other end of the seal protrudes enough to pull the seal out with a pair of pliers (photos).

6   Clean all sealant and foreign material from the cylinder bearing cap and case. Do not use an abrasive cleaner for this.

7   Inspect components for nicks, scratches or burrs at all sealing surfaces.

8   Coat the seal lips of the new seal with light engine oil. Do not get oil on the seal mating ends.

9   Included in the purchase of the rear main oil seal should be a small plastic installation tool. If not included, make your own by cutting an old feeler gauge blade as shown in Fig. 2.15.

10   Position the narrow end of this installation tool between the crankshaft and the seal seat. The idea is to protect the new seal from being damaged by the sharp edge of the seal seat.

11   Raise the new upper half of the seal into position with the seal lips facing towards the front of the engine. Push the seal onto its seat, using the installation tool as a protector against the seal contacting the sharp edge.

12   Roll the seal around the crankshaft, all the time using the tool as a 'shoehorn' for protection. When both ends of the seal are flush with the engine block, remove the installation tool being careful not to withdraw the seal as well.

13   Install the lower half of the oil seal to the bearing cap, again using the installation tool to protect the seal against the sharp edge. Make sure the seal is firmly seated, then withdraw the installation tool (photo).

14   Smear a bit of sealant to the bearing cap areas immediately adjacent to the seal ends (photo).

15   Install the bearing cap (with seal) and torque the attaching bolts to

34.1 Inspecting the ring gear teeth on the drive plate (flywheel)

35.5 A centerpunch is used to put small marks on bearing caps to identify each for reassembly in their original positions

35.4 Lifting a main bearing cap and bearing off the crankshaft

35.5 Lifting the crankshaft out of the engine block

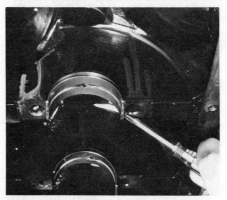

35.7 A screwdriver can be used to gently pry the main bearings from the engine block

36.3 Lowering the rear main bearing cap away from the crankshaft

36.4 The lower half of the rear main bearing seal

36.5A A hammer and brass drift should be used to push the upper seal half around the crankshaft

36.5B Once the seal protrudes, it can be pulled free with needle-nose pliers

36.13 Using a protector tool (arrow) when pushing the main seal into place

36.14 Sealant should be used where the rear main cap touches the engine block

37.7 Measuring the inside of a cylinder

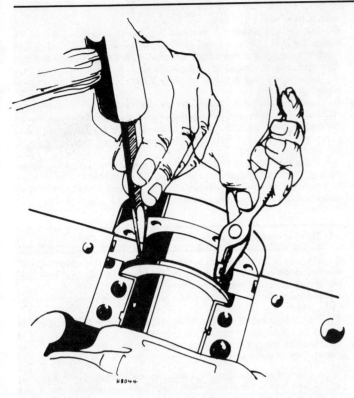

Fig. 2.13 Removing crankshaft rear oil seal (upper half) with engine in car (Sec 36)

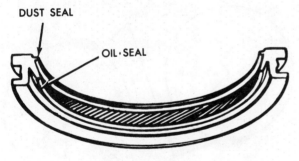

Fig. 2.14 Crankshaft oil (rear main) seal (Sec 36)

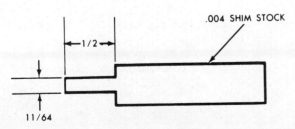

Fig. 2.15 Protective tool used for installing crankshaft rear oil seal (rear main) in engine (Sec 36)

about 10-12 ft. lb only. Now tap the end of the crankshaft first rearward, then forward to line up the thrust surfaces. Retorque the bearing cap bolts to the proper specification.

37 Cylinder block – inspection

1   It is important that the cylinder block be inspected carefully and as described. The cylinder block was designed to operate with exacting tolerances, and if the engine is reassembled without first properly inspecting the block, all work and cost involved in the rebuild may be for nothing.

2   Clean the cylinder block as necessary to remove built-up sludge and grime. Clean all excess gasket material from the sealing surfaces.

3   Inspect the cylinder block for cracks in the cylinder walls, water jacket, valve lifter bores and main bearing webs. Use a flashlight where necessary. In most cases, cracks will require that a new engine block be purchased.

4   The cylinder bores must be examined for taper, ovality, scoring and scratches. These checks are important for proper operation of the pistons and piston rings.

5   Scoring and scratches can usually be seen with the naked eye and felt with the fingers. If they are deep, the engine block may have to be replaced with a new one. If the imperfections are slight, a qualified machine shop should be able to hone or bore the cylinders to a larger size.

6   There are two indicators for excessive wear of the cylinders. First, if the vehicle was emitting blue smoke from the exhaust system before engine dismantling. This blue smoke is caused by oil seeping past the piston rings due to the wear of the cylinder walls. Second, the thickness of the ridge at the top of the cylinder (which may have been removed during piston removal) can give an indication about overall cylinder wear.

7   Using an internal-type dial gauge, measure each bore at three different points (photos). Take a measurement near the top of the bore and then near the bottom of the bore. Finally, measure at the center. Jot down all measurements to determine the taper of the cylinder (slightly larger at the top than the bottom or vice versa).

8   An out of round condition can be found in a similar fashion, except measure the cylinder first parallel with the engine centerline and then turn the micrometers until they are perpendicular with the centerline (180 degrees from first measurement).

9   Where the cylinder bores are worn beyond the permitted tolerances as shown in the Specifications Section, the block will have to be replaced with a new one, honed or bored.

10 A final check of the cylinder block would include an inspection for warpage. This is done with a straightedge and feeler gauges in the same manner as for the cylinder heads. The tolerances described in Section 17 also apply to the cylinder block. If warpage is slight, a machine shop can resurface the block.

38 Engine – rebuilding alternatives

1   At this point in the engine rebuilding process the home mechanic is faced with a number of options for completing the overhaul. The decision to replace the cylinder block, piston/rod assemblies and crankshaft depend on a number of factors with the number one consideration being the condition of the cylinder block. Other considerations are: cost, competent machine shop facilities, parts availability, time available to complete the project and experience.

2   Some of the rebuilding alternatives are as follows:

Individual parts – If the inspection procedures prove that the engine block and most engine components are in reusable condition, this may be the most economical alternative. The block, crankshaft and piston/rod assemblies should all be inspected carefully. Even if the block shows little wear, the cylinder bores should receive new camshaft bearings and a finish hone; both jobs for a machine shop.

Master kit (crankshaft kit) – This rebuild package usually consists of a reground crankshaft and a matched set of pistons and connecting rods. The pistons will come already installed with new piston pins to the connecting rods. Piston rings and the necessary bearings may or may not be included in the kit. These kits are commonly available for standard cylinder bores, as well as for engine blocks which have been bored to a regular oversize.

Short block – A short block consists of a cylinder block with a crankshaft and piston/rod assemblies already installed. All new bearings are incorporated and all clearances will be within tolerances. Depending on where the short block is purchased, a guarantee may be included. The existing camshaft, valve mechanism, cylinder heads and ancillary parts can be bolted to this short block with little or no machine shop work necessary for the engine overhaul.

Long block – A long block, called a 'Target or Target Master' engine by GM dealerships consists of a short block plus oil pump, oil pan, cylinder heads, valve covers, camshaft and valve mechanism, camshaft gear, timing chain and crankcase front cover. All components are installed with new bearings, seals and gaskets incorporated throughout. The installation of manifolds and ancillary parts is all that is necessary. Some form of guarantee is usually included with purchase.

3   Give careful thought to which method is best for your situation and discuss the alternatives with local machine shop owners, parts dealers or GM dealership partsmen.

39 Crankshaft and bearings – inspection and servicing

1   Examine the crankpin and main journal surfaces for scoring, scratches or corrosion. If evident, then the crankshaft will have to be reground professionally.
2   Using a micrometer, test each journal and crankpin at several different points for ovality (photo). If this is found to be more than 0.001 inch then the crankshaft must be reground. Undersize bearings are available as listed in Specifications to suit the recommended reground diameter, but normally your GM dealer will supply the correct matching bearings with the reconditioned crankshaft.
3   After a high mileage, the main bearings and the connecting rod bearings may have worn to give an excessive running clearance. The correct running clearance for the different journals is given in the Specifications.
    The clearance is best checked using a product such as 'Plastigage' having refitted the original bearings and caps and tightened the cap bolts to the torque settings specified in Specifications. *Never attempt to correct excessive running clearance by filing the caps but always fit new shell bearings, having first checked the crankshaft journals and crankpins for ovality and to establish whether their diameters are of standard or reground sizes.*
4   Checking the connecting rod bearings is carried out in a similar manner to that described for the main bearings. The correct running clearance is given in the Specifications.
5   It is good practice to check the running clearance of rod and main bearings even if new bearings are installed. The use of 'Plastigage' is described in Section 43.
6   The crankshaft endplay should be checked by forcing the crankshaft to the extreme front position, then using a feeler gauge at the front end of the rear main bearing. Refer to the Specifications for the permissible clearance. This procedure is detailed in Section 45.
7   The connecting rod side-clearance should be measured with a feeler gauge between the connecting rod caps. If the side clearance is outside the specified tolerance, replace the rod assembly. This procedure is detailed in Section 44.

40 Piston and connecting rod assemblies – cleaning and inspection

1   In most cases where the engine has seen high mileage, the original pistons will have to be replaced with new ones. This is because the cylinders will have to be bored to a larger size to compensate for normal wear. If however the cylinder walls require only a slight finish honing, the old pistons may be reused if they are in good condition.
2   Wash the connecting rods and pistons in a cleaning solvent and dry with compressed air, if available.
3   Don't use a wire brush or any abrasive cleaning tools on any part of the piston.
4   Clean the ring grooves of the piston with a groove cleaner tool and make sure the oil ring holes and slots are clean (photo).
5   Check the rods for twist and bending and inspect the rods for nicks or cracks. If any of the above items are found, the rod must be replaced

with a new one.
6   Inspect the piston for cracked ring lands, skirts or pin bosses. Check for worn or wavy ring lands, scuffed or damaged skirts and eroded areas at the top of the piston. Replace any pistons that are damaged or show signs of excessive wear.
7   Inspect the ring grooves for nicks which may cause the rings to hang up.
8   With the piston still connected to the connecting rod, swivel the rod back and forth and noting the degree of difficulty. Compare all piston/rod assemblies. If the rods seem loose on the piston pins, and move with little or no drag, the piston pins have worn and the piston pin must be replaced.
9   If the cylinder block is in need of any machine work, even finish honing, chances are that the machinist will want the pistons on hand to check piston-to-bore clearance as the cylinder walls are cut. This measurement is critical and should be left to the machine shop.

41 Pistons and piston rings – assembly

1   The piston should be attached to its appropriate connecting rod. As mentioned previously, this is a job for a professional equipped with the proper supports and an arbor press.
2   The new piston rings should be comparable in size to the piston being used.
3   The installation of the piston rings on the piston is critical to the overall performance of the rebuilt engine.
4   Measure the ring end gap of each ring before it is installed in the piston. This is done as follows:

a) *Arrange the piston rings into sets for each piston. The set will contain a top ring, 2nd ring and a three-piece oil control ring (two rails and a spacer).*
b) *Slip a top ring into the appropriate cylinder bore. Push the ring into the cylinder bore about $\frac{1}{4}$ inch below the upper limit*

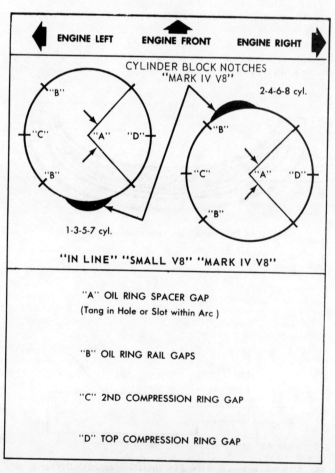

Fig. 2.16 Piston ring gap locations (Sec 41)

of ring travel (a total of about 1 inch below block deck). Push the ring down into position with the top of a piston to make sure the ring is square with the cylinder wall (photo).

c) Using a feeler gauge, measure the gap between the ends of the ring (photo). If the gap is less than specified (see Specifications), remove the ring and try another top ring for fit.

d) Check all top rings in the same manner and if necessary use a fine file to remove a slight amount of material from the ends of the ring(s). If inadequate end gap is used, the rings will break during operation.

e) Measure the end gap of each 2nd ring and oil control ring as described above.

5   Check the fit of each piston ring into its groove by holding the ring next to the piston and then placing the outer surface of the ring into its respective groove. Roll the ring entirely around the piston and check for any binding. If the binding is due to a distorted ring, replace the ring with a new one. Perform this check for the top and 2nd rings of each piston.

6   Install the piston rings as follows:

a) Study Fig. 2.16 thoroughly to understand exactly where each ring gap should be located in relation to the piston and other rings. The location of each ring gap is important (photo).

b) If a piston ring expander tool is available, use this to install the rings (photo). If not, small lengths of tin can be used to prevent the rings from entering the wrong groove (see Section 32 on piston ring removal).

c) Install the bottom oil ring spacer in its groove and insert the anti-rotation tang in the oil hole (photo). Hold the spacer ends butted and install the lower steel oil ring rail with the gap properly located. Install the upper steel oil ring rail and properly set its gap. Flex or squeeze the oil ring assembly to make sure it is free in the groove. If not, dress the groove with a file or replace the oil control ring assembly as necessary.

d) Install the end ring and properly locate its gap.

e) Install the top ring with gap properly positioned.

f) Repeat the above procedures for all piston assemblies.

7   Proper clearance of the piston rings in their grooves is very important. Clearance between the ring and its groove is checked with a blade feeler gauge, sliding the appropriately sized feeler gauge (see Specifications) between the top of the ring and the inside of the groove (photo). Rotate the feeler blade all the way around the piston, checking for proper clearance. Replace rings or clean and dress the groove as necessary for proper clearance.

42 Engine assembly – general information

1   Before assembling any parts to the engine block, the block should have all necessary machine work completed and the engine block should be thoroughly cleaned. If machine work was performed, chances are that the block was hot-tanked afterward to remove all traces of the machined cuttings.

2   The oil galleys and water passages of the block should also be thoroughly clean and free from dirt or machining leftovers. It's good practice to install new freeze plugs in the engine whenever it is stripped for a total overhaul. These plugs are difficult to replace once the engine has been assembled and installed. If the engine was sent out for machine work and hot-tanking, it may be best to let the machine shop remove and install new plugs. If they are to be done at home, proceed as follows:

a) Use a hammer and punch to press one side of the plug into the block (photo).

b) Use pliers to pry the old freeze plug out of its recess (photo).

c) Place a suitable replacement plug into position and hammer into place until flush with the engine block. Special installation tools are available for pressing the plug into place, however a suitable sized socket will work fine (photo).

3   Clean and examine all bolts, nuts and fasteners. Replace any that are damaged.

4   Clean and cover all engine components to keep dirt and dust away from them until they can be installed.

5   Have assembly grease and an oil can filled with engine oil handy to lubricate parts as they are installed.

6   Lay out all necessary tools and a reliable torque wrench on a clean work table for easy retrieval.

7   New gaskets and seals must be used throughout. These are commonly available together in a master rebuild gasket set.

8   In almost all cases, parts to be replaced during a major overhaul include: camshaft bearings, connecting rod bearings, main bearings, piston rings, timing chain, spark plugs and oil filter. These are in addition to any parts found damaged or excessively worn during dismantling or the various inspection processes.

43 Main bearings and rod bearings – checking clearance

1   **Note**: *There are three precautions to take when working with Plastigage. These are:*

a) *Plastigage is soluble in oil, so all oil and grease should be removed from the crankshaft and bearing surfaces while the testing is done.*

b) *Do not rotate the crankshaft while the Plastigage is installed in the engine as this may cause damage to the crankshaft or bearing surfaces.*

c) *Remove all traces of the Plastigage when testing is complete. Be very careful not to harm the crankshaft or bearing surfaces as the Plastigage is removed. Do not use sharp tools or abrasive cleaners, instead, remove the used Plastigage with your fingernail or a blunt wood stick.*

2   Whenever an engine is overhauled the bearing clearances should be checked. This should be done for reused bearings as well as for new bearings.

3   The procedure is basically the same for both the main bearings and the connecting rod bearings.

4   With the crankshaft set into the engine block, install the main bearings into the engine block and the main bearing caps (photo).

5   Remove all oil, grime and foreign materials from the crankshaft and bearing surfaces.

6   Place a piece of Plastigage (available at most auto supply shops) along the length of each main bearing journal on the crankshaft.

7   Install each main bearing cap and tighten the attaching bolts to specifications (photo). The arrow on each cap should face toward the front of the engine.

8   Now remove each bearing cap and measure the width of the Plastigage strip which will have flattened out when the caps were tightened. A scale is provided on the Plastigage envelope for measuring the width of the Plastigage strip, and thus, bearing clearance (photo).

9   If the Plastigage is flattened more at the ends than in the middle, or vice versa, this is an indication of journal taper which can be checked in the Specifications Section.

10   To test for an out of round condition, remove all traces of the Plastigage (be careful not to damage the crankshaft or bearing surfaces) and rotate the crankshaft 90 degrees. With the crankshaft rotated to this point, use the Plastigage to check the clearances again. Compare these measurements with those taken previously to arrive at eccentricity or out of round.

11   To check connecting rod bearing clearances, install each piston/rod assembly (Section 46) and use the Plastigage as described above (photos).

12   Connecting rod side clearance (Section 44) can also be checked at this time.

13   If the bearings have shown to be within all tolerances, they may be installed following the steps outlined in the appropriate sections.

14   If not within specifications, the bearings should be replaced with the correctly sized bearings. Upper and lower bearings should always be replaced as a unit.

44 Connecting rod side clearance – checking

1   Side clearance can be checked with the piston/rod assemblies temporarily installed for bearing clearance checking.

2   With the piston/rod assemblies installed and the bearing caps tightened to specifications, use feeler gauges to check the clearance

39.2 Measuring a crankshaft journal

40.4 Cleaning the piston ring grooves with a special tool made especially for this purpose

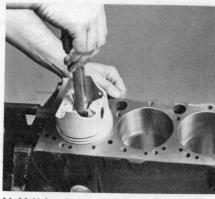

41.4A Using the top of a piston to push a piston ring into a cylinder bore for measuring

41.4B Measuring the piston ring end gap with a feeler gauge

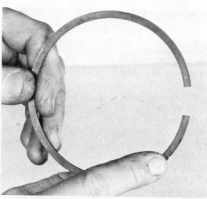

41.6A Most piston rings will be marked with a small dimple to indicate the top side

41.6B A piston ring expanding tool eases ring removal and installation

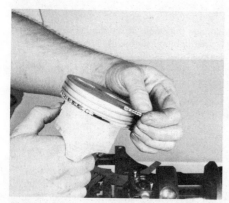

41.6C Installing the bottom oil control spacer

41.7 Using a feeler gauge to measure the clearance between piston ring and piston groove

42.2A A hammer and centerpunch can be used to push the freeze plug into the engine block

42.2B Pliers are then used to pull the freeze plug out of the engine block

42.2C A special installation tool or a suitably sized socket can be used to force the new freeze plugs into their bores

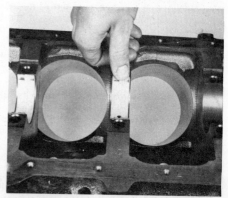

43.4 Installing a main bearing half into the engine

43.7 Tightening a main bearing cap bolt

43.8 The flattened Plastigage is then measured using the scale printed on the package

43.11A A length of Plastigage on the crankshaft journal, in preparation of the rod cap and bearing to be installed on top of it

43.11B Measuring the flattened Plastigage for connecting rod bearing clearance

44.2 A feeler gauge is used to measure connecting rod side clearance once the piston/rod assemblies are installed

45.4 Oil from a squirt can is used to lubricate the bearings

between the sides of the connecting rods and the crankshaft (photo).

3   If the clearance at this point is below the minimum tolerance, the rod may be machined for more clearance at this area.

4   If the clearance is too excessive, a new rod must be used or the crankshaft must be reground or replaced with a new one.

45 Crankshaft, main bearings and oil seal – installation

1   Note: *If a new or reground crankshaft is being installed, or if the original crankshaft has been reground, make sure the correct bearings are being used.*

2   Install the rear main bearing oil seal. The upper half of the seal should be positioned on its cylinder block seat and the lower half on the rear main bearing cap. Install with the lips toward the front of the engine. Where two lips are incorporated, install lip with helix towards the front of the engine. Use the protector installation tool when installing the seal halves. (See Section 36 for use of installation tool and further information).

3   Lubricate the seal lips with engine oil.

4   Install the main bearings in the cylinder block and main bearing caps. Lubricate the bearing surfaces with engine oil (photo).

5   Lower the crankshaft into position, being careful not to damage the bearing surfaces (photo).

6   Apply a thin coat of brush-on sealer to the block mating surface and the corresponding surface of the bearing cap. Do not allow sealer to get on the crankshaft or seal (see Section 36).

7   Install the main bearing caps (with bearings) over the crankshaft and onto the cylinder block. The arrows should point toward the front of the engine.

8   Torque all main bearing cap attaching bolts to the proper specification, except the rear bearing cap. Torque the rear bearing cap bolts to about 10 to 12 ft. lb only at this time. Tap the end of the crankshaft with a lead hammer, first to the rear and then to the front to line up the rear bearing properly. Now retorque all bearing cap bolts to the proper specification.

9   To measure crankshaft end play, force the crankshaft as far forwards as it will go and use a feeler gauge to measure the gap between the front of the rear main bearing and the crankshaft thrust surface (photo).

10 Install the flywheel as described in Section 33 to ease in engine rotation during reassembly.

46 Pistons, connecting rods and bearings – installation

1   With the pistons complete with piston rings and connecting rods, they can be installed in the engine.

2   Make sure the cylinder bores are perfectly clean. Wipe the cylinder walls several times with a light engine oil and a clean, lint-free cloth (photo).

3   Lubricate the connecting rod bearings and install them into their appropriate rod and rod cap.

4   Lightly coat the pistons, rings and cylinder walls with light engine oil.

5   Install a length of rubber or plastic tubing over the connecting rod studs on one rod assembly. This will prevent the threaded bolts from possibly damaging the cylinder wall or crankshaft journal as the piston/rod assembly is pushed into place (photo).

6   Check that all the piston ring gaps are positioned properly (see Section 41).

7   Check that the piston/rod assembly is properly positioned. Most pistons will be marked with an 'F' or a drilled out area indicating the piston should be installed with these marks toward the front of the engine (photo). The rod bearing tang slots should be towards the outside of the engine block once installed.

8   Place a piston ring compressor around the piston, with the base of the compressor flush with the cylinder block (photo). Tighten the compressor until the rings are flush with the piston surface and then push the piston assembly into the bore. A wooden hammer handle can be used to tap the top of the piston slightly (photo). Hold the ring compressor solidly against the cylinder block until all rings are inside

45.5 Lowering the crankshaft into position

45.9 Measuring crankshaft end play with a feeler gauge between rear cap and rear throw

46.2 The cylinder bores should be lubricated with oil. Use your hands to prevent foreign matter from entering engine block

46.5 Short pieces of rubber hose are again used to protect the cylinder walls and crankshaft as the piston/rod assemblies are pushed into place

46.7 Most pistons will be marked in some way to indicate installation toward the front of the engine

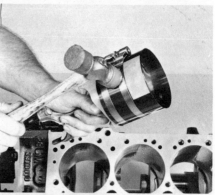

46.8A With the piston ring compressor around the piston, it is sometimes necessary to tap the compressor lightly to seal the rings

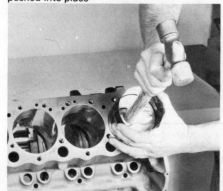

46.8B A wood hammer handle can be used to push the piston/connecting rod assembly into the engine block

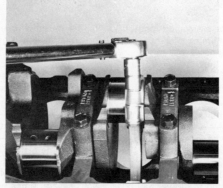

46.10 Tightening a connecting rod nut

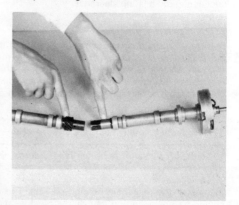

47.6 The pre-oiling tool (right) has the gear and the advance weights ground off

47.7 A common drill motor connects to the modified distributor to turn the oil pump

47.8 Oil and/or assembly grease will spurt from the rocker arms to indicate that the oiling system is functioning properly

the bore. Continue pushing until the connecting rod is near its installed position.

9   Ensure that all bearing surfaces and the crankshaft journal are coated with engine oil and remove the tubing protector pieces. Install the connecting rod bearing cap (with bearing) to the connecting rod.

10 Torque the nuts to specification (photo).

11 Repeat this procedure for all cylinders, using the rubber or plastic tubing on each assembly to prevent damage as the pistons are pushed into place. Rotate the crankshaft as necessary to make the connecting rod nuts accessible for tightening.

47 Engine – final assembling and pre-oiling after overhaul

1   After the crankshaft, piston/rod assemblies and the various associated bearings have been installed in the engine block, the remainder of the components (cylinder heads, oil pump, camshaft, etc.) can be installed following the installation procedures located in the various sections of this Chapter.

2   Follow the engine disassembly sequence in the reverse order of installation, using new gaskets where necessary.

3   Adjust the valve lash as described in Section 22.

4   After a major overhaul it is a good idea to pre-oil the engine before it is installed and initially started. This will tell you if there are any faults in the oiling system at a time when corrections can be made easily and without major damage. Pre-oiling the engine will also allow the parts to be lubricated thoroughly in a normal fashion, but without heavy loads placed upon them.

5   The engine should be assembled completely with the exception of the distributor and the valve covers.

6   A modified distributor will be needed for this job. This pre-oil tool is a distributor body with the bottom gear ground off and the counterweight assembly removed from the top of the shaft (photo).

7   Place the pre-oiler into the distributor shaft access hole at the rear of the intake manifold and make sure the bottom of the shaft mates with the oil pump. Clamp the modified distributor into place just as you would an ordinary distributor. Now attach an electric drill motor to the top of the shaft (photo).

8   With the oil filter installed, all oil galley-ways plugged (oil pressure sending unit at rear of block) and the crankcase full of oil as shown on the dipstick, rotate the pre-oiler with the drill. Make sure the rotation is in a clockwise direction. Soon, oil should start to flow from the rocker arms, signifying that the oil pump and oiling system is

functioning properly (photo). It may take 2 to 3 minutes for the oil to flow to each rocker arm. Allow the oil to circulate throughout the engine for a few minutes.

9   Check for oil leaks at all locations and correct as necessary.

10 Remove the pre-oiler and install the normal distributor and valve covers.

48 Engine start-up after major repair or overhaul

1   With the engine in place in the vehicle and all components connected, make a final check that all pipes and wiring have been connected and that no rags or tools have been left in the engine compartment.

2   Connect the negative battery cable. If it sparks or arcs, power is being drawn from someplace and all accessories and wiring should be checked.

3   Fill the cooling system with the proper mixture and amount of coolant (Chapter 3).

4   Fill the crankcase with the correct quantity and grade of oil (Chapter 1).

5   Check the tension of all drive belts (Chapter 1).

6   Remove the high tension wire from the center tower of the distributor cap (1970 – 1974) or the 'BAT' wire connection from the HEI distributor (1975 – 1980) to prevent the engine from starting. Now crank the engine over for about 15 to 30 seconds. This will allow the oil pump to distribute oil and the fuel pump to start pumping fuel to the carburetor.

7   Now connect the high tension lead at the distributor and start the engine. Immediately check all gauges and warning lights for proper readings and check for leaks of coolant or oil.

8   If the engine does not start immediately, check to make sure fuel is reaching the carburetor. This may take a while.

9   After allowing the engine to run for a few minutes at low speed, turn it off and check the oil and coolant levels.

10 Start the engine again and check the ignition timing, emission control settings and carburetor idle speeds (Chapter 1).

11 Run the vehicle easily during the first 500 to 1000 miles (break-in period) then check the torque settings on all major engine components, particularly the cylinder heads. Tighten any bolts which may have loosened.

12 If the vehicle is equipped with mechanical lifters, these should be reset with the engine running and hot.

Chapter 3 Cooling system

Contents

Specifications

System type .... Pressurized, with thermostatic control, and pump and fan assistance

Pressure cap setting .... 15 lbf/in^2

Thermostat type .... Wax pellet

Thermostat rating .... 195°F (180°F for 402 cu in 375 HP)

Water pump .... Impeller type

Radiator type .... Crossflow

Cooling fan .... Belt driven from engine
Automatic fluid clutch fan on later models

Coolant capacity

	U.S. quarts
1970 w/307, 350 cu in engine	16 qts*
w/402 cu in engine	24 qts**
1971–1974 w/307, 350 cu in engine	15.5 qts*
w/402 cu in engine	24 qts**
1975 (all V8)	17 qts*
1976 – 1978 (all V8)	17.5 qts*
1979 (all V8)	17 qts*
1980 w/267, 305 cu in engine	15 qts
w/350 cu in engine	16 qts

* With air conditioning add 1 qt
**With air conditioning add 2 qts

Torque specifications

	lb-ft
Water outlet bolts	30
Water pump bolts	30
Temperature sender unit	20
Radiator mounting bolts	20
Fan fluid hub bolts	25

1 General description

The engine cooling system is of the pressurized type with pump and fan assistance. It comprises a radiator, flow and return water hoses, water pump, thermostat and vehicle interior heater.

The system is pressurized by means of a spring loaded radiator filler cap which prevents premature boiling by increasing the boiling point of the coolant. If the coolant temperature goes above this increased boiling point, the extra pressure in the system forces the radiator cap internal spring loaded valve off its seat and exposes the overflow pipe down which displaced coolant escapes.

It is important to check that the radiator cap is in good condition and that the spring behind the sealing washer has not weakened or corroded. Most service stations have a machine for testing that the cap operates at the specified pressure.

On vehicles built after 1972, a coolant recovery system is provided. This consists of a plastic reservoir into which the coolant which normally escapes down the overflow pipe is retained. When the engine cools and the coolant contracts, coolant is drawn back into the radiator and thus maintains the system at full capacity.

This is a continuous process and provided the level in the reservoir is correctly maintained, no topping-up of the radiator or cooling system will be necessary.

The cooling system functions in the following manner. The water pump discharges engine coolant to each bank of cylinders; this flows from the front of each bank around each cylinder and towards the rear of the block. Passages in the block and cylinder head direct coolant around the inlet and exhaust ports and around the exhaust valve guide inserts. A metered amount of coolant is also diverted to cool the spark plug region.

When the thermostat is closed, coolant is re-directed through a small passage in the front right-hand cylinder head and block to a mating hole in the bottom of the water pump runner. At normal running temperature, the thermostat is open and coolant is directed from the intake manifold through the coolant outlet and thermostat to the radiator.

The radiator is of the crossflow type. Hot engine coolant enters the radiator at the top left-hand side, is cooled by the inrush of cold air throuh the core (this is created by the fan and ram-effect of air, resulting from forward motion of the vehicle) and returns to the engine via the outlet at the right-hand side.

Later models are fitted with a fluid type fan coupling. This is a sealed unit, thermostatically controlled which 'slips' the fan blades according to engine temperature and speed, to avoid overcooling with consequent loss of fuel economy.

2 Coolant level

Note: *If the radiator cap has to be removed when the engine is hot, rotate the cap slowly counter-clockwise to the detent and allow the residual pressure to escape. Do not press the cap down until all hissing has stopped and take extreme care that the hands are not scalded.*

Vehicles without expansion reservoir
1   The level of the coolant in the radiator should be maintained at 3 inches below the bottom of the filler neck. Carry out this check when the engine and coolant are cold.

Vehicles with expansion reservoir
2   The level of the coolant in the expansion reservoir should be maintained at the 'FULL HOT' mark. Any checking and topping-up

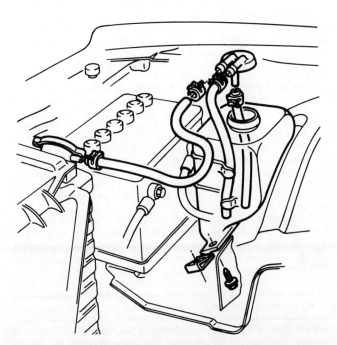

Fig. 3.1 Typical coolant recovery reservoir (Sec 2)

should be carried out with the engine and cooling system at normal operating temperature.

3 Antifreeze and inhibiting solutions

1   It is recommended that the cooling system is filled with a water/ethylene glycol based antifreeze solution which will give protection down to at least – 20°F at all times. This provides protection against corrosion and increases the coolant boiling point. When handling antifreeze, take care that it is not spilled on the vehicle paintwork, since it will invariably cause damage if not removed immediately.
2   The coolng system should be drained, flushed and refilled every alternate Fall. The use of antifreeze solutions for periods of longer than two years is likely to cause damage and encourage the formation of rust and scale due to the corrosion inhibitors gradually losing their efficiency.
3   Before adding antifreeze to the system, check all hose connections and check the tightness of the cylinder head bolts as such solutions are searching.
4   The exact mixture of antifreeze to water which you should use depends upon the relative weather conditions. The mixture should contain at least 50 percent antifreeze, offering protection to –34°F. Under no circumstances should the mixture contain more than 70 percent antifreeze.

4 Thermostat – removal and installation

1   The thermostat is basically a restriction valve which is actuated by a thermostatic element. It is mounted inside a housing on the engine and is designed to open and close at predetermined temperatures to allow coolant to warm-up the engine or cool it.
2   To remove the thermostat for replacement or testing, begin by disconnecting the negative battery cable.
3   Remove the air cleaner for better working access.
4   Drain the coolant into a suitable container for disposal. See Chapter 1 for more information on this. It is not necessary to drain the coolant from the engine.
5   Disconnect the upper radiator hose from the thermostat housing (photo).
6   Remove the thermostat housing bolts and the housing from the engine (photo). On some models, the alternator mounting bracket will have to be disconnected first, as this bracket is attached to the housing mounting stud. Also, late model vehicles may have a TVS switch installed in the thermostat housing. If this is the case, disconnect each of the vacuum hoses on the switch (noting their installed positions) and then unscrew the switch from the housing.
7   After lifting the thermostat housing from the engine, the thermostat will be visible and can be removed from the engine (photo). Note how the thermostat sits in the recess, as it must be replaced in this same position.
8   Before installation, use a gasket scraper or putty knife to carefully remove all traces of the old gasket on the thermostat housing and the engine sealing surface. Do not allow the gasket particles to drop down into the intake manifold.
9   Place a $\frac{1}{8}$-inch bead of RTV or equivalent sealer around the sealing surface on the engine and place the thermostat into its recess.
10 Immediately place the thermostat housing with sealer and a new gasket into position and torque-tighten the attaching bolts.
11 Where applicable, install the alternator brace and/or the TVS switch and vacuum hoses.
12 Connect the upper radiator hose and tighten- the hose clamp securely.
13 Connect the negative battery cable and fill the radiator with the proper amount of antifreeze and water (see Chapter 1).
14 With the radiator cap removed, start the engine and run, until the upper radiator hose becomes hot. When this hose is hot, the thermostat should be in the open position. At this point, add more coolant if necessary to reach the top of the filler neck.
15 Install the radiator cap, making sure the arrows are aligned with the overflow hose.

4.5 Disconnecting the upper radiator hose from the thermostat housing

4.6 As the housing is lifted away from the engine, the thermostat becomes visible

4.7 Lift the thermostat out of its bore, noting how it is installed

5   Thermostat – testing

1   The only way to test the operation of the thermostat is with the unit removed from the engine. In most cases if the thermostat is suspect it is more economical to merely buy a replacement thermostat as they are not very costly.

2   To test, first remove the thermostat as described in Section 4.

3   Inspect the thermostat for excessive corrosion or damage. Replace the thermostat with a new one if either of these conditions is found.

4   Place the thermostat in hot water 25 degrees above the temperature stamped on the thermostat. Since nearly all Chevrolet V8 engines use a 195-degree thermostat, the water temperature will be approximately 220. When submerged in this water (which should be agitated thoroughly), the valve should be fully open.

5   Now remove the thermostat using a piece of bent wire and place it in water which is 10 degrees below the temperature on the thermostat. In most cases this cooler water temperature should be 185 degrees. At this temperature the thermostat valve should close fully.

6   Reinstall the thermostat if it checks out OK, or purchase a new thermostat of the same temperature rating. See Section 4 for installing the thermostat.

6   Radiator – removal and installation

1   Disconnect the negative battery cable.

2   Drain the radiator referring to Chapter 1.

3   Disconnect the radiator upper and lower hoses and the automatic transmission cooling lines if applicable (photo).

4   Disconnect the radiator shroud and hang it over the fan. The

shroud is attached with screws going into the radiator with clips or staples across the bottom (photos).

5   Remove the upper metal panel at the top of the radiator (photo).

6   Lift the radiator straight up and out of the engine compartment (photo). Be careful not to scratch the paint on the front nosepiece. If coolant drips on any body paint, immediately wash it off with clear water as the antifreeze solution can damage the finish.

7   With the radiator removed, it can be inspected for leaks or damage. If in need of repairs, have a professional radiator shop or dealer perform the work as special welding techniques are required.

8   Bugs and dirt can be cleaned from the radiator by using compressed air and a soft brush. Do not bend the cooling fins as this is done.

9   Inspect the rubber mounting pads which the radiator sits on and replace as necessary.

10   Lift the radiator into position making sure it is seated in the mounting pads.

11   Install the upper panel, shroud and hoses in the reverse order of removal.

12   Connect the negative battery cable and fill the radiator as described in Chapter 1.

13   Start the engine and check for leaks. Allow the engine to reach normal operating temperature (upper radiator hose hot) and add coolant until the level reaches the bottom of the filler neck.

14   Install cap with arrows aligned with the overflow tube.

7   Water pump – testing

1   A failure in the water pump can cause serious engine damage due to overheating. The pump will not be able to circulate cooled water through the engine.

2   There are three ways in which to check the operation of the water pump while it is still installed on the engine. If the pump is suspect, it should be replaced with a new or factory-rebuilt unit.

3   With the engine warmed up to normal operating temperature, squeeze the upper radiator hose. If the water pump is working properly, a pressure surge should be felt as the hose is released.

4   Water pumps are equipped with 'weep' or vent holes (photo). If a failure occurs to the bladder of the pump, small amounts of water will leak from these 'weep' holes. In most cases it will be necessary to use a flashlight from under the car to see evidence of leakage from this point in the pump body.

5   If the water pump shaft bearings fail there may be a squealing sound at the front of the engine while it is running. Shaft wear can be felt if the water pump pulley is forced up and down. Do not mistake drive belt slippage, which also causes a squealing sound, for water pump failure.

8   Water pump – removal and installation

Note: *It is not economical or practical to overhaul a water pump. If failure occurs, a new or rebuilt unit should be purchased to replace the faulty water pump.*

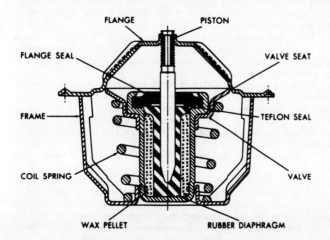

Fig. 3.2 Sectional view of thermostat (Sec 5)

6.3 Disconnecting the lower radiator hose from the bottom of the radiator

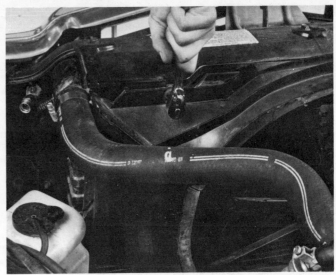

6.4A Screws secure the fan shroud to the radiator

6.4B With the shroud disconnected, hang it over the fan, away from the radiator

6.5A The radiator top panel is secured by bolts across the top

6.5B Lifting the radiator top plate away from the radiator

6.6 With the top plate removed, the radiator can be lifted from the engine compartment

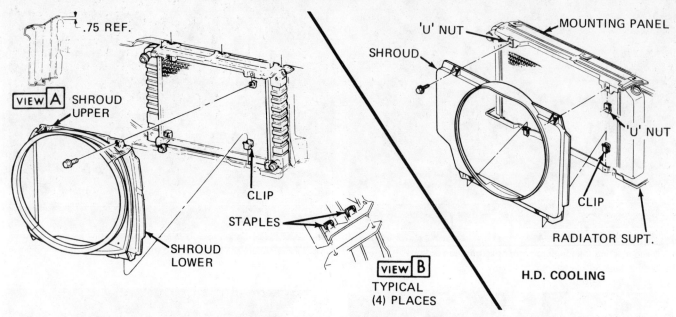

Fig. 3.3 Fan shroud mountings (Sec 6)

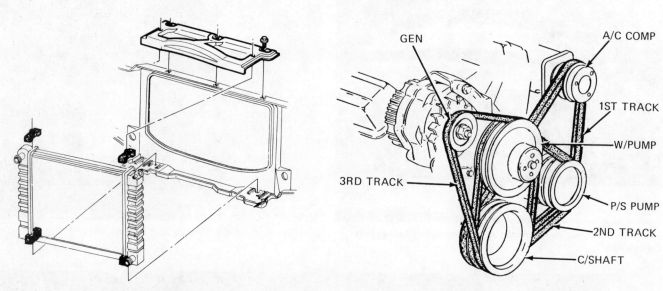

Fig. 3.4 Radiator mounting (Sec 6)

Fig. 3.5 Typical drive belt routings (Sec 8)

1   Disconnect the negative battery cable.

2   Drain the radiator, referring to Chapter 1 if necessary.

3   Reaching inside the radiator shroud, remove the bolts which secure the fan to the water pump hub. Remove the fan and spacer (if equipped) (photo). A thermostatic fan clutch must remain in the 'in-car' position.

4   Remove the bolts which secure the radiator shroud to the radiator and lift the shroud up and out of the engine compartment (see Section 6).

5   Loosen the two mounting bolts for the alternator. There is an adjusting strap bolt located in the slotted bracket and a long pivot bolt under the alternator.

6   Push the alternator inward to relieve tension on the drive belt and then remove the drive belt from the alternator and water pump pulleys.

7   Remove the water pump pulley from the hub (photo).

8   Completely remove the alternator strap bolt and pivot the alternator away from the water pump. Now remove the alternator mounting bracket which is secured at the thermostat housing on the top of the engine with one of the water pump bolts. Remove the negative battery cable and then lift the mounting bracket off the

engine (photo).

9   Disconnect the wiring at the rear of the alternator using identifying pieces of tape if necessary to help in reinstallation.

10   Remove the alternator pivot bolt and lift the alternator off the engine (photo).

11   Loosen the two mounting bolts for the AIR pump. Completely remove the bracket which is attached to the water pump, then pivot the AIR pump away from the engine (photo). On some models, the AIR pump pulley must first be removed from the pump to gain access to the bracket bolts.

12   If equipped with power steering, loosen the adjusting bolt and completely remove the pivot bolt which passes through the water pump (photo). Swing the pump away from the engine as far as possible without crimping the hoses.

13   Disconnect the lower radiator hose, heater hose and by-pass hose (if equipped) from the water pump housing (photos).

14   Remove the remaining bolts which secure the water pump to the front of the engine block. Lift the water pump away from the engine and out of the engine compartment (photo).

15   If installing a new or rebuilt water pump, transfer the heater hose

7.4 The 'weep' hole out of which water leaks when the internal bladder has failed

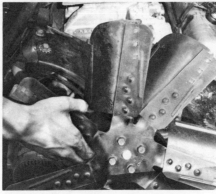
8.3 Removing the fan from the engine compartment

8.7 Lifting the drive belt pulley from the water pump shaft

8.8 The alternator bracket must be removed for access to the water pump

8.10 Removing the alternator from its brackets

8.11 This bracket for the AIR pump mounts to the water pump and so must be removed

8.12 The long pivot bolt for the power steering pump also mounts to the water pump

8.13A Disconnecting the lower radiator hose from the water pump

8.13B Disconnecting the heater hose from the top of the water pump

8.14 Removing the water pump from the engine

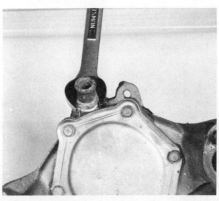
8.15 If a replacement pump is used, transfer all hose fittings from the old pump to the new

8.16 The gasket surfaces must be perfectly clean before the replacement water pump is installed

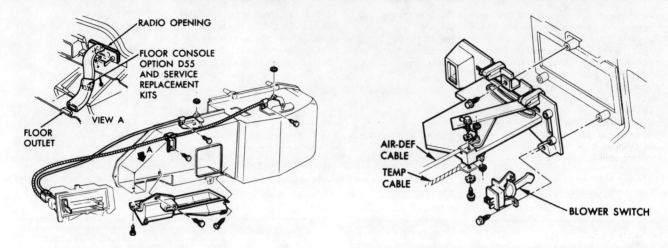

Fig. 3.6 Heater distribution assembly (Sec 10)   Fig. 3.7 Heater control head assembly (Sec 10)

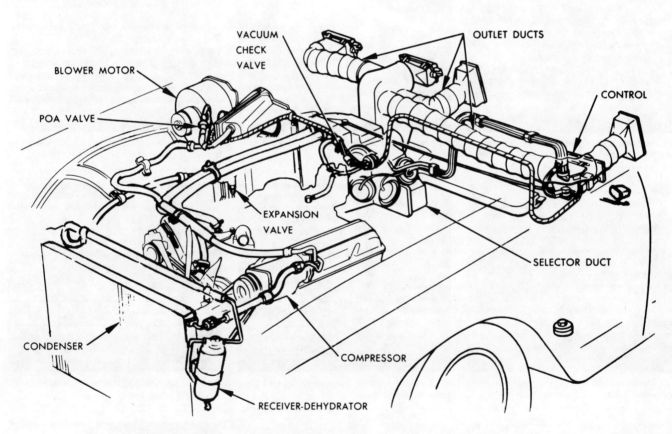

Fig. 3.8 Typical air conditioning system components (Sec 11)

fitting from the old pump to the new one (photo).

16 Clean the gasket surfaces of the engine of all excess gasket material using a gasket scraper or putty knife (photo).

17 Use a thin coat of gasket sealer on the new gaskets and install to the new pump. Place the pump into position on the engine and secure with the bolts. Do not toruqe-tighten these bolts until the power steering pump bracket and air pump brackets have been installed, as these brackets are secured with the water pump bolts.

18 Install the engine components in the reverse order of removal, tightening the appropriate fasteners to torque specifications.

19 Adjust all drive belts to the proper tension (see Chapter 1).

20 Connect the negative battery cable and fill the radiator with a mixture of ethylene glycol antifreeze and water in a 50/50 mixture.

Start the engine and allow to idle until the upper radiator hose gets hot. Check for leaks. With engine hot, fill with more coolant mixture until the level is at the bottom of the filler neck. Install radiator cap and check coolant level periodically over the next few miles of driving.

---

9   Water temperature sender – fault diagnosis and replacement

1 The indicator system comprises a lamp mounted on the instrument panel and a sender unit which is located on the left-hand cylinder head.

2 In the event of an unusual indication or a fault developing, check

the coolant level in the system and then ensure that the connecting wiring between the gauge and the sender unit is secure.

3   When the ignition switch is turned on and the starter motor is turning, the indicator lamp should be illuminated (overheated engine indication). If the lamp is not on, the bulb may be burned out, the ignition switch may be faulty or the circuit may be open.

4   As soon as the engine starts, the lamp should go out and remain so unless the engine overheats. Failure of the lamp to go out may be due to the wiring being grounded between the lamp and the sender unit, a defective temperature sender unit or a faulty ignition switch.

5   If the sender unit is to be replaced it is simply unscrewed from the left-hand cylinder head and a replacement installed. There will be some coolant spillage, so check the level after the replacement has been installed.

10 Heater components – removal and installation

Blower assembly

1   Disconnect the battery ground cable then remove all wiring, hoses, etc. to the right-hand fender skirt.

2   Raise the vehicle.

3   Remove the 8 rearmost fender skirt to fender attaching screws.

4   Pull outwards then down on the fender skirt and place a 2 x 4 inch wooden block between the skirt and fender.

5   Remove the blower wheel retaining nut and separate the wheel from the blower.

6   Pass the blower through the fender skirt opening (paragraph 4).

7   Installation is the reverse of the removal procedure, but ensure that the blower wheel is fitted with the open end away from the motor.

Air distribution duct and core

8   Disconnect the battery ground cable.

9   Drain the radiator (refer to Chapter 1, if necessary).

10 Disconnect the heater hoses at the core connections. Temporarily plug the core tubes to prevent coolant spillage.

11 Remove the nuts from the heater distributor studs on the engine side of the dashpanel (firewall).

12 Remove the glovebox and door assembly.

13 Using a $\frac{1}{4}$ inch drill, drill out the lower right-hand distributor stud from beneath the dash.

14 Pull the distributor assembly from the dash panel mounting, taking care not to kink the bowden cables. When clearance is obtained, disconnect the bowden cables and resistor wires and remove the distributor assembly from the vehicle.

15 Remove the core assembly from the distributor assembly.

16 When installing, reverse the removal procedure, ensuring that the hose from the water pump goes to the top heater core pipe. Ensure that the case sealer is intact before fitting the core; if necessary fit a new sealer. Replace the drilled-out stud with a new screw and pall (stamped) nut.

17 After filling the cooling system, run the engine and check for coolant leaks.

Control head

18 Disconnect the battery ground cable.

19 Remove the ashtray assembly.

20 Remove the six steering column trim panel screws and lower the panel and control as an assembly.

21 Disconnect all cables and wires at the control head.

22 Remove control head attaching screws and remove control head.

23 Installation is a reversal of removal, however make sure of cable operation before completing assembly.

11 Air conditioner – general description

1   Three types of systems may be encountered. The Four-Season System in which both the heating and cooling functions are performed by the one system. Air entering the vehicle, passes through the cooling unit (evaporator) and then around the heating unit so following the 'reheat' system principle.

2   The evaporator cools the air passing through it and by means of its built-in thermostatic switch, controls the operation of the compressor.

3   The system operates by air (outside or recirculated) entering the evaporator core by the action of the blower, where it receives maximum cooling if the controls are set for cooling. When the air leaves the evaporator, it enters the heater/air conditioner duct assembly and by means of a manually controlled deflector, it either passes through or bypasses the heater core in the correct proportions to provide the desired vehicle interior temperature.

4   Distribution of this air is then regulated by a vacuum actuated deflector and passes through the various outlets according to requirements.

5   When during the cooling operation, the air temperature is cooled too low for comfort, it is warmed to the required level by the heater. When the controls are set to 'HEATING ONLY', the evaporator will cease to function and ambient air will be warmed by the heater in a similar manner to that just described.

6   The main units of the system comprise the evaporator, an engine driven compressor and the condenser.

7   In view of the toxic nature of the chemicals and gases employed in the system, no part of the system must be disconnected by the home mechanic. Due to the need for specialized evacuating and charging equipment, such work should be left to your GM dealer or a refrigeration specialist.

8   The Comfortron System is essentially the same as the Four Season System except that it is fully automatic in operation.

9   The GM Air Conditioner is a dealer installed unit and operates independently of the vehicle heater using only recirculated air.

12 Air conditioner – checks and maintenance

1   Regularly inspect the fins of the condenser (located ahead of the radiator) and if necessary, brush away leaves and bugs.

2   Clean the evaporator drain tubes free from dirt.

3   Check the condition of the system hoses and if there is any sign of deterioration or hardening, have them replaced by your dealer.

4   At similar intervals, check and adjust the compressor drive belt as described in Chapter 1.

Chapter 4 Fuel and exhaust systems

Refer to Chapter 13 for specifications and information related to 1981 models

Contents

Specifications

System	Rear mounted fuel tank, mechanically operated fuel pump and 2 or 4 barrel carburetor
Fuel type	Unleaded or low leaded fuels (vehicles without a catalytic converter)

Fuel tank capacity
1970	19.0 gals
w/Evaporative control system	18.0 gals
1971	17.0 gals
1972–1973	18.0 gals
1974–1978	21.0 gals
1979–1980	20.8 gals

Carburetor specifications Rochester 2GV (1970)

Engine displacement (cu in)	307	350
Float level	27/32	23/32
Float drop	$1\frac{3}{4}$	$1\frac{3}{8}$
Accelerator pump stroke	$1\frac{1}{8}$	1 17/32
Fast idle (rpm)	2200 to 2400 (one turn)	2200 to 2400 (one turn)
Choke rod	0.060	0.085
Choke vacuum break	0.125	0.200
Choke unloader	M 0.160 A 0.215	M 0.275 A 0.325
Main metering jet		
manual	0.051	0.059
auto	0.051	0.060
* Curb idle speed rpm		
manual	700	700
auto	600	600

M – Manual transmission
A – Automatic transmission
* Refer also to relevant text for intermediate speed levels to be set during adjustment procedure. Also see vehical decal.

Carburetor specifications Rochester 2GV (1971 thru 1974)

Engine displacement (cu in)	1971 307	1971 350	1972 307	1972 350	1973 307	1973 350	1974 350
Float level	13/16	23/32	25/32	23/32	21/32	19/32	19/32
Float drop	1 3/4	1 3/8	1 31/32	1 9/32	1 9/32	1 9/32	1 9/32
Accelerator pump stroke	1 3/64	1 5/32	1 5/16	1 1/2	1 5/16	1 7/16	M 1 9/32 A 1 3/16
Fast idle (rpm)	2200 to 2400 (one turn)	2200 to 2400 (one turn)	1850	M 2200 A 1850	1600	1600	1600
Choke rod	M 0.075 A 0.040	0.100	M 0.75 A 0.40	0.100	0.150	0.200	M 0.200 A 0.245
Choke vacuum break	M 0.110 A 0.080	0.180	M 0.110 A 0.080	0.180	0.80	0.140	M 0.140 A 0.130
Choke unloader	0.215	0.325	0.215	0.325	0.215	0.250	M 0.250 A 0.325
*Curb idle speed (rpm) manual initial	700	700	1000	1050	950	1050	1000
manual final	600	600	900	900	900	900	900
auto initial	580	580	650	650	630	630	630
auto final	550	550	600	600	600	600	600
Maximum CO at idle	0.5%	0.5%	0.5%	0.5%	0.5%	0.5%	0.5%

M – Manual transmission
A – Automatic transmission
* Refer also to relevant text for intermediate speed levels to be set during adjustment procedure. Also see vehicle decal.

Carburetor specifications Rochester 2GC (1975 thru 1976)

Engine displacement (cu in)	1975 350	1976 305, 350	1977 305	1978 305
Float level	21/32	9/16	19/32	15/32
Float drop	31/32	1 9/32	1 9/32	1 9/32
Accelerator pump stroke	1 5/8	1 11/16	1 21/32	1 21/32
Fast idle (rpm)	1600	1600	1600	1600

Engine displacement (cu in)	1975 350	1976 305, 350	1977 305	1978 305
Choke rod	0.400	0.260	0.260	0.260
Choke vacuum break	0.130	0.140	0.140	0.140
Choke unloader	0.350	0.325	0.325	0.325
Curb idle speed manual initial	1000	650	650	650
final	900	600‡	600	600
auto initial	650	550	550	550
final	600	500†	500	500
Maximum CO at idle	see Decal	see Decal	see Decal	see Decal

Note: *The use of a twist drill of suitable diameter will provide a substitute for a gauge when carrying out many of the carburetor adjustments.*

† *With solenoid adjuster 700 rpm*
‡ *With solenoid adjuster 650 rpm*
M − Manual transmission
A − Automatic transmission

Carburetor specifications Rochester M2ME and E2ME (1979, 1980)

Engine displacement (cu in)	267, 305
Float level	5/16
Float drop	−
Accelerator pump stroke	1/4
Fast idle (rpm)	1300 (manual trans) 1600 (auto trans)
Choke rod	24.5°
Choke vacuum break	21° (front) 30° (rear)
Choke unloader	38°
Curb idle speed manual initial	See Emissions decal inside engine compartment
final	
auto initial	
final	
Max. CO at idle	See Decal

Carburetor specifications Rochester 4MV (1970)

Engine displacement (cu in)	350, 402
Float level	1/4
Accelerator pump stroke	5/16
Fast idle (rpm)	1500 (Man) 1800 (Auto)
Choke rod	0.100
Choke vacuum break	M 0.275 A 0.245
Choke unloader	0.450
Air valve spring	(350) 7/16 (402) 13/16
Air valve dashpot	0.020
§Curb idle speed (rpm) manual	700
auto	600

§*Refer also to relevant text for intermediate speed levels to be set during adjustment procedure.*

All carburettors: Primary throttle bore 1 3/8   Secondary throttle bore 2 1/4.   M − Manual transmission   A − Automatic transmission

Carburetor specifications Rochester 4MV (1971 thru 1974)

	1971	1972	1973	1974
Engine displacement (cu in)	350, 402	350, 402	350	350
Float level	1/4	1/4	7/32	1/4
Accelerator pump stroke	3/8	3/8	13/32	13/32
Fast idle (rpm)	M 1350 A 1500	M 1350 A 1500	M 1300 A 1600	M 1300 A 1600
Choke rod	0.100	0.100	0.430	0.430
Choke vacuum break	M 0.275 A 0.260	(350) 0.215 (others) 0.250	0.250	0.220
Choke unloader	0.450	0.450	0.450	0.450
Air valve spring	13/16	13/16	–	–
Air wind up valve	–	–	1/2	7/8
Air valve dashpot	0.020	0.020	0.020	–
§Curb idle speed (rpm) } manual initial	675	750†	920	950
final	600	750*†	900‡*	900
auto initial	630	600*	620*	650
final	600	600	600	600
Maximum CO at idle	1%	1%	1%	0.5%

Refer also to relevant text for intermediate speed levels to be set during adjustment procedure
All carburetors: Primary throttle bore 1 3/8
Secondary throttle bore 2 1/4
M – Manual transmission
A – Automatic transmission
‡ With solenoid adjuster 650 rpm
† 350 cu in engine Initial 1000 rpm Final 900 rpm
* On vehicles equipped with Air Injector Reactor system, turn mixture screw 1/4 turn from lean roll point for final carburetor setting

Carburetor Specifications – Holley 4150 (1970 thru 1972)

Engine displacement (cu in)	350, 402
Float level Primary	0.350
Secondary	0.50
Accelerator pump stroke	0.015
Fast idle (rpm)	2200 (0.25)
Choke vacuum break	0.300
Choke unloader	0.350
Main metering jets Primary	70 68 (1972
Secondary	76 73 only)
Primary throttle bore	1 11/16
Secondary throttle bore	1 11/16
Secondary stop	1/2 turn open
Curb idle } manual initial	750*
speed (rpm) } automatic initial	700*

* Set 1/4 turn rich from lean roll position for curb (final) speed

Carburetor specifications Rochester M4MCA, M4MC, M4ME (1975 thru 1980)

Engine displacement (cu in)	350 1975, M4MCA	305, 350 1976 on, M4MC and M4ME
Float level	15/32	13/32 (1976 – 1977) 15/32 (1978 – 1979) 7/16 (1980)
Accelerator pump stroke	0.275	9/32
Fast idle (rpm)	1600	1600
Choke rod	0.300	0.325
Choke vacuum break	Front 0.180 Rear 0.170	0.185
Choke unloader	0.325	0.325
Spring wind up	7/8	7/8 (350)
Air valve dashpot	0.015	0.015
Choke coil lever	0.120	0.120
* Curb idle speed (rpm) manual initial	900	900
final	800	800
auto initial	650	650
final	600	600

* Use preferred figures from individual vehicle Decal.

Torque specifications

	lb-in
Two barrel carburetor	
Throttle body to bowl	72
Bowl cluster	46
Fast idle cam	58
Metering jet	40
Choke lever	14
Choke housing to throttle body	46
Choke housing cover	26
Air horn to bowl	46
Vacuum break unit	26
Choke shaft	14
Fuel inlet nut	400
Fuel inlet needle seat	45
Four barrel carburetor	
Throttle body to bowl	46
Choke lever	14
Choke housing	46
Choke housing cover	26
Air horn to bowl (large)	46
(small)	26
Air horn to throttle body	46
Choke lever	14
Vacuum break unit	26
Solenoid bracket	71
Fuel inlet nut	400

Manifold bolts	lb-ft
Intake	30
Exhaust except 350 engine inner bolts	20
350 engine inner bolts	30
Exhaust pipe to manifold bolts	15
Catalytic converter fill plug	50

1 General description

1 The fuel system of all models comprises a rear fuel tank, a mechanically operated fuel pump, a carburetor and an air cleaner.
2 The carburetor may be of dual or four barrel type depending upon the engine capacity and the date of production of the vehicle.
3 All models are equipped with some form of emission control equipment. The later the date of the vehicle, the more complex and sophisticated do the carburetor and the emission control system become.

2 Air cleaner – servicing

Non-temperature-controlled type (paper element)

1 At the intervals specified in Chapter 1, unscrew the top of the air cleaner cover and remove the cover.
2 Remove the cleaner element and discard it, then wipe clean the interior of the casing, insert a new element and install the cover.

Non-temperature-controlled type (oil bath)

3 With this type of air cleaner, release the clamp screw at the base of the reservoir and lift the cleaner assembly from the carburetor.
4 Remove the wing nut and take off the cover and element.
5 Release the clamp screw and remove the air intake horn from the carburetor. Loosen the stud wing nut to allow removal of the reservoir.
6 Drain the oil from the reservoir and clean all components in a suitable solvent.
7 Reassemble and install the air cleaner components. Fill the reservoir with SAE 50 engine oil when operating in above freezing temperatures, or SAE 20 below freezing.

Temperature-controlled (thermostatic) air cleaner (TAC)

8 If a plain paper air cleaner element is used, replace it as described in paragraphs 1 and 2 of this Section.
9 If a Polywrap element is used, remove the Polywrap band from the paper element and discard the element. If the band is in good undamaged condition, rinse it clean in kerosene and squeeze it dry. Dip the band in clean engine oil and gently squeeze out the excess. Install the band to a new paper element and reassemble.
10 Any malfunction in the temperature-controlled air cleaner should first be checked out by starting the engine (cold) and observing the position of the deflector flap valve, using a mirror to look up the intake nozzle of the cleaner. This should be closed to cold air but open to warm air. Conversely, once the engine has warmed up, the flap should be open to cold and closed to warm. Both tests are carried out with the engine idling.
11 The vacuum unit can be removed from the air cleaner by drilling out the two spotwelds to remove the retaining strap. The new vacuum unit repair pack will contain the necessary sheet metal screws to hold the retaining strap in position when reassembling.
12 The sensor can be removed by prying up the tabs on the sensor retaining clip.

3 Fuel pump – description and testing

1 The fuel pump is a sealed type and is actuated from the engine camshaft. A pushrod is used between the camshaft and the pump rocker.
2 No servicing can be carried out as the unit is sealed, but if the pump is suspected of being faulty, carry out the following test.
3 Verify that gas is in the fuel tank. Disconnect the primary wire which runs between the coil and the distributor to prevent the engine firing when the starter motor is actuated. (1970 – 1974 models only). For 1975 – 1980 models, disconnect the distributor wiring marked 'BAT'.
4 Disconnect the fuel inlet pipe from the carburetor and place its open end in a container.
5 Operate the starter motor and check that well-defined spurts of fuel are being ejected from the open end of the pipe. If so, the pump is operating correctly; if not, replace the pump as described in the following section.

4 Fuel pump – removal and installation

1 To remove the pump, remove the fuel inlet and outlet pipes. Use two wrenches to prevent damage to the pump and connections (photo).
2 Remove the fuel pump mounting bolts, the pump, and the gasket (photos).
3 If the pushrod is to be removed, first remove the pipe plug or the pump adapter and gasket, as appropriate (photo).
4 When installing, first install the pushrod using the gasket sealant on the pipe plug or gasket (where applicable). Retain the pushrod in position using heavy grease (photo).
5 Install the pump using a new gasket. Use gasket sealant on the screw threads (photos).
7 Connect the fuel pipes, start the engine and check for leaks.

5 Fuel filters – replacement

1 See Chapter 1 for the step-by-step process.

6 Fuel tank – removal and installation

1 The fuel tank located between the frame rails and behind the rear axle is held in place by two steel straps. These straps are hinged at either the front or the rear end (with a bolt through the hinge) and secured at the opposite end with a bolt and nut assembly.
2 Disconnect the battery before performing any servicing operations involving the fuel supply.

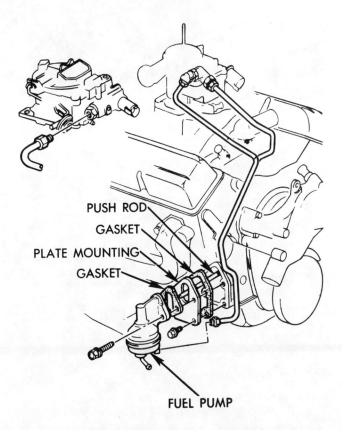

PUSH ROD
GASKET
PLATE MOUNTING
GASKET
FUEL PUMP

Fig. 4.1 Fuel pump and fuel line (Sec 4)

4.1 Use two wrenches to disconnect the fuel pipe from the fuel pump

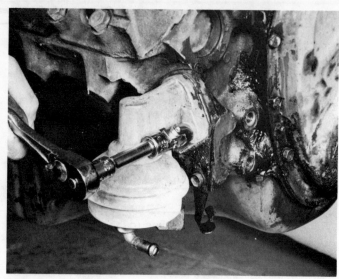

4.2A Removing the fuel pump attaching bolts

4.2B Removing the fuel pump from the engine block

4.3 The fuel pump push rod is located behind the fuel pump

4.4 When installing the push rod, use heavy grease to keep it secure inside its bore

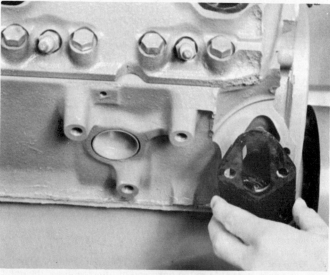

4.5A If a spacer plate is used, it should be installed after the push rod

4.5B Installing the fuel pump

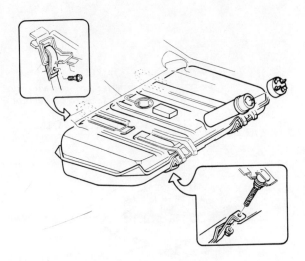

Fig. 4.2 Fuel tank installation (Sec 6)

3   Disconnect the fuel gauge wiring to the top of the tank. On early models, the wire should be disconnected from inside the trunk and then fed through the trunk floorpan with the rubber grommet pushed out of place.
4   Raise the vehicle for access underneath the car.
5   Drain all fuel from the tank into a clean container. Since there are no drain plugs for the Camaro, it is necessary to siphon the fuel through the filler neck, or drain the fuel through the fuel feed line running to the carburetor. Do not start the siphoning process with your mouth as serious personal injury could result. Also make sure that no open flames, lighted cigarettes or sparks are in the area as they could ignite the fuel vapor.
6   Disconnect the fuel hose and/or vapor return hose at the top of the tank.
7   Remove the gauge ground wire attached to the underbody.
8   Disconnect the filler neck at the tank.
9   Support the bottom of the tank using an adjustable jack and a piece of wood to spread the load.
10 Remove the tank strap bolts and carefully lower the tank checking that all connections are free of the tank as it is lowered. Read the following section for important repair and storage information.
11 Installation is a reversal of the removal process. Make sure all electrical connections are clean and properly installed and all hoses are tightened securely to the tank.

7   Fuel tank – repairs and storage

1   Any repairs to the fuel tank or filler neck should be carried out by a professional who has experience in this critical and potentially dangerous work. Even after cleaning and flushing of the fuel system, explosive fumes can remain and ignite during the repairing of the tank.
2   If the fuel tank is removed from the vehicle, it should not be placed in any area where sparks, or open flames could ignite the fumes coming out of the tank. Be especially careful inside garages where a water heater is located as the pilot light of the heater could cause an explosion.

8   Carburetors – description

Note: *For information on carburetor identification, refer to Chapter 13.*
1   Reference should be made to the Specifications Section of Chapter 1 for the general application of the different types of carburetors installed during the production run of vehicles covered by this manual. It is emphasized that the information given is not intended

to identify a particular carburetor with a specific vehicle, and the actual carburetor fitted to your engine should be checked out by recording the number stamped on the unit, and checking it with your partsman. It is very important not to use an incorrect unit, nor to modify the jets or internal components by substituting parts with different manufacturer's part numbers from those originally used.
2   All units have automatic chokes, either stove (hot air) heated from the manifold, or electrically heated.
3   Depending upon engine capacity, the carburetor may be of dual or four-barrel downdraft type.
4   Overhaul of a worn carburetor is not difficult, but always obtain a repair kit in advance, which will contain all the necessary gaskets and replaceable items.
5   If a carburetor has seen considerable use, and is obviously well worn, it will probably be more economical to replace it with a new, or factory reconditioned unit.

Rochester 2G series carburetor
6   This carburetor is a dual barrel, side bowl design.
7   Units fitted to manual and automatic transmission vehicles are similar but vary in calibration.
8   The main metering jets are of a fixed type, calibration being accomplished through a system of air bleeds.
9   A power enrichment valve assembly is incorporated by which power mixtures are controlled by air velocity past the boost venturi according to engine demands.
10 On later model vehicles, an electrically-operated throttle closing solenoid (controlled through the ignition switch) is used to ensure that the throttle valve closes fully after the ignition is switched off, to prevent running-on (dieseling).
11 The choke is automatic and is operated by an exhaust manifold heated coil.

Rochester 4MV (Quadrajet) series carburetor
12 This is a downdraft two stage unit. The primary side uses a triple venturi system. The secondary side has two large bores and one metering system which supplements the primary main metering system and receives fuel from a common float chamber.

Rochester M4MC (Quadrajet) series carburetor
13 This is also downdraft two stage unit and is very similar to the 4 MV unit.

Holley 4150 series carburetor
14 This 4 barrel carburetor is fitted to early high-performance vehicles only.
15 The 4150 is a center inlet carburetor with a temperature sensing choke coil mounted on the intake manifold.

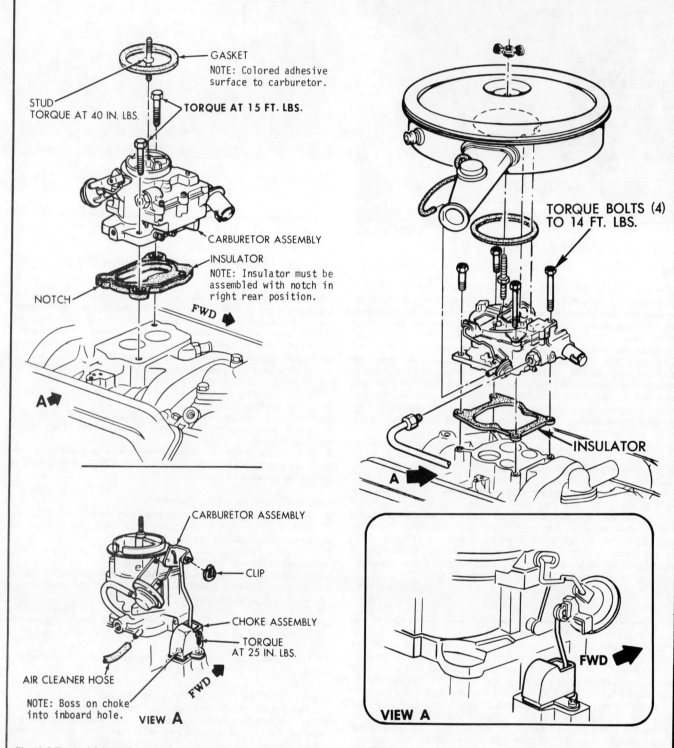

GASKET
NOTE: Colored adhesive surface to carburetor.

STUD
TORQUE AT 40 IN. LBS.

TORQUE AT 15 FT. LBS.

CARBURETOR ASSEMBLY

INSULATOR
NOTE: Insulator must be assembled with notch in right rear position.

NOTCH

FWD

A

TORQUE BOLTS (4) TO 14 FT. LBS.

INSULATOR

A

CARBURETOR ASSEMBLY

CLIP

CHOKE ASSEMBLY

TORQUE AT 25 IN. LBS.

AIR CLEANER HOSE

NOTE: Boss on choke into inboard hole.

FWD

VIEW A

VIEW A

FWD

Fig. 4.3 Typical 2-barrel carburetor and choke mounting (Sec 9)

Fig. 4.4 Typical 4-barrel carburetor and choke mounting (Sec 9)

9 Carburetors – removal and installation

1 Remove the air cleaner.
2 Disconnect the fuel and vacuum pipes from the carburetor.
3 Disconnect the choke rod or electrical wire (M4ME and M2ME carburetors).
4 Disconnect the accelerator linkage.
5 Disconnect the throttle valve linkage or downshift cable (automatic transmission).
6 Remove all hoses and electrical connections, making **very careful note** of where they were removed from. Tags or coded pieces of tape will help.
7 Remove the carburetor attaching nuts and/or bolts.
8 Lift away the carburetor.
9 Remove the gasket and/or insulator.
10 Installation is the reverse of the removal procedure, but the following points should be noted:

   a) By filling the carburetor bowl with fuel, the initial start-up will be easier and less drain on the battery will occur.
   b) New gaskets should be used.
   c) Idle speed and mixture settings should be checked, and adjusted if necessary.

10 Carburetor (Rochester 2GV) – idle adjustment

1 Idle speed adjustment must be carried out after the engine has fully warmed up. The air cleaner must be fitted, except where otherwise specified, and it is essential that the ignition timing and dwell angle are correctly set. All emission control systems must also be functioning correctly. In order to check engine speed, an external tachometer must be connected, following the manufacturer's instructions. **Note:** If the information given on the Decal label has superseded the information given in Specifications, the Decal label should be assumed to be correct.

1970 models
2 Disconnect and plug the distributor vacuum line and disconnect the 'Fuel Tank' line from the vapor canister.

3 Turn the mixture screws in gently until they seat and then back them out four turns.
4 Adjust the idle speed screw to obtain 800 rpm (manual transmission in neutral) or the solenoid screw to obtain 630 rpm (automatic transmission in 'Drive').
5 Now adjust the two mixture screws equally to obtain 700 rpm (manual) or 600 rpm (automatic).
6 On vehicles with automatic transmission, disconnect the electrical lead from the solenoid and then set the idle speed screw on the carburetor to obtain 450 rpm.
7 Reconnect the distributor vacuum line and the solenoid lead.

1971 models
8 Disconnect and plug the distributor vacuum line.
9 Disconnect the 'Fuel Tank' line from the vapor canister.
10 Adjust the idle speed screw on the carburetor to obtain 600 rpm (manual transmission in neutral) and air conditioning off (if fitted). With automatic transmission, adjust to 550 rpm (transmission in Drive) with the air conditioning (if fitted) on. Do not adjust the idle solenoid screw on automatic transmission vehicles.
11 The idle mixture screws on these carburetors are preset and should not be tampered with, which, in any event, cannot be accomplished without first breaking their limiter caps (refer to paragraph 24).

1972 models
12 The operators are similar to those described in paragraphs 8 to 11 for 1971 models except that with air conditioning off, the idle stop solenoid screw should be adjusted to give an idle speed of 900 rpm (manual transmission in Neutral) or 600 rpm (automatic transmission in Drive).

1973 and 1974 models
13 Disconnect and plug the distributor vacuum pipe.
14 Disconnect the 'Fuel Tank' line from the vapor canister.
15 With air conditioning off, adjust the idle stop solenoid screw to obtain 900 rpm (manual in Neutral) or 600 rpm (automatic in Drive).
16 Now de-energize the idle stop solenoid and with the idle cam screw on the low step of the cam, adjust the cam screw to obtain 400 rpm (automatic transmission in Drive) or 500 rpm (manual transmission in Neutral).
17 Reconnect the vacuum and fuel tank lines.

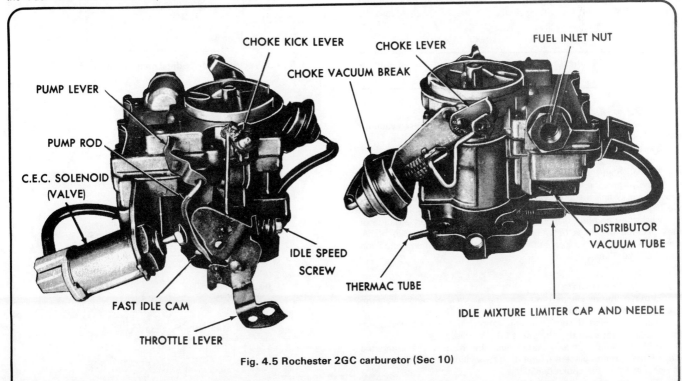

PUMP LEVER
PUMP ROD
C.E.C. SOLENOID (VALVE)
FAST IDLE CAM
THROTTLE LEVER
CHOKE KICK LEVER
CHOKE VACUUM BREAK
IDLE SPEED SCREW
THERMAC TUBE
CHOKE LEVER
FUEL INLET NUT
DISTRIBUTOR VACUUM TUBE
IDLE MIXTURE LIMITER CAP AND NEEDLE

Fig. 4.5 Rochester 2GC carburetor (Sec 10)

Idle mixture adjustment (1971 on)

18 The idle mixture screws are fitted with limiter caps as already described and any minor adjustment should be restricted to turning the screws within the extent of their travel ($\frac{1}{2}$ to $\frac{3}{4}$ turn clockwise). Turning the screws in leans the mixture.

19 If after overhaul or replacement of carburetor internal components, it is essential to adjust the mixture screws, carry out the following operations:

20 Disconnect the fuel tank vent hose from the vapor canister.

21 Disconnect and plug the distributor vacuum line.

22 Switch off the air conditioning (if fitted).

23 Set transmission in Neutral (manual) or Drive (automatic).

24 Using a pair of pliers break off the tabs on the mixture screw limiter cap.

25 Refer to Specifications and set the engine idle speed to the initial idle speed (lean drop method) given in Specifications Section.

26 Now turn out the mixture screws equally until maximum idle speed is achieved. Readjust the initial speed to that given in the Specifications.

27 Now turn both mixture screws in equally until the final idle speed is obtained as given in the Specifications Section.

28 Reconnect the hoses and fit new limiter caps with the cap stops at the fully rich (backed out) position.

29 An alternative method of setting the idle mixture adjustment is to connect a CO meter (exhaust gas analyzer) in accordance with the maker's instructions and then turn the mixture screws in or out until the CO level is within the maximum shown in the Specifications Section, consistent with smooth idling.

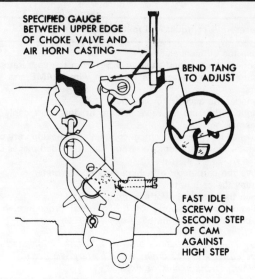

Fig. 4.6 Choke rod adjustment diagram (Sec 11)

11 Carburetor (Rochester 2GV) – choke rod adjustment

Note: *The following adjustment will normally only be required after overhaul or repair of the carburetor.*

1   Turn the idle stop screw in until it just touches the bottom step of the fast idle cam, then screw it in exactly one full turn.

2   Position the idle screw so that it is on the second stop of the fast idle cam against the shoulder of the high step.

3   Hold the choke valve plate towards the closed position (using a rubber band to keep it in place) and check the gap between the upper edge of the choke valve plate and the inside wall of the air horn.

4   Adjust to the specified gap, if necessary, by bending the tang on the upper choke lever. The setting should provide the specified fast idle speeds.

12 Carburetor (Rochester 2GV) – choke vacuum break adjustment

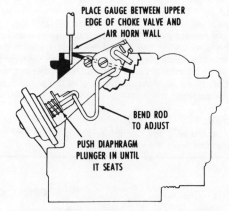

Fig. 4.7 Vacuum break adjustment diagram (Sec 12)

Pre 1972 models

1   Remove the air cleaner and plug the air cleaner sensor vacuum take-off port in the carburetor.

2   Start the engine or apply suction to the diaphragm vacuum tube.

3   Remove the choke rod from the lever and install a rubber band to the lever to hold the choke towards the closed position.

4   Slowly open the accelerator until the choke is closed as far as the vacuum break link reaction will permit, and the idle is determined by the high step of the fast idle cam. Release the accelerator.

5   With the condition of paragraph 4 maintained, insert a gauge of the specified thickness between the air horn and the choke blade. Bend the rod or tang as necessary to obtain the specified dimension (see Specifications Section).

1972 models onwards

6   Remove the air cleaner and plug the air cleaner sensor vacuum take-off port in the carburetor.

7   Using an external suction source, apply suction to the vacuum break diaphragm until the plunger is fully seated.

8   With the diaphragm fully seated, push the choke valve towards the closed position and place a gauge of the specified thickness between the air horn and the choke blade.

9   Bend the vacuum break rod if necessary to obtain the specified dimension (see Specifications Section).

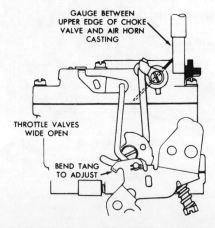

Fig. 4.8 Choke unloader adjustment diagram (Sec 13)

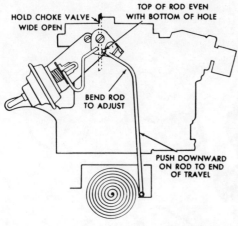

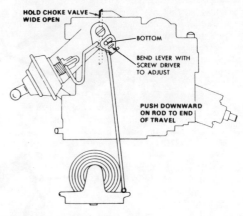

Fig. 4.9 Choke coil rod adjustment diagram (Sec 14)

13 Carburetor (Rochester 2GV) – choke unloader adjustment

1   Hold the throttle valve plates in the fully open position.
2   Hold the choke valve plate towards the closed position using a rubber band to keep it in place.
3   Check the gap between the upper edge of the choke valve plate and the inside wall of the air horn.
4   Bend the tang on the throttle lever to adjust the gap to the specified value, if necessary, as given in Specifications Section.

14 Carburetor (Rochester 2GV) – choke coil rod adjustment

Pre-1972 models
1   Hold the choke valve open then pull down on the coil rod to the end of its travel.
2   The top of the rod end which slides in the hole in the choke lever, should be even with the bottom of the choke lever hole. Bend the rod at the point shown to adjust.
3   Connect the rod to the choke lever and install the retaining clip. Check that the choke operates freely.

1972 models onwards
4   Hold the choke valve plate fully open.
5   Disconnect the thermostatic coil rod from the upper lever and push down on the rod as far as it will go. The top of the rod should be level with the bottom of the hole in the choke lever.
6   Adjust if necessary by bending the rod.

15 Carburetor (Rochester 2GV) – accelerator pump adjustment

1   Unscrew the idle speed screw.
2   Close both throttle valve plates completely and measure from the top surface of the air horn ring to the top of the pump rod.
3   Bend the rod to obtain the specified dimension.

16 Carburetor (Rochester 2GV) – overhaul

1   When a carburetor develops faults after a considerable mileage, it is usually more economical to replace the complete unit, rather than to completely dismantle it and replace individual components. Where, however, it is decided to strip and rebuild the unit, first obtain a repair kit which will contain all the necessary gaskets and other needed items, and proceed in the following sequence.
2   Bend back the lockwasher tabs then remove the idle stop solenoid (where applicable) from the carburetor.
3   Remove the choke lever from the vacuum break diaphragm link and the vacuum break link from the diaphragm plunger. The diaphragm plunger stem spring need not be removed.
4   Disconnect the vacuum break hose from the tube then remove the

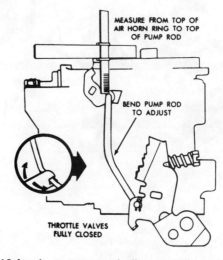

Fig. 4.10 Accelerator pump rod adjustment diagram (Sec 15)

diaphragm from the air horn by unscrewing two retaining screws.
5   Remove the fuel inlet filter nut, filter, spring and two gaskets.
6   Remove the pump rod from the throttle lever after removing the retaining clip. Rotate the upper pump lever counter-clockwise, then remove the pump rod from the lever by aligning the rod 'pip' with the lever notch.
7   Remove the fast idle cam retaining screw, rotate the cam and remove it from the rod.
8   Hold the choke open, rotate the upper end of the choke rod towards the pump lever and remove the rod from the upper choke lever.
9   Remove the air horn from the float bowl (8 screws).
10 Remove the float hinge pin, float, splash shield and float needle.
11 Unscrew the float needle seat and remove the gasket.
12 Remove the air horn to float bowl gasket.
13 Depress the power piston shaft, and allow the spring to snap sharply and eject the piston from the casting.
14 Remove the inner pump lever retaining screw then remove the outer pump lever and plastic washer from the air horn. Place the plunger in gasoline to prevent the rubber from drying out.
15 Rotate the pump plunger stem out of the hole in the inner lever if it is required to remove it. Do not bend the tang on the inner lever.
16 If the choke shaft or the valve need replacement, remove the two staked screws, remove the valve, then remove the shaft and lever from the air horn.
17 Remove the pump plunger return spring from the pump well, followed by the inlet check ball (where applicable).
18 Remove the pump inlet screen from the bottom of the float bowl (where applicable).
19 Unscrew the main jets, power valve and gaskets.
20 Remove the cluster and gasket (3 screws and washers). Note the fiber washer on the center screw.

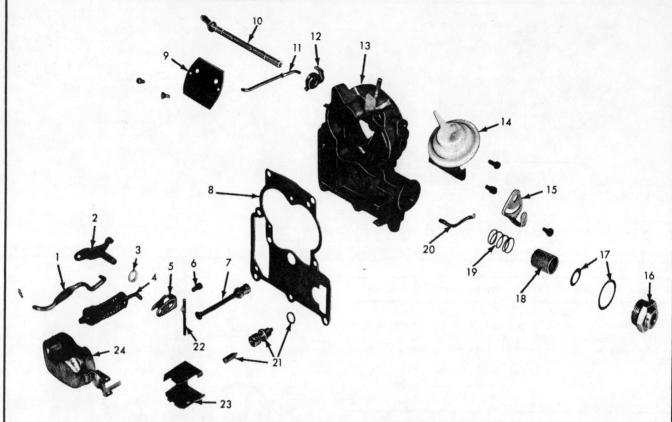

Fig. 4.11 Exploded view of air horn (Sec 16)

1 Accelerator pump rod	10 Shaft
2 Pump outer lever	11 Choke rod
3 Washer	12 Choke kick lever
4 Accelerator pump	13 Air horn
5 Pump inner lever	14 Vacuum diaphragm
6 Lever retainer	15 Choke lever
7 Power piston	16 Fuel inlet nut
8 Gasket	17 Gaskets
9 Choke valve plate	

18 Fuel filter
19 Filter spring
20 Diaphragm link
21 Fuel inlet needle and seat
22 Float hinge pin
23 Splash shields
24 Float

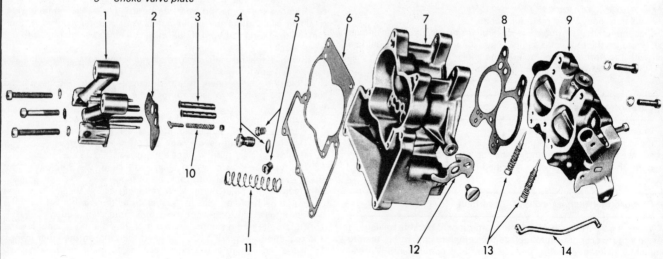

Fig. 4.12 Exploded view of throttle body and fuel bowl (Sec 16)

1 Venturi cluster	7 Bowl	11 Accelerator pump
2 Gasket	8 Gasket	12 Fast idle cam
3 Main well splash shield	9 Throttle body	13 Idle mixture screw
4 Power valve	10 Pump discharge check assembly	14 Choke rod
5 Main jets		
6 Gasket		

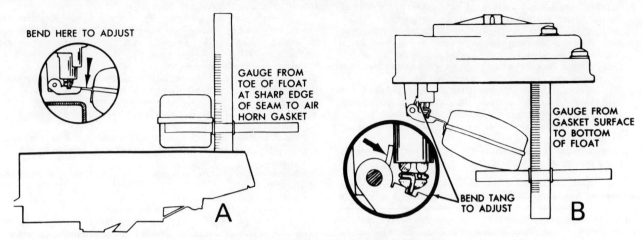

Fig. 4.13 Brass float adjustment diagram (Sec 16)

A   Float level   B   Float drop

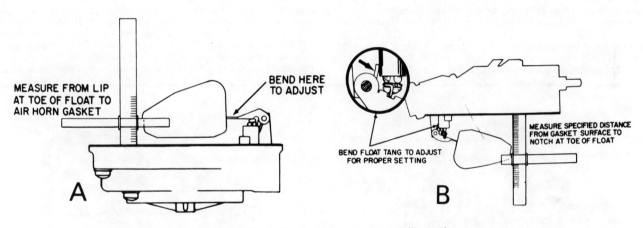

Fig. 4.14 Plastic float adjustment diagram (Sec 16)

A   Float level   B   Float drop

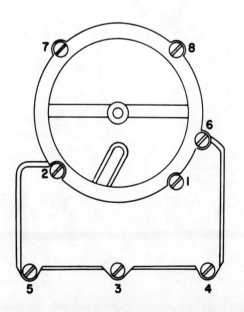

Fig. 4.15 Air horn screw tightening sequence – 2GV and 2GC carburetors (Secs 16 and 24)

21 Remove the pump discharge spring retainer, the spring and the check ball.

22 Remove the throttle body to bowl attaching screws. Remove the body and gasket.

23 Further dismantling is not recommended. If it is essential to remove the idle mixture needles, pry out the plastic limiter caps, then count the number of turns to bottom the needles and fit replacements in exactly the same position. New limiter caps should be fitted after running adjustments have been made.

24 Clean all metal parts in a suitable cold solvent. Do not immerse rubber parts, plastic parts, the vacuum break assembly, or the idle stop solenoid, or permanent damage will result. Do not probe the jets, but blow them through with clean, dry compressed air. Examine all fixed and moving parts for cracks, distortion, wear and other damage; replace as necessary. Discard all gaskets and fuel inlet filter.

25 Assembly is essentially the reverse of the removal procedure, but the following points should be noted:

a)   If new idle mixture screws are used, and the original setting was not noted, install the screws finger-tight to seat them, then back-off 4 full turns (3 full turns for 1970 models).

b)   When installing the choke valve on the seat, the letters 'RP' face upwards. Ensure that there is 0.020 inch clearance between the choke kick lever on the air horn before tightening the choke valve screws.

c)   Brass float: With the air horn inverted and the air horn gasket *installed, measure the distance from the gasket to the edge of the float seam at the outer edge of the float pontoon. Adjust the float level to the specified dimension by bending the float arm. With the air horn assembly upright and float freely suspended, measure from the gasket to the bottom of the float pontoon. Adjust the float drop to the specified dimension by bending the tang adjacent to the float needle.*

d) Plastic float: Refer to the procedure for the brass float, but note that for float level and float drop, the dimension is taken from the lip at the toe of the float in both instances.

e) Install and tighten the air horn screws evenly in the order shown.

f) After reassembly, carry out all the settings and adjustments listed previously in this Chapter.

17 Carburetor (Rochester 2GC) – idle adjustment

Note: *If the information given on the Decal label has superseded the information given in the Specifications, the Decal label should be assumed to be correct.*

Idle speed – 1975 models

1   Have the engine at normal operating temperature with the ignition settings correct.
2   Disconnect the fuel tank hose from the vapor canister.
3   Connect a tachometer to the engine and switch the air conditioning off.
4   Turn the idle speed screw until the engine is running at the speeds specified in Specifications Section with manual transmission in Neutral and automatic transmission in Drive.

Idle mixture – 1975 models

5   The mixture screws are fitted with limiter caps which restrict their movement between ½ and ¾ turn lean. Any adjustment should be kept to this but where the carburetor has been overhauled or new components fitted then the caps should be broken off and the following operations carried out.
6   Have the engine at normal operating temperature with air conditioning off and a tachometer connected to the engine.
7   Disconnect the fuel tank hose from the vapor canister.
8   Adjust the idle speed screw until the initial idle speed (see Specifications Section) is obtained.
9   Now unscrew the mixture screws equally until maximum idle speed is achieved. Readjust the idle speed screw again to obtain initial idle speed.
10   Screw in the mixture screws equally until final idle speed (lean drop) is obtained.

Idle speed – 1976 models and later

11   Have the engine at normal operating temperature with ignition settings correct and emission control systems operating correctly.
12   Set the idle speed screw on the low step of the fast idle cam.
13   Turn the idle speed screw to set the curb (initial idle speed) to specification (see Specifications Section or vehicle Decal).
14   *Where a solenoid is fitted to the carburetor,* carry out the operations described in paragraphs 11 and 13 and then with (i) the solenoid energized, (ii) the lead disconnected from the air conditioner compressor, (iii) the air conditioner on, open the throttle to allow the solenoid plunger to extend fully. Turn the solenoid hexagonal headed bolt until the idle speed is 700 rpm (manual) or 650 rpm (automatic). Reconnect the compressor lead on completion.
15   2GC carburetors are fitted with a solenoid when the vehicle is

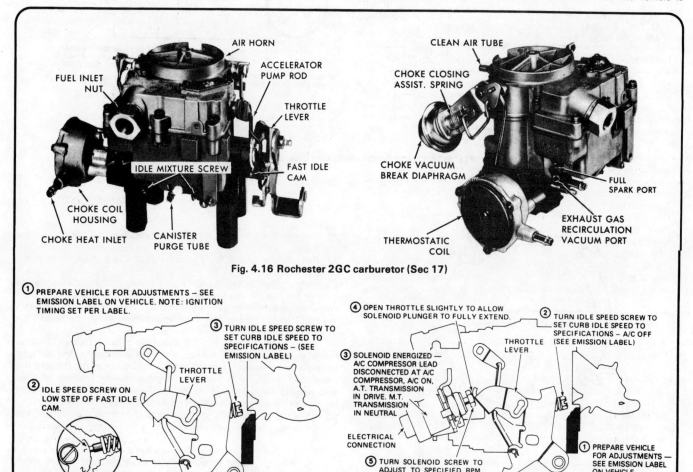

Fig. 4.16 Rochester 2GC carburetor (Sec 17)

Fig. 4.17 Idle speed adjustment diagram without solenoid (Sec 17)

Fig. 4.18 Idle speed adjustment diagram with solenoid (Sec 17)

equipped with automatic transmission or air conditioning.

Idle mixture – 1976 models and later
16 Refer to paragraphs 5 to 10 of this Section.

18 Carburetor (Rochester 2GC) – accelerator pump rod adjustment

1 The procedure is as for 2GV carburetor (Section 15).

19 Carburetor (Rochester 2GC) – choke coil lever adjustment

1 Remove three screws and retainers and remove the thermostatic coil cover, gasket and inside baffle plate assembly.
2 Place the idle speed screw on the highest step of the fast idle cam.
3 Close the choke valve by pushing up on the intermediate choke lever.
4 The edge of the coil lever inside the choke housing must align with the edge of the gauge.
5 If necessary, bend the choke rod to adjust.

20 Carburetor (Rochester 2GC) – fast idle cam adjustment

1 Place the idle speed screw on the second step of the cam, against the high step.
2 Check the dimension between the upper edge of the choke valve and the air horn wall.
3 If adjustment is necessary to obtain the specified dimension, bend the choke lever tang.

21 Carburetor (Rochester 2GC) – choke unloader adjustment

1 Hold the throttle valve open with the fingers.
2 Using a suitable gauge, check that the clearance between the edge of the choke valve plate and the air horn wall is as specified (see Specifications Section).
3 If necessary, bend the tang to adjust.

22 Carburetor (Rochester 2GC) – vacuum break adjustment

1 Using a separate source of suction, such as the mouth or a small hand pump, seat the vacuum break diaphragm.
2 Cover the vacuum break bleed hole with a piece of masking tape.
3 Place the idle speed screw on the high step of the fast cam idle.
4 Hold the choke coil lever inside the choke housing towards the closed choke position.
5 Check the dimension between the upper edge of the choke valve and the air horn wall. If adjustment is required to obtain the specified dimension (see Specifications Section) bend the vacuum break rod.
6 Remove the masking tape on the vacuum unit bleed hole and reconnect the vacuum hose.

23 Carburetor (Rochester 2GC) – automatic choke coil adjustment

1 Place the idle speed screw on the highest step of the fast idle cam.
2 Loosen the choke coil cover retaining screws.
3 Rotate the cover against the coil tension until the choke begins to close. Continue rotating until the index mark aligns with the specified point on the choke housing, which is between the center and $\frac{1}{2}$ notch lean.
4 Tighten the choke cover retaining screws.

24 Carburetor (Rochester 2GC) – overhaul

Note: *When a carburetor develops faults after a considerable mileage, it is usually more economical to replace the complete unit rather than*

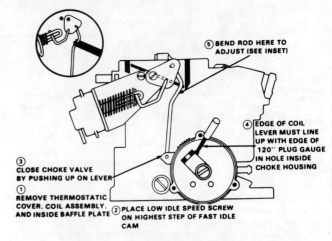

Fig. 4.19 Choke coil lever adjustment diagram (Sec 19)

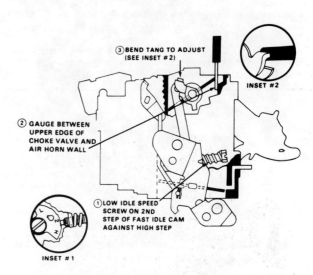

Fig. 4.20 Fast idle cam adjustment diagram (Sec 20)

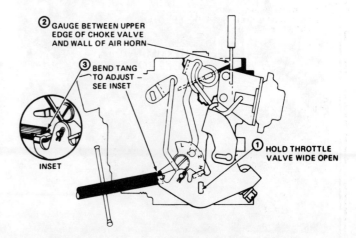

Fig. 4.21 Choke unloader adjustment diagram (Sec 21)

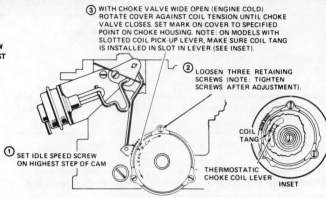

③ STEM PULLED OUT UNTIL SEATED

④ GAUGE BETWEEN UPPER EDGE OF CHOKE VALVE AND WALL OF AIR HORN

① PLACE IDLE SPEED SCREW ON HIGHEST STEP OF FAST IDLE CAM

VACUUM DIAPHRAGM SEATED

⑤ BEND ROD TO ADJUST

NOTE: PLUG END COVER WITH A PIECE OF MASKING TAPE MAKING SURE TO COVER PURGE BLEED HOLE. REMOVE TAPE AFTER ADJUSTMENT.

② USE OUTSIDE VACUUM SOURCE

Fig. 4.22 Choke vacuum break adjustment diagram (Sec 22)

③ WITH CHOKE VALVE WIDE OPEN (ENGINE COLD) ROTATE COVER AGAINST COIL TENSION UNTIL CHOKE VALVE CLOSES. SET MARK ON COVER TO SPECIFIED POINT ON CHOKE HOUSING. NOTE: ON MODELS WITH SLOTTED COIL PICK-UP LEVER, MAKE SURE COIL TANG IS INSTALLED IN SLOT IN LEVER (SEE INSET).

② LOOSEN THREE RETAINING SCREWS (NOTE: TIGHTEN SCREWS AFTER ADJUSTMENT).

① SET IDLE SPEED SCREW ON HIGHEST STEP OF CAM

COIL TANG

THERMOSTATIC CHOKE COIL LEVER

INSET

Fig. 4.23 Automatic choke coil adjustment diagram (Sec 23)

SPRING CLIP

Fig. 4.24 Disconnnecting lower end of pump rod (Sec 24)

VACUUM BREAK LEVER

Fig. 4.25 Removing vacuum break lever (Sec 24)

VACUUM BREAK LEVER

INTERMEDIATE CHOKE ROD

Fig. 4.26 Removing intermediate choke rod (Sec 24)

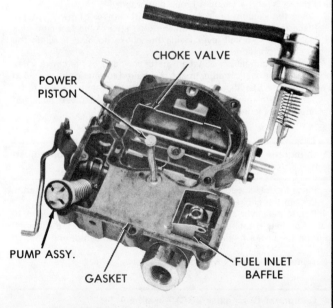

CHOKE VALVE

POWER PISTON

PUMP ASSY.

GASKET

FUEL INLET BAFFLE

Fig. 4.27 Removing the power piston (Sec 24)

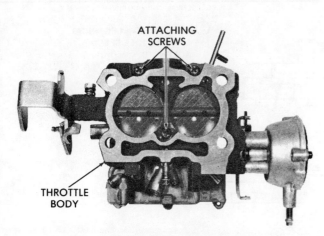

Fig. 4.28 Throttle body screws (Sec 24)

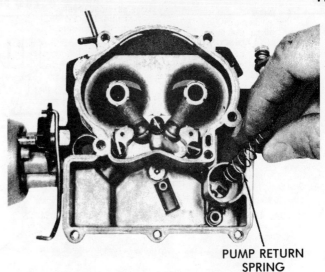

Fig. 4.29 Removing the pump return spring (Sec 24)

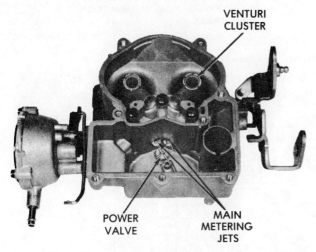

Fig. 4.30 Removing the main metering jets and venturi cluster (Sec 24)

Fig. 4.31 Removing the pump discharge spring retainer (Sec 24)

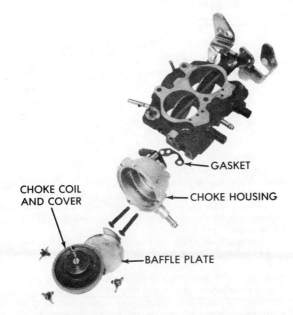

Fig. 4.32 The choke housing assembly (Sec 24)

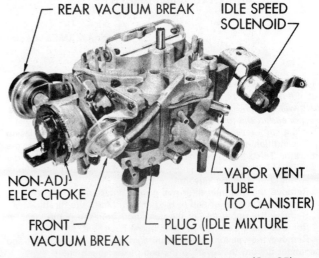

Fig. 4.33 Rochester model M2ME carburetor (Sec 25)

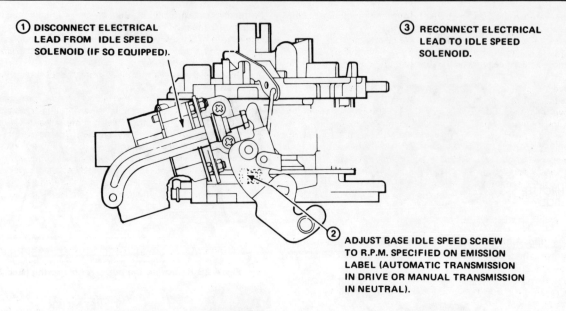

Fig. 4.34 Adjusting M2ME series carburetor idle speed (Secs 25 and 28)

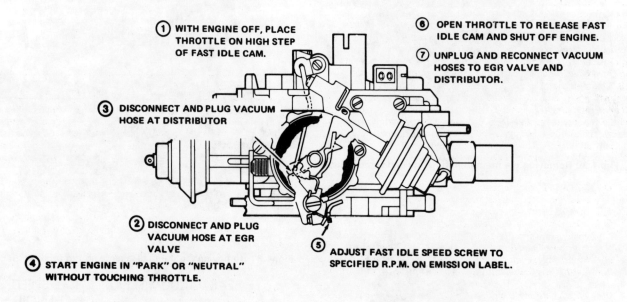

Fig. 4.35 Adjusting M2ME series carburetor fast idle speed (Secs 26 and 29)

to completely dismantle it and replace individual components. However, if it is decided to strip and rebuild the unit, first obtain a repair kit which will contain all the necessary gaskets and other needed items, and proceed in the following sequence.

1 If the carburetor is fitted with a solenoid (automatic transmission or air conditioning) this should be removed before dismantling the carburetor. To do this, bend back the lockwasher tabs and unscrew the large nut which holds the solenoid to the bracket. Avoid immersion of the solenoid in cleaning solvent.

2 Remove the fuel inlet filter nut, gasket, filter and spring.

3 Disconnect the lower end of the pump rod from the throttle lever.

4 Remove the upper end of the pump rod from the pump lever.

5 Remove the vacuum break diaphragm hose.

6 Remove the vacuum break diaphragm assembly (2 screws) and disconnect it from the lever on the end of the choke shaft.

7 Remove the vacuum break lever from the end of the choke shaft (1 screw), then remove the intermediate choke rod from the vacuum

break lever on the coil housing.

8 Remove the fast idle cam retaining screw, then remove the cam from the end of the choke rod. The upper end of the rod cannot be removed until the air horn has been removed from the float bowl.

9 Remove the 8 air horn attaching screws and lockwashers, then lift off the air horn.

10 Remove the float hinge pin and lift off the float. The float needle and pull clip (where applicable) can now be removed from the float arm.

11 Unscrew the float needle seat and remove the gasket.

12 Depress the power piston and release it to allow it to snap free.

13 Remove the pump plunger assembly and inner pump lever from the shaft by loosening the set screws on the inner lever.

14 If the pump assembly is to be overhauled, break off the flattened end of the pump plunger stem; the service pump uses a grooved pump plunger stem and retaining clip. After removng the inner pump lever and pump assembly, remove the outer lever and shaft assembly from

the air horn. Remove the plastic washer from the pump plunger shaft.

15 Remove the gasket from the air horn.

16 Remove the fuel inlet baffle (next to the needle seat).

17 Taking care not to bend the choke shaft, remove the choke valve. The retaining screws may need to be suitably dressed to permit removal.

18 Remove the choke valve shaft. Remove the fast idle cam rod and lever from the shaft.

19 Remove the pump plunger return spring from the float bowl pump well, then invert the bolt and remove the aluminium ball.

20 Remove the main metering jets, power valve and gasket from inside the float bowl.

21 Remove the three screws which retain the venturi cluster; remove the cluster and gasket.

22 Use needle-nosed pliers to remove the pump discharge spring retainer, then remove the spring and check ball from the discharge passage.

23 Remove the three large throttle body to bowl attaching screws and lockwashers. Remove the throttle body and gasket.

24 Remove the thermostatic choke coil cover (3 screws and retainers) and gasket from the choke housing. Do not remove the cap baffle from beneath the coil cover.

25 Remove the choke housing baffle plate.

26 From inside the choke housing, remove the 2 attaching screws; remove the housing and gasket.

27 Remove the screw from the end of the intermediate choke shaft, then remove the choke lever from the shaft. Remove the inner choke coil lever and shaft assembly from the choke housing, followed by the rubber dust seal.

28 Further dismantling is not recommended, particularly with regard to the throttle valves or shaft since it may be impossible to reassemble the valves correctly in relation to the idle discharge orifices. If it is essential to remove the idle mixture needles, break off the plastic limiter caps then count the number of turns to bottom the needles and fit replacements in exactly the same position. New limiter caps should be fitted after running adjustments have been made.

29 Clean all metal parts in a suitable cold solvent. Do not immerse rubber parts, plastic parts, diaphragm assemblies or pump plungers, as permanent damage will result. Do not probe the jets, but blow through with clean, dry compressed air. Examine all fixed and moving parts for cracks, distortion, wear and other damage; replace as necessary. Discard all gaskets and the fuel inlet filter.

30 Assembly is essentially the reverse of the removal procedure, but the following points should be noted:

a) If new idle mixture screws were used, and the original setting was not noted, install the screws finger-tight to seat them, then back off 4 full turns.

b) When installing the rubber dust seal in the choke housing cavity, the seal lip faces towards the carburetor after the housing is installed.

c) Before installing the choke cover coil and baffle plate assembly, carry out the Choke Coil Lever adjustment (Section 19).

d) When installing the choke coil and cover assembly, the end of the coil must be below the plastic tang on the inner choke housing lever. At this stage carry out the Automatic Choke Coil adjustment (Section 23).

e) When installing the venturi cluster, ensure that a gasket is fitted on the center screw.

f) Install the choke valve with the letters 'RP' or the part number, facing upwards.

g) Carry out float level and float drop checks as specified for the 2GV carburetor in Section 16 for plastic floats.

h) Install and tighten the air horn screws as shown for 2GV carburetors.

j) After reassembly, carry out the relevant settings and adjustments listed previously in this Chapter.

25 Carburetor (M2ME) – idle adjustment

1 Idle speed adjustment must be carried out after the engine has fully warmed up. The air cleaner must be fitted, except where otherwise specified, and it is essential that the ignition timing and dwell angle are correctly set. All emission control systems must also

be functioning correctly. In order to check engine speed, an external tachometer must be connected, following the manufacturer's instructions. **Note:** *if the information given on the Decal label has superseded the information given in Specifications, the Decal label should be assumed to be correct.*

2 Disconnect the electrical lead from the idle speed solenoid (if so equipped).

3 Adjust the base idle speed screw to the rpm specified on the emission label. The shift selector on automatic transmissions should be in Drive, and manual transmissions should be in Neutral.

4 The idle mixture screws have been preset at the factory and sealed. The only time the mixture screws will need adjusting is in the case of a major carburetor overhaul, throttle body replacement or in the case of a high emissions reading by official inspections. Because the mixture screws are sealed, an artificial enrichment procedure using propane gas is required to check the mixture. Adjusting the mixture by any other means may be a violation of law.

26 Carburetor (M2ME) – fast idle adjustment

1 With the engine turned off, place the throttle on the high step of the fast idle cam.

2 Disconnect and plug the vacuum hose at the EGR valve.

3 Disconnect and plug the vacuum hose at the distributor.

4 Start the engine in 'Park' or 'Neutral' without touching the accelerator pedal.

5 Adjust the fast idle speed screw to the rpm specified on the emission Decal.

6 Open the throttle to release the fast idle cam and turn off the engine.

7 Unplug and reconnect the vacuum hoses to the EGR valve and distributor.

27 Carburetor (M2ME) – overhaul

1 When a carburetor develops faults after a considerable mileage, it is usually more economical to replace the complete unit, rather than to completely dismantle it and replace individual components. Where, however, it is decided to strip and rebuild the unit, first obtain a repair kit which will contain all the necessary gaskets and other needed items and proceed in the following sequence.

2 Remove the solenoid (if equipped) from the float bowl. Screws secure the solenoid and bracket assembly. Do not immerse the solenoid in any type of carburetor cleaner.

3 Remove the choke lever at the top of the carburetor by removing the retaining screw. Then rotate the choke lever to remove the choke rod from its slot in the lever.

4 To remove the choke rod from the lower lever, hold the lower lever outward and twist the choke rod in a counterclockwise direction.

5 Note the position of the accelerator pump rod on its lever. Then remove the pump lever by driving the pivot pin inwards slightly until the lever can be removed from the air horn.

6 Remove the seven screws which attach the top air horn assembly to the bowl. Two of them are countersunk near the center of the carburetor. Lift the air horn straight up and off the float bowl.

7 From the air horn assembly, remove the vacuum break hose followed by the vacuum break control and bracket assembly. Do not immerse the vacuum break assembly in carburetor cleaner.

8 Lift the air horn gasket from the top of the float bowl assembly being careful not to distort the spring holding the main metering rods in place.

9 Remove the pump plunger from the pump well. Following the plunger from the well will be the plunger return spring.

10 Remove the power piston and metering rods from the well. Do this by pressing down on the piston and releasing it quickly with a snap. This procedure may have to be repeated many times. Do not remove the piston with pliers on the metering rod hanger. The A.P.T. metering rod adjustment screw is pre-set and should not be changed. If float bowl replacement is necessary the new float bowl will be supplied with a new A.P.T. metering screw.

11 Remove the metering rods from the power piston by disconnecting the spring from the top of each rod. Rotate the rod to remove from the hanger.

12 Remove the plastic filler block over the float valve.
13 Remove the float assembly and float needle by pulling up on the retaining pin. Also remove the needle, seat and gasket.
14 Remove the main metering jets only if necessary to replace.
15 Remove the pump discharge check ball retainer and check ball.
16 Remove the pump well fill slot baffle.
17 The choke cover is held in place with rivets to discourage tampering. It is removed by drilling out the rivet heads with a .159-inch drill bit.
18 Remove the choke assembly retainers, cover gasket and choke cover assembly from the main housing. Do not remove the baffle beneath the choke cover coil.
19 The choke housing can be removed from the float bowl by removing the retaining screw inside the housing.
20 Remove the rear vacuum break rod from the intermediate choke lever.
21 To remove the intermediate choke shaft, remove the retaining screw inside the choke housing and the coil lever from the flats on the shaft. Slide the intermediate shaft outward and remove the fast idle cam from the shaft.
22 Remove the cup seal from the float bowl insert. Do not remove the cup seal from the float bowl insert. Do not remove the insert itself.
23 Turn the float bowl upside down and remove the choke lever from inside the cavity.

24 From the float bowl assembly, remove the fuel inlet nut, gasket, check valve filter and spring.
25 The throttle body can be separated from the float bowl by removing the attaching screws.
26 Remove the pump rod from the throttle lever.
27 Do not remove the plugs covering the idle mixture needles unless it is necessary to replace the mixture screws. The mixture passages should clean with normal soaking and air pressure.
28 Clean all metal parts in a suitable cold solvent. Do not immerse rubber parts, plastic parts, the vacuum break assembly or the idle stop solenoid. Do not probe the jets, but blow them through with clean, dry compressed air. Examine all fixed and moving parts for cracks, distortion, wear and other damage. Replace parts as necessary. Discard all gaskets and the fuel inlet filter.
29 Assembly is essentially the reverse of the removal procedure, but the following points should be noted:

a) *Do not install the choke coil cover assembly until the inside coil lever is adjusted. With the fast idle cam follower on the high step, push up on the coil tang until the choke valve is closed. Insert a .120-inch plug gauge and bend the choke rod near the lever until the lower edge of the lever just contacts the plug gauge.*

b) *With the float bowl components assembled, adjust the float*

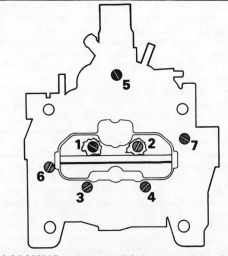

Fig. 4.36 M2ME carburetor air horn screw tightening sequence (Sec 27)

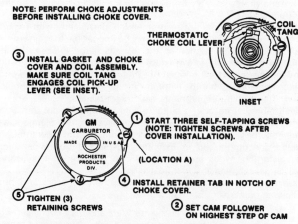

NOTE: PERFORM CHOKE ADJUSTMENTS BEFORE INSTALLING CHOKE COVER.

③ INSTALL GASKET AND CHOKE COVER AND COIL ASSEMBLY. MAKE SURE COIL TANG ENGAGES COIL PICK-UP LEVER (SEE INSET).

① START THREE SELF-TAPPING SCREWS (NOTE: TIGHTEN SCREWS AFTER COVER INSTALLATION).

(LOCATION A)

④ INSTALL RETAINER TAB IN NOTCH OF CHOKE COVER.

⑤ TIGHTEN (3) RETAINING SCREWS

② SET CAM FOLLOWER ON HIGHEST STEP OF CAM

THERMOSTATIC CHOKE COIL LEVER

COIL TANG

INSET

GM CARBURETOR MADE IN U.S.A. ROCHESTER PRODUCTS DIV.

INSTALLATION OF CHOKE COVER

Fig. 4.37 M2ME choke assembly (Sec 27)

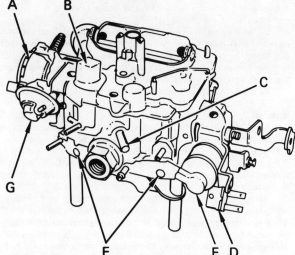

Fig. 4.38 Rochester model E2ME carburetor (Sec 30)

A Electric choke	E Idle speed solenoid
B Mixture control solenoid	F Plug (idle mixture needle)
C Vapor vent tube	G Front vacuum break
D Wide open throttle switch	

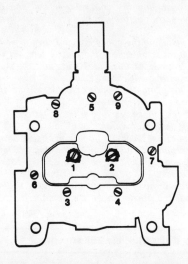

Fig. 4.39 E2ME carburetor air horn screw tightening sequence (Sec 30)

level. Hold down the float retainer firmly and push the float down tightly against the needle. Measure from the top of the float bowl (without gasket) to the top of the float, about $\frac{3}{16}$" back from the toe. Bend the float arm as necessary.

    c) *Tighten the seven air horn attaching screws evenly in the sequence given.*

28 Carburetor (E2ME) – idle speed

1   The procedure for setting idle speed on the E2ME carburetor is the same as that for the M2ME. Refer to Section 25.

29 Carburetor (E2ME) – fast idle adjustment

1   The procedure for adjusting the fast idle on the E2ME is the same as that for the M2ME. Refer to Section 26.

30 Carburetor (E2ME) – overhaul

1   When a carburetor develops faults after a considerable mileage, it is usually more economical to replace the complete unit, rather than to completely dismantle it and replace individual components. Where, however, it is decided to strip and rebuild the unit, first obtain a repair kit which will contain all the necessary gaskets and other needed items, and proceed in the following sequence:

2   Remove the screws holding the wide open throttle and idle solenoid and bracket assembly to the float bowl. Do not immerse these parts in carburetor cleaner.

3   Remove the upper choke lever from the end of the shaft by removing the retaining screw and rotating the lever.

4   Remove the choke rod from the lower lever inside the float bowl casting. Do this by holding the lever outward and twisting the rod counterclockwise.

5   Use a drift to drive the pump lever pivot pin inward until the lever can be removed from the air horn. Note the position of the accelerator pump rod in the lever and then remove the pump lever from the pump rod.

6   Remove the vacuum break hose from the tube on the float bowl.

7   Remove the nine air horn attaching screws. Two of them are countersunk near the center of the carburetor. Lift the air horn straight up and off the float bowl.

8   From the air horn assembly, remove the vacuum break control with its bracket. Do not immerse this in carburetor cleaner.

9   Remove the pump plunger stem seal by inverting the air horn and using a small screwdriver to remove the staking. Remove and discard the retainer and seal.

10 The air horn assembly includes an idle air bleed valve which is pre-set at the factory. The air valve and seals should not be removed from the air horn unless replacement is necessary. The air horn assembly should not be immersed or cleaned in carburetor cleaner in the normal manner as this may damage the O-rings which seal the idle air bleed valve.

11 Holding down on the pump plunger stem, raise the corner of the air horn gasket still attached to the float bowl and remove the pump plunger from its well.

12 Remove the solenoid metering rod plunger by lifting straight up.

13 Remove the rubber seal from around the mixture control solenoid plunger.

14 Remove the air horn gasket from the float bowl.

15 Remove the pump return spring from the well.

16 Remove the plastic filler block over the float valve.

17 Carefully lift out each metering rod assembly. Make sure the return spring comes with the assembly.

18 Remove the mixture control solenoid from the float bowl. Do this by first removing the two attaching screws. Do not remove the solenoid connector at this time. Turn the mixture control screw counterclockwise and remove the screw. Carefully lift the solenoid and connector assembly from the float bowl. The solenoid and connector are serviced as an assembly only.

19 Remove the plastic insert from the cavity in the float bowl under the solenoid connector.

20 Remove the solenoid screw tension spring next to the float hanger clip.

21 Remove the float assembly and float needle by pulling up on the retaining clip. Remove the needle and seat.

22 Remove the large mixture control solenoid spring from the bottom of the float bowl.

23 Remove the main metering jets, if necessary.

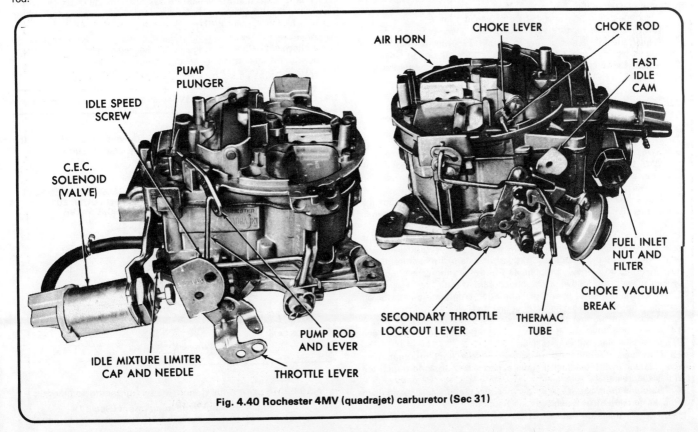

Fig. 4.40 Rochester 4MV (quadrajet) carburetor (Sec 31)

24 Remove the pump discharge check ball retainer and check ball.
25 Remove the pump well fill slot baffle, if necessary for replacement.
26 Remove the rear vacuum break control, along with its attaching bracket. Do not immerse this in carburetor cleaner.
27 The non-adjustable choke is designed to be a permanent fixture. Rivets are used to secure the cover. If disassembly is necessary, see the overhaul instructions for the M2ME, as the choke mechanisms are the same.
28 Remove the fuel inlet nut, gasket, check valve filter assembly and spring from the float bowl.
29 Remove the four throttle body attaching screws and remove the throttle body assembly.
30 Remove the pump rod from the throttle lever by rotating the rod until the tang aligns with the slot in the lever.
31 Do not remove the plugs covering the idle mixture needles unless they must be replaced, which is not common in a standard overhaul.
32 Clean all metal parts in a suitable cold solvent. Do not immerse rubber parts, plastic parts, the vacuum break assembly, wide-open throttle switch, solenoid or air horn assembly. Do not probe the jets, but blow them through with clean, dry compressed air. Examine all fixed and moving parts for cracks, distortion, wear and other damage. Replace parts as necessary. Discard all gaskets and the fuel filter.
33 Assembly is essentially the reverse of the removal procedure, but the following points should be noted:

    a) To make the float level adjustment, hold the float retaining clip firmly in place and push down lightly on the float arm. Measure from the top of the float bowl casting (without gasket) to the top of the float about $\frac{3}{16}''$ back from the toe. Bend the float arm as necessary for adjustment.

    b) Tighten the nine air horn attaching screws securely in the sequence give.

31 Carburetor (Rochester 4MV) – idle adjustment

1970 models (350, 402 cu in engines)
Note: *If the information given on the Decal label has superseded the information given in the Specifications, the Decal label should be assumed to be correct.*
1 Have the engine at the normal operating temperature with a tachometer connected.
2 Disconnect and plug the distributor vacuum line.
3 Gently seat the mixture screws and then unscrew four turns.
4 Adjust the idle speed screw to obtain 775 rpm (manual transmission in Neutral) or 630 rpm (automatic transmission in Drive).
5 Adjust the mixture screws equally until the engine speed is 700 rpm (manual) 600 rpm (automatic).

1971 and 1972 models (350, 402 cu in engines)
6 Disconnect the distributor vacuum line from the distributor and plug the line. Connect a tachometer to the engine.
7 Disconnect the fuel tank line from the vapor canister.
8 Switch the air conditioning off.
9 With the engine at the normal operating temperature, adjust the idle stop solenoid screw to obtain 900 rpm (manual transmission in Neutral) or 600 rpm (automatic transmission in Drive).
10 Place the fast idle cam follower on the second step of the cam and adjust the fast idle to 1350 rpm (manual) or 1500 rpm (automatic in Park).
11 The mixture screws fitted to these vehicles have limiter caps which restrict their movement to between $\frac{1}{2}$ and $\frac{3}{4}$ turn lean. Any adjustment should be confined to this but where the carburetor has been overhauled or new components fitted, then the caps should be broken off and the following operations carried out.
12 Have the engine at the normal operating temperature with the air conditioning off and a tachometer connected.
13 Disconnect the fuel tank hose from the vapor canister.
14 Adjust the idle speed screw until the initial idle speed (see Specifications Section) is obtained.
15 Now unscrew the mixture screws equally until maximum idle speed is achieved. Readjust the idle speed screw again to obtain the initial idle speed.
16 Screw in the mixture screws equally until the final idle speed (lean drop) is obtained (see Specifications Section).
17 If an Air Injection Reactor System is fitted, now turn the mixture screws $\frac{1}{4}$ turn out equally.
18 If the carburetor is fitted with a solenoid, the final idle speed should be adjusted to complete the turning procedure by de-energizing the solenoid and turning the solenoid Allen screw to attain 450 rpm.
19 An alternative method of adjusting the mixture is to connect a CO meter (exhaust gas analyzer) in accordance with the maker's instructions and adjust the screws equally until the emission level is within the maximum permitted (see Specifications Section).
20 Install new limiter caps to the mixture screws so that any travel will be in the lean direction (screw in) only.

1973 and 1974 models (350, 400 cu in engines)
21 The operations are similar to those described in the preceding paragraphs except to refer to Specifications Section for initial, final and fast idle settings.

32 Carburetor (Rochester 4MV) – choke rod adjustment

1 Place the cam follower on the second step of the fast idle cam and against the high step.
2 Rotate the choke valve towards the closed position by turning the external lever counterclockwise.
3 Check that the dimension between the lower edge of the choke valve and the air horn wall (at the lever end) is as specified. Bend the choke rod if adjustment is required.

33 Carburetor (Rochester 4MV) – choke vacuum break adjustment

Pre-1972 models
1 Refer to Section 12.

1972 models onwards
2 Using an external source of suction, seat the choke vacuum break diaphragm.
3 Open the throttle slightly so that the cam follower clears the fast idle cam steps, then rotate the vacuum break lever towards the closed direction. Ensure that the vacuum break rod is in the outer end of the slot in the diaphragm plunger. A rubber band can be used to hold the vacuum break lever in position.
4 Measure the distance from the lower edge of the choke valve to the air horn wall. Check this against the figure shown in Specifications Section and if adjustment is needed, bend the link rod.

34 Carburetor (Rochester 4MV) – choke coil rod adjustment

Pre-1972 models
1 Hold the choke valve closed then pull down on the coil rod to the end of its travel. The rod should contact the bracket surface.

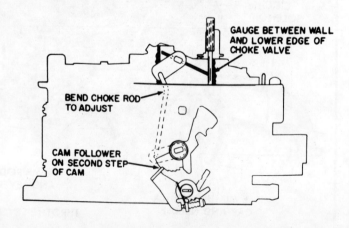

Fig. 4.41 Choke rod adjustment (Sec 32)

2   Bend the choke coil rod, if necessary, so that the top of the rod aligns with the bottom of the holes.
3   Connect the coil rod to the choke lever and install the retaining clip. Check that the choke operates freely over its full range of travel.

1972 models onwards

4   Rotate the choke coil lever counterclockwise to fully close the choke.
5   With the coil rod disconnected and the cover removed, push down on the rod until it contacts the bracket surface.
6   The coil rod must fit in the choke lever notch; bend the rod to adjust if necessary.
7   Install the choke coil cover.
8   Install the coil rod in the choke coil lever slot and install the retaining clip.
9   Check that the choke operates freely over its full range of travel.

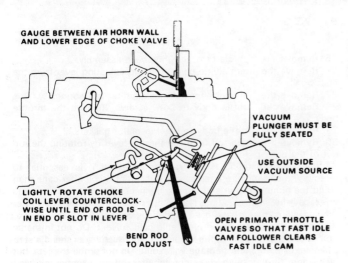

Fig. 4.42 Choke vacuum break adjustment (Sec 33)

35 Carburetor (Rochester 4MV) – air valve dashpot adjustment

Pre-1972 models

1   Seat the vacuum break diaphragm, and check that the specified clearance exists between the dashpot and the end of the slot in the air valve lever, when the air valve is fully closed.
2   If adjustment is necessary, bend the rod at the air valve end.

1972 models onwards

3   Seat the choke vacuum break diaphragm using an outside source of suction, then measure the dimension between the end of the slot in the vacuum break plunger lever and the air valve when the air valve is fully closed.
4   If adjustment is necessary, bend the rod at the air valve end.

36 Carburetor (Rochester 4MV) – overhaul

1   When a carburetor develops faults after a considerable mileage, it is usually more economical to replace the complete unit rather than to completely dismantle it and replace individual components. However, if it is decided to strip and rebuild the unit, first obtain a repair kit which will contain all the necessary gaskets and other needed items, and proceed in the following sequence.
2   Bend back the lockwasher tabs, then remove the idle stop solenoid.
3   Remove the larger idle stop solenoid bracket screw from the float bowl.
4   Remove the clip from the upper end of the choke rod, disconnect the rod from the upper choke shaft lever and remove the rod from the lower lever in the bowl.
5   Drive the pump lever pivot inwards to remove the roll pin then remove the pump lever from the air horn and pump rod.
6   Remove 2 long screws, 5 short screws and 2 countersunk head screws retaining the air horn to the float bowl.
7   Remove the vacuum break hose, and the diaphragm unit from the bracket.
8   Disconnect the choke assist spring.
9   Remove the metering rod hanger and secondary rods after removing the small screw at the top of the hanger.
10 Lift off the air horn, but leave the gasket in position. Do not attempt to remove the air bleed tubes or accelerating well tubes.
11 If the choke valve is to be replaced, remove the valve attaching

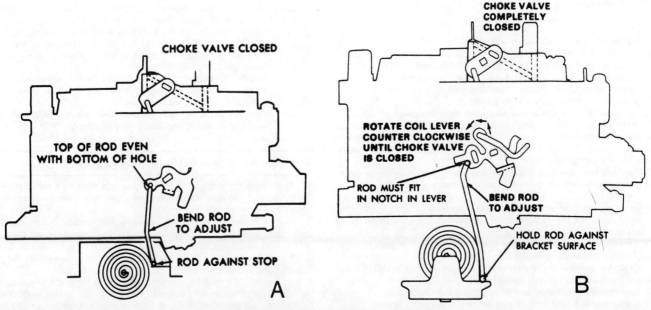

Fig. 4.43 Choke coil rod adjustment (Sec 34)

A   Thru 1971   B   1972 on

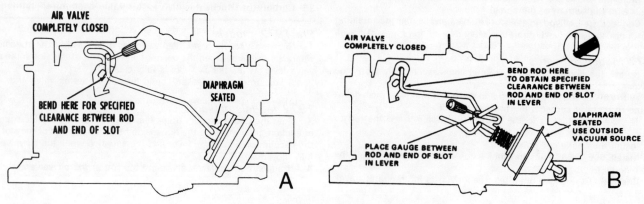

Fig. 4.44 Air valve dashpot adjustment (Sec 35)

A   Thru 1971   B   1972 on

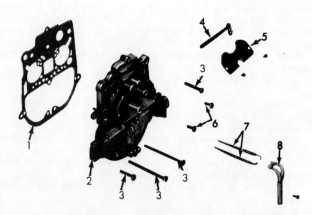

Fig. 4.45 Exploded view of the 4MV air horn (Sec 36)

1 Gasket	*6 Countersunk retaining*
2 Air horn	* screw*
3 Air horn retaining screw	*7 Secondary metering rods*
4 Choke shaft and lever	*8 Metering rod hanger*
5 Choke valve plate	

screws, then measure the valve and shaft.

12 The air valves and air valve shaft are calibrated and should not be removed. A shaft spring repair kit is available, and contains all the necessary instructions, if these parts require replacement.

13 Remove the pump plunger from the well.

14 Carefully remove the air horn gasket.

15 Remove the pump return spring from the pump well.

16 Remove the plastic filler over the float valve.

17 Press the power piston down and release it to remove it. Remove the spring from the well. Note the power piston plastic retainer which is used for ease of assembly.

18 Remove the metering rods from the power piston by disconnecting the spring from the top of each rod, then rotating the rod to remove it from the hanger.

19 Remove the float assembly by pulling up on the retaining pin until it can be removed, then sliding the float towards the front of the bowl to carefully disengage the needle pull clip.

20 Remove the pull clip and the fuel inlet needle, then unscrew the needle seat and remove the gasket.

21 Unscrew the primary metering jets; do not attempt to remove the secondary metering jets.

22 Remove the discharge ball retainer and the check ball.

23 Remove the baffle from the secondary side of the bowl.

24 Remove the choke assembly after removing the retaining screw on the side of the bowl. Remove the secondary locknut lever from the cast boss on the bowl.

25 Remove the fast idle cam and the choke assembly.

26 Remove the intermediate choke rod and actuating lever from the float bowl.

27 Remove the fuel inlet filter nut, gasket, filter and spring.

28 Remove the throttle body to bowl screws. Remove the throttle body.

29 Remove the throttle body to bowl insulator gaskets.

30 Remove the pump rod from the throttle lever by rotating the rod out of the primary lever.

31 Further dismantling is not recommended. If it is essential to remove the idle mixture needles, pry out the plastic limiter caps then count the number of turns to bottom the needles and fit replacements in exactly the same position. New limiter caps should be fitted after running adjustments have been made (see Section 31).

32 Clean all metal parts in a suitable cold solvent. Do not immerse rubber parts, plastic parts, the vacuum break assembly or the idle stop solenoid, or permanent damage will result. Do not probe the jets, but blow them through with clean dry compressed air. Examine all fixed and moving parts for cracks, distortion, wear and other damage; replace as necessary. Discard all gaskets and the fuel inlet filter.

33 Assembly is essentially the reverse of the removal procedure, but the following points should be noted:

a) *If new idle mixture screws are used, and the original setting was not noted, install the screws finger-tight to seat them, then back off 4 full turns (see Section 31).*

b) *Having installed the float, measure from the top of the float bowl gasket surface (gasket not fitted) to the top of the float at a point $\frac{3}{16}$ inch from the toe. Bend the float up, or down, to obtain the specified dimension.*

c) *Tighten the air horn retaining screws in the sequence shown.*

d) *When connecting the pump lever to the upper pump rod, install the rod in the inner hole.*

e) *After reassembly, carry out all the relevant settings and adjustments listed previously in this chapter.*

37 Carburetor (Holley 4150) – idle adjustment

1   Connect a tachometer to the engine and then as a basic starting point, seat the idle mixture screws gently and then unscrew them three complete turns.

2   With the engine at normal operating temperature, turn the idle speed screw until the specified idle speed (see Specifications Section) is obtained with manual transmission in Neutral or automatic in Drive.

3   Refer to the vehicle Decal for instructions whether the air conditioning system should be on or off.

4   Adjust the idle mixture screws to obtain the highest idle speed. On vehicles fitted with an idle solenoid adjust the idle speed to 600 rpm by turning the solenoid hexagon headed screw. Disconnect the lead from the solenoid and check the idle speed. Now adjust the idle speed screw as necessary to obtain 400 rpm.

5   With or without a solenoid fitted, adjust the mixture screw inwards

to give a 20 rpm drop in engine speed (lean roll).
6 Unscrew the mixture screw $\frac{1}{4}$ of a turn.
7 Repeat the operations described in paragraphs 5 and 6 for the second mixture screw (where fitted).
8 Readjust the idle speed screw if necessary to obtain the specified idle speed (see Specifications Section).

38 Carburetor (Holley 4150) – float adjustment

1 Remove the air cleaner then unscrew the fuel level sight plugs.
2 Start the engine and allow it to idle.
3 With the vehicle on a level surface the fuel level should be within $\pm \frac{1}{32}$ inch of the threads at the bottom of the sight plug port.
4 If adjustment is required, loosen the inlet needle lockscrew and turn the adjusting nut clockwise to lower, or counterclockwise to raise, the fuel level. Tighten the lockscrew afterwards. (1/6 turn of the nut gives approximately $\frac{1}{16}$ inch fuel level change).
5 Allow approximately one minute for the fuel level to stabilize, then re-check.
6 To ensure a proper secondary float level setting, open the primary throttles slightly, and hand operate the secondary throttles.
7 Install the sight plug and air cleaner on completion.

39 Carburetor (Holley 4150) – secondary throttle valve stop screw adjustment

1 Back off the adjustment screw until the throttle plates are fully closed.
2 Rotate the adjustment screw until it *just* touches the throttle lever then rotate it an additional half-turn.

40 Carburetor (Holley 4150) – accelerator pump adjustment

1 Hold the throttle lever wide open (using a rubber band to keep it in place), then fully compress the pump lever – i.e., lever pressed down.
2 Measure the gap between the spring adjusting nut and the pump lever arm. Adjust, if necessary, to obtain a gap of 0.015 in by turning the nut or screw while preventing the opposite end from turning.
3 After adjustment, close the throttle lever then partly open it again. Any movement of the throttle lever should be noticed at the operating lever spring end, indicating correct pump tip-in.

41 Carburetor (Holley 4150) – choke unloader adjustment

1 Hold the throttle lever wide open (using a rubber band to keep it in place).
2 Hold the choke valve towards the closed position against the unloader tang of the throttle shaft. Measure the gap between the choke valve lower edge and main body. Adjust, if necessary, to obtain the specified gap by bending the choke rod at the offset bend.

42 Carburetor (Holley 4150) – vacuum break adjustment

1 Hold the choke valve closed (using a rubber band to keep it in place).
2 Hold the vacuum break against the stop then measure the gap between the choke valve lower edge and the main body. Adjust, if necessary, to obtain the specified gap by bending the vacuum break link.

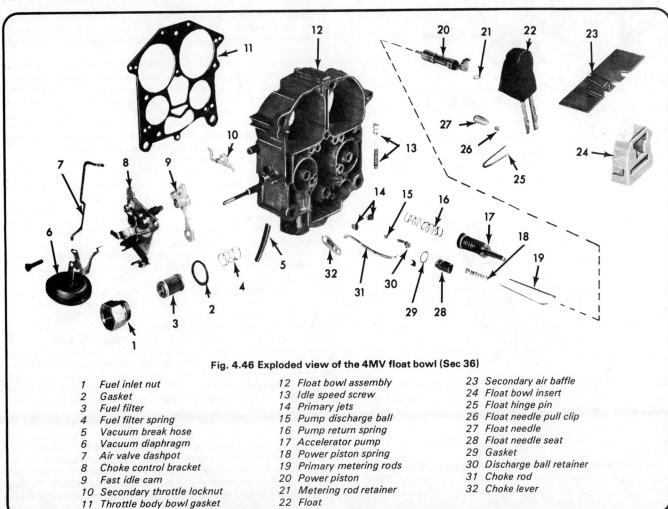

Fig. 4.46 Exploded view of the 4MV float bowl (Sec 36)

1 Fuel inlet nut	12 Float bowl assembly	23 Secondary air baffle
2 Gasket	13 Idle speed screw	24 Float bowl insert
3 Fuel filter	14 Primary jets	25 Float hinge pin
4 Fuel filter spring	15 Pump discharge ball	26 Float needle pull clip
5 Vacuum break hose	16 Pump return spring	27 Float needle
6 Vacuum diaphragm	17 Accelerator pump	28 Float needle seat
7 Air valve dashpot	18 Power piston spring	29 Gasket
8 Choke control bracket	19 Primary metering rods	30 Discharge ball retainer
9 Fast idle cam	20 Power piston	31 Choke rod
10 Secondary throttle locknut	21 Metering rod retainer	32 Choke lever
11 Throttle body bowl gasket	22 Float	

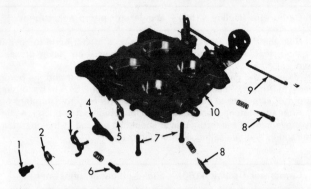

Fig. 4.47 Exploded view of the 4MV throttle body (Sec 36)

1	Shouldered retaining screw	6	Fast idle screw
2	Torsion spring	7	Throttle body bowl screws
3	Fast idle adjusting lever	8	Idle mixture needle
4	Fast idle cam lever	9	Accelerator pump rod
5	Choke unloader lever	10	Throttle body assembly

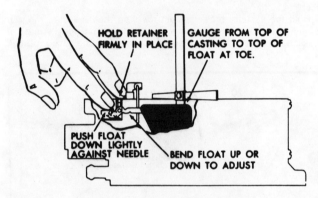

Fig. 4.48 Float adjustment (Sec 36)

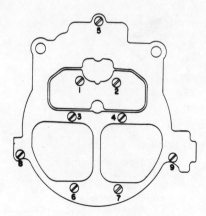

Fig. 4.49 4MV air horn screw tightening sequence (Sec 36)

43 Carburetor (Holley 4150) – fast idle cam adjustment

1   Open the throttle slightly then close the choke plate, positioning the fast idle lever against the top step of the fast idle cam.
2   Adust the fast idle to give the specified throttle opening on the idle transfer side of the carburetor. Adjust, if necessary, by bending the fast idle lever.

44 Carburetor (Holley 4150) – overhaul

1   When a carburetor fault develops after a considerbale mileage, it is usually more economical to replace the complete unit rather than to replace individual components. However, if it is decided to strip and rebuild the unit, first obtain a repair kit which will contain all the necessary gaskets and other needed items, and proceed in the following manner:
2   Initially loosen the fuel inlet fitting, fuel bowl sight plugs, and the needle and seat lockscrews.
3   Remove the primary fuel bowl (4 screws), the metering body, splash shield and gasket.
4   Remove the secondary fuel bowl (4 screws), the metering body and gasket.
5   Disconnect the secondary throttle operating rod at the throttle lever, followed by the throttle operating assembly and gasket.
6   Disconnect the hose at the vacuum break.
7   Remove the throttle body to main body screws, the throttle body and the gasket.
8   Loosen the inlet needle and seat lockscrew, then turn the adjusting nut counterclockwise to remove the needle and seat assembly.
9   Remove the hinge pin retainer and slide out the float. Remove the spring if necessary.
10   Remove the sight plug and gasket, and the inlet fitting, fuel filter, spring and gaskets.
11   From the primary bowl remove the air valve assembly (where applicable) and the pump diaphragm screws, pump housing, diaphragm and spring. Check the pump inlet ball for damage and correct operation; if unserviceable, a new bowl assembly will be required.
12   Using a wide bladed screwdriver, remove the main metering jets. Remove the power valves using a 1 in. 12 point socket. From the primary side only, remove the idle mixture screws and seals.
13   To disassemble the secondary throttle operating assembly, remove the diaphragm cover, spring and diaphragm.
14   From the main body, remove the vacuum break retaining screws. Remove the assembly, disconnecting the link at the choke lever.
15   Remove the choke lever retaining clip followed by the lever itself and the fast idle cam.
16   Remove the pump discharge nozzle screw, nozzle and gasket, then invert the body to remove the discharge check valve.
17   If further dismantling is required, file off the staked ends of the shaft screws and remove them. Remove the choke rod (upwards, through the seal), followed by the seal. Remove the valve from the shaft slot and slide the shaft from the main body.
18   To disassemble the throttle body, if required, remove the pump operating lever assembly and disassemble the spring bolt and nut.
19   Remove the idle speed screw and spring.
20   Remove the secondary throttle shaft diaphragm lever and the primary throttle shaft fast idle cam lever.
21   Remove the key and disconnect the secondary locknut throttle connecting link from the shaft levers.
22   File off the staked ends of the throttle plate attaching screws, then remove the screws and plates. Remove any burrs from the shafts and withdraw them out of the flange.
23   Remove the throttle lever accelerator pump cam and the vacuum break hose.
24   Clean all metal parts in a suitable cold solvent (this includes the choke rod seal – see paragraph 17). Do not immerse rubber parts, plastic parts (eg: secondary throttle shaft bushings and accelerator pump cam), vacuum break unit and other non-metallic parts. Do not probe the jets, but blow through them with clean, dry compressed air. Examine all fixed and moving parts for cracks, distortion, wear and other damage; replace as necessary. Discard all gaskets. Check the

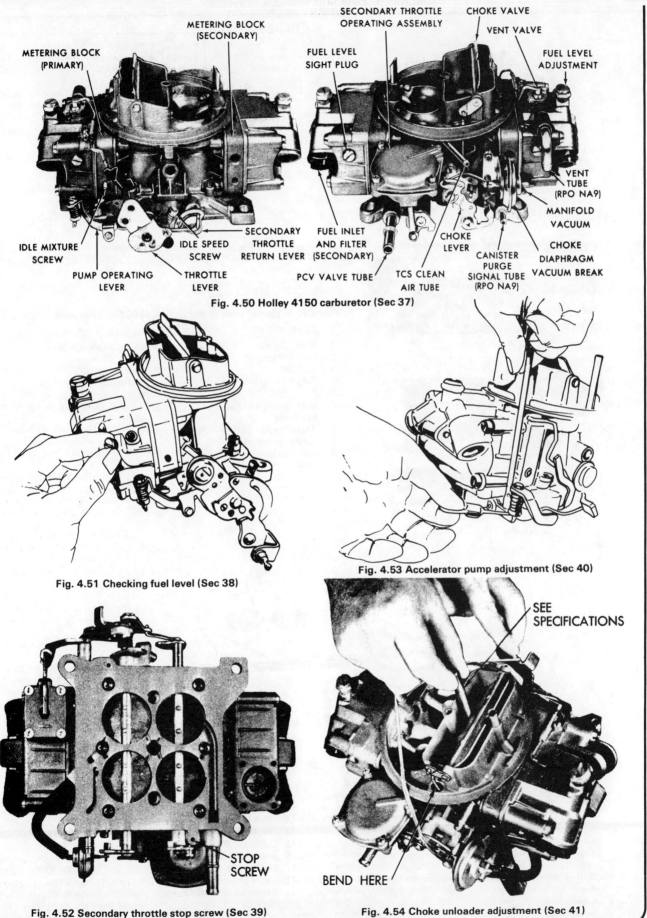

METERING BLOCK (PRIMARY)

METERING BLOCK (SECONDARY)

SECONDARY THROTTLE OPERATING ASSEMBLY

FUEL LEVEL SIGHT PLUG

CHOKE VALVE

VENT VALVE

FUEL LEVEL ADJUSTMENT

IDLE MIXTURE SCREW

PUMP OPERATING LEVER

IDLE SPEED SCREW

THROTTLE LEVER

SECONDARY THROTTLE RETURN LEVER

FUEL INLET AND FILTER (SECONDARY)

PCV VALVE TUBE

TCS CLEAN AIR TUBE

CHOKE LEVER

CANISTER PURGE SIGNAL TUBE (RPO NA9)

VENT TUBE (RPO NA9)

MANIFOLD VACUUM

CHOKE DIAPHRAGM VACUUM BREAK

Fig. 4.50 Holley 4150 carburetor (Sec 37)

Fig. 4.51 Checking fuel level (Sec 38)

Fig. 4.53 Accelerator pump adjustment (Sec 40)

STOP SCREW

Fig. 4.52 Secondary throttle stop screw (Sec 39)

SEE SPECIFICATIONS

BEND HERE

Fig. 4.54 Choke unloader adjustment (Sec 41)

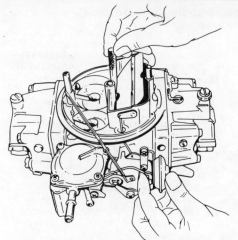

Fig. 4.55 Vacuum break adjustment (Sec 42)

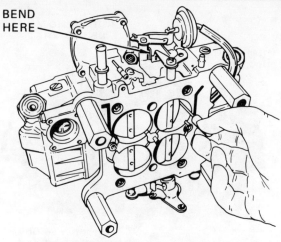

Fig. 4.56 Fast idle cam adjustment (Sec 43)

BEND HERE

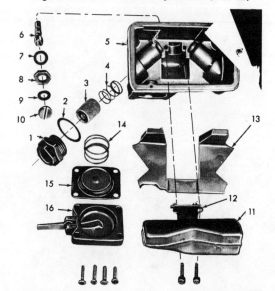

Fig. 4.57 Exploded view of the Holley 4150 fuel bowl assembly (Sec 44)

1   Fuel inlet nut
2   Inlet nut gasket
3   Fuel filter
4   Fuel filter spring
5   Fuel bowl
6   Inlet needle and seat assembly
7   Adjusting nut gasket
8   Fuel inlet adjusting nut
9   Inlet nut lock screw gasket
10 Inlet nut lock screw
11 Float
12 Float hinge pin
13 Fuel displacement block
14 Pump diaphragm spring
15 Pump diaphragm (primary only)
16 Pump cover

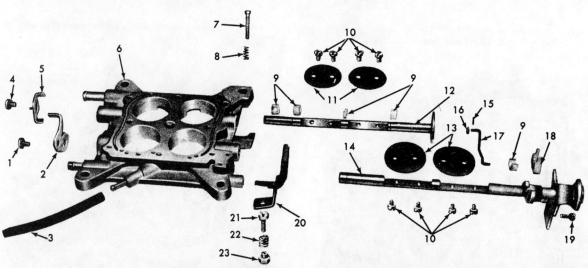

Fig. 4.58 Exploded view of the Holley 4150 throttle body assembly (Sec 44)

1   Screw (fast idle cam lever)
2   Fast idle cam lever
3   Hose (vacuum break)
4   Screw (secondary throttle) lever
5   Lever (secondary throttle operating)
6   Throttle body
7   Screw (idle speed)
8   Spring (idle speed screw)
9   Bushing (throttle shaft)
10 Screw (throttle plate)
11 Throttle plate (secondary)
12 Throttle shaft (secondary)
13 Throttle plate (primary)
14 Throttle shaft (primary)
15 Cotter pin (throttle link)
16 Washer (throttle link)
17 Link (throttle connector)
18 Cam (accelerator pump)
19 Screw (accelerator pump cam)
20 Pump operating lever
21 Screw (pump lever adjusting)
22 Spring (pump lever adjusting screw)
23 Nut (pump lever adjusting)

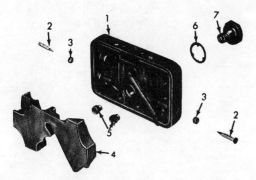

Fig. 4.59 Holley 4150 metering body (Sec 44)

1 Metering body
2 Idle mixture needle
3 Seal
4 Fuel displacement block
   (where fitted)
5 Main metering jets
6 Power valve gaskets
7 Power valve

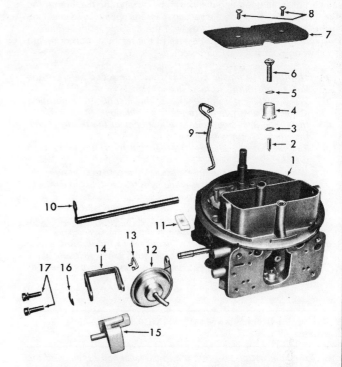

Fig. 4.60 Exploded view of the Holley 4150 main body (Sec 44)

1 Main body assembly
2 Pump discharge needle
3 Gasket (pump discharge nozzle)
4 Pump discharge nozzle
5 Gasket (pump discharge nozzle screw)
6 Screw (pump discharge nozzle)
7 Choke valve
8 Screw (choke valve)
9 Choke rod
10 Choke shaft and lever
11 Seal (choke rod)
12 Vacuum break
13 Link (vacuum break)
14 Choke lever
15 Fast idle cam
16 Retainer (choke lever)
17 Screw (vacuum break)

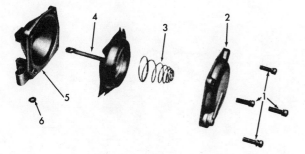

Fig. 4.61 Holley 4150 secondary throttle operating housing (Sec 44)

1 Screw
2 Cover
3 Spring
4 Diaphragm
5 Housing
6 Gasket

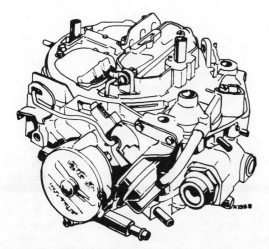

Fig. 4.62 Rochester M4MC (Quadrajet) carburetor (Sec 45)

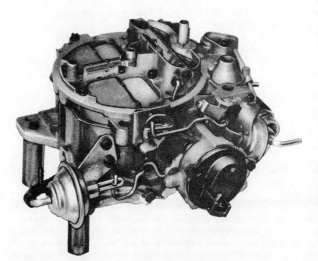

Fig. 4.63 Rochester M4ME (Quadrajet) carburetor (Sec 45)

secondary throttle operating diaphragm by moving the diaphragm rod to the up position, plugging the vacuum passage opening and checking that the diaphragm holds upwards until the passage is unplugged.

25 Assembly is essentially the reverse of the removal procedure, but the following points should be noted:

a) *Throttle shaft plastic bushings should be rolled between the finger and thumb to help shape them.*

b) *When installing throttle valves, the identification numbers should be downwards (to the manifold side).*

c) *Install the idle speed screw to just contact the throttle lever, then turn 1½ turns further.*

d) *Ensure that the choke valve can fall freely under its own weight.*

e) *When installing the idle mixture screws, use new seals. Preliminary adjustment is made by screwing them in lightly to just seat, then screwing out one turn.*

f) *Adjust the floats by inverting the fuel bowls and turning the adjustable needle seat until the top of the float is the specified distance from the top of the fuel bowl.*

g) *On completion of assembly, install the carburetor and adjust the float, the secondary throttle stop valve, fast idle cam, accelerator pump, choke unloader and vacuum break, as necessary.*

45 Carburetor (Rochester M4MC/M4MCA/M4ME) – idle adjustment

Note: *If the information given on the Decal label has superseded the information given in Specifications, the Decal label should be assumed to be correct.*

1975 on

1 Have the engine at normal operating temperature, air cleaner in position and air conditioning off. Connect a reliable tachometer to the engine.

2 Disconnect the fuel tank hose from the vapor canister.

3 Disconnect the lead from the idle stop solenoid.

4 With automatic in Drive or manual in Neutral, turn the idle speed screw to obtain the curb (final) idle speed shown in the Specifications Section.

5 Reconnect the solenoid, crack open the throttle slightly to extend the solenoid plunger.

6 Now turn the solenoid plunger screw to set the curb (initial) idle speed shown in Specifications Section.

7 Remove the tachometer and reconnect the fuel tank hose.

8 The idle mixture screws are pre-set and fitted with limiter caps which allow them to be turned about one turn lean to rectify uneven idling. If after carburetor overhaul or replacement of components, the mixture must be adjusted beyond the limit of travel of the caps, carry out the following operations:

9 Repeat the procedure described in paragraphs 1 and 2.

10 Break off the cap on the mixture screws.

11 Set the idle speed to the curb (initial) figure using the solenoid plunger.

12 Unscrew each of the mixture screws equally until the highest idle speed is achieved. Reduce the speed if necessary to curb (initial) specifications using the solenoid plunger.

13 Now screw in each of the mixture screws equally until the curb (final) idle speed is obtained.

14 Reconnect the fuel tank hose and switch off the engine.

46 Carburetor (Rochester M4M series) – accelerator pump rod adjustment

1 With the fast idle cam follower off the steps of the fast idle cam, back out the idle speed screw until the throttle valves are completely closed in the bore. Make sure that the secondary actuating rod is not restricting movement; bend the secondary closing tang if necessary then readjust it after pump adjustment.

2 Place the pump rod in the inner hole in the lever.

3 Measure from the top of the choke valve wall (next to the vent stack) to the top of the pump stem.

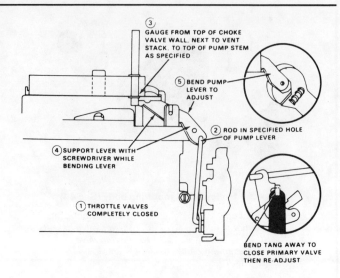

Fig. 4.64 Pump rod adjustment diagram for M4MC/M4MCA models (Sec 46)

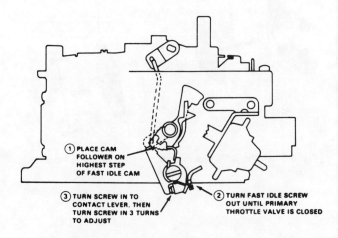

Fig. 4.65 Fast idle adjustment diagram (carburetor removed) for M4M series (Sec 47)

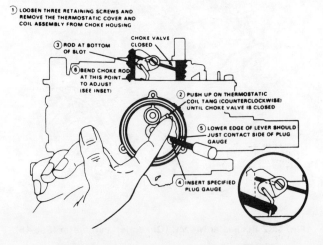

Fig. 4.66 Choke coil lever adjustment (Sec 48)

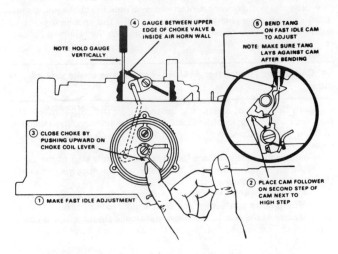

Fig. 4.67 Fast idle cam (choke rod) adjustment (Sec 49)

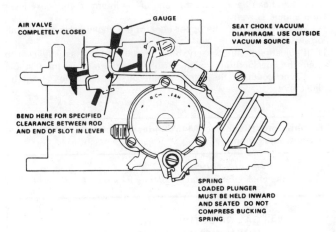

Fig. 4.68 Air valve dashpot adjustment (Sec 50)

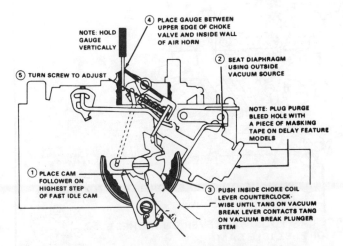

Fig. 4.69 Front vacuum break adjustment (Sec 51)

4   If necessary, adjust to obtain the specified dimension (see Specifications Section) by bending the lever while supporting it with a screwdriver.
5   Adjust the idle speed (Section 45).

47 Carburetor (Rochester M4M Series) – fast idle adjustment

Carburetor removed
1   Place the cam follower lever on the highest step of the fast idle cam.
2   Turn the fast idle screw out until the primary throttle valves are closed.
3   Turn in the fast idle screw to contact the lever then screw in a further 3 full turns.

Carburetor in vehicle
4   Connect a tachometer to the engine which should be at the normal operating temperature.
5   Place the transmission in Park or Neutral.
6   Disconnect and plug the vacuum hose at the EGR valve.
7   Position the cam follower on the highest step of the fast idle cam.
8   Turn the fast idle screw to achieve the specified fast idle (see Specifications Section).
9   Remake the original connections, remove the tachometer and switch off the engine.

48 Carburetor (Rochester M4M Series) – choke coil lever adjustment

1   Loosen the 3 retaining screws and remove the cover and coil assembly from the choke housing.
2   Push up on the thermostatic coil tang (counterclockwise) until the choke valve is closed.
3   Check that the choke rod is at the bottom of the slot in the choke lever.
4   Insert a plug gauge (an unmarked drill shank is suitable) of the specified size in the hole in the choke housing.
5   The lower edge of the choke coil lever should just contact the side of the plug gauge.
6   If necessary, bend the choke rod at the point shown.

49 Carburetor (Rochester M4M Series) – fast idle cam (choke rod) adjustment

Note: Always adjust choke coil lever before carrying out the following operations.
1   Turn the fast idle screw in until it contacts the fast idle cam follower lever, then turn in 3 full turns more.
2   Place the lever on the second step of the fast idle cam against the rise of the high step.
3   Push upwards on the choke coil lever inside the housing to close the choke valve.
4   Measure between the upper edge of the choke valve and the air horn wall.
5   If necessary, bend the tang on the fast idle cam to adjust, but ensure that the tang lies against the cam after bending
6   Re-check the fast idle adjustment.

50 Carburetor (Rochester M4M Series) – air valve dashpot adjustment

1   Using an external source of suction, seat the front vacuum break diaphragm. Suction from the mouth or a small hand pump is normally adequate.
2   Ensure that the air valves are completely closed then measure between the air valve dashpot and the end of the slot in the air valve lever. This dimension should be 0.015 in.
3   Bend the air valve dashpot rod at the point shown, if adjustment is necessary.

51 Carburetor (Rochester M4M Series) – front vacuum break adjustment

1   Loosen the 3 retaining screws and remove the choke coil cover and coil assembly from the choke housing.
2   Place the cam follower lever on the highest step of the fast idle cam.
3   Using an outside source of suction, seat the diaphragm unit.
4   Push up on the inside choke coil lever until the tang on the vacuum break lever contacts the tang on the plunger.
5   Measure between the upper edge of the choke valve and the inside of the air horn wall.
6   Turn the adjustment screw on the vacuum break plunger to obtain the specified dimension.
7   Install the vacuum hose on completion.

52 Carburetor (Rochester M4M Series) – rear vacuum break adjustment

1   Initially follow the procedure of Paragraphs 1 thru 3 in the previous Section, but additionally plug the bleed hose in the end cover of the vacuum break unit using adhesive tape.
2   Push up on the choke coil lever inside the choke housing towards the closed choke position.
3   With the choke rod in the bottom of the slot in the choke lever, measure between the upper edge of the choke valve and the air horn wall.
4   If necessary, bend the vacuum break rod at the point shown to obtain the specified dimension.
5   On completion, remove the adhesive tape and install the vacuum hose.

53 Carburetor (Rochester M4MC and M4MCA) – automatic choke coil adjustment

1   With the hot air heater type of choke, install the choke coil and cover assembly with a gasket between the cover and housing. The tang in the coil must be installed in the slot inside the choke coil lever pick-up arm.

2   Place the fast idle cam follower on the highest step of the fast idle cam then rotate the cover counterclockwise until the choke just closes.
3   Align the index mark on the cover with the specified point (2 notches lean) on the choke housing then tighten the retaining screws.

54 Carburetor (Rochester M4ME) – automatic choke coil adjustment

1   With this type of electrically heated automatic choke, make sure that with the coil assembly inside the choke housing, the coil tang contacts the bottom side of the inner face of the choke coil lever pick-up arm.
2   Position the fast idle cam follower on the high step of the cam.
3   Rotate the cover and coil assembly counterclockwise until the choke valve just closes.
4   Align the index marks (center) and install the cover and screws.
Note: *The ground contact for the electrically heated choke is through a metal plate at the rear of the choke assembly. Do not install a gasket between the cover and housing or this will interrupt the circuit.*

55 Carburetor (Rochester M4M Series) – unloader adjustment

1   Adjust the choke coil, as described in the previous section.
2   Hold the throttle valves wide open and the chokes fully closed. A rubber band can be used on the tang of the intermediate choke lever if the engine is warm.
3   Measure between the upper edge of the choke valve and the air horn wall.
4   If adjustment is necessary, bend the tang on the fast idle lever to obtain the specified dimension. Ensure that the tang on the fast idle cam lever contacts the center point of the fast idle cam after adjustment.

56 Carburetor (Rochester M4M Series) – secondary throttle valve lock-out adjustment

Lock-out lever clearance
1   Hold the choke valves and secondary lock-out valves closed then

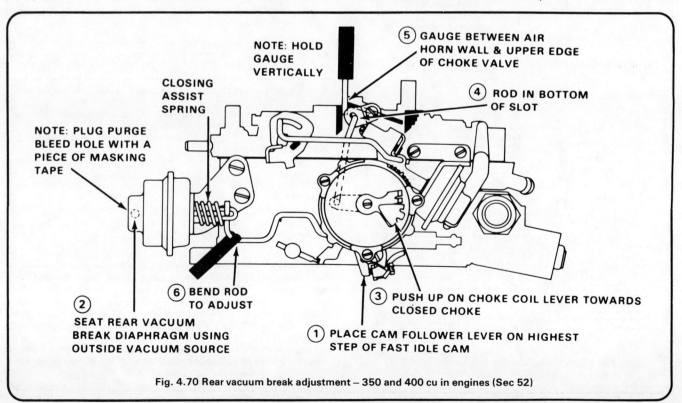

Fig. 4.70 Rear vacuum break adjustment – 350 and 400 cu in engines (Sec 52)

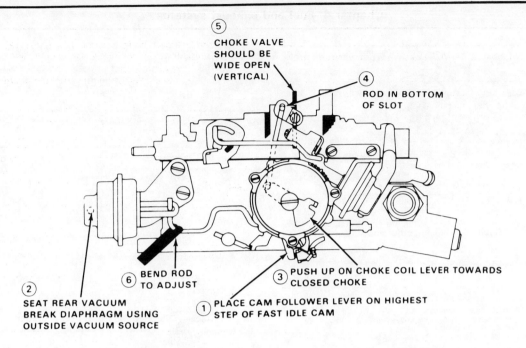

Fig. 4.71 Rear vacuum break adjustment – 454 cu in engine (Sec 52)

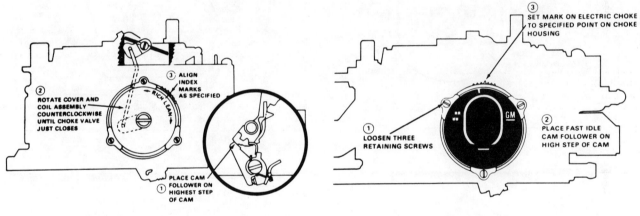

Fig. 4.72 Automatic choke coil adjustment – Rochester M4MC and M4MCA models only (Sec 53)

Fig. 4.73 Automatic choke coil adjustment for model M4ME only (Sec 53)

Fig. 4.74 Choke unloader adjustment (Sec 55)

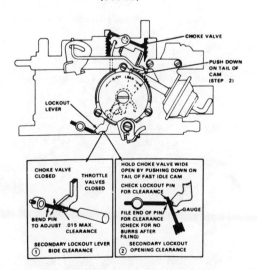

Fig. 4.75 Secondary throttle valve lock-out adjustment (Sec 56)

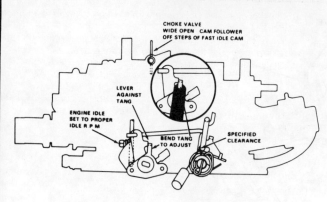

CHOKE VALVE
WIDE OPEN   CAM FOLLOWER
OFF STEPS OF FAST IDLE CAM

LEVER
AGAINST
TANG

ENGINE IDLE
SET TO PROPER
IDLE RPM

BEND TANG
TO ADJUST

SPECIFIED
CLEARANCE

Fig. 4.76 Secondary closing adjustment (Sec 57)

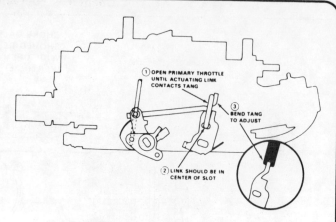

① OPEN PRIMARY THROTTLE
UNTIL ACTUATING LINK
CONTACTS TANG

③ BEND TANG
TO ADJUST

② LINK SHOULD BE IN
CENTER OF SLOT

Fig. 4.77 Secondary opening adjustment (Sec 58)

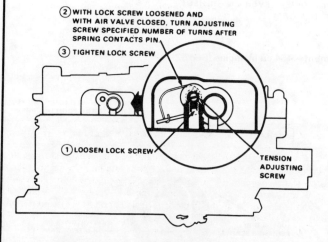

② WITH LOCK SCREW LOOSENED AND
WITH AIR VALVE CLOSED, TURN ADJUSTING
SCREW SPECIFIED NUMBER OF TURNS AFTER
SPRING CONTACTS PIN.

③ TIGHTEN LOCK SCREW

① LOOSEN LOCK SCREW

TENSION
ADJUSTING
SCREW

Fig. 4.78 Air valve wind-up adjustment (Sec 59)

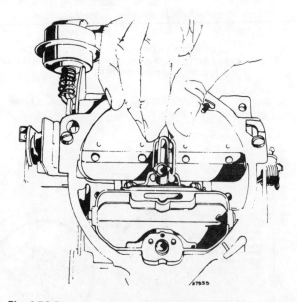

Fig. 4.79 Removing the secondary metering rods (Sec 60)

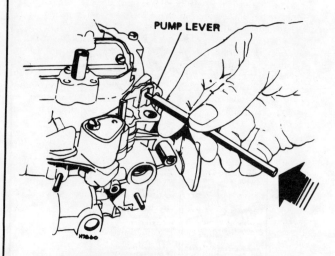

PUMP LEVER

Fig. 4.80 Removing the pump lever (Sec 60)

Fig. 4.81 Air horn retaining screws (Sec 60)

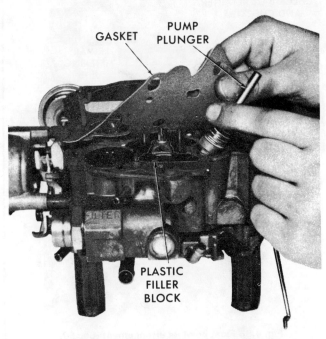

Fig. 4.82 Removing the pump plunger (Sec 60)

GASKET   PUMP PLUNGER

PLASTIC FILLER BLOCK

Fig. 4.83 Removing the power piston and metering rods (Sec 60)

measure the clearance between the lock-out pin and lock-out lever.
2   If adjustment is necessary, bend the lock-out pin to obtain the specified clearance (0.015 inch).

Opening clearance
3   Push down on the tail of the fast idle cam to hold the choke wide open.
4   Hold the secondary throttle valve partly open then measure between the end of the lock-out pin and the toe of the lock-out lever. (This should be 0.015 inch).
5   If adjustment is necessary, file the end of the lock-out pin but ensure that no burrs remain afterwards.

57 Carburetor (Rochester M4M Series) – secondary closing adjustment

1   Adjust the engine idle speed, as described previously in this Chapter.

2   Hold the choke valve wide open with the cam follower lever off the steps of the fast idle cam.
3   Measure the clearance between the slot in the secondary throttle valve pick-up lever and the secondary actuating rod.
4   If adjustment is necessary, bend the secondary tang on the primary throttle lever to obtain the specified clearance (0.020 inch).

58 Carburetor (Rochester M4M Series) – secondary opening adjustment

1   Lightly open the primary throttle lever until the link just contacts the tang on the secondary lever.
2   Bend the tang on the secondary lever, if necessary, to position the link in the center of the secondary lever slot.

59 Carburetor (Rochester M4M Series) – air valve spring wind-up adjustment

1   Remove the front vacuum break diaphragm unit and the air valve dashpot rod.
2   Using a suitable hexagonal wrench loosen the lock screw then turn the tension adjusting screw counterclockwise until the air valve is partly open.
3   Hold the air valve closed then turn the tension adjusting screw clockwise the specified number of turns after the spring contacts the pin (Air Valve Spring Wind-up, see Specifications Section).
4   Tighten the lockscrew and install the air valve dashpot rod, and the front vacuum break diaphragm unit and bracket.

60 Carburetor (Rochester M4M Series) – overhaul

1   When a carburetor fault develops after a considerable mileage, it is usually more economical to replace the complete unit rather than to completely dismantle it and replace individual components. However, if it is decided to strip and rebuild the unit, first obtain a repair kit which will contain all the necessary gaskets and other needed items, and proceed in the following manner.
2   If the carburetor has an idle stop solenoid, remove the bracket retaining screws and lift away the solenoid and bracket assembly.
3   Remove the upper choke lever from the end of the choke shaft (1 screw) then rotate the lever to remove it, and disengage it from the choke rod.
4   Remove the choke rod from the lower lever inside the float bowl by holding the lever outwards with a small screwdriver and twisting the rod counterclockwise.
5   Remove the vacuum hose from the front vacuum break unit.
6   Remove the small screw at the top of the metering rod hanger, and remove the secondary metering rods and hanger.
7   Using a suitable drift, drive the small pump lever pivot roll pin inwards to permit removal of the lever.
8   Remove 2 long screws, 5 short screws and 2 countersunk head air horn screws to detach the float bowl. Remove the secondary air baffle deflector (where applicable) from beneath the 2 center air horn screws.
9   Remove the float bowl but leave the gasket in position at this stage. Do not attempt to remove the small tubes protruding from the air horn.
10   Remove the front vacuum break bracket screws and lift off the unit. Detach the air valve dashpot rod from the diaphragm assembly and the air valve lever.
11   If considered necessary, remove the staked choke valve attaching screws then remove the choke valve and shaft from the air horn. Do not remove the air valve and the air valve shaft. The air valve closing spring or center plastic cam can be replaced by following the instructions in the appropriate repair kit.
12   Remove the air horn gasket from the float bowl taking care not to distort the springs holding the main metering rods.
13   Remove the pump plunger and pump return spring from the pump well.
14   Depress the power piston stem and allow it to snap free, withdrawing the metering rods with it. Remove the power piston spring from the well.
15   Taking care to prevent distortion, remove the metering rods from

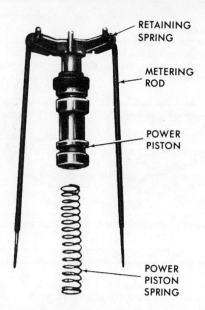

RETAINING
SPRING

METERING
ROD

POWER
PISTON

POWER
PISTON
SPRING

Fig. 4.84 Power piston and metering rods (Sec 60)

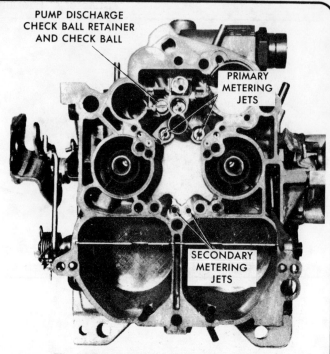

PUMP DISCHARGE
CHECK BALL RETAINER
AND CHECK BALL

PRIMARY
METERING
JETS

SECONDARY
METERING
JETS

Fig. 4.85 Float bowl jet arrangement (Sec 60)

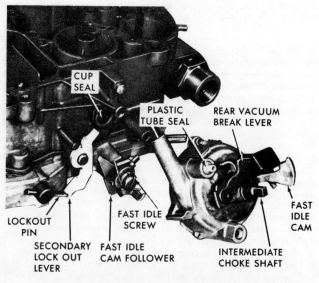

CUP
SEAL

PLASTIC
TUBE SEAL

REAR VACUUM
BREAK LEVER

LOCKOUT
PIN

SECONDARY
LOCK OUT
LEVER

FAST IDLE
CAM FOLLOWER

FAST IDLE
SCREW

INTERMEDIATE
CHOKE SHAFT

FAST
IDLE
CAM

Fig. 4.86 Choke assembly (Sec 60)

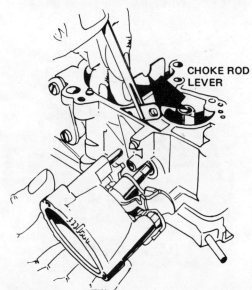

CHOKE ROD
LEVER

Fig. 4.87 Connecting the choke rod lever (Sec 60)

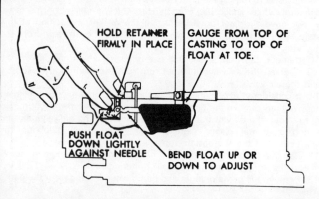

HOLD RETAINER
FIRMLY IN PLACE

GAUGE FROM TOP OF
CASTING TO TOP OF
FLOAT AT TOE.

PUSH FLOAT
DOWN LIGHTLY
AGAINST NEEDLE

BEND FLOAT UP OR
DOWN TO ADJUST

Fig. 4.88 Float level adjustment (Sec 60)

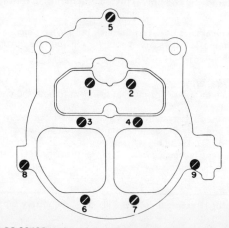

Fig. 4.89 M4M series air horn tightening sequence (Sec 60)

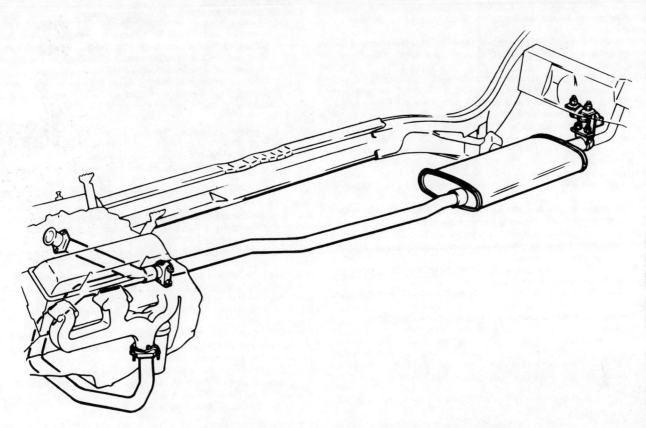

Fig. 4.90 Typical single exhaust system without catalytic converter (Sec 61)

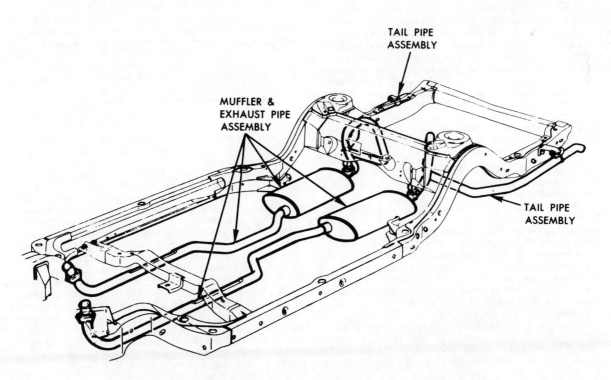

TAIL PIPE
ASSEMBLY

MUFFLER &
EXHAUST PIPE
ASSEMBLY

TAIL PIPE
ASSEMBLY

Fig. 4.91 Typical dual exhaust system without catalytic converter (Sec 61)

the power piston by disconnecting the tension springs then rotating the rods.

16 Remove the plastic filler block over the float valve then remove the float assembly and needle by pulling up on the pin. Remove the needle seat and gasket.

17 Remove the 2 cover screws and carefully lift out the metering rod and filler spool (metering rod and aneroid on M4MCA carburetors) from the float bowl. **Note:** *The adjustable part throttle (APT) metering rod assembly is extremely fragile and must not be interfered with. If replacement is necessary, refer to paragraphs 35 thru 44.*

18 Remove the primary main metering jets. Do not attempt to remove the APT metering jet or secondary metering orifice plates.

19 Remove the pump discharge check ball retainer and the ball.

20 Remove the rear vacuum break hose and the bracket retaining screws. Remove the vacuum break rod from the slot in the plunger head.

21 Press down on the fast idle cam and remove the vacuum break rod. Move the end of the rod away from the float bowl, then disengage the rod from the hole in the intermediate lever.

22 Remove the choke cover attaching screws and retainers. Pull off the cover and remove the gasket.

23 Remove the choke housing assembly from the float bowl by removing the retaining screw and washer.

24 Remove the secondary throttle valve lock-out lever from the float bowl.

25 Remove the lower choke lever by inverting the float bowl.

26 Remove the plastic tube seal from the choke housing.

27 If it is necessary to remove the intermediate choke shaft from the choke housing, remove the coil lever retaining screw and withdraw the lever. Slide out the shaft and (if necessary), remove the fast idle cam.

28 Remove the fuel inlet filter nut, gasket and filter from the float bowl.

29 If necessary, remove the pump well fill slot baffle and the secondary air baffle.

30 Remove the throttle body attaching screws and lift off the float bowl. Remove the insulator gasket.

31 Remove the pump rod from the lever on the throttle body.

32 If it is essential to remove the idle mixture needles, pry out the plastic limiter caps then count the number of turns to bottom the needles and fit replacements in exactly the same position. New limiter caps should be fitted after running adjustments have been made.

33 Clean all metal parts in a suitable cold solvent. Do not immerse rubber parts, plastic parts, pump plungers, filler spools or aneroids, or vacuum breaks. If the choke housing is to be immersed, remove the cup seal from inside the choke housing shaft hole. If the bowl is to be immersed remove the cup seal from the plastic insert; do not attempt to remove the plastic insert. Do not probe the jets, but blow through with clean, dry compressed air. Examine all fixed and moving parts for cracks, distortion, wear and other damage; replace as necessary. Discard all gaskets and the fuel inlet filter.

34 Assembly is essentially the reverse of the removal procedure, but the following points should be noted:

   a) *If new idle mixture screws were used, and the original setting was not noted, install the screws finger-tight to seat them, then back off 4 full turns.*

   b) *The lip on the plastic insert cup seal (on the side of the float bowl) faces outward.*

   c) *The lip on the inside choke housing shaft hole cup seal faces inwards towards the housing.*

   d) *When installing the assembled choke body, install the choke rod lever into the cavity in the float bowl. Install the plastic tube seal into the housing cavity before installing the housing. Ensure that the intermediate choke shaft engages into the lower choke lever. The choke coil is installed at the last stage of assembly.*

   e) *Where applicable, the notches on the secondary float bowl air baffle are towards the top, and the top edge of the baffle must be flush with the bowl casting.*

   f) *To adjust the float, hold the retainer firmly in place and push*

down lightly against the needle. Measure from the top of the float bowl casting (air horn gasket removed) to a point on the top of the float $\frac{1}{16}$ inch back from the toe. Bend the float arm to obtain the specified dimension by pushing on the pontoon.

   g) *Tighten the air horn screws in the order shown.*

   h) *On completion of assembly, adjust the front and rear vacuum breaks, fast idle cam (choke rod), choke coil lever and automatic choke coil.*

APT metering rod replacement

35 Replacement of the metering rod must only be carried out if the assembly is damaged or the aneroid has failed.

36 Lightly scribe the cover to record the position of the adjusting screw slot.

37 Remove the cover screws then carefully lift out the rod and cover assembly.

38 Hold the assembly upright then turn the adjusting screw counter-clockwise, counting the number of turns until the metering rod bottoms in the cover.

39 Remove the E-clip from the threaded end of the rod then turn the rod clockwise until it disengages from the cover.

40 Install the tension spring on the new metering rod assembly and screw the rod and spring assembly into the cover until the assembly bottoms.

41 Turn the adjusting screw clockwise the number of turns noted at Paragraph 38.

42 Install the E-clip. **Note:** *It will not matter if the scribed line (Paragraph 36) does not align exactly provided that the assembly sequence has been followed.*

43 Carefully install the cover and metering rod assembly onto the float bowl, aligning the tab on the cover assembly with the float bowl slot closest to the fuel inlet nut.

44 Install the cover attaching screws and nut.

61 Exhaust system – general description

1 The exact exhaust system installed will depend on a number of factors, most notably the engine size, geographic area where the car will be driven and the year of production. Typical components of an exhaust system are: the exhaust manifold connected to the engine, a muffler, a catalytic converter (1975 and later) and exhaust pipe to route the gases through the components and out the rear of the car.

2 Information concerning the catalytic converter can be found in Chapter 6 dealing with the emission system.

3 The exhaust system should be periodically checked for leaks which could prove hazardous to persons inside the car. Leaks can be detected by placing your hand along the pipes before the system has warmed up. After driving, the exhaust system can cause injury if touched. A leaking exhaust system can also become apparent by excessive noise during operation.

4 As a general rule, the components of the exhaust system are secured by U-shaped clamps. After removing the clamps, the exhaust pipes (which are of a slightly different diameter) can be pulled away from each other. Due to the high temperatures and exposed location of the exhaust pieces, rust and corrosion can 'freeze' the parts together. Liquid penetrating oils are available to help loosen the connections; however, it is often necessary to cut the parts with a hack saw or cutting torch. The later method should be employed only by a person experienced in this work.

5 The exhaust system is often a cause of mysterious rattles and noises heard from inside the car. The rubber-insulated hangers which suspend the system should be checked for deterioration and damage. No exhaust components should come in contact with other vehicle parts.

6 When replacing exhaust system parts, do not tighten the clamp bolts until the complete system has been installed and clearances checked. Then tighten from the front to the rear.

Chapter 5 Ignition

Refer to Chapter 13 for specifications and information related to 1981 models

Contents

Specifications

System type	12V, negative ground
Battery (Energizer type)	Lead acid
Distributor type	
Thru 1974	Mechanical contact breaker
1975 on	Breakerless. Designated High Energy Ignition (HEI).
Distributor direction of rotation	Clockwise
Mechanical contact breaker gap (initial setting prior to checking dwell angle)	0.019 in
Firing order	1-8-4-3-6-5-7-2
Condenser capacity (thru 1974)	0.18 to 0.23 mfd
Coil (with breaker type distributor)	
Primary resistance	1.77 to 2.05 Ohms
Secondary resistance	3000 to 20 000 Ohms
Resistor	1.35 Ohms
Coil (with breakerless distributor)	
Primary resistance	0.41 to 0.51 Ohms
Secondary resistance	3000 to 20 000 Ohms
Resistor	0.43 to 0.68 Ohms
Alternator (generator)	
Type (according to year of manufacture)	Delcotron Series 1D, 10SI or 10DN Series 100B
Field current	2.2/2.6 amps at 80°F (pre-1973)
	4.0/4.5 amps at 80°F (1973 onwards)
Output current	Varies according to vehicle specification and alternator type
Voltage regulator (used with Series 1D and 10DN Series 100B Delcotron)	
Type	Double contact
Field relay	
Air gap	0.015 in
Point opening	0.030 in
Closing voltage	1.5/3.2 volts
Regulator	
Air gap	0.067 in
Point opening	0.014 in
Voltage setting	13.8/14.8 V at 85°F
Starter motor	
Voltage	9V
Current	Varies with model application

Spark plugs

Year and engine	Spark plug	Electrode gap
1970		
307	AC R4Y	0.035 in
350	AC R44	0.035 in
402 (350 HP)	AC R42TS	0.035 in
402 (375 HP)	AC R43TS	0.035 in
1971		
307	AC R45TS	0.035 in
350 (2 barrel)	AC R45TS	0.035 in
350 (4 barrel)	AC R44TS	0.035 in
402	AC R44TS	0.035 in
1972 thru 1974		
All engines	Standard AC R44T Cold AC R43T }	0.035 in
1975		
All engines	AC R44TX	0.060
1976		
All engines	Standard AC R45TS Cold AC R44TS	0.045
1977 thru 1980		
All engines	AC R45TS	0.045

Distributor application

Year and engine	Distributor No.	Centrifugal advance crank degrees @ engine rpm	Vacuum advance crank degrees @ in hg	Dwell angle degrees	Ignition timing at engine idle degrees BTDC	Transmission type
1970						
307 cu in 200 HP	1111995	0 @ 1000 3 @ 1200 10 @ 1600 28 @ 4300	0 @ 6 15 @ 12	29 to 31	2	Manual
307 cu in 200 HP	1112005	0 @ 800 2 @ 1200 12 @ 2200 24 @ 4300	0 @ 8 20 @ 17	29 to 31	8	Automatic
350 cu in 250 HP	1112001	0 @ 800 3 @ 1000 15 @ 1800 36 @ 4100	0 @ 7 24 @ 17	29 to 31	TDC	Manual
350 cu in 250 HP	1112002	0 @ 900 2 @ 1100 8 @ 1400 32 @ 4400	0 @ 7 24 @ 17	29 to 31	4	Automatic
350 cu in 300 HP	1111996	0 @ 950 14 @ 1400 20 @ 1800 30 @ 4700	0 @ 10 15 @ 17	29 to 31	TDC	Manual
350 cu in 320 HP (Z-28)	1112019	0 @ 1150 14 @ 2100 26 @ 5000	0 @ 8 15 @ 15.5	29 to 31	8	All
402 cu in 350 HP	1111998	0 @ 900 9 @ 1250 15 @ 15.5 17 @ 2000 32 @ 5000	0 @ 8	29 to 31	4	Automatic
402 cu in 350 HP	1111999	0 @ 900 13 @ 1275 21 @ 2000 36 @ 5000	0 @ 8 15 @ 15.5	29 to 31	TDC	Manual
402 cu in 350 HP and 375 HP	1112000	0 @ 900 9 @ 1250 17 @ 2000 32 @ 5000	0 @ 6 15 @ 12	29 to 31	4	Automatic or Manual

Year and engine	Distributor No.	Centrifugal advance crank degrees @ engine rpm	Vacuum advance crank degrees @ in hg	Dwell angle degrees	Ignition timing at engine idle degrees BTDC	Transmission type
1971						
307 cu in 200 HP	1112039	0 @ 680 2 @ 1320 20 @ 4200	0 @ 8 20 @ 17	29 to 31	8	Automatic
307 cu in 200 HP	1112005	0 @ 800 2 @ 1200 12 @ 2200 24 @ 4300	0 @ 8 20 @ 17	29 to 31	4	Manual
350 cu in 245 HP	1112042	0 @ 880 2 @ 1120 10 @ 1600 15 @ 2200 28 @ 4300	0 @ 8 20 @ 17	29 to 31	2	Manual
350 cu in 245 HP	1112005	0 @ 800 2 @ 1200 12 @ 2200 24 @ 4300	0 @ 8 20 @ 17	29 to 31	6	Automatic
350 cu in 270 HP	1112044	0 @ 840 2 @ 1160 10 @ 1800 15 @ 2400	0 @ 8 15 @ 15.5	29 to 31	4	Manual
350 cu in 270 HP	1112045	0 @ 865 2 @ 1335 11 @ 2400 18 @ 4200	0 @ 8 15 @ 15.5	29 to 31	8	Automatic
350 cu in (Z-28)	112049	0 @ 1070 2 @ 1330 16 @ 2250 24 @ 5000	0 @ 8 15 @ 15.5	29 to 31	8	Manual
350 cu in (Z-28)	112074	0 @ 1034 2 @ 1366 12 @ 2200 20 @ 5000	0 @ 8 15 @ 15.5	29 to 31	12	Automatic
402 cu in 300 HP	1112057	0 @ 930 2 @ 1260 16 @ 2400 30 @ 4400	0 @ 8 20 @ 17	29 to 31	8	Automatic or Manual
454 cu in 365 HP	1112052	0 @ 857 2 @ 1143 14 @ 2000 22 @ 3900	0 @ 8 20 @ 17	29 to 31	8	Automatic or Manual
1972						
307 cu in 200 HP	1112039	0 @ 680 2 @ 1320 20 @ 4200	0 @ 8 20 @ 17	29 to 31	8	Automatic
307 cu in 200 HP	1112005	0 @ 800 2 @ 1200 12 @ 2200 24 @ 4300	0 @ 8 20 @ 17	29 to 31	4	Manual
350 cu in 165 HP	1112005	0 @ 800 2 @ 1200 12 @ 2200 24 @ 4300	0 @ 8 20 @ 17	29 to 31	6	Automatic or Manual
350 cu in 175 HP	1112044	0 @ 840 2 @ 1160 10 @ 1800 15 @ 2400	0 @ 8 15 @ 15.5	29 to 31	4	Manual
350 cu in 175 HP	1112045	0 @ 865 2 @ 1335 11 @ 2400 18 @ 4200	0 @ 8 15 @ 15/5	29 to 31	8	Automatic

Year and engine	Distributor No.	Centrifugal advance crank degrees @ engine rpm	Vacuum advance crank degrees @ in hg	Dwell angle degrees	Ignition timing at engine idle degrees BTDC	Transmission type
350 cu in 255 HP	1112049	0 @ 1070 2 @ 1330 16 @ 2250 24 @ 5000	0 @ 8 15 @ 15.5	29 to 31	8	Automatic
350 cu in 255 HP	1112095	0 @ 1090 2 @ 1310 21 @ 2350 28 @ 5000	0 @ 8 15 @ 15.5	29 to 31	4	Manual
402 cu in 240 HP	1112057	0 @ 930 2 @ 1260 16 @ 2400 30 @ 4400	0 @ 8 20 @ 17	29 to 31	8	Automatic or Manual
1973 307 cu in 115 HP	1112102	0 @ 1000 2 @ 1320 10 @ 2100 20 @ 4200	0 @ 6 15 @ 12	29 to 31	8	Automatic
307 cu in 115 HP	1112227	0 @ 1000 2 @ 1200 12 @ 2200 24 @ 4300	0 @ 6 15 @ 12	29 to 31	4	Manual
350 cu in 145 HP	1112168	0 @ 1000 2 @ 1300 10 @ 2600 20 @ 4200	0 @ 4 14 @ 7	29 to 31	8	Automatic or Manual
350 cu in 175 HP	1112094	0 @ 1100 2 @ 1550 6 @ 2410 12 @ 3300 14 @ 4200	0 @ 6 15 @ 14	29 to 31	12	Automatic
350 cu in 175 HP	1112093	0 @ 1100 2 @ 1320 6 @ 1800 11 @ 2400 18 @ 4200	0 @ 6 15 @ 14	29 to 31	8	Manual
350 cu in (Z-28)	1112148	0 @ 1200 2 @ 1460 12 @ 2200 20 @ 5000	0 @ 6 15 @ 12	29 to 31	8	Automatic
1974 350 cu in 145 HP	1112168	0 @ 1000 20 @ 2400	0 @ 2 to 4 14 @ 7.5 to 8.5	29 to 31	TDC (Manual) 8 (Automatic)	Automatic or Manual
350 cu in 160 HP	1112847	0 @ 1100 11 @ 2400 18 @ 4200	0 @ 2 to 4 14 @ 7.5 to 8.5	29 to 31	4 (Manual) 8 (Automatic)	Automatic
350 cu in 185 HP	1112849	0 @ 1000 10 @ 1800 15 @ 2400 22 @ 4200	0 @ 2 to 4 14 @ 7.5 to 8.5	29 to 31	8 (4 Manual California)	Automatic or Manual
350 cu in (Z-28)	1112093	0 @ 1100 11 @ 2400 18 @ 4200	0 @ 5 to 7 15 @ 13 to 14	29 to 31	8	All
350 cu in (Z-28)	1112852	0 @ 1200 2 @ 1460 12 @ 2200 20 @ 5000	0 @ 2 to 4 14 @ 7.5 to 8.5	29 to 31	8	All
1975 350 cu in 145 HP	1112880	0 @ 1200 12 @ 2000 22 @ 4200	0 @ 4 18 @ 12	HEI Ignition	6	Automatic or Manual

Year and engine	Distributor No.	Centrifugal advance crank degrees @ engine rpm	Vacuum advance crank degrees @ in hg	Dwell angle degrees	Ignition timing at engine idle degrees BTDC	Transmission type
350 cu in 195 HP	1112888	0 @ 1100 12 @ 1600 22 @ 4200	0 @ 4 18 or 12	HEI Ignition	6	Automatic or Manual
350 cu in (Z-28)	1112883	0 @ 110 12 @ 1600 16 @ 2400 22 @ 4600	0 @ 4 15 @ 10	HEI Ignition	6	Automatic or Manual
1976 305 cu in 140 HP	1112977	0 @ 1000 10 @ 1700 20 @ 3800	0 @ 4 18 @ 12	HEI Ignition	6 (Manual) 8 (Automatic)	Automatic or Manual
305 cu in 140 HP	1112999	0 @ 1000 10 @ 1700 20 @ 3800	0 @ 4 10 @ 8	HEI Ignition	0	Automatic (California)
350 cu in 145 HP	1112880	0 @ 1200 12 @ 2000 22 @ 4200	0 @ 4 18 @ 12	HEI Ignition	6	Automatic
350 cu in 165 HP	1112888	0 @ 1100 12 @ 1600 16 @ 2400 22 @ 4600	0 @ 4 18 @ 12	HEI Ignition	8	Automatic or Manual
350 cu in 165 HP	1112905	0 @ 1200 12 @ 2000 22 @ 4200	0 @ 6 15 @ 12	HEI Ignition	6	Automatic or Manual (California)
1977 305 cu in 140 HP	1103239	0 @ 1200 15 @ 2700 20 @ 4200	0 @ 4 15 @ 10	HEI Ignition	8	Automatic or Manual
305 cu in 140 HP	1103244	0 @ 1000 10 @ 1700 20 @ 3800	0 @ 4 20 @ 10	HEI Ignition	6	Automatic (California)
350 cu in 165 HP	1103246	0 @ 1200 12 @ 2000 22 @ 4200	0 @ 4 18 @ 12	HEI Ignition	8	Automatic or Manual
350 cu in 165 HP	1103248	0 @ 1200 12 @ 2000 22 @ 4200	0 @ 4 10 @ 8	HEI Ignition	8	Automatic or (California)
1978 305 cu in	1103281	0 @ 1000 10 @ 1700 20 @ 3800	0 @ 4 18 @ 12	HEI Ignition	4	Manual
305 cu in	1103282	0 @ 1000 10 @ 1700 20 @ 3800	0 @ 4 20 @ 10	HEI Ignition	4	Automatic
350 cu in	1103337	0 @ 1100 12 @ 1600 16 @ 2400	0 @ 4 24 @ 10	HEI Ignition	6	Manual or Automatic
350 cu in	1103353	0 @ 1100 12 @ 160 16 @ 2400	0 @ 4 20 @ 10	HEI Ignition	6	Manual or Automatic
350 cu in	1103285	0 @ 1200 12 @ 2000 22 @ 4200	0 @ 4 10 @ 8	HEI Ignition	8	Automatic (California)
1979 305 cu in	1103281	0 @ 1000 10 @ 1700 20 @ 3800	0 @ 4 18 @ 12	HEI Ignition	4	Manual

Year and engine	Distributor No.	Centrifugal advance crank degrees @ engine rpm	Vacuum advance crank degrees @ in hg	Dwell angle degrees	Ignition timing at engine idle degrees BTDC	Transmission type
305 cu in	1103379	0 @ 1000 10 @ 1700 20 @ 3800	0 @ 3 20 @ 8.5	HEI Ignition	4	Automatic
305 cu in	1103285	0 @ 1200 12 @ 2000 22 @ 4200	0 @ 4 10 @ 8	HEI Ignition	4	Automatic (California)
350 cu in	1103353	0 @ 1100 12 @ 1600 16 @ 2400 22 @ 4600	0 @ 4 20 @ 10	HEI Ignition	6	Manual or Automatic
350 cu in	1103285	0 @ 120 12 @ 2000 22 @ 4200	0 @ 4 10 @ 8	HEI Ignition	8	Automatic (California)

1980

Year and engine	Distributor No.	Centrifugal advance crank degrees @ engine rpm	Vacuum advance crank degrees @ in hg	Dwell angle degrees	Ignition timing at engine idle degrees BTDC	Transmission type
267 cu in	1103371	0 @ 1000 8 @ 1700 22 @ 4400	0 @ 3 24 @ 10	HEI Ignition	4	Automatic
305 cu in	1103282	0 @ 1000 10 @ 1700 20 @ 3800	0 @ 4 20 @ 11	HEI Ignition	4	Manual
305 cu in	1103379	0 @ 1000 10 @ 1700 20 @ 3800	0 @ 3 20 @ 8.5	HEI Ignition	4	Automatic
305 cu in	1103368	0 @ 1000 10 @ 1700 20 @ 3800	0 @ 4 10 @ 8	HEI Ignition	4	Automatic (California)
350 cu in	1103353	0 @ 1100 12 @ 1600 16 @ 2400 22 @ 4600	0 @ 4 20 @ 10	HEI Ignition	6	Manual
350 cu in	1103337	0 @ 1100 12 @ 1600 16 @ 2400 22 @ 4600	0 @ 4 24 @ 11	HEI Ignition	6	Automatic

Torque specifications

	lb-ft
Spark plugs	15

1 General description – ignition system

In order that the engine can run correctly it is necessary for an electrical spark to ignite the fuel/air mixture in the combustion chamber at exactly the right moment in relation to engine speed and load. The ignition system is based on feeding low tension (LT) voltage from the battery to the coil where it is converted to high tension (HT) voltage. The high tension voltage is powerful enough to jump the spark plug gap in the cylinders many times a second under high compression pressures, providing that the system is in good condition and that all adjustments are correct.

The ignition system fitted to all pre-1975 cars as standard equipment is the conventional distributor with mechanical contact breaker and coil type. For 1975 models a breakerless high energy ignition (HEI) system is used.

Pre-1975 ignition systems

The ignition system is divided into two circuits: the low tension circuit and the high tension circuit.

The low tension (sometimes known as the primary) circuit consists of the battery lead to the starter motor, lead to the ignition switch, calibrated resistance wire from the ignition switch to the low tension or primary coil winding, and the lead from the low tension coil windings to the contact breaker points and condenser in the distributor.

The high tension circuit consists of the high tension or secondary coil windings, the heavy ignition lead from the center of the coil to the center of the distributor cap, the rotor, and the spark plug leads and spark plugs.

The system functions in the following manner. Low tension voltage is changed in the coil into high tension voltage by the opening and closing of the contact breaker points in the low tension circuit. High tension voltage is then fed via the brush in the center of the distributor cap to the rotor arm of the distributor cap, and each time it comes in line with one of the 8 segments in the cap, which are connected to the spark plug leads, the opening and closing of the contact breaker points causes the high tension voltage to build up, jump the gap from the rotor arm to the appropriate segment and so, via the spark plug lead to the spark plug, where it finally jumps the spark plug gap before going to ground.

The ignition advance is controlled both mechanically and by a vacuum operated system. The mechanical governor mechanism comprises two weights, which move out from the distributor shaft as the engine speed rises due to centrifugal force. As they move outwards they rotate the cam relative to the distributor shaft, and so advance the spark. The weights are held in position by two light springs and it is the tension of the springs which is largely responsible for correct spark advancement.

The vacuum control consists of a diaphragm, one side of which is connected via a small bore tube to the carburetor, and the other side to the contact breaker plate. Depression in the inlet manifold and carburetor, which varies with engine speed and throttle opening, causes the diaphragm to move, so moving the contact breaker plate, and advancing or retarding the spark. A fine degree of control is achieved by a spring in the vacuum assembly.

On some models, a Transmission Controlled Spark (TCS) system has an effect on vacuum advance. Further information on this system can be found in Chapter 6.

1975 and later ignition systems

The high energy ignition (HEI) system is a pulse triggered, transistor controlled, inductive discharge system.

A magnetic pick-up inside the distributor contains a permanent magnet, pole-piece and pick-up coil. A time core, rotating inside the pole piece, induces a voltage in the pick-up coil, and when teeth on the timer and pole piece line up, a signal passes to the electronic module to open the coil primary circuit. The primary circuit current decreases and a high voltage is induced in the coil secondary winding; this is then directed to the spark plugs by the distributor rotor as with the conventional system. A capacitor is fitted to suppress radio interference.

The system features a longer spark duration and the dwell period automatically increases with engine speed. These features are desirable for firing lean and EGR diluted mixtures (refer to Chapter 6).

The ignition coil, somewhat smaller than the coil in a conventional system, and the elctronic module are both housed in the distributor cap. The distributor does not require routine servicing.

Spark advancement is by mechanical and vacuum means, as described for conventional systems. The TCS system is not used.

If the need arises for the vehicle to be cranked remotely using jumper cables from another battery source, the distributor BAT terminal must be disconnected.

2 Battery – maintenance

1 Every week, check the level of the battery electrolyte. The method of doing this depends upon the type of battery. Some batteries have a 'Delco eye' which glows if the level is low. Others have a split ring in the filler opening with which the electrolyte should be level.
2 On later vehicles (1977) a 'Freedom' battery is used which does not require topping up.

3 Clean the top of the battery, removing all dirt and moisture (photos). As well as keeping the terminals clean and covered with petroleum jelly, the top of the battery, and especially the top of the cells, should be kept clean and dry. This helps prevent corrosion and ensures that the battery does not become partially discharged by leakage through dampness and dirt. On some models a felt ring is used under the battery terminals. This should be oiled.
4 Once every three months, remove the battery and inspect the battery securing bolts, the battery clamp plate, and battery leads for corrosion (white fluffy deposits on the metal which are brittle to touch). If any corrosion is found, clean off the deposits with an ammonia or soda solution. After cleaning, smear petroleum jelly on the battery terminals and lead connectors. Application of a zinc-base primer and/or underbody paint wil help to prevent recurrence of corrosion on body panel metal.
5 If topping-up the battery becomes excessive and the case has been inspected for cracks that could cause leakage, but none are found, the battery is beng over-charged and the alternator will have to be tested and if necessary serviced as described later in this Chapter.
6 If any doubt exists about the state of charge of a battery, a hydrometer should be used to test it by withdrawing a little electrolyte from each cell in turn.
7 The specific gravity of the electrolyte at the temperature of 80°F (26.7°C) will be approximately 1.270 for a fully charged battery. For every 10°F (5.5°C) that the electrolyte temperature is above that stated, add 0.04 to the specific gravity or subtract 0.04 if the temperature is below that stated.
8 A specific gravity reading of 1.240 with an electrolyte temperature of 80°F (26.7°C) indicates a half-charged battery.
9 With the 'Freedom' type of battery, a charge indicator is built into it which uses a color system to relay the state of charge of the battery.

3 Battery charging

1 In winter time when heavy demand is placed upon the battery, such as when starting from cold, and much electrical equipment is continually in use, it is a good idea to occasionally have the battery fully charged from an external source at the rate of 3.5 to 4 amps.
2 Continue to charge the battery at this rate until no further rise in specific gravity is noted over a four hour period.
3 Alternatively, a trickle charger charging at the rate of 1.5 amps can be safely used overnight.
4 Special rapid boost charges which are claimed to restore the power of the battery in 1 to 2 hours are most dangerous as they can cause serious damage to the battery plates. This type of charge should only be used in a 'crisis' situation.
5 On vehicles equipped with the "Freedom" type battery, do not charge the battery if the built-in hydrometer on the top of the battery is a clear or light yellow color. This coloring indicates that the battery needs replacement.

4 Battery – removal and installation

1 The battery is located at the front of the engine compartment. It is held in place by either a hold-down rod running across the top of the battery or a clamp near the bottom of the battery case.
2 As hydrogen gas is produced by the battery, keep open flames or lighted cigarettes away from the battery at all times.
3 Avoid spilling any of the electrolyte battery fluid on the vehicle or yourself. Always keep the battery in the upright position. Any spilled electrolyte should be immediately flushed with large quantities of water. Wear eye protection when working with a battery to prevent serious eye damage from splashed fluid.
4 Always disconnect the negative (–) battery cable first, followed by the positive (+) cable.
5 After the cables are disconnected from the battery, remove the hold-down mechanism, be it a rod or bottom clamp.
6 Carefully lift the battery from its tray and out of the engine compartment.
7 Installation is a reversal of removal, however make sure that the hold-down clamp or rod is securely tightened. Do not over-tighten, however, as this may damage the battery case. The battery posts and cable ends should be cleaned prior to connection.

2.3A All corrosion should be removed from the battery terminals

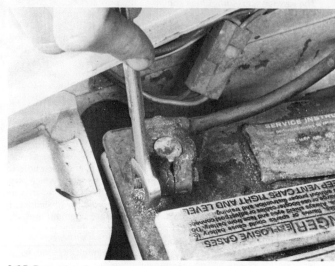

2.3B Removing the cable connector from the terminal

2.3C A special wire-brush cleaning tool is used here to clean the battery terminal

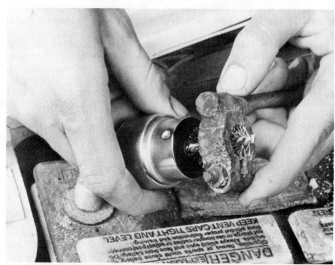

2.3D The wire brush is also used to clean the corrosion from the inside of the cable connector

5   Condenser (capacitor) – testing, removal and installation (1970–1974)

1   The condenser ensures that when the contact breaker points open, the sparking between them is not excessive to cause severe pitting. The condenser is fitted in parallel and its failure will automatically cause failure of the ignition system as the points will be prevented from interrupting the low tension circuit.

2   Testing for an unserviceable condenser may be done by switching on the ignition and separating the contact points by hand. If this action is accompanied by a blue flash then condenser failure is indicated. Difficult starting, missing of engine after several miles running or badly pitted points are other indications of a faulty condenser.

3   The surest test is by substitution with a new unit.

4   To replace the condenser, remove the distributor cap, rotor and RFI shield.

5   Disconnect the condenser lead and remove the condenser retaining screw. Slide the condenser from the bracket.

6   Installation is the reverse of the removal procedure.

6   Distributor cap – replacement (1970–1974)

Note: *It is imperative that the spark plug wires be installed in the correct order on the distributor cap.*

1   Purchase a replacement distributor cap for the particular model year and engine size.

2   Release the old cap from the distributor body by pushing downward on the slotted latches and then turning the latches $\frac{1}{4}$ turn.

3   Place the new cap next to the old one. Use the metal window and the two latches as reference points to get the new cap in the same relative position.

4   Begin transferring the spark plug wires one at a time from the old cap to the new one. Do not pull on the wire insulation, but rather grab the rubber boot, twist slightly and then pull the plug wire free by the boot.

5   Push the plug wires and boots firmly onto the new distributor cap.

6   Place the new cap and plug wires into position over the top of the distributor and lock it in place by pushing and turning the latches. Make sure the cap is firmly seated.

Measuring plug gap. A feeler gauge of the correct size (see ignition system specifications) should have a slight 'drag' when slid between the electrodes. Adjust gap if necessary

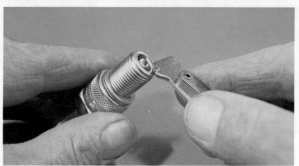

Adjusting plug gap. The plug gap is adjusted by bending the earth electrode inwards, or outwards, as necessary until the correct clearance is obtained. Note the use of the correct tool

Normal. Grey-brown deposits, lightly coated core nose. Gap increasing by around 0.001 in (0.025 mm) per 1000 miles (1600 km). Plugs ideally suited to engine, and engine in good condition

Carbon fouling. Dry, black, sooty deposits. Will cause weak spark and eventually misfire. Fault: over-rich fuel mixture. Check: carburettor mixture settings, float level and jet sizes; choke operation and cleanliness of air filter. Plugs can be re-used after cleaning

Oil fouling. Wet, oily deposits. Will cause weak spark and eventually misfire. Fault: worn bores/piston rings or valve guides; sometimes occurs (temporarily) during running-in period. Plugs can be re-used after thorough cleaning

Overheating. Electrodes have glazed appearance, core nose very white – few deposits. Fault: plug overheating. Check: plug value, ignition timing, fuel octane rating (too low) and fuel mixture (too weak). Discard plugs and cure fault immediately

Electrode damage. Electrodes burned away; core nose has burned, glazed appearance. Fault: pre-ignition. Check: as for 'Overheating' but may be more severe. Discard plugs and remedy fault before piston or valve damage occurs

Split core nose (may appear initially as a crack). Damage is self-evident, but cracks will only show after cleaning. Fault: pre-ignition or wrong gap-setting technique. Check: ignition timing, cooling system, fuel octane rating (too low) and fuel mixture (too weak). Discard plugs, rectify fault immediately

7.6A A special distributor wrench is available for loosening the distributor lock bolt

7.6B The hold-down bolt and retainer used at the base of the distributor

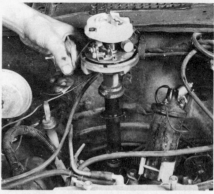

7.7 Once the bottom retainer is removed, the distributor can be lifted straight out of the engine. Carefully note position of rotor as described in text

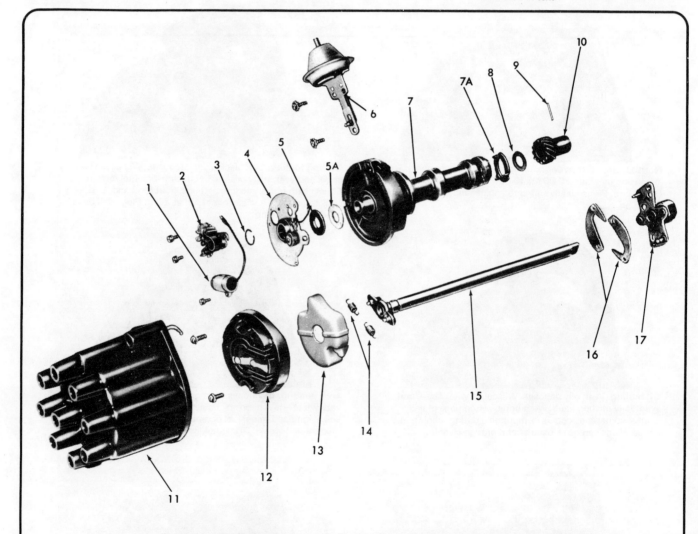

Fig. 5.1 Exploded view of mechanical breaker type distributor (1970 – 1974) (Sec 7)

1	Condenser	9	Drive gear pin
2	Contact point assembly	10	Drive gear
2a	Cam lubricator	11	Cap
3	Retaining ring	12	Rotor
4	Breaker plate	13	Radio frequency
5	Felt washer		interference shield
5a	Plastic seal	14	Weight springs
6	Vacuum unit	15	Mainshaft
7	Housing	16	Advance weights
7a	Tanged washer	17	Cam weight base assembly
8	Shim washer		

7 Distributor – removal and overhaul (1970–1974)

1 Release the two latches on the distributor cap by pressing them downward with a screwdriver and then turning them $\frac{1}{4}$ turn. Move the cap (with the spark plug wires still attached) out of the way. Use wire or tape if necessary.

2 Disconnect the distributor primary wiring lead from the coil terminal.

3 At this point it is important to mark the position of the rotor and distributor housing for easier reassembly. At the very bottom of the distributor, scribe a mark on the distributor base and another mark in line with the base mark on the engine block. Also note the direction in which the rotor contact is pointed. Make a mark on the distributor housing in-line with the rotor contact strip.

4 Disconnect the vacuum line at the distributor.

5 Note the position of the vacuum advance mechanism (canister from which vacuum hose was just disconnected) relative to the engine.

6 Remove the distributor hold-down bolt and clamp from the base of the distributor. A special curved distributor wrench is best for this purpose (photos).

7 Lift the distributor straight up and out of the engine (photo).

8 Avoid rotating the engine with the distributor removed as the ignition timing will be changed.

9 To disassemble, remove the rotor (2 screws), the advance weight springs and the weights. Where applicable, also remove the radio frequency interference (RFI) shield.

10 Drive out the roll pin retaining the gear to the shaft then pull off the gear and spacers.

11 Ensure that the shaft is not burred, then slide it from the housing.

12 Remove the cam weight base assembly.

13 Remove the screws retaining the vacuum unit and lift off the unit itself.

14 Remove the spring retainer (snap-ring) then remove the breaker plate assembly.

15 Remove the contact points and condenser, followed by the felt washer and plastic seal located beneath the breaker plate.

16 Wipe all components clean with a solvent moistened cloth and examine them for wear, distortion and scoring. Replace parts as necessary. Pay particular attention to the rotor and distributor cap to ensure that they are not cracked.

17 Fill the lubricating cavity in the housing with general purpose grease then fit a new plastic seal and felt washer.

18 Install the vacuum unit, the breaker plate in the housing and the spring retainer on the upper bushing.

19 Lubricate the cam weight base and slide it on the mainshaft; install the weights and springs.

20 Insert the mainshaft in the housing then fit the shims and drive-gear. Install a new roll-pin.

21 Install the contact point set (Chapter 1).

22 Install the rotor, aligning the round and square pilot holes.

23 Instal the distributor as described in Section 8.

8 Distributor – installation (1970–1974)

If engine was not rotated after removal

1 Turn the rotor about $\frac{1}{8}$ turn in a clockwise direction past the mark made on the distributor housing upon removal.

2 Lower the distributor down into the engine, positioning the vacuum advance mechanism in the approximate position as removal. To mesh the gears at the bottom of the distributor it may be necessary to turn the rotor slightly.

3 With the base of the distributor all the way down against the engine block, the rotor should be pointed to the mark made on the distributor housing. If these two marks are not in alignment, repeat the previous steps.

4 Now turn the distributor housing until the scribed marks at the bottom of the distributor are in alignment.

5 Place the clamp into position and tighten the clamp bolt securely.

6 Connect the vacuum hose to the distributor and connect the primary wire to the coil terminal.

7 Install the distributor cap.

8 Check the ignition timing as described in Chapter 1.

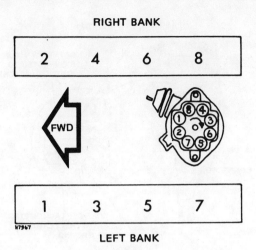

Fig. 5.2 Spark plug wire connection (1970 – 1974) diagram (Sec 8)

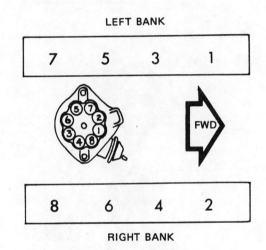

Fig. 5.3 Spark plug wire connection (Mark IV, big-block engine, 1970 – 1974) diagram (Sec 8)

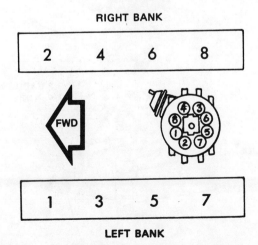

Fig. 5.4 Spark plug wire connection (1975 – 1980) diagram (Sec 9)

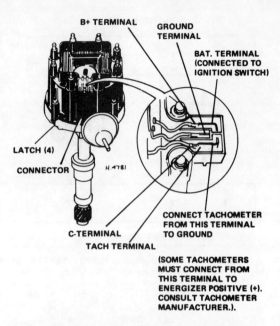

Fig. 5.5 Breakerless type distributor coil connections (Sec 9)

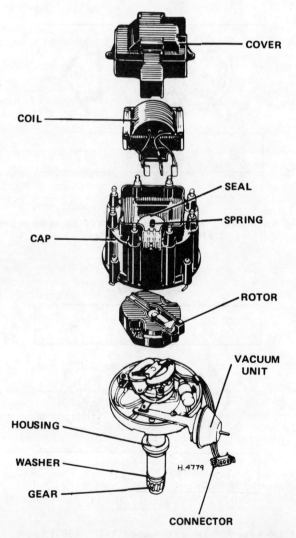

Fig. 5.6 Components of the HEI (breakerless) distributor (Sec 10)

If engine was rotated after removal

9 Turn the crankshaft by applying a wrench to the crankshaft pulley bolt at the front of the engine until the number 1 piston is at top-dead-center (TDC). This can be ascertained by removing the number 1 spark plug and feeling the compression being generated. If you are careful not to scratch' the cylinder, you can also use a length of stiff wire to feel the piston come to the top of the cyinder.

10 With the number 1 piston at TDC (as indicated by the timing marks on the front cover), the distributor should be firing this cylinder.

11 Hold the distributor over its recess with the vacuum advance unit in its 'installed' position. It should be pointed towards the front of the right-hand cylinder head.

12 Point the metal contact on the rotor towards the number 1 cylinder and lower the distributor into place.

13 With the distributor fully seated to the engine (it may be necessary to turn the rotor slightly to mesh the gears), the rotor contact should be in-line with the number 1 spark plug wire in the distributor cap. To find out if this is true, temporarily install the cap to the distributor, checking the rotor contact and the number 1 spark plug terminal.

14 Install the clamp and the hold-down bolt at the bottom of the engine. Leave the bolt loose enough to enable you to turn the distributor.

15 Start the engine and adjust the timing as described in Chapter 1.

16 *On Mark IV engines,* there is a punch mark on the drive gear which represents the position of the contact end of the rotor. This enables the distributor to be installed with the cap in place.

17 Once installed, turn the distributor until the contact points are just about to open and tighten the clamp bolt.

18 Tighten all connections and install the distrubutor caps.

19 Check and adjust the dwell angle and the timing as soon as the engine has been run to normal operating temperature.

9   Distributor – removal and installation (1975–1980)

1 The procedures for removing and installing the breakerless distributor are basically the same as for the conventional unit described in Sections 7 and 8. Follow the sequence given in Sections 7 and 8 with the following exceptions:

  a) Disconnect the wiring connector on the outside of the distributor.

  b) The spark plug wires are connected to a ring around the top of the distributor cap. This retaining ring can be removed once the latches are disengaged.

  c) Ignore all references to the contact points and setting the dwell angle as this does not apply to the breakerless distributor.

  d) Set the ignition timing after installation.

10 Distributor (breakerless type) – overhaul

1 Remove the distributor as previously described.

2 Remove the rotor (2 screws) (photo).

3 Remove the 2 screws retaining the module. Move the module aside and remove the connector from the 'B' and 'C' terminals. (photo).

4 Remove the connections from the 'W' and 'G' terminals (photos).

5 Carefully drive out the roll pin from the drive gear (photo).

6 Remove the gear, shim and tanged washer from the distributor shaft (photo).

7 Ensure that the shaft is not burred, then remove it from the housing.

8 Remove the washer from the upper end of the distributor housing.

9 Remove 3 screws and take out the pole-piece, magnet and pick-up coil (photo).

10 Remove the lock ring, then take out the pick-up coil retainer, shim and felt washer.

11 Remove the vacuum unit (2 screws).

12 Disconnect the capacitor lead and remove the capacitor (1 screw).

13 Disconnect the wiring harness from the distributor housing.

14 Wipe all components clean with a solvent moistened cloth and examine them for wear, distortion and other damage. Replace parts as necessary.

15 To assemble, position the vacuum unit to the housing and secure

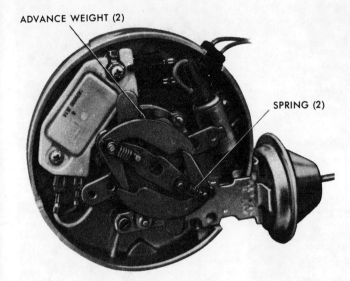

ADVANCE WEIGHT (2)

SPRING (2)

Fig. 5.7 Advance mechanism – HEI distributor (Sec 10)

with the 2 screws.
16 Position the felt washer over the lubricant reservoir at the top of the housing then position the shim on top of the felt washer.
17 Position the pick-up coil retainer to the housing. The vacuum advance arm goes over the actuating pin of the advance mechanism. Secure it with the lock-ring.
18 Install the pick-up coil magnet and pole-piece. Loosely install the 3 screws to retain the pole-piece.
19 Install the washer to the top of the housing. Install the distributor shaft then rotate it and check for equal clearance all round between the shaft projections and pole-piece. Secure the pole-piece when correctly positioned.
20 Install the tanged washer, shim and drivegear. Align the gear and install a new roll pin.
21 Loosely install the capacitor with one screw.
22 Install the connector to the 'B' and 'C' terminals on the module with the tab at the top.
23 Apply silicone grease to the base of the module and secure it with 2 screws. This grease is essential to ensure good heat conduction.
24 Position the wiring harness with the grommet in the housing notch then connect the pink wire to the capacitor stud and the black wire to the capacitor mounting screw. Tighten the screw.
25 Connect the white wire from the pick-up coil to the module 'W' terminal and the green to the 'G' terminal.
26 Install the advance weights, weight retainer (dimple downwards), and springs.
27 Install the rotor and secure with the 2 screws. Ensure that the notch on the side of the rotor engages with the tab on the cam weight base.
28 Install the distributor as previously described.

11 Ignition coil – removal and installation

Thru 1974
1 This is a straightforward operation, requiring only the removal of the electrical connections and the two mounting screws (photo). It is a good policy to mark the connections before removal to ensure that they are re-installed correctly.

1975 on
2 Disconnect the battery wire and harness connector from the distributor cap.
3 Remove the coil cover (3 screws) and the coil assembly (4 screws) from the distributor cap (photo).
4 Note the position of each wire, duly marking them if necessary.

Remove the coil ground wire then push the leads from the underside of the connectors. Remove the coil from the distributor cap (photo).
5 Installation is the reverse of the removal procedure, but ensure that the leads are connected to their original positions (photo).

12 Spark plugs

1 Properly functioning spark plugs are a necessity if the engine is to perform properly. At the intervals specified in Chapter 1 or your owner's manual, the spark plugs should be replaced with new ones. Removal and installation information can be found in the Tune-up and Basic Maintenance Chapter.
2 It is important to replace spark plugs with new ones of the same heat range and type. A series of numbers and letters are stamped on the spark plug to help identify each variation.
3 The spark plug gap is of considerable importance as, if it is too large or too small the size of the spark and its efficiency wil be seriously impaired. To set it, measure the gap with a feeler gauge, and then bend open, or close, the outer plug electrode until the correct gap is achieved. The center electrode should never be bent as this may crack the insulation and cause plug failure, if nothing worse.
4 The condition and appearance of the spark plugs will tell much about the condition and tune of the engine. If the insulator nose of the spark plug is clean and white with no deposits, this is indicative of a weak mixture, or too hot a plug (a hot plug transfers heat away from the electrode slowly – a cold plug transfers it away quickly.
5 If the tip and insulator nose is covered with hard black looking deposits, then this is indicative that the mixture is too rich. Should the plug be black and oily, then it is likely that the engine is fairly worn, as well as the mixture being too rich.
6 If the insulator nose is covered with light tan to greyish brown deposits, then the mixture is correct and it is likely that the engine is in good condition.
7 If there are any traces of long brown tapering stains on the outside of the white portion of the plug, then the plug will have to be replaced with a new one, as this shows that there is a faulty joint between the plug body and the insulator, and compression is being allowed to leak away.
8 Always tighten a spark plug to the specified torque – no tighter.

13 General description – charging system

The charging system is made up of the alternator, voltage regulator and the battery. These components work together to supply electrical power for the engine ignition, lights, radio, etc.
The alternator is turned by a drive belt at the front of the engine, Thus, when the engine is operating, voltage is generated by the internal components of the alternator to be sent to the battery for storage.
The purpose of the voltage regulator is to limit the alternator voltage to a pre-set value. This prevents power surges, circuit overloads, etc. during peak voltage output. 1970 – 1972 vehicles have an external voltage regulator mounted to the inner fender panel. 1973 and later models have the voltage regulator built into the alternator housing.
The charging system does not ordinarily require periodic maintenance. The drive belts, electrical wiring and connections should, however, be inspected during normal tune-ups (see Chapter 1).

14 Alternator – maintenance and special precautions

1 The alternator fitted to all models is a Delco-Remy Delcotron. Three types have been used, the 5.5 inch Series 1D, 10DN Series 100B and the Series 10SI. The first types require a separate voltage regulator; the last type has an integral regulator.
2 Alternator maintenance consists of occasionally wiping away any dirt or oil which may have collected.
3 Check the tension of the driving belt (refer to Chapter 1, Section 41).
4 No lubrication is required as alternator bearings are grease sealed for the life of the unit.
5 Take extreme care when making circuit connections to a vehicle fitted with an alternator and observe the following. When making

10.1 A typical HEI distributor removed from the engine

10.2 The HEI rotor is held in position by two screws

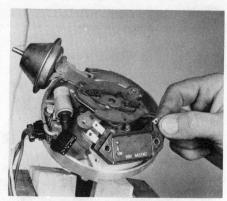

10.3 The electronic module is secured to the inside of the distributor with two screws

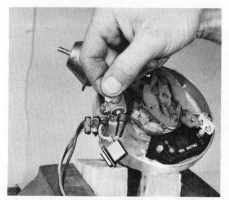

10.4 Disconnecting the wiring connectors on the inside of the distributor

10.5 Using a hammer and punch to drive out the roll pin from the bottom of the distributor shaft

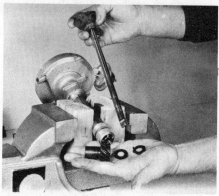

10.6 The shaft, gear, shim and tanged washer removed from the distributor

10.9 The pole-piece and washer removed from the upper end of the distributor body

11.1 1970 – 1974 ignition coil being lifted away from the top of the engine

11.3 The coil cover being lifted off the top of the distributor cap (1975 – 1980)

11.4 The coil is then removed from its recess in the top of the distributor cap

11.5 Before installing new coil, ensure that center electrode is in good condition

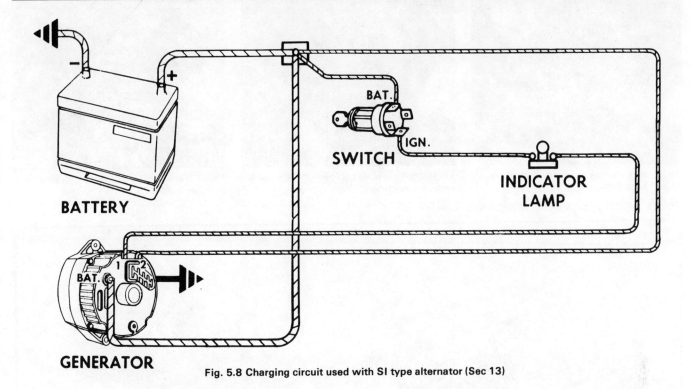

Fig. 5.8 Charging circuit used with SI type alternator (Sec 13)

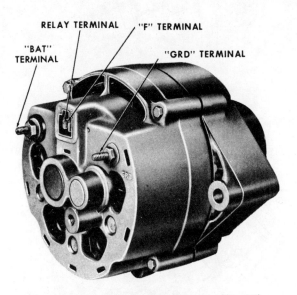

Fig. 5.9 Series 1D Delcotron alternator (Sec 14)

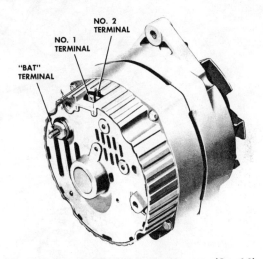

Fig. 5.10 Series 10 SI Delcotron alternator (Sec 14)

connections to the alternator from a battery always match correct polarity. Before using electric-arc welding equipment to repair any part of the vehicle, disconnect the connector from the alternator and disconnect the positive battery terminal. Never start the car with a battery charger connected. Always disconnect both battery leads before using a mains charger. If boosting from another battery, always connect in parallel using heavy cable. It is not recommended that testing of an alternator should be undertaken at home due to the testing equipment required and the possibility of damage occurring during testing. It is best left to automotive electrical specialists.

15 Alternator – removal and installation

1   Disconnect both leads from the battery terminals.
2   Disconnect the leads from the rear face of the alternator, marking them first to ensure correct installation (photo).

3   Loosen the alternator mounting and adjuster link bolts, push the unit in towards the engine as far as possible, and slip off the drivebelts (photos).
4   Remove the mounting bolts and lift the alternator from the engine compartment.
5   Installation is a reversal of removal; adjust the drivebelt tension.
Note: *New alternators are not usually supplied with pulleys. The old one should therefore be removed if a new unit is to be purchased. To do this, hold the alternator shaft still with an Allen wrench while the pulley nut is unscrewed.*

16 Alternator – overhaul

Note: *Due to the critical nature of the disassembly and testing of the various alternator components it may be advisable for the home mechanic to simply replace a faulty unit with a new or factory rebuilt*

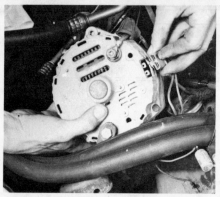

15.2 Disconnecting the wiring from the rear side of the alternator

15.3A The long pivot bolt for the alternator is under the housing

15.3B The adjusting strap bolt is located inside a slotted bracket

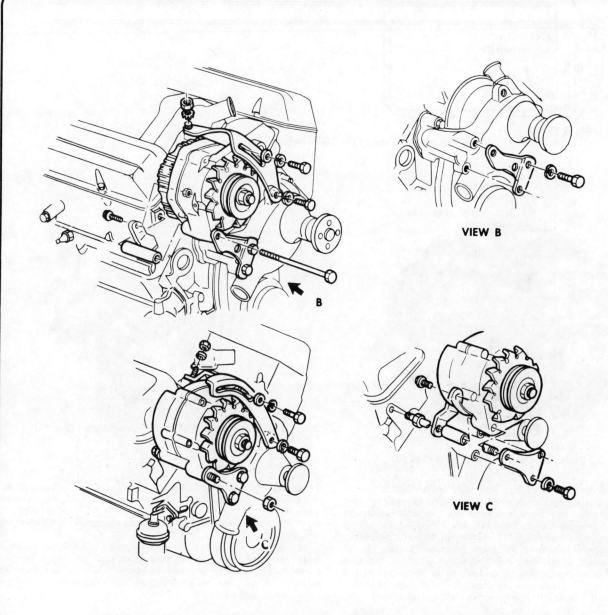

Fig. 5.11 Typical Delcotron alternator installation — (upper) small V8, (lower) Mark IV V8 (Sec 15)

VIEW B

VIEW C

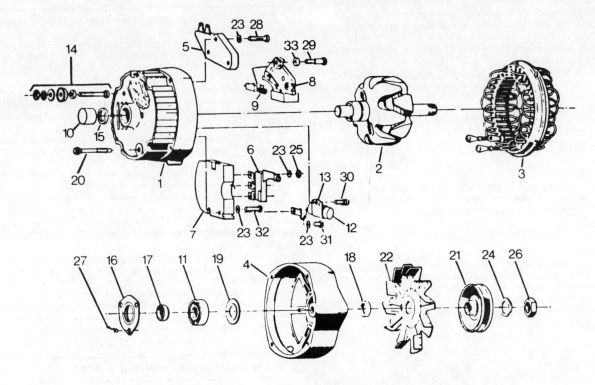

Fig. 5.12 Exploded view of 10 SI Delcotron alternator (Sec 26)

1 Slip ring end frame	11 Bearing	20 Through bolt
2 Rotor	12 Capacitor	21 Pulley
3 Stator	13 Bracket	22 Fan
4 Drive end frame	14 Terminal components	23 Washer
5 Regulator	15 Seal	24 Washer
6 Diode	16 Plate	25 Nut
7 Rectifier bridge	17 Collar	26 Nut
8 Brush assembly	18 Collar	27 to 32 Screws
9 Brush holder	19 Washer	33 Washer
10 Bearing		

POINT OPENING

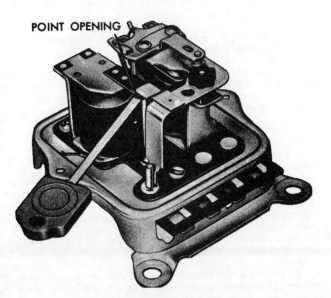

Fig. 5.13 Checking field relay point opening (Sec 17)

AIR GAP
(Check With Points Just Touching)

Fig. 5.14 Checking field relay air gap (Sec 17)

model. If it is decided to perform the overhaul procedure make sure that replacement parts are available before proceeding.

1   Remove the alternator and pulley as described in the preceding Section.
2   Secure the alternator in the jaws of a vice, applying the pressure to the mounting flange.
3   Remove the four through-bolts, and separate the slip-ring, end frame and stator assembly from the drive-end and rotor assembly. Use a screwdriver to lever them apart and mark the relative position of the end frames to facilitate reassembly.
4   Remove the stator lead securing nuts and separate the stator from the end frame.

1D series

5   Extract the screws and remove the brush holder assembly.
6   Remove the heat sink from the end frame after extracting the BAT and GRD terminals and single securing screw.

10 SI series

7   Continue dismantling, by removing the rectifier bridge, securing screw and the BAT terminal screw. Disconnect the capacitor lead and remove the rectifier bridge from the end-frame.
8   Unscrew the two securing screws and remove the brush holder and regulator. Carefully retain the insulating sleeves and washers.
9   Remove the capacitor (one screw) from the end-frame.

All models

10 If the slip ring end-frame bearing is dry or noisy when rotated, it must be replaced (not greased). Greasing will not extend its service life. Press out the old bearing and discard the oil seal. Press in the new bearing, squarely, until the bearing is flush with the outside of the end-frame. Install a new oil seal. During these operations, support the end-frame adequately to prevent cracking or distorting the frame.
11 Now insert a $\frac{5}{16}$ inch Allen wrench into the socket in the center of the shaft at the drive pulley end. Using this to prevent the shaft from rotating, unscrew the pulley retaining nut and remove the washer, pulley, fan and the spacer.
12 Remove the rotor and spacers from the drive end-frame.
13 If the bearing in the drive end-frame is dry or noisy it must be replaced. Do not grease it in the hope that this will extend its life. Access to the bearing is obtained after removing the retainer plate bolts and separating the plate/seal assembly. Press the bearing out using a piece of tube applied to the inner race and press the new one in by applying the tube to the outer race. Make sure that the slinger is correctly located and recommended grease is applied to the bearing before installation.
14 With the alternator completely dismantled, wipe all components clean (do not use solvent on the stator or rotor windings), and examine for wear or damage. Purchase new components as necessary.
15 If the slip rings are dirty they should be cleaned by spinning the rotor and holding a piece of 400 grain abrasive paper against them. This method will avoid the creation of flat spots on the rings. If the rings are badly scored, out-of-round or otherwise damaged, the complete rotor assembly must be replaced.
16 Check the brushes for wear. If they are worn halfway or more in length, do not re-use them. Purchase new springs only if they appear weak or are distorted.
17 Reassembly is a reversal of dismantling but observe the following points:

(a) *Tighten the pulley nut to the specified torque. Take great care to position the insulating washers and sleeves correctly on the brush clip screws*
(b) *Clean the brush contact surfaces before installing the slip ring end-frame and hold the brushes up in their holders by passing a thin rod through the opening in the slip ring end-frame to permit the brushes to pass over the slip rings*
(c) *Finally make sure that the marks on the slip ring and drive end-frame (which were made before dismantling) are in alignment.*

17 Voltage regulator (externally mounted type) – removal, servicing and installation

1   A discharged battery will normally be due to a fault in the voltage regulator but before testing the unit, check the following:
2   Check the drivebelt tension.
3   Test the condition of the battery.
4   Check the charging circuit for loose connections and broken wires.
5   Make sure that lights or other electrical accessories have not been left switched on inadvertently.
6   Check the generator indicator lamp for normal illumination with the ignition switched on and off, and with the engine idling and stationary.
7   Disconnect the battery ground cable and the harness connector. Remove the screws securing the unit to the vehicle.
8   Under no circumstances should the voltage regulator contacts be cleaned since any abrasive materials will destroy the contact material. Relay point and air-gap adjustments can be checked using a feeler gauge to obtain approximate settings if they are thought to be requiring attention.
9   The field relay point opening may be adjusted by bending the stop. The air gap is checked with the points just touching and is adjusted by bending the flat contact spring. **Note:** *The field relay will normally operate satisfactorily even if the air-gap is outside the specified limits, and should be adjusted when the system is functioning satisfactorily.*
10 Installation is the reverse of the removal procedure, but ensure that the rubber gasket is in place on the regulator base.

18 General description – starting system

The function of the starting system is to crank the engine. This system is composed of a starting motor, solenoid and battery. The battery supplies the electrical energy to the solenoid which then completes the circuit to the starting motor which does the actual work of cranking the engine.

The solenoid and starting motor are mounted together on a pad at the side of the engine. No periodic lubrication or maintenance is required to the starting system components.

The electrical circuitry of the vehicle is arranged so that the starter motor can only be operated when the clutch pedal is fully depressed (manual transmission) or the transmission selector lever is at 'P' or 'N' (automatic transmission).

The starter motor fitted to the Camaro range has remained almost unchanged throughout the production run of the vehicle. However, with the introduction of the HEI ignition system in 1975, the 'R' terminal on the solenoid was removed.

19 Starter motor – testing in vehicle

1   If the starter motor does not rotate at all when the switch is operated, check that the speed selector lever is in 'N' or 'P' (automatic transmission) and that the front seat belts are connected (starter interlock system) and also that the clutch pedal is depressed (where applicable).
2   Check that the battery is well charged and all cables, both at the battery and starter solenoid terminals, are secure.
3   If the motor can be heard spinning but the engine is not being cranked, then the overrunning clutch in the starter motor is slipping and the assembly must be removed from the engine and dismantled.
4   If, when the switch is actuated, the starter motor does not operate at all but the solenoid plunger can be heard to move with a loud 'click' then the fault lies in the main solenoid contacts or the starter motor itself.
5   If the solenoid plunger cannot be heard to move when the switch is actuated then the solenoid itself is defective or the solenoid circuit is open.
6   To check out the solenoid, connect a jumper lead between the battery (+) terminal and the terminal on the solenoid to which the purple cable is attached. If the starter motor now operates, the solenoid is OK and the fault must lie in the ignition or neutral start switches or in their interconnecting wiring.
7   If the starter motor still does not operate, remove the starter/solenoid assembly for dismantling, testing and repair.

20.4A Removing the bolts which secure the starting motor to the engine block

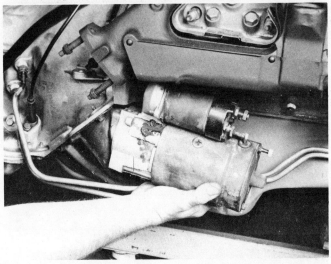

20.4B The starter motor and solenoid being drawn away from flywheel

8 If the starter motor cranks the engine at an abnormally slow speed, first ensure that the battery is fully charged and all terminal connections are tight, also that the engine oil is not too thick a grade and that the resistance is not due to a mechanical fault within the power unit.

9 Run the engine until normal operating temperature is attained, shut it off and disconnect the coil to distributor LT wire or 'BAT' connection on HEI distributors so that the engine will not fire during cranking.

10 Connect a voltmeter positive lead to the starter motor terminal of the solenoid and then connect the negative lead to ground.

11 Actuate the ignition switch and take the voltmeter readings as soon as a steady figure is indicated. Do not allow the starter motor to turn for more than 30 seconds at a time. A reading of 9 volts, or more, with the starter motor turning at normal cranking speed proves it to be in good condition. If the reading is 9 volts, or more, but the cranking speed is slow, then the motor is faulty. If the reading is less than 9 volts and the cranking speed is slow, the solenoid contacts are probably at fault and should be replaced as described later in this Chapter.

20 Starter motor – removal and installation

1 Disconnect the ground cable from the battery.

2 Raise the vehicle to a satisfactory working height.

3 Disconnect the leads at the starter solenoid marking each with a coded piece of tape for easy identification upon reassembly. Temporarily replace each of the securing nuts to the terminals as they have various thread types which could cause damage to the stubs if not properly re-installed.

4 Loosen the starter motor front bracket nut and then remove the two mount bolts (photos).

5 Remove the front bracket bolt, rotate the bracket so that the starter motor can be withdrawn by lowering its front end.

6 Installation is a reversal of removal but tighten the mount bolts first to the specified torque and then tighten the front bracket bolt and nut.

7 Install each of the wires to the solenoid terminals using your identification coding.

21 Starter motor – dismantling and component testing

Note: *Due to the critical nature of the disassembly and testing of the starter motor it may be advisable for the home mechanic to simply purchase a new or factory-rebuilt unit. If it is decided to overhaul the starter, check on the availability of singular replacement components before proceeding.*

1 Disconnect the starter motor field coil connectors from the solenoid terminals.

2 Unscrew and remove the through bolts.

3 Remove the commutator end-frame, field frame assembly and the armature from the drive housing.

4 Slide the two-section thrust collar off the end of the armature shaft and then using a piece of suitable tube drive the stop/retainer up the armature shaft to expose the snap-ring.

5 Extract the snap-ring from its shaft groove and then slide the stop/retainer and overrunning clutch assembly from the armature shaft.

6 Dismantle the brush components from the field frame.

7 Release the V-shaped springs from the brushholder supports.

8 Remove the brushholder support pin and then lift the complete brush assembly upwards.

9 Disconnect the leads from the brushes if they are worn down to half their original length and they are to be replaced.

10 The starter motor is now completely dismantled except for the field coils. If these are found to be defective during the tests described later in this Section removal of the pole shoe screws is best left to a service station who will have the necessary pressure driver.

11 Clean all components and replace any obviously worn components.

12 *On no account attempt to undercut the insulation between the commutator segments on starter motors having the molded type commutators.* On commutators of conventional type, the insulation should be undercut (below the level of the segments) by 1/32 inch. Use an old hacksaw blade to do this and make sure that the undercut is the full width of the insulation and the groove is quite square at the bottom. When the undercutting is completed, brush away all dirt and dust.

13 Clean the commutator by spinning it while a piece of number '00' sandpaper is wrapped round it. On no account use any other type of abrasive material for this work.

14 If necessary, because the commutator is in such bad shape, it may be turned down in a lathe to provide a new surface. Make sure to undercut the insulation when the turning is completed.

15 *To test the armature for ground:* use a lamp-type circuit tester. Place one lead on the armature core or shaft and the other on a segment of the commutator. If the lamp lights then the armature is grounded and must be replaced.

16 *To test the field coils for open circuit:* place one test probe on the insulated brush and the other on the field connector bar. If the lamp does not light, the coils are open and must be replaced.

17 *To test the field coils for ground:* place one test probe on the connector bar and the other on the grounded brush. If the lamp lights then the field coils are grounded.

18 The overrunning clutch cannot be repaired and if faulty, it must be replaced as a complete assembly.

22 Starter motor – reassembly and adjustment

1   Install the brush assembly to the field frame as follows:

2   Install the brushes to their holders.

3   Assemble the insulated and grounded brushholders together with the V-spring and then locate the unit on its support pin.

4   Push the holders and spring to the bottom of the support and then rotate the spring to engage the V in the support slot.

5   Connect the ground wire to the grounded brush and the field lead wire to the insulated brush.

6   Repeat the operations for the second set of brushes.

7   Smear silicone oil onto the drive end of the armature shaft and then slide the clutch assembly (pinion to the front) onto the shaft.

8   Slide the pinion stop/retainer onto the shaft so that its open end is facing away from the pinion.

9   Stand the armature vertically on a piece of wood and then position

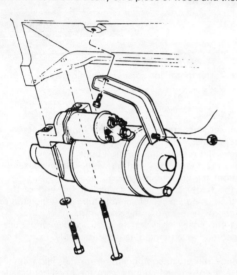

Fig. 5.15 Starter motor mounting (Sec 20)

the snap-ring on the end of the shaft. Using a hammer and a piece of hardwood, drive the snap-ring onto the shaft.

10 Slide the snap-ring down the shaft until it drops into its groove.

11 Install the thrust collar on the shaft so that the shoulder is next to the snap-ring. Using two pairs of pliers, squeeze the thrust collar and stop/retainer together until the snap-ring fully enters the retainer.

12 Lubricate the drive housing bushing with silicone oil and after ensuring that the thrust collar is in position against the snap-ring, slide the armature and clutch assembly into the drive housing so that at the same time, the shift lever engages with the clutch.

13 Position the field frame over the armature and apply sealing compound between the frame and the solenoid case.

14 Position the field frame against the drive housing taking care not to damage the brushes.

15 Lubricate the bushing in the commutator end-frame using silicone oil; place the leather brake washer on the armature shaft and then slide the commutator end-frame onto the shaft.

16 Reconnect the field coil connectors to the MOTOR terminal of the solenoid.

17 Now check the pinion clearance. To do this, connect a 6 volt battery between the solenoid S terminal and ground and at the same time fix a heavy connecting cable between the MOTOR terminal and ground (to prevent any possibility of the starter motor rotating). As the solenoid is energized it will push the pinion forward into its normal cranking position and retain it there. With the fingers, push the pinion away from the stop/retainer in order to eliminate any slack and then check the clearance between the face of the pinion and the face of stop/retainer using a feeler gauge. The clearance should be between 0.010 and 0.140 inch to ensure correct engagement of the pinion with the flywheel (or driveplate – automatic transmission) ring-gear. If the clearance is incorrect, the starter will have to be dismantled again and any worn or distorted components replaced, no adjustment being provided for.

23 Starter motor solenoid – removal, repair and installation

1   After removing the starter/solenoid unit as described in Section 20 disconnect the connector strap from the solenoid MOTOR terminal.

2   Remove the two screws which secure the solenoid housing to the end-frame assembly.

3   Twist the solenoid in a clockwise direction to disengage the flange

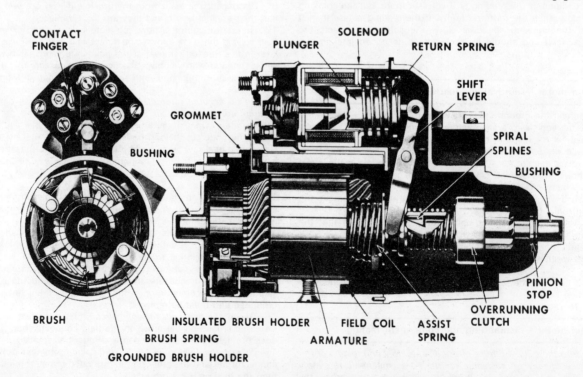

Fig. 5.16 Cutaway view of typical starter motor (Sec 21)

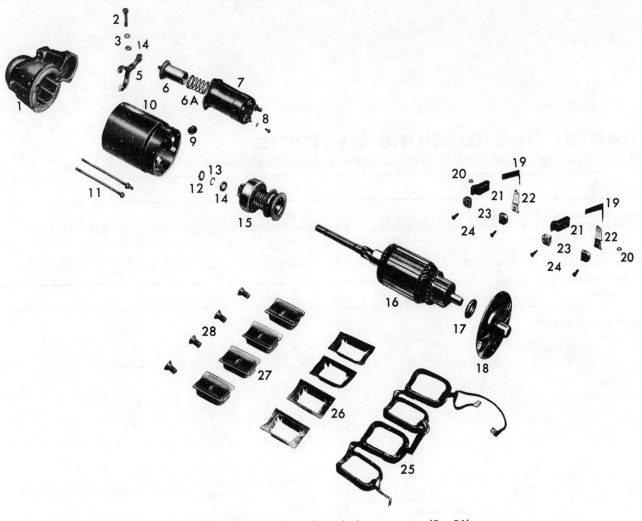

Fig. 5.17 Exploded view of a typical starter motor (Sec 21)

1 Drive housing	10 Field frame	20 Washer
2 Pivot bolt	11 Tie bolts	21 Brush holders
3 Washer and nut	12 Thrust collar	22 Grounded brush holders
4 Pin	13 Snap ring	23 Brushes
5 Shift lever	14 Retainer	24 Screws
6 Solenoid plunger	15 Clutch assembly	25 Field coils
6a Spring	16 Armature	26 Insulators
7 Solenoid body	17 Brake washer	27 Pole shoes
8 Screw and lockwasher	18 Commutator end frame	28 Screws
9 Grommet	19 Brush springs	

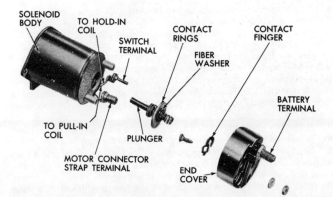

Fig. 5.18 Exploded view of starter motor solenoid (Sec 23)

key and then withdraw the solenoid.

4   Remove the nuts and washers from the solenoid terminals and then unscrew the two solenoid end-cover retaining screws and washers and pull off the end-cover.

5   Unscrew the nut washer from the battery terminal on the end-cover and remove the terminal.

6   Remove the resistor bypass terminal and contactor.

7   Remove the motor connector strap terminal and solder a new terminal in position.

8   Use a new battery terminal and install it to the end-cover. Install the bypass terminal and contactor.

9   Install the end-cover and the remaining terminal nuts.

10 Install the solenoid to the starter motor by first checking that the return spring is in position on the plunger and then insert the solenoid body into the drive housing and turn the body counterclockwise to engage the flange key.

11 Install the two solenoid securing screws and connect the MOTOR connector strap.

Chapter 6 Emissions Systems

Refer to Chapter 13 for specifications and information related to 1981 models

Contents

Specifications

Torque specifications	lb-ft	lb-in
Diverter valve to air pump		90
Air pump mounting bolts	20 to 35	
Air pump pulley bolts	24	
Exhaust manifold		
(inner bolts)	20	
(outer bolts)	30	
Actuator mounting bolts		25
Thermal vacuum switches	15	
Catalytic converter fill plug	28	

1 General description

1   Despite the general bad feelings towards emission controls, they play a necessary and integral role in the overall operation of the internal combustion engine. Your car is designed to operate with its pollution control systems, and disconnecting them or failing to properly maintain the components is illegal, not to mention being potentially harmful to the engine.

2   Through the years as smog standards have become more stringent, emission control systems have had to become more diverse and complex to keep pace. Where once the anti-pollution devices incorporated were installed as peripheral components to the main engine, later model engines work closely with, and in some cases are even controlled by, the emission control systems. Nearly every system in the make-up of a modern-day automobile is affected in some fashion by the emission systems.

3   This is not to say that the emission systems are particularly difficult for the home mechanic to maintain and service. You can perform general operational checks, and do most (if not all) of the regular maintenance easily and quickly at home with common tune-up and hand tools.

4   While the end result from the various emission systems is to reduce the output of pollutants into the air (namely hydrocarbons [HC] carbon Monoxide [CO], and oxides of Nitrogen [NOx]) the various systems function independently toward this goal. This is the way in which this chapter is divided.

2 Positive crankcase ventilation system (all 1970 – 1980)

General description

1   The positive crankcase ventilation, or PCV as it is more commonly calld, reduces hydrocarbon emissions by circulating fresh air through the crankcase to pick up blow-by gases which are then re-routed through the carburetor or intake manifold to be reburned by the engine.

2   The main components of this simple system are vacuum hoses and a PCV valve which regulates the flow of gases according to engine speed and manifold vacuum.

Positive crankcase ventilation system – checking

3   The PCV system can be checked for proper operation quickly and easily. This system should be checked regularly as carbon and gunk deposited by the blow-by gases will eventually clog the PCV valve and/or system hoses. When the flow of the PCV system is reduced or stopped, common symptoms are rough idling or a reduced engine speed at idle.

4   To check for proper vacuum in the system, remove the top plate of the air cleaner and locate the small PCV filter on the inside of the air cleaner housing.

5   Disconnect the hose leading to this filter. Be careful not to break the molded fitting on the filter

6   With the engine idling, place your thumb lightly over the end of the hose. Leave it there for about 30 seconds. You should feel a slight pull or vacuum (photo). The suction may be heard as your thumb is released. This will indicate that air is being drawn all the way through the system. If a vacuum is felt, the system is functioning properly. Check that the filter inside the air cleaner housing is not clogged or dirty. If in doubt, replace the filter with a new one, which is an inexpensive safeguard.

7   If there is very little vacuum, or none at all, at the end of the hose, the system is clogged and must be inspected further.

8   Shut off the engine and locate the PCV valve. Carefully pull it from its rubber grommet. Shake it and listen for a clicking sound. If the valve does not click freely , replace the valve with a new one.

9   Now start the engine and run it at idle speed with the PCV valve removed. Place your thumb over the end of the valve and feel for a suction (photo). This should be a relatively strong vacuum which will

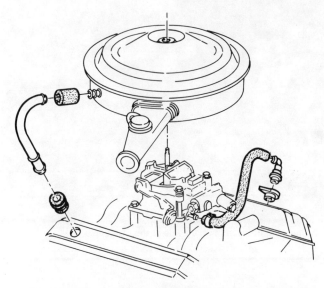

Fig. 6.1 Typical components of a Positive Crankcase Ventilation (PCV) system (Sec 2)

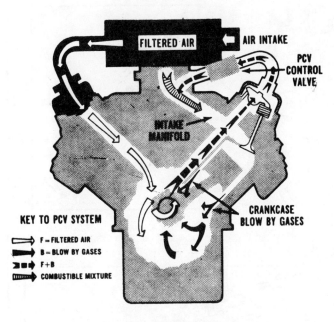

Fig. 6.2 PCV system operation (Sec 2)

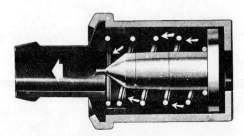

Fig. 6.3 Sectional view of a PCV valve (Sec 2)

be felt immediately.

10 If little or no vacuum is felt at the PCV valve, turn off the engine and disconnect the vacuum hose from the other end of the valve. Run the engine at idle speed and check for vacuum at the end of the hose just disconnected. No vacuum at this point indicates that the vacuum hose or inlet fitting at the engine is plugged. If it is the hose which is blocked, replace it with a new one or remove it from the engine and blow it out sufficiently with compressed air. A clogged passage at the carburetor or manifold requires that the component be removed and thoroughly cleaned of carbon build-up. A strong vacuum felt going into the PCV valve, but little or no vacuum coming out of the valve, indicates a failure of the PCV valve requiring replacement with a new one.

11 When purchasing a new PCV valve make sure it is the proper one. Each PCV valve is metered for specific engine sizes and model years. An incorrect PCV valve may pull too much or too little vacuum, possibly causing damage to the engine.

12 Information on removing and installing the PCV valve can be found in Chapter 1.

3 Air injection reactor system (all 1970 – 1980)

General description

1   The function of the air injection reactor system is to reduce hydrocarbons in the exhaust. This is done by pumping fresh air directly into the exhaust manifold ports of each engine cylinder. The fresh oxygen-rich air helps combust the unburned hydrocarbons before they are expelled as exhaust.

2   This system operates at all engine speeds and will bypass air only for a short time during deceleration and at high speeds. In these cases the additional fresh air added to the over-rich fuel/air mixture may cause backfiring or popping through the exhaust.

3   This system as it is used on GM engines consists of: the air injection pump (with supporting brackets and drivebelt) at the front of the engine, an air diverter valve attached to the pump housing, the manifold and injection tubes running into each port at the exhaust manifolds, and a check valve for each hose leading from the pump to the injection tubes on either side of the engine.

Air injection reactor system – checking

4   Properly installed and adjusted air injection systems are fairly reliable and seldom cause problems. However, a malfunctioning system can cause engine surge, backfiring and over-heated spark plugs. The air pump is the most critical component of this system and the belt at the front of the engine which drives the pump should be your first check. If the belt is cracked or frayed, replace it with a new one. Check the tension of the drivebelt by pressing it with your finger. There should be about $\frac{1}{2}$ inch of play in the belt when pushed half-way between the pulleys.

5   The adjusting or replacement procedures for the drivebelt depend on the mounting of the air pump. On some models, a single belt is used for both the air pump and the alternator. If this is the case, loosen the mounting bolt and the adjusting bolt for the alternator and then push against the alternator to tighten the belt. Hold in this position while the two bolts are tightened. The procedure is basically the same for air pumps which use their own belt, except it will be the air pump which will be loosened.

6   To check for proper air delivery from the pump, follow the hoses from the pump to where they meet the injection tube/manifold assembly on each side of the engine (photo). Loosen the clamps and disconnect the hoses.

7   Start the engine and with your fingers or a piece of paper, check that air is flowing out of these hoses (photo). Accelerate the engine and observe the air flow, which should increase in relation to engine speed. If this is the case, the pump is working satisfactorily. If air flow was not present, or did not increase, check for crimps in the hoses, proper drivebelt tension, and for a leaking diverter valve which can be heard with the pump operating.

8   To check the diverter valve, sometimes called the 'gulp' valve or anti-backfire valve, make sure all hoses are connected and start the engine. Locate the muffler on the valve which is a canister unit with holes in it (photo).

9   Being careful not to touch any of the moving engine components,

2.6 Checking for vacuum in the PCV hose where it connects to the air cleaner

2.9 Checking for vacuum in the line at the PCV valve

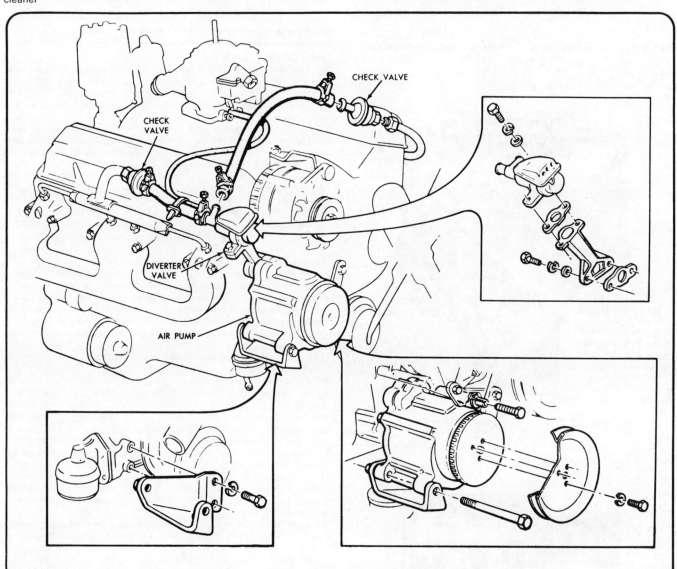

Fig. 6.4 Typical AIR injection Reactor (AIR) system (Sec 3)

3.6 One of the two check valves used in the AIR system for V8 engines

3.7 With the hose disconnected from the check valve, air should be felt with the engine running

3.8 The diverter valve with its by-pass muffler is mounted to the AIR pump at the front of the engine

3.10 A small diameter hose leads to the diverter valve. This is the vacuum signal hose to be disconnected during testing

3.17 Removing the AIR pump pulley

3.18A The pump is held to the engine by brackets and attaching bolts

3.18B Lifting the pump and diverter valve away from the engine

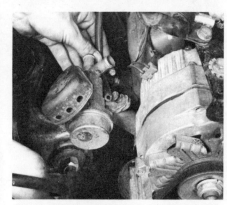

3.29 A slightly different type of diverter valve shown here with the air delivery hoses and vacuum hose disconnected

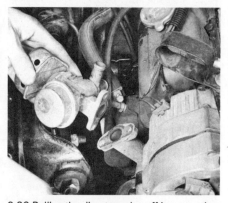

3.30 Pulling the diverter valve off its mounting base on the pump

3.36 The air delivery manifold has threaded fittings in the exhaust manifold. Shown is a flare nut wrench which wraps around the fitting to prevent rounding off the flats

3.38 An exhaust manifold, injection tubes fitted inside the ports and the air delivery manifold

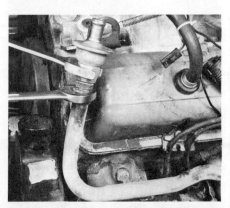

3.44 Two wrenches should be used to loosen the check valve from the manifold

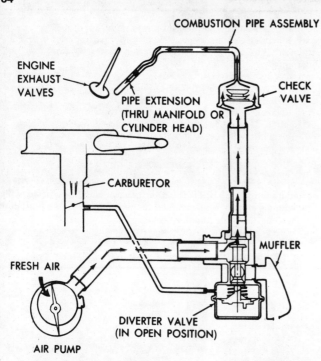

Fig. 6.5 AIR system operation during normal driving (Sec 3)

Fig. 6.6 AIR system operation during deceleration and high engine vacuum (Sec 3)

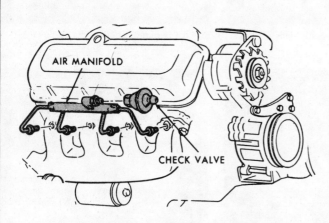

Fig. 6.7 Typical injection tube mounting (Sec 3)

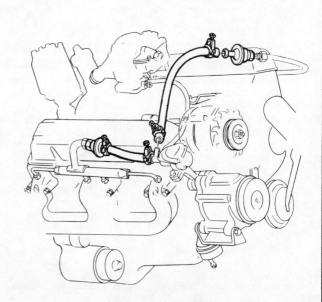

Fig. 6.8 AIR system hose routings (Sec 3)

4.17 The idle solenoid is located on the left side of the carburetor and has an electrical connector attached

4.18 The solenoid has a bolt at one end which contacts the throttle linkage. Adjusting this bolt changes the engine idle speed

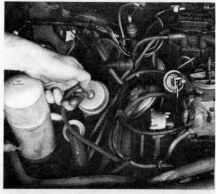

5.11 Checking for vacuum at the hose which leads to the actuator

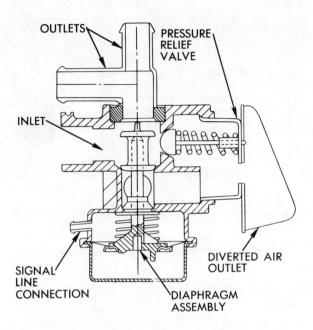

OUTLETS

PRESSURE
RELIEF
VALVE

INLET

SIGNAL
LINE
CONNECTION

DIAPHRAGM
ASSEMBLY

DIVERTED AIR
OUTLET

Fig. 6.9 Sectional view of the AIR diverter valve (Sec 3)

place your hand near the muffler outlet holes and check that no air is escaping with the engine at idle speed. Now have an assistant depress the accelerator pedal to accelerate the engine and then quickly let off the pedal. A momentary blast of air should be felt discharging through the diverter valve muffler.

10 If no air discharge was felt, disconnect the smaller vacuum hose at the diverter valve (photo). Place your finger over the end of the hose and again have your assistant depress the accelerator and let it off. As the engine is decelerating, a vacuum should be felt. If vacuum was felt, replace the diverter valve with a new one. If no vacuum was felt, the vacuum hose or engine vacuum source is plugged, requiring a thorough cleaning to eliminate the problem.

11 The check valves are located on the air manifold assembly and their function is to prevent exhaust gases from flowing back into the air pump. To find out if they are functioning properly, disconnect the two air supply hoses where they attach to the check valves. Start the engine, and being careful not to touch any moving engine components place your hand over the outlet of the check valve. The valve can be further checked by turning off the engine, allowing it to cool, and orally blowing through the check valve (toward the air manifold). Then attempt to suck back through it. If the valve is allowing you to suck back towards the air pump, it is bad and should be replaced.

12 Another check for this system is for leaks in the hose connection and/or hoses themselves. Leaks can often be detected by sound or feel with the pump in operation. If a leak is suspected, use a soapy water solution to verify this. Pour or sponge the solution of detergent and water on the hoses and connections. With the pump running, bubbles will form if a leak exists. The air delivery hoses are of a special design to withstand engine temperatures, so if they are replaced make sure the new hoses are of the proper standards.

Air pump – removal and installation

13 As mentioned earlier, some air pumps share a common drivebelt with the alternator where others use their own belt. This will affect the removal and installation procedure somewhat.

14 Disconnect the air delivery hoses at the air pump. Note the position of each hose for reassembly.

15 Disconnect the vacuum source hose at the diverter valve.

16 Compress the drivebelt to keep the air pump pulley from turning, and remove the bolts and washers securing the pulley to the pump.

17 To get some slack in the belt, loosen the alternator adjusting bolt and the pivot bolt. Push the alternator inward until the belt and air

pump pulley can be removed from the pump (photo).

18 Remove the bolts which secure the air pump to its brackets and then lift the pump and diverter valve assembly from the engine compartment (photos).

19 If the diverter valve is to be installed onto the new air pump, remove the bolts securing it to the pump and separate the two components.

20 Check the pump for evidence that exhaust gas has entered it, indicating a failure of one or both the check valves.

21 Install the diverter valve to the new air pump using a new gasket. Torque the attaching bolts to specifications.

22 Install the air pump to its engine mounting brackets with the attaching bolts loose. The exception to this is on models where the mounting bolts are inaccessible with the pulley installed. In this case, the pump mounting bolts should be fully tightened to specifications at this point.

23 Install the pump pulley with the bolts only hand tight.

24 Place the drive belt into position on the air pump pulley and adjust the belt by gently prying on the alternator until about $\frac{1}{2}$ inch of play is felt in the belt when pushed with your fingers half-way between the pulleys. Tighten the alternator bolts, keeping the belt tension at this point.

25 Keep the pump pulley from turning by compressing the drive belt and torque the pulley bolts to specifications.

26 Connect the hoses to the air pump and diverter valve. Make sure the connections are tight.

27 Tighten the mounting bolts for the pump to specifications.

28 Check the operation of the air pump as outlined previously.

Diverter valve – removal and installation

29 Disconnect the vacuum signal line and air delivery hoses at the diverter valve. Note the position of each for assembly (photo).

30 Remove the bolts which secure the valve to the air pump and remove the diverter valve from the engine compartment (photo).

31 When purchasing a new diverter valve, keep in mind that although many of the valves are similar in appearance, each is designed to meet particular requirements of various engines therefore be sure to install the correct valve.

32 Install the new diverter valve to the air pump or pump extension with a new gasket. Torque the securing bolts to specification.

33 Connect the air delivery and vacuum source hoses and check the operation of the valve as outlined previously.

Air manifold and injection tubes – removal and installation

34 Due to the high temperatures at this area, the connections at the exhaust manifold may be difficult to loosen. Commercial penetrating oil applied to the threads of the injection tubes may help in the removal procedure.

35 Disconnect the air delivery hoses at the manifold check valves.

36 Loosen the threaded connectors on the exhaust manifold at each exhaust port (photo). Slide the connectors upwards on the injection tubes so the threads are out of the exhaust manifold.

37 Pull the injection tube/air manifold assembly from the engine exhaust manifold and out of the engine compartment. Depending on the model year, injection tube extensions leading inside the engine may come out with the assembly.

38 On models where the extension tubes remain inside the exhaust manifold, they must be pressed out after the exhaust manifold is removed from the engine (photo).

39 If the exhaust manifold was removed from the engine to clean or replace the extensions, reinstall the manifold with extensions to the engine using a new gasket. Torque to the proper specifications.

40 Thread each of the injection tube connectors loosely into the exhaust manifold, using an anti-seize compound on the threads. After each of the connectors is sufficiently started, tighten each securely.

41 Connect the air supply hoses to the check valves.

42 Start the engine and check for leaks as previously described.

Check valve – removal and installation

43 Disconnect the air supply hose at the check valve.

44 Using two wrenches on the flats provided, remove the check valve from the air manifold assembly (photo). Be careful not to bend or twist the delicate manifold or injection tubes as this is done.

45 Installation is a reversal of the removal procedure.

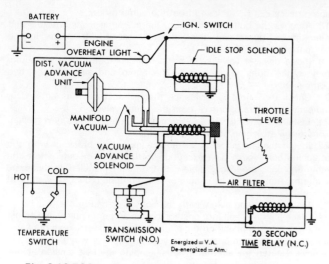

Fig. 6.10 TCS system operation with engine off (Sec 4)

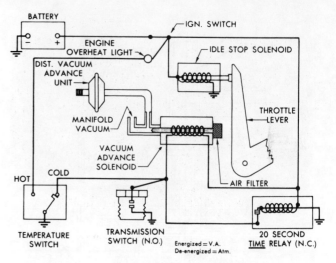

Fig. 6.11 TCS system operation with engine cold (Sec 4)

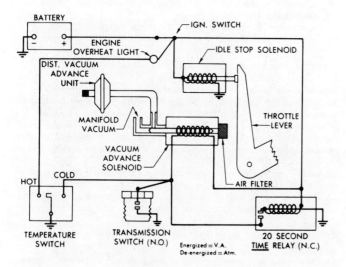

Fig. 6.12 TCS system operation with engine warm and transmission in low gear (Sec 4)

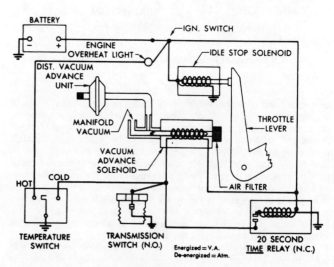

Fig. 6.13 TCS system operation with engine warm and transmission in high gear (Sec 4)

4   Transmission controlled spark system (some 1970 – 1974)

General description

1   This system is designed to eliminate the vacuum advance at the distributor under certain driving conditions. The system is incorporated on all Camaros 1970 – 1972, vehicles with manual transmissions, and the 307-cubic-inch engine with automatic transmission in 1973, and only vehicles with manual transmission in 1974. The transmission controlled spark (TCS) system used for 1971 models is also known as the combination emission control (CEC) system.

2   Vacuum for the advancing mechanism in the distributor is shut off until the transmission is in 'Hi' gear or 3rd and 4th gears with the 4-speed transmission. Vacuum is also allowed in 'Reverse' for the Turbo Hydramatic automatic transmissions.

3   This system is made up of: a transmission switch; engine coolant temperature switch; time delay relay; vacuum advance solenoid; and an idle stop solenoid. Although this system is somewhat more difficult to service, check and maintain than the other emissions systems, when each component is examined individually the operation of the TCS system can be easily understood.

Transmission switch

4   On manual transmissions, the electrical switch is actuated by the internal shifter shaft. The switch is located on the outside of the transmission case, adjacent to the shifter shaft.

5   Automatic transmissions use a pressure-sensitive switch which is actuated by the fluid pressure as the transmission reaches 'Hi' gear (and 'Reverse' in the case of the Turbo Hydramatics). This switch is located on the outside of the transmission on Powerglide and Turbo Hydramatic 350 transmissions. Turbo Hydramatic 400 transmissions have the switch mounted internally in the transmission.

6   When activated in the proper transmission gears, the switch sends an electrical input to the vacuum advance solenoid. This TCS component has remained basically unchanged through the four years in which it was used.

Temperature switch

7   The function of this switch is to sense the engine temperature and send a signal to the vacuum advance solenoid. It is the same switch which operates the dashboard-mounted warning light or water temperature gauge. The switch is located in the left cylinder head, between the number 1 and number 3 exhaust ports on small-block V8 engines, and between the number 3 and number 5 exhaust ports on Mark IV big-block engines.

8   The temperature switch monitors engine coolant temperatures and sends electrical current to the vacuum advance solenoid. On 1970 – 1972 vehicles, the temperature switch reacts with the vacuum advance solenoid to allow full vacuum advance whenever the engine

Fig. 6.14 Typical location of TCS transmission switch (Sec 4)

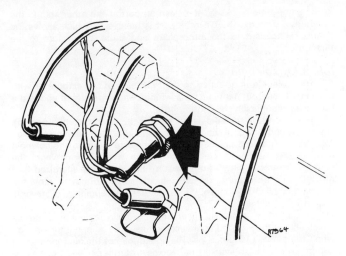

Fig. 6.15 Location of TCS coolant temperature switch in engine cylinder head (Sec 4)

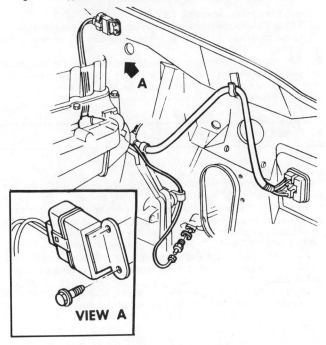

Fig. 6.16 Typical location of TCS time relay on engine compartment firewall (Sec 4)

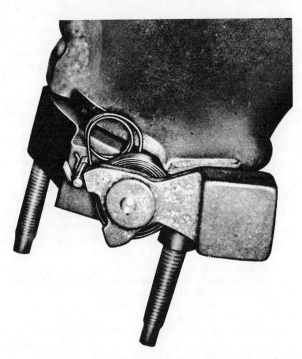

Fig. 6.17 Heat riser location at connection between the exhaust manifold and exhaust pipe (Sec 5)

temperature is below 82 degrees. For 1973 and 1974 this temperature was raised to 93 degrees. This means that regardless of the transmission gear or any other engine condition, the TCS system is not functional and should have no affect on engine operation until the engine has warmed up to these operating temperatures.

Time delay relay

9   This electrically-operated relay has undergone some changes in the various TCS systems. In each model year, however, its main function is to delay the operation of the vacuum advance solenoid.

10 In all years except 1972, the time delay relay will allow full distributor vacuum advance during the first 20 seconds of engine operation. This means that every time the ignition switch is turned on, no matter if the engine is warm or cold, the delay relay will render the TCS system inoperative for the first 20 seconds.

11 On 1972 models the delay relay performs a different function. The relay does not come into play until the transmission reaches 'Hi' gear as signalled by the transmission switch. When this happens, the time relay delays the operation of the vacuum advance solenoid for about 23 seconds. In other words, the engine distributor does not receive full vacuum until about 20 seconds after the transmission reaches 'Hi' gear.

12 It should also be noted that the 1972 delay relay automatically recycles whenever the transmission is taken out of 'Hi' gear, as in a downshift or when put into passing gear. Once the transmission is back into 'Hi', it will again take about 20 seconds to achieve full vacuum advance at the distributor.

13 The 1972 relay is located under the dashboard, on the center reinforcement brace. For the other years, the relay is mounted inside the engine compartment, on the firewall.

Vacuum advance solenoid

14 This is the heart of the TCS system, with its function being to supply or deny vacuum to the distributor.

15 This canister-shaped unit is located on the right side of the engine, attached to the intake manifold. It can be readily located by simply following the vacuum hose out of the distributor vacuum advance unit.

16 In the energized position, the plunger inside the solenoid opens the vacuum port from the carburetor to the vacuum advance unit, and

at the same time blocks off the clean air port at the other end. In the de-energized mode, the clean air port is uncovered which allows the distributor to vent to the atmosphere and shuts off vacuum to the distributor.

Idle stop solenoid

17 This solenoid is attached to the right side of the carburetor with brackets. It can be identified by a wiring connector at one end and a bolt-head plunger on the other (photo).

18 The idle stop solenoid is an electrically operated, two-position control. It is used to provide a predetermined throttle setting (photo).

19 In the energized position, the plunger extends from the solenoid body and contacts the carburetor throttle lever. This prevents the carburetor throttle plates from closing fully. When de-energized (key off), the solenoid plunger retracts into the solenoid body to allow the throttle plates to fully close, which 'starves' the engine and prevents run-on or 'dieseling'.

20 The 1971 system also incorporates a solid state timing device which allows the air conditioning compressor (if equipped) to come on when the ignition is turned off. The added load of the air conditioning compressor helps to shut off the engine to further prevent dieseling.

Transmission controlled spark – checking

21 This system is difficult to check due to the fact that the vehicle must be in full operation. This means that the checks must be made with the car travelling at speed.

22 If a problem in this system is suspected, first check that all electrical wires and connections are in good condition and intact. Also inspect the vacuum hoses at the vacuum advance solenoid and the distributor vacuum advance unit. A blown fuse in the fuse box can also cause problems in this system.

23 To ascertain if the TCS system is in fact malfunctioning, connect a vacuum gauge in the hose between the solenoid and the distributor. A length of vacuum hose must be used to enable you to route the gauge inside the passenger's compartment. Make sure the hose is not crimped and will not be damaged by moving or hot engine parts.

24 Drive the car and have an assistant watch the vacuum gauge. Make a log of vacuum gauge readings and transmission gears. If the system is functioning properly, the following conditions will be met:

  a) *When the engine is cold, vacuum will show on the gauge until the engine has warmed to operating temperature.*
  b) *Vacuum should be present on the gauge during the first 20 seconds after the engine is started, regardless of temperature.*
  c) *At normal operating temperature there should be vacuum showing on the gauge in 'Hi' gear only.*

25 The system should be tested with the engine cold, and also after it has reached normal operating temperature. Don't forget about the time delay function and how it relates to your particular vehicle.

26 The above test will tell you if the system as a whole is functioning properly. The following are test procedures for the individual TCS components if a fault is detected in the driving test.

Idle stop solenoid

27 Have an assistant turn the ignition switch on as you watch the idle stop solenoid plunger. With the key on, the plunger should extend against the throttle linkage. With the key off, the plunger should retract into the solenoid.

Transmission switch

28 With the engine warm and running, have an assistant put the transmission in a low forward gear (make sure the front wheels are blocked, parking brake is on and the assistant has the brake pedal depressed). There should be no vacuum going to the distributor. If there is vacuum going to the distributor, remove the transmission switch connection. Replace the transmission switch if the vacuum stops when the transmission switch connection was removed.

Temperature switch

29 When the engine is cold, there should be vacuum going to the distributor. If this is not the case, ground the wire from the cold terminal of the temperature switch. If the vacuum advance solenoid energizes, replace the temperature switch with a new one.

30 A failure of the temperature switch may also show up on the driving test with the engine at different operating temperatures, as

well as a malfunction of the temperature gauge or dash warning light.

Vacuum advance solenoid

31 Check the vacuum running into the solenoid from the intake manifold or carburetor. You should be able to feel this vacuum with the engine running.

32 Now reconnect the vacuum inlet hose and disconnect the vacuum hose leading to the distributor. Disconnect the electrical connectors at the solenoid and run a 12-volt jumper wire to the solenoid. The solenoid should be energized, allowing vacuum to reach the distributor.

Time delay relay (1972)

33 With the ignition on, check for 12 volts at the tan colored lead to the relay. Use a test light for this.

34 Install a 12-volt jumper wire to the terminal with the tan lead, and ground the terminal with the black lead. If, after 26 seconds, the advance solenoid does not energize (meaning vacuum to the distributor), replace the delay relay.

Time delay relay (except 1972)

35 Remove the temperature switch connector at the time delay relay.

36 Check to make sure the relay is cool, then turn the ignition to the on position.

37 The vacuum advance solenoid should energize for about 20 seconds and then de-energize. If it does not de-energize, remove the blue lead from the time relay. If this causes the solenoid to de-energize, the relay is bad.

---

5 Forced air pre-heat system (all 1970 – 1980)

General description

1 While coming under different names, the end result from this system is the same – to improve engine efficiency and reduce hydrocarbon emissions during the initial warm-up period of the car.

2 There are two different methods used to achieve this goal. First, a thermostatic air cleaner (Thermac) is used to draw warm air from the exhaust manifold directly into the carburetor. Second, some form of exhaust valve is incorporated inside the exhaust pipe to recirculate warm exhaust gases which are then used to pre-heat the carburetor and choke.

3 It is during the first few miles of driving (depending on outside temperature) when this system has its greatest effect on engine performance and emissions output. Once the engine has reached normal operating temperature, the flapper valves in the exhaust pipe and air cleaner open, allowing for normal engine operation.

4 Because of this cold-engine only function, it is important to periodically check this system to prevent poor engine performance when cold, or over-heating of the fuel mixture once the engine has reached operating temperatures. If either the exhaust heat valve or air cleaner valve sticks in the 'no heat' position, the engine will run poorly, stall and waste gas until it has warmed up on its own. A valve sticking in the 'heat' position causes the engine to run as if it is out of tune due to the constant flow of hot air to the carburetor.

5 The components which make up this system include: a heat valve inside the exhaust pipe on the right side of the engine (called a heat riser on 1970 – 1974 models), an actuator and thermal vacuum switch (on 1975 – 1980 models to control the heat valve) and a thermostatic air cleaner consisting of a temperature sensor, vacuum diaphragm and heat stove (all models 1970 – 1980). Initial checking procedures can be found in Chapter 1.

Forced air pre-heat system – checking

6 The conventional heat riser, installed on cars built up until 1975, should be checked often for free operation. Because of the high exhaust temperatures and its location which is open to the elements, corrosion frequently keeps the valve from operating freely, or even freezes it in position.

7 To check the heat riser operation, locate it on the exhaust manifold (it can be identified by an external weight and spring) and with the engine cold, try moving the counter-weight. The valve should move freely with no binding. Now have an assistant start the engine (still cold) while the counter-weight is observed. The valve should move to

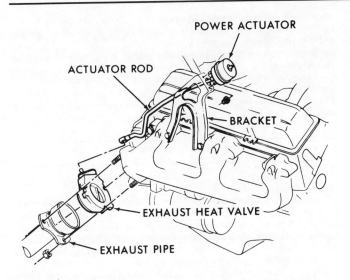

Fig. 6.18 Components and locations of EFE system (Sec 5)

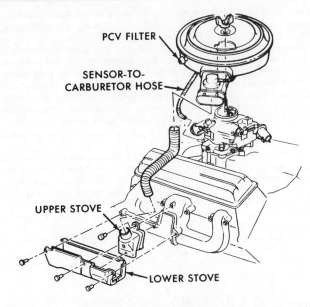

Fig. 6.19 Hoses and mountings of Thermac assembly (Sec 5)

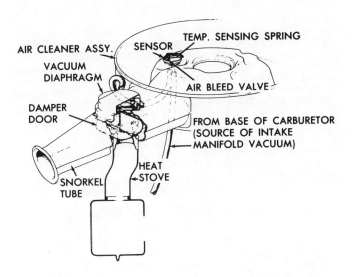

Fig. 6.20 Component of Thermac assembly (Sec 5)

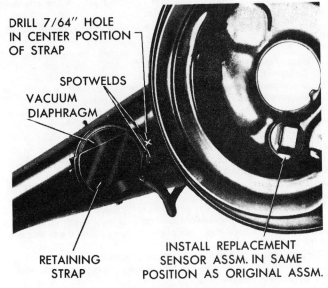

Fig. 6.21 Thermac vacuum diaphragm and sensor replacement (Sec 5)

the closed position and then slowly open as the engine warms.

8 A stuck or binding heat riser valve often can be loosened by soaking the valve shaft with solvent as the counter-weight is moved back and forth. Light taps with a hammer may be necessary to free a tightly stuck valve. If this proves unsuccessful the heat riser must be replaced with a new one after disconnecting it from the exhaust pipe.

9 In 1975, Chevrolet introduced a replacement for the heat riser which they called the Early Fuel Evaporation System. This system provides the same function, but uses manifold vacuum to open and close the heat valve.

10 To check this system, locate the actuator and rod assembly which is on a bracket attached to the right exhaust manifold. With the engine cold, have an assistant start the engine. Observe the movement of the actuator rod which leads to the heat valve inside the exhaust pipe. It should immediately operate the valve to the closed position. If this is the case, the system is operating corrrectly.

11 If the actuator rod did not move, disconnect the vacuum hose at the actuator and place your thumb over the open end (photo). With the engine cold and at idle, you should feel a suction indicating proper vacuum. If there is vacuum at this point, replace the actuator with a new one.

12 If there is no vacuum in the line, this is an indication that either the hose is crimped or plugged, or the thermal vacuum switch threaded into the water outlet is not functioning properly. Replace the hose or switch as necessary.

13 To make sure the Early Fuel Evaporation System is disengaging once the engine has warmed, continue to observe the actuating rod as the engine reaches normal operating temperature (approximately 180 degrees depending on engine size). The rod should again move, indicating the valve is in the open position.

14 If after the engine has warmed, the valve does not open, pull the vacuum hose at the actuator and check for vacuum with your thumb. If there is no vacuum, replace the actuator. If there is vacuum, replace the TVS switch on the water outlet housing.

Thermac assembly – checking

15 The thermostatic air cleaner components can be quickly and easily checked for proper operation. Routine checking procedures and illustrations can be found in Chapter 1.

16 With the engine off, observe the damper door inside the air cleaner snorkel. If this is difficult because of positioning, use a mirror. The

valve should be open, meaning that in this position all air would flow through the snorkel and none through the exhaust manifold hot-air duct at the underside of the air cleaner housing.

17 Now have an assistant start the engine and continue to observe the flapper door inside the snorkel. With the engine cold and at idle the damper door should close off all air from the snorkel allowing heated air from the exhaust manifold to enter the air cleaner as intake. As the engine warms to operating temperature the damper door should move, allowing outside air through the snorkel to be included in the mixture. Eventually, the door should recede to the point where most of the incoming air is through the snorkel and not the exhaust manifold passage.

18 If the damper door did not close off snorkel air when the cold engine was first started, disconnect the vacuum hose at the snorkel vacuum motor and place your thumb over the hose end, checking for vacuum. If there is vacuum going to the motor, check that the damper door and link are not frozen or binding within the air cleaner snorkel. Replace the vacuum motor if the hose routing is correct and the damper door moves freely.

19 If there was no vacuum going to the motor in the above test, check the hoses for cracks, crimps or disconnections. If the hoses are clear and in good condition, replace the temperature sensor inside the air cleaner housing.

Actuator and rod assembly – replacement

20 Disconnect the vacuum hose from the actuator.
21 Remove the two nuts which attach the actuator to the bracket.
22 Disconnect the rod from the heat valve and remove the actuator and rod from the engine compartment.
23 Install the actuator and rod in the reverse order, tightening the attaching nuts to specifications.

Exhaust heat valve – replacement

24 Remove the crossover exhaust pipe.
25 Disconnect the actuating rod from the heat valve.
26 Remove the valve from inside the exhaust pipe.
27 Installation is a reversal of removal; however, make sure all attaching fasteners are tightened to proper specifications.

Thermal vacuum switch (TVS) – replacement

28 Drain the engine coolant until the fluid level is below the engine water outlet (thermostat) housing.
29 Disconnect the hoses from the TVS switch making note of their positions for reassembly.
30 Using a suitable wrench, remove the TVS switch.
31 Apply a soft setting sealant uniformly to the threads of the new TVS switch. Be careful that none of the sealant gets on the sensor end of the switch.
32 Install the switch and tighten to specifications.
33 Connect the vacuum hoses to the switch in their original positions and add coolant as necessary.

Air cleaner vacuum motor – replacement

34 Remove the air cleaner assembly from the engine and disconnect the vacuum hose from the motor.
35 Drill out the two spot welds which secure the vacuum motor retaining strap to the snorkel tube.
36 Remove the motor attaching strap.
37 Lift up the motor, cocking it to one side to unhook the motor linkage at the control damper assembly.
38 To install, drill a 7/64 inch hole in the snorkel tube at the center of the retaining strap.
39 Insert the vacuum motor linkage into the control damper assembly.
40 Using the sheet metal screw supplied with the motor service kit, attach the motor and retaining strap to the snorkel. Make sure the sheet metal screw does not interfere with the operation of the damper door.
41 Connect the vacuum hose to the motor and install the air cleaner assembly.

Air cleaner temperature sensor – replacement

42 Remove the air cleaner from the engine and disconnect the vacuum hoses at the sensor.
43 Carefully note the position of the sensor. The new sensor must be

installed in exactly the same position.
44 Pry up the tabs on the sensor retaining clip and remove the sensor and clip from the air cleaner.
45 Install the new sensor with a new gasket in the same position as the old one.
46 Press the retaining clip on the sensor. Do not damage the control mechanism in the center of the sensor.
47 Connect the vacuum hoses and install the air cleaner to the engine.

6   Fuel evaporative system (all 1970 – 1980)

General description

1   Although the evaporative control system is one of the most complex looking, it is in actuality one of the most basic and trouble-free portions of the emissions network. Its function is to reduce hydrocarbon emissions. Basically, this is a closed fuel system which reroutes wasted fuel back to the gas tank and stores fuel vapors instead of venting them to the atmosphere.
2   Due to its very nature of having few moving parts, the evaporative control system requires no periodic maintenance except for a replacement of the oiled fiberglass filter in the bottom of the charcoal canister at the recommended intervals.
3   A tip-off that this system is not operating properly is the strong smell of fuel vapors or if the engine starves from lack of fuel during acceleration.
4   A pressure vacuum gasoline filler cap must be used, as a standard cap may render the system ineffective and could possibly collapse the fuel tank. Other components which make up this system include: a special gas tank with fill limiters and vent connections, a charcoal canister with integral purge valve and filter which stores vapor from the fuel tank to be burned by the carburetor, a carburetor bowl vent valve and various hoses linking the main components.

Fuel evaporative system – checking

5   As mentioned earlier, this system requires little maintenance, however, if a problem is suspected the system should be inspected.
6   With the engine cold and at room temperature, disconnect the fuel tank line at the charcoal canister. On all models the canister is located inside the engine compartment behind the left headlight. Each of the

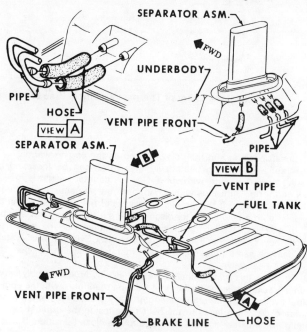

Fig. 6.22 Fuel tank components and connections of fuel evaporative system (Sec 6)

hose connections are duly labeled.

7   As this hose is disconnected, check for the presence of liquid fuel in the line. Fuel in this vapor hose is an indication that the vent controls or pressure-vacuum relief valve in the gas cap are not functioning properly.

8   Hook up a pressure suction device on the end of the fuel vapor line. Apply 15 psi pressure to the line and observe for excessive loss of pressure.

9   Check for a fuel vapor smell in the engine compartment and around the gas tank.

10 Remove the fuel filler cap and check for pressure in the gas tank.

11 If there is a large loss of pressure or a fuel odor, inspect all lines for leaks or deterioration.

12 With the fuel filler cap removed, apply pressure again and check for obstructions in the vent line.

13 To check the purge valve built into the canister, start the engine and disconnect the vacuum signal line running from the engine to the canister. With your thumb over the end of the hose, raise the engine speed to about 1500 rpm and check for vacuum. If there is no vacuum signal, check the EGR operation as described in this chapter. The vacuum signal for the canister and the EGR valve originate from the same source.

14 The purge line to the charcoal canister functions with the PCV vacuum source, so if there is no vacuum when this hose is disconnected from the canister check the PCV valve vacuum.

Charcoal canister and filter – replacement

15 Chapter 1 contains all information concerning the servicing of the fuel evaporation system, in particular the replacement of the canister filter.

7   Exhaust gas recirculation (EGR) system (all 1973 – 1980)

General description

1   This system is used to reduce oxides of nitrogen (NOx) emitted from the exhaust. Formation of these pollutants takes place at very high temperatures; consequently, it occurs during the peak temperature period of the combustion process. To reduce peak temperatures, and thus the formation of NOx, a small amount of exhaust gas is taken from the exhaust system and recirculated in the combustion cycle.

2   To tap this exhaust supply without an extensive array or pipes and connections in the exhaust system, additional exhaust pasages are cast into the intricate runner system of the intake manifold. Because of this arrangement, most of the EGR routing components are hidden from view under the manifold.

3   Very little maintenance other than occasionally inspecting the vacuum hoses and the EGR valve is required. Besides the heart of the system – the EGR valve – the only moving part which can wear out is a thermal vacuum switch (TVS) which controls the vacuum signal to the EGR valve at varying engine temperatures.

4   The EGR system does not recirculate gases when the engine is at idle or during deceleration. The system is also regulated by the thermal vacuum switch which does not allow the system to operate until the engine has reached normal operating temperature.

5   Common engine problems associated with the EGR system are: rough idling or stalling when at idle, rough engine performance upon light throttle application and stalling on deceleration.

Exhaust gas recirculation system – checking

6   Locate the EGR valve located on the right side of the intake manifold, adjacent to the carburetor (photo). Initial checking with illustrations can be found in Chapter 1.

7   Place your finger under the EGR valve and push upwards on the diaphragm plate. The diaphragm should move freely from the open to the closed position. If it doesn't, replace the EGR valve.

8   Now start the engine and run at idle speed. With your finger, manually depress the EGR diaphragm. If the valve or adjacent accessories are hot, wear gloves to prevent burning your fingers. When the diaphragm is pressed (valve closed to recirculate exhaust), the engine should lose speed, stumble or even stall. If the engine did not change speed, the EGR passages should be checked for blockage. This will require that the intake manifold be removed (see Chapter 2 for engine strip-down).

9   Now allow the engine to reach normal operating temperature. Have an assistant depress the accelerator slightly and hold the engine speed constant above idle.

10 Pull off the vacuum signal line at the EGR valve and check for the diaphragm plate to move downward, accompanied by an increase in engine speed.

11 Reinstall the vacuum line to the valve and the diaphragm plate should move upward with a decrease in engine speed.

12 If the diaphragm did not move, make sure the engine was at operating temperature. Repeat the test if in doubt.

13 Your next check would be that vacuum is reaching the EGR valve. Pull off the vacuum hose at the valve and with the engine running and accelerator slightly pressed, check for vacuum at the end of the hose with your thumb (photo). If there is vacuum, replace the EGR valve with a new one. If there is no vacuum signal, follow the vacuum hose to its source, inspecting for disconnections, cracks, breaks or blockage in the lines.

14 On all model years except 1973, the EGR system uses a thermal vacuum switch to regulate EGR valve operation in relation to engine temperature. 1973 vehicles have the vacuum source routed directly to the carburetor.

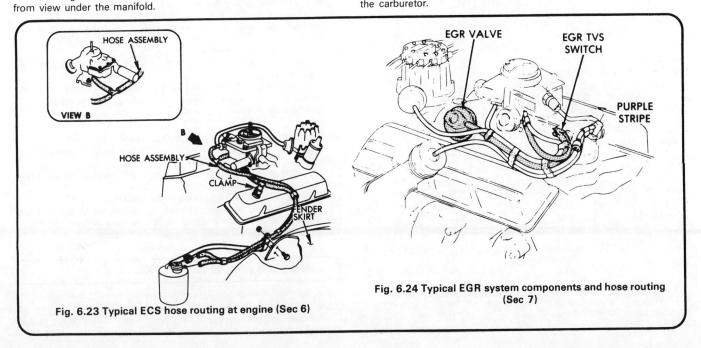

Fig. 6.23 Typical ECS hose routing at engine (Sec 6)

Fig. 6.24 Typical EGR system components and hose routing (Sec 7)

7.6 The EGR valve is a disc-shaped diaphragm bolted to the intake manifold, adjacent to the carburetor

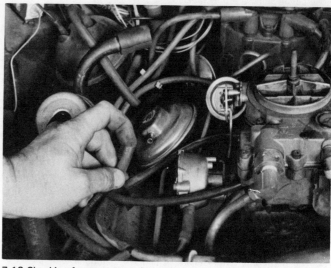

7.13 Checking for vacuum at the end of the hose which attaches to the EGR valve

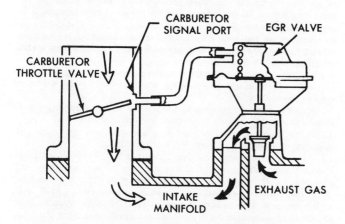

Fig. 6.25 Operation of EGR system (Sec 7)

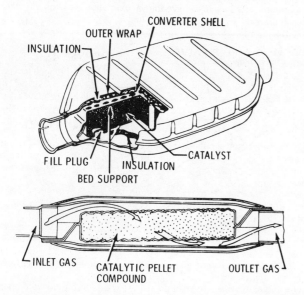

Fig. 6.26 Sectional view of an underfloor converter (Sec 8)

15 This vacuum switch opens as the coolant temperature increases, allowing vacuum to reach the EGR valve. The exact temperature varies from year to year, but is indicative of the normal operating temperature of the particular engine.

16 The best way to test the switch is with a vacuum gauge, checking the vacuum signal with the engine hot.

17 Disconnect the vacuum hose at the EGR valve, connect the vacuum gauge to the disconnected end of the hose and start the engine. Note the reading on the vacuum gauge with the engine at an idle and then have an assistant depress the accelerator slightly and note this reading. As the accelerator is depressed, the vacuum reading should increase.

18 If the gauge does not respond to the throttle opening, disconnect the hose which leads from the carburetor to the thermal vacuum switch. Repeat the test with the vacuum gauge installed in the vacuum hose end at the switch. If the vacuum gauge responds to accelerator opening, the thermal vacuum switch is defective and should be replaced with a new one.

19 If the gauge still does not respond to an increase in throttle opening, check for a plugged hose or defective carburetor.

EGR valve – replacement

20 Disconnect the vacuum hose at the EGR valve.

21 Remove the nuts or bolts which secure the valve to the intake manifold.

22 Lift the EGR valve from the engine.

23 Clean the mounting surfaces of the EGR valve. Remove all traces of gasket material.

24 Place the new EGR valve, with new gasket, on the intake manifold. Install the spacer, if used. Tighten the attaching bolts or nuts.

25 Connect the vacuum signal hose.

Thermal vacuum switch – replacement

26 Drain the engine coolant until the coolant level is beneath the switch.

27 Disconnect the vacuum hoses from the switch, noting their positions for reassembly.

28 Using a suitable wrench, remove the switch.

29 When installing the switch, apply thread sealer to the threads being careful not to allow the sealant to touch the bottom sensor.

30 Install the switch and tighten it to specifications.

8 Catalytic converter (all 1975 – 1980)

General description

1 The catalytic converter is an emission control device added to the exhaust system to reduce hydrocarbon and carbon monoxide pol-

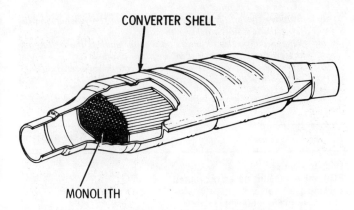

Fig. 6.27 Sectional view of a monolith catalytic converter (Sec 8)

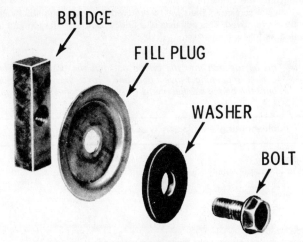

Fig. 6.29 Fill plug components of bead-type catalytic converter (Sec 8)

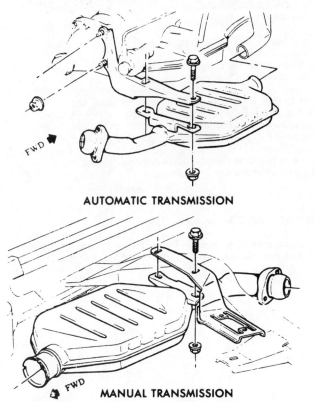

Fig. 6.28 Typical installation of a catalytic converter (Sec 8)

lutants. This converter contains beads which are coated with a catalytic substance containing platinum and palladium.

2   It is imperative that only unleaded gasoline be used in a vehicle equipped with a catalytic converter. Unleaded fuel reduces combustion chamber deposits, corrosion and prevents lead contamination of the catalyst.

3   Periodic maintenance of the catalytic converter is not required; however, if the car is raised for other service it is advisable to inspect the overall condition of the catalytic converter and related exhaust components.

4   If the catalytic converter has been proven by an official inspection station to be ineffective, the converter can be replaced with a new one or the coated beads drained and replaced. Physical damage or the use of leaded fuels are the main causes of a malfunctioning catalytic converter.

5   It should be noted that the catalytic converter can reach very high temperatures in operation. Because of this, any work performed to the converter or in the general area where it is located should be done only after the system has sufficiently cooled. Also, caution should be exercised when lifting the vehicle with a hoist as the converter can be damaged if the lifting pads are not properly positioned.

6   There are no functional tests which the home mechanic can make to determine if the catalytic converter is performing its task.

Catalytic converter – replacement

7   While the removal of the catalytic converter will be a rare occurrence, it can be successfully separated from the exhaust system for replacement.

8   Raise the car and support firmly with jack stands. The converter and exhaust system should be cool before proceeding.

9   Disconnect the converter at the front and rear. On most models a flange is used with four bolts and nuts to secure the converter to its mating exhaust pipes. If the fasteners are frozen in place due to the high temperatures and corrosion, apply a penetrating oil liberally and allow to soak in. As a last resort, the fasteners will have to be carefully cut off with a hacksaw.

10   Gently separate the inlet and outlet converter flanges from the exhaust pipes and remove the converter from under the vehicle.

11   Installation is a reversal of the removal process; however, always use new nuts and bolts.

Catalyst – replacement

12   There are two types of catalytic converters now being used on vehicles. The monolith converter has coated rods which cannot be serviced. If failure occurs, the entire converter must be replaced with a new one. The catalyst in bead type converters can be changed by draining and filling the beads through a plug at the bottom of the converter.

13   With specialized equipment, the beads can be replaced with the converter still positioned under the car. This is definitely a job for a dealer who has the equipment and training necessary to perform this operation.

14   Bead replacement is more easily done with the converter removed from the car. Follow the sequence outlined in the preceding paragraphs to do this.

15   With the converter on a suitable work bench, remove the pressed fill plug. This is done by driving a small chisel between the converter shell and the fill plug lip. Deform the lip until pliers can be used to remove the plug. Be careful not to damage the converter shell surface where the plug seals.

16   Once the plug is removed, drain the beads into a suitable container for disposal. Shake the converter vigorously to remove all beads.

17   To fill the catalytic converter with new beads, raise the front of the converter to approximately 45 degrees and pour the beads through the fill hole. Tapping lightly on the converter belt with a hammer as the beads are poured in will help to settle them. Continue tapping and

pouring until the converter is full.

18 A special service fill plug will be required to replace the stock one which was removed. This consists of a bridge, bolt and fill plug and is installed as follows:

a) *Install the bolt into the bridge and put the bridge into the converter opening. Move it back and forth to loosen the beads until the bridge sits flat on the inside of the converter, straight across the opening (bolt centered).*

b) *Remove the bolt from the bridge and put the washer and fill plug, dished side out, over the bolt.*

c) *While holding the fill plug and washer against the bolt head, thread the bolt 4 or 5 turns into the bridge.*

d) *After fill plug has seated against the converter housing, tighten the bolt to 28 ft lbs.*

19 Install the converter, start the engine and check for leaks.

9 Troubleshooting – emission systems

Condition	Possible cause
Engine idles abnormally rough and/or stalls	EGR valve vacuum hoses misrouted Leaking EGR valve EFE valve malfunctioning PCV system clogged or hoses misrouted TCS system malfunctioning
Engine runs rough on light throttle acceleration	Malfunctioning EGR valve EFE valve malfunctioning TCS system malfunctioning
Engine stalls and/or backfires during deceleration	Restriction in EGR vacuum hoses Sticking EGR valve Malfunctioning AIR diverter valve Malfunctioning TCS system
Engine detonation	EGR control valve blocked or air flow restricted Binding EFE (heat riser) valve Malfunctioning or restricted operation of Thermac air cleaner Clogged PCV valve and/or hoses
Engine dieseling on shut-off	TCS idle stop solenoid improperly adjusted Thermac valve sticking
Excessive engine oil consumption	Clogged PCV valve and or hoses
Poor high gear performance	Malfunctioning TCS switch
Fuel odor	Evaporative emission system hoses clogged; hoses disconnected or cracked; charcoal canister filter in need of replacement

Chapter 7 Part A Manual Transmission

Contents

Specifications

Transmission type	3 or 4 forward speeds (all synchromesh) and reverse. Floor or steering column shift.

Application

1970 – 1980 3 speed	Saginaw
1970 – 1973 4-speed	Saginaw, Muncie
1974	Saginaw, Muncie, Warner
1975 4-speed	Warner
1976 4-speed	Saginaw
1977 – 1980 4-speed	Saginaw, Warner

Oil capacity

3 speed units	2.0 US pts
4 speed units	3.0 US pts

Torque specifications

lb-ft

Three-speed Saginaw

Clutch gear retainer to case bolts	15
Side cover to case bolts	15
Extension to case bolts	45
Shift lever to shifter shaft bolts	25
Lubrication filler plug	18
Transmission case to clutch housing bolts	75
Crossmember to frame nuts	25
Crossmember to mount bolts	40
Mount to transmission bolts	32

Four-speed Saginaw

Clutch gear retainer to case bolts	15
Side cover to case bolts	15
Extension to case bolts	45
Shift lever to shifter shaft bolts	25
Lubrication filler plug	18
Transmission case to clutch housing bolts	75
Crossmember to frame nuts	25
Crossmember to mount and mount to extension bolts	40
Mount to transmission bolts	32

Four-speed Muncie

Clutch gear bearing retainer to case bolts	25
Cover to case bolts	20
Extension and retainer to case bolts	
(Upper)	20
(Lower)	30

	lb-ft
Lubrication filler plug	30
Shift lever to shifter shaft nut	20
Mount to transmission bolts	32

Four-speed Warner

Clutch gear retainer to case bolts	18
Side cover to case bolts	18
Extension to case bolts	40
Shift lever to shifter shaft bolts	20
Lubrication filler plug	15
Transmission case to clutch housing bolts	52
Crossmember to mount and mount to extension bolts	25
Rear bearing retainer to case bolts	25
Extension to rear bearing retainer bolts (short)	25
Retainer to case bolt	35
Transmission drain plug	20

1 General description

1 Manual transmissions have been available for the Camaro since its inception. The only exception to this is for cars built for California during the later years where the automatic is required.
2 Manual transmissions may be of the three or four-speed type manufactured by Muncie, Saginaw or Warner. Gearshift is by column or floor-mounted lever according to model.
3 The forward speeds on all versions are of the synchromesh type.
4 No provision is made for periodic oil changing but the oil level should be checked at the specified intervals and topped up as necessary.

2 Shift linkage – adjustment

Column shift

1 Place the shift lever in 'Reverse' and the ignition switch in the 'Lock' position.
2 Raise the vehicle for access beneath, then loosen the shift control swivel locknuts. Pull down slightly on the 1st/Reverse control rod attached to the column lever to remove any slackness, then tighten the locknut at the transmission lever.
3 Unlock the ignition switch and shift the column lever to Neutral. Position the column lower levers in the 'Neutral' position, align the gauge holes in the levers and insert a $\frac{3}{16}$ inch diameter gauge pin.
4 Support the rod and swivel to prevent movement, then tighten the 2nd/3rd shift control rod locknut.
5 Remove the alignment tool from the column lower levers and check the operation. Place the column shift lever in 'Reverse' and check the interlock control. It must not be possible to obtain 'Lock' except in 'Reverse'.
6 Lower the vehicle to the ground.

Floor shift

7 Switch the ignition to 'Off' then raise the vehicle for access beneath.
8 Loosen the swivel locknuts on the shift rods. Check that the rods pass freely through the swivels.
9 Set the shift levers to 'Neutral' at the transmission.
10 Move the shift control lever into the 'Neutral' detent position, align the control assembly levers, and insert the locating gauge into the lever alignment slot.
11 Tighten the shift rod swivel locknuts then remove the gauge.
12 Shift the transmission control lever into 'Reverse' and place the ignition switch in the 'Lock' position. Loosen the locknut at the back drive control rod swivel, then pull the rod down slightly to remove any slack in the column mechanism. Tighten the clevis jam nut.
13 Check the interlock control; the key should move freely to, and from, the 'Lock' position when the adjustment is correct. 14 Check the transmission shift control and readjust if necessary.
15 Lower the vehicle to the ground.

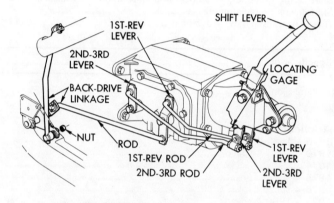

Fig. 7.1 3-speed floorshift linkage (Sec 2)

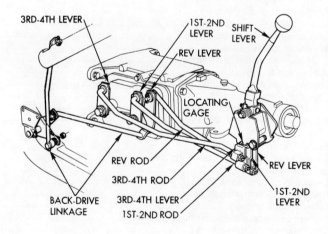

Fig. 7.2 4-speed floorshift linkage (Sec 2)

3 Transmission mounts – checking

1   Raise the car for access beneath and support firmly with stands. Make sure the vehicle is secured, as you must jostle the vehicle somewhat to check the mounts.
2   Push upward and pull downward on the transmission extension housing and observe the transmission mount.
3   If the extension can be pushed upwards but cannot be pulled down, this is an indication that the rubber is worn and the mount is bottomed out.
4   If the rubber portion of the mount separates from the metal plate, this also means that the mount should be changed.
5   Check that all of the attaching screws or nuts are tight on the crossmember and the transmission.

4 Floorshift transmission backdrive linkage – adjustment

1   Shift the transmission into 'Reverse' and turn the ignition switch to the 'Lock' position.
2   Raise the vehicle for access beneath.
3   Loosen the backdrive control rod swivel locknut, pull down on the column linkage to remove any slackness, then tighten the clevis jam nut.
4   Check that the ignition key moves freely through the 'Lock' position; readjust if necessary at the bellcrank.

5   Lower the vehicle to the ground.

5 Shift control assembly – removal and installation

Column shift models
1   Refer to Chapter 11 in conjunction with steering column dismantling.

Floor shift (3 and 4-speed)
2   With the shift lever in the Neutral position, remove the shift lever knob and center console trim plate.
3   Raise the vehicle and support firmly on stands.
4   Disconnect the shift rods from the shift control levers. They are secured with retaining clips. Mark each rod and its appropriate lever for easy reinstallation, and take care not to lose any special washers used.
5   Remove the bolts which secure the shift control unit to its support assembly.
6   Rotate the control assembly and pull it down past the crossmember and remove it from under the vehicle.
7   To reinstall, slide the control assembly up into the rubber boot and position it against the support. Install the retaining bolts.
8   Place the control levers in the Neutral position and insert a $\frac{1}{4}$-inch gauge pin (see Section 2, 'Shift linkage – adjustment').
9   Connect the shift rods to the control levers and install the appropriate washers and retaining pins.

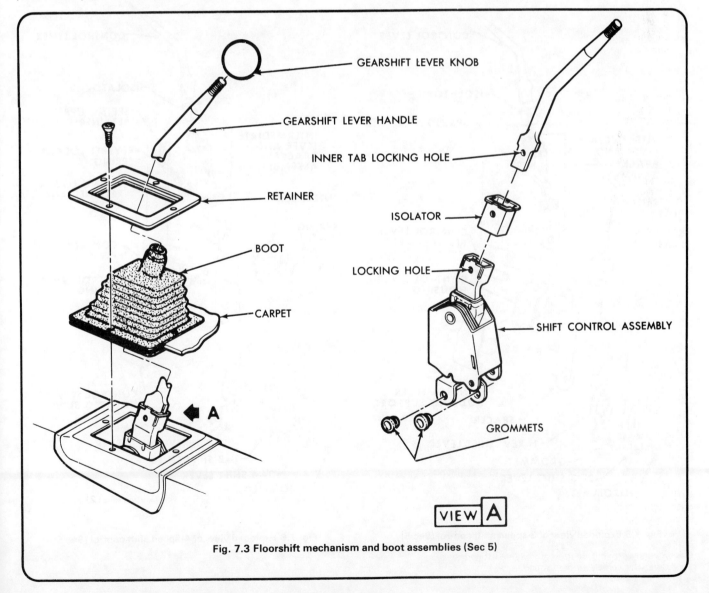

Fig. 7.3 Floorshift mechanism and boot assemblies (Sec 5)

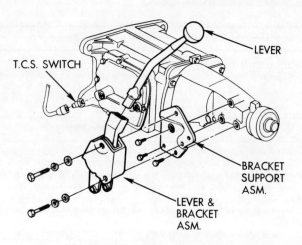

Fig. 7.4 Floorshift lever and bracket attachment (Sec 5)

10 Lower the vehicle and check for proper operation. Make the necessary adjustment referring to the proper sections in this chapter.

6 Transmission oil seals – replacement

1 The following oil seals can be replaced without removing the transmission from the car.

Speedometer gear seal

2 Raise the vehicle for access beneath. Set firmly on stands.
3 Disconnect the speedometer cable, remove the lockplate to extension bolt and lockwasher, then remove the lockplate.
4 Insert a screwdriver in the lockplate fitting, and pry the fitting gear and shaft from the extension.
5 Pry out the O-ring.
6 Installation is the reverse of removal, but lubricate the new seal with transmission lubricant and hold the assembly so that the slot in the fitting is towards the lockplate boss on the extension.

Extension oil seal

7 Remove the drive shaft, as described in Chapter 8. Remove any ancillary items necessary to provide additional clearance.

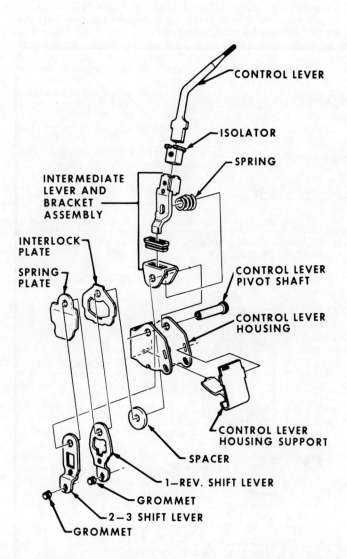

Fig. 7.5 Exploded view of 3-speed shift control (Sec 5)

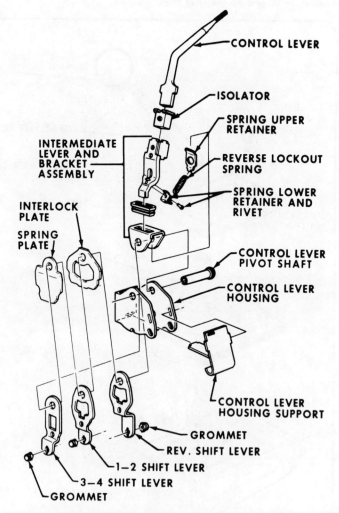

Fig. 7.6 Exploded view of 4-speed shift control (Sec 5)

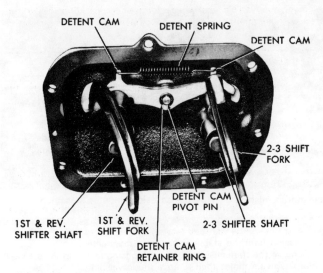

Fig. 7.7 3-speed Saginaw transmission side cover (Sec 7)

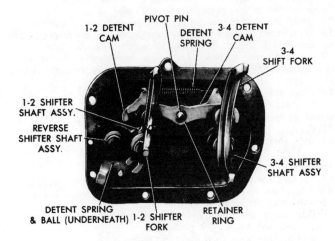

Fig. 7.8 4-speed Saginaw transmission side cover (Sec 8)

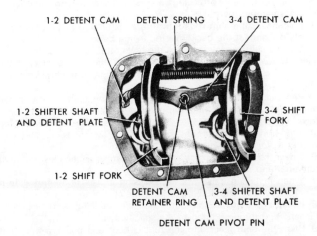

Fig. 7.9 4-speed Muncie transmission side cover (Sec 8)

8   Carefully pry out the old seal.
9   Carefully clean the counterbore and examine for any damage.
10 Pre-lubricate between the lips of the new seal with transmission lubricant and coat the outer diameter with a suitable sealant.
11 Carefully install the seal, lips inwards, until the flange seats, ideally a tubular spacer should be used for this job (photo).
12 Reinstall the drive shaft (refer to Chapter 8) and any other ancillary items removed.

7   Transmission side cover (3 speed Saginaw) – overhaul

1   Shift transmission into 'Neutral' and raise the vehicle for access beneath. Set firmly on stands.
2   Disconnect the control rods from the levers on the side of the transmission.
3   Remove the cover assembly from the transmission case and allow the oil to drain.
4   Remove both shift forks from the shifter shaft assemblies and both shifter shaft assemblies from the cover.
5   Pry out shaft O-ring seals if replacement is required.
6   Remove the detent cam spring and pivot retainer C-clip. Remove both detent cams.
7   Inspect all parts for damage and wear, and replace as necessary.
8   With the detent spring tang projecting up over the 2nd/3rd shifter shaft cover opening, install the 1st/Reverse detent cam onto the detent cam pivot pin. With the detent spring tang projecting up over the first and reverse shifter shaft cover hole, install the 2nd/3rd detent cam.
9   Install the C-clip to the pivot shaft and hook the spring into the detent cam notches.
10 Install the shifter shaft assemblies carefully into the cover and the shift forks to the shifter shaft assemblies. Lift up the detent cam to allow the forks to seat properly.
11 Set the shifter levers into the Neutral detent (center position) and position the gasket on the case.
12 Carefully position the side cover, ensuring that the shift forks are aligned with their appropriate mainshaft clutch sliding sleeves.
13 Install and torque tighten the cover bolts to the specified value.
14 Top-up the oil in the transmission and lower the vehicle to the ground.

8   Transmission side cover (4 speed Saginaw and Muncie) – overhaul

1   Shift Saginaw models into 'Neutral' and Muncie models into 'Second' gear.
2   Raise the vehicle for access beneath. Set firmly on stands.
3   Remove the shift levers from the shifter shafts.
4   Remove the cover assembly and allow the oil to drain.
5   Remove the outer shifter levers.
6   Remove the shift forks from the shifter shaft assemblies, and the three shifter shaft assemblies from the cover.
7   If necessary, pry out the O-ring on the 1st/2nd and Reverse shafts.
8   On Saginaw models remove the Reverse shifter shaft detent ball and spring.
9   Remove the detent cam spring and the pivot pin C-clip. Mark the cams for identification on reassembly, then remove them.
10 Inspect all the parts for damage and wear and replace as necessary.
11 With the detent spring tang projecting up over the 3rd/4th shifter shaft cover opening, install the 1st/2nd detent cam onto the detent cam pivot pin. With the detent spring tang projecting up over the 1st/2nd shifter shaft cover hole, install the 3rd/4th detent cam.
12 Install the detent cam C-clip to the pivot shaft and hook the spring into the cam notches.
13 Install the 1st/2nd and 3rd/4th shifter shaft assemblies carefully into the cover.
14 Install the shift forks to the shifter shaft assemblies, lifting up on the detent cam to permit the forks to seat.
15 Install the Reverse detent ball and spring, then install the Reverse shifter shaft assembly to the cover.
16 Move the shifter levers into 'Neutral' (Saginaw) or 'Second' (Muncie).

6.11 Extension housing oil seal

10.1 Speedometer drive cable at transmission

10.4 Transmission mount to crossmember bolt

17 Position the cover gasket on the case and carefully position the side cover, ensuring that the shift forks are aligned with their appropriate mainshaft clutch sliding sleeves.
18 Screw in the side cover bolts and tighten to the specified torque.
19 Top-up the transmission oil and then lower the car to the ground.

9 Transmission side cover (4 speed Warner) – overhaul

1   Shift the transmission into 2nd gear.
2   Raise the car to provide access to the side cover. Set firmly on stands.
3   Disconnect the wiring from the TCC switch.
4   Remove the shift levers from the shifter shafts.
5   Unscrew and remove the nine cover screws, remove the cover and allow the oil to drain.
6   Remove the TCS from the cover.
7   Remove the outer shifter lever nuts and pull the levers from the shafts.
8   Push the shifter shafts into the cover allowing the detent balls to fall free. Extract the shifter shafts.
9   Remove the interlock sleeve, the interlock pin and poppet spring.
10 Inspect and replace components as necessary.
11 Reassemble by reversing the overhaul procedure.
12 Before installing the side cover, move the shifter levers to 2nd gear position.
13 Locate a new gasket on the transmission.
14 Move the side cover into position making sure that the shift forks are aligned with their respective synchronizer sliding sleeve grooves.
15 Insert the cover bolts and tighten to the specified torque wrench setting.
16 Connect the shift levers and the TCS switch wiring.
17 Add lubricant to level of the filler plug hole.
18 Lower the car to the ground.

10 Transmission – removal and installation

1970 thru 1972
1   Raise the vehicle for access beneath, then disconnect the speedometer cable, back-up lamp switch and TCS switch, as appropriate (photo).
2   Remove the drive shaft assembly (refer to Chapter 8) and then support the engine/transmission by placing a jack under the oil pan. Use a block of wood as an insulator.
3   Remove the crossmember to frame attaching bolts. On 4-speed and floor shift transmission, also remove the crossmember to control lever support attaching bolts.
4   Remove the bolt retaining the transmission mount to the crossmember (photo).
5   Raise the engine slightly until the crossmember can be moved rearwards.
6   Remove the shift levers at the transmission side cover. On 4-speed and floorshift transmissions, also remove the stabilizer to control lever assembly retaining nut. Push the bolt towards the

transmission until the stabilizer can be disconnected.
7   Remove the transmission to clutch housing retaining bolts, install guide pins in the holes then remove the lower bolts.
8   Lower the engine until the transmission can be withdrawn rearwards and removed.
9   When installing, raise the transmission into position, then slide it forwards, piloting the clutch gear into the clutch housing.
10 Install the transmission retaining bolts and lockwashers, then torque-tighten to the specified value.
11 Install the shift levers and the stabilizer rod (where applicable).
12 Support the engine and raise it slightly until the crossmember can be repositioned. Install and torque-tighten the retaining bolts.
13 Remove the engine jack then install the transmission crossmember to mount retaining bolts and the crossmember to control lever support attaching bolts (where applicable).
14 Install the drive shaft (refer to Chapter 8).
15 Connect the speedometer cable, TCS switch and back-up switch wiring, as appropriate.
16 Fill the transmission with the correct quantity and grade of lubricant, then lower the vehicle to the ground.

1973 and later models
17 Remove the shift lever knob, and on 4-speed models the spring and T-handle.
18 Raise the vehicle for access beneath.
19 Disconnect the speedometer cable and TCS switch on the transmission (photo).
20 Remove the drive shaft (refer to Chapter 8).
21 Support the engine/transmission by placing a jack and block of wood as an insulator under the oil pan.
22 Remove the transmission mount to crossmember bolts and crossmember to frame attaching bolts. Support the engine and remove the crossmember (photo).
23 Disconnect the shift rods from the transmission and on floorshift models disconnect the backdrive rod at the bellcrank.
24 On floorshift models, remove the bolts attaching the shift control assembly to the support; then carefully pull the unit down until the shift lever clears the rubber boot. Remove the assembly from the vehicle.
25 Remove the transmission to clutch housing upper bolts. Install guide pins in the holes, then remove the lower bolts.
Note: *On some later models it may be necessary to remove the catalytic converter to permit removal of the transmission. (Refer to Chapter 6, for further information).*
26 Lower the supporting jack until the transmission can be withdrawn rearwards and removed.
27 When installing, raise the transmission into position and slide it forwards, guiding the clutch gear into the clutch housing.
28 Install the transmission clutch housing retaining bolts and lockwashers, and torque-tighten to the specified value.
29 Slide the shift lever into the rubber boot and position the shaft control to the support. Install and torque-tighten the retaining bolts.
30 Connect the shift rods to the transmission and torque-tighten the bolts. Connect the backdrive rod to the bellcrank.
31 Raise the engine and position the crossmember. Install and torque-tighten the transmission mount and crossmember retaining

bolts.
32 Install the drive shaft (refer to Chapter 8).
33 Connect the speedometer cable and TCS switch wiring.
34 Install the T-handle and spring (4-speed), and the shift knob on floorshift models.
35 Fill the transmission with the correct quantity and grade of lubricant, then lower the vehicle to the ground.

11 Three-speed (Saginaw) transmission — overhaul

1 Remove the transmission, drain the oil and remove the side cover assembly (refer to Section 7).
2 Remove the drive-gear bearing retainer and gasket.
3 Remove the drive-gear bearing stem snap-ring, then pull out the gear until a large screwdriver can be used to lever the drive-gear bearing from its location.
4 Remove the speedometer driven gear from the rear extension, then remove the extension retaining bolts.
5 Remove the reverse idler shaft E-ring.
6 Withdraw the drive-gear, mainshaft and extension assembly together through the rear casing.
7 From the mainshaft, detach the drive-gear, needle bearings and synchronizer ring.
8 Expand the snap-ring in the rear extension which retains the rear bearing and then withdraw the rear extension.
9 Using a dummy shaft or special tool (J22246) drive the countershaft (complete with Woodruff key) out of the rear of the transmission case. Carefully remove the dummy shaft and extract the countergear, bearings and thrust washers from the interior of the transmission case.
10 Drive the reverse idler shaft out of the rear of the transmission case using a long drift.

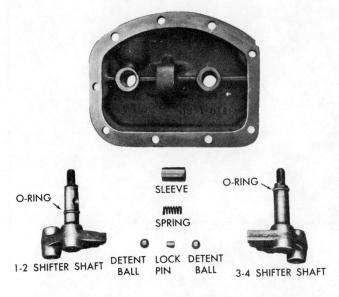

SLEEVE

SPRING

O-RING

O-RING

1-2 SHIFTER SHAFT

DETENT BALL   LOCK PIN   DETENT BALL

3-4 SHIFTER SHAFT

Fig. 7.10 4-speed Warner transmission side cover (Sec 9)

Fig. 7.11 Cutaway view of 3-speed Saginaw transmission (Sec 11)

1 Drive gear bearing	13 1st speed synchro snap ring	21 Rear oil seal	30 Countergear roller bearings
2 Bearing retainer	14 Reverse gear	22 Retainer oil seal	31 Anti-lash plate assembly
3 Pilot bearings	15 Reverse gear thrust and spring washers	23 Snap ring (bearing to gear)	32 Magnet
4 Case	16 Snap ring (bearing to mainshaft)	24 Drive gear bearing	33 2nd/3rd synchro sleeve
5 3rd speed blocker ring	17 Extension	25 Snap ring (bearing to case)	34 Countergear
6 2nd/3rd synchro snap ring	18 Vent	26 Thrust washer (front)	35 Countershaft
7 2nd/3rd synchro hub	19 Speedo drive gear and clip	27 Thrust washer (rear)	36 Reverse idler shaft
8 2nd speed blocker ring	20 Mainshaft	28 Snap ring (bearing to extension)	37 1st speed synchro sleeve
9 2nd speed gear		29 Rear bearing	38 E-ring
10 1st speed gear			39 Reverse idler gear
11 1st speed blocker ring			40 Woodruff key
12 1st speed synchro hub			

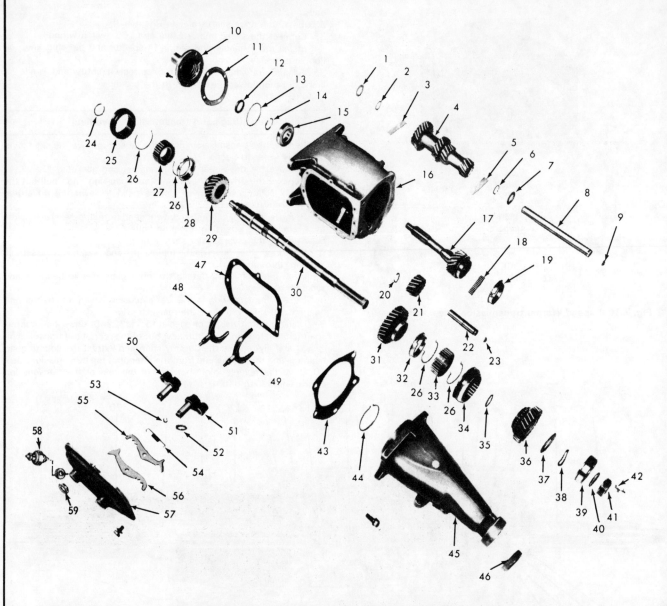

Fig. 7.12 Exploded view of 3-speed Saginaw transmission (Sec 11)

1 Thrust washer (front)	16 Case	32 1st speed blocker ring	45 Extension
2 Bearing washer	17 Drive gear	33 1st/2nd synchro hub assembly	46 Oil seal
3 Needle bearings	18 Pilot bearings	34 1st/2nd synchro sleeve	47 Gasket
4 Countergear	19 3rd speed blocker ring	35 Snap ring (hub to shaft)	48 2nd/3rd shift fork
5 Needle bearings	20 E-ring	36 Reverse gear	49 1st/reverse shift fork
6 Bearing washer	21 Reverse idler gear	37 Thrust washer	50 2nd/3rd shifter shaft assembly
7 Thrust washer (rear)	22 Reverse idler shaft	38 Spring washer	51 1st/reverse shifter shaft assembly
8 Countershaft	23 Woodruff key	39 Rear bearing	
9 Woodruff key	24 Snap ring (hub to shaft)	40 Snap ring (bearing to shaft)	52 O-ring seal
10 Bearing retainer	25 2nd/3rd synchro sleeve	41 Speedo drive gear	53 E-ring
11 Gasket	26 Synchro key spring	42 Retaining clip	54 Spring
12 Oil seal	27 2nd/3rd synchro hub assembly	43 Gasket	55 2nd/3rd detent cam
13 Snap ring (bearing to case)	28 2nd speed blocker ring	44 Snap ring (rear bearing to extension)	56 1st/reverse detent cam
14 Snap ring (bearing to gear)	29 2nd speed gear		57 Side cover
15 Drive gear bearing	30 Mainshaft		58 TCS switch and gasket
	31 1st speed gear		59 Lip seal

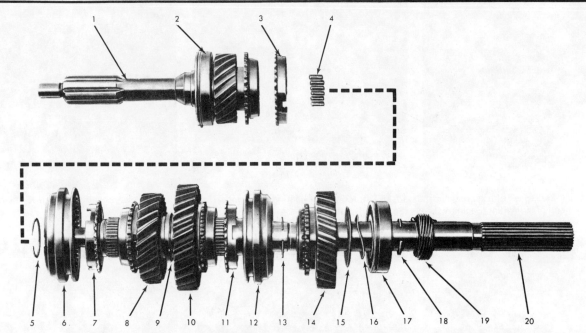

Fig. 7.13 Clutch drive gear and mainshaft assembly of 3-speed Saginaw transmission (Sec 11)

1	Drive gear	7	2nd speed blocker ring	12	1st speed synchro assembly	16	Spring washer
2	Drive gear bearing	8	2nd speed gear	13	Snap ring	17	Rear bearing
3	3rd speed blocker ring	9	Shoulder (part of mainshaft)	14	Reverse gear	18	Snap ring
4	Mainshaft pilot bearings (14)	10	1st speed gear	15	Reverse gear thrust	19	Speedo drive gear and clip
5	Snap ring	11	1st speed blocker ring		washer	20	Mainshaft
6	2nd/3rd synchro assembly						

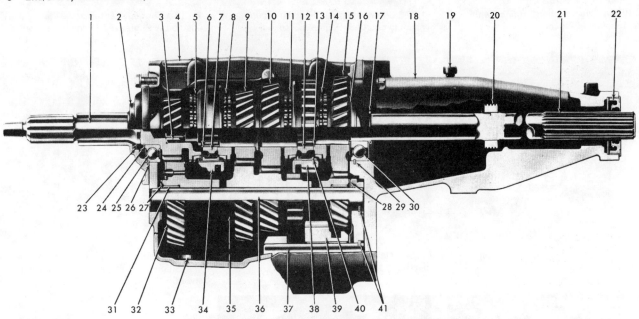

Fig. 7.14 Cutaway view of 4-speed Saginaw transmission (Sec 12)

1	Drive gear	14	1st speed blocker ring	24	Snap ring (bearing to gear)	33	Magnet
2	Bearing retainer	15	First gear	25	Drive gear bearing	34	3rd/4th synchro sleeve
3	Pilot bearings	16	Reverse gear thrust and spring washers	26	Snap ring (bearing to case)	35	Countergear assembly
4	Case	17	Snap ring (bearing to mainshaft)	27	Thrust washer (front)	36	Countershaft
5	4th speed blocker ring	18	Extension	28	Thrust washer (rear)	37	Reverse idler shaft
6	3rd/4th synchro snap ring	19	Vent	29	Snap ring (bearing to extension)	38	1st/2nd speed synchro sleeve and reverse gear
7	3rd/4th synchro snap ring	20	Speedo drive gear and clip	30	Rear bearing	39	Reverse idler gear (sliding)
8	3rd speed blocker ring	21	Mainshaft	31	Countergear roller bearings	40	Clutch key
9	3rd speed gear	22	Rear oil seal	32	Anti-lash plate assembly	41	Woodruff key
10	2nd speed gear	23	Retainer oil seal				
11	2nd speed blocker ring						
12	1st/2nd speed synchro hub						
13	1st/2nd speed synchro snap ring						

11.13 Removing 2nd speed blocker ring and gear from front end of mainshaft (Saginaw 3-speed)

11.15 Extracting rear bearing snap-ring (Saginaw 3-speed)

11.32A Assembling countergear rollers (Saginaw 3-speed)

11.32B Countergear rollers retained with grease (Saginaw 3-speed)

11.32C Countergear needle roller retaining washer in position (Saginaw 3-speed)

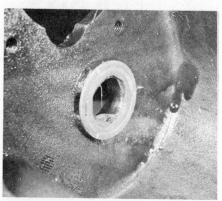

11.32D Countergear thrust washer held in position with grease (Saginaw 3-speed)

11.33 Reverse idler gear and shaft (Saginaw 3-speed)

11.34 Installing countershaft (Saginaw 3-speed)

11.35A Mainshaft rear bearing outer snap-ring in position in extension housing (Saginaw 3-speed)

11.35B Expanding rear bearing outer snap-ring (Saginaw 3-speed)

11.36 Mainshaft pilot bearings retained with grease (Saginaw 3-speed)

11.3A Installing clutch drive gear, mainshaft and extension (Saginaw 3-speed)

11.38B Countergear anti-lash plate (Saginaw 3-speed)

11.40 Clutch drive gear bearing outer snap-ring (Saginaw 3-speed)

11.41 Installing clutch drive gear bearing shaft snap-ring (Saginaw 3-speed)

11.42 Installing clutch drive gear bearing retainer and gasket (Saginaw 3-speed)

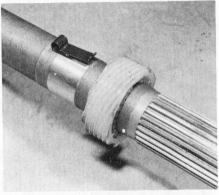

12.5 Removing speedometer drive gear from mainshaft (Saginaw 4-speed)

12.6 Extracting rear bearing snap-ring from mainshaft (Saginaw 4-speed)

12.7 Removing wave washer, thrust washer and 1st gear from mainshaft (Saginaw 4-speed)

12.8A Removing 1st/2nd blocker ring (Saginaw 4-speed)

12.8B Extracting 1st/2nd synchro hub snap-ring (Saginaw 4-speed)

12.8C Removing 1st/2nd synchro sleeve (incorporating reverse gear) – Saginaw 4-speed

12.9 Removing 2nd speed blocker ring and gear (Saginaw 4-speed)

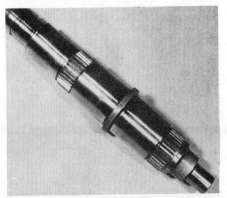

12.11A Mainshaft showing fixed shoulder (Saginaw 4-speed)

11 The mainshaft should only be dismantled if a press or bearing puller is available: otherwise take the assembly to your Chevrolet dealer. Be careful to keep all components separated and in order for easier reassembly.

12 Remove the 2nd/3rd synchro hub snap-ring from the mainshaft. Do not mix up the synchro unit components; although identical, the components of each unit are matched in production.

13 Remove the synchro unit, 2nd speed blocker ring and 2nd speed gear from the front end of the mainshaft (photo).

14 Depress the speedometer drive-gear retaining clip and remove the gear from the mainshaft.

15 Remove the rear bearing snap-ring from its mainshaft groove (photo).

16 Support the reverse gear and press the mainshaft out of the rear bearing, and snap-ring from the rear end of the mainshaft.

17 Remove 1st/reverse synchro hub snap-ring from the mainshaft and remove the synchro unit.

18 Remove the 1st speed blocker ring and 1st speed gear from the rear end of the mainshaft.

19 Clean all components in solvent and dry thoroughly. Check for wear or chipped teeth. If there has been a history of noisy gearshifts or the synchro facility could easily be 'beaten' then replace the appropriate synchro unit.

20 Extract the oil seal from the rear end of the rear extension and drive in a new one with a tubular drift.

21 Clean the transmission case inside and out and check for cracks, particularly around the bolt holes.

22 Extract the drive-gear bearing retainer seal and drive in a new one.

23 Commence rebuilding the transmission by first reassembling the mainshaft. Install 2nd speed gear so that the rear face of the gear butts against the flange on the mainshaft.

24 Fit the blocker ring, followed by the 2nd/3rd synchro assembly (shift fork groove nearer rear end of the mainshaft). Make sure that the notches of the blocker ring align with the keys of the synchro assembly.

25 Fit the snap-ring which retains the synchro hub to the mainshaft.

26 To the rear end of the mainshaft, install the 1st speed gear, followed by the blocker ring.

27 Install the 1st/reverse synchro unit (shift fork groove nearer the front end of the mainshaft), again making sure that the notches of the blocker ring align with the keys of the synchro unit.

28 Install the snap-ring, reverse gear thrust washer and spring washer.

29 Install the mainshaft rear ball bearing with the outer snap-ring groove nearer the front of the shaft.

30 Install the rear bearing shaft snap-ring.

31 Fit the speedometer drive gear and retaining clip.

32 Insert a dummy shaft through the countergear, and stick the roller bearings (27 at each end), needle retainer washers and the transmission case thrust washers, in position using thick grease. Note that the tangs on the thrust washers are away from the gear faces. **Note:** *If no dummy shaft is available, carefully stick the roller bearings in place, but when installing the shaft (paragraph 34), take care that they are not dislodged (photos).*

33 Install reverse idler gear and shaft with Woodruff key from the rear of the transmission case. Do not install the idler shaft E-ring at this time (photo).

34 Install the countergear assembly from the rear of the transmission case and then insert the countershaft so that it picks up the roller bearings and the thrust washers, at the same time displacing the dummy shaft or tool (if used). The countershaft should be inserted so that its slot is at its rear end when installed (photo).

35 Expand the snap-ring in the rear extension and locate the extension over the rear end of the mainshaft and onto the rear bearing. Make sure that the snap-ring seats in the rear bearing groove (photo).

36 Insert the mainshaft pilot bearings (14 of them) into the clutch gear cavity and then assemble the 3rd speed blocker ring onto the clutch drive gear (photo).

37 Locate the clutch drive gear, pilot bearings and 3rd speed blocker ring over the front of the mainshaft. Do not fit the drive gear bearing at this time; also make sure that the notches in the blocker ring align with the keys in the 2nd/3rd synchro unit.

12.11B Installing 3rd speed gear to mainshaft (Saginaw 4-speed)

12.12A Installing 3rd/4th blocker ring (Saginaw 4-speed)

12.12B Installing 3rd/4th synchro assembly (Saginaw 4-speed)

12.13 Installing 3rd/4th synchro hub snap-ring (Saginaw 4-speed)

12.15 Installing 1st/2nd synchro assembly (Saginaw 4-speed)

12.21 Mainshaft pilot bearings retained with grease (Saginaw 4-speed)

38 Stick a new gasket (using grease) to the rear face of the transmission case and then, from the rear, insert the combined clutch drive gear mainshaft and rear extension. Make sure that the 2nd/3rd synchro sleeve is pushed fully forward so that the clutch drive gear engages with the countergear anti-lash plate (photos).

39 Install the rear extension to transmission case bolts. Torque tighten to specifications.

40 Fit the outer snap-ring to the clutch drive gear bearing and install the bearing over the drive gear and into the front of the transmission case (photo).

41 Fit the clutch drive gear bearing shaft snap-ring (photo).

42 Install the clutch drive gear bearing retainer and its gasket making sure that the oil return hole is at the bottom (photo).

43 Now install the reverse idler gear 'E' ring to the shaft.

44 With the synchronizer sleeves in the neutral position, install the side cover, gasket and fork assembly (Section 7). Torque-tighten all the bolts

45 Install the speedometer driven gear in the rear extension.

12 Four speed (Saginaw) transmission – overhaul

1 Carry out the operations of paragraph 1 thru 9 of Section 11 but note than an E-ring is not fitted to the reverse idler shaft.

2 Remove the reverse idler gear stop-ring (where applicable), the use a long drift to drive the reverse idler shaft out of the rear of the transmission case.

3 Remove the 3rd/4th synchro hub snap-ring from the mainshaft. Do not mix up the synchro unit components, which although identical in appearance are matched in production.

4 Remove the synchro unit, 3rd gear blocker ring and 3rd speed gear from the front end of the mainshaft.

5 Depress the speedometer drive-gear retaining clip and remove the gear from the mainshaft (photo).

6 Remove the rear bearing snap-ring from its mainshaft groove (photo).

7 Support 1st gear and press the mainshaft out of the rear bearing. Remove the snap-ring, the rear bearing, the wave washer, thrust washer and 1st gear from the rear end of the mainshaft (photo).

8 Remove the blocker ring and 1st/2nd synchro hub snap-ring from the mainshaft and remove the synchro unit/reverse gear (photos).

9 Remove the 2nd speed blocker ring and 2nd speed gear from the rear end of the mainshaft (photo).

10 Carry out the operations of paragraphs 19 thru 22 of Section 11.

11 Commence rebuilding the transmission by first reassembling the mainshaft. Install 3rd speed gear so that the rear face of the gear butts against the flange on the mainshaft (photos).

12 Install the blocker ring, followed by 3rd/4th synchro assembly (shift fork groove nearer mainshaft flange). Make sure that the notches of the blocker ring align with the keys of the synchro assembly (photos).

13 Install the snap-ring which retains the synchro hub to the mainshaft (photo).

14 To the rear end of the mainshaft, install the 2nd speed gear followed by the blocker ring.

15 Install the 1st/2nd synchro unit (shift fork groove nearer the front of the mainshaft), again making sure that the notches of the blocker ring align with the keys of the synchro unit. Install the snap-ring and blocker ring (photo).

16 Install 1st gear, the steel thrust washer and the wave washer.

17 Install the mainshaft rear ball bearing with the outer snap-ring groove nearer the front of the shaft.

18 Install the rear bearing shaft snap-ring.

19 Fit the speedometer drive-gear and retaining clip.

20 Carry out the operations of paragraphs 32 thru 35 of Section 11 but ignore the reference to the E-ring.

21 Insert the mainshaft pilot bearings (14 of them) into the clutch cavity and then assemble the 4th speed blocker ring onto the clutch drive-gear (photo).

22 Locate the clutch drive-gear, pilot bearings and 4th speed blocker ring over the front of the mainshaft. Do not fit the drive-gear bearing at this time; also make sure that the notches in the blocker ring align with the keys in the 3rd/4th synchro unit.

23 Carry out the operations of paragraphs 38 thru 42 and paragraph 44 of Section 11. Note that the reference at paragraph 38 to 2nd/3rd synchro sleeve will now be 3rd/4th synchro sleeve.

13 Four speed (Muncie) transmission – overhaul

1 Remove the transmission, drain the oil and remove the transmission side cover (refer to Section 8).

2 Remove the bolts and lockstrips securing the front bearing retainer. Remove the retainer and gasket.

3 Lock-up the transmission by selecting 2 gears then use a suitable wrench (Chevrolet tool J.933 is designed for this purpose) to remove the drive-gear retaining nut.

4 Select neutral, then drive out the lockpin from the reverse shifter lever boss. Pull the shifter shaft out about $\frac{1}{8}$ inch to disengage the reverse shift fork.

5 Remove the 6 case extension retaining bolts then tap the extension rearwards using a soft hammer. Move the extension to the left when the reverse idler is out as far as it will go. This will permit the extension to be removed.

6 Remove the reverse idler, flat thrust washer, shaft and roll pin.

7 Remove the speedometer gear and reverse gear using a suitable extractor.

8 Slide the 3rd/4th synchronizer sleeve forwards into 4th gear position, then carefully remove the rear bearing retainer and mainshaft assembly from the case by tapping the retainer with a soft hammer.

9 Remove the 17 bearing rollers from the main drive-gear, and the 4th speed synchronizer blocker ring.

10 Lift the front half of the reverse idler and its thrust washer from the case.

11 Press the drive-gear from the front bearing into the case.

12 Tap out the front bearing and snap-ring from inside the case.

13 Using a dummy shaft or special tool (J.22379), press out the countershaft, then remove the countergear and both tanged washers.

14 Remove the 112 rollers, six 0.070 spacers and the roller spacer from the countergear.

15 Remove the mainshaft front snap-ring and slide the 3rd/4th speed clutch assembly, 3rd gear and synchronizing ring from the mainshaft.

16 Remove the rear bearing snap-ring and press the mainshaft out of the retainer.

17 If no press or suitable extractor is available, this may be the limit of the dismantling and you may have to contact your dealer if you need to go further.

18 Remove the mainshaft rear snap-ring then, while supporting on the second speed gear, press on the rear of the mainshaft to remove the 1st gear and sleeve, 1st gear synchronizing ring, 1st/2nd speed synchronizing clutch assembly, 2nd speed synchronizing ring and second speed gear.

19 Remove the reverse shift fork from the shifter shaft, then carefully drive the shaft inwards to allow the detent ball to drop out. Remove the shaft and ball detent spring.

20 Carry out the operations of paragraphs 19 thru 21 of Section 11.

21 Place the reverse shifter shaft detent spring into its hole in the extension then install the shifter shaft until the detent plate butts against the inside of the extension housing.

22 Commence reassembly by placing the detent ball on the spring and hold it down while moving the shifter shaft away from the case until the ball drops into the detent on the shaft detent plate.

23 Install the fork but do not lock it at this stage.

24 To the rear of the mainshaft, assemble the 2nd gear, hub towards the rear of the shaft.

25 Install the 1st/2nd synchronizer clutch assembly to the mainshaft (hub towards the front), together with a synchronizing ring on each side. Align the keyways with the clutch keys.

26 Press the 1st gear sleeve onto the mainshaft using a $1\frac{3}{4}$ inch inside-diameter pipe or similar.

27 Install the 1st gear (hub towards the front) and, using a $1\frac{5}{8}$ inch inside-diameter pipe, press on the rear bearing.

28 Select a snap-ring to give 0 to 0.005 inch from the mainshaft groove to the rear face of the mainshaft rear bearing. New snap-rings are available in sizes of 0.087, 0.090, 0.093 and 0.096 inch.

29 Install the 3rd gear (hub to the front of the transmission) and the 3rd gear synchronizing ring (notches to the front of the transmission).

30 Install the 3rd/4th gear clutch assembly with the sleeve taper and hub towards the front. Ensure that the hub keys align with the synchronizing ring notches.

31 Install the snap-ring in the mainshaft groove in front of the 3rd/4th speed clutch assembly, with the ends seated behind the spline teeth.

32 Install the rear bearing retainer. Spread the snap-ring in the plate

to allow it to drop around the rear bearing and press on the end of the mainshaft until it engages the groove in the rear bearing.

33 Install the reverse gear.

34 Install the speedometer gear, pressing it on to obtain a dimension of $4\frac{7}{8}$ inch from the forward side of the gear to the flat surface of the rear bearing retainer.

35 Install the tubular spacer in the counter gear.

36 Using heavy grease to retain the rollers, install one spacer, 28 rollers, one spacer, 28 rollers and one more spacer in *each* end of the counter gear.

37 Insert the dummy-shaft into the counter gear.

38 Lay the transmission case on its side with the cover opening towards you, then put the tanged washers in place, retaining them with grease.

39 Position the countergear, making sure that the thrust washers do not move, then position the transmission case so that it is resting on its front face.

40 Lubricate the countershaft with transmission oil and insert it in the rear of the case. Turn the countershaft so that the flat on the end is horizontal and facing the bottom of the case.

41 Align the countergear and shaft, and press in the shaft, ejecting the dummy-shaft out of the front of the case. Ensure that the thrust-washers are still in place.

42 Check the overall countergear endplay using a dial gauge or similar. If in excess of 0.025 inch, new thrust washers must be used.

43 Install the cage and 17 rollers into the main drive-gear – retaining them with heavy grease. Install the oil slinger on the main drive-gear concave side towards the gear.

44 Install the main drive-gear and pilot bearings through the side cover opening and into position in the transmission front bore.

45 Position the gasket on the front face of the rear bearing retainer.

46 Install the 4th speed synchronizing ring on the main drive-gear with the notches towards the rear of the transmission.

47 Position the reverse idler gear tanged thrust washer on the machined face of the ear cast in the case for the reverse idler shaft, and retain with heavy grease. Position the front reverse idler gear next

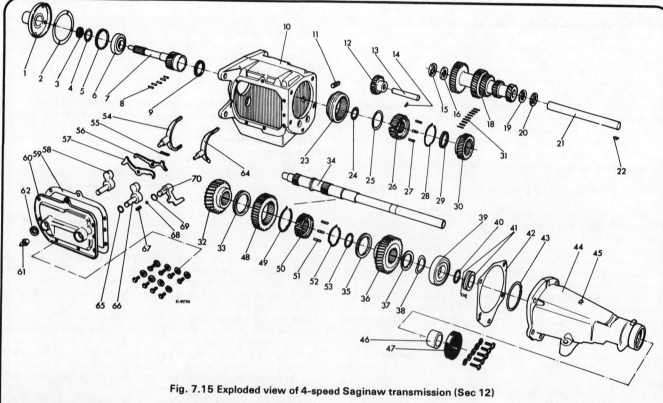

Fig. 7.15 Exploded view of 4-speed Saginaw transmission (Sec 12)

1 Bearing retainer	20 Thrust washer (rear)	39 Rear bearing	54 3rd/4th shift fork
2 Gasket (retainer to case)	21 Countershaft	40 Snap ring (bearing to	55 Detent spring
3 Oil seal	22 Woodruff key	shaft)	56 3rd/4th detent cam
4 Snap ring (bearing to shaft)	23 Synchro sleeve	41 Speedo drive gear and	57 1st/2nd detent cam
5 Snap ring (bearing to case)	24 Snap ring (hub to shaft)	clip)	58 3rd/4th shifter shaft
6 Drive gear bearing	25 Key retainer	42 Gasket (extension to case)	59 Gasket (cover to case)
7 Drive gear	26 3rd/4th synchro hub	43 Snap ring (extension to	60 Cover
8 Mainshaft pilot bearings	27 Clutch keys	rear bearing)	61 TCS switch and gasket
9 4th speed blocker ring	28 Key retainer	44 Extension	62 Lip seal
10 Case	29 3rd speed blocker ring	45 Vent	63 Detent cam retainer
11 Filler plug	30 3rd speed gear	46 Bushing	64 1st/2nd shift fork
12 Reverse idler gear	31 Needle bearings	47 Oil seal	65 O-ring
13 Reverse idler shaft	32 2nd speed gear	48 1st/2nd synchro sleeve	66 1st/2nd shift shaft
14 Woodruff key	33 2nd speed blocker ring	and reverse gear	67 Spring
15 Thrust washer (front)	34 Mainshaft	49 Key retainer	68 Ball
16 Needle retainer washer	35 1st speed blocker ring	50 1st/2nd synchro hub	69 O-ring
17 Needle bearings	36 1st speed gear	51 Clutch keys	70 Reverse shifter shaft
18 Countergear	37 Thrust washer	52 Key retainer	and fork
19 Needle retainer washer	38 Wave washer	53 Snap ring (hub to shaft)	

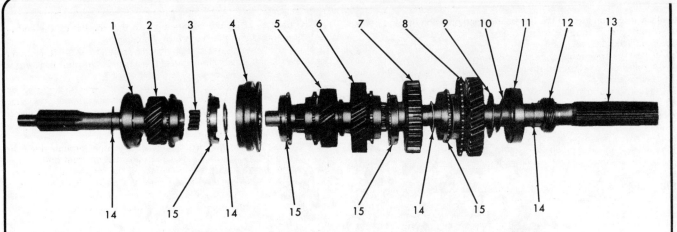

Fig. 7.16 Clutch gear and mainshaft of 4-speed Saginaw transmission (Sec 12)

1 Drive gear bearing
2 Drive gear
3 Mainshaft pilot bearings
4 3rd/4th synchro assembly

5 3rd speed gear
6 2nd speed gear
7 1st/2nd synchro and reverse gear assembly

8 1st speed gear
9 Thrust washer
10 Spring washer
11 Rear bearing

12 Speedo drive gear
13 Mainshaft
14 Snap ring
15 Synchro blocker ring

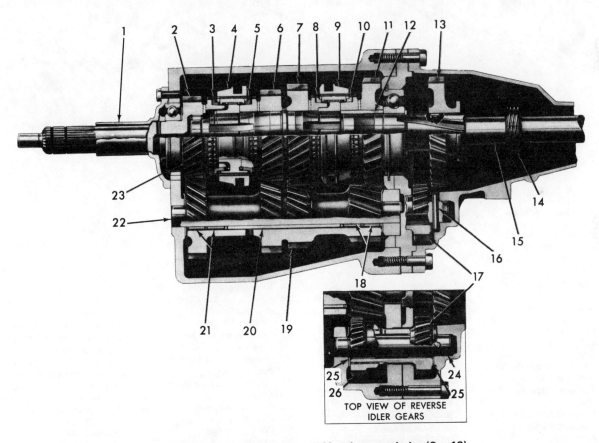

Fig. 7.17 Cutaway view of 4-speed Muncie transmission (Sec 13)

1 Bearing retainer
2 Main drive gear
3 4th speed synchro ring
4 3rd/4th speed clutch
5 3rd speed synchro ring
6 3rd speed gear
7 2nd speed gear
8 2nd speed synchro ring

9 1st/2nd speed clutch assembly
10 1st speed synchro ring
11 1st speed gear
12 1st speed gear sleeve
13 Reverse gear
14 Speedo drive gear
15 Mainshaft

16 Reverse idler shaft rollpin
17 Reverse idler gear (rear)
18 Countergear bearing roller
19 Countergear
20 Counter bearing roller spacer

21 Countershaft bearing roller
22 Countergear shaft
23 Oil slinger
24 Reverse idler shaft
25 Thrust washer
26 Reverse idler gear (front)

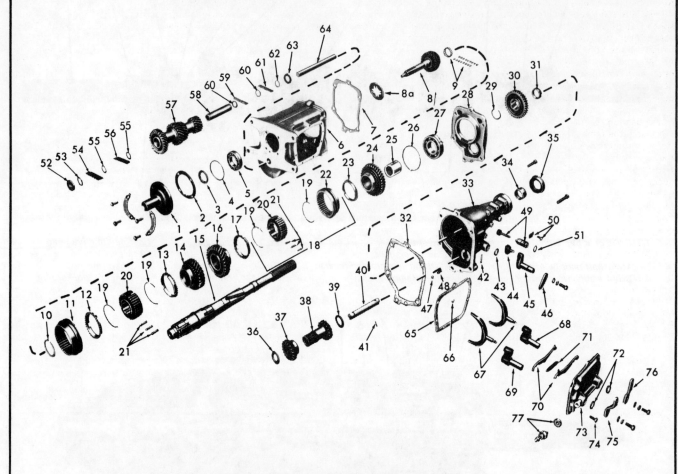

Fig. 7.18 Exploded view of 4-speed Muncie transmission (Sec 13)

1	Bearing retainer	19	Clutch key spring
2	Gasket	20	Clutch hub
3	Bearing retaining nut	21	Clutch keys
4	Bearing snap ring	22	1st/2nd speed clutch sliding sleeve
5	Main drive gear bearing	23	1st speed gear synchro ring
6	Transmission case		
7	Rear bearing retainer gasket	24	1st speed gear
		25	1st speed gear sleeve
8	Main drive gear	26	Rear bearing snap ring
8a	Oil slinger	27	Rear bearing
9	Bearing rollers (17) and cage	28	Rear bearing retainer
		29	Selective fit snap ring
10	Snap ring	30	Reverse gear
11	3rd/4th speed clutch sliding sleeve	31	Speedo drive gear
		32	Gasket
12	4th speed gear synchro ring	33	Case extension
		34	Extension bushing
13	3rd speed synchro ring	35	Rear oil seal
14	3rd speed gear	36	Thrust washer (tanged)
15	Mainshaft	37	Reverse idler gear (front)
16	2nd speed gear	38	Reverse idler gear (rear)
17	2nd speed gear synchro ring	39	Thrust washer (flat)
		40	Reverse idler shaft
18	1st/2nd speed clutch assembly		

41	Reverse idler shaft rollpin	58	Countergear roller spacer
42	Reverse shifter shaft lock pin	59	Bearing rollers (28)
		60	Spacer
43	Reverse shifter shaft lip seal	61	Bearing rollers (28)
		62	Spacer
44	Reverse shift fork	63	Washer (tanged)
45	Reverse shifter shaft and detent plate	64	Countershaft
		65	Gasket
46	Reverse shifter lever	66	Detent cams retainer ring
47	Reverse shifter shaft detent ball	67	Forward speed shift forks
		68	1st/2nd speed gear shifter shaft and detent plate
48	Reverse shifter shaft ball detent spring		
		69	3rd/4th speed gear shifter shaft and detent plate
49	Speedo driven gear and fitting		
		70	Detent cams
50	Retainer and bolt	71	Detent cam spring
51	O-ring	72	Lip seals
52	Washer (tanged)	73	Side cover
53	Spacer	74	Headed cam pin
54	Bearing rollers (28)	75	3rd/4th speed shifter lever
55	Spacer	76	1st/2nd speed shifter lever
56	Bearing rollers (28)	77	TCS switch and gasket
57	Countergear		

to the thrust washer, with the hub facing towards the rear of the case.

48 Slide the 3rd/4th synchronizing clutch sleeve forward into the 4th speed detent position, then lower the mainshaft assembly into the case. Ensure that the notches on the 4th speed synchronizing ring align with the keys in the clutch assembly.

49 Align the rear bearing retainer guide pin with the hole in the rear of the case then tap the retainer into place with a soft faced hammer.

50 From the rear of the case, insert the rear reverse idler gear, engaging the splines with the portion of the front gear inside the case.

51 Use heavy grease to retain the gasket in position with the rear face of the bearing retainer.

52 Install the remaining flat thrust washer on the reverse idler shaft. If a new shaft is being used, drive out the old roll pin and press it into the new shaft.

53 Install the reverse idler shaft, roll pin and thrust washer into the gears and the front boss of the case, picking up the front thrust washer. The roll pin must be vertical.

54 Pull the reverse shifter shaft to the left side of the extension and rotate the shaft to bring the shift fork forwards to the reverse detent position. Move the extension onto the transmission case while slowly pushing in on the shifter shaft to engage the shift fork with the reverse gear shift collar. Now lead the reverse idler shaft into the extension housing, allowing the extension to slide onto the transmission case.

55 Install the 6 extension and retainer attaching bolts and torque tighten them.

56 Move the reverse shifter shaft to align the shaft groove with the holes in the boss, then drive in the lock pin. Install the shifter lever.

57 With the snap-ring groove to the front, press the main drive-gear bearing onto the shaft and into the case until at least 3 threads are exposed.

58 Lock the transmission in two gears at once, then install the main drive-gear retaining nut and draw it up tight, using the special wrench. With the bearing seating on the gear shoulder, torque-tighten the nut (40 lb ft) and lock it by staking in several places. Take care not to damage the shaft screw threads.

59 Install the bearing retainer, gasket, 4 attaching bolts and 2 lockstrips, using a suitable sealant on the screw threads. Torque-tighten the bolts.

60 Shift the mainshaft 3rd/4th sliding clutch sleeve into neutral and 1st/2nd sliding clutch sleeve forward into the second gear detent. Shift the side cover 3rd/4th shifter lever into the neutral detent and the 1st/2nd shifter lever into the 2nd gear detent.

61 Install the side cover gasket and carefully position the side cover to ensure proper alignment. Install the attaching bolts and torque-tighten evenly to the specified value.

14 Four speed (Warner) transmission – overhaul

1 With the transmission removed from the car, clean away all external dirt.

2 Shift the transmission into 2nd gear, remove the drain plug and drain the lubricant.

3 Unscrew and remove the side cover bolts, then withdraw the cover and gasket. Remove the shift forks.

4 From the front of the transmission, unbolt and remove the drive gear bearing retainer and gasket.

5 Remove the lock pin from the reverse shifter lever boss, pull the shifter shaft partially out to disengage the reverse shifter fork from the reverse gear.

6 Remove the rear extension housing bolts and tap the extension to the rear with a soft-faced hammer, but only enough to start it moving.

7 Pull the extension until the reverse idler shaft clears the reverse idler gears. Rotate the extension to free the shift fork from the collar of reverse gear, and then withdraw the extension completely. Remove the gasket.

8 Extract the speedometer gear snap-ring, slide the speedometer

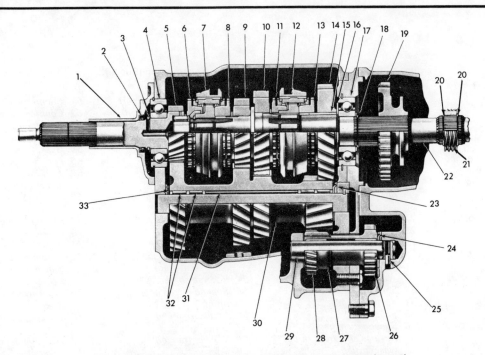

Fig. 7.19 Cutaway view of 4–speed Warner transmission (Sec 4)

1	Bearing retainer	9	3rd speed gear
2	Lip seal	10	2nd speed gear
3	Snap ring and washer	11	2nd speed synchro ring
4	Clutch gear bearing	12	1st/2nd speed clutch assembly
5	Clutch gear	13	1st speed synchro ring
6	4th speed synchro ring	14	1st speed gear
7	3rd/4th speed clutch assembly	15	1st speed gear bushing
8	3rd speed synchro ring	16	Spacer

17	Rear main bearing	26	Rear idler gear
18	Snap ring and washer	27	Spacer
19	Reverse gear	28	Front idler gear
20	Snap rings	29	Reverse idler shaft
21	Speedo gear	30	Countergear
22	Mainshaft	31	Countergear sleeve
23	Thrust washer	32	Countergear bearing rollers
24	Thrust washer	33	Thrust washers
25	Idler shaft rollpin		

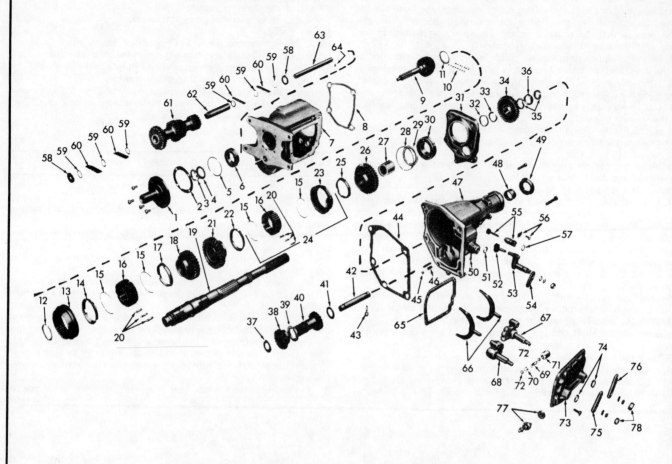

Fig. 7.20 Exploded view of 4-speed Warner transmission (Sec 14)

1	Bearing retainer	21	2nd speed gear
2	Gasket	22	2nd speed gear synchro
3	Selective fit snap ring		ring
4	Spacer washer	23	1st/2nd speed clutch
5	Bearing snap ring		sliding sleeve
6	Main drive gear bearing	24	1st/2nd speed clutch
7	Transmission case		assembly
8	Rear bearing retainer	25	1st speed gear synchro
	gasket		ring
9	Main drive gear	26	1st speed gear
10	Bearing rollers (16)	27	1st speed gear sleeve
11	Washer	28	Rear bearing snap ring
12	Snap ring	29	Thrust washer
13	3rd/4th speed clutch	30	Rear bearing
	sliding sleeve	31	Rear bearing retainer
14	4th speed gear synchro	32	Washer
	ring	33	Selective fit snap ring
15	Clutch key spring	34	Reverse gear
16	Clutch hub	35	Snap ring
17	3rd speed gear synchro	36	Speedo drive gear
	ring	37	Reverse idler front thrust
18	3rd speed gear		washer (flat)
19	Mainshaft	38	Reverse idler gear (front)
20	Clutch keys (3)	39	Snap ring

40	Reverse idler gear (rear)	61	Countergear
41	Thrust washer (tanged)	62	Countergear roller spacer
42	Reverse idler shaft	63	Countershaft
43	Lock pin and welch plug	64	Countershaft Woodruff key
44	Gasket	65	Gasket
45	Detent ball	66	Forward speed shift forks
46	Ball detent spring	67	1st/2nd speed gear shifter
47	Extension case		shaft and detent plate
48	Extension bushing	68	3rd/4th speed gear shifter
49	Rear oil seal		shaft and detent plate
50	Lock pin	69	Poppet spring
51	O-ring seal	70	Interlock pin
52	Reverse shift fork	71	Interlock sleeve
53	Reverse shifter shaft	72	Detent balls
	and detent plate	73	Side cover
54	Reverse shifter lever	74	Lip seals
55	Speedo driven gear and	75	3rd/4th speed shifter
	fitting		lever
56	Retainer and bolt	76	1st/2nd speed shifter
57	O-ring seal		lever
58	Washer (tanged)	77	TCS switch and gasket
59	Spacer	78	Lever attaching nuts
60	Bearing rollers (28)		

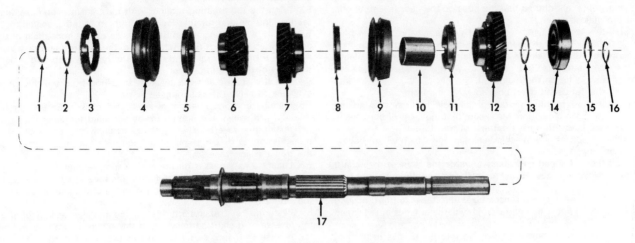

Fig. 7.21 4–speed Warner mainshaft (Sec 14)

1	Washer	5	3rd speed synchro ring	9	1st/2nd speed clutch	13	Washer

1 Washer
2 Snap ring
3 4th speed synchro ring
4 3rd/4th speed clutch assembly

5 3rd speed synchro ring
6 3rd speed gear
7 2nd speed gear
8 2nd speed synchro ring

9 1st/2nd speed clutch assembly
10 1st gear bushing
11 1st speed synchro ring
12 1st gear

13 Washer
14 Rear bearing
15 Washer
16 Snap ring
17 Mainshaft

Fig. 7.22 Rear extension sealed bolt (4–speed Warner) (Sec 14)

gear from the mainshaft then extract the remaining snap-ring.
9 Slide the reverse gear from the mainshaft and then pull the reverse idler gear from the rear face of the transmission case.
10 Extract the snap-ring and spacer washer from the front bearing.
11 Using a suitable extractor, withdraw the front main drive gear bearing from the transmission case.
12 Remove the rear retainer lockbolt.
13 Move 1st/2nd and 3rd/4th synchronizer sleeves forward to provide enough clearance for removal of the mainshaft assembly.
14 Withdraw the mainshaft and rear bearing retainer from the transmission case.
15 Remove the front reverse idler gear and thrust washer from the case.
16 Using a dummy shaft (or special tool J-24658) drive the countershaft out of the transmission case, then remove the countergear and tanged thrust washers. Retrieve any needle bearings from the bottom of the case.
17 Unless a suitable press or extractors are available, dismantling the mainshaft should be left to your GM dealer. If suitable tools are available, proceed in the following way.
18 Extract the snap-ring from the front of the 3rd/4th synchro unit. Slide the washer, synchro unit, synchro ring and 3rd speed gear from the mainshaft.
19 Expand the rear bearing retainer snap-ring and slide the retainer

from the mainshaft.
20 Extract the snap-ring from the rear of the mainshaft rear bearing.
21 Support the front face of 2nd gear and press the mainshaft out of the rear bearing, 1st gear and sleeve. 1st/2nd synchro unit and 2nd gear.
22 With all components removed, inspect for wear or damage, and replace as necessary.
23 The synchronizer units should be dismantled only after having marked their hub to sleeve relationship.
24 Replace the extension housing and drive gear bearing retainer oil seals, as a matter of routine, at major overhaul.
25 To replace the reverse shifter shaft O-ring oil seal, remove the shift fork and carefully drive the shifter shaft into the extension housing allowing the detent ball to drop into the case. Remove the detent spring.
26 Extract the O-ring seal from the shaft.
27 When reassembling, place the detent spring into the hole and start the reverse shifter shaft into its hole in the boss. Hold the ball down and push the shaft into position turning it until the ball drops into place in the detent on the shaft detent plate.
28 Fit a new O-ring and install the shift fork, but do not drive the shifter shaft lock pin into place until the extension housing has been installed.
29 Replacement of the reverse idler shaft can be carried out if the welch plug and roll pin in the extension housing is first driven into the shaft, and the shaft then extracted.
30 Fit the new idler shaft, drive in a new roll pin and finally tap in a new welch plug smeared with sealer.
31 Overhaul of the transmission side cover assembly is covered in Section 9.
32 The countergear end-play should be checked in the following way. Stick the thrust washers into the case using some thick grease.
33 Assemble the countergear rollers and spacers. Divide the rollers into four equal quantities, and then into each end of the countergear install rollers, spacer, rollers and spacer. Hold them in position using thick grease and insert the dummy shaft. Offer the assembly into position in the case without disturbing the thrust washers and insert the countershaft from the rear end of the case. The dummy shaft will be displaced. Make sure that the slot for the Woodruff key is correctly aligned but do not fit the key itself if case removal is required to change the thrust washers.
34 Using feeler gauges or a dial gauge check the end-float of the countergear. If it exceeds 0.025 in, new thrust washers are required. If the end-play is correct, the countershaft and gear can remain undisturbed pending reassembly of the transmission.

35 Commence reassembly of the mainshaft by installing the 2nd speed gear to its rear end so that the boss on the gear faces the rear end of the mainshaft.

36 Install the 1st/2nd synchronizer unit with a synchro ring on both sides. Make sure that the taper is towards the rear of the mainshaft.

37 Locate the 1st gear sleeve on the mainshaft and press the sleeve onto the shaft until the 2nd gear, the synchro unit and the sleeve contact the shoulder on the mainshaft.

38 Install the 1st speed gear (boss towards the front).

39 Apply pressure to the inner race of the mainshaft rear bearing and press the bearing into position. Make sure that the snap-ring groove in the outer race is towards the front end of the shaft.

40 Install the spacer and the thickest snap-ring which will fit behind the rear bearing.

41 Install the 3rd speed gear (boss towards the front of mainshaft) and the 3rd speed gear synchronizer ring (notches to front of mainshaft).

42 Install the 3rd/4th speed synchronizer unit (taper to front) making sure that the keys in the hub correspond with the notches in 3rd speed ring.

43 Install the thickest possible snap-ring into the groove in front of the 3rd/4th synchronizer unit.

44 Install the rear bearing retainer over the end of the mainshaft. Expand the snap-ring to drop it round the rear bearing and into its groove.

45 Install reverse gear to the mainshaft so that the shift collar is to the rear.

46 Install a snap-ring, the speedometer drive gear and the second snap-ring.

47 To reassemble the transmission, install the countergear and countershaft as described in paragraphs 32 and 33 (if not already done). Fit the Woodruff key.

48 Install the front reverse idler gear (teeth facing forward) and thrust washer into the transmission case.

49 Using heavy grease, install the sixteen roller bearings and washer into the main drive gear. Engage the main drive gear with the mainshaft assembly front end.

50 Push the 3rd/4th synchro sleeve forward.

51 Locate a new gasket for the rear bearing retainer on the rear of the transmission case and then carefully install the mainshaft/drive gear assembly into the transmission case.

52 Align the rear bearing retainer with the transmission case, install the locating pin and retainer lockbolt. Tighten to the specified torque.

53 Locate a snap-ring around the outside of the front main bearing and then tap it into position in the front of the transmission case. Apply pressure to the inner race and make sure that the snap-ring is nearer the front of the bearing.

54 Install a spacer and the thickest snap-ring from the thicknesses available to secure the bearing.

55 Install the front bearing retainer and gasket. Smear the bolt threads with sealer and tighten to the specified torque.

56 Install the reverse idler gear up against the rear face of the transmission so that the splines engage with the reverse gear inside the transmission case.

57 Locate a new gasket on the rear bearing retainer.

58 Install the tanged thrust washer on the reverse idler shaft, so that the tang of the washer engages in the notch of the idler thrust face of the extension.

59 Place the 1st/2nd and 3rd/4th synchro unit sleeves in neutral. Pull the reverse shift shaft partially out of the extension housing and push the reverse shift fork as far forward as possible. Offer the extension housing to the mainshaft, at the same time pushing the shifter shaft in to engage reverse shift fork with reverse gear shift collar.

60 When the fork engages, rotate the shifter shaft to move reverse gear rearward so enabling the extension to butt against the transmission case.

61 Install the reverse shifter shaft lock pin.

62 Install the extension housing retaining bolts and the shorter rear bearing retainer bolts. It is vital that the bolt indicated in the illustration has sealer applied to its threads before installation. Tighten all bolts to the specified torque (Fig. 7.22).

63 Set the 1st/2nd speed synchro sleeve to the 2nd gear position and 3rd/4th to neutral.

64 Locate the forward shift forks in the sliding sleeves.

65 Set the 1st/2nd speed gear shifter shaft and detent plate on the transmission side cover in 2nd gear position and install the side cover, using a new gasket to which sealer has been applied on both sides.

66 Check the gear selection. Refill the transmission with oil after it has been installed in the car.

Chapter 7 Part B Automatic transmission

Refer to Chapter 13 for specifications and information related to 1981 models

Contents

Specifications

Transmission type	2-speed or 3-speed fully automatic depending upon model and engine. Shift control is by either a steering column mounted rod or by a floor-mounted, cable-operated shifter.

Applications

1970 – 1972	Powerglide (2-speed)
	Turbo Hydra-Matic 350 (3-speed)
	Turbo Hydra-Matic 400 (3-speed)
1973 – 1974	Turbo Hydra-Matic 350 (3-speed)
	Turbo Hydra-Matic 400 (3-speed)
1975 – 1980	Turbo Hydra-Matic 350 (3-speed)

Fluid capacities

Powerglide

* Routine fluid change	$1\frac{1}{2}$ US qts
Filling from dry (overhaul)	9.0 US qts

Turbo Hydra-Matic 350

* Routine fluid change	$2\frac{1}{2}$ US qts
Filling from dry (overhaul)	10.0 US qts

Turbo Hydra-Matic 400

* Routine fluid change	3.75 US qts
Filling from dry (overhaul)	11 US qts

* The small quantity required at routine fluid changing is due to the fact that the fluid in the torque converter cannot be drained unless dismantled.

Torque specifications

	lb-ft

Powerglide

Transmission case to engine	35
Transmission oil pan to case	8
Transmission extension to case	25
Speedometer driven gear fitting retainer	4
Servo cover to transmission case bolts	20
Front pump to transmission case bolts	15
Front pump cover to body attaching bolts	20
Pinion shaft lockplate attaching screws	$2\frac{1}{2}$
Governor body to hub attaching bolts	7
Governor hub drive screw	8
Governor support to transmission case bolts	10
Valve body to transmission case bolts	15
Valve body suction screen attaching screws	$2\frac{1}{2}$
Upper valve body plate bolts	5
Lower to upper valve body attaching bolts	15
Inner control lever Allen head screw	$2\frac{1}{2}$
Parking lock pawl reaction bracket attaching bolts	10
Oil cooler plugs at transmission case	5
Pressure test point plugs	5
Low band adjustment locknut	15
Converter to flexplate bolts	35
Under pan to transmission case	$7\frac{1}{2}$

	lb-ft	lb-in
Oil cooler pipe connectors to transmission case or radiator	10	
Oil cooler pipe to connectors	10	
Vacuum modulator to transmission case	15	
Oil pan drain plug	20	
Parking brake lock and range selector inner lever Allen head screw ..	2½	

Turbo Hydra-Matic 350

	lb-ft	lb-in
Pump cover to pump body	17	
Pump assembly to case	18½	
Valve body and support plate		130
Parking lock bracket	29	
Oil suction screen		40
Oil pan to case		130
Extension to case	25	
Modulator retainer to case		130
Inner selector lever to shaft	25	
Detent valve actuating bracket		52
Converter to flexplate bolts	35	
Under pan to transmission case		110
Transmission case to engine	35	
Oil cooler pipe connectors to transmission case or radiator	15	
Oil cooler pipe to connectors	10	
Gearshift bracket to frame	15	
Gearshift shaft to swivel	20	
Manual shaft to bracket	20	
Detent cable to transmission		75
Intermediate band adjust nut	15	

Turbo Hydra-Matic 400

	lb-ft	lb-in
Pump cover bolts	18	
Parking pawl bracket bolts	18	
Center support bolts	23	
Pump to case attaching bolts	18	
Extension housing to case attaching bolts	23	
Rear servo cover bolts	18	
Detent solenoid bolts	7	
Control valve body bolts	8	
Bottom pan attaching screws	12	
Modulator retainer bolt	18	
Governor cover bolts	18	
Manual lever to manual shaft nut	8	
Manual shaft to inside detent lever	18	
Linkage swivel clamp nut	43	
Converter dust shield screws		93
Transmission to engine mounting bolts	35	
Converter to flexplate bolts	32	
Rear mount to transmission bolts	40	
Rear mount to cross-member bolt	40	
Cross-member mounting bolts	25	
Line pressure take-off plug	13	
Strainer retainer bolt	10	
Oil cooler pipe connectors to transmission case or radiator	14	
Oil cooler pipe to connector	10	
Gearshift bracket to frame	15	
Gearshift shaft to swivel	20	
Manual shaft to bracket	20	
Downshift switch to bracket	30	

1 General description

1 Fully automatic transmissions have been available on Camaro models since their introduction. The type depends upon the year of manufacture, and the engine size and output.
2 *Powerglide* The Powerglide is a fully automatic 2-speed transmission which changes speed depending on load and throttle position. A forced downshift facility is provided for immediate change to low speed for rapid acceleration.
3 *Turbo Hydra-Matic* These are fully automatic 3-speed transmissions and although they differ in basic design, operate on the same principle as the Powerglide.
4 Automatic transmissions comprise a 3-element hydrokinetic torque converter coupling capable of torque multiplication in an infinitely variable ratio between approximately 2 : 1 and 1 : 1, and a

torque/speed responsive hydraulically epicyclic gearbox.
5 In view of the need for special tools and equipment to carry out overhaul and repair operations to any of these automatic transmission units, the information in this chapter is restricted to maintenance and adjustment procedures; also the removal and installation of the transmission which will enable the home mechanic to install a new or rebuilt unit which, after a high mileage, is probably the most economical method of repair when a fault develops.

2 Identification

1 Besides checking the transmission serial number, there is a quick way to determine which of the three automatic transmissions a particular vehicle is fitted with. Read the following transmission oil pan descriptions and see Fig. 7.26 to identify the various models.

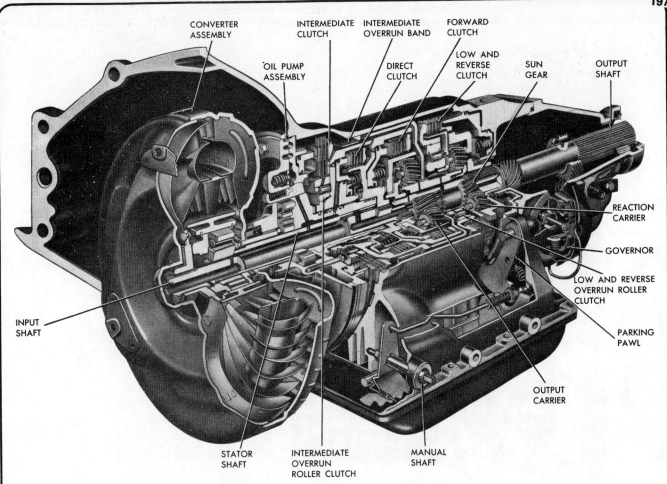

CONVERTER ASSEMBLY

OIL PUMP ASSEMBLY

INTERMEDIATE CLUTCH

DIRECT CLUTCH

INTERMEDIATE OVERRUN BAND

FORWARD CLUTCH

LOW AND REVERSE CLUTCH

SUN GEAR

OUTPUT SHAFT

REACTION CARRIER

GOVERNOR

LOW AND REVERSE OVERRUN ROLLER CLUTCH

PARKING PAWL

INPUT SHAFT

OUTPUT CARRIER

STATOR SHAFT

INTERMEDIATE OVERRUN ROLLER CLUTCH

MANUAL SHAFT

Fig. 7.23 Typical Turbo Hydra-Matic 350 type automatic transmission

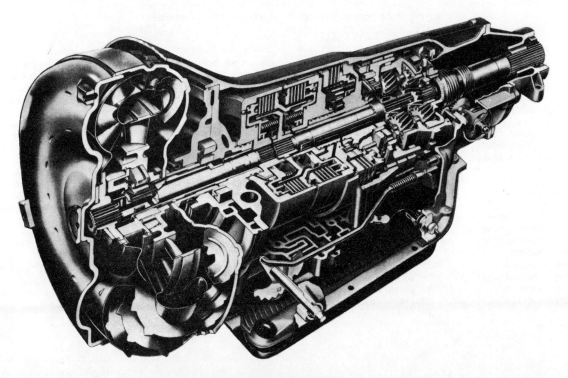

Fig. 7.24 Typical Turbo Hydra-Matic 400 type transmission

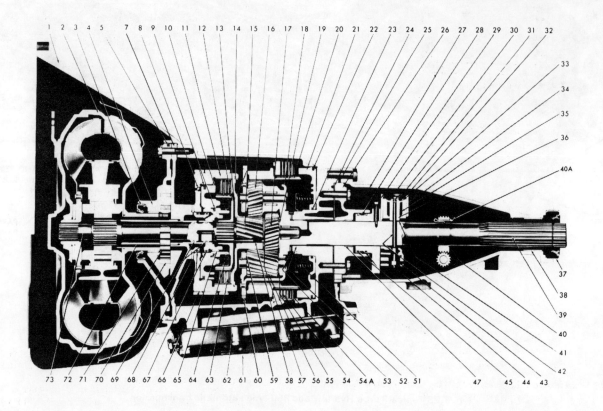

Fig. 7.25 Typical Powerglide type automatic transmission

1 Transmission case
2 Welded converter
3 Oil pump seal assembly
4 Oil pump body
5 Oil pump body square ring seal
7 Oil pump cover
8 Clutch relief valve ball
9 Clutch piston inner and outer seal
10 Clutch piston
11 Clutch drum
12 Clutch hub
13 Clutch hub thrust washer
14 Clutch flange retainer ring
15 Low sun gear and clutch flange assembly
16 Planet short pinion
17 Planet input sun gear
18 Planet carrier
19 Planet input sun gear thrust washer
20 Ring gear

21 Reverse piston
22 Reverse piston outer seal
23 Reverse piston inner seal
24 Governor support gasket
25 Extension seal ring
26 Governor support
27 Extension
28 Governor hub
29 Governor hub drive screw
30 Governor body
31 Governor shaft retainer clip
32 Governor outer weight retainer ring
33 Governor inner weight retainer ring
34 Governor outer weight
35 Governor spring
36 Governor inner weight
37 Extension rear oil seal
38 Extension rear bushing
39 Output shaft

40 Speedometer drive and driven gear
40A Speedometer driven gear retaining clip
41 Governor shaft urethane washer
42 Governor shaft
43 Governor valve
44 Governor valve retaining clip
45 Governor hub seal rings
47 Governor support bushing
51 Reverse piston return springs, retainer and retainer ring
52 Transmission rear case bushing
53 Output shaft thrust bearing
54 Reverse clutch pack
54A Reverse clutch cushion spring (waved)
55 Pinion thrust washer

56 Planet long pinion
57 Low sun gear needle thrust bearing
58 Low sun gear bushing (splined)
59 Pinion thrust washer
60 Parking lock gear
61 Transmission oil pan
62 Valve body
63 High clutch pack
64 Clutch piston return spring retainer and retainer ring
65 Clutch drum bushing
66 Low brake band
67 High clutch seal rings
68 Clutch drum thrust washer (selective)
69 Turbine shaft seal rings
70 Oil pump driven gear
72 Oil pump drive gear
72 Stator shaft
73 Input shaft

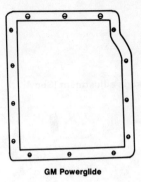

GM Powerglide

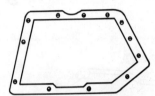

GM Turbo Hydra-Matic 250, 350, 375B

GM Turbo Hydra-Matic 400

Fig. 7.26 Transmission fluid pan shapes for identifying automatic transmission type (Sec 2)

Powerglide

2   The Powerglide transmission case is made of either cast iron or aluminum. The word 'Powerglide' is plainly stamped on the case. The shift quadrant indicator is set up in one of two ways: P-N-D-L-R or P-R-N-D-L.

Turbo Hydra-Matic 350

3   This transmission is a two-piece design with a downshift cable running from the accelerator to the right side of the transmission case. The oil pan has 13 bolts and is square-shaped with one corner angled (notched).

Turbo Hydra-Matic 400

4   The case of the 400 is also two-piece, but the downshifting is electrically controlled from a switch at the carburetor to the left side of the transmission. The oil pan also has 13 securing bolts. The shape of the pan is elongated and irregular.

3   Extension housing oil seal – replacement

1   This operation can be carried out without removing the transmission from the vehicle.
2   Place the vehicle over a pit or jack it up to gain access to the transmission. Support the vehicle with jack stands.
3   Disconnect the drive shaft from the transmission as described in Chapter 8.
4   Pry out the defective seal using a screwdriver or chisel as a lever.
5   Apply jointing compound to the outer edge of the new seal and drive it into position using a piece of tubing as a drift.
6   Install the driveshaft and check the fluid level in the transmission unit.

4   Column shift linkage – checking and adjustment

1   The selector linkage will be in need of adjustment if at any time 'Low' or 'Reverse' can be obtained without first having to lift the shift control lever to enable it to pass over the mechanical stop.
2   If adjustment is required, release the control rod swivel or clamp and set the lever on the side of the transmission in the 'Drive' or L2 detent. This can be clearly defined by placing the lever in L or L1 and moving the lever back one detent (click).
3   Position the shift control lever up against the 'Drive' stop and then tighten the swivel or clamp on the control rod.
4   Check all selector positions especially 'Park'. In some cases, especially with worn linkage it may be necessary to readjust slightly in order to ensure that the 'Park' detent is fully engaged.
5   Check that the ignition key can be moved freely to the 'Lock' position when the shift lever is in 'Park' and not in any other position.

5   Floor shift linkage – checking and adjustment

Powerglide

1   Place the shift lever in the 'Park' position.
2   Rotate the ignition key to the 'Lock' position.
3   Raise the vehicle and loosen the retaining screw located on the end of the shaft attached to the steering column.
4   Remove all lash in the column by rotating the shift lever in a downward direction. Then tighten the rod retaining screw.
5   Lower the vehicle and check for proper operation.

Turbo Hydra-Matic 1970 thru 1972

6   The operations are as described in earlier paragraphs of this section for the Powerglide transmission.

Turbo Hydra-Matic 1973 on

7   Move the shift control lever (J) (Fig. 7.29) into each speed range position and check that the lever (C) on the side of the transmission is in the corresponding detent position.
8   With the ignition key in 'Run' and shift lever in 'Reverse' check that the key cannot be removed also that that the steering wheel is unlocked.
9   Turn the key to 'Lock' and move the shift lever to 'Park' and check that the key can be withdrawn but the steering wheel is locked.
10 If adjustment is required, loosen screw (E) on the swivel (B) so that the rod (A) is free to move.
11 Set the shift lever in 'Drive' and then loosen the nut (G) so that the pin (F) is free to move in the slot of the transmission lever (C).
12 Set the transmission lever (C) in 'Drive'. Do this by moving the lever on the side of the transmission counterclockwise to the L1 detent and then back two detents ('clicks') to 'Drive'.
13 Tighten the nut (G) to 20 lb ft.
14 Set the shift control lever (J) in 'Park' and turn the ignition key to 'Lock'.
15 Pull down on the rod (A) lightly against the lockstop and then tighten screw (E) to 20 lb ft.

6   Turbo Hydra-Matic 350 – downshift (detent) cable adjustment

1970 – 1971 models

1   Disengage the snap lock of the detent cable.
2   Manually place the carburetor in the wide open throttle position with the lever fully against the stop. On vehicles with four barrel carburetors it will be necessary to disengage the secondary locknut before moving the throttle lever.
3   Make sure that the detent cable has passed through its detent position and holding the throttle lever fully open, press the snap lock on the detent cable downward until its top is flush with the cable.

1972 models

4   Insert a screwdriver on each side of the snap lock and pry upward to release.
5   Compress the locking tabs and disconnect the snap lock assembly from its bracket.

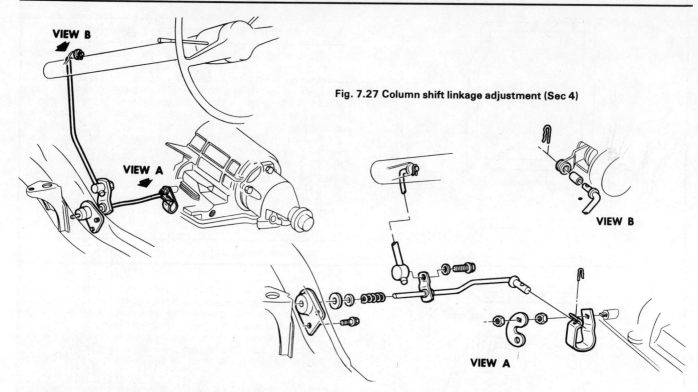

Fig. 7.27 Column shift linkage adjustment (Sec 4)

VIEW B

VIEW A

VIEW B

VIEW A

6   Manually set the carburetor in the fully open position with the throttle lever fully against its stop. Vehicles with four barrel carburetors require the secondary lockout to be disengaged before doing this.
7   With the carburetor in the fully open position push the snap lock on the detent cable downward until it is flush with the cable.

1973 – 1980 models
8   This will normally only be required after installation of a new cable.
9   Depress accelerator pedal to the fully open position. The cable ball will slide into the sleeve of the cable and automatically adjust the setting of the detent cable.

7   Turbo Hydra-Matic 400 – downshift (detent) switch adjustment

1970 thru 1971
1   Pull the detent switch driver rearwards until the hole in the switch body aligns with the hole in the driver. Insert a pin (0.092 in diameter) into the holes to a depth of .10 in to hold the driver in position.
2   Loosen the switch mounting bolt.
3   Depress the accelerator fully and then move the switch forward until the driver contacts the accelerator lever.
4   Tighten the switch bolt and extract the alignment pin.

1972 on
5   The switch is mounted on the pedal bracket as shown.
6   The switch is set by pushing the plunger as far forward as possible. At the first full depression of the accelerator pedal, the switch is automatically adjusted.

8   Turbo Hydra-Matic – neutral start switch adjustment (1970 thru 1972)

Column shift
1   Set the shift lever in 'Drive' and hold the lever tang against the selector plate. Release the switch screws.
2   Align the slot in the contact support with the hole in the switch and then insert a $\frac{3}{32}$ in diameter pin.
3   Place the contact support drive slot over the shifter tube drive tang and tighten the screws.

4   Withdraw the alignment pin.

Floor shift
5   Release the switch mounting screws and then set the shift lever in 'Drive' and align the hole in the contact support with the one in the switch and then insert a $\frac{3}{32}$ in diameter pin.
6   Place the contact support drive slot over the drive tang and tighten the switch mounting screws.
7   Withdraw the alignment pin.
8   With both types of switch, check the operation with the ignition switched on. The starter should only operate in shift positions N or P.

9   Turbo Hydra-Matic – combined neutral start/back-up lamp/seat belt warning switch adjustment – 1973 on

Column shift
1   If a new switch is being installed, set the shift lever against the 'Neutral' gate by rotating the lower lever on the shift tube in a counterclockwise direction as viewed from the driver's seat.
2   Locate the switch actuating tang in the shifter tube slot and then tighten the securing screws.
3   Connect the wiring harness and switch on the ignition and check that the starter motor will actuate.
4   If the switch operates correctly, move the shift lever out of neutral which will cause the alignment pin (fitted during production of the switch) to shear.
5   If an old switch is being installed or readjusted, use a pin (0.093 to 0.097 in diameter) to align the hole in the switch with the actuating tang. Insert the pin to a depth of $\frac{1}{4}$ inch. Remove the pin before moving the shift lever out of neutral.

Floor shift
6   This is similar to the procedure just described for column shift except that the shift lever should be set in 'Park' not 'Neutral'.
7   Access to the switch is obtained after removal of the trim plate and shift control assembly.

10   Powerglide transmission – removal and installation

1   Raise the vehicle or place it over an inspection pit for access beneath. Drain the transmission oil.

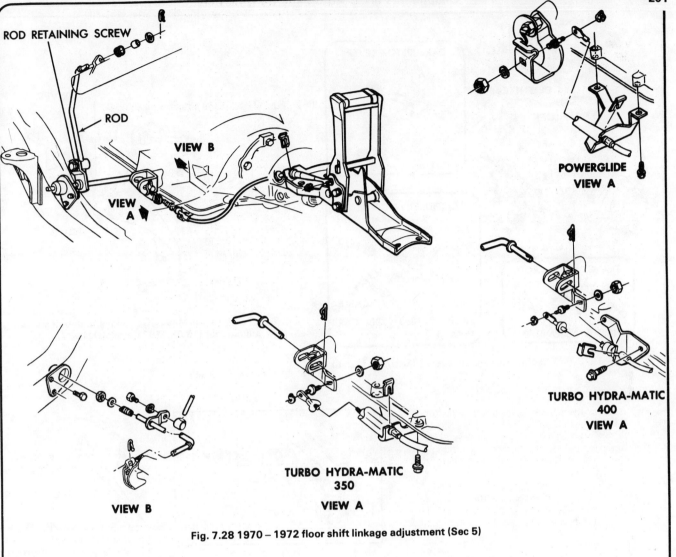

ROD RETAINING SCREW

ROD

VIEW B

VIEW A

POWERGLIDE
VIEW A

TURBO HYDRA-MATIC
400
VIEW A

VIEW B

TURBO HYDRA-MATIC
350
VIEW A

Fig. 7.28 1970 – 1972 floor shift linkage adjustment (Sec 5)

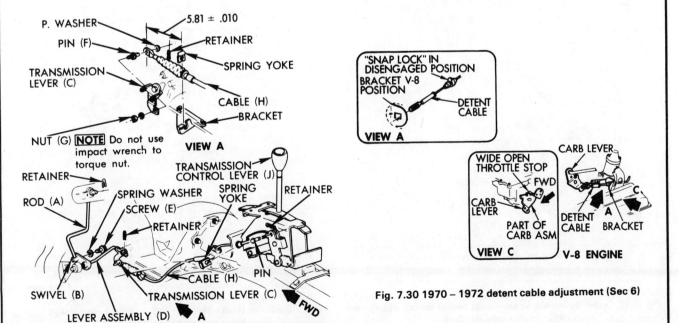

P. WASHER

5.81 ± .010

PIN (F)

RETAINER

SPRING YOKE

TRANSMISSION
LEVER (C)

CABLE (H)

BRACKET

NUT (G) **NOTE** Do not use
impact wrench to
torque nut.

VIEW A

RETAINER

TRANSMISSION
CONTROL LEVER (J)

ROD (A)

SPRING WASHER

SPRING
YOKE

RETAINER

SCREW (E)

RETAINER

CABLE (H)

PIN

SWIVEL (B)

TRANSMISSION LEVER (C)

FWD

LEVER ASSEMBLY (D)   A

Fig. 7.29 1973 – 1980 floor shift linkage adjustment (Sec 5)

"SNAP LOCK" IN
DISENGAGED POSITION
BRACKET V-8
POSITION

DETENT
CABLE

VIEW A

WIDE OPEN
THROTTLE STOP

CARB LEVER

FWD

CARB
LEVER

DETENT
CABLE

BRACKET

PART OF
CARB ASM

VIEW C

V-8 ENGINE

Fig. 7.30 1970 – 1972 detent cable adjustment (Sec 6)

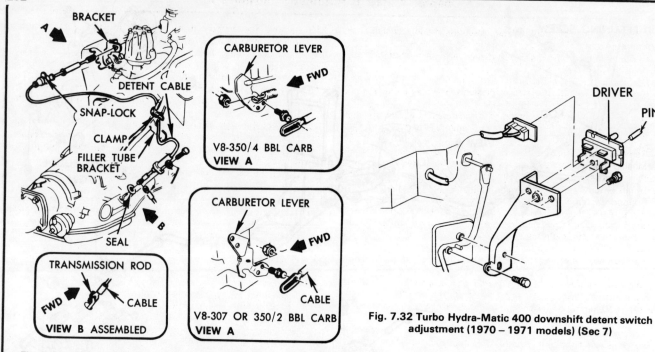

Fig. 7.31 1973 – 1980 downshift detent cable adjustment (Sec 6)

Fig. 7.32 Turbo Hydra-Matic 400 downshift detent switch adjustment (1970 – 1971 models) (Sec 7)

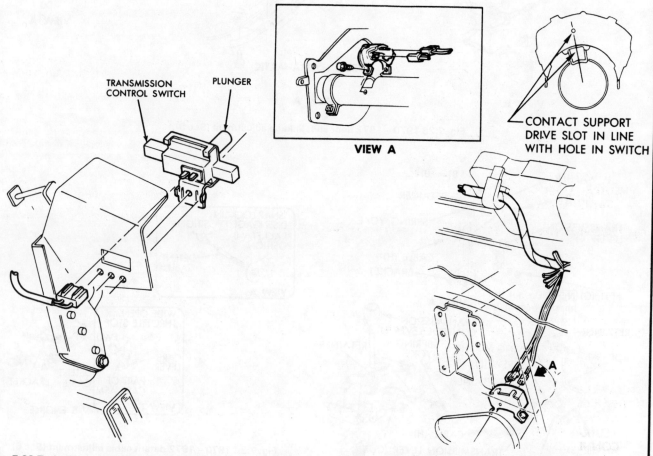

Fig. 7.33 Turbo Hydra-Matic downshift detent switch adjustment (1972 – 1980 models) (Sec 7)

Fig. 7.34 Turbo Hydra-Matic (1970 – 1972) column shift neutral start switch adjustment (Sec 8)

2   Disconnect the oil cooler lines, vacuum modulator line, and speedometer cable.
3   Disconnect the throttle valve and manual control rods from the transmission.
4   Disconnect the driveshaft (refer to Chapter 8).
5   Support the weight of the transmission using a suitable jack and spacers.
6   Disconnect the rear mount on the transmission extension, then disconnect the transmission support crossmember and slide it rearwards.
7   Remove the converter underpan, scribe the converter/flexplate relationship for assembly, then remove the flexplate to converter attaching bolts. These can be brought into view, one at a time if the crankshaft is turned using a wrench applied to the pulley bolt.
8   Support the engine at the oil pan rail with a suitable jack, then lower the rear of the transmission slightly so that the upper housing attaching bolts can be reached using a suitable socket and extension. Take care that the distributor does not touch the firewall as the transmission is being lowered.
9   Remove the upper attaching bolts first, then the remainder of the bolts.
10 Remove the transmission rearwards and downwards, and away from the engine. If necessary, pry it free from the flexplate. Keep the rear of the transmission downwards at all times or the converter will fall out. This can be retained using a holding strap.
11 When installing, remove the converter holding strap, keep the rear of the transmission slightly downwards then raise the transmission into place.
12 Install the upper attaching bolts, followed by the remaining bolts; torque-tighten to the specified value.

13 Remove the support from beneath the engine then raise the transmission into its installed position.
14 Align the scribe marks and install the converter to the flexplate. Torque-tighten the bolts to the specified value.
15 Install the converter underpan.
16 Install the support crossmember to the transmission and frame.
17 Remove the lifting equipment then connect the driveshaft (refer to Chapter 7).
18 Connect the manual and throttle valve control lever rods, the oil cooler lines, vacuum modulator line and speedometer drive cable.
19 Refill the transmission (Chapter 1), check for proper operation and examine for leaks.
20 Lower the vehicle and check the transmission fluid level.

11 Turbo Hydra-Matic transmission – removal and installation

1   Disconnect the battery ground cable and release the parking brake.
2   Raise the vehicle on a hoist or place it over an inspection pit.
3   Disconnect the speedometer cable, detent cable, electrical leads, modulator vacuum line and oil cooler pipes, as appropriate.
4   Disconnect the shift control linkage.
5   Disconnect the driveshaft (Chapter 8).
6   Support the transmission with a suitable jack, and disconnect the rear mount from the frame crossmember.
7   Remove the two bolts at each end of the crossmember then remove the crossmember.
8   Remove the converter underpan.
9   Loosen the exhaust downpipe bolts a1t the manifold and unscrew them about $\frac{1}{4}$ inch.
10 Mark the relationship of the flexplate to the torque converter and then unscrew the connecting bolts. These are accessible through the front of the torque converter housing but will have to be brought into view one at a time by applying a wrench to the torsional damper center bolt.
11 Lower the transmission as far as possible without causing any engine or transmission components to come into contact with the engine compartment firewall.
12 Remove the transmission to engine connecting bolts and remove the oil filler tube at the transmission.
13 Raise the transmission to its normal position, support the engine with the jack and slide the transmission rearwards from the engine. Keep the rear of the transmission downwards so that the converter does not fall off. Use a holding strap similar to the one described in Section 10.
14 Installation is the reverse of the removal procedure, but additionally ensure that the weld nuts on the converter are flush with the flexplate and that the converter rotates freely in this position. Tighten all bolts finger-tight before torque-tightening to the specified value.

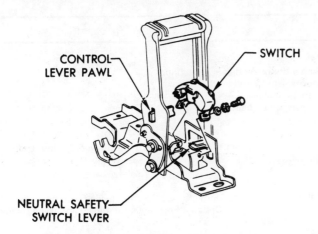

Fig. 7.35 Turbo Hydra-Matic (1970 – 1972) floor shift neutral start switch adjustment (Sec 8)

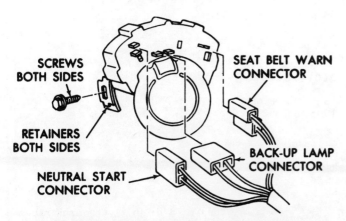

Fig. 7.36 Turbo Hydra-Matic (1973 – 1980) combined neutral start/back-up lamp/seat belt warning switch adjustment (Sec 9)

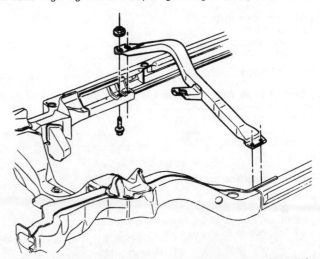

Fig. 7.37 Typical transmission crossmember support (Sec 11)

Chapter 8 Driveline

Contents

Specifications

Clutch
Clutch type .... Single dry plate, diaphragm spring
Clutch actuation .... Mechanical by rod
Clutch pedal free-play (measured at center of pedal pad) .... 1 to 1½ inches
Clutch throwout (release) bearing type .... Grease sealed ball

Driveshaft
Driveshaft type .... Open, single section, tubular steel with two universal joints and one slip joint

Rear axle
Rear axle type .... Salisbury, semi-floating with cast carrier having overhung hypoid pinion and ring gear. Optional Positraction (limited slip) axle available on all models
Rear axle ring gear diameter .... 8½ inch

Lubricant capacity
1970 thru 1971
Light duty axle .... 4.5 pints
Heavy duty axle .... 4.9 pints

1973 thru 1980 .... 4.25 pints

B and O type axles (see Section 13, this Chapter)
Axleshaft end-play .... 0.001 to 0.022 in
Pinion bearing pre-load:
    New .... 15 to 30 in lbs
    Used .... 10 to 15 in lbs

Torque specifications
Clutch
	lb-ft
Clutch pressure plate bolts	35
Transmission case to clutch bellhousing bolts	55
Clutch bellhousing to engine bolts	30

Driveshaft
Universal joint to companion flange:
1970 − 1976	15
1977 − 1980	70

Rear axle

1970 thru 1971

Differential carrier cover bolts	30
Ring gear bolts	85
Differential bearing cap bolts	60
Oil filler plug	20
Differential pinion lock	20

1972

Differential carrier cover bolts	25
Ring gear bolts	85
Differential bearing caps	60
Oil filler plug	25
Differential pinion lock	20

1973 on

As 1972 except for

Ring gear bolts	90

1 General description – clutch

1 All models are fitted with a single dry plate, diaphragm spring type clutch. Operation is by means of a pendant foot pedal and rod linkage. The unit comprises a pressure plate assembly which contains the pressure plate, diaphragm spring and fulcrum rings. The assembly is bolted to the rear face of the flywheel.

2 The driven plate (friction disc) is free to slide along the gearbox input shaft and it is held in place between the flywheel and pressure plate faces by the pressure exerted by the diaphragm spring. The friction lining material is riveted to the driven plate which incorporates a spring-cushioned hub designed to absorb transmission rotational shocks and to assist in ensuring smooth take-offs.

3 The circular diaphragm spring assembly is mounted on shouldered pins and held in place in the cover by fulcrum rings. The spring itself is held in place by spring steel clips. On high performance vehicles, or where a heavy duty clutch is required, the diaphragm spring has bent fingers, whereas the standard version has flat fingers. The bent finger design is used to gain a centrifugal boost to aid rapid re-engagement of the clutch at high rotational speeds.

4 Depressing the clutch pedal pushes the throwout-bearing, mounted on its hub retainer, forward to bear against the fingers of the diaphragm spring. This action causes the diaphragm spring outer edge to deflect and so move the pressure plate rearwards to disengage the pressure plate from the driven plate.

5 When the clutch pedal is released, the diaphragm spring forces the pressure plate into contact with the friction linings of the driven plate and at the same time pushes the drive plate fractionally forward on its splines to ensure full engagement with the flywheel. The driven plate is now firmly sandwiched between the pressure plate and the flywheel and so the drive is taken up.

2 Clutch – adjustment

1 The free-play at the clutch pedal should be approximately 1 inch.

2 There is only one linkage adjustment to compensate for all normal clutch wear.

3 To check for correct adjustment, apply the parking brake, block the front wheels and start the engine. Hold the clutch pedal approximately $\frac{1}{2}$ inch from the floor and move the shift lever between 'First' and 'Reverse' gears several times. If the shift is not smooth, clutch adjustment is necessary.

4 Raise the car to permit access to the clutch linkage under the car. Place firmly on jack stands.

5 Disconnect the return spring at the clutch fork.

6 Rotate the clutch lever and shaft assembly until the clutch pedal is firmly against the rubber bumper on the dashboard brace. If in doubt about this, have an assistant check this from inside the car.

7 Push the outer end of the clutch fork rearward until the release bearing lightly contacts the pressure plate fingers.

8 Keep the fork in this position while the push rod is removed from its holes in the shaft. Now place the rod in the gauge hole of the shaft,

directly above the normal operating hole.

9 With the push rod in the gauge hole, loosen the locking nut and turn the rod to increase its length. Increase the length of the rod until all lash is removed from the system.

10 Remove the rod from the gauge hole and return it to the lower operating hole in the shaft. Install the retainer and then carefully tighten the nut, being sure the length of the rod is not changed.

11 Connect the return spring and check the pedal free-play as described previously. Lower the vehicle, then check for correct operation and free travel.

3 Clutch pedal – removal and installation

1 Disconnect the return spring for the clutch pedal.

2 Disconnect the clutch pedal push rod where it meets the pedal arm. This is held in place at the top of the pedal with a lock pin.

3 Disconnect the electrical coupler for the neutral start switch. Then remove the switch from the top of the clutch pedal.

4 The pivot shaft which runs through the clutch and brake pedals must now be removed. It is held in place with a retaining nut on one end. Remove the nut and slide the shaft until it clears the pedal support. Now insert a dummy shaft in the support to hold the brake pedal components in place while the pivot shaft is removed.

5 Remove the pivot shaft, pedal arm and bushings.

6 Inspect all parts and replace as necessary. Do not clean the nylon bushings with cleaning agent, simply wipe them clean with a cloth. Lubricate the bushings and all moving parts.

7 To reinstall the pedal, push the bushings into place and then the pivot shaft and pedal arm.

8 Install the retaining nut to the end of the shaft.

9 Install the neutral start switch and connect its wiring coupler.

10 Connect the push rod to the pedal arm. Make sure it is securely fastened.

11 Connect the return spring and check for free travel. Adjust the components as required.

4 Clutch cross-shaft – removal and installation

1 Remove the linkage return and lower linkage springs. Disconnect the clutch pedal and fork push rods from their respective cross-shaft levers.

2 Loosen the outboard ball stud nut and slide the stud out of the slot in the bracket.

3 Move the cross-shaft outboard far enough to clear the inboard ball stud, then lift it out and remove it from the vehicle.

4 Check the ball stud seats on the cross-shaft, the engine bracket ball stud assembly and the anti-rattle spring for damage and wear; replace parts as necessary.

5 When installing, reverse the removal procedure. Lubricate the ball studs and seat with graphite grease on assembly and finally adjust the clutch (Section 2).

5 Clutch – removal, servicing and installation

1 Access to the clutch is normally obtained by removing the transmission, leaving the engine in the car. If, of course, the engine is being removed for major overhaul, then the opportunity should always be taken to check the clutch assembly for wear at the same time.

2 Disconnect the clutch fork push rod and spring then remove the clutch housing from the engine cylinder block.
3 Slide the clutch fork from the ball stud and remove the fork from the dust boot.
4 If necessary, the ball stud can be removed from the clutch housing by unscrewing (photo).
5 If there are no alignment marks on the clutch cover (an X-mark or white-painted letter) scribe or center-punch marks for indexing purposes during installation.
6 Unscrew the bolts securing the pressure plate and cover assembly one turn at a time in a diagonal sequence to prevent distortion of the clutch cover.
7 With all the bolts and lockwashers removed, carefully lift the

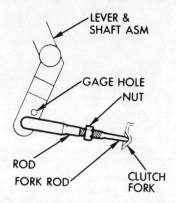

Fig. 8.1 Clutch adjustment diagram (Sec 2)

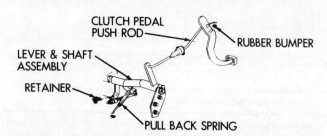

Fig. 8.2 Clutch pedal components (Sec 3)

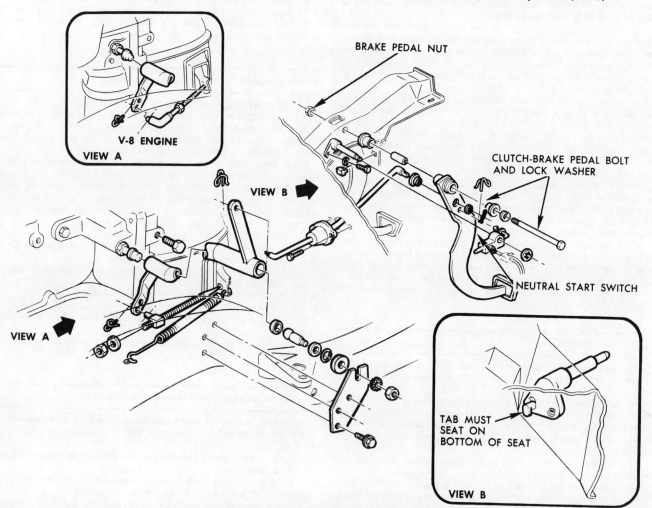

Fig. 8.3 Clutch pedal and cross-shaft components (Sec 3)

5.4 Front face of transmission showing the clutch fork ball stud

5.7 Removing the clutch assembly

5.19 Centralizing the clutch driven plate using an old clutch drive gear

5.24A Engagement of clutch fork with throwout bearing

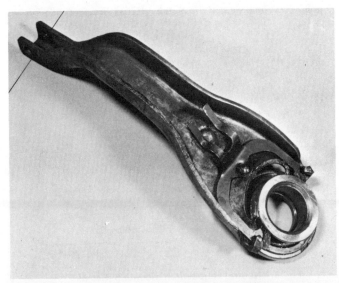

5.24B Rear view of the clutch fork and throwout bearing

5.24C Clutch fork and throwout bearing installed

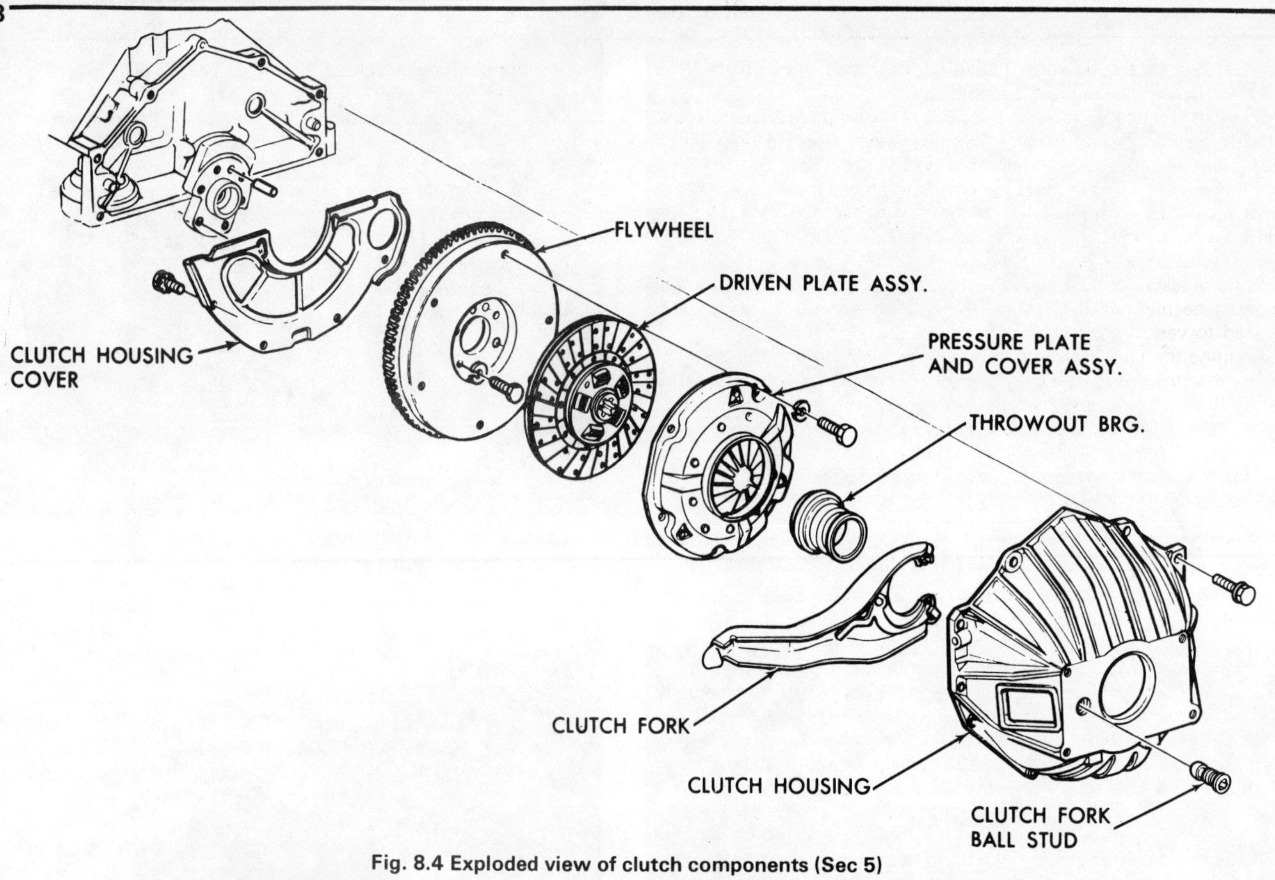

FLYWHEEL

DRIVEN PLATE ASSY.

PRESSURE PLATE
AND COVER ASSY.

CLUTCH HOUSING
COVER

THROWOUT BRG.

CLUTCH FORK

CLUTCH HOUSING

CLUTCH FORK
BALL STUD

Fig. 8.4 Exploded view of clutch components (Sec 5)

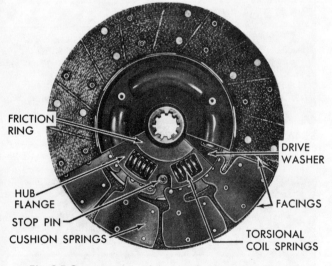

FRICTION
RING

DRIVE
WASHER

HUB
FLANGE

FACINGS

STOP PIN

CUSHION SPRINGS

TORSIONAL
COIL SPRINGS

Fig. 8.5 Cutaway view of the clutch driven plate (Sec 5)

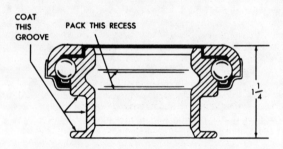

COAT
THIS
GROOVE

PACK THIS RECESS

1¼

Fig. 8.6 Sectional view of the clutch release (throwout) bearing (Sec 5)

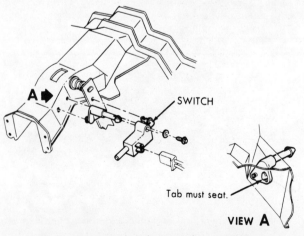

A▶

SWITCH

Tab must seat.

VIEW **A**

Fig. 8.7 Neutral start switch mounting (Sec 6)

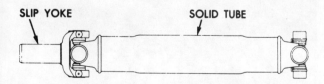

SLIP YOKE

SOLID TUBE

Fig. 8.8 Typical drive shaft (propeller shaft)

clutch away from the flywheel taking care that the driven plate does not fall or become damaged (photo).

8   It is not practicable to dismantle the pressure plate assembly and the term 'dismantling' is usually used for simply fitting a new clutch driven plate and pressure plate (if necessary).

9   If a new clutch driven plate is being fitted it is a false economy not to replace the throwout bearing at the same time. This will preclude having to replace it at a later date when wear on the clutch linings is still very small.

10 If the pressure plate assembly requires replacement, an exchange unit must be purchased. This will have been accurately set up and balanced to very fine limits.

11 Examine the clutch plate friction linings for wear and loose rivets, and the disc for rim distortion, cracks, broken hub springs, and worn splines. The surface of the friction linings may be highly glazed, but as long at the clutch material pattern can be clearly seen this is satisfactory. Compare the amount of lining wear with a new clutch disc at the stores in your local service station. If worn, the driven plate must be replaced.

12 Check the machined faces of the flywheel and the pressure plate. If either are grooved they should be machined until smooth, or replaced.

13 If the pressure plate is cracked or split, it is essential that an exchange unit is fitted; also if the pressure of the diaphragm spring is suspect, this should be checked and replaced if necessary.

14 Check the throwout bearing for smoothness of operation. There should be no harshness or slackness in it. It should spin reasonably freely bearing in mind it has been pre-packed with grease. If in doubt, replace the bearing with a new one.

15 It is important that no oil or grease gets on the clutch plate friction linings, or the pressure plate and flywheel faces. It is advisable to replace the clutch with clean hands and to wipe down the pressure plate and flywheel faces with a clean dry rag before assembly begins.

16 Place the driven plate against the flywheel making sure that the longer splined boss faces towards the flywheel (thicker torsional spring assembly projection towards the transmission).

17 Install the pressure plate and clutch cover assembly so that the marks made on dismantling are in alignment. Tighten the bolts only finger-tight so that the driven plate is gripped, but can still be slid sideways.

18 The clutch plate must now be centralized so that when the engine and transmission are mated, the clutch shaft splines will pass through the splines in the center of the driven plate hub.

19 Centralization can be carried out quite easily by inserting a round bar or long screwdriver through the hole in the center of the clutch, so that the end of the bar rests in the small hole in the end of the crankshaft containing the input shaft pilot bushing. Ideally an old clutch drive gear or centralizing tool should be used (photo).

20 Using the clutch shaft bearing bushing as a fulcrum, moving the bar sideways or up and down will move the clutch plate in whichever direction is necessary to achieve centralization.

21 Centralization is easily judged by removing the bar and viewing the driven plate hub in relation to the hole in the center of the clutch cover plate diaphragm spring. When the hub appears exactly in the center of the hole, all is correct. Alternatively, the clutch shaft will fit the bushing and center of the clutch hub exactly, obviating the need for visual alignment. On pressure plate covers which have cutaway edges, the center plate can be centralized simply by lining up its edges with the edge of the flywheel, just using the fingers.

22 Tighten the clutch cover bolts firmly in a diagonal sequence to ensure that the cover plate is pulled down evenly and without distortion to the flange. Torque the bolts to specifications.

23 Lubricate the clutch fork fingers at the throwout bearing end, and the ball and socket, with a high melting point grease. Also lubricate the throwout bearing collar and groove (see Fig. 8.6).

24 Install the clutch fork and dust boot into the clutch housing and install the throwout bearing to the fork (photos).

25 Install the clutch housing.

26 Install the transmission. Refer to Chapter 2 or Chapter 7, as necessary.

27 Connect the fork push rod and spring, lubricating the spring and push rod ends.

28 Adjust the shift linkage (Chapter 7) and the clutch linkage (Section 2).

---

6   Neutral start switch – removal and installation

1   This switch is a safety device intended to prevent the vehicle from being started without the clutch pedal being fully depressed. The small switch mounts to the clutch pedal mounting bracket and is activated by a plastic shaft which is part of the switch.

2   Disconnect the electrical coupler at the switch.

3   Compress the switch actuating shaft retainer and remove the shaft, with the switch attached, from the bracket.

4   To install, slide the switch onto the bracket and make sure the tab is fully seated. Then rotate the switch actuating shaft until it aligns with the hole in the clutch pedal arm and pop the shaft into the hole.

5   Connect the electrical coupler to the switch.

6   The switch is self-aligning, meaning that there is no need for adjustments.

---

7   General description – driveshaft

1   The driveshaft is of a one piece tubular steel construction having a universal joint at each end to allow for vertical movement of the rear axle. At the front end of the shaft is a sliding sleeve which engages with the transmission unit splined output shaft.

2   Early models were fitted with Cleveland or Saginaw type universal joints. The Cleveland type is retained with snap-rings outboard of the universal joint but the Saginaw type is retained by a nylon material which is injected into a groove in the yoke during manufacture. The latter type of joint can be serviced by the use of a repair kit which utilizes snap-rings inboard of the yoke when the joint is reassembled. Some later models (1974 on) are fitted with a constant velocity joint at the axle end. The complete joint can be removed as an assembly by following the procedure given for the early type universal joint. The constant velocity joint has a centering ball which can be serviced (see Section 12).

3   Some driveshafts incorporate a vibration damper. This item is not serviced separately, and in the event of replacement being necessary, the damper and sleeves are to be replaced as an assembly.

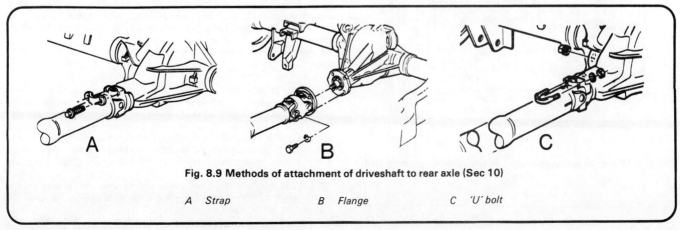

Fig. 8.9 Methods of attachment of driveshaft to rear axle (Sec 10)

A   Strap   B   Flange   C   'U' bolt

4   The driveshafts are finely balanced during manufacture and it is recommended that an exchange unit is obtained rather than dismantling the universal joints when wear is evident. However, this is not always possible and provided care is taken to mark each individual yoke in relation to the one opposite, then the balance will usually be maintained. Do not drop the assembly during operations.

8   Universal joints – testing for wear

1   Wear in the needle roller bearings is characterized by vibration in the transmission, 'clonks' on taking up the drive, and in extreme cases of lack of lubrication, metallic squeaking and ultimately grating and shrieking sounds as the bearings break up.
2   It is easy to check if the needle roller bearings are worn with the shaft in position, by trying to turn it with one hand, the other hand holding the rear axle flange when the rear universal joint is being checked, and the front half coupling when the front universal joint is being checked. Any movement between the shaft and the couplings is indicative of considerable wear.
3   A further test for wear is to attempt to lift the shaft and note any movement between the yokes of the joints.
4   If wear is evident, either fit a new propeller shaft assembly complete or replace the universal joints, as described later in this chapter.

9   Driveshaft out-of-balance – correction

1   Vibration of the driveshaft at certain roadspeeds may be caused by any of the following:

   a) Undercoating or mud on the shaft
   b) Loose rear strap attachment bolts
   c) Worn universal joints
   d) Bent or dented driveshaft

2   Vibrations which are thought to be emanating from the drive shaft are sometimes caused by improper tire balance. This should be one of your first checks.
3   If the shaft is in a good, clean, undamaged condition, it is worth disconnecting the rear end attachment straps and turning the shaft 180 degrees to see if an improvement is noticed. Be sure to mark the original position of each component before disassembly so the shaft can be returned to the same location.
4   If the vibration persists after checking for obvious causes and changing the position of the shaft, the entire assembly should be checked out by a professional shop or replaced.

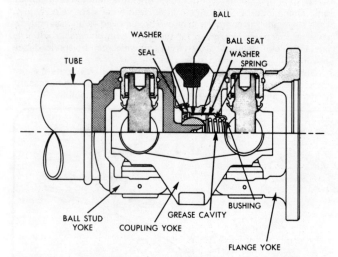

Fig. 8.10 A typical constant velocity joint with a centering ball (Sec 12)

10   Driveshaft – removal and installation

1   Raise the rear of the vehicle and support it securely on blocks or axle-stands.
2   Mark the relationship of the driveshaft to the companion flange on the rear axle pinion (photo).
3   Disconnect the rear universal joint by unscrewing and removing the nuts from the U-bolts or strap retaining bolts, or by removing the flange bolts. Where U-bolts or retaining straps are used, wrap adhesive tape around the bearing cups to prevent them being displaced and the needle rollers dropping out (photos).
4   Lower the rear end of the driveshaft and then withdraw the complete shaft assembly to the rear. The front splined sliding sleeve section will be drawn off the transmission output shaft during the removal operation and a small amount of lubricant may be lost from vehicles equipped with manual transmission (photo).
5   Installation is a reversal of removal but remember to align the shaft to flange mating marks and take care not to damage the transmission extension oil seal with the sliding joint splines (photo).
6   Check the transmission oil level when installation is complete.

11   Universal joints – dismantling and reassembly

Cleveland type joint
1   Clean away all dirt from the ends of the bearings on the yokes so that the snap-rings can be removed using a pair of snap-ring pliers. If the snap-rings are very tight, tap the end of the bearing cup (inside the snap-ring) to relieve the pressure (photo).
2   Support the trunnion yoke on a short piece of tube or the open end of a socket then use a suitably sized socket to press out the cross (trunnion) by means of a vise (photo).
3   Press the trunnion through as far as possible then grip the bearing cup in the jaws of a vise to fully remove it. Repeat the procedure for the remaining cups (photo).
4   On some models, the slip yoke at the transmission end has a vent hole. When dismantling, ensure that this vent hole is not blocked.
5   A universal joint repair kit will contain a new trunnion, seals, bearings, cups and snap-rings.
6   Commence reassembly by packing each of the reservoirs at the trunnion ends with lubricant.
7   Make sure that the dust seals are correctly located on the trunnion so that the cavities in the seals are nearer the trunnion.
8   Using a vise, press one bearing cup into the yoke so that it1 enters by not more than one quarter-inch.
9   Using a thick grease, stick each of the needle rollers inside the cup (photo).
10   Insert the trunnion into the partially fitted bearing cup taking care not to displace the needle rollers.
11   Stick the needle bearings into the opposite cup and then holding the trunnion in correct alignment, press both cups fully home in the jaws of the vise.
12   Install the new snap-rings.
13   Repeat the operations on the other two bearing cups.
14   In extreme cases of wear or neglect, it is possible that the bearing cup housings in the yoke will have worn so much that the cups are a loose fit in the yokes. In such cases, replace the complete driveshaft assembly.
15   Always check the wear in the sliding sleeve splines and replace the sleeve if worn.

Saginaw type joint
16   Where a Saginaw joint is to be disassembled, the procedure given in the previous section for pressing out the bearing cup is applicable. If the joint has been previously repaired it will be necessary to remove the snap-rings inboard of the yokes; if this is to be the first time that servicing has been carried out, there are no snap-rings to remove, but the pressing operation in the vise will shear the plastic molding material.
17   Having removed the cross (trunnion), remove the remains of the plastic material from the yoke. Use a small punch to remove the material from the injection holes.
18   Reassembly is similar to that given for the Cleveland type joint

10.2 Marking the position of the drive shaft and universal joint components. All parts must be reinstalled in their original positions

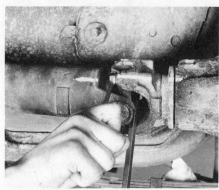

10.3A Hold the drive shaft from turning as the securing bolts are loosened

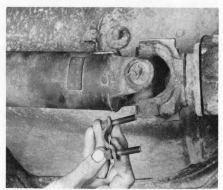

10.3B The securing strap and bolts removed from the rear axle assembly

10.4 Lower the rear of the driveshaft slightly and then pull front out of transmission

10.5 When reinstalling, be careful not to damage the seal at the rear of the transmission

11.1 Removing the snap-rings from the bearing cup surface

11.2 Pressing out trunnion (cross) using a vise and sockets. One socket should be slightly smaller than the bearing cup and the socket on the other side slightly larger

11.3 The trunnion (cross) removed from the driveshaft yoke

11.9 The inside of the bearing cup showing the small roller bearings

except that the snap-rings are installed inside the yoke. If difficulty is encountered, strike the yoke firmly with a hammer to assist in seating.

12 Double cardan type constant velocity joint – overhaul

1   An inspection kit containing two bearing cups and two retainers is available to permit the joint to be dismantled to the stage where the joint can be inspected. Before any dismantling is commenced, mark the flange yoke and coupling yoke so that they can be reassembled in the same relative position.

2   Dismantle the joint by removing the bearing cups in a similar way to that described in the preceding section according to type.

3   Disengage the flange yoke and trunnion from the centering ball. Pry the seal from the ball socket and remove the washers, springs and the 3 ball seats.

4   Clean the ball seat insert bushing and inspect for wear. If evident the flange yoke and trunnion assembly must be replaced.

5   Clean the seal, ball seats, spring and washers and inspect for wear. If excessive wear is evident or parts are broken, a replacement service kit must be used.

6   Remove all plastic material from the groove of the coupling yoke (if this type of joint is used).

7   Inspect the centering ball, if damaged it must be replaced.

8   Withdraw the centering ball from the stud using a suitable extractor. Provided that the ball is not to be re-used, it will not matter if it is damaged.

9   Press a new ball onto the stud until it seats firmly on the stud shoulder. It is extremely important that no damage to the ball occurs during this stage and suitable protection must be given to it.

10 Using the grease provided in the repair kit, lubricate all the parts and insert them into the ball seat cavity in the following order: spring, washer (small OD), 3 ball seats (largest opening outwards to receive the ball), washer (large OD) and the seal.

11 Lubricate the seal lips and press it (lip inwards) into the cavity. Fill the cavity with the grease provided.

13.4 The rear axle identification number stamped onto the surface of the right axle tube

14.4 The pinion shaft lock screw and the pinion shaft being removed from the differential assembly

14.5 The C-lock being withdrawn from the differential

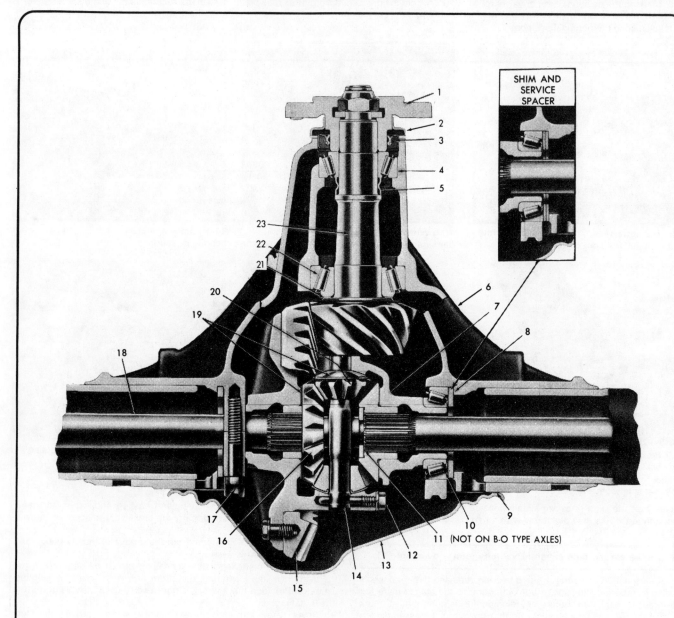

SHIM AND SERVICE SPACER

Fig. 8.11 Typical rear axle differential cross-section (Sec 13)

1 Companion flange	6 Differential carrier	11 "C" lock
2 Deflector	7 Differential case	12 Pinion shaft lock bolt
3 Pinion oil seal	8 Shim	13 Cover
4 Pinion front bearing	9 Gasket	14 Pinion shaft
5 Pinion bearing spacer	10 Differential bearing	15 Ring gear

16 Side gear	21 Shim
17 Bearing cap	22 Pinion rear bearing
18 Axle shaft	23 Drive pinion
19 Thrust washer	
20 Differential pinion	

11 (NOT ON B-O TYPE AXLES)

12 Install the flange yoke to the centering ball, ensuring that the alignment marks are correctly positioned.
13 Install the trunnion caps as described previously for the Cleveland or Saginaw types.

13 General description and identification – rear axle

1 The rear axle is of hypoid, semi-floating type. The differential carrier is a casting with a pressed steel cover and the axle tubes are of steel construction.
2 Due to the need for special gauges and equipment and to the fact that individual differential components are no longer supplied (only a complete rear axle unit) the servicing and repair operations should be confined to those described in this chapter.
3 An optional 'Positraction' (limited slip) differential unit has been available since the earliest models. Basically, the inclusion of clutch cones or plates and springs slow the rotation of the differential case when one wheel is on a firm surface and the other on a slippery one. This slowing action applies additional force to the pinion gears and through the medium of the cone which is splined to the axleshafts, exerts equalizing rotational power to the axleshaft which is driving the wheel under traction.
4 In order to be able to undertake certain operations, particularly removal of the axleshafts, it is important to know the axle identification number. This is located on the front face of the right-hand axle tube about 3 inches from the differential cover. After the dirt and road grime has been brushed away, the code can be read (photo). A typical General Motors axle code for 1971 and later models will read: CA C 150 N W.
5 The first two letters, in this case CA, are the axle code. By using the axle code and ratio chart which follows you can determine the gear ratios installed in the axle assembly. In 1970 only, a three-letter axle ratio code was used, this being the only difference between 1970 and later models.

6 The third letter of the code identifies the manufacturer of the axle. This is important, as axle design varies slightly between manufacturers. This single-letter code will be one of the following: B-Buick, C-Chevrolet (Buffalo), G-Chevrolet gear and axle, K-GM of Canada, M-GM of Canada, O-Oldsmobile or P-Pontiac. Manufacturers code letters B or O, indicate that the wheel bearings are pressed onto the axleshafts whereas all other letters have bearings pressed into the axle tubes and the axleshafts are retained with C-locks.
7 Following the manufacturer's code letter will be varying numbers which indicate which day of the year that the axle was built. Letter D or N following the date code represents day or night shift.
8 The last letter of the code is a locking axle (Positraction) identification. Vehicles built with this type of axle will have one of the following code letters: E-Eaton, G-Chevrolet, O-Oldsmobile, or W-Borg-Warner.
9 The following axle code chart identifies the gear ratio and year of each axle assembly. Axle assemblies built for 1978 and later vehicles may have the axle ratio stamped on the housing rather than the two-letter (three-letter in 1970) axle code.

CA	3.08 non-locking	1971 – 1974
CB	3.36 non-locking	1971 – 1974
CG	3.36 locking	1971 – 1974
CJ	3.42 non-locking	1971 – 1972
CK	3.42 non-locking	1971 – 1972
CL	3.42 non-locking	1973 – 1974
CM	3.42 locking	1973 – 1974
GX	3.55 locking	1971 – 1974
GY	3.08 locking	1971 – 1974
GZ	2.73 non-locking	1971 – 1974
PA	2.73 non-locking	1975 – 1978
PC	3.08 non-locking	1975 – 1978
PE	3.42 non-locking	1978

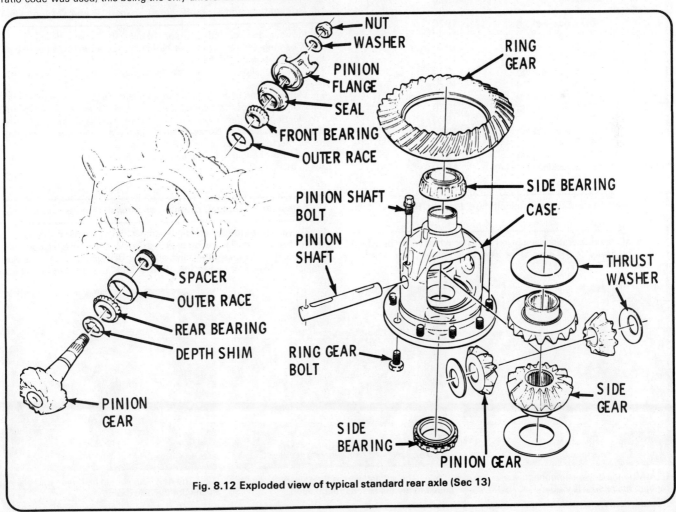

Fig. 8.12 Exploded view of typical standard rear axle (Sec 13)

PF	3.73 non-locking	1978
PH	2.56 non-locking	1975, 1977
PJ	2.41 non-locking	1978
PM	3.23 non-locking	1978
PP	3.23 locking	1978
PS	2.41 locking	1978
PT	2.56 locking	1975, 1977
PU	2.73 locking	1975 – 1978
PW	3.08 locking	1975 – 1978
PY	3.42 locking	1975, 1978
PZ	3.42 non-locking	1975
PZ	3.73 locking	1978
COA	2.56 non-locking	1970
COB	2.56 non-locking	1970
COC	2.73 non-locking	1970
COD	2.73 locking	1970
COE	3.08 non-locking	1970
COF	3.08 locking	1970
COG	3.36 non-locking	1970
COH	3.36 locking	1970
COI	3.08 non-locking	1970
COJ	3.08 locking	1970
COK	3.36 non-locking	1970
COL	3.36 locking	1970
COM	2.56 non-locking	1970
CON	2.56 locking	1970
COO	4.10 non-locking	1970
COP	2.73 locking	1970
COR	2.73 locking	1970
COS	3.07 non-locking	1970
COT	3.07 locking	1970
COU	3.31 non-locking	1970
COV	3.31 locking	1970
COW	3.55 non-locking	1970
COX	3.55 locking	1970
COY	3.73 non-locking	1970
COZ	3.73 locking	1970
CRA	3.07 non-locking	1970
CRB	3.31 non-locking	1970
CRC	3.55 non-locking	1970
CRD	3.73 non-locking	1970
CRE	4.10 non-locking	1970
CRF	2.56 non-locking	1970
CRG	2.56 locking	1970
CRH	3.08 non-locking	1970
CRI	3.08 locking	1970
CRX	2.73 non-locking	1970
CRY	2.73 locking	1970

14 Axleshaft – removal and installation (except B and O type axles)

1   The following operations apply to rear axles which have the wheel bearings pressed into the ends of the axle casing tubes (third letters of axle code – C, G, K, P, M).

2   Raise the rear of the vehicle and support securely and remove the wheel and brake drum.

3   Unscrew and remove the pressed steel cover from the differential carrier and allow the oil to drain into a suitable container.

4   Unscrew and remove the lock screw from the differential pinion shaft. Remove the pinion shaft (photo).

5   Push the outer (flanged) end of the axleshaft inwards and remove the C-ring from the inner end of the shaft (photo).

6   Withdraw the axleshaft taking care not to damage the oil seal in the end of the axle housing as the splined end of the axleshaft passes through it.

7   Installation is a reversal of removal but tighten the lock screw to the specified torque.

8   Always use a new cover gasket and tighten the cover bolts to the specified torque.

9   Refill the unit with the correct quantity and grade of lubricant.

15 Axleshaft oil seal – replacement (except B and O type axles)

1   Remove the axleshaft as described in the preceding section.

2   Pry out the old oil seal from the end of the axle casing, using a large screwdriver or the inner end of the axleshaft itself as a lever (photos).

3   Apply high melting point grease to the oil seal recess and tap the seal into position so that the lips are facing inwards and the metal face is visible from the end of the axle housing. When correctly installed, the face of the oil seal should be flush with the end of the axle casing (photo).

4   Installation of the axleshaft is as described in the preceding section.

16 Axleshaft bearing – replacement (except B and O type axles)

1   Remove the axleshaft (Section 14) and the oil seal (Section 15).

2   A bearing extractor will now be required or a tool made up which will engage behind the bearing.

3   Attach a slide hammer and extract the bearing from the axle casing.

4   Clean out the bearing recess and drive in the new bearing using a piece of tubing *applied against the outer bearing track*. Lubricate the new bearing with gear lubricant. Make sure that the bearing is tapped in to the full depth of its recess and that the numbers on the bearing are visible from the outer end of the casing.

5   Discard the old oil seal and install a new one and install the axleshaft.

17 Axleshaft – removal, overhaul and installation (B and O type)

1   The usual reason for axleshaft removal on this type of axle is that the shaft end play has become excessive. To check this, remove the road wheel and brake drum and attach a dial gauge with its stylus against the axleshaft end flange. If the shaft is then moved in and out

15.2A After the brake components are removed, the oil seal is visible

15.2B The splined end of the axleshaft can be used to pry the seal out of position

15.3 The new seal should be driven into place, flush with the axle casing

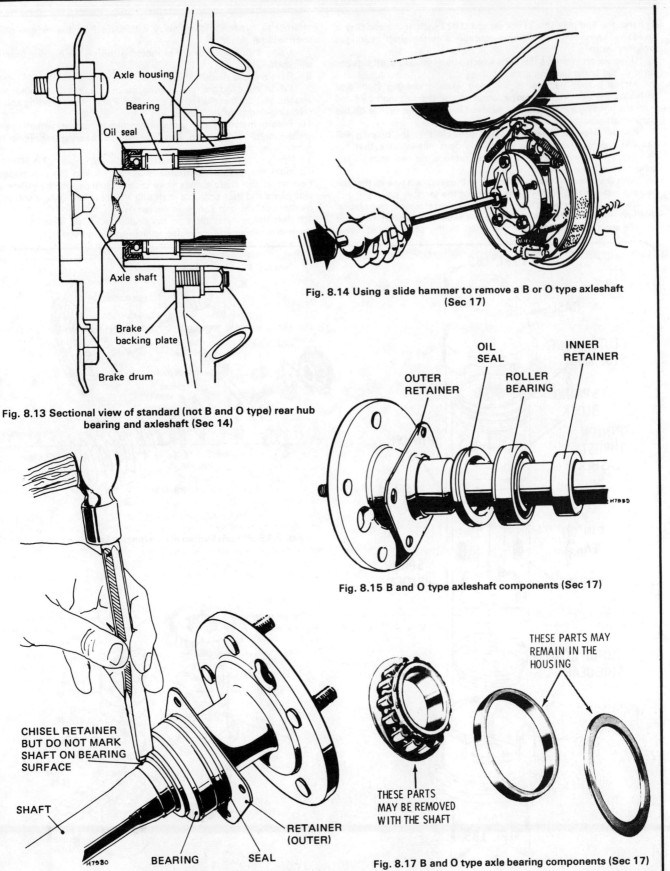

Fig. 8.13 Sectional view of standard (not B and O type) rear hub bearing and axleshaft (Sec 14)

Axle housing

Bearing

Oil seal

Axle shaft

Brake backing plate

Brake drum

Fig. 8.14 Using a slide hammer to remove a B or O type axleshaft (Sec 17)

OUTER RETAINER

OIL SEAL

ROLLER BEARING

INNER RETAINER

Fig. 8.15 B and O type axleshaft components (Sec 17)

CHISEL RETAINER BUT DO NOT MARK SHAFT ON BEARING SURFACE

SHAFT

BEARING

SEAL

RETAINER (OUTER)

Fig. 8.16 Spreading bearing retaining ring on B and O type axleshaft (Sec 17)

THESE PARTS MAY REMAIN IN THE HOUSING

THESE PARTS MAY BE REMOVED WITH THE SHAFT

Fig. 8.17 B and O type axle bearing components (Sec 17)

by hand, the end play should not exceed 0.022 inch. If the end play is excessive, carry out the following operations as the shaft bearing is probably worn.

2   Unscrew and remove the bolts which attach the axleshaft retainer plate to the brake backing plate.

3   Attach a slide hammer to the road wheel mounting studs and withdraw the axleshaft. Do not attempt to pull the axleshaft by hand from the housing as you will only succeed in pulling the vehicle off the support stands.

4   As the axleshaft is removed, it is possible that the bearing will become separated into three parts. This does not indicate that the bearing is unserviceable. If this happens, remove the two sections left behind from the axle tube.

5   With the axleshaft removed, hold it in the jaws of a vise so that the bearing retainer ring rests on the edges of the jaws.

6   Using a hammer and a sharp chisel, nick the retainer in two places. This will have the effect of spreading the retainer so that it will slide off the shaft. Do not damage the shaft in the process and never

attempt to cut the retainer away with a torch as the temper of the shaft will be ruined.

7   Using a suitable press or extractor, withdraw the bearing from the axleshaft.

8   Remove and discard the oil seal.

9   When installing the new bearing, make sure that the retainer plate and the seal are installed to the shaft first. Press on the bearing and the retaining ring tight up against it.

10   Before installing the axleshaft assembly, smear wheel bearing grease onto the bearing end and to the bearing recess in the axlehousing tube.

11   Apply rear axle oil to the axleshaft splines.

12   Hold the axleshaft horizontal and insert it into the axle housing. Feel when the shaft splines have picked up those in the differential side gears and then push the shaft fully into position, using a soft faced hammer on the end flange as necessary.

13   Bolt the retainer plate to the brake backplate, install the brake drum and wheel and lower the vehicle to the ground.

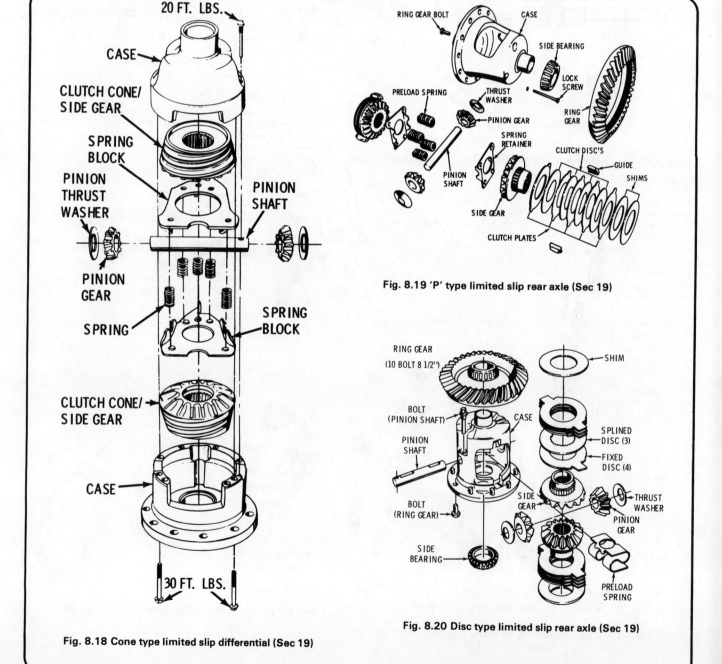

Fig. 8.18 Cone type limited slip differential (Sec 19)

Fig. 8.19 'P' type limited slip rear axle (Sec 19)

Fig. 8.20 Disc type limited slip rear axle (Sec 19)

18 Pinion oil seal (all axles) – replacement

1   Place the vehicle over an inspection pit or raise the rear end to provide adequate working clearance.

2   Disconnect the driveshaft as described in Section 10 and tie it to the body sideframe. Do not allow it to slide out of the transmission.

3   Using a torque wrench check the torque required to rotate the pinion and record this for use later.

4   Scribe or dot punch alignment marks on the pinion stem, nut and flange so that they can be refitted in the same relative position.

5   Count the number of threads visible between the end of the nut and the end of the pinion stem and record for use later.

6   A suitable tool must now be used to hold the pinion flange quite still while the self-locking pinion nut is removed. This can easily be made by drilling two holes at the end of a length of flat steel bar and bolting it to the frame.

7   Unscrew and remove the pinion nut.

8   Withdraw the companion flange. If this is tight, use a two or three legged extractor engaged behind the flange. On no account attempt to lever behind the deflector or to hammer on the end of the pinion stem.

9   Pry out the old seal and discard it.

10   Lubricate the lips of a new seal with extreme pressure lithium based grease and tap it into position making sure that it enters the housing squarely and to its full depth.

11   Align the mating marks made before dismantling and install the companion flange. If necessary, use a piece of tubing as a spacer and screw on the pinion nut to force the flange fully home on the stem. *On no account, attempt to hammer the flange home.*

12   Smear a non-hardening jointing compound on the ends of the splines which are visible in the center of the companion flange so that any oil seepage will be sealed in.

13   Install the thrust-washer and nut but tighten the nut carefully so that the original number of threads is exposed.

14   Now measure the torque required to rotate the pinion and tighten the nut fractionally until the figure compares with that recorded before dismantling. In order to compensate for the drag of the new oil seal, the nut should be further tightened so that the rotational torque of the pinion exceeds that recorded before dismantling by between 1 and 5 lbf-in. The rotational torque (pinion bearing preload) is normally between 15 and 30 lb-in with new bearings and 10 and 15 lb-in with bearings which have been in service.

15   Reconnect the driveshaft, install the brake drum and wheel and lower the vehicle.

19 Positraction (limited slip) type axles – description, testing, precautions

1   This type of axle incorporates a special type of differential unit.

Essentially the device provides more driving force to the wheel with traction when one wheel begins to spin.

2   Two types of assembly are used, one having clutch plates and the other having cones. Some makes of Positraction are not repairable and in the event of a fault occurring or wear developing, the complete assembly must be replaced.

3   An on-vehicle check can be carried out in the following way. If equipped with manual transmission, shift into 'Neutral'.

4   Raise the rear of the vehicle until the wheels are off the ground. Remove one wheel.

5   Using a suitable adaptor connect a torque wrench to the axleshaft flange. Alternatively, a spring balance can be used.

6   Have an assistant hold the wheel still in position on the opposite hub quite firmly to prevent it from rotating, then measure the torque required to start the axleshaft (opposite to the one to which the torque wrench is attached) moving. A minimum of 40 lb-ft should be required for an axle which has seen considerable service and 70 lb-ft for a new, or nearly new assembly.

7   Always use fluid lubricant for topping up a Positraction type axle.

8   Never run the engine when one rear wheel is off the ground as the vehicle may obtain traction through the remaining wheel and jump off the jacks or support stands.

20 Rear axle assembly – removal and installation

1   Raise the rear of the vehicle and support it securely on stands placed under the body frame rails.

2   Position an adjustable floor jack under the differential housing and just take up the weight. Do not raise sufficiently to take the weight of the vehicle from the frame stands.

3   Disconnect the lower shock absorber mountings (Chapter 11).

4   Remove the driveshaft.

5   Remove the rear wheels and brake drums. See Chapter 9 for information if difficulty is experienced in removing the brake drums.

6   Disconnect the hydraulic brake lines from their clips on the axle housing.

7   Unbolt and remove the differential cover, allowing the fluid to drain into a suitable container.

8   Remove the axle shafts as described in Section 14 or Section 17 of this chapter, depending on type.

9   Depending on axle type, unbolt the brake backing plates, carefully withdraw the brake assemblies and wire them up to the frame without bending the hydraulic pipes or disconnecting them.

10   Remove the leaf springs as described in Chapter 11.

11   Withdraw the axle assembly from under the vehicle.

12   Installation is a reversal of removal but tighten all suspension bolts and nuts to the specified torque (refer to Chapters 9 and 11). Fill the axle assembly with the proper grade and amount of lubricant (see Specifications, this chapter, and Chapter 1).

Chapter 9 Braking system

Refer to Chapter 13 for specifications and information related to 1981 models

Contents

Specifications

System type

Four wheel hydraulic, dual circuit. All models, 1970 – 1980, have front disc brakes as standard with rear drum brakes. All brakes self-adjusting. Power booster option. Foot-operated parking brake by cables to the rear.

Drum size

Front	9.5 x 2.5 in
Rear	9.5 x 2.0 in
Maximum refinish internal diameter	9.560 in
Wear limit	9.590 in

Fluid type

DOT-3, GM No. 11 or equivalent

Brake pedal free travel (without booster)

1/16 to 1/4 in

Torque specifications

	lb-ft	lb-in
Master cylinder to dash	24	
Master cylinder to booster	24	
Booster to dash	25	
Brake line nuts		150
Bleeder valves		110
Brake shoe anchor pin	120	
Wheel cylinder to flange plate		110
Caliper mounting bolt	35	
Flexible hose to caliper	22	
Shield to steering knuckle		140
Brake pedal pivot bolt	30	

1 General description

The hydraulic system comprises two separate front and rear circuits.

The master cylinder is of tandem type with separate reservoirs for two circuits and in the event of a leak or failure in one hydraulic braking circuit, the other circuit will remain fully operative. A visual warning of circuit failure or air in the system is given by a warning lamp activated by displacement of the piston in the brake distribution (pressure differential warning) switch from its normal 'in balance' position.

The parking brake operates mechanically to the rear brakes only. It is operated by a foot operated pedal to the left of the steering column.

A combination valve is fitted into the hydraulic circuit and provides the following three services:

Metering valve: This prevents the front disc brakes from operating until the rear shoes have contacted the drum.

Failure warning switch: This switch operates if either front or rear brakes fail to operate and a dash warning lamp then operates.

Proportioner: This reduces rear brake system pressure during rapid deceleration, reducing the tendency for rear wheel skidding.

A power brake booster, which utilizes engine manifold vacuum and atmosphere pressure to provide assistance to the hydraulically operated brakes, is available as an option.

All brakes are self adjusting.

2 Maintenance and inspection

1   See Chapter 1 for maintenance and inspection procedures

3 Drum brakes – lining inspection and replacement

1   Jack up the rear of the vehicle and remove the roadwheel. Fully release the parking brake.
2   Mark the position of the brake drum in relation to one of the wheel studs so that the drum can be installed in the same relative attitude.
3   Remove the brake drums (photo). If the brake drums are stuck tight due to severe wear (causing the shoes to be 'locked' in grooves in the drum interior) and cannot be removed by gently tapping with a soft faced hammer or hardwood block, then the lanced area of the brake drum must be chiselled or knocked out. Rotate the drum until the adjuster lever can be released from the sprocket by pulling it outwards with a thin rod inserted through the aperture. The sprocket can then be backed-off to release the drum. **Note:** *If the lanced area in the drum is knocked out, ensure that all metal is removed from the brake compartment. Install a metal hole cover afterwards to prevent contamination of the brakes.*
4   Brush away any accumulations of dust, taking great care not to inhale it as it contains asbestos and is injurious to health.
5   Inspect the thickness of the friction material. If it has worn down to within $\frac{1}{32}$ in of the lining rivets or the metal backing plate of the shoe, then the shoes must be replaced (photo). It is recommended that new or factory exchange shoes are obtained rather than attempt to reline the old ones yourself. Perform work on one brake assembly at a time, using the other side for reference.
6   Unhook the brake shoe pull-back springs from the anchor pin and link end (photos).
7   Remove the actuator return spring, the link, the hold-down pins and the springs (photo).
8   Remove the actuator assembly but do not dismantle unless parts are broken.
9   Separate the brake shoes. This is achieved by removing the adjustment screw and spring. If the shoes are to be re-installed, mark the positions in which they are fitted (photo).
10 Remove the parking brake lever from the secondary brake shoe (photos).
11 If there is any sign of hydraulic oil leakage at the wheel cylinders, the cylinder should be replaced or overhauled.
12 Check the flange plate attaching bolts for tightness. Clean any rust and dirt from the shoe contact faces on the flange plate.
13 When installing, ensure that no grease or oil contact the linings and that they are free from nicks and burrs.
14 Lubricate the parking brake cable and the fulcrum end of the parking brake lever with brake lube. Attach the lever to the secondary shoe and ensure that it moves freely (photo).
15 Put a smear of brake lube on the contact point of the pads and flange plate, and the threads of the brake adjusting screw (photos).
16 Connect the brake shoes together with the adjusting screw spring, then place the screw, socket and nut in position. **Note:** *Adjusting screws are marked 'L' or 'R' (left or right side of vehicle). The sprocket (star-wheel) should only be installed next to the secondary shoe and the adjusting screw spring inserted to prevent interference with the sprocket. Ensure that the sprocket lines up with the adjusting hole in the flange plate.*
17 Connect the parking brake cable to the lever.
18 Secure the primary shoe (short lining forward) first with the hold down pin and spring using pliers, and at the same time engage the shoes with the wheel cylinder connecting links (photo).
19 Install the actuator assembly and secondary shoe with the hold down pin and spring using needle-nosed pliers. Position the parking brake strut and strut spring (photo).
20 Install the guide plate over the anchor pin, then install the wire link. The wire link is connected to the actuator assembly first then placed over the anchor pin stud while holding the adjuster assembly fully down (photo).
21 Install the actuator return spring, easing it in place with a screwdriver or similar tool.
22 Hook the pull back springs into the shoes then install the spring from the primary shoe over the anchor pin and then the spring from the

secondary shoe over the wire link end (photo).
23 Ensure that the actuating lever functions by moving it by hand, then turn the sprocket back $1\frac{1}{4}$ turns to retract the shoes (photos).
24 Install the drum and roadwheel, ensuring that the drum locating tang is in line with the locating lobe in the hub.
25 Lower the vehicle to the ground.
26 Make numerous forward and reverse stops to finally adjust the brakes, until a satisfactory pedal action results.

4 Disc pads – inspection and replacement

1   At the intervals specified in Chapter 1, remove the front road-wheels and inspect the thickness of the pad material remaining. Check the ends of the outboard shoes by looking in at each end of the caliper. The inboard shoe can be checked by looking down through the inspection hole at the top of the caliper. Pads should be replaced when they are worn down to $\frac{1}{32}$ inch thickness over the rivet heads.
2   In addition to the visual inspection, most models are equipped with an audible warning device which will indicate that the disc pads have worn down to their safe limit. The device is essentially a spring steel tang which emits a squeal by rubbing on the disc when the friction material has worn down to 0.030 in.
3   To replace the disc pads, first check that the brake fluid reservoir is no more than $\frac{1}{3}$ full. Siphon off fluid above this level and discard it.
4   Raise the front end of the vehicle and remove the wheels. Perform disc pad replacement on one brake brake assembly at a time, using the assembled brake for reference if necessary.
5   Push the piston back into its bore. If necessary a C-clamp can be used but a flat bar will usually do the job. As the piston is depressed to the bottom of the caliper bore, so the fluid in the master cylinder reservoir will rise. Ensure that it does not overflow (photo).
6   Using an Allen key remove the 2 mounting bolts which attach the caliper to the support, then lift off the caliper (photos).
7   Remove the shoes, then position the caliper so that the brake hose will not have to support the caliper weight. If the disc pads are to be re-installed, mark their position (photo).
8   Remove the shoe support spring from the piston.
9   Remove the 2 sleeves from the inboard ears of the caliper.
10 Remove the 4 rubber bushings from the grooves in each caliper ear (photo).
11 Clean the holes and bushing grooves in the caliper ears.
12 Examine the inside of the caliper for signs of fluid leakage. If evident, the caliper should be overhauled.
13 When installing, ensure that the caliper is clean and that the dust boot is undamaged.
14 Lubricate new sleeves, rubber bushings, bushing grooves and the end of the mounting bolts using Delco Silicone Lube or equivalent.
15 Install the rubber bushings on the caliper ears.
16 Install the sleeves to the inboard ears so that the end towards the shoe is flush with the machine surface of the ear (photo).
17 Install the shoe support spring and inboard shoe in the center off the piston cavity. Push down until the shoe is flat against the caliper (photos).
18 Position the outboard shoe in the caliper with the ears at the top of the shoe over the caliper ears and the tab at the bottom of the shoe engaged in the caliper cutout. If equipped with wear sensor, it will go towards the rear of the caliper.
19 With the shoes installed, lift up the caliper and rest the bottom edge of the outboard lining on the outer edge of the disc to make sure that no clearance exists between the tab at the bottom and the caliper abutment.
20 Position the caliper over the disc, lining up the holes in the caliper ears and mounting bracket.
21 Install the mounting bolts, ensuring that they pass under the retaining ears of the inboard shoe and through the holes in the outboard shoe and caliper ears, then into the mounting bracket.
22 Torque-tighten the mounting bolts.
23 Pump the brake pedal to seat the linings on the disc then bend the upper ears of the outboard shoe until no radial clearance exists between the shoe and the caliper housing.
24 Install the front wheel and lower the vehicle.
25 Service the other side using the same procedures.
26 Add brake fluid to the master cylinder reservoir until it is $\frac{1}{4}$ inch from the top.
27 Pump the brake pedal several times until a satisfactory pedal

3.2 Pulling a brake drum off the axle studs

3.5 Measuring the thickness of the brake shoe lining

3.6A A brake servicing tool is used here to disconnect the return spring for the primary brake shoe. A common screwdriver can also be used to pry the spring loose

3.6B The return spring for the secondary (rear) shoe also has a stiff wire link

3.7 To remove the anchor spring assemblies, compress the spring and then turn the end of the pin at the center of the spring

3.9 The primary shoe is held to the secondary shoe by a spring just behind the adjusting 'starwheel'

3.10A Removing the parking brake strut which runs between the shoes, behind the axle flange. Pay attention to how it is installed for reassembly

3.10B Pliers are used to disconnect the secondary shoe from the parking brake cable

3.14 After lubricating the parking brake cable, pull back the spring and connect the lever

3.15A Grease should be applied to the raised portions of the backing plate to prevent squeaks. These areas contact the brake shoes

3.15B Grease is also applied to the anchor pin

3.15C The adjustment 'starwheel' should be lubricated to ensure easy adjustments

3.18 The primary shoe installed by the anchor spring assembly

3.19A The actuating spring is located just ahead of the parking brake lever

3.19B The parking brake strut has recesses in it to fit in the brake shoe cutouts

3.20 Use the brake tool or a screwdriver to force the wire link over the anchor pin

3.22 The installed position of the primary shoe return spring

3.23A The adjusting mechanism sprocket must be toward the rear shoe

3.23B The brakes are adjusted by lifting the lever away from the sprocket and then turning the adjusting mechanism. The brakes do this automatically when traveling in reverse

4.5 A C-clamp is used to force the caliper piston back into its bore

4.6A An Allen head wrench is needed to remove the caliper mounting bolts from the inboard side

4.6B A caliper mounting bolt being removed from the caliper housing

4.7 Once the caliper is removed from the rotor, the pads are easily pulled from the caliper

4.10 Rubber sleeves are located inside grooves and can be pried out with a screwdriver for replacement

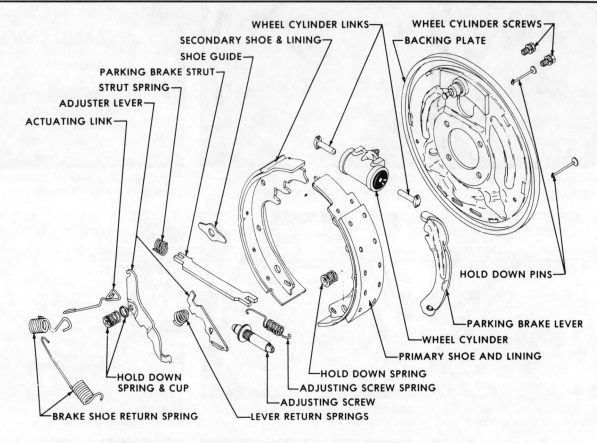

WHEEL CYLINDER LINKS
SECONDARY SHOE & LINING
SHOE GUIDE
PARKING BRAKE STRUT
STRUT SPRING
ADJUSTER LEVER
ACTUATING LINK
WHEEL CYLINDER SCREWS
BACKING PLATE
HOLD DOWN PINS
PARKING BRAKE LEVER
WHEEL CYLINDER
PRIMARY SHOE AND LINING
HOLD DOWN SPRING
ADJUSTING SCREW SPRING
ADJUSTING SCREW
LEVER RETURN SPRINGS
HOLD DOWN SPRING & CUP
BRAKE SHOE RETURN SPRING

Fig. 9.1 Typical drum brake assembly (Sec 3)

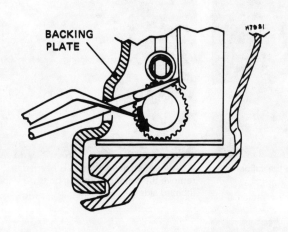

BACKING PLATE

Fig. 9.2 Adjusting brake shoes inward to remove a stuck brake drum (Sec 3)

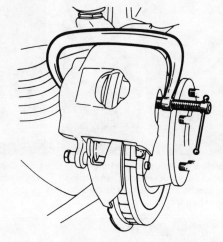

Fig. 9.3 Using a 'C' clamp to depress caliper piston (Sec 4)

action is obtained then top up the master cylinder reservoir again (if necessary).

5   Wheel cylinder (drum brake) – removal, overhaul and installation

1   Raise the vehicle and remove the wheel.
2   Remove the brake drum. See 'Note' in Section 3.
3   Clean around the hydraulic connection to the wheel cylinder then disconnect the line. Plug the end of the line to prevent fluid loss and dirt contamination.
4   Remove the brake shoe pull back springs.

5   Remove the cylinder to flange plate securing screws and disengage the push rods from the brake shoes. Remove the cylinder (photos).
6   Using pliers, remove the boots from the cylinder and discard them.
7   Remove and discard the piston cups.
8   Inspect the cylinder bore and pistons for corrosion and pitting. Discard if pitted, but where there is staining, the surface may be polished with crocus cloth working around the circumference (not along the length).
9   Ensure your hands are clean, dry and free from grease, gasoline, kerosene or cleaning solvents then clean the metal parts in new brake fluid or denatured alcohol.
10   Shake off the surplus fluid for ease of handling.

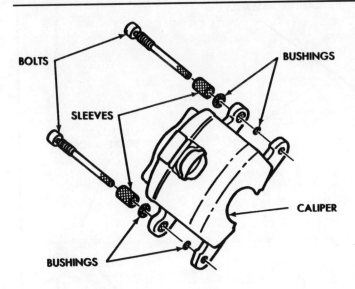

LUBRICATE AREAS INDICATED

Fig. 9.4 Caliper lubrication points (Sec 4)

BOLTS

BUSHINGS

SLEEVES

BUSHINGS

CALIPER

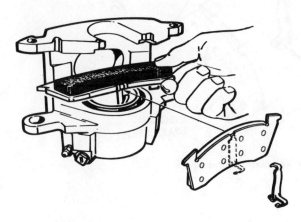

Fig. 9.5 Installing disc shoe support spring (Sec 4)

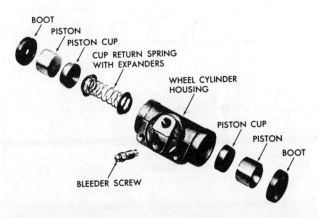

BOOT
PISTON
PISTON CUP
CUP RETURN SPRING
WITH EXPANDERS
WHEEL CYLINDER
HOUSING
PISTON CUP
PISTON
BOOT
BLEEDER SCREW

Fig. 9.6 Exploded view of typical drum brake wheel cylinder (Sec 5)

11 Lubricate the cylinder with clean brake fluid and insert the spring expander assembly.

12 Insert new cups which must be clean and dry and **not** lubricated. The flat surface must be forward to enter ends of the cylinder. Use only the fingers to manipulate the cups.

13 Install the pistons, flat surface uppermost. Do **not** lubricate them before installation.

14 Press new boots into the cylinder counterbores. **Do not** lubricate them before installation.

15 When installing the wheel cylinder, position the wheel cylinder on the brake flange plate and install screws loosely.

16 Install the push rods and pull back springs, then connect the hydraulic line to the cylinder, moving the cylinder as necessary to prevent stripping the threads.

17 Tighten the cylinder mounting screws.

18 Install the brake drum and wheel.

19 Bleed the braking system (Section 10) then lower the vehicle to the ground.

6 Disc caliper – overhaul

1 Remove the disc pads as described in Section 4. Disconnect the brake flexible hose from the rigid brake line at the support bracket. Cap the line to prevent loss of fluid.

2 Unbolt and remove the caliper (also as described in Section 4) complete with flexible hose. Unscrew the hose from the caliper noting the copper sealing gaskets which should be replaced when the hose is reconnected.

3 To disassemble, clean the exterior of the caliper using brake fluid (never use gasoline, kerosene or cleaning solvents) then place the assembly on a clean workbench.

4 Drain the fluid from the caliper and then place a cloth pad between the caliper piston and body then apply air pressue to the fluid inlet hole to free the piston; a small hand pump is adequate. If this method proves unsuccessful at dislodging the piston, hydraulic fluid pressure must be used. With the brake pads removed, reconnect the caliper to the brake line on the vehicle and have an assistant slowly depress the brake pedal. The fluid will force the piston out of its bore. Be careful that the piston is not damaged.

5 Carefully pry the dust boot out of the caliper bore.

6 Using a small piece of wood or plastic, remove the piston seal from its groove in the caliper piston bore. Metal objects may cause bore damage.

7 Remove the caliper bleeder valve, then remove and discard the sleeves and bushings from the caliper ears. Also discard all rubber parts.

8 Clean the remaining parts in brake fluid. Allow them to drain and then shake them vigorously to remove as much fluid as possible.

9 Carefully examine the piston for scoring, nicks and burrs and loss of plating. If surface defects are present, parts must be replaced. Check the caliper bore in a similar way, but light polishing with crocus cloth is permissible to remove light corrosion and stains. Discard the mounting bolts if they are corroded or damaged.

10 When assembling, lubricate the piston bores and seal with clean brake fluid; position the seal in the caliper bore groove.

11 Lubricate the piston with clean brake fluid then assemble a new boot in the piston groove with the fold towards the open end of the piston (photo).

12 Insert the piston squarely into the caliper bore then apply force to bottom the piston in the bore (photo).

13 Position the dust boot in the caliper counterbore then use a suitable drift to drive it into its location (Chevrolet tool no J-22904 is available for this purpose). Ensure that the boot is installed below the caliper face and evenly all round.

14 Install the bleeder screw.

15 The remainder of the procedure for installation is the reverse of the removal procedure. Always use new copper gaskets when connecting the brake hose and finally bleed the system of air (Section 10).

7 Master cylinder – removal, overhaul and installation

1 As many types and sizes of master cylinders were installed on the Camaro, it may be wise to take all components with you to the auto parts store for proper fitting.

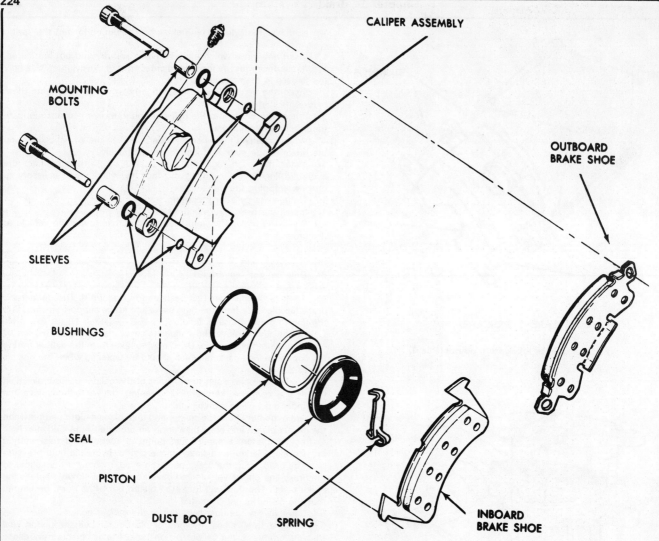

MOUNTING
BOLTS

CALIPER ASSEMBLY

OUTBOARD
BRAKE SHOE

SLEEVES

BUSHINGS

SEAL

PISTON

DUST BOOT

SPRING

INBOARD
BRAKE SHOE

Fig. 9.7 Exploded view of caliper brake assembly (Sec 6)

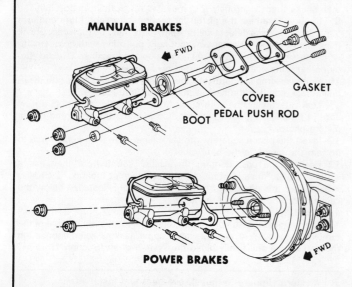

MANUAL BRAKES

◄ FWD

GASKET

COVER

BOOT PEDAL PUSH ROD

POWER BRAKES

FWD ►

Fig. 9.8 Master cylinder mounting – typical (Sec 7)

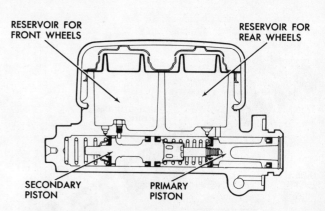

RESERVOIR FOR
FRONT WHEELS

RESERVOIR FOR
REAR WHEELS

SECONDARY
PISTON

PRIMARY
PISTON

Fig. 9.9 Typical hydraulic system in a master cylinder (Sec 7)

4.16 Lubricate the caliper bushings and push them into position

4.17A The shoe support spring installed in the center of the new disc pad

4.17B The inboard shoe being installed in the caliper. The extended portion of the support spring fits inside the piston

4.18 The outboard shoe is installed with its flange fitting in the caliper cutout area

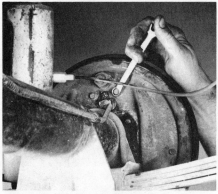

5.5A The two screws which mount the wheel cylinder are located on the inboard side of the backing plate

5.5B Removing the wheel cylinder from the backing plate

6.11 The piston boot should be installed in the groove, with the fold toward the open end of the piston

6.12 Forcing the piston back into the caliper

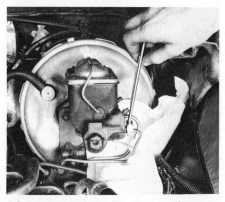

7.2 It is best to use a flared nut to disconnect the hydraulic lines at the master cylinder

7.4 Removing the master cylinder. Be careful not to spill the fluid

7.7 The stop bolt is located at the bottom of the reservoir

7.8A Depress the piston assembly with a screwdriver as the retaining ring is pried free with a screwdriver

7.8B A wire hook can be used to draw out the piston assembly

7.11A After a screw is threaded into the tube seat, two screwdrivers are used to pry the tube seat out of its bore

7.11B A new tube seat being installed

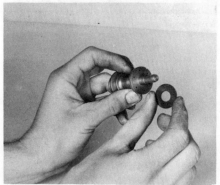

7.12A Fitting a new seal to the secondary piston

7.12B A new seal at the other end of the secondary piston

7.14A All parts should be liberally coated with fresh brake fluid during assembly

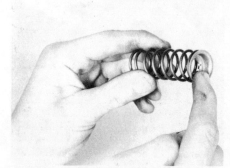

7.14B Installing the spring retainer to the end of the spring

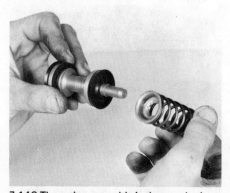

7.14C The spring assembly is then pushed onto the secondary piston assembly

7.15 The piston/spring assembly is then pushed into the master cylinder bore

2   Remove the hydraulic lines at the master cylinder (photo). Collect any fluid spillage with dry cloths and plug the ends of the hydraulic lines to prevent fluid loss or dirt from entering the system.
3   On manual brakes, disconnect the push rod at the brake pedal inside the car.
4   Unbolt and remove the master cylinder from the firewall or power booster (photo). Be careful that no brake fluid is accidently dripped on any painted surface as it will ruin the finish.
5   Drain all fluid from the master cylinder and place the unit in a vise. Use wood blocks to cushion the jaws of the vise.
6   On manual brakes remove the push rod retaining ring.
7   Remove the secondary stop bolt from the bottom of the front fluid reservoir (Delco Moraine) or from the base of the master cylinder body (Bendix) (photo).
8   Remove the retaining ring from the groove and take out the primary piston assembly (photo). Following the primary piston out of the bore will be the secondary piston, spring and retainer. A piece of

bent stiff wire can be used to draw these assemblies out of the cylinder bore (photo).
9   Examine the inside surface of the master cylinder and the secondary piston. If there is evidence of scoring or 'bright' wear areas, the entire master cylinder should be replaced with a new one.
10   If the components are in good condition, wash in clean hydraulic fluid. Discard all the rubber components and the primary piston. Purchase a rebuild kit which will contain all the necessary parts for the overhaul.
11   Inspect the tube seats which are located in the master cylinder body where the fluid pipes connect. If they appear damaged they should be replaced with new ones which come in the overhaul kit. They are forced out of the body by threading a screw into the tube and then prying outwards (photo). The new ones are forced into place using a spare brake line nut (photo). All parts necessary for this should be included in the rebuild kit.
12   Place the new secondary seals in the grooves of the secondary

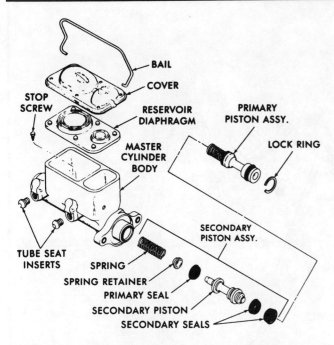

Fig. 9.10 Exploded view of typical power brake master cylinder (Sec 7)

BAIL
COVER
STOP SCREW
RESERVOIR DIAPHRAGM
PRIMARY PISTON ASSY.
LOCK RING
MASTER CYLINDER BODY
SECONDARY PISTON ASSY.
TUBE SEAT INSERTS
SPRING
SPRING RETAINER
PRIMARY SEAL
SECONDARY PISTON
SECONDARY SEALS

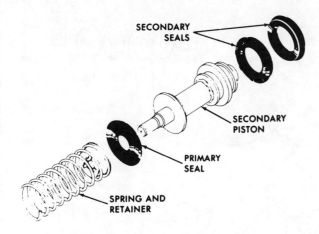

Fig. 9.11 Exploded view of Delco secondary piston (Sec 7)

SECONDARY SEALS
SECONDARY PISTON
PRIMARY SEAL
SPRING AND RETAINER

piston (photos).

13 Assemble the primary seals and seal protector over the end of the secondary piston.

14 Lubricate the cylinder bore and secondary piston with hydraulic fluid (photo). Insert the spring retainer into the spring then place the retainer and spring over the end of the secondary piston (photos). The retainer should locate inside the primary seal lips.

15 With the master cylinder vertical, push the secondary piston into the bore to seat its spring (photo).

16 Coat the seals of the primary piston with brake fluid and fit it into the cylinder bore. Hold it down while the retaining ring is installed in the cylinder groove.

17 Continue to hold the piston down while the stop screw is installed.

18 Install the reservoir diaphragm into the reservoir cover plate making sure it is fully collapsed inside the recessed lid.

19 Install the master cylinder in the reverse order of removal, torque-tightening the attaching nuts to specifications.

20 Fill the master cylinder with fresh brake fluid and bleed the master cylinder and complete hydraulic system as outlined in Section 10.

8 Hydraulic brake hoses – inspection, removal and installation

1 Periodically, examine all hydraulic brake lines, both rigid and flexible, for rusting, chafing and general deterioration. Also check the security of the connections.

2 If the hoses or pipes have to be disconnected, extensive loss of fluid can be avoided if the vent holes in the master cylinder fluid reservoir cap are taped over to create a vacuum.

Drum brakes

3 Using a back-up wrench on the hose fitting, unscrew the connector from the hose fitting.

4 Remove the U-shaped retainer from the hose fitting, withdraw the hose fitting from the support bracket, turn it out of the wheel cylinder and remove the copper gasket.

5 When installing, use a new copper gasket, moisten the screw threads with brake fluid and torque-tighten to the wheel cylinder.

6 With the weight on the suspension and the wheels 'straight-ahead', insert the female end of the hose through the support bracket, allow it to seek its own position without kinking then install the U-shaped retainer and secure the hose in the bracket.

7 Turn the wheels from lock-to-lock to ensure that the hose does not contact other parts (reposition the female end if necessary).

8 Place the tubular steel connector in the hose fitting and torque-tighten, using a back-up wrench on the hose fitting.

9 Remove the tape from the master cylinder reservoir, top-up with new brake fluid and then bleed the system of air.

Disc brakes

10 To disconnect a rigid line from a flexible hose, unscrew the connector out of the hose end fitting. These connectors are located at the support brackets. Always hold the flexible hose and fitting quite still by using an open-ended wrench.

11 To remove the flexible hose, extract the retainer from t1he hose and fitting and pull the hose from the support bracket.

12 Remove the hose to caliper bolt, remove the center connector and the hose.

13 Installation is a reversal of removal but always use new copper gaskets in conjunction with the flexible hose end fittings and always let the flexible hose take up its natural curvature; never secure it in a twisted or kinked position.

Rigid lines

14 Rigid lines which need to be replaced can be purchased at many service stations. Take the old pipe as a pattern and make sure that the pipes are fitted with the correct connectors and that the ends are double-flared.

9 Hydraulic system pressure valves and switches

1 On all models a combination distribution block, or combination valve is installed in the hydraulic line (photo). It is located adjacent to the master cylinder or on the inside of the body frame rail and its functions are as follows:

The metering valve holds off full pressure to the front disc brakes until a certain pressure level is reached. This allows the pressure in the rear brake circuit to build up sufficiently to overcome the force of the shoe retracting springs and ensure balanced braking between front and rear wheels.

The warning switch incorporates a piston which normally remains in a central position (in balance) when the front and rear independent hydraulic pressures are equal. In the event of a failure in either circuit, the piston is displaced and completes an electrical circuit through a switch terminal and lights a warning lamp in the vehicle interior.

The proportioning valve limits hydraulic pressure to the rear brakes to prevent them locking before full braking effort is obtained by the front disc brakes.

2 The following tests should be carried out periodically.

Brake warning lamp check

3 Disconnect the electrical lead from the switch terminal and connect the lead to ground.

4 Turn the ignition switch 'ON' and the brake failure warning lamp should light up. If it does not, check for burned out bulb or faulty

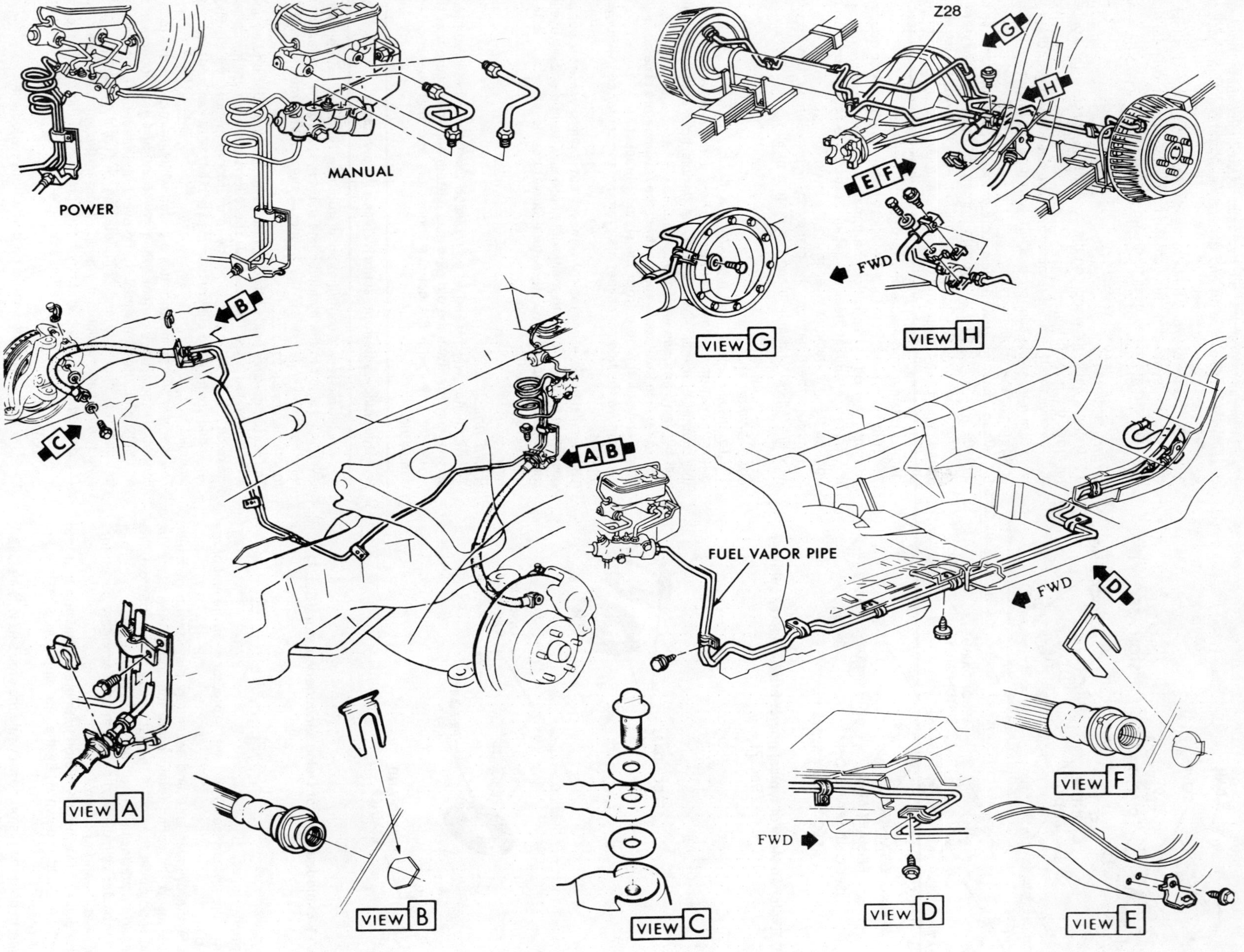

VIEW F

VIEW E

VIEW D

VIEW H

VIEW G

VIEW C

VIEW B

VIEW A

FWD

FWD

FWD

FWD

D

E|F

G

H

A|B

B

C

A

Z28

MANUAL

POWER

FUEL VAPOR PIPE

Fig. 9.12 Brake pipe and hose routing (Sec 8)

wiring.

Warning switch operation check

5   The operation of the switch can be checked by switching on the ignition and with the help of an assistant, bleeding first a front caliper and then a rear wheel cylinder as described in the following Section. The warning lamp should light immediately the bleeder valve is released and heavy pressure applied to the brake foot pedal.

6   Any fault detected in the switch can only be rectified by replacement of the complete valve/switch assembly.

7   Bleed the hydraulic system (both circuits) on completion as described in the next Section.

10 Hydraulic system – bleeding

Note: *Never allow the hydraulic fluid to come in contact with the paint work of the vehicle as it acts as an efficient paint stripper.*

1   Whenever the hydraulic system is disconnected (to remove or install a component) air will enter the fluid lines and bleeding must be carried out. This is not a routine operation and if air enters the system without any repair operations having been carried out, then the cause must be sought and the fault rectified.

2   When applying the foot brake pedal, if the first application causes the pedal to go down further than usual but an immediate second or third application (pumping) reduces the pedal travel and improves the braking effect, this is a sure sign that there is air in the system.

3   Use only clean hydraulic fluid (which has remained unshaken for 24 hours and has been stored in an airtight container) for topping-up the master cylinder reservoirs during the following operations. Make sure that the reservoirs are kept topped-up during the whole of the bleeding operations otherwise air will be drawn into the system and the whole sequence of bleeding will have to be repeated (photo). Where power brakes are fitted, depress the brake pedal several times to destroy any residual vacuum.

4   If the master cylinder is equipped with bleeder valves, do these valves first and then move to the wheel closest to the master cylinder (photo). Proceed to each wheel, working away from the master cylinder.

5   Push a length of hose onto the bleeder valve and then immerse the open end of the hose in a jar containing sufficient brake fluid to keep the end of the hose well covered (photo).

6   Unscrew the bleeder valve $\frac{3}{4}$ turn and have an assistant depress the brake pedal. Just before the pedal reaches the floor, close the bleeder valve and allow the pedal to be released. Bubbles will flow from the tube as air is expelled and the operation must be repeated until the bubbles cease.

7   Repeat the operation on the other front caliper then transfer operations to the rear brakes. At all times remember to maintain the fluid level as stated in paragraph 3.

8   On vehicles equipped with a combination valve the pin in the end of the metering part of the valve must be held in the open position. This can be carried out using the official tool (J 23709) or a similar device clamped under the mounting bolt which should have been temporarily loosened. The pin must be pushed, and held in.

9   If any difficulty is experienced in bleeding the hydraulic system or if the help of an assistant cannot be obtained, a pressure bleeding kit is a worthwhile investment. If connected in accordance with the makers' instructions, each bleed valve can be opened in turn to allow the system fluid to be pressure ejected until clear of air bubbles without the need to replenish the master cylinder reservoir during the process.

10   If the front or rear hydraulic circuit has been 'broken' beyond the distribution block then only the particular circuit concerned need be bled. If the master cylinder has been removed and replaced or its connecting pipelines, then both circuits must be bled.

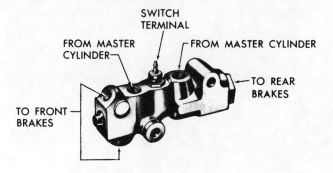

Fig. 9.13 Combination valve and switch (Sec 9)

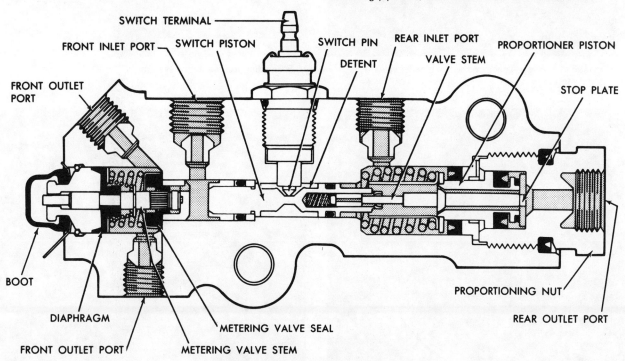

Fig. 9.14 Combination valve components (Sec 9)

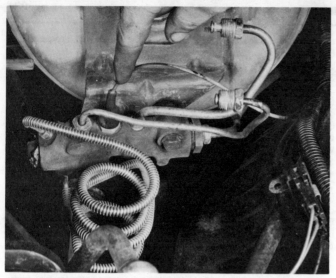

9.1 The combination valve is located just under the master cylinder in most models. The electrical wire is for the dashboard warning light

10.3 Always keep the master cylinder full of fresh fluid when bleeding the brakes

10.4 Most master cylinders are equipped with a bleeder valve. The procedure is the same

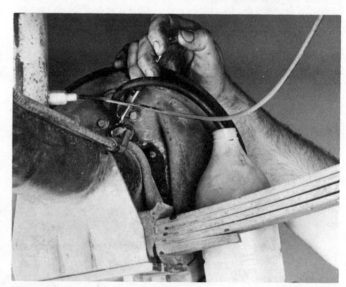

10.5 Bleeding the rear brake system

11.3 Using a dial indicator to check for faults in the front disc assembly

14.3 The parking brake is adjusted from under the car. The threaded rod allows plenty of adjustment

11 Disc and drum – inspection and renovation

1   Whenever the disc brake pads are inspected for wear, take the opportunity to check the condition of the disc (rotor) surfaces. Light scoring or grooving is normal but deep grooves or severe erosion are not. 1974 and earlier models have a single deep groove in the rotor called a 'squeal' groove. Do not be fooled into thinking this groove is due to damage.
2   If vibration has been noticed during application of the brake pedal, suspect disc runout.
3   To check this, a dial gauge will be required or the use of feeler blades between the disc and a fixed point (photo).
4   Turn the disc slowly and check that the runout does not exceed 0.004 in.
5   Sometimes the different wearing characteristics of the disc material may cause it to wear to uneven thickness. Any variation in thickness over 0.0005 in will also cause vibration during brake application.
6   Discs usually have the wear limit and refinish thickness dimensions cast into them.
7   If your dealer cannot refinish a disc to come within the specified tolerances then a new disc must be installed (refer to front suspension, Chapter 11).
8   Whenever a brake drum is removed for lining inspection, check the drum for cracks, scoring or out of round.
9   An out of round drum will usually give rise to a pulsating feeling of the brake pedal as the brakes are applied. The internal diameter should be checked at several different points using an internal micrometer. Drums can be refinished internally provided the wear and refinish sizes cast into it are not exceeded.

12 Brake pedal – removal and installation

1   Disconnect the battery ground cable.
2   Disconnect the clutch pedal return spring if a manual transmission is fitted.
3   Remove the clip retainer from the push rod pin which travels through the pedal arm.
4   Remove the nut from the pedal shaft bolt. Slide the shaft out far enough to clear the brake pedal arm.
5   The brake pedal can now be removed, along with the spacer and bushing. The clutch pedal (if equipped) will remain in place.
6   When installing, lubricate the spacer and bushings with brake lube and tighten the pivot nut to specifications.

13 Stop lamp switch – replacement and adjustment

1   This switch is located on a flange or bracket protruding from the brake pedal support.
2   With the brake pedal in the fully released position, the plunger on the body of the switch should be fully pressed in. When the pedal is pushed in, the plunger releases and sends electrical current to the stop lights at the rear of the car.
3   Electrical contact should be made when the pedal is depressed .38 to .64 inches. If this is not the case, the switch can be adjusted by turning it in or out as required.
4   To replace the switch if it is faulty, disconnect the electrical coupler (two couplers if car is equipped with cruise control) and loosen the switch lock nut until the switch can be unscrewed from the bracket. Installation is a reversal of this procedure.

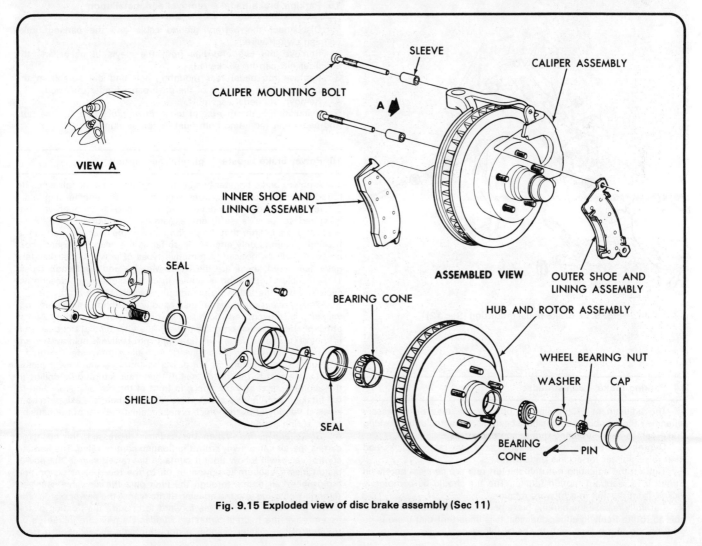

Fig. 9.15 Exploded view of disc brake assembly (Sec 11)

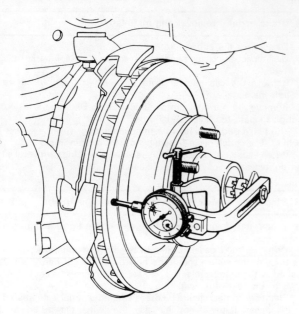

Fig. 9.16 Checking rotor for lateral runout (Sec 11)

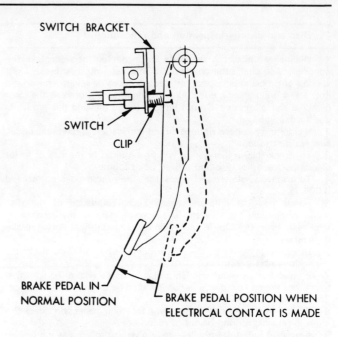

Fig. 9.18 Stoplamp switch (Sec 13)

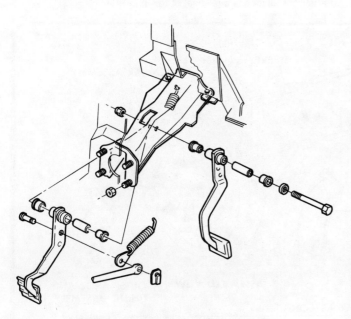

Fig. 9.17 Brake pedal mounting (Sec 12)

14 Parking brake – adjustment

1   The adjustment of the parking brake cable may be necessary whenever the rear brake cables have been disconnected or the parking brake cables have stretched due to age and stress.
2   Depress the parking brake pedal exactly two ratchet clicks and then raise the car for access underneath.
3   Tighten the adjusting nut until the left rear tire can just barely be turned in a rearward motion (photo). The tire should be completely locked from moving in a forward rotation.
4   Carefully release the parking brake pedal and check that the tire is able to rotate freely in either direction. It is important that there is no drag on the rear brakes with the pedal released.

15 Parking brake pedal – removal and installation

1   Disconnect the battery ground cable and the parking brake warning switch wire.
2   Remove the clip and ball from the clevis (if necessary, the equalizer nut can be slackened).
3   Remove the pedal rear mounting bolt and the nuts from the mounting studs at the front of the dash panel (under the hood).
4   Remove the pedal assembly.
5   Installation is the reverse of the removal procedure, but the nuts and pedal rear mounting bolt must be torque tightened.

16 Power brake booster – general description

1   A power brake booster has been an option on all models since its introduction. The booster utilizes vacuum from the engine manifold.
2   In the event of a fault developing in the booster, enough vacuum is stored to provide sufficient assistance for two or three brake applications and after that the performance of the hydraulic part of the braking system is only affected in so far as the need for higher pedal pressures will be noticed. Alternative types of power brake boosters have been used; these are the Delco-Moraine and the Bendix types. The principle of operation is similar in each case, and the descriptive cycle given in the following paragraph is applicable to both types.
3   *Brakes released:* In the 'at rest' condition with the engine running, vacuum is present on both sides of the power piston. Air at atmospheric pressure, entering through the filter behind the push rod, is shut off at the air valve. The floating control valve is held away from the seat in the power piston insert. Any air in the system is drawn through a small passage in the power piston, past the power piston insert valve seat to the insert itself. It then travels through a drilling in the support plate, into the space in front of the power piston then to the intake manifold via a check valve. Vacuum therefore exists on both sides of the power piston which is held against the rear of the housing under spring action.
4   *Brake application:* When the pedal is depressed, the push rod carries the air valve away from the floating control valve. The floating control valve will follow until it contacts the raised seat in the power piston insert; vacuum is now shut off to the rear power piston and atmospheric air enters through the filter past the air valve seat and through a passage into the housing at the rear of the power piston. The power piston therefore moves forward to operate the floating piston assembly of the hydraulic master cylinder. As pressure increases on the end of the master cylinder piston, the hydraulic reaction plate is

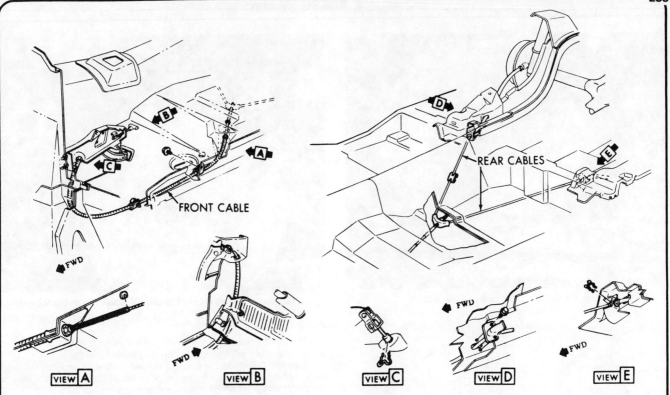

Fig. 9.19 Parking brake assembly (Sec 14)

FRONT CABLE

REAR CABLES

FWD

VIEW A   VIEW B   VIEW C   VIEW D   VIEW E

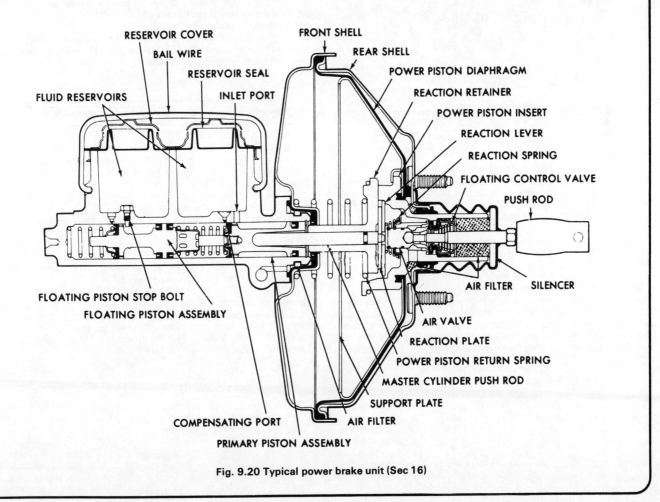

RESERVOIR COVER

BAIL WIRE

RESERVOIR SEAL

INLET PORT

FLUID RESERVOIRS

FRONT SHELL

REAR SHELL

POWER PISTON DIAPHRAGM

REACTION RETAINER

POWER PISTON INSERT

REACTION LEVER

REACTION SPRING

FLOATING CONTROL VALVE

PUSH ROD

AIR FILTER   SILENCER

AIR VALVE

REACTION PLATE

POWER PISTON RETURN SPRING

MASTER CYLINDER PUSH ROD

SUPPORT PLATE

AIR FILTER

FLOATING PISTON STOP BOLT

FLOATING PISTON ASSEMBLY

COMPENSATING PORT

PRIMARY PISTON ASSEMBLY

Fig. 9.20 Typical power brake unit (Sec 16)

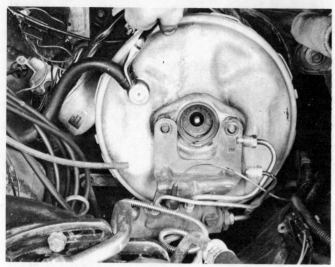

17.2 Disconnecting the vacuum hose to the power booster

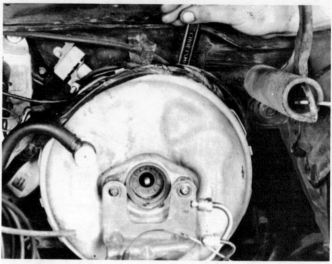

17.3 The attaching nuts for the booster assembly are at the firewall

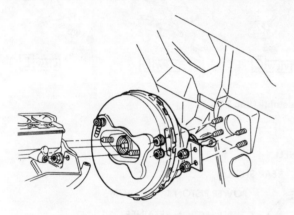

Fig. 9.21 Power brake booster mounting

The hydraulic pressure in the brake system is released as the floating piston assembly returns to the normal position.

7   *Vacuum failure:* In the event of vacuum failure, ie; engine switched off or failure of the vacuum line, application of the brake pedal moves the pedal push rod which in turn contacts the master cylinder push rod and the brakes are applied. This gives a condition as found in the standard braking system, and a correspondingly higher pedal pressure is required.

8   The power brake unit requires no special maintenance apart from periodic inspection of the hoses and inspection of the air filter beneath the boot at the pedal push rod end.

9   Dismantling of the power brake unit requires the use of special tools and in the event of a fault developing, it is recommended that a new or factory-exchange unit is fitted rather than attempt to overhaul the original booster.

17 Power brake booster – removal and installation

1   Remove the securing nuts which hold the master cylinder to the power brake unit. Position the master cylinder out of the way, being careful not to strain the hydraulic lines leading to the master cylinder. If there is any doubt as to the flexibility of the fluid lines disconnect them at the cylinder and plug the ends.

2   Disconnect the vacuum hose leading to the front of the power brake booster. Cover the end of the hose.

3   Loosen the four nuts that secure the booster to the firewall. Do not remove these nuts at this time.

4   Inside the car, disconnect the power brake push rod from the brake pedal. Do not force the push rod to the side when disconnecting.

5   Now fully remove the four booster mounting nuts and carefully lift the unit out of the engine compartment.

6   When installing, loosely install the four mounting nuts and then connect the push rod to the brake pedal. Torque-tighten the attaching nuts and reconnect the vacuum hose and master cylinder. If the hydraulic brake fluid lines were disconnected, the master cylinder as well as the entire braking system should be bled to eliminate any air which has entered the system (see Section 10).

moved off its seat on the lower piston and contacts the reaction levers. These levers swing on their pivots and bear against the end of the air valve operating rod assembly to provide a feed back (approximately 30% of the master cylinder load) to the pedal. This enables the driver to 'feel' the degree of brake application.

5   *Brake holding:* When the desired braking force is achieved the power piston moves forward until the floating control valve again seats on the air valve. The power piston will now remain stationary until there is a change in applied pedal pressure.

6   *Brakes released:* When the pedal pressure is released the air valve is forced back to contact the power piston under spring action. As it moves, the floating control valve is pushed off its seat on the power piston insert by the air valve. Atmospheric air is shut off by the air valve seating on the floating control valve. As the floating control cable lifts from its seat, it opens the rear of the power piston to intake manifold vacuum, and the power piston returns to the rear housing.

Chapter 10 Electrical system

Refer to Chapter 13 for specifications and information related to 1981 models

Contents

Specifications

Wiper motor
Type .... 2 speed, non-depressed park
Gear ratio .... 51 : 1
Current:
    low speed 6.0A
    high speed 4.5A
    Stall .... 18A max

Windshield washer
Type .... Positive displacement, piston type
Mounting .... Integral with wiper motor

Fuses
Circuit   Rating (amp)
1970
Radio, tape player, accessories 10
Turn signal, heater, back up lamps, cruise control 20
Instrument lamps 4
Tail, parking, side marker lamps 20
Stop, hazard warning lamps 20
Courtesy, dome, cigar lighter, clock lamps 20
Gauges, tell tale lamps 10
Windshield wiper motor 20
Air conditioning, TCS system 25

1971 thru 1973
Radio, TCS System, rear defogger Hydra-Matic downshift 10
Windshield wiper 25
Stop lamps, hazard flasher 20
Heater, air conditioner 25
Turn signal, back-up lamps, Cruise master, power windows 20

Fuses

Circuit	Rating (amp)
Instrument lamps, heater dial	3
Instrument panel lamps, gauges	10
Clock, courtesy lights, cigar lighter, anti-diesel valve, glove box lamp, light watch system	20
Tail, parking, rear license, dome and side marker lamp	20
Air conditioner high speed blower fuse	30
(in-line fuse located between horn relay and air conditioner relay)	

1974 on

	Rating (amp)
Radio, TCS system, anti-diesel valve, Hydra-Matic downshift, pulse wiper	10
Windshield wiper	25
Stop lamps, hazard flasher	20
Heater, air conditioner	25
Turn signal, back-up lamps, side marker, blocking relay (air conditioner), power windows	20
Instrument and floor shift lamps, heater dial	4
Gauges, instrument panel warning, rear defogger, Cruise control, seat belt buzzer	10
Clock, courtesy lamp, cigar lighter, trunk, glove box, dome lamp	20
Tail, rear license, side marker lamps	20
Air conditioner high speed blower fuse (in-line fuse located between horn relay and air conditioner relay)	30

Bulbs

Lamp	Candlepower/watts	Bulb No
1970 thru 1973		
Headlamp outer		
high	60W	6014
low	50W	Sealed beam
Parking, directional (front and rear)	32/3	1157
Rear license plate	4	67
Back-up lamp	32	1156
Glove compartment	2	1895
Instrument panel lamps	2	194
Side marker	2	194
Heater control	2 7 (1972-up)	1895 1445 (1972-up)
Interior dome	12	211
Map lamp	4	563
Courtesy lamp	6	631
Radio dial	2	1893
(AM)	2	293
Washer fluid level indicator	3	168
Trunk lamp	15	1003
Underhood lamp	15	93
Radio dial (except stereo and tape player)	3	1816
Radio dial (stereo and tape player)	3	564
Rear seat courtesy	6	212
1974 on		
Headlamp –		
outer high beam	60W	6014
low beam	50W	Sealed beam
Front turn and parking	24/2.2	1157 NA
Rear tail, stop, turn	32/3	1157
Rear license plate	33	168
Glove compartment	2	1891
Indicator and warning lamps	2	194
Instrument panel cluster lamps	3	168
Side marker	2	194
Heater, air conditioner panel lamps	2	194
Interior dome lamp	12	561
Trunk lamp	15	1003
Underhood lamp	15	93
Courtesy lamp	6	631
Radio dial lamp (excluding stereo and tape)	1	1893
Radio dial lamp (stereo and tape)	2	1893
Reading lamp	15	1004
Radio indictor	+ LED	D5410

Torque specifications

	lb-ft
Starter motor mountings bolts	30
Alternator pulley unit	45

1 General description

The electrical system is of the 12 volt, negative ground type.

Power for the lighting system and all electrical accessories is supplied by a lead/acid type battery which is charged by an alternator.

This chapter covers repair and service procedures for the various lighting and electrical components not associated with the engine. Information on the battery, alternator, voltage regulator and starter motor can be found in Chapter 5.

It should be noted that whenever portions of the electrical system are worked on, the negative battery cable should be disconnected to prevent electrical shorts and/or fires.

2 Fuses

1   The electrical circuits of the car are protected by a combination of fuses, circuit breakers and fusible links.

2   The fuse panel or fuse box is located in most models underneath the dashboard, on the left side of the vehicle. It is easily accessible for fuse inspection or replacement without completely removing the box from its mounting.

3   Each of the fuses is designed to protect a specific circuit, and the various circuits are identified on the fuse panel itself.

4   If an electrical component has failed, your first check should be the fuse. A fuse which has 'blown' can be readily identified by inspecting the element inside the glass tube. If this metal element is broken, the fuse is inoperable and must be replaced with a new one.

5   When removing and installing fuses it is important that metal objects are not used to pry the fuse in or out of the holder. Plastic fuse pullers are available for this purpose.

6   It is also important that the correct fuse be installed. The different electrical circuits need varying amounts of protection, indicated by the amperage rating on the fuse. See the Specifications Section of this Chapter for the correct amperage needs of each circuit.

7   At no time should the fuse be bypassed by using metal or foil. Serious damage to the electrical system could result.

8   If the replacement fuse immediately fails do not replace again until the cause of the problem is isolated and corrected. In most cases this will be a short circuit in the wiring system caused by a broken or deteriorated wire.

3 Fusible links

1   In addition to fuses, the wiring system incorporates fusible links

for overload protection. These links are used in circuits which are not ordinarily fused, such as the ignition circuit.

2   Although the fusible links appear to be of a heavier gauge than the wire they are protecting, this appearance is due to the heavy insulation. All fusible links are four wire gauges smaller than the wire they are incorporated into.

3   The exact locations of the four fusible links used may differ slightly but their protective circuits are the same. They are as follows:

a)   A 14-gauge fusible link protecting the 10-gauge battery charging circuit. This may be located at the 'Bat' terminal of the starter solenoid or as a pigtail lead at the battery positive cable.

b)   A 16-gauge link to protect all unfused wiring of 12-gauge or larger. This is located at the horn relay or junction block.

c)   A 20-gauge link is used to protect the generator warning light and the field circuitry which is of 16-gauge thickness. This link is also located at the junction block. Later models also have another fusible link at the horn relay for this purpose.

d)   Two fusible links are used to protect the ammeter circuit. They are 20-gauge and located at the junction block and horn relay.

4   The fusible links cannot be repaired, but rather a new link of the same wire size and Hypalon insulation can be put in its place. This process is as follows:

5   Disconnect the battery ground cable.

6   Disconnect the fusible link from the starter solenoid.

7   Cut the damaged fusible link out of the wiring system. Do this just behind the connector.

8   Strip the insulation from the circuit wiring approximately $\frac{1}{2}$ inch.

9   Position connector on the new fusible link and crimp into place in the wiring circuit.

10 Use rosin core solder at each end of the new link to obtain a good solder joint.

11 Use plenty of electrical tape around the soldered joint. No exposed wiring should show.

12 Connect the fusible link at the starter solenoid. Connect the battery ground cable. Test circuit for proper operation.

4 Circuit breakers

1   A circuit breaker is used to protect the headlight wiring, and located in the light switch. An electrical overload in the system will cause the lights to go on and off, or in some cases to remain off. If this happens, check the entire headlight wiring system immediately. Once the overload condition is corrected the circuit breaker will function

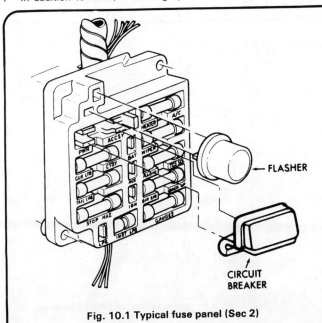

Fig. 10.1 Typical fuse panel (Sec 2)

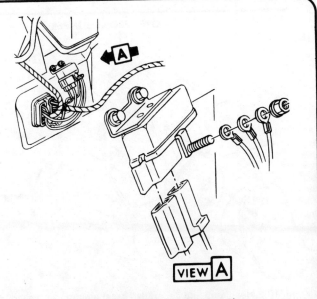

Fig. 10.2 Typical horn relay (Sec 6)

normally.

2   Vehicles equipped with power windows and/or power door locks will also have a circuit breaker for protection of electrical overloads to these circuits. They are located on the bulkhead of the engine compartment.

5   Turn signal and hazard flashers

1   Small canister-shaped flasher units are incorporated into the electrical circuits for the directional signals and hazard warning lights.
2   When the units are functioning properly an audible click can be heard with the circuit in operation. If the turn signals fail on one side only, and the flasher unit cannot be heard, a faulty bulb is indicated. If the flasher click can be heard, a short in the wiring is indicated.
3   If the turn signals fail on both sides, the fault may be due to a blown fuse, faulty flasher unit or switch, or a broken or loose connection. If the fuse has blown, check the wiring for a short before installing a new fuse.
4   The hazard warning lamps are checked in the same manner as paragraph 3 above.
5   The hazard warning flasher unit is located in the fuse box located under the dashboard on the left side. The turn signal flasher may be mounted in the fuse box or under the lower lip of the instrument panel.
6   When replacing either of these flasher units it is important to buy a replacement of the same capacity. Vehicles of model years 1970 – 1977 have 2-lamp turn signal flashers and 4-lamp hazard units. 1978 and later models have 2-lamp turn signal units and 6-lamp hazard flashers. Check the new flasher against the old one to be assured of the proper replacement.

6   Horns – fault testing

1   If the horn proves inoperable, your first check should be the fuse. A blown fuse can be readily identified at the fuse box under the lower left side of the dashboard.
2   If the fuse is in good condition, disconnect the electrical lead at the horn. Run a jumper wire from a 12-volt source (+ battery terminal) to the wiring terminal on the horn. If the horn does not blow, the fault lies in the grounding of the horn or the horn itself.
3   If current is not reaching the horn, indicated by the horn sounding from the above test, there is a failure in the circuit before the horn.
4   In most cases a failure of the horn relay is indicated if the circuit before the horn is at fault. Other checks would include bent metal contacts on the horn actuator or loose or broken wires in the system.
5   The horn relay is located in the wiring system, usually under the dashboard near the fuse box. When checking or replacing the horn

relay be aware that the threaded stud is always hot and shorting of this stud to ground could destroy a fusible link, disabling the vehicle until the link is replaced.

7   Headlight sealed beam unit – removal and installation

1   Whenever replacing the headlight, do not turn the spring-loaded adjusting screws of the headlight, as this will alter the aim.
2   Remove the headlight bezel screws and remove the decorative bezel (photo).
3   Use a cotter pin removal tool or similar device to unhook the spring from the retaining ring.
4   Remove the two screws which secure the retaining ring and withdraw the ring. Support the light as this is done (photo).
5   Pull the sealed beam unit outward slightly and disconnect the electrical connector from the rear of the light. Remove the light from the vehicle (photo).
6   Position the new unit close enough to connect the electrical connector. Make sure that the numbers molded into the lens are at the top.
7   Install the retaining ring with its mounting screws and spring.
8   Install the decorative bezel and check for proper operation. If the adjusting screws were not altered, the new headlight will not need to have the aim adjusted.

8   Headlamps – adjustment

1   Adjustment screws are provided at the front of the lamp to alter the lamp beam in both the horizontal and vertical planes.
2   It is strongly recommended that this work is left to a service station having modern beam setting equipment, any adjustment at home being regarded as a temporary, emergency operation.

9   Bulb replacement – front end

Parking lamp
1970 – 1973

1   Remove the screws which secure the lens to the body. Carefully extract the lens, being careful not to damage the fiber gasket (photo).
2   Push in on the bulb and turn it $\frac{1}{4}$ turn counterclockwise. Remove the bulb from the socket (photo).
3   Check that the electrical contacts and wiring are in a useable condition and push the new bulb into place. This is done with a twisting motion.

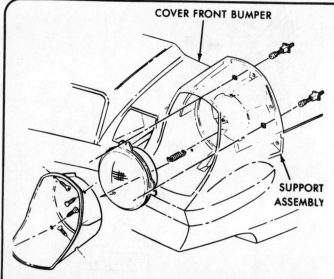

Fig. 10.3 Headlamp and decorative bezel mounting – typical installation (Sec 7)

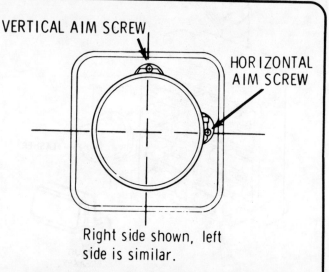

Fig. 10.4 Adjustment screw locations for single headlamp installations (Sec 8)

7.2 Removing the decorative bezel around the headlamp

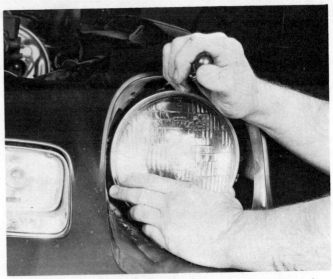

7.4 Support the headlamp as the retaining ring screws are removed

7.5 Pull outwards on the headlamp until the electrical connector can be disconnected

9.1 On most models the entire parking light assembly is withdrawn from the body for access to the bulb

9.2 The bulb is located inside a socket which is twisted out of the light housing

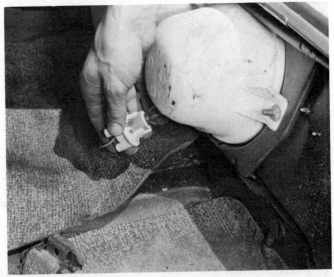

10.2 The rear bulbs are located in sockets which are twisted out of position. Access is through trunk

Fig. 10.5 Front side marker lamp installation (Sec 9)

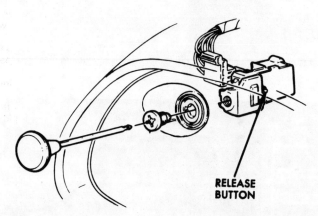

RELEASE
BUTTON

Fig. 10.6 Headlamp switch mounting (Sec 13)

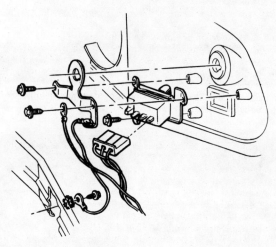

Fig. 10.7 Windshield, wiper/washer switch mounting (Sec 14)

4   Check the operation of the new bulb and if satisfactory, install the lens covering.

1974 – 1980
5   The bulb is housed in a metal socket which is located behind the grille.
6   Twist the socket out of the rear of the housing and replace the bulb as described for earlier vehicles.

Side marker lamps
All models
7   The bulb is located inside a twist socket at the rear of the housing.

Twist the socket on the inner fender panel $\frac{1}{4}$ turn and disengage the socket and bulb from the housing. The old bulb can then be released from the socket and a new one put in its place.

10 Bulb replacement – rear end

1   All the various bulbs for the rear end lighting are accessible from inside the trunk. The bulbs are located inside a metal socket which is secured to the rear of the particular housing.
2   The lamp bulb socket for all the lamps except the license plate is removed by twisting the socket $\frac{1}{4}$ turn. The bulb inside the socket can then be replaced and the socket re-installed (photo).
3   In most cases the license plate sockets must be pried out of the rear of the housing. Use a screwdriver to carefully lift the socket and bulb out of the hole in the housing. Replace the bulb and then push the socket back into position.

11 Bulb replacement – interior lamps

Center console lamps
1   Pry up the switch assembly from the console and remove the bulb from its socket.
2   The courtesy lamp bulb is accessible after extracting the lens screws and removing the lens.

Automatic floor shift quadrant lamps
3   Remove the quadrant trim plate from the console and withdraw the lamp socket.

Interior (roof) lamp
4   Pinch the sides of the plastic lamp lens together and remove it.
5   The festoon type bulb can now be carefully pried from between the spring contacts.

12 Bulb replacement – instrument panel

1   All of the instrument illumination and telltale bulbs are mounted in twist sockets on the rear of the printed circuit instrument panel.
2   Most of the sockets can be reached without removing the instrument panel. For better access it is recommended that the steering column trim cover be removed from the lower portion of the dashboard. On most models there are a total of six screws retaining this panel, with two of those screws hidden above the ashtray. If, with the trim cover removed, the upper bulbs are still inaccessible, then the instrument cluster will have to be removed (See Section 17).

13 Headlamp switch – removal and installation

1   Disconnect the negative cable at the battery.
2   Remove the steering column cover from the bottom of the dashboard for better access.
3   With the headlights in the 'full on' position, reach up under the dashboard and depress the lighting switch shaft retainer while pulling gently on the lighting knob. Remove the shaft and knob assembly.
4   Remove the nut which secures the lighting switch to the carrier.
5   For better access to the switch, remove the screws which secure the instrument cluster carrier and tilt the cluster.
6   Unplug the electrical connector at the switch and remove the switch.
7   Installation is a reversal of removal, however, make sure that all ground connections are refastened and that the switch shaft is fully seated in the switch. The shaft retainer should lock the shaft into place.

14 Windshield wiper-washer control – removal and installation

1   Remove the negative battery cable at the battery.
2   Remove the steering column trim cover with the air conditioning lap cooler attached to it. Two of the securing screws are hidden above

the ash tray.

3   Remove the screws securing the instrument cluster and pull the cluster outward slightly to gain better access to the switch (see Section 17).

4   Disconnect the electrical connector from the rear of the switch.

5   Remove the screws securing the switch to the instrument cluster and remove the switch.

6   Installation is a reversal of removal, however, make sure that all ground wires are reconnected.

15 Cigar lighter assembly – removal and installation

1   Disconnect the negative battery cable at the battery.

2   Reach up under the dashboard and disconnect the electrical connector at the rear of the lighter housing. On some early models it may be necessary to remove the steering column trim panel at the bottom of the dashboard for better access.

3   Grip the retainer from the rear of the instrument carrier and unscrew the lighter housing from the front. A rubber thumb cover will help during this operation.

4   When installing make sure the grounding ring is between the lighter housing and the retainer.

16 Speedometer cable – replacement

1   Disconnect the negative battery cable.

2   Reach up under the dashboard and disconnect the speedometer cable casing from the speedometer head. This is done by pressing the retaining spring clip towards the front of the instrument cluster and then pulling back on the speedometer cable casing.

3   Remove the dash panel sealing plug from the casing.

4   Using pliers, pull the old core out of the top of the casing. If the inner cable has broken, it will be necessary to remove the lower piece of cable from under the vehicle. Some models come equipped with a two-piece speedometer cable, while some have a single cable leading all the way from the speedometer head to the transmission. Ascertain which type you have and disconnect the lower end as necessary to pull out the remaining broken piece of inner cable.

5   When installing a new speedometer cable core always lubricate it the entire length with special lubricant designed for this purpose. Do not use oil.

6   Push the core into the casing, using a twisting motion when necessary. Make sure the end of the core is fully engaged in the pinion gear inside the transmission.

7   Reinstall the dash sealing plug and connect the casing to the rear of the instrument cluster. As in removal, push in on the retaining clip and then push the casing fully into the rear of the gauge.

8   Road test the vehicle and check for proper operation of the speedometer.

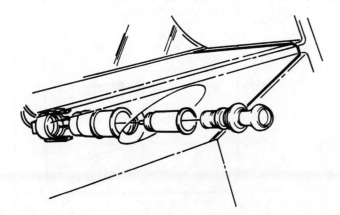

Fig. 10.8 Cigar lighter mounting (Sec 15)

17 Instrument cluster – removal and installation

1970 – 1979

1   Disconnect the battery ground cable.

2   Remove the steering column trim cover beneath the dashboard. This is held in place by six screws. Two of these screws are hidden above the ashtray (photo).

3   Reach up under the dash and depress the headlamp switch shaft retainer button while gently pulling outward on the shaft and knob.

4   Remove the headlamp switch retaining nut.

5   Remove the cigar lighter element.

6   Reach up under the lower edge of the cluster and remove the two mounting screws. One is on each side of the steering column, about three inches from the column center.

7   Remove the four screws visible at the front side of the carrier.

8   Remove the ground screw for the wiper switch. If applicable, it will be located near the top left corner of the switch.

9   Tilt the carrier outwards for access to the electrical connectors for the wiper and headlamp switches. Disconnect the electrical connectors at these switches, as well as the cigar lighter (photo).

10 Disconnect the transmission shift indictor from the steering column.

11 Disconnect the speedometer cable at the rear of the cluster. It is held in place by a tang which must be pushed forward as the cable is drawn away.

12 Disconnect the various electrical connectors attached to the rear printed circuit board and clock. Remove the wiring harness from its securing clips.

13 Remove the instrument cluster from the dash. Place on a bench for the remainder of the strip down (see following sections which are appropriate). The installation is a reversal of the removal procedure, however make sure that all ground connections are replaced in their original positions.

1980 models

14 Disconnect the battery ground cable.

15 Remove the six cluster bezel attaching screws.

16 Reach up under the dashboard and depress the headlamp retaining button while at the same time pulling gently on the headlamp switch knob.

17 Remove the headlamp switch retaining nut.

18 Disconnect the electrical couplers at the rear of the headlamp switch and windshield wiper switch. Remove the headlamp switch from the mounting hole in the bezel. Remove the windshield wiper switch which is held in place by two attaching screws.

19 Remove the cigar lighter element and disconnect the electrical connector. Unscrew the retainer from the housing and then remove the cigar lighter housing from the bezel.

20 The bezel is now free to be removed by pulling rearward.

21 Remove the cluster to carrier attaching screws and pull the instrument cluster rearward slightly for better access.

22 Disconnect the printed circuit electrical connector at the rear of the instrument cluster.

23 Disconnect the speedometer cable and wiring clips. The speedometer cable is held to the gauge by a retaining clip which must be pushed inward while the cable is pulled free.

24 Remove the instrument cluster.

25 Installation is a reversal of the removal procedure, however, make sure that all electrical connectors are firmly in place.

18 Gauge printed circuit board – replacement

1   Disconnect the negative battery cable.

2   Remove the instrument cluster as described in Section 17.

3   With the instrument cluster on a clean workbench, twist each of the illumination bulbs out of their sockets and remove the gauge securing nuts. Lift the printed circuit off the rear of the instrument cluster.

4   Place the new printed circuit into position, securing it with the illumination bulbs and gauge nuts.

5   Reinstall the instrument cluster referring to Section 17.

6   Connect the negative battery cable.

17.2 Removing the steering column trim panel from under the dashboard

17.9 Tilting the instrument cluster outward from the dashboard opening

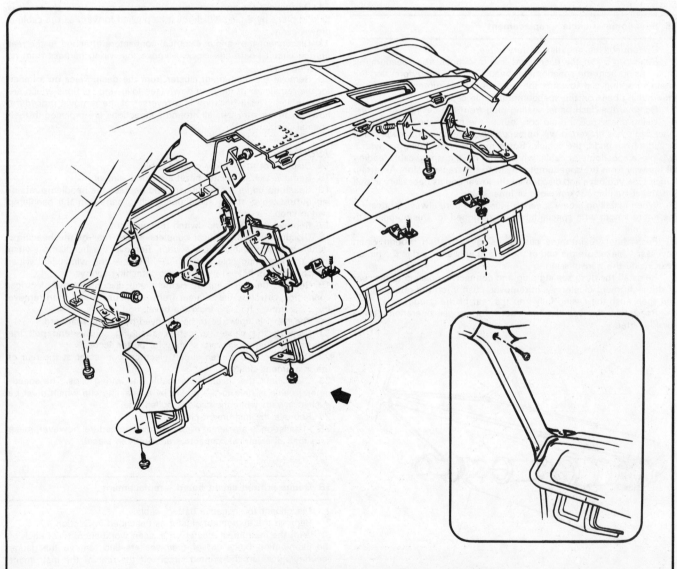

Fig. 10.9 Instrument panel – shown from inside the car (Sec 17)

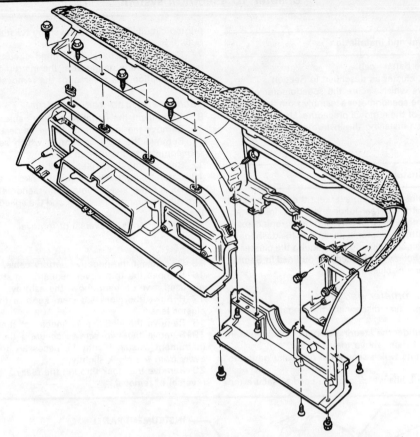

Fig. 10.10 Instrument panel and pad – shown from behind dashboard (Sec 17)

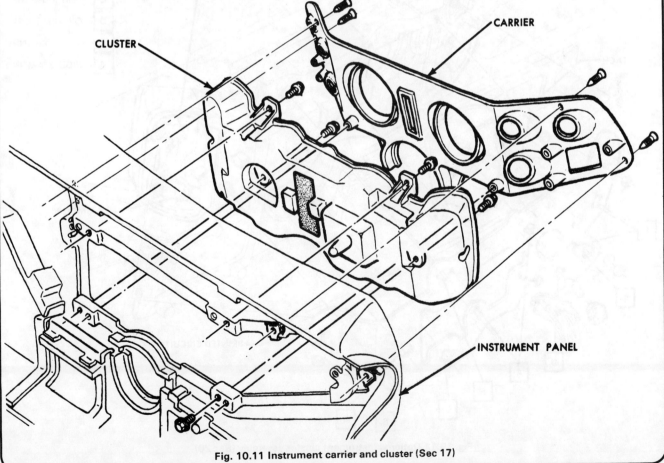

CLUSTER

CARRIER

INSTRUMENT PANEL

Fig. 10.11 Instrument carrier and cluster (Sec 17)

19 Speedometer – removal and installation

1 Disconnect the negative battery cable.
2 Remove the instrument cluster as described in Section 17.
3 Remove the two screws which secure the speedometer case to the rear of the cluster. Lift the speedometer assembly from the cluster.
4 Installation is a reversal of the removal procedure. Use Section 17 as a guide if necessary when installing the instrument cluster.

20 Optional instrument cluster – servicing

1 All of the illumination bulbs, instruments (except the speedometer) and the printed circuit board are rear-loaded into the instrument cluster. This means that most of the servicing and replacement operations can take place with the cluster in position in the dashboard.
2 Vehicles equipped with air conditioning may require the cluster be removed for greater access. Follow the procedures outlined in Section 17 for removal of the instrument cluster.

Fuel, temperature and ammeter gauges

3 To remove these gauges, first disconnect the negative battery cable.
4 Remove the trim cover under the steering column. This is held in place with six screws, two of them above the ash tray.
5 Remove the screws or nuts which secure the particular gauge to the rear of the cluster.
6 Remove the illumination bulbs which also are used to secure the

printed circuit. They are removed by twisting them $\frac{1}{4}$ turn and pulling outwards.
7 Carefully peel back the printed circuit enough to enable you to remove the faulty gauge from the instrument cluster.
8 Installation is a reversal of the removal operations.

Tachometer and speedometer

9 Disconnect the negative battery cable.
10 Remove the instrument cluster as described in Section 17.
11 Remove the nuts or screws which secure the tachometer and speedometer to the printed circuit.
12 Remove the illumination bulbs.
13 Carefully lay back the printed circuit and remove the attaching screws for the instruments. The tachometer can then be removed through the rear of the cluster and the speedometer pulled out through the front.
14 Installation is a reversal of removal.

Clock

15 Disconnect the negative battery cable.
16 Remove the trim cover beneath the steering column. Six screws are used, two of them above the ashtray.
17 Remove the clock set stem knob at the front of the instrument cluster lens.
18 Remove the electrical connector at the rear of the clock.
19 Remove the two screws securing the clock to the rear of instrument cluster. It may be necessary to move the printed circuit away from the clock slightly.
20 Remove the clock through the rear of the cluster. Installation is a reversal of removal.

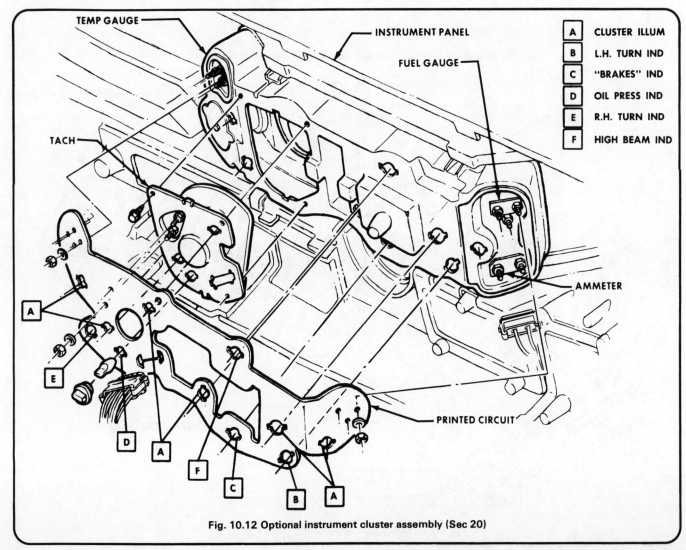

Fig. 10.12 Optional instrument cluster assembly (Sec 20)

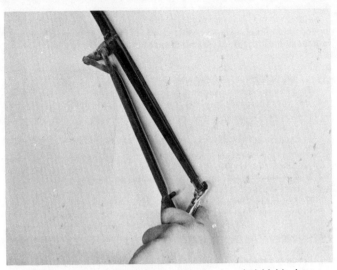

22.3 Using pliers to pinch the locking tabs on the windshield wiper blades

24.3 The splined windshield wiper arm and the small metal locking clip which must be depressed

21 Windshield wiper system – general description

1   A two-speed wiper motor is installed as standard equipment and incorporates the gear train and the self-parking mechanism.
2   The wiper arms will only park when the motor is operating in low speed.
3   The drive from the wiper motor to the wiper arms is by means of a crank arm and a strut to the transmission shafts.
4   On all models, the windshield wiper motor incorporates the drive system for the windshield washers.
5   Two types of windshield wiper assemblies may be encountered according to vehicle model. On one type, the wiper arms park parallel with and about two inches above the windshield molding while on the other type, the blades park in a depressed position against a step on the windshield lower molding.

22 Wiper blade element – replacement

1   Two methods are used to retain the rubber wiper blade element to the blade assembly. This 'refill', as it is sometimes called, can be replaced without removing or disassembling the wiper mechanism.
2   One method uses a press-type button, in most cases colored red.

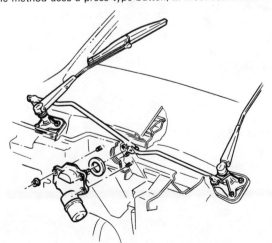

Fig. 10.13 Windshield wiper and motor assembly (Sec 26)

Depress the button and then slide the rubber element off of the wiper blade. To install a new element, press the button and slide the new piece into place. Once centered on the blade, it will lock into place.
3   The other method incorporates a spring-type retainer clip at the end of the removable element. When the retainer is pinched together, the element can slide out of the blade assembly. A small air of pliers can be used to squeeze the retainer. When installing a new element, be certain that the metal insert passes through all of the retaining tabs of the blade assembly (photo).

23 Windshield wiper blades – removal and installation

1   Pull the wiper arm/blade assembly away from the windshield glass against the tension of the wiper arm spring.
2   Depress the small tab which lies just below the wiper arm at the blade connector socket and pull the blade from the arm. **Note:** *On some models a coil spring blade retainer is used. To remove the blade, insert a screwdriver on top of the spring and push downwards.*
3   Installation is a reversal of removal; make sure that the connector is pushed fully onto the arm so that the small locating 'pip' is secure in the hole in the connector.

24 Windshield wiper arm – removal and installation

1   Make sure that the wiper arms are in the self-parked position, the motor having been switched off in the low speed mode.
2   Note carefully the position of the wiper arm in relation to the windshield lower reveal moulding. Use tape on the windshield to mark the exact location of the wiper arm on the glass.
3   Using a suitable hooked tool or a small screwdriver, pull aside the small spring tang which holds the wiper arm to the splined transmission shaft and at the same time pull the arm from the shaft (photo).
4   Installation is a reversal of removal but do not push the arm fully home on the shaft until the alignment of the arm has been checked. If necessary, the arm can be pulled off again and turned through one or two serrations of the shaft to correct the alignment without the necessity of pulling aside the spring tang.
5   Finally, press the arm fully home on its shaft and then wet the windshield glass and operate the motor on low speed to ensure that the arc of travel is correct.

25 Wiper motor – removal and installation

1   Raise the hood and remove the cowl screen at the base of the windshield.

2   Reaching through the opening, loosen the transmission drive link to crank arm attaching nuts.
3   Remove the transmission drive links from the crank arm of the motor.
4   Disconnect the washer hoses and electrical wiring at the motor.
5   Remove the three bolts which secure the motor to the firewall cowling. Push the crank arm through its mounting hole and then withdraw the motor.
6   Installation is a reversal of removal, however, make sure that the motor is in the 'Park' position.

26 Windshield wiper motor/transmission – servicing

1   The unit has a very long operating life and when it has finally worn so much that dismantling and repair is necessary, consideration should be given to the purchase of a new or reconditioned unit, particularly if the major components require replacement.

27 Washer assembly – removal, servicing and installation

1970 thru 1974 (rectangular motor type)

1   The washer pump can be removed independently, leaving the wiper motor in the vehicle. Disconnect the washer hoses and electrical wiring.
2   Remove the washer pump mounting screws and lift off the pump from the wiper motor.
3   Pull off the four lobe washer pump drive cam. This is a press fit and may require prying.

4   Remove the felt washer from the wiper shaft.
5   Remove the ratchet dog retaining screw, then hold the spring loaded solenoid plunger in position and lift the solenoid assembly and ratchet dog off the pump frame. Separate the dog from the mounting plate if necessary.
6   To remove the ratchet wheel, move the spring out of the shaft groove and slide the ratchet wheel off its shaft.
7   To separate the pump and pump actuator plate from the frame, pull the pump housing towards the valve end until the grooves in the housing clear the frame.
8   Reassembly is the reverse of the dismantling procedure.
9   Installation is the reverse of the removal procedure.

1970 on (round motor type)

10   Disconnect the washer hoses from the pump and disconnect the wires from the pump relay.
11   Remove the plastic pump cover.
12   Remove the frame screws and withdraw the pump and frame.
13   Extract the screw and lift the ratchet dog from the mounting plate.
14   Disengage the pawl spring from the pawl and then slide the pawl from the cam follower pin.
15   Pry the ratchet spring out the slot in the shaft, hold the relay armature against the relay coil and slide the ratchet wheel off the shaft.
16   Pry off the retainer and slide the cam off the shaft.
17   Remove the relay armature and spring.
18   Chisel off the four tabs that secure the coil mounting bracket. Remove the relay coil and terminal board.
19   To remove the plastic pump housing, pull it towards the valve end

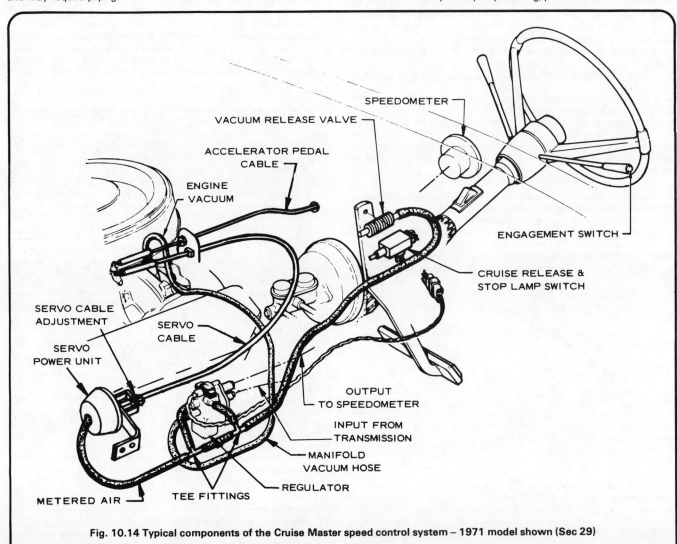

Fig. 10.14 Typical components of the Cruise Master speed control system – 1971 model shown (Sec 29)

until the grooves in the housing clear the base. Detach the assembly from the cam follower pin. The piston and plastic housing are serviced as an assembly.

20 The valve can be removed from the pump housing after extracting the four screws but make sure to mark the relative position of the valve to the housing before separating.

21 Reassembly is a reversal of dismantling but note that the wiper motor must be in the 'Park' position before assembling the pump and the wiper motor.

28 Modified pulse (programmed) wiper/washer system – description, removal, dismantling, reassembly, installation

1 This system which is fitted to some models as optional equipment is designed to provide (i) a low speed single wipe cycle delay of up to 10 seconds and (ii) wash/wipe cycle comprising squirts, wiping and switching off in the 'Park' position.

2 To remove the washer pump, first withdraw the complete wiper/washer assembly from the vehicle.

3 Remove the plastic tab from the opening under the terminals and pull the plastic cover from the mounting post.

4 Disconnect the electrical leads and extract the three screws that attach the pump to the wiper transmission.

5 The valve assembly can be removed after extracting the four securing screws.

6 Slide the cam from the shaft after first removing the retainer.

7 Remove the pulse relay timing device, holding switch and override switch (one screw) from the washer frame.

8 Disconnect the red and yellow leads from the pulse relay and detach it from the locator pins.

9 Remove the dog spring assembly and the ratchet pawl retaining ring. Disconnect the pawl spring and slide the pawl from the cam follower shaft.

10 Disconnect the relay armature spring and remove the armature.

11 Release the ratchet gear spring from the groove in the shaft and slide the ratchet gear from the shaft.

12 To release the pump housing from its sheet metal hose, pull it towards the valve assembly until the grooves in the plastic pump housing clear the base. Detach the assembly from the cam follower pin.

13 Bend or chisel off the four bent over tabs that secure the coil mounting bracket to its base.

14 Reassembly is a reversal of dismantling but observe the following points.

15 When installing the pulse relay onto the switch base locator pins, rotate the drive cam counter clockwise and secure the complete assembly with the screw. Remember to insert the sealing rings between the housing and valve body.

29 Cruise master – description, adjustment and component replacement

1 This cruising speed control system is optionally available on certain models and allows the driver to maintain a constant highway speed without the necessity of continual adjustment of foot pressure on the accelerator pedal.

2 The system employs a servo unit connected to the intake manifold, a speedometer cable-driven regulator and various switches.

3 An override capability is built in.

4 Any malfunction in the performance of the system should first be checked out by inspecting the fuse, the security of the leads and terminals, and the vacuum pipes and connections.

5 The following adjustments should then be checked and if necessary altered to conform to those specified.

6 The servo operating rod which connects to the carburetor throttle linkage should be adjusted by turning the link on the rod until there is 0.02 to 0.04 inches of free play at the carburetor.

7 *The regulator* can be adjusted by turning the orifice tube in or out *(never remove it as it cannot be re-installed)*. If the vehicle cruises below the engagement speed, screw the orifice tube out. If the vehicle cruises above the engagement speed, screw the orifice tube in. Each $\frac{1}{4}$ turn of the orifice tube will change the cruise speed by about 1 mph. Tighten the locknut after each adjustment.

8 *The brake release switch* contacts must open when the brake

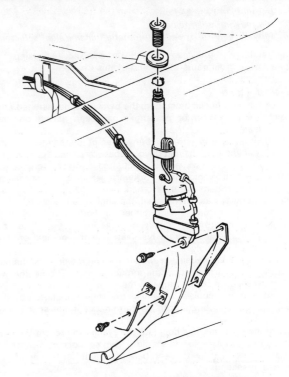

Fig. 10.15 Power radio antenna (Sec 30)

pedal is depressed between 0.38 and 0.64 inch measured at the pedal pad.

9 The vacuum valve plunger must clear the pedal arm when the arm is moved $\frac{5}{16}$ inch measured at the switch.

10 *The column mounted engagement switch* is non-adjustable, and is serviced only as part of the complete turn signal lever assembly.

11 Faulty components should be replaced as complete assemblies after disconnecting electrical leads, vacuum hoses and control cables from them as necessary.

30 Power radio antenna – removal and installation

1 Lower the antenna mast fully by turning off the radio or ignition key switch. If the unit has failed with the antenna mast in the 'up' position, it may be advisable to cut off the mast portion to make replacement easier.

2 Disconnect the negative battery cable.

3 Access to the power antenna motor is through the inner fender panel. Raise the vehicle and remove the front tire for better access if necessary.

4 Remove the fender skirt attaching screws and pull down on the rear edge of the skirt. Use a piece of 2x4-inch lumber as a spacer to keep the skirt pulled away as work is performed.

5 Remove the escutcheon nut at the fender.

6 Disconnect the electrical leads and remove the antenna and motor assembly through the fender skirt opening.

7 When installing a new unit, be sure that the mast is fully retracted and the lower bracket attachment is secured by the fender skirt attaching screw.

31 Seat belt warning systems

1972 thru 1973

1 This sytem combined with the ignition key buzzer, provides for both visual and audible warnings if, with the weight of a person in either of the front seats, the following actions are taken without the seat belts having been fastened:

(i)   the ignition switched on
(ii) the parking brake released
(iii) forward gear (or speed – automatic transmission) selected

Any faults in the system should be checked out using the appropriate wiring diagrams at the end of this Chapter.

1974 thru 1976

2   Before the vehicle can be started, the belts must be fastened *after* the weight of the driver or passenger has been placed on their respective seats.

3   A warning system is actuated if any attempt is made to start the vehicle without the belts having been properly fastened.

4   The warning system will again be actuated if, after the engine has been started and the vehicle is in a forward gear or speed range, the occupied front seat belts are unfastened.

5   Once the engine has been started, the engine can be switched off and subsequently restarted with either or both front seat belts unfastened provided the driver only remains in his seat. Once the driver's weight is removed from his seat then the original starting procedure will again apply.

6   In order to facilitate vehicle maintenance and repair, a mechanic's start position is incorporated in the ignition switch. The engine will then start irrespective of the mode of the front seat belts or whether either front seat is occupied. Whenever the engine is started by this method, the warning buzzer can be terminated if the seat buckle switch is cycled.

7   An anti-bounce device is built into the system to prevent the non-start mode being re-established should a front seat occupant raise his weight from his seat (with seat belt fastened) for a period not exceeding ten seconds.

8   An override relay is incorporated in the system to permit starting the engine in the event of complete system failure. The relay is mounted within the engine compartment and to bring the relay into use, carry out the following operations:

9   Turn the ignition 'ON'.

10   Open the hood and depress and then release the button on the override relay. The engine can now be started and the vehicle driven until such time as the ignition key is turned to the 'OFF' or 'LOCK'

position, when the override relay will return to its de-energized position.

1977 on

11   The system used on these later vehicles incorporates a timer-controlled buzzer and warning lamp which operate for a few seconds after the ignition is switched on without the seat belts having been fastened.

12   With this system, the fastening of safety belts is left to the driver and abandons the need for complicated starter interlock and other devices used in earlier systems.

32 Radio – removal and installation

1   Disconnect the negative battery cable.

2   Pull off the radio control knobs and bezels. These are not held on with lock nuts, but are merely pushed onto the shafts.

3   Using a deep socket, remove the control shaft lock nuts now visible at the base of the shafts.

4   Look up under the dashboard, at the rear of the radio unit. Any obstructions, commonly a center air duct or hoses, should be disconnected and removed for access.

5   Remove the screws or nuts securing the rear mounting bracket to the radio.

6   Push the radio forward until the shafts are clear of the dashboard and then lower the unit enough to remove the electrical connections at the rear of the radio. Also disconnect the antenna lead-in cable.

7   Carefully lower the radio unit and remove.

8   Installation is a reversal of the removal operation, however, always attach the speaker wiring harness before applying power to the radio.

33 Power door lock system

1   This optional system incorporates a solenoid actuator inside each door. The solenoid is electrically operated from a control switch on the instrument panel and operates the lock through a linkage. Each actuator has an internal circuit breaker which may require one to three

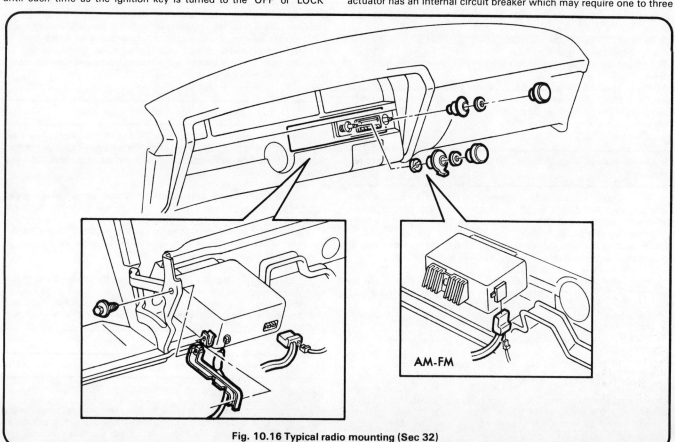

Fig. 10.16 Typical radio mounting (Sec 32)

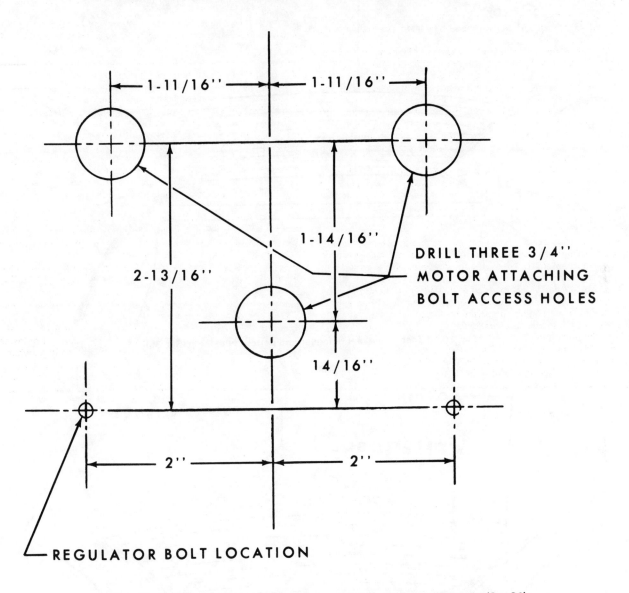

ALIGN TEMPLATE WITH APPROPRIATE REGULATOR
LOWER ATTACHING BOLTS ON DOOR

1-11/16''   1-11/16''

1-14/16''

DRILL THREE 3/4''
MOTOR ATTACHING
BOLT ACCESS HOLES

2-13/16''

14/16''

2''   2''

REGULATOR BOLT LOCATION

Fig. 10.17 Template used for gaining access to the power window motor bolts (Sec 34)

minutes to reset.

2   To remove the solenoid, raise the door window and remove the door panel trim pad as described in Chapter 12.

3   After prying away the water shield, the solenoid can be seen through the large access hole. The solenoid can be mounted to either the rear door lock pillar or the inner metal door panel.

4   Early models use attaching screws through the door panel and into the solenoid bracket. Later models use rivets to secure the solenoid to the pillar. These must be drilled out using a $\frac{1}{4}$ inch drill bit.

5   Once the securing devices are removed, disconnect the wiring harness at the solenoid and the actuating link held in place with a metal clip. Remove the solenoid from the door cavity.

6   To install, place the solenoid in position and connect the electrical connector and actuating link. If rivets were drilled out, new aluminum rivets ($\frac{1}{4}$ x 0.500'' size) can be used upon reassembly. Optionally, $\frac{1}{4}$ –

20 screws and U nuts can be used.

7   Check the operation of the door locks before installing the water shield and trim panel.

34 Power window system

1   This system incorporates an electric motor and an independent control switch for each of the door windows. The driver's door has a master control switch permitting operation of all the windows.

2   The electric motor which powers the window regulator is a reversible-direction motor and operates with 12 volts. It features an internal circuit breaker for protection. The motor is secured to the regulator with bolts.

3   The electrical motor can be removed from the regulator with the

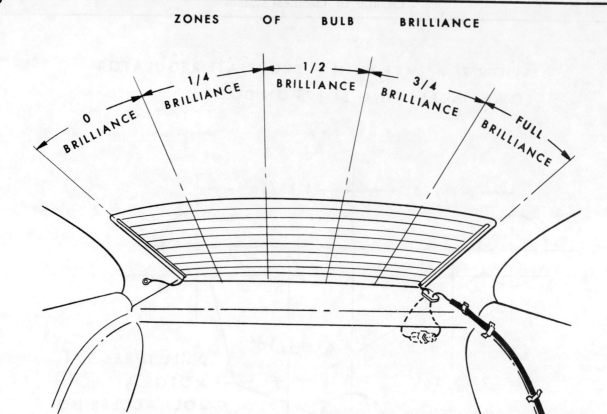

Fig. 10.18 Testing the rear defogger grid pattern with lamp (Sec 35)

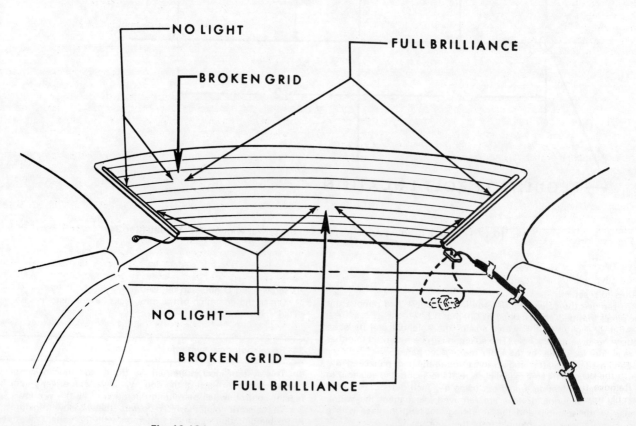

Fig. 10.19 Lamp brilliance with broken defogger grid lines (Sec 35)

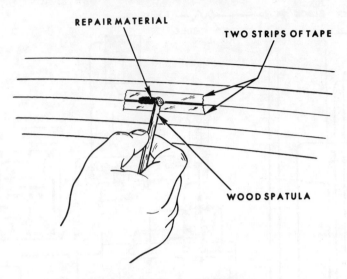

Fig. 10.20 Repairing window defogger grid (Sec 35)

remainder of the window system intact only if the door glass is intact and attached to the regulator. If the door glass is broken or removed from the door, the motor must be separated after the regulator is removed from inside the door.

Glass intact and attached

4   Raise the window and remove the door trim panel and water shield as described in Chapter 12.
5   Reach inside the door access cavity and disconnect the wiring harness at the motor.
6   It is imperative at this point that the window glass be taped or blocked in the up position. This will prevent the glass from falling into the door and possibly causing injury or damage.
7   Since the bolts used to secure the motor to the regulator are inaccessible, it is necessary to drill three large access holes in the metal door inner panel. The position of these holes is critical. Use the full-size template shown as Fig. 10.17. This template should be positioned on the door with tape after properly aligning it with the regulator attaching rivets (late models) or bolts (early models).
8   Use a center punch to dimple the panel at the center of the template access holes and then drill the ¾-inch holes with a hole saw.
9   Reach in through the access hole and support the motor as the attaching bolts are removed. Remove the motor through the access hole, being careful that the window glass is firmly supported in the up position.
10   Before installation, the motor drive gear and regulator sector teeth should be lubricated.
11   Upon positioning of the motor, make sure that the drive gear properly engages with the regulator sector teeth. Install remaining components in the reverse order of removal. Waterproof tape can be used to seal the three access holes drilled in the metal inner panel.

Glass broken or not attached

12   Remove the window regulator as described in Chapter 12. Make sure that the wiring harness to the motor is disconnected first.
13   It is imperative that the regulator sector gear be locked into position before removing the motor from the regulator. The control arms are under pressure and can cause serious injury if the motor is removed without performing the following operation.
14   Drill a hole through the regulator sector gear and backplate. Install a bolt and nut to lock the gear in position. Do not drill closer than ½ inch to the edge of the sector gear or backplate.
15   Remove the three motor attaching bolts and remove the motor assembly from the regulator.
16   Prior to installation, the motor drive gear and regulator sector teeth should be lubricated. The lubricant should be cold weather approved to at least –20 degrees Fahrenheit. Lubriplate Spray Lube 'A' is recommended by GM.
17   When installing the motor to the regulator make sure that the

sector gear teeth and drive gear teeth properly mesh.
18   Once the motor attaching bolts are tightened, the locking nut and bolt can be removed. Install the regulator as described in Chapter 12. Don't forget to connect the motor wiring.

35 Electric grid-type rear defogger – testing and repair

1   This option consists of a rear window with a number of horizontal elements that are baked into the glass surface during the glass forming operation.
2   Small breaks in the element system can be successfully repaired without removing the rear window.
3   To test the grids for proper operation, start the engine and turn on the system.
4   Ground one lead of a test lamp and lightly touch the other prod to each grid line.
5   The brilliance of the test lamp should increase as the probe is moved across the element from right to left. If the test lamp glows brightly at both ends of the grid lines, check for a loose ground wire for the system. All of the grid lines should be checked in at least two places.
6   To repair a break in a grid line it is recommended that a repair kit specifically for this purpose be purchased from a GM dealer. Included in the repair kit will be a decal, a container of silver plastic and hardener, a mixing stick and instructions.
7   To repair a break, first turn off the system and allow it to de-energize for a few minutes.
8   Lightly buff the grid line area with fine steel wool and then thoroughly clean the area with alcohol.
9   Use the decal supplied in the repair kit, or use electrician's tape above and below the area to be repaired. The space between the pieces of tape should be the same as existing grid lines. This can be checked from outside the car. Press the tape tightly against the glass to prevent seepage.
10   Mix the hardener and silver plastic thoroughly.
11   Using the wood spatula, apply the silver plastic mixture between the pieces of tape, overlapping the damaged area slightly on either end.
12   Carefully remove the decal or tape and apply a constant stream of hot air directly to the repaired area. A heat gun set at 500 to 700 degrees Fahrenheit is recommended. Hold the gun asbout 1 inch from the glass for 1 to 2 minutes.
13   If the new grid line appears off color, tincture of iodine can be used to clean the repair and bring it back to the proper color. This mixture should not remain on the repair for more than 30 seconds.
14   Although the defogger is now fully operational, the repaired area should not be disturbed for at least 24 hours.

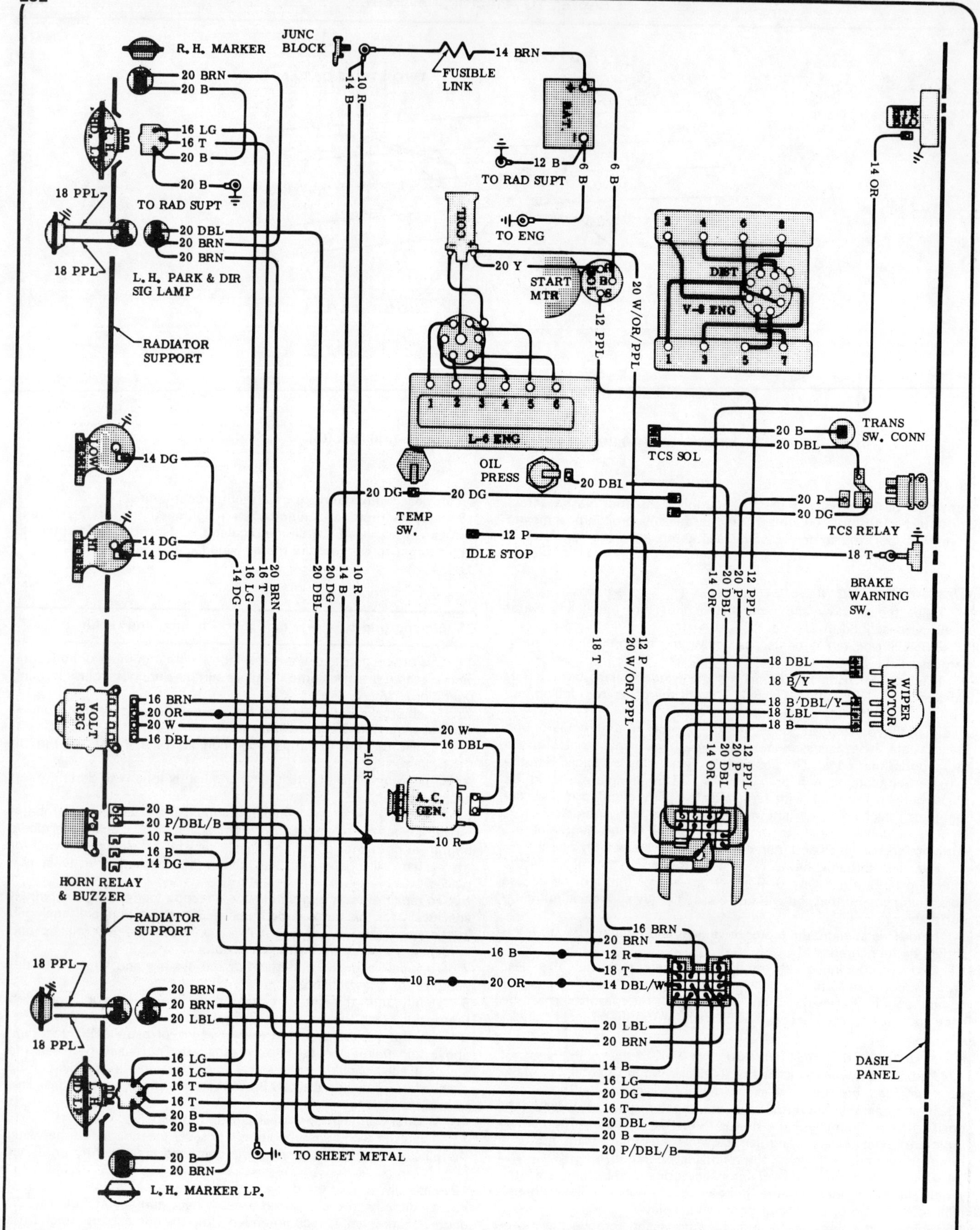

Fig. 10.21 Wiring diagram for 1970 engine compartment
(key to wiring diagram on pages 310 and 311)

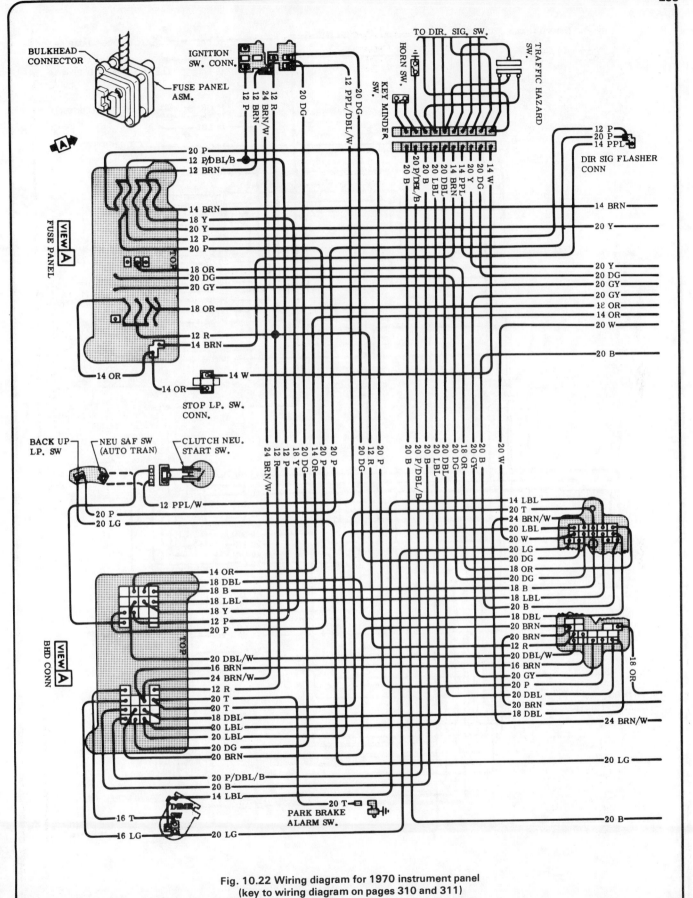

Fig. 10.22 Wiring diagram for 1970 instrument panel
(key to wiring diagram on pages 310 and 311)

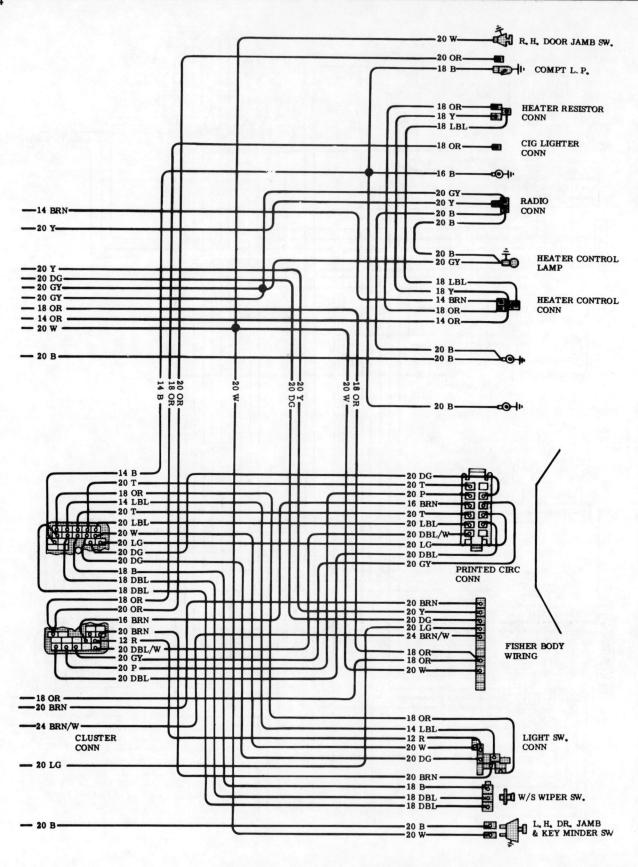

Fig. 10.23 Wiring diagram for 1970 instrument panel
(key to wiring diagram on pages 310 and 311)

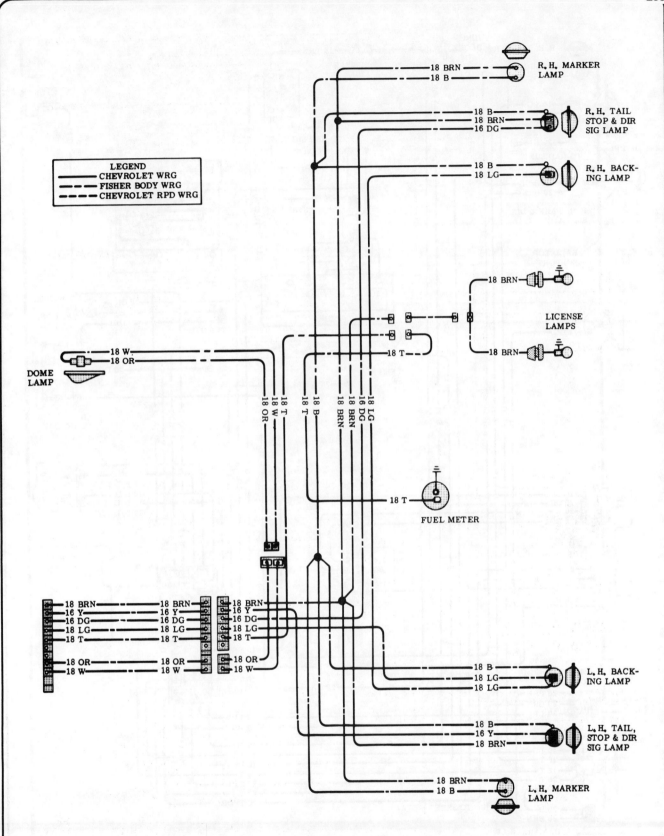

Fig. 10.24 Wiring diagram for 1970 body and rear lighting
(key to wiring diagram on pages 310 and 311)

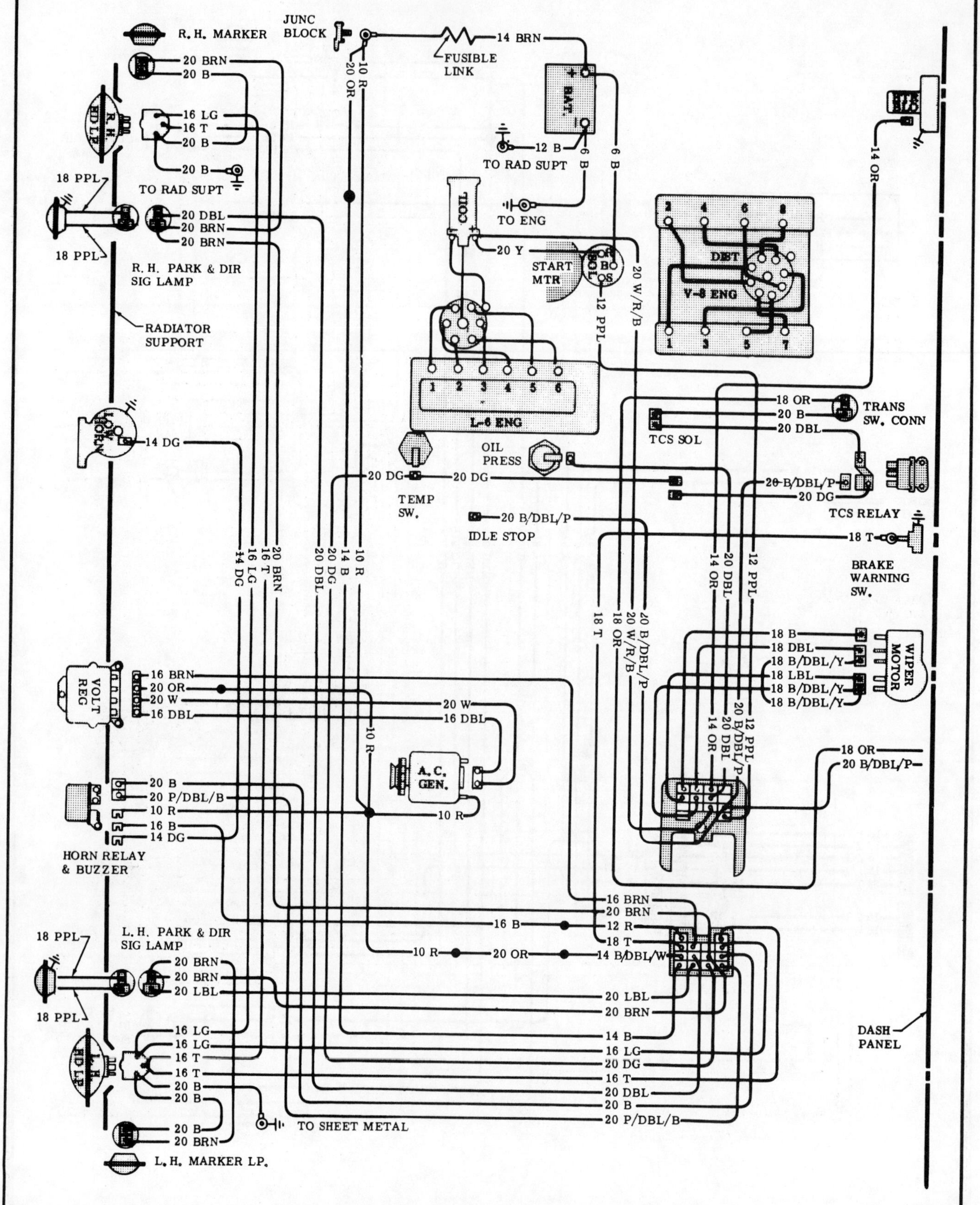

Fig. 10.25 Wiring diagram for 1971 engine compartment
(key to wiring diagram on pages 310 and 311)

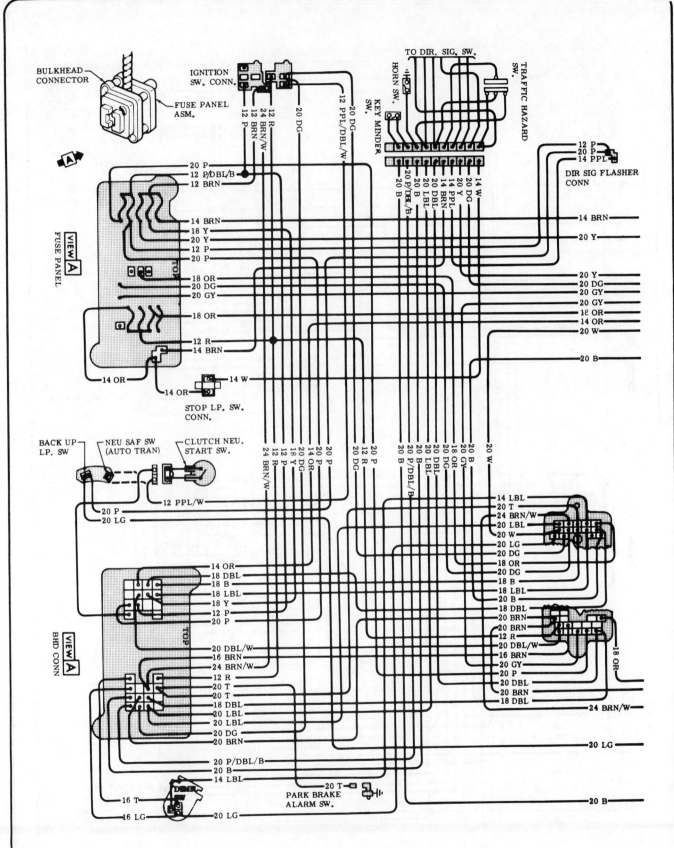

Fig. 10.26 Wiring diagram for 1971 instrument panel
(key to wiring diagram on pages 310 and 311)

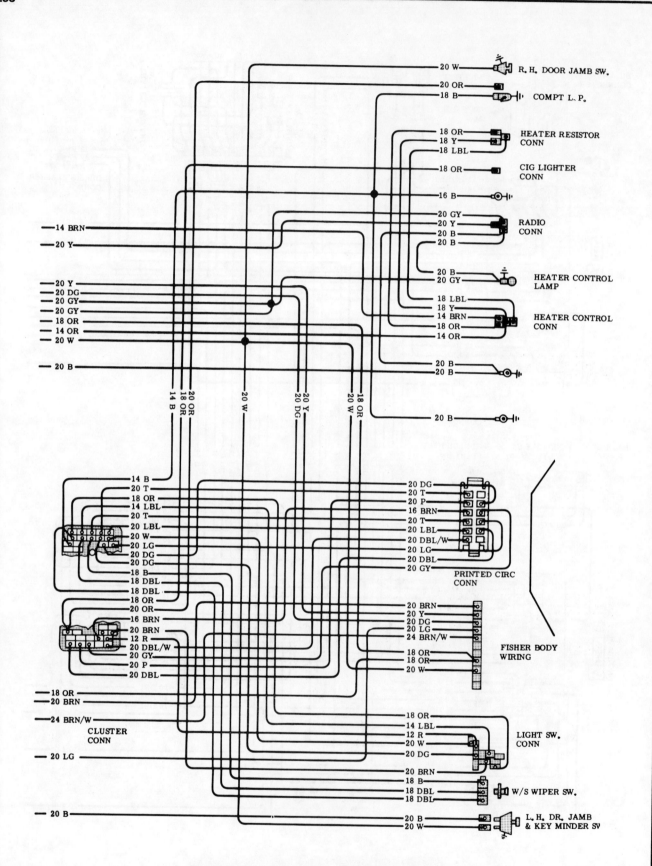

Fig. 10.27 Wiring diagram for 1971 instrument panel
(key to wiring diagram on pages 310 and 311)

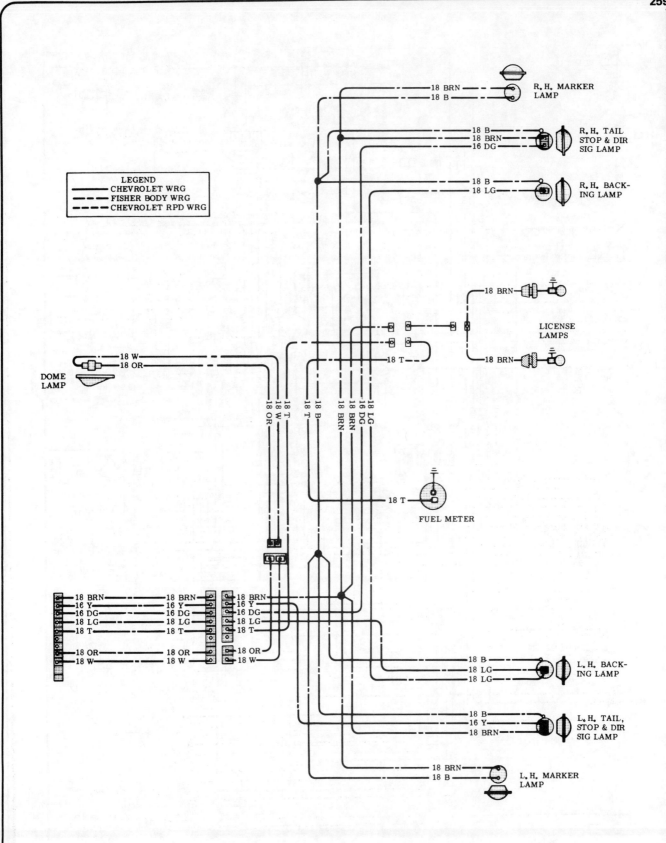

Fig. 10.28 Wiring diagram for 1971 body and rear lighting
(key to wiring diagram on pages 310 and 311)

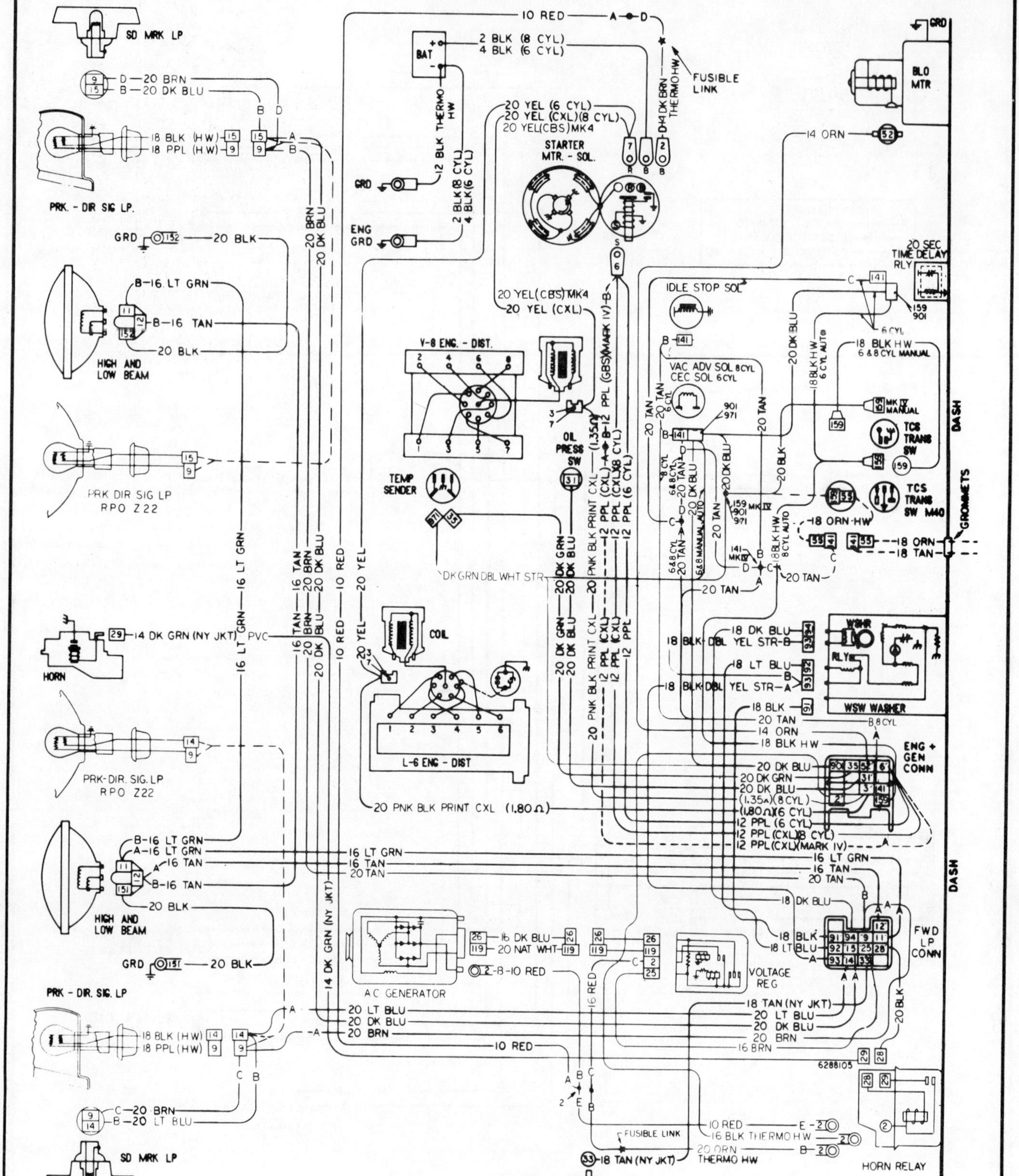

Fig. 10.29 Wiring diagram for 1972 engine compartment
(key to wiring diagram on pages 310 and 311)

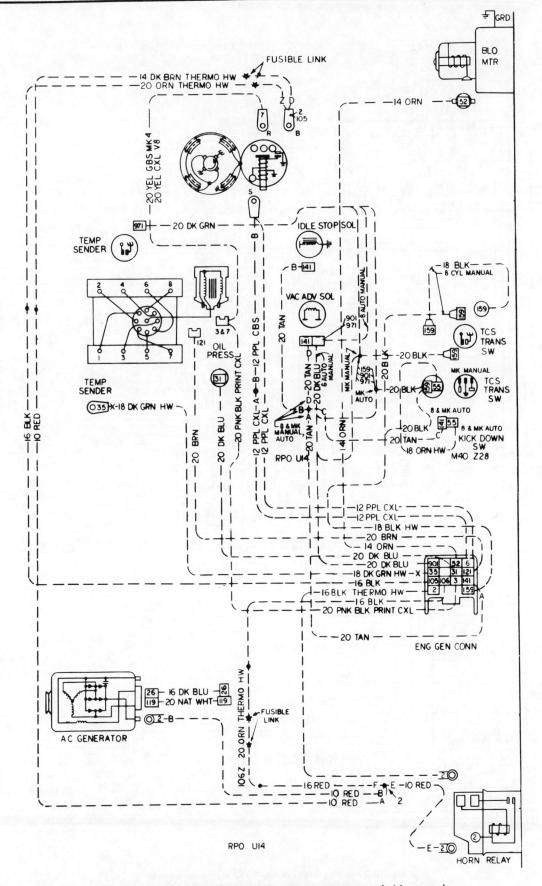

Fig. 10.30 Wiring diagram for 1972 engine compartment (with gauges)
(key to wiring diagram on pages 310 and 311)

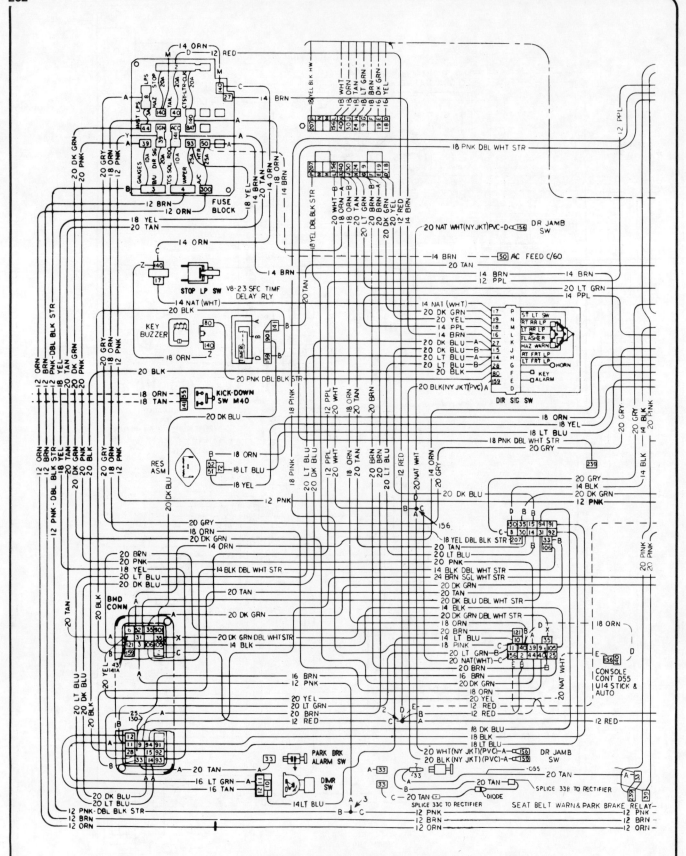

**Fig. 10.31 Wiring diagram for 1972 instrument panel
(key to wiring diagram on pages 310 and 311)**

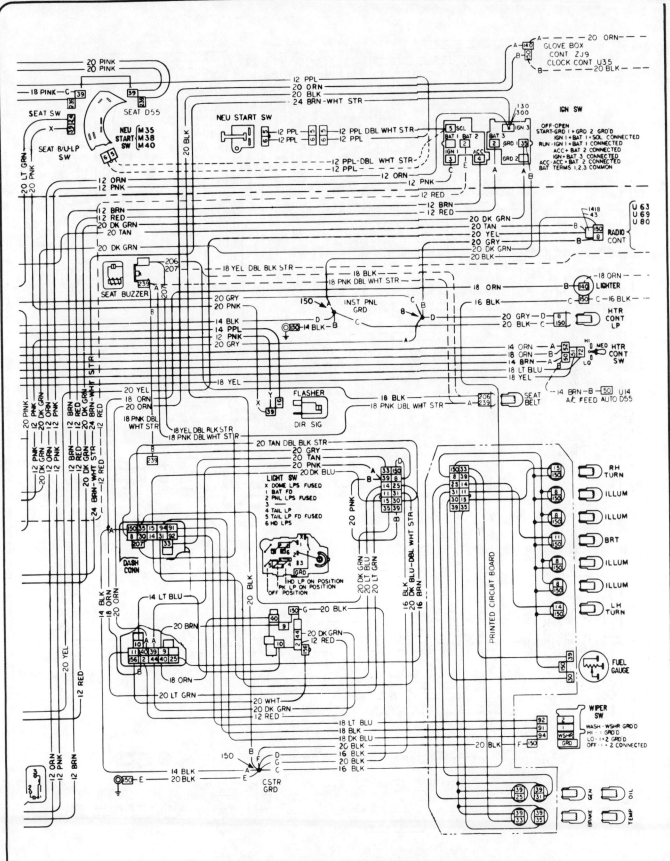

**Fig. 10.32 Wiring diagram for 1972 instrument panel
(key to wiring diagram on pages 310 and 311)**

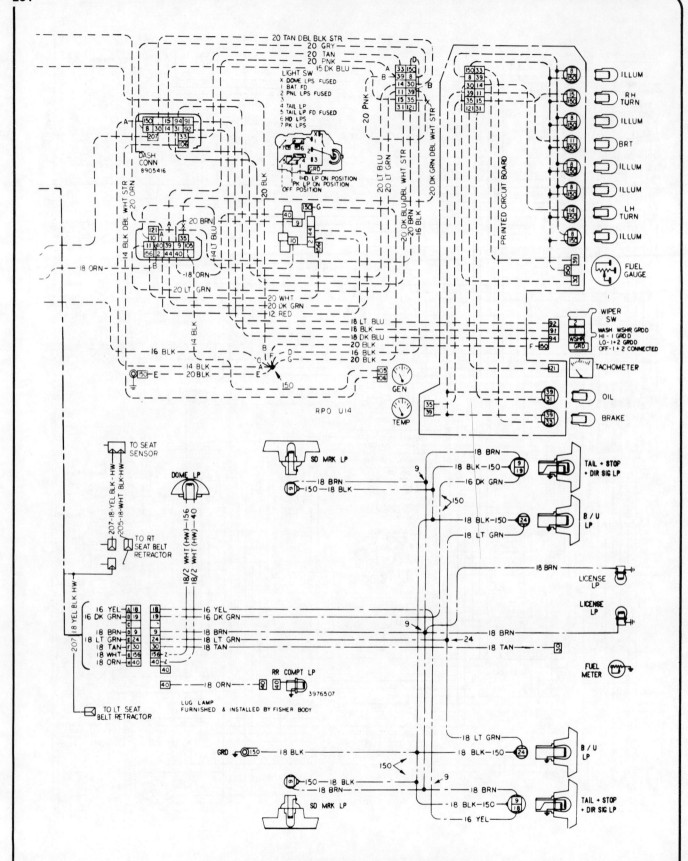

Fig. 10.33 Wiring diagram for 1972 body and rear lighting
(key to wiring diagram on pages 310 and 311)

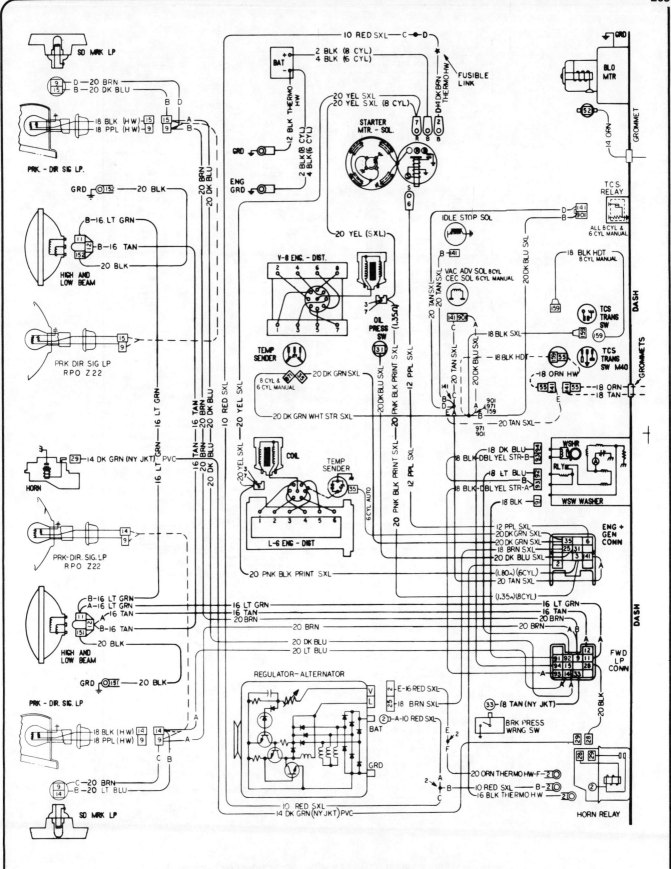

Fig. 10.34 Wiring diagram for 1973 engine compartment
(key to wiring diagram on pages 310 and 311)

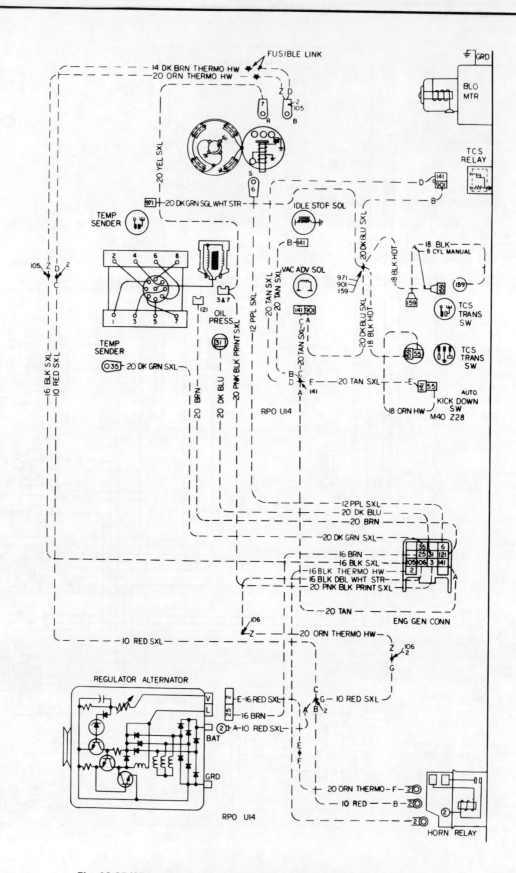

**Fig. 10.35 Wiring diagram for 1973 engine compartment (with gauges)
(key to wiring diagram on pages 310 and 311)**

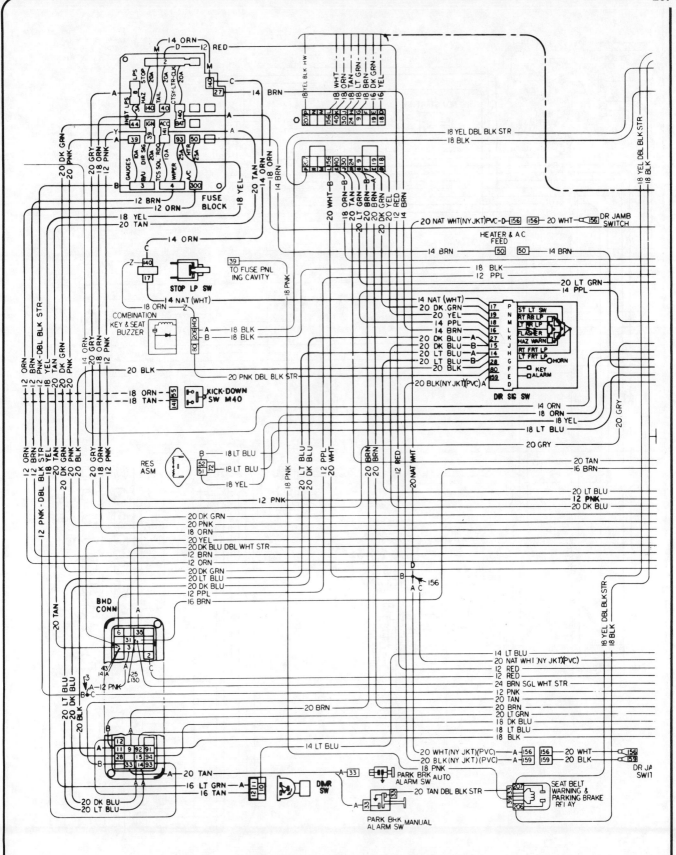

Fig. 10.36 Wiring diagram for 1973 instrument panel
(key to wiring diagram on pages 310 and 311)

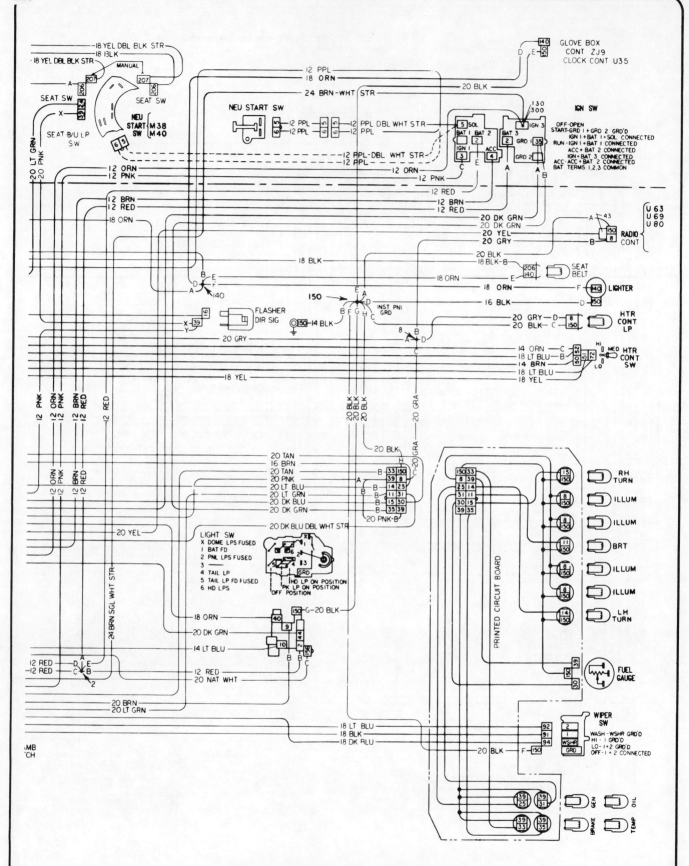

**Fig. 10.37 Wiring diagram for 1973 instrument panel
(key to wiring diagram on pages 310 and 311)**

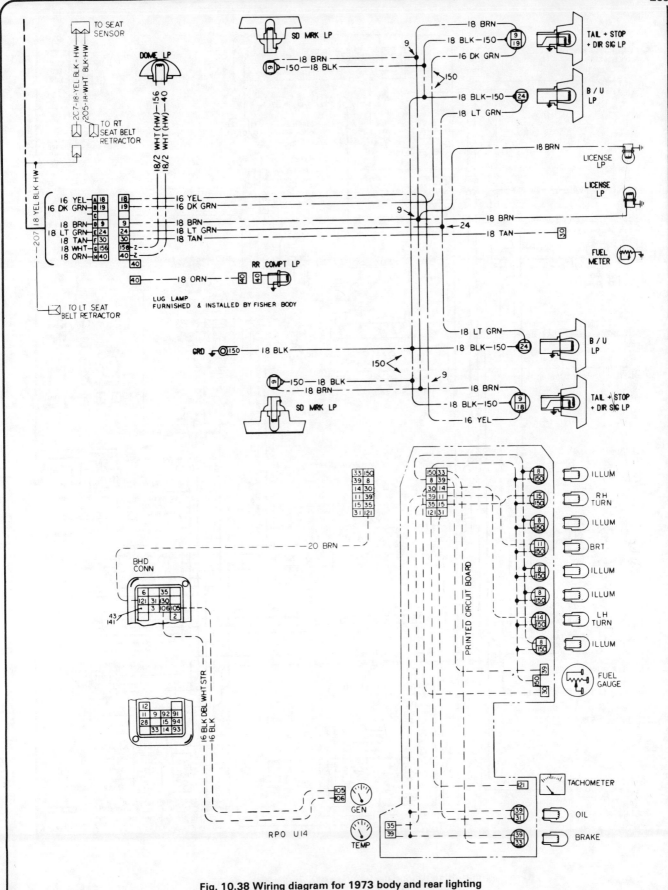

**Fig. 10.38 Wiring diagram for 1973 body and rear lighting
(key to wiring diagram on pages 310 and 311)**

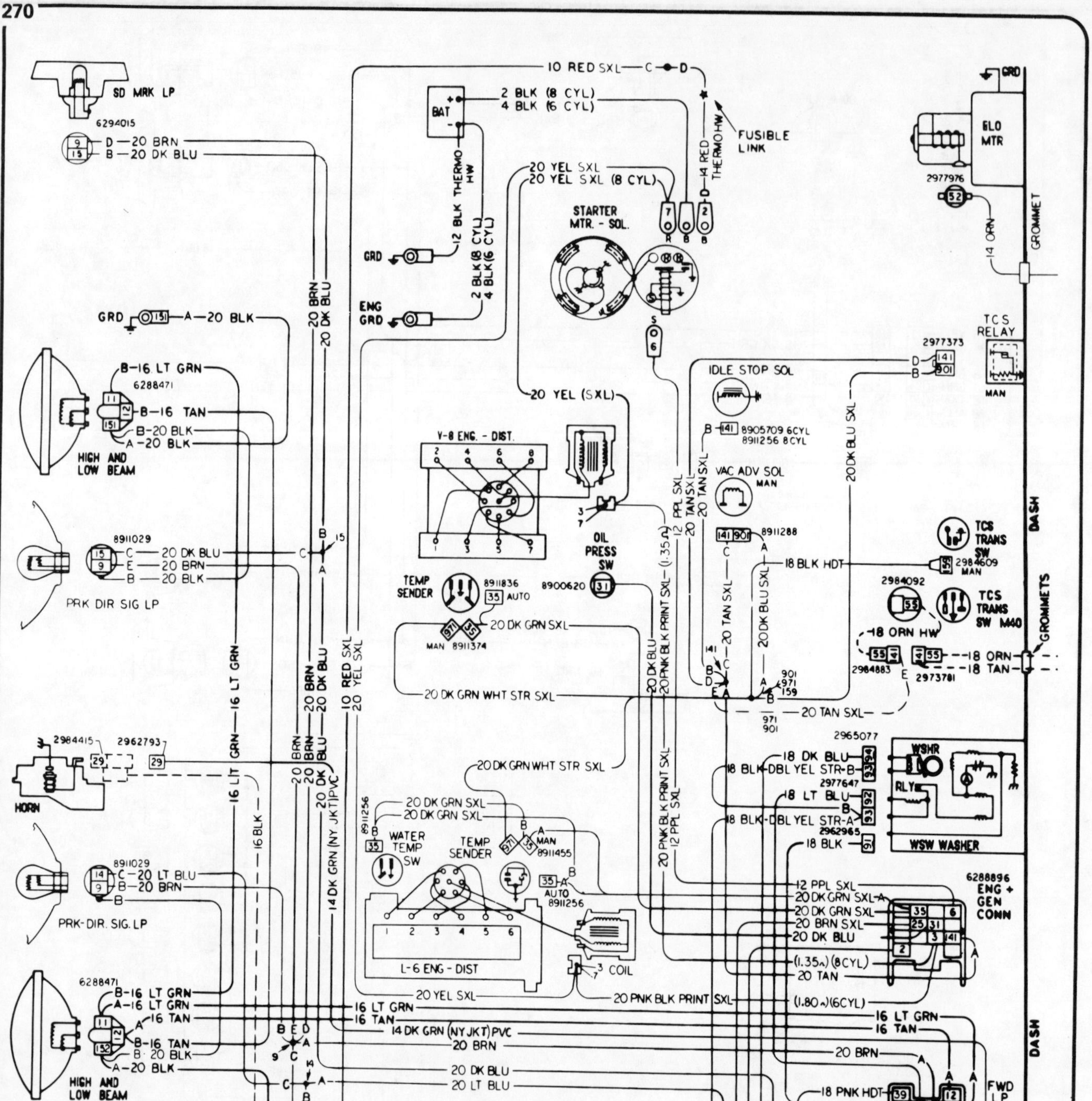

Fig. 10.39 Wiring diagram for 1974 engine compartment
(key to wiring diagram on pages 310 and 311)

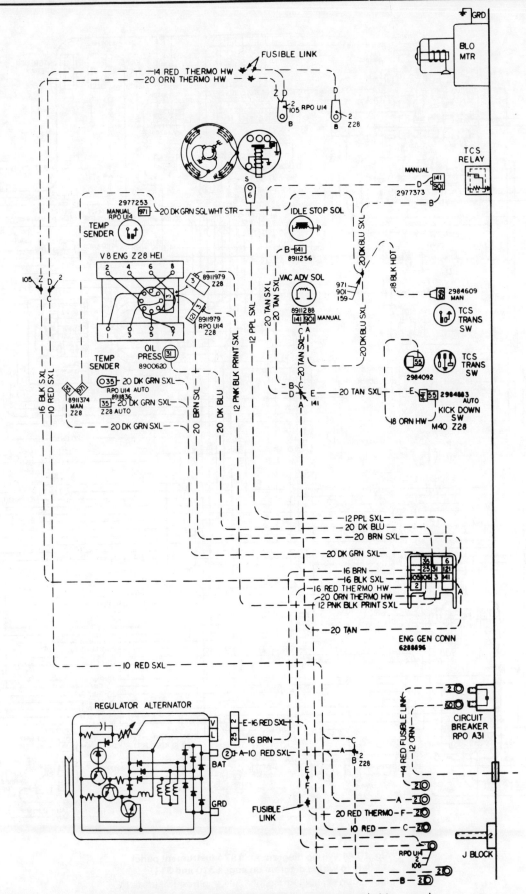

Fig. 10.40 Wiring diagram for 1974 engine compartment (with gauges)
(key to wiring diagram on pages 310 and 311)

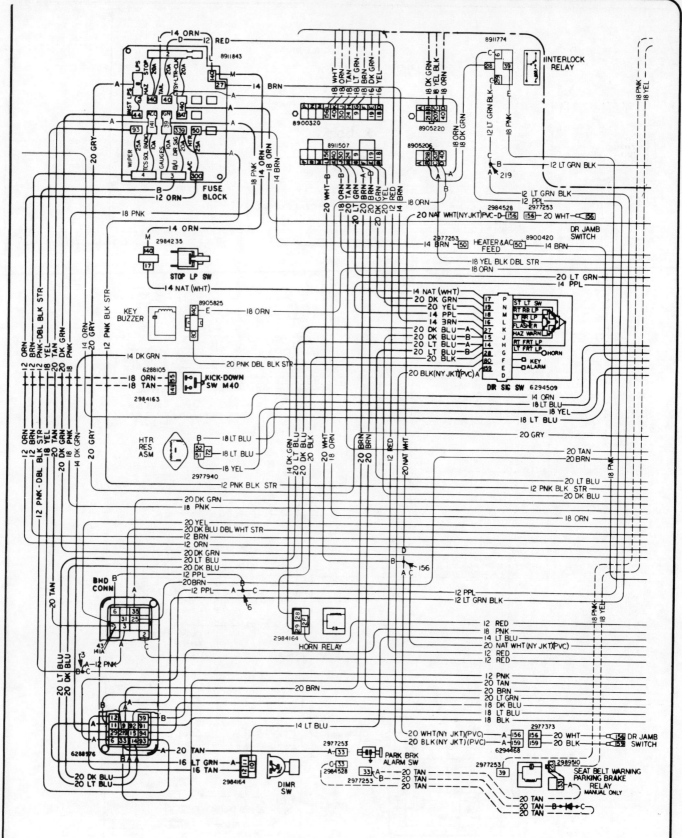

Fig. 10.41 Wiring diagram for 1974 instrument panel
(key to wiring diagram on pages 310 and 311)

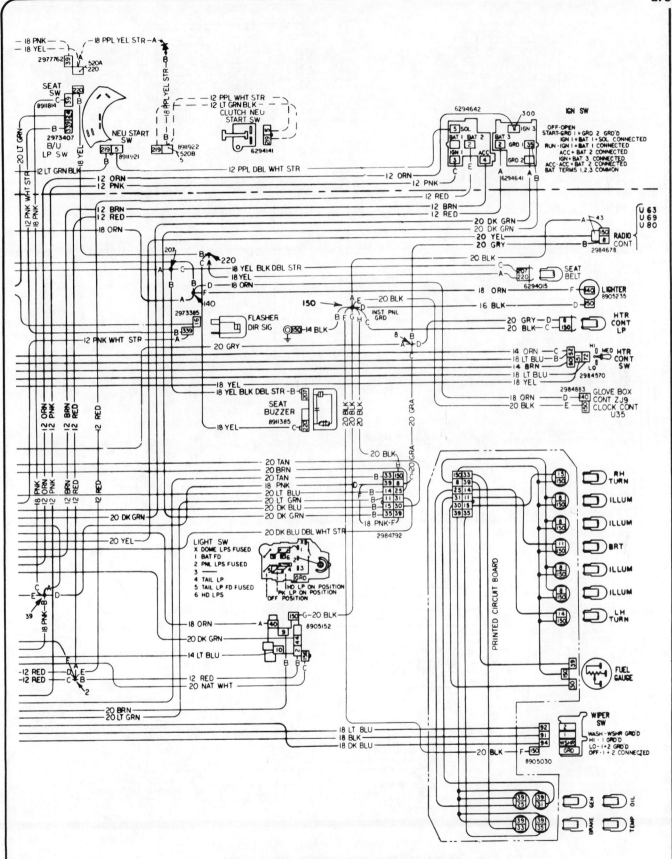

Fig. 10.42 Wiring diagram for 1974 instrument panel
(key to wiring diagram on pages 310 and 311)

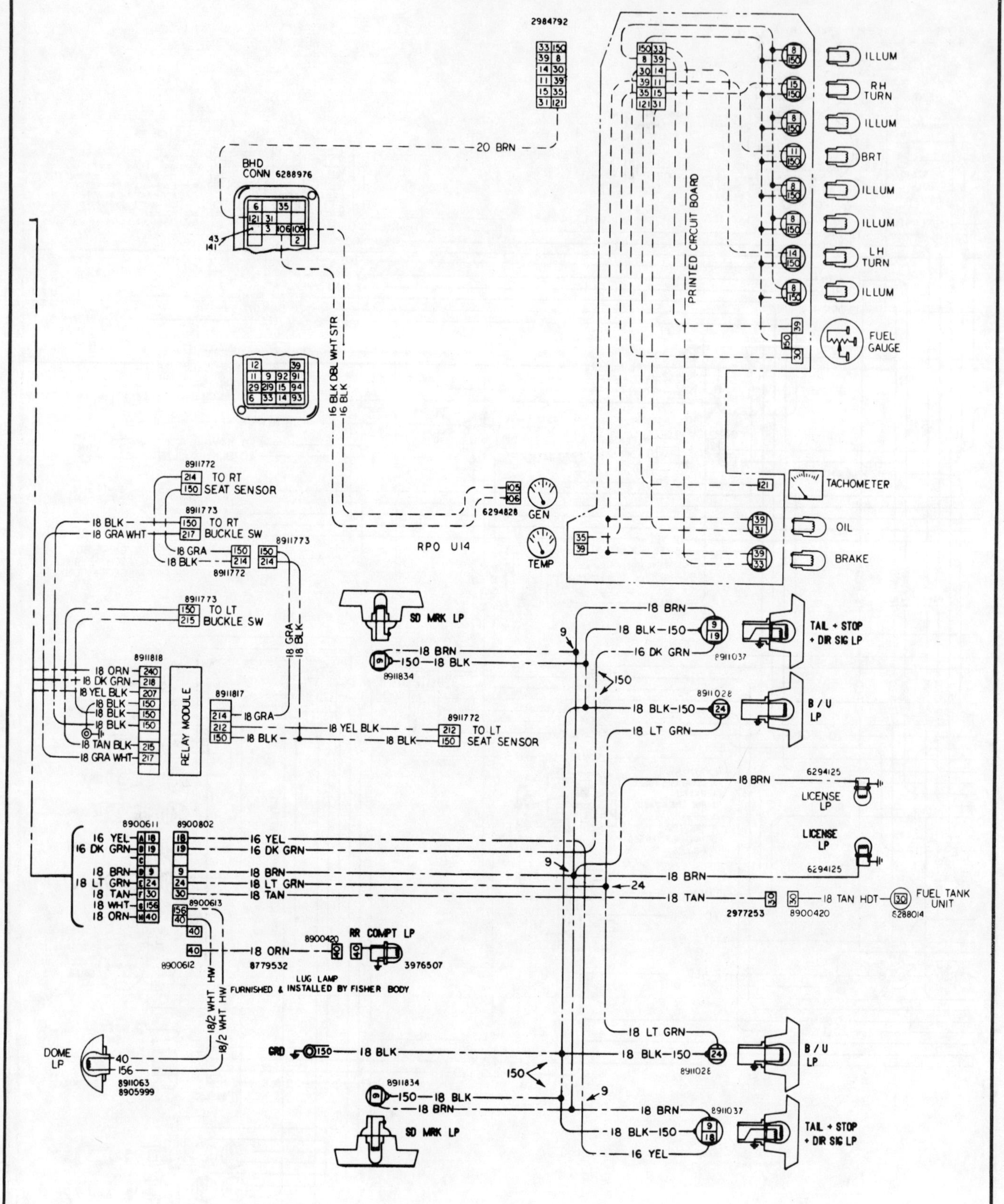

**Fig. 10.43 Wiring diagram for 1974 body and rear lighting
(key to wiring diagram on pages 310 and 311)**

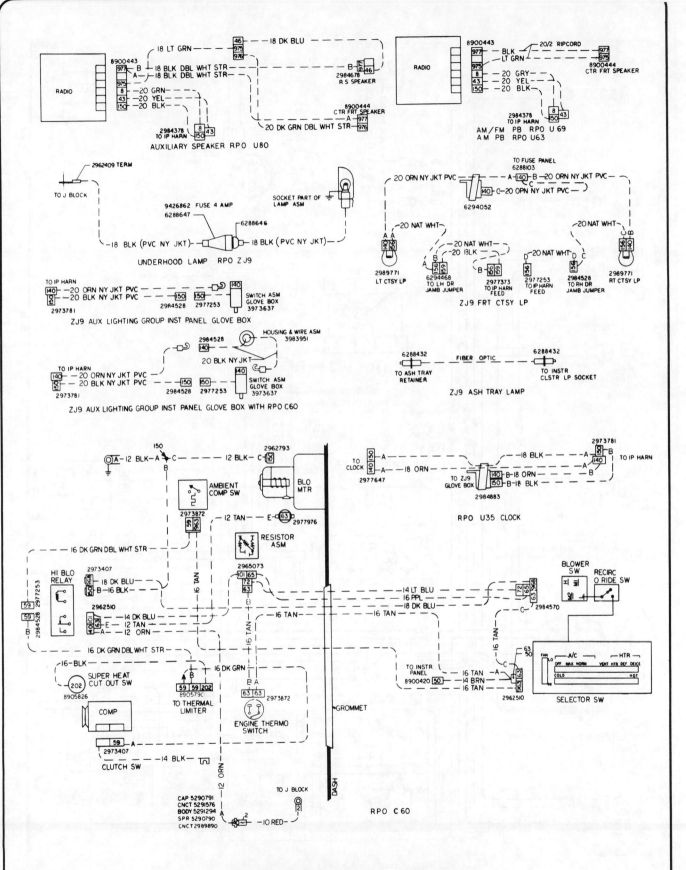

**Fig. 10.44 Wiring diagram for 1974 optional circuits
(key to wiring diagram on pages 310 and 311)**

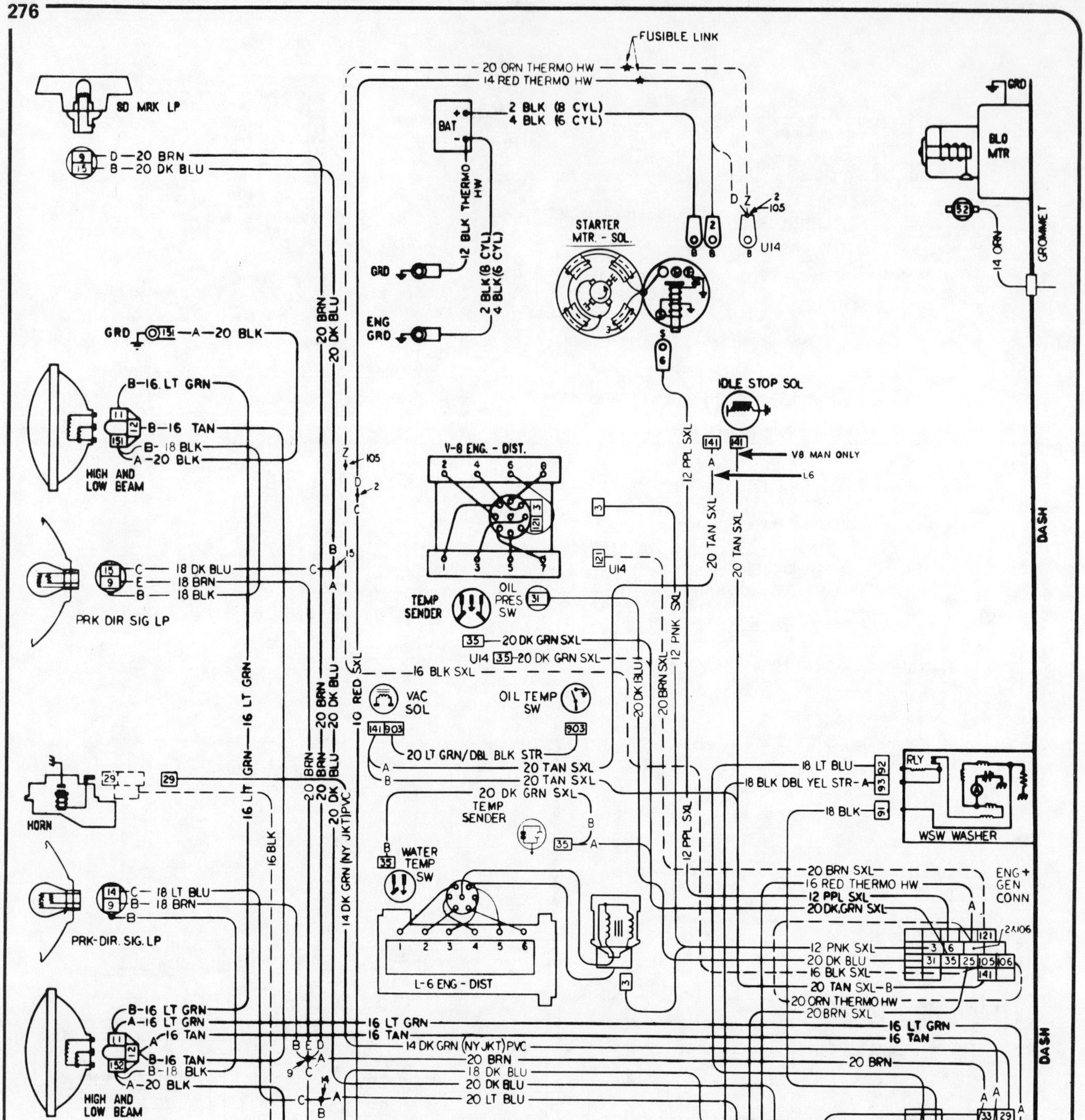

Fig. 10.45 Wiring diagram for 1975 engine compartment
(key to wiring diagram on pages 310 and 311)

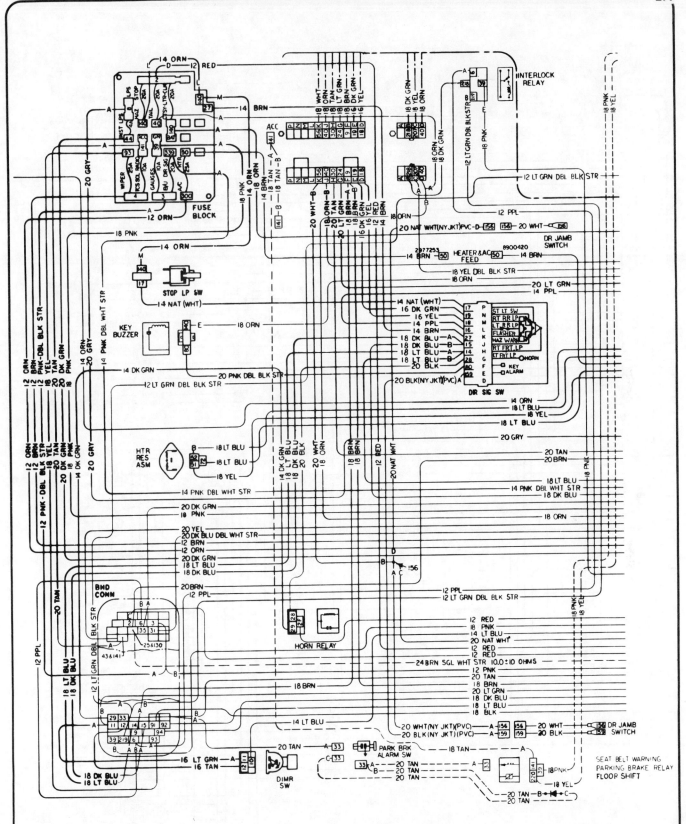

Fig. 10.46 Wiring diagram for 1975 instrument panel
(key to wiring diagram on pages 310 and 311)

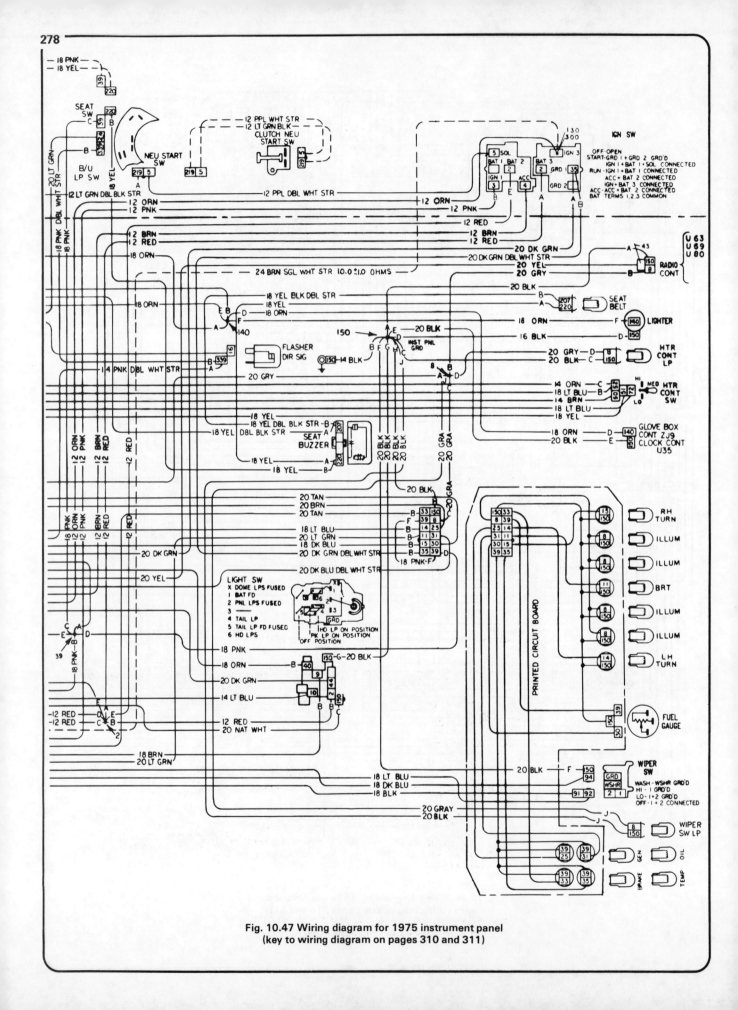

Fig. 10.47 Wiring diagram for 1975 instrument panel
(key to wiring diagram on pages 310 and 311)

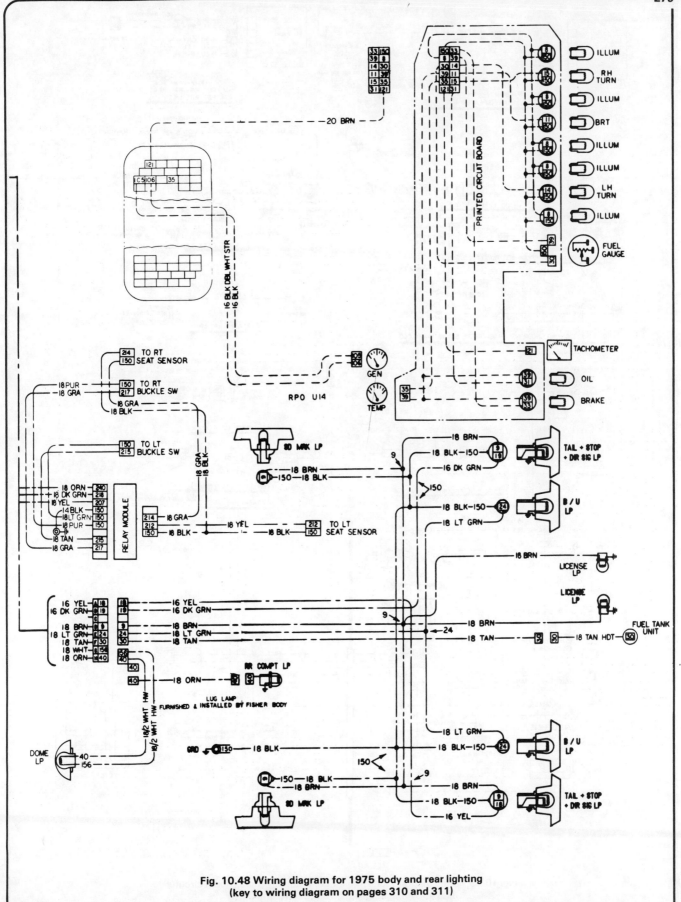

Fig. 10.48 Wiring diagram for 1975 body and rear lighting
(key to wiring diagram on pages 310 and 311)

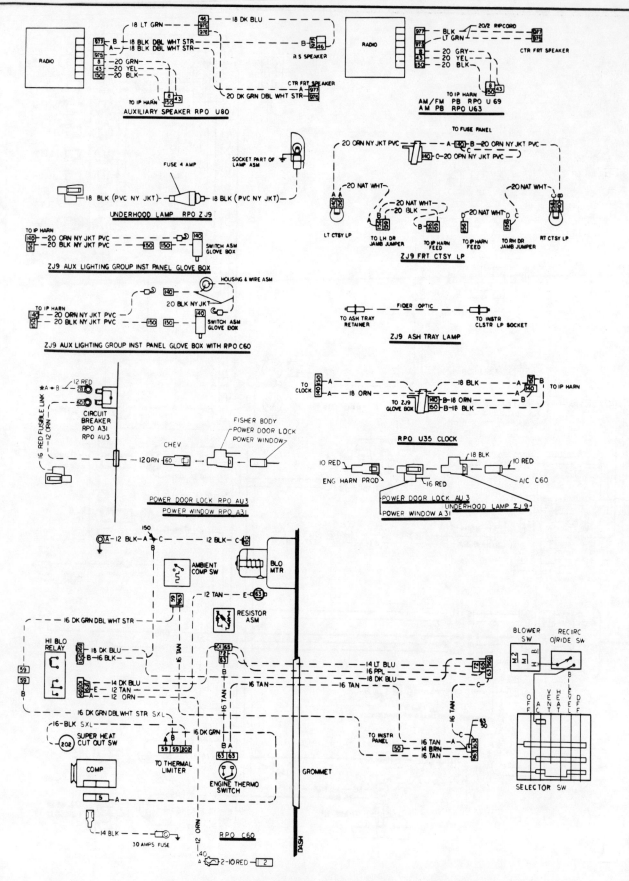

Fig. 10.49 Wiring diagram for 1975 air conditioning and optional circuits (key to wiring diagram on pages 310 and 311)

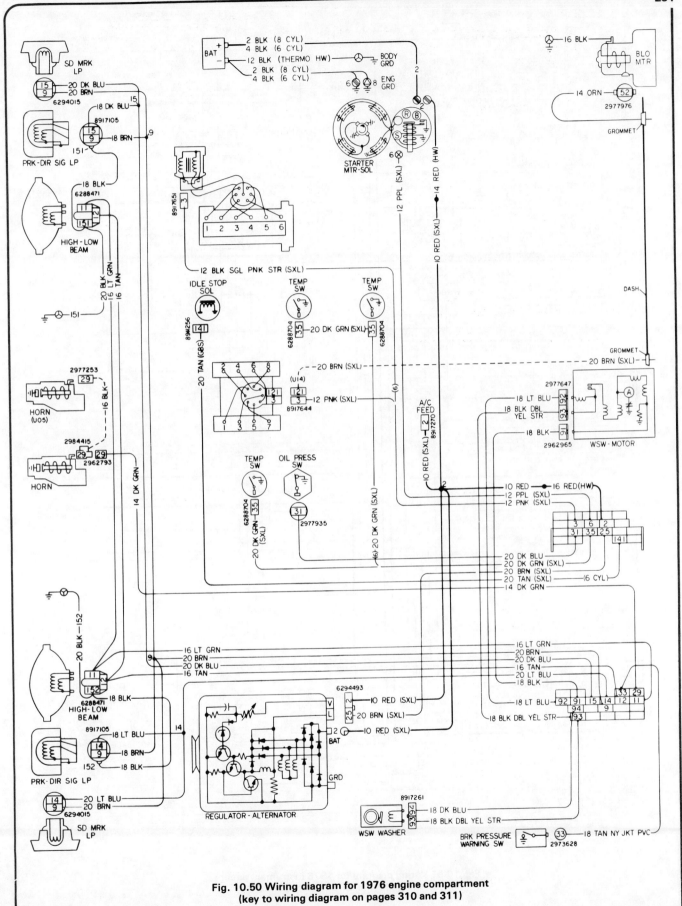

Fig. 10.50 Wiring diagram for 1976 engine compartment
(key to wiring diagram on pages 310 and 311)

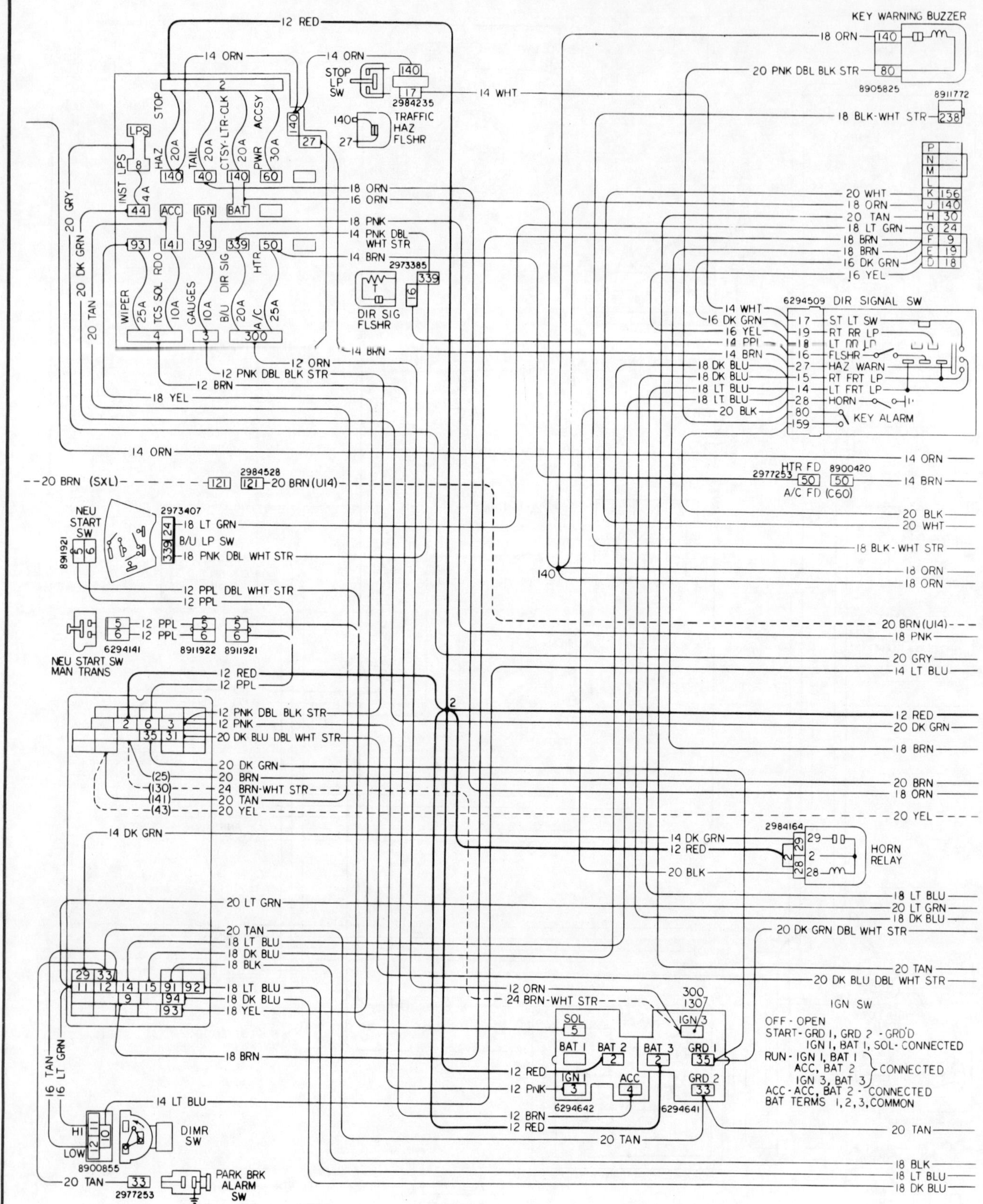

Fig. 10.51 Wiring diagram for 1976 instrument panel (key to wiring diagram on pages 310 and 311)

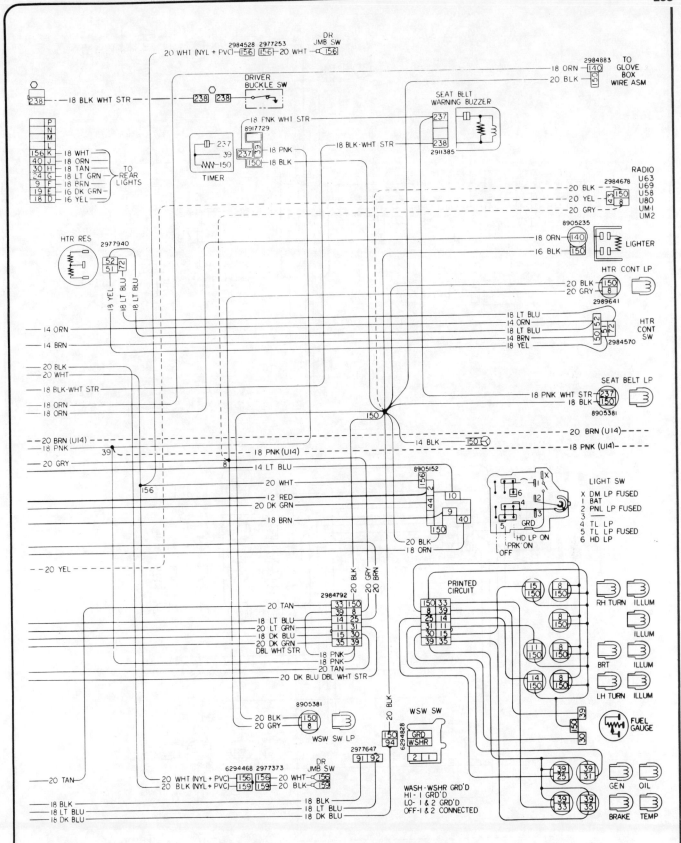

Fig. 10.52 Wiring diagram for 1976 instrument panel
(key to wiring diagram on pages 310 and 311)

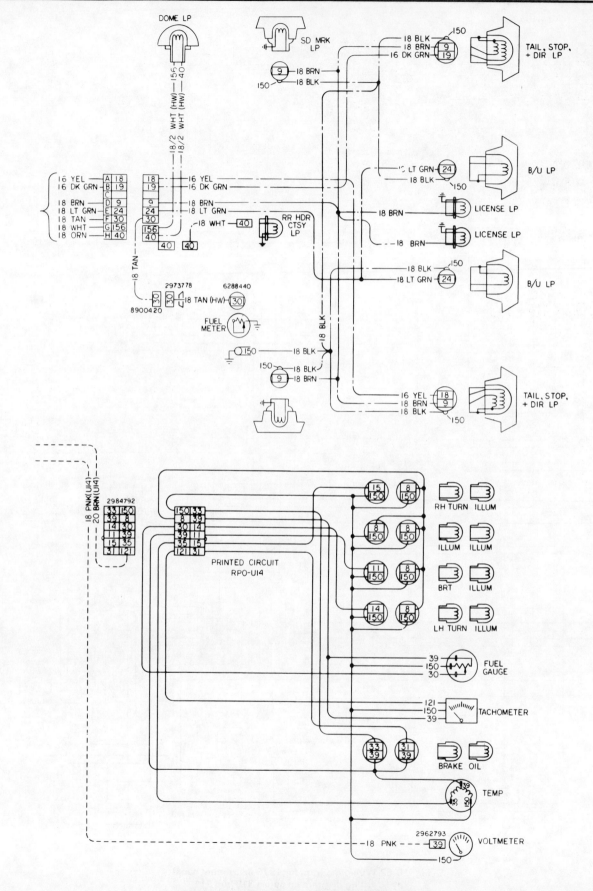

Fig. 10.53 Wiring diagram for 1976 body and rear lighting
(key to wiring diagram on pages 310 and 311)

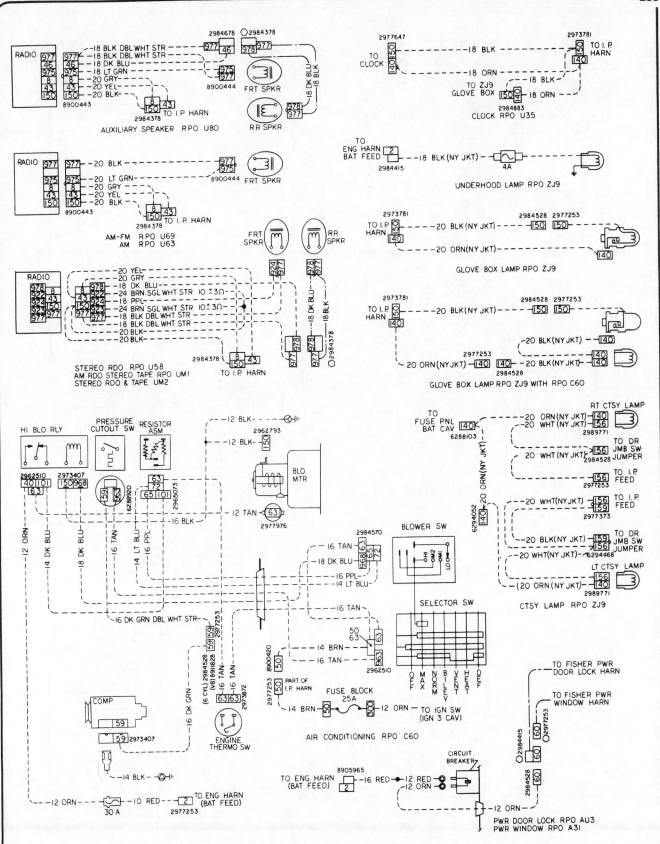

Fig. 10.54 Wiring diagram for 1976 air conditioning and optional circuits (key to wiring diagram on pages 310 and 311)

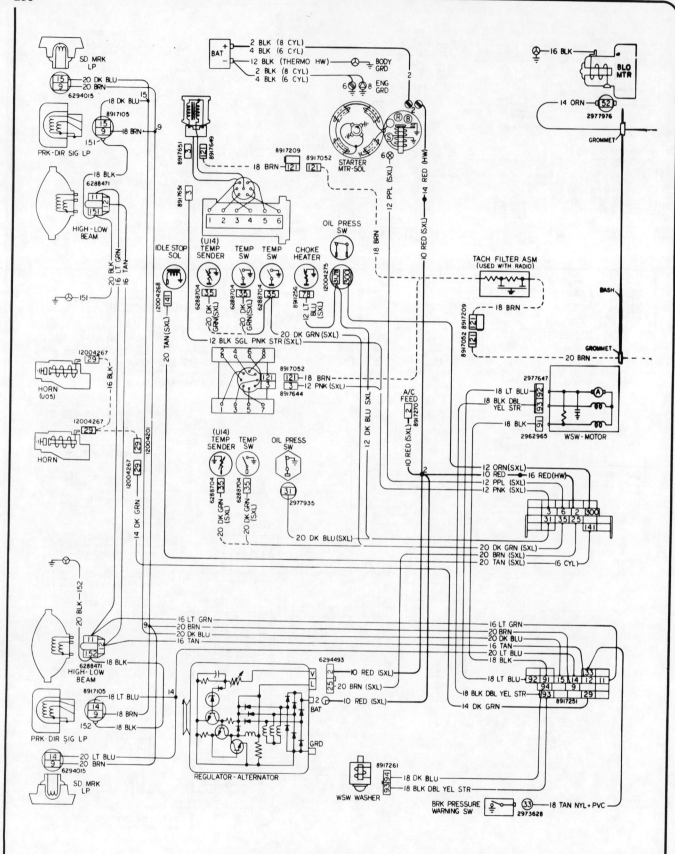

Fig. 10.55 Wiring diagram for 1977 engine compartment
(key to wiring diagram on pages 310 and 311)

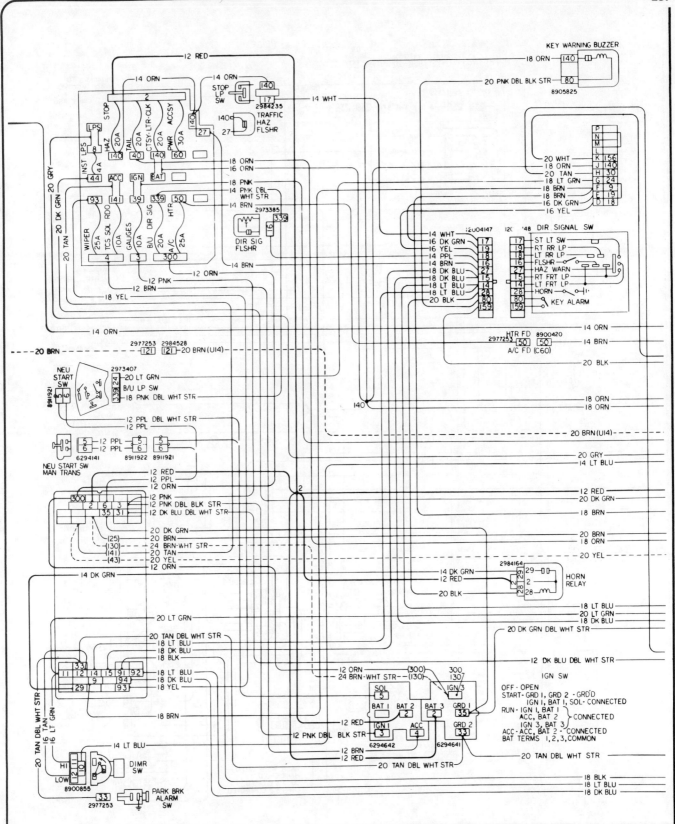

Fig. 10.56 Wiring diagram for 1977 instrument panel
(key to wiring diagram on pages 310 and 311)

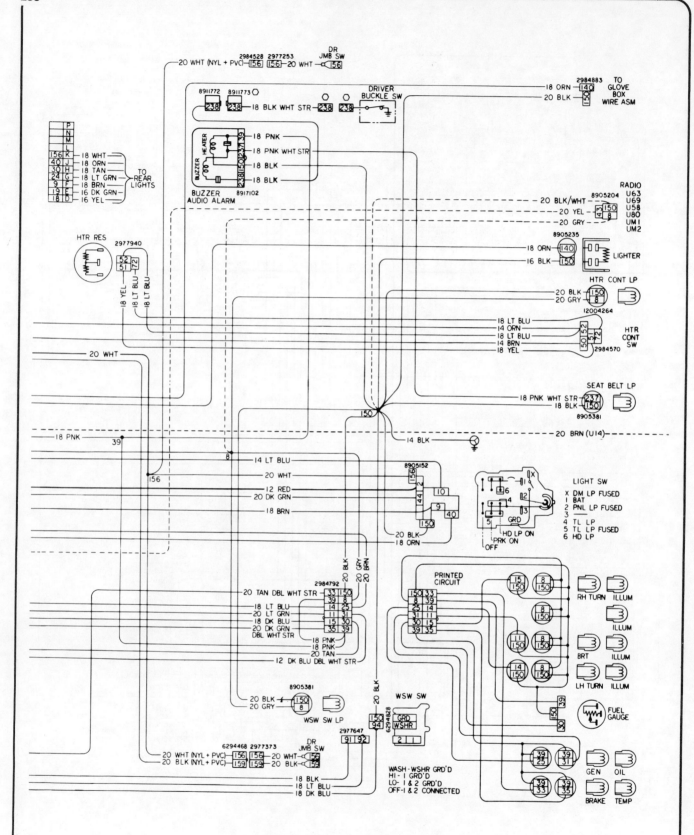

Fig. 10.57 Wiring diagram for 1977 instrument panel
(key to wiring diagram on pages 310 and 311)

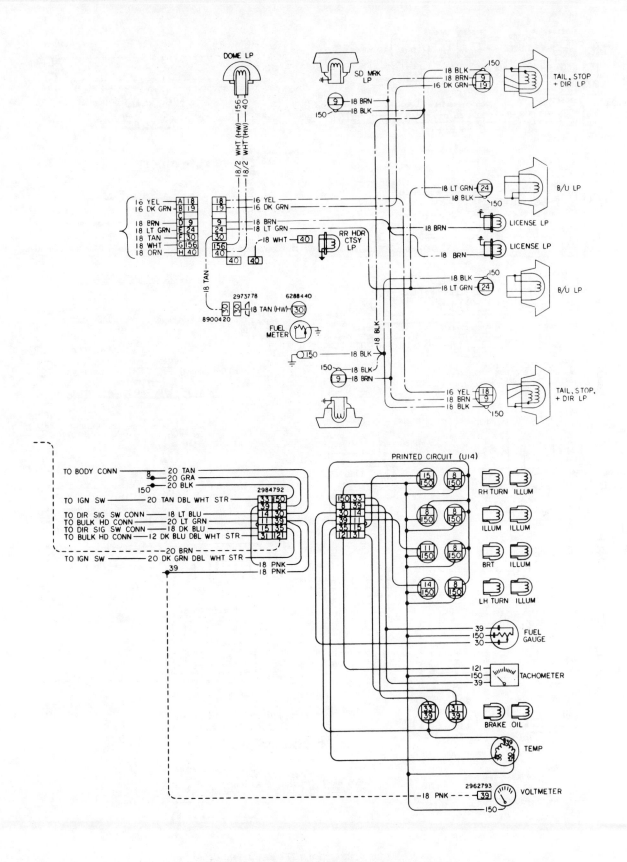

Fig. 10.58 Wiring diagram for 1977 body and rear lighting
(key to wiring diagram on pages 310 and 311)

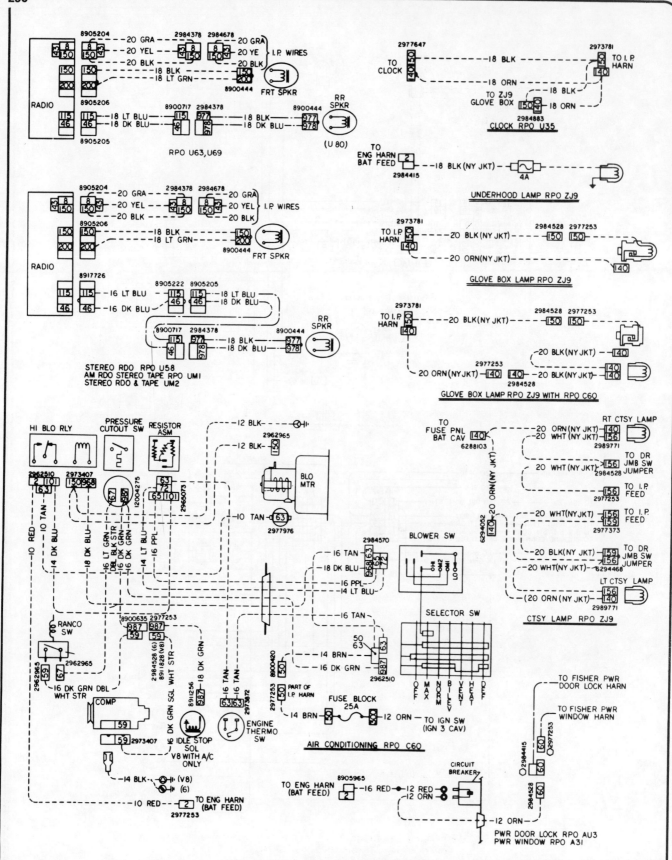

Fig. 10.59 Wiring diagram for 1977 air conditioning and optional circuits (key to wiring diagram on pages 310 and 311)

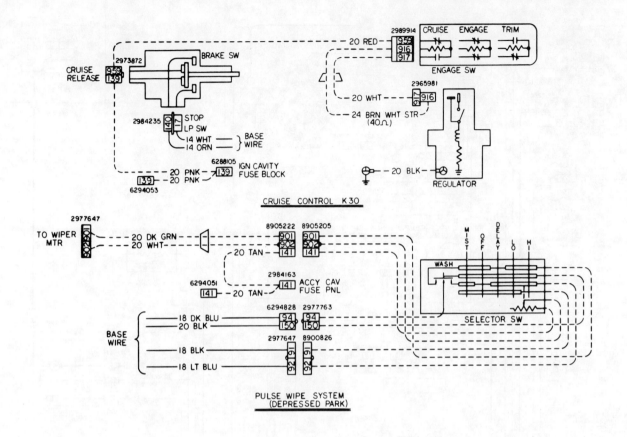

CRUISE CONTROL K 30

PULSE WIPE SYSTEM
(DEPRESSED PARK)

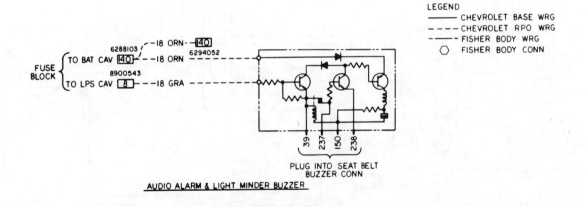

LEGEND
—— CHEVROLET BASE WRG
----- CHEVROLET RPO WRG
---- FISHER BODY WRG
◯ FISHER BODY CONN

AUDIO ALARM & LIGHT MINDER BUZZER

Fig. 10.60 Wiring diagram for 1977 optional accessory circuits
(key to wiring diagram on pages 310 and 311)

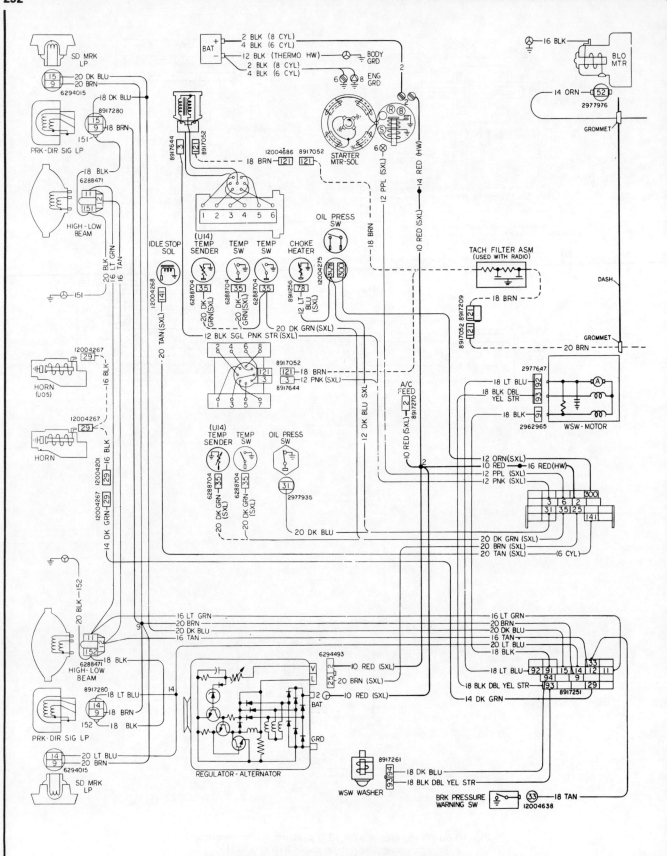

**Fig. 10.61 Wiring diagram for 1978 engine compartment
(key to wiring diagram on pages 310 and 311)**

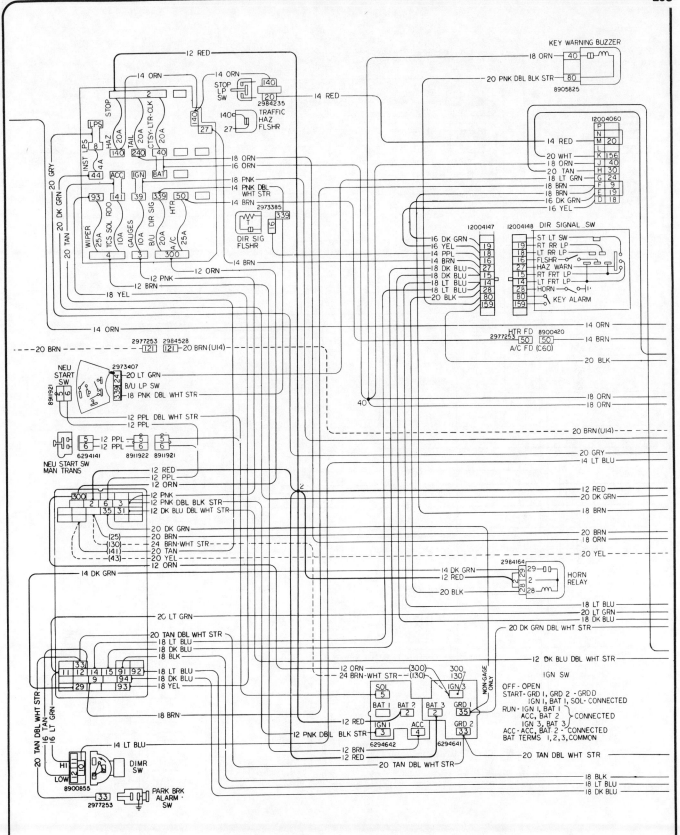

Fig. 10.62 Wiring diagram for 1978 instrument panel
(key to wiring diagram on pages 310 and 311)

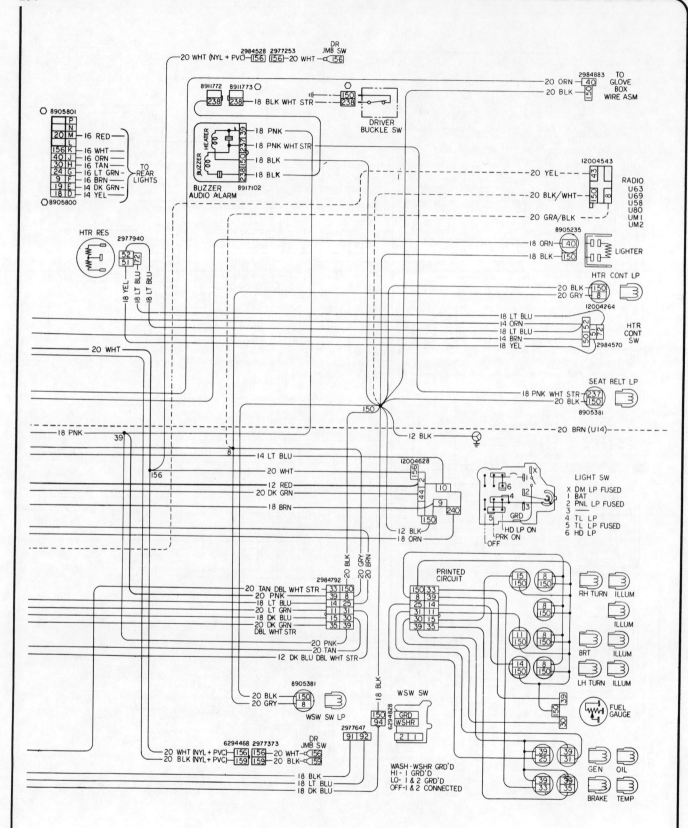

Fig. 10.63 Wiring diagram for 1978 instrument panel
(key to wiring diagram on pages 310 and 311)

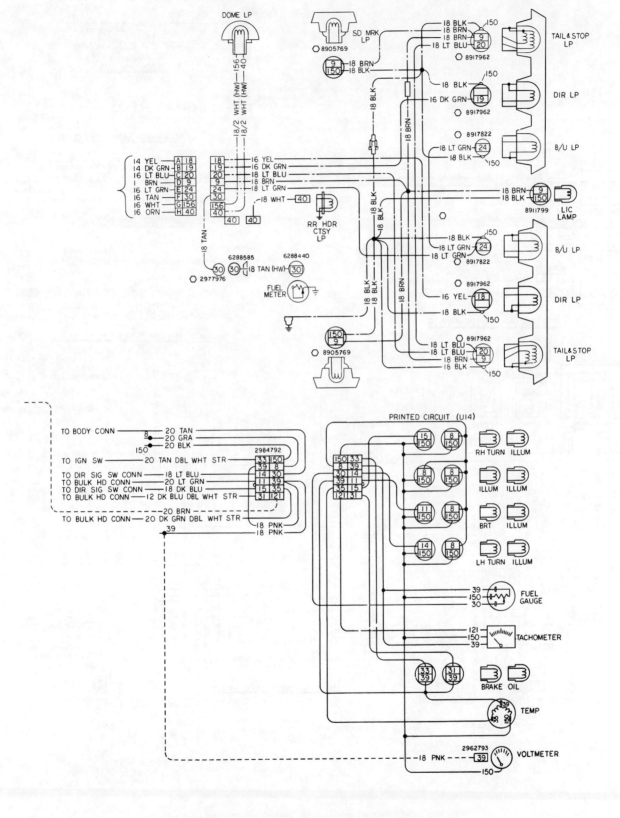

Fig. 10.64 Wiring diagram for 1978 body and rear lighting (key to wiring diagram on pages 310 and 311)

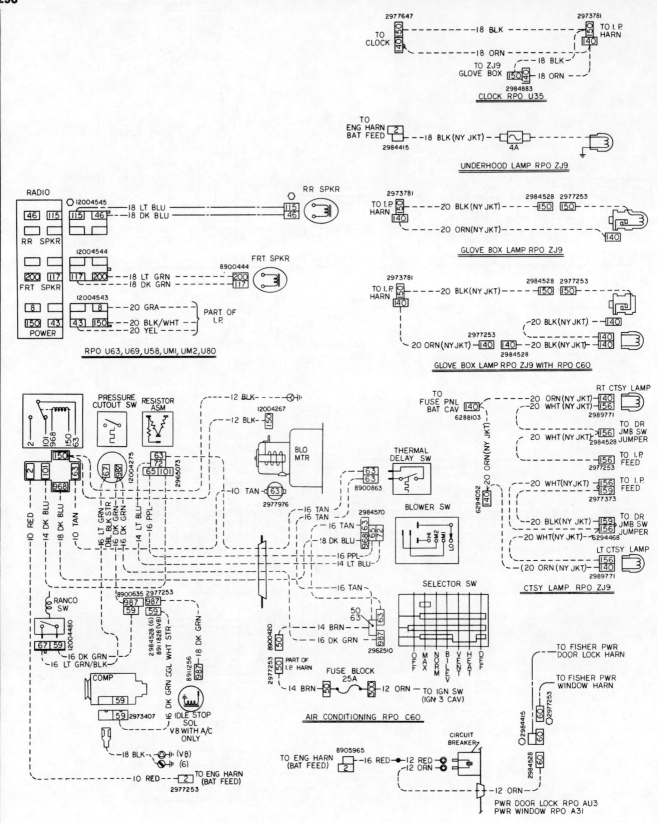

**Fig. 10.65 Wiring diagram for 1978 air conditioning and optional circuits
(key to wiring diagram on pages 310 and 311)**

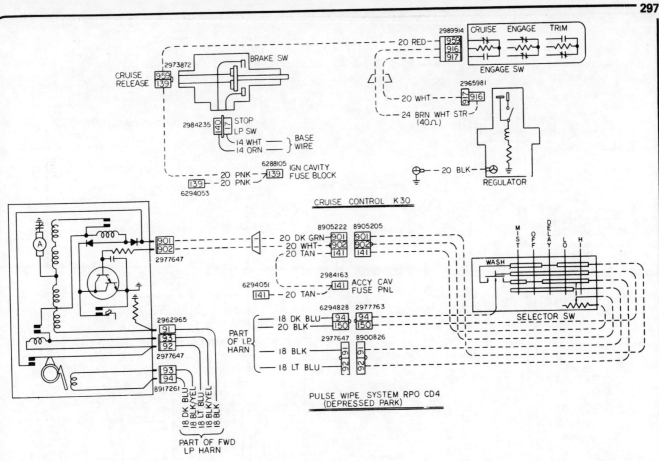

CRUISE CONTROL K30

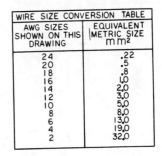

PULSE WIPE SYSTEM RPO CD4
(DEPRESSED PARK)

WIRE SIZE CONVERSION TABLE	
AWG SIZES SHOWN ON THIS DRAWING	EQUIVALENT METRIC SIZE mm²
24	.22
20	.5
18	.8
16	1.0
14	2.0
12	3.0
10	5.0
8	8.0
6	13.0
4	19.0
2	32.0

LEGEND

——— CHEVROLET BASE WRG
- - - CHEVROLET RPO WRG
—·— FISHER BODY WRG
⬡ FISHER BODY CONN

SYM	STUD		
⑊	2	⚹	1/4
⊖	4	⬟	5/16
◇	6	⊘	3/8
⊗	8	⊕	7/16
⊕	10	✳	1/2
⊕	12	✴	5/8

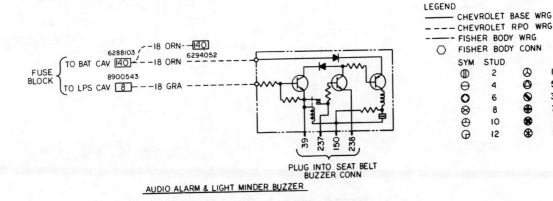

AUDIO ALARM & LIGHT MINDER BUZZER

Fig. 10.66 Wiring diagram for 1978 optional accessory circuits
(key to wiring diagram on pages 310 and 311)

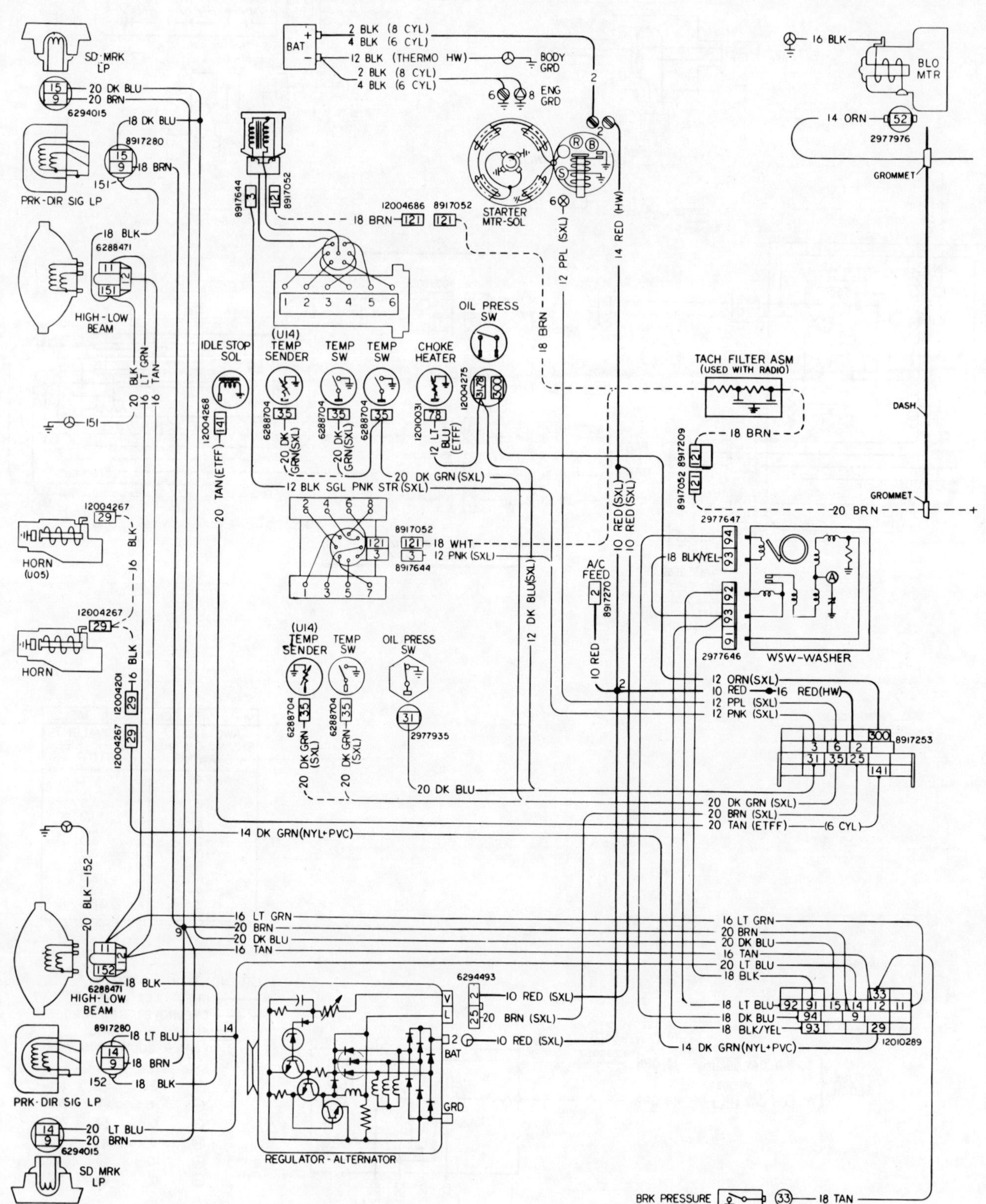

Fig. 10.67 Wiring diagram for 1979 engine compartment
(key to wiring diagram on pages 310 and 311)

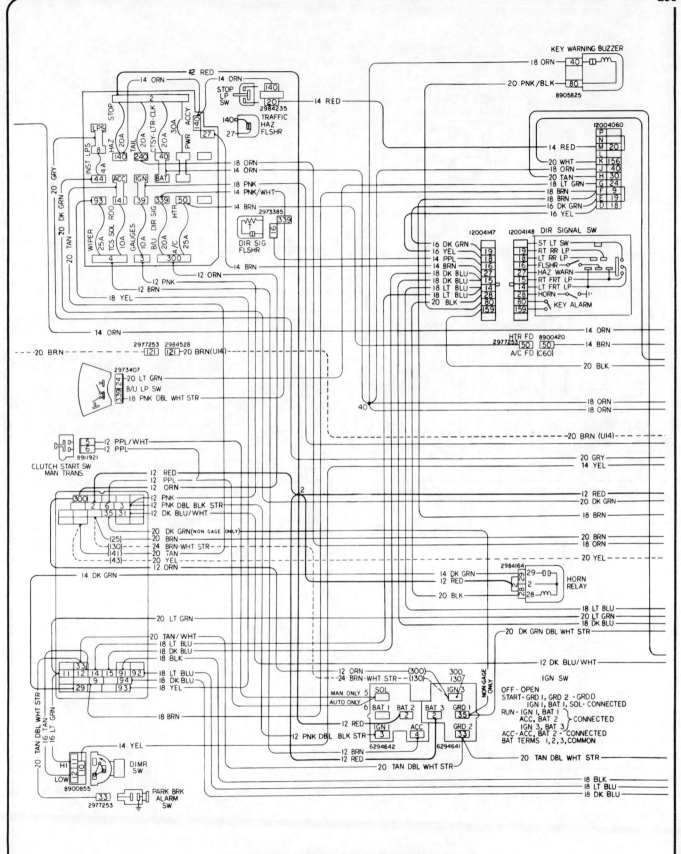

**Fig. 10.68 Wiring diagram for 1979 instrument panel
(key to wiring diagram on pages 310 and 311)**

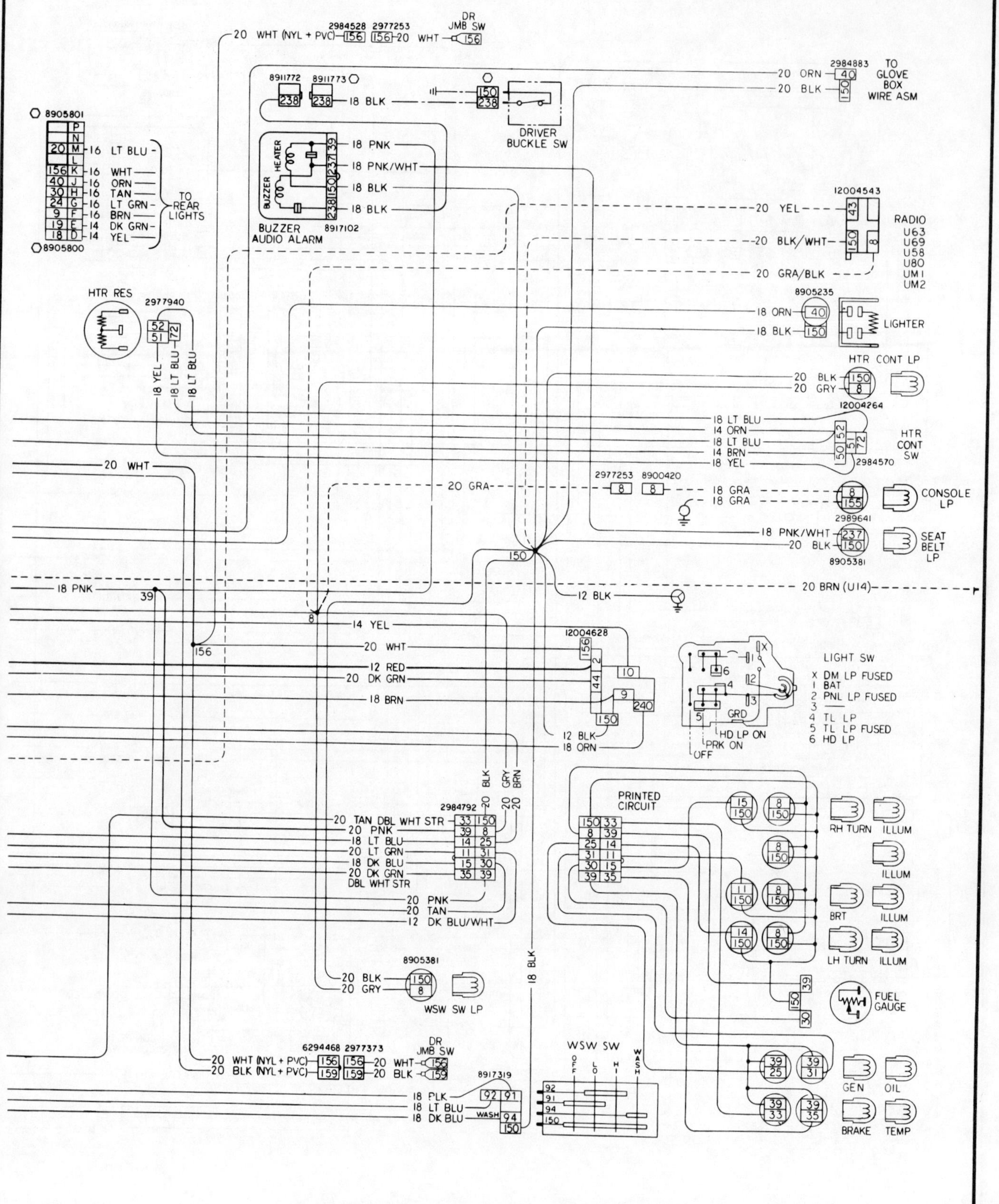

Fig. 10.69 Wiring diagram for 1979 instrument panel
(key to wiring diagram on pages 310 and 311)

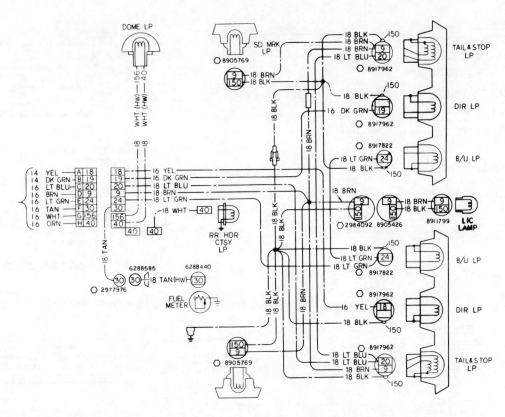

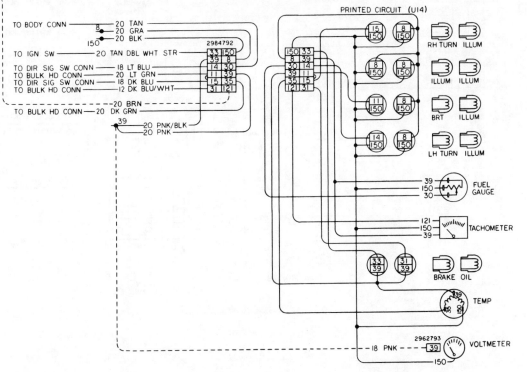

**Fig. 10.70 Wiring diagram for 1979 body and rear lighting
(key to wiring diagram on pages 310 and 311)**

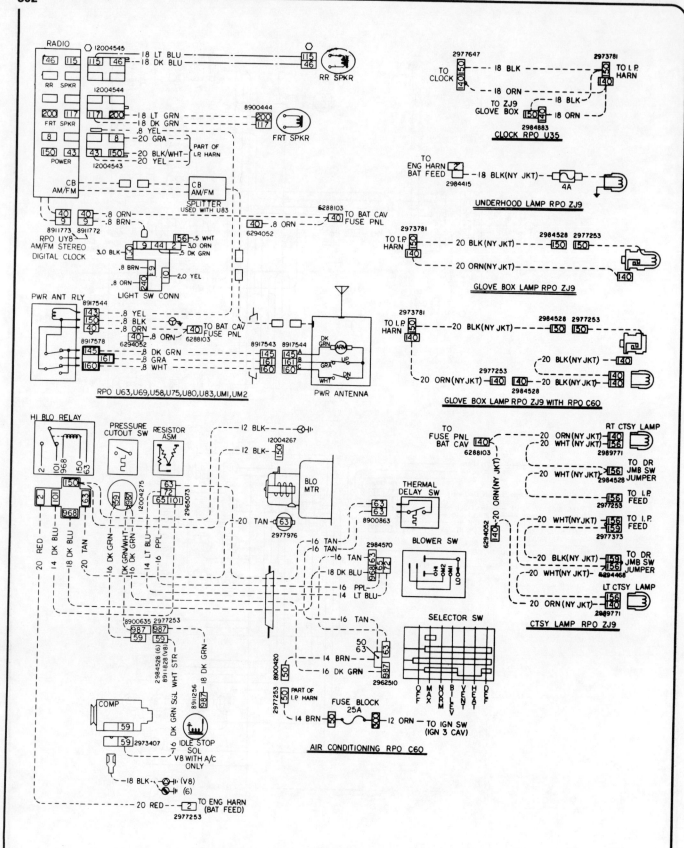

Fig. 10.71 Wiring diagram for 1979 air conditioning and optional circuits
(key to wiring diagram on pages 310 and 311)

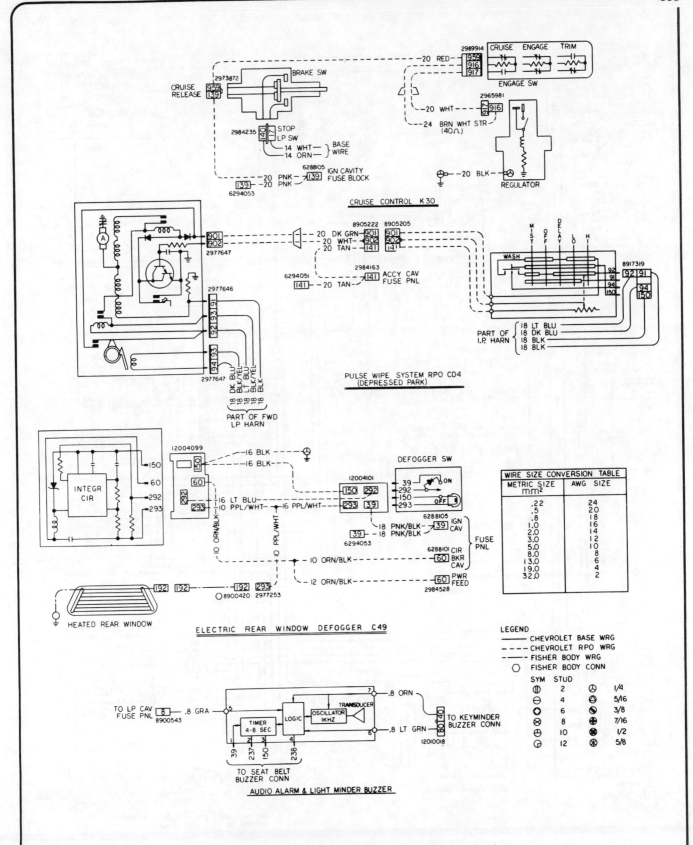

**Fig. 10.72 Wiring diagram for 1979 optional accessory circuits
(key to wiring diagram on pages 310 and 311)**

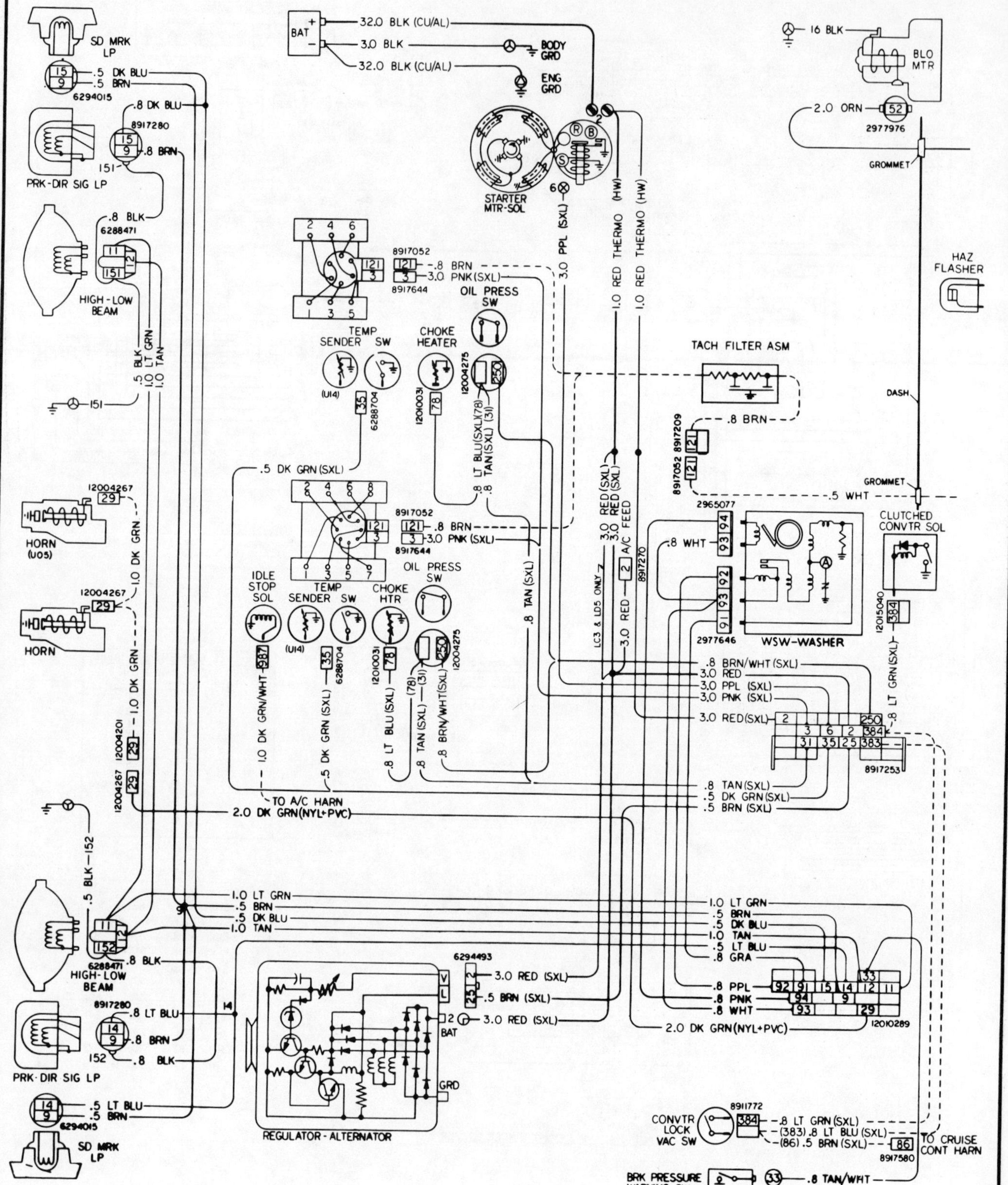

SD MRK LP

15 9 | .5 DK BLU
.5 BRN
6294015

PRK-DIR SIG LP
15 9 | .8 BRN
8917280
151

HIGH-LOW BEAM
6288471
151
1 2
.8 BLK

151

.5 BLK
1.0 LT GRN
1.0 TAN

HORN (U05)
12004267 29
1.0 DK GRN

HORN
12004267 29

12004201
1.0 DK GRN
12004267 29

HIGH-LOW BEAM
6288471
.5 BLK — 152
.8 BLK
152

PRK·DIR SIG LP
8917280
14 9 | .8 LT BLU
.8 BRN
152
.8 BLK

14 9 | .5 LT BLU
.5 BRN
6294015

SD MRK LP

+ BAT —
32.0 BLK (CU/AL)
3.0 BLK — BODY GRD
32.0 BLK (CU/AL) — ENG GRD

R B
S
STARTER MTR-SOL
6

3.0 PPL (SXL)
1.0 RED THERMO (HW)
1.0 RED THERMO (HW)

2 4 6
1 3 5
8917052
121 3 | .8 BRN
3 | 3.0 PNK (SXL)
8917644
OIL PRESS SW
121

TEMP SENDER SW
(U14)
CHOKE HEATER
12004275
35 6288704
78
120003J
.8 LT BLU (SXL)(78)
.8 TAN (SXL) (31)

.5 DK GRN (SXL)

2 4 6
1 3 5 7
8917052
121 3 | .8 BRN
3 | 3.0 PNK (SXL)
8917644
OIL PRESS SW

IDLE STOP SOL
1.0 DK GRN/WHT
TEMP SENDER SW (U14)
.5 DK GRN (SXL)
35 6288704
CHOKE HTR
78
120003J
.8 LT BLU (SXL)
.8 TAN (SXL) (78) (3) 12004275
.8 BRN/WHT(SXL)

TO A/C HARN
2.0 DK GRN (NYL+PVC)

6294493
251 2 | 3.0 RED (SXL)
.5 BRN (SXL)
2 | 3.0 RED (SXL)
BAT
GRD
REGULATOR - ALTERNATOR

CONVTR LOCK VAC SW
8911772
384
.8 LT GRN (SXL)
(383) .8 LT BLU (SXL)
(86) .5 BRN (SXL)
86
8917580

BRK PRESSURE WARNING SW
33 | .8 TAN/WHT
12004638

16 BLK
BLO MTR

2.0 ORN
52
2977976

GROMMET

HAZ FLASHER

TACH FILTER ASM
.8 BRN
121

8917052 8917209
121
2965077

DASH

GROMMET
.5 WHT

CLUTCHED CONVTR SOL
120150040
384
LT GRN (SXL)

.8 WHT
93 94
WSW-WASHER
91 93 92
A
2977646

LC3 & LD5 ONLY
3.0 RED (SXL)
3.0 RED (SXL)
2 | RED (SXL)
A/C FEED
8917270
.8 TAN (SXL)

.8 BRN/WHT (SXL)
3.0 RED
3.0 PPL (SXL)
3.0 PNK (SXL)
3.0 RED (SXL)
2 3 6 2 250
31 35 25 383 384
8917253

.8 TAN (SXL)
.5 DK GRN (SXL)
.5 BRN (SXL)

1.0 LT GRN
.5 BRN
.5 DK BLU
1.0 TAN
.5 LT BLU
.8 GRA
.8 PPL
.8 PNK
.8 WHT
2.0 DK GRN (NYL+PVC)

92 91 15 14 33
94 9 12 11
29
12010289

TO CRUISE CONT HARN

Fig. 10.73 Wiring diagram for 1980 engine compartment
(key to wiring diagram on pages 310 and 311)

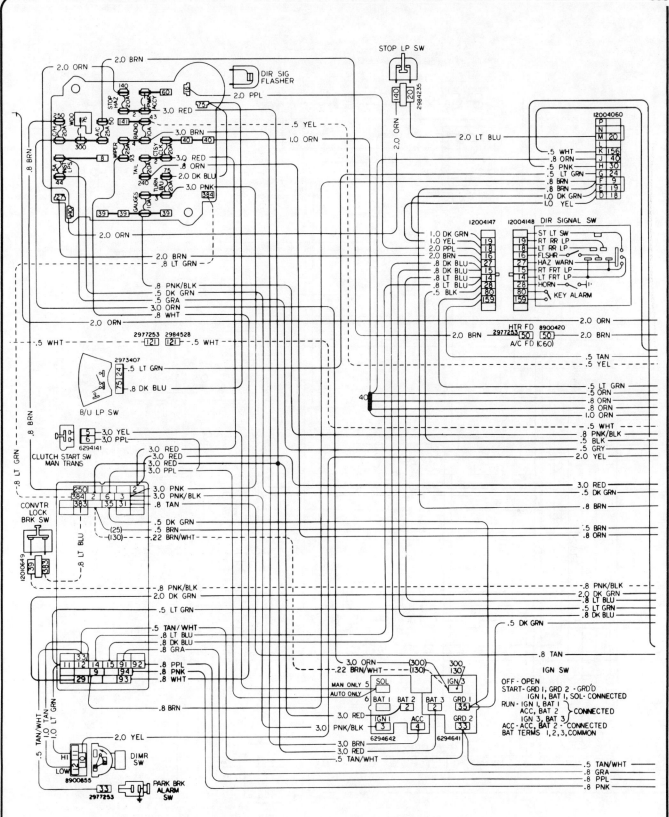

**Fig. 10.74 Wiring diagram for 1980 instrument panel
(key to wiring diagram on pages 310 and 311)**

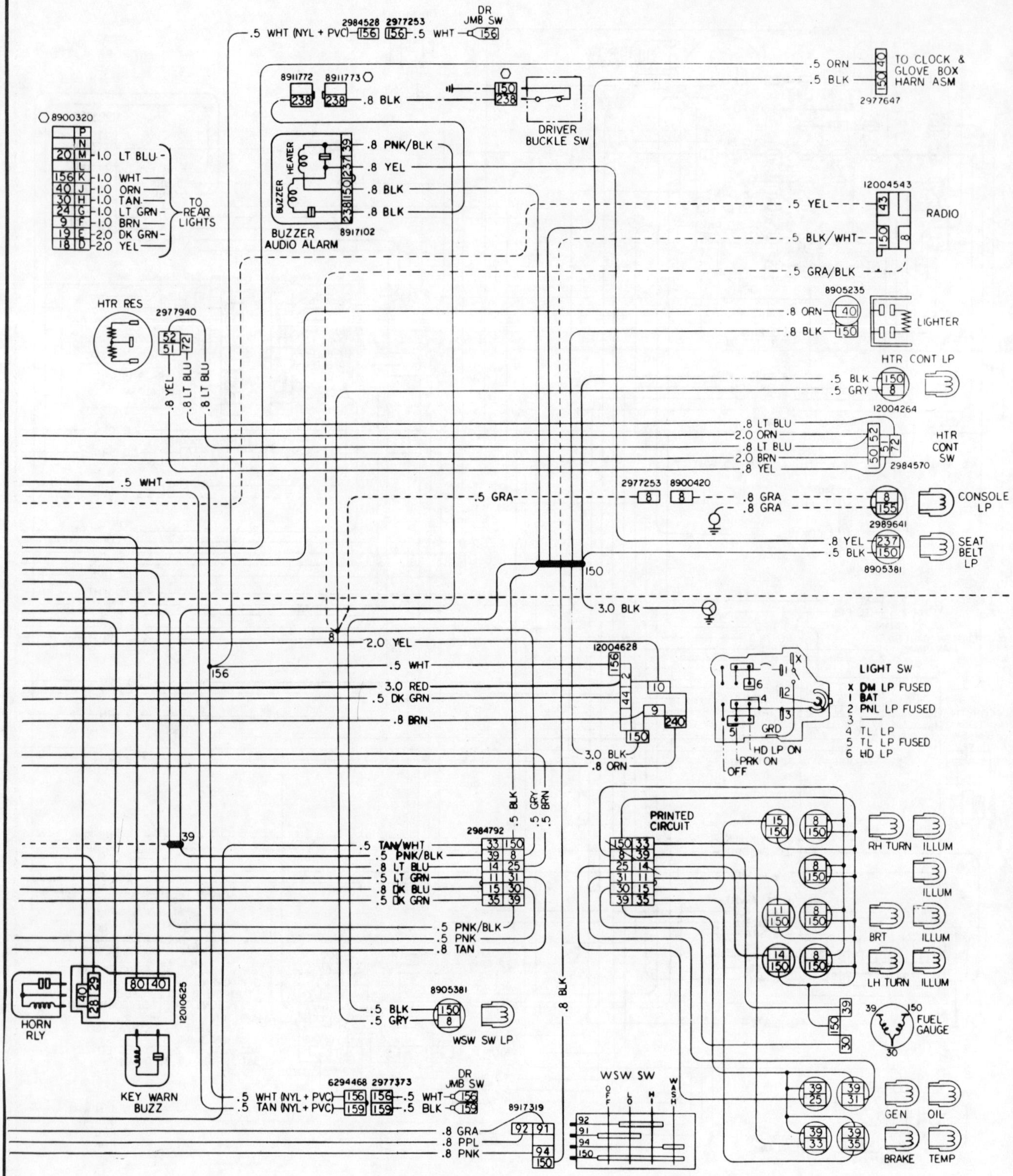

.5 WHT (NYL + PVC) 156 156 .5 WHT

DR JMB SW 156

2984528 2977253

8911772 8911773 8900320 8911772 8911773

238 238 .8 BLK 150 238

DRIVER BUCKLE SW

.5 ORN 150 40 TO CLOCK & GLOVE BOX HARN ASM
.5 BLK 150 8
2977647

8900320

	P
	N
20 M	1.0 LT BLU
	L
156 K	1.0 WHT
40 J	1.0 ORN
30 H	1.0 TAN
24 G	1.0 LT GRN
9 F	1.0 BRN
19 E	2.0 DK GRN
18 D	2.0 YEL

TO REAR LIGHTS

HEATER
238 150 237 39
.8 PNK/BLK
.8 YEL
.8 BLK
.8 BLK
BUZZER AUDIO ALARM
8917102

12004543
.5 YEL 43 RADIO
.5 BLK/WHT 150 8
.5 GRA/BLK

8905235
.8 ORN 40 LIGHTER
.8 BLK 150

HTR CONT LP
.5 BLK 150
.5 GRY 8
12004264

HTR RES 2977940
52 72
51 51
.8 YEL
.8 LT BLU
.8 LT BLU

.8 LT BLU
2.0 ORN
.8 LT BLU
2.0 BRN
.8 YEL
HTR CONT SW
150 52
51 72
2984570

.5 WHT

.5 GRA

2977253 8900420
8 8
.8 GRA
.8 GRA
8 155 CONSOLE LP
2989641

.8 YEL 237 SEAT BELT LP
.5 BLK 150
8905381

150

3.0 BLK

2.0 YEL
.5 WHT
3.0 RED
.5 DK GRN
.8 BRN

156

12004628
156 2
44 10
9 240
150

LIGHT SW
X DM LP FUSED
I BAT
2 PNL LP FUSED
3 TL LP
4 TL LP
5 TL LP FUSED
6 HD LP
HD LP ON
PRK ON
OFF
GRD

3.0 BLK
.8 ORN

39

.5 TAN/WHT 33 150
.5 PNK/BLK 39 8
.8 LT BLU 14 25
.5 LT GRN 11 11
.8 DK BLU 15 30
.5 DK GRN 35 39
2984792

.5 PNK/BLK
.5 PNK
.8 TAN

.5 BLK
.5 GRY

PRINTED CIRCUIT
15 150 | 8 150 RH TURN ILLUM
150 33 | 8 150
25 14 | 8 150 ILLUM
31 11 | 11 150
30 15 | 11 150 BRT ILLUM
39 35 | 14 150
| 15 150 LH TURN ILLUM

39 150 FUEL GAUGE
30

HORN RLY 40 29 80 40 28 29 12010625

KEY WARN BUZZ

DR JMB SW
6294468 2977373
.5 WHT (NYL + PVC) 156 156 .5 WHT 159
.5 TAN (NYL + PVC) 159 159 .5 BLK 159

8917319
.8 GRA 92 91
.8 PPL 91
.8 PNK 94
150

8905381
150 8
WSW SW LP

WSW SW
OFF LO HI WSH
92
91
94
150

150 39
30

39 32 | 39 39 GEN OIL
25 | 31

39 33 | 39 39 BRAKE TEMP
35

Fig. 10.75 Wiring diagram for 1980 instrument panel
(key to wiring diagram on pages 310 and 311)

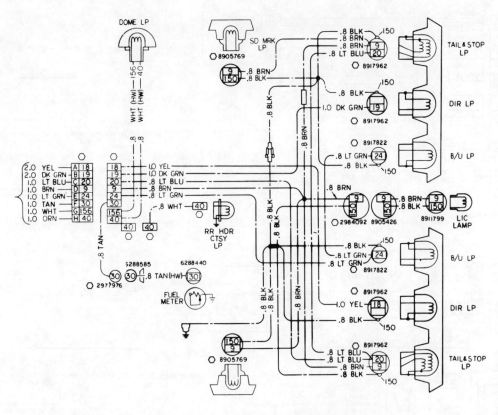

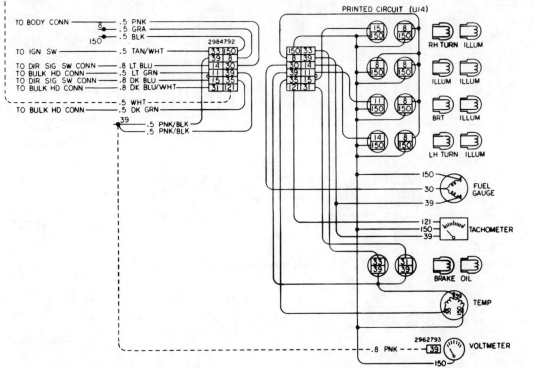

**Fig. 10.76 Wiring diagram for 1980 body and rear lighting
(key to wiring diagram on pages 310 and 311)**

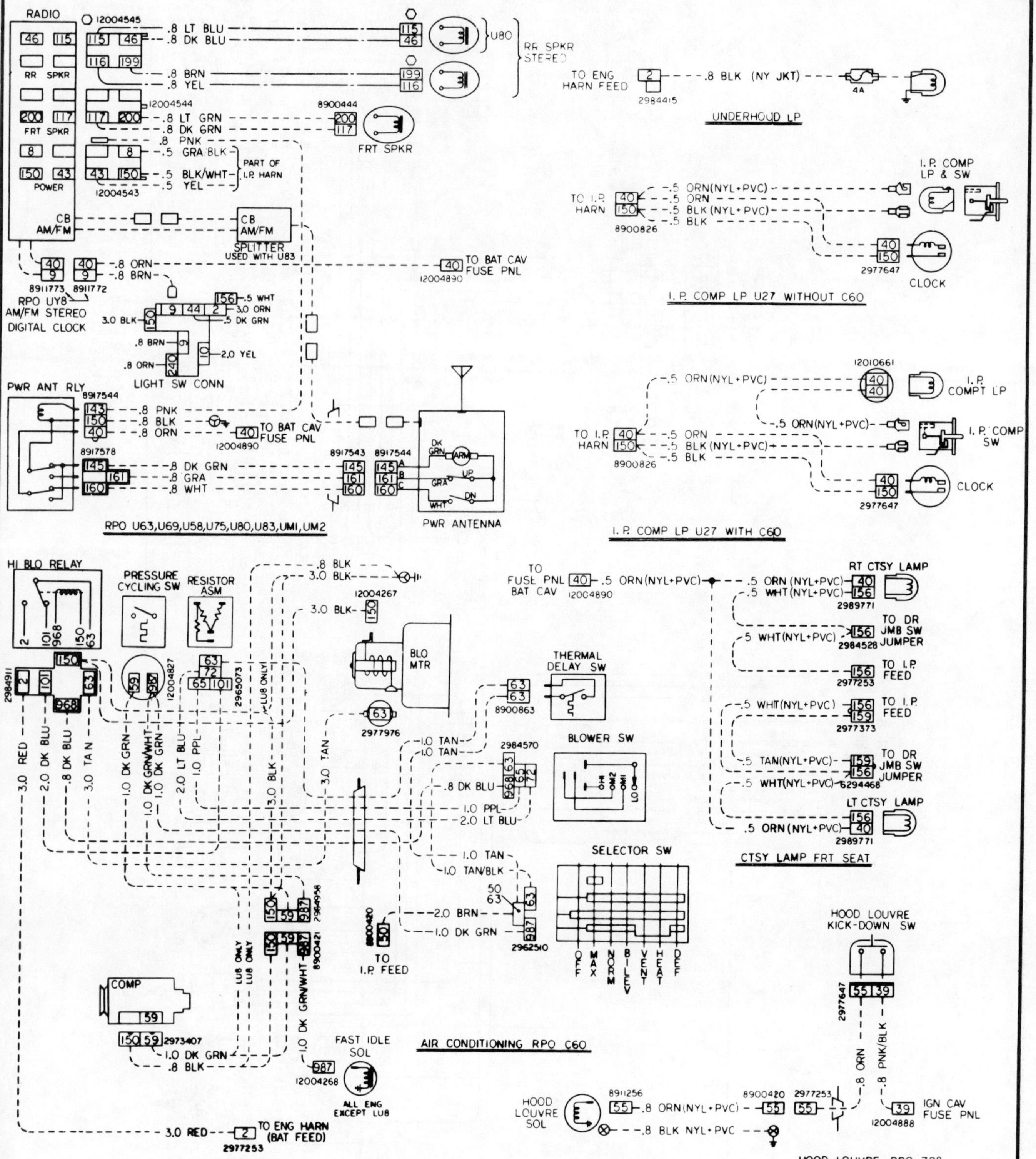

Fig. 10.77 Wiring diagram for 1980 air conditioning and optional circuits
(key to wiring diagram on pages 310 and 311)

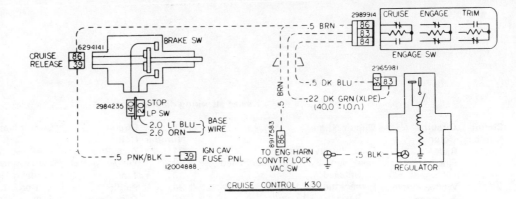

CRUISE CONTROL K30

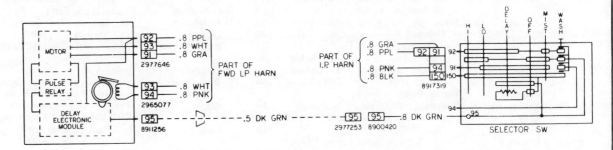

PULSE WIPE SYSTEM RPO CD4

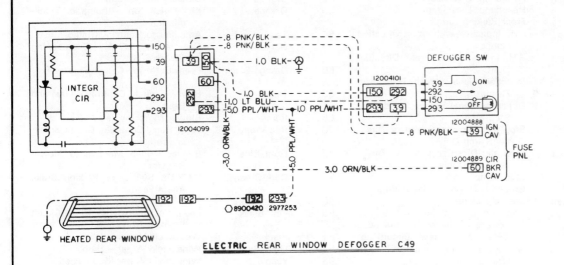

ELECTRIC REAR WINDOW DEFOGGER C49

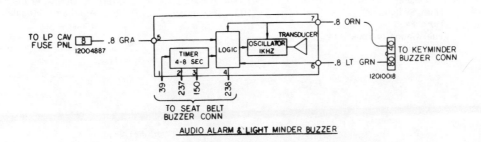

AUDIO ALARM & LIGHT MINDER BUZZER

**Fig. 10.78 Wiring diagram for 1980 optional accessory circuits
(key to wiring diagram on pages 310 and 311)**

Key to all wiring diagrams

Circuit Number	Circuit Color	Circuit Name	Circuit Number	Circuit Color	Circuit Name
2	Red	Feed, Battery – Unfused	31	Dark Blue	Oil Pressure – Engine
3	Pink	Feed, Ign. Sw. "On" Controlled – Unfused	32	Yellow	Map Light
3	White,–Purple & Orange	Primary Ignition Voltage – Dropping Resistor. .38 ohm/ft.	33	Tan	Warning Light – Brake Alarm
3	White–Red & Black	Primary Ignition Voltage – Dropping Resistor 30 ohm./ft.	34	Purple	Fog or Drive Lamp
4	Brown	Feed, Ign. Sw. Accy. Controlled – Unfused	35	Dark Green	Telltale Temp. Gauge (Hot), or Std. Temp. – Readable Gauge.
5	Purple	Neutral Safety Switch Feed or Neutral Safety Switch to Relay (Truck) or Relay to Ignition Switch (Truck) (Auto. Trans.)	38	Dark Blue	Flasher, Fuse Feed
			39	Pink-Black	Feed, Ign.Sw. "On" Controlled Fused
			40	Orange	Feed, Battery – Fused
6	Purple	Starter Solenoid Feed	41	Brown-White	Feed, Ign. Sw. Accsy. Controlled – Fused
7	Yellow	Primary Ignition Resistance Bypass	43	Yellow	Radio Feed
8	Gray	Instrument and Panel Lights, (Fused No. 44 Circuit)	44	Dark Green	Instrument and Panel Lights, Feed (Usually Light Switch to Fuse)
9	Brown	Tail and License Lamp, Forward Side Marker Lamps	45	Black	Marker and Clearance Lamps (Trailers – ICC Requirement)
		Tail, Clearance and Marker Lamps (Trailers)	46	Dark Blue	Rear Seat Speaker Feed from Radio Single or Rt. Stereo
10	Light Blue	Dimmer Switch Feed	47	Dark Blue	Auxiliary Circuits (Trailer)
11	Light Green	Headlamp, High beam	49	Gray	Mod. Assembly to Control
12	Tan	Headlamp, Low Beam	50	Brown	Blower Switch – Feed
13	Purple	Front Parking Lamps	51	Yellow	Blower Feed – Low
14	Light Blue	L.H. Indicator and Front Direction Light	52	Orange	Blower Feed – High
15	Dark Blue	R.H. Indicator and Front Direction Light	55	Orange	Kick-Down on Automatic Transmission
16	Purple	Direction Signal Switch, Feed from Flasher	56	Tan	Amplifier to Heatsink (Radio)
17	White	Direction Signal Switch, Feed from Stop Switch	59	Dark Green	Compressor to Air Conditioning Switch
18	Yellow	Stop and Direction Lamp or Direction Lamp Only-Rear L.H.	60	Orange-Black	Feed, Battery – Circuit Breaker Protected
19	Dark Green	Stop and Direction Lamp, or Direction Lamp Only – Rear R.H.	63	Tan	Blower-Switch Control – Low and Feed
20	Red	Stop Lamp (Trailer)	65	Purple	Blower Motor to Relay
22	White	Ground – Direct (Trailer Wiring)	70	Red-White	Feed, Relay Controller Circuit Breaker Protected
24	Light Green	Back-Up Lamp	72	Light Blue	Blower Switch Medium to Blower Resistor
25	Brown	Generator or Generator Armature to Voltage Regulator "A" (Includes Generator Telltale Circuit) or Regulator to Ignition Switch (Truck)	75	Dark Green	Back-Up Switch or Parking Brake Alarm Feed
			80	Pink-Black	Feek-Key Warning Buzzer
			90	Pink-Black	Feed, Cutout Sw. Controlled Circuit Breaker Protected
26	Dark Blue	Field Circuit (F) (Gen. Reg.)	91	Black	Windshield Wiper – Low
27	Brown	Traffic Hazard Switch, Feed from Flasher	92	Light Blue	Windshield Wiper – High
			93	Yellow	Windshield Wiper Motor Feed
28	Black	Horn Switch	94	Dark Blue	Windshield Washer Switch to Windshield Washer
29	Dark Green	Horn Feed	101	Dark Blue	Resistor Output to Blower Relay
30	Tan	Fuel Gauge to Tank Unit	102	White	S1 Alternator Regulator Sensing Circuit

Key to all wiring diagrams

Circuit Number	Circuit Color	Circuit Name
105	Black	Ammeter – Generator
106	Black-White	Ammeter – Battery
107	Dark Blue	Over-Speed Warning Light
111	Black	Buzzer to Low Air Pressure or Vacuum Switch
112	Dark Green White	Telltail Temperature Gauge (Hot)
119	White	Generator (Alternator) to Regulator
120	Black	Power Trans. Relay to Thermo Switch (Truck)
121	Brown	Tachometer to Coil
124	Black	Switch on Shift Lever to Adaptor, or to Motor on Rear Axle (Low), or to Adaptor (Low) (Truck)
125	Light Green	Switch to Diff. Lock-Out Valve (Truck)
126	Brown	Diesel Ignition – Buzzer to No. 4 "L" on Voltage Regulator (Truck)
127	Dark Green	Two-Speed Axle – Switch on Shift Lever to Motor on Rear Axle (High) (Truck)
130	Color depends on Resonator Brown-White Black-Pink	Generator (Alternator) External Resistance 2 ohms per foot 1 ohm per foot
131	Brown	Low Vacuum to Air Pressure Warning Light to Switch (Truck)
139	Pink-Black	Feed, Ign. Sw. "On" Controlled – Fused
140	Orange	Feed, Battery – Fused
141	Brown-White	Feed Ign. Sw. Accsy. Controlled Fused
150	Black	Ground Circuit – Direct
151	Black	Ground Circuit – Direct
152	Black	Ground Circuit – Direct
152	Black	Ground Circuit – Direct
154	Black	Ground Circuit – Direct
155	Black	Ground Circuit – Direct
156	White	
167	White Black	Ground Circuit – Sw. Controlled – Body Interior Lamps – such as
158	White-Dark Green	Dome, Courtesy, Map, Warning, etc.
159	Black-Purple	Ground – Key Warning Buzzer
162	Gray	Power Top-Up
163	Purple	Power Top-Down
164	Dark Blue	Window Control-L.F. – Up
165	Brown	Window Control-L.F. – Down
166	Dark Blue White	Window Control-R.F. – Up

Circuit Number	Circuit Color	Circuit Name
167	Tan	Window Control-R.F. – Down
168	Dark Green	Window Control-L.R. – Up
169	Purple	Window Control-L.R. – Down
170	Light Green	Window Control-R.R. – Up
171	Purple-White	Window Control-R.R. – Down
178	Dark Green	Power Seat – 6-W – Fore and Aft
179	Tan	Power Seat – 6-W – Solenoid – Rear – Up and Down
180	Light Green	Power Seat – 6-W – Solenoid – Frt – Up and Down
181	Light Blue	Power Seat – Solenoid – Fore and Aft
182	Yellow	Power Seat – 6-W – Aft and Down
183	Light Blue	Tailgate – Window – Up
184	Tan-White	Tailgate – Window – Down
189	Dark Green	Power Seat – 4-W – Fore and Down
190	Yellow	Power Seat – 4-W – Aft and Up
191	Light Green	Power Seat – 4-W – Solenoid – Up and Down
192	Purple	Defogger – High or Single Speed
193	White-Purple & Orange	Defogger – Low Speed – .38 ohm/ft.
198	Light Green	In-Car Sensor to Control
199	Brown	Rear Seat Speaker – Feed from Radio Left Stereo
200	Light Green	Front Speaker – Feed from Radio – Single or Right Stereo
201	Tan	Front Speaker – Feed from Radio – Left Stereo
202	Black	Compressor Overheat Switch to Thermal Limiter
203	Red/White	Rear Air Conditioning Potentiometer Feed
204	Brown	Ambient Temperature Switch to Thermal Limiter (Feed)
205	White/Black	Seat Belt Seat Sensor to Belt Retractor (Grd.)
206	Black	Neutral Start Switch to Buzzer and Lamp
207	Yellow/Black	Seat Sensor to Neutral Start Switch
208	Black	Switch Controlled Ground (TCS)
209	Purple	Parking Brake Warning Lamp
239	Pink-Black	Feed, Ign. Sw. "On" Controlled – Fused
240	Orange	Feed, Battery – Fused
241	Brown-White	Feedd Ign. Sw. Accsy. Controlled – Fused
252	Gray	Electric Door Lock (Unlock)
253	Light Green	Electric Door Lock (Lock)
340	Orange	Feed, Battery – Fused

NOTE: *Ground circuit numbers used in the order as listed, depending on the number of circuits at any one time. *When No. 35 circuit does not apply (normally on Vehicles with both Telltale Light and Standard Temperature Gauge.)*

Key to all wiring diagrams pages 252 and 309 inclusive

Chapter 11 Suspension

Contents

Specifications

Front suspension

Type .... Independent, upper and lower control arms with coil springs, telescopic shock absorbers and stabilizer bar

Steering geometry

Vehicle	Caster	Camber	Steering axle inclination	Toe-in
1970	$+\frac{1}{2}° \pm \frac{1}{2}°$	$+1° \pm \frac{1}{2}°$	$10\frac{1}{2}° \pm \frac{1}{2}°$	$\frac{1}{8}$ to $\frac{1}{4}$ in
1971 – 1972	$0° \pm \frac{1}{2}°$	$1° \pm \frac{1}{2}°$	$9\frac{1}{2}° \pm \frac{1}{2}°$	$\frac{1}{8}$ to $\frac{1}{4}$ in
1973 – 1974	$0° \pm \frac{1}{2}°$	$1° \pm \frac{1}{2}°$	$9\frac{1}{2}° \pm \frac{1}{2}°$	$\frac{3}{16} \pm \frac{1}{16}$ in
1975	$0° \pm \frac{1}{2}°$	$1° \pm \frac{1}{2}°$	–	$\frac{1}{16} \pm \frac{1}{16}$ in
1976 – 1977	$1° \pm \frac{1}{2}°$	$1° \pm \frac{1}{2}°$	–	$\frac{1}{16} \pm \frac{1}{16}$ in
1978 – 1980	$1° \pm \frac{1}{2}°$	$1° \pm \frac{1}{2}°$	–	$\frac{1}{8} \pm \frac{1}{16}$ in

Rear suspension

Type .... Leaf springs with telescopic shock absorbers

Steering

Type .... Recirculating ball with impact absorbing column. Optional power steering and tilt column on certain models

Manual steering adjustment data

	1970 thru 1972	1973 thru 1974	1975 on
Worm bearing preload	5 to 8 lb-in	4 to 6 lb-in	5 to 8 lb-in
Over center preload	4 to 10 lb-in	5 to 9 lb-in	4 to 10 lb-in
Total steering gear preload	14 lb-in	16 lb-in	16 lb-in

Power steering adjustment data

	1970 thru 1974	1975 on
Ball bearing drag	3 lb-in	3 lb-in
*Thrust bearing preload	$\frac{1}{2}$ to 2 lb-in	3 to 4 lb-in
**Over center preload	3 to 6 lb-in	4 to 5 lb-in
Total gear preload	14 lb-in	14 lb-in

*In excess of valve assembly drag
**In excess of combined ball drag and thrust bearing preload

Torque specifications   **lb-ft**

Front suspension

1970

Upper swivel joint ballstud nut	50
Lower swivel joint ballstud nut	80
Swivel joint securing bolts (replacement only)	25
Shock absorber upper mounting nut	8
Shock absorber lower mounting	20
Stabilizer bar bracket bolts	24
Stabilizer bar link nuts	12
Lower control arm inner pivot nuts	80
Upper control arm mounting nuts	80
Upper control arm collar bolts	70

1971 thru 1973

Upper swivel joint ballstud nut	50
Lower swivel joint ballstud nut	90
Swivel joint securing bolts (replacement only)	25
Control arm pivot to frame	
(upper)	85
(lower)	90
Upper control arm pivot shaft nuts	60
Shock absorber upper mounting	8
Shock absorber lower mounting	20
Stabilizer bar bracket bolts	24
Stabilizer bar link nuts	13
Disc caliper mounting bolts	35

1974 on

Swivel joint upper ballstud nut	60
Swivel joint lower ballstud nut	85
Swivel joint securing bolts (replacement only)	10
Control arm pivot to frame (upper)	75
Control arm pivot to frame (lower)	100
Upper control arm pivot shaft nuts	75
Shock absorber upper mounting	12
Shock absorber lower mounting	20
Stabilizer bar link nuts	13
Stabilizer bar bracket bolts	24
Disc brake caliper mounting bolts	35

Rear suspension
All

Spring to axle retainer	40
Front eye bolt	75
Front mounting bracket to body	25
Rear shackle bolts	50
Shock absorber upper	18
Shock absorber lower	8
Pinion nose bumper	8
Axle tube rebound bumper	35

Steering
1970 thru 1976

	lb-ft
Steering gear mounting bolts	70
Pitman shaft nut	
(to 1973)	140
(1974 on)	185
Steering wheel nut	
(standard)	30
(tilt column)	5
Steering flexible coupling flange bolts	20
Steering flexible coupling pinch bolts	30
Tie-rod end ballstud nut	35
Tie-rod clamp nut	16
Idler arm mounting nut	35
Dash panel bracket to column	15
Dash panel bracket to dash	20
Power steering pump pulley nut	60
Power steering pump mounting bolts	25
Idler arm to relay rod	50
Power steering hose end fittings	25

1977 on as for earlier models except:

Column support to column bracket stud nuts	25
Flexible coupling flange bolts	20
Idler arm mounting nuts	60
Idler arm to relay rod	40

Wheels
Wheel nuts

1970	65
1971 thru 1975	70
1976 on	80

1 General description

1 The front suspension is of the independent type incorporating upper and lower suspension arms, coil springs, hydraulic telescopic shock absorbers and a stabilizer bar.

2 The rear leaf spring suspension is attached to a solid rear axle assembly. The front of each leaf spring is attached to the frame with rubber bushings. At the rear, a shackle is used which allows the spring to flex and change its length slightly while the car is in motion. The rear telescopic shock absorbers are staggered, meaning that the left shock is behind the axle housing and the right one is forward of the housing.

3 The steering gear is of the recirculating ball type with an energy absorbing column. An ignition lock is built into the steering column. All model years offered power steering as an option. A tilt steering column was available as an option for late models only.

2 Maintenance and inspection (balljoints)

1 At the intervals specified in Chapter 1 check all the steering and suspension joints for wear or deterioration of the rubber bushings or dust excluders. With the help of an assistant check for 'lost' movement between the steering wheel at the front roadwheels which must be due to wear or looseness of the components.

2 Lower suspension arm balljoint wear must be checked in one of the following ways:

Vehicles built thru 1973, support the weight of the lower suspension control arm with a jack, then measure the distance from the grease fitting to the end of the lower threaded balljoint stud. Apply leverage under the tire to seat the lower balljoint stud internally, then remeasure. If the difference between these measurements is greater than $\frac{1}{16}$ inch the joint is worn and must be replaced.

Vehicles built from 1974 on, check the wear indicators for indication or excessive lower balljoint wear. When new, a dimension of 0.050 inch should exist from the grease nipple fitting to the balljoint cover surface; if the fitting is flush, or has receded inside the cover, the balljoint must be replaced.

3 Front wheel bearings – lubrication, replacement and adjustment

1 See Chapter 1, Section 24 for complete details on servicing the front wheel bearings.

4 Shock absorber – removal, inspection and installation

Any sign of oil on the outside of shock absorber bodies will indicate that the seals have started to leak and the units must be replaced as assemblies. Where the shock absorber has failed internally, this is more difficult to detect although rear axle patter or tramp, particularly on uneven road surfaces may provide a clue. When a shock absorber is suspected to have failed, remove it from the vehicle and holding it in a vertical position operate it for the full length of its stroke eight or ten times. Any lack of resistance in either direction will indicate the need for replacement.

Front shock absorber

1 Raise the front end of the vehicle. Use an open-ended wrench to prevent the upper (squared) end from turning, then remove the upper stem retaining nut, retainer and rubber grommet.

2 Remove the 2 bolts retaining the lower shock absorber pivot to the control arm (photo).

3 Pull the assembly out from the bottom.

4 When installing, fit the lower retainer and rubber grommet in place over the upper stem.

5 Install the shock absorber in the fully extended position up through the lower control arm and spring.

6 Fit the upper rubber grommet, retainer and attaching nut after the shock absorber upper stem has passed through the upper control arm frame bracket.

7 Using an open-ended wrench, hold the upper stem and torque-tighten the retaining nut.

8 Install the bolts at the shock absorber lower pivot, torque tighten, then lower the vehicle.

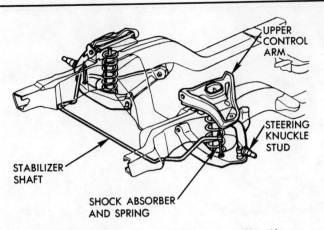

Fig. 11.1 Front suspension components (Sec 1)

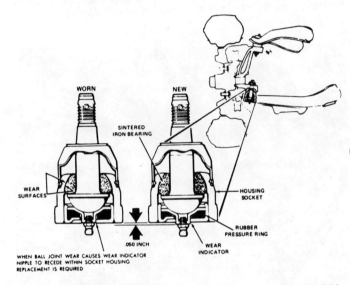

Fig. 11.2 Front suspension balljoint wear indicator – 1973 – 1980 models only (Sec 2)

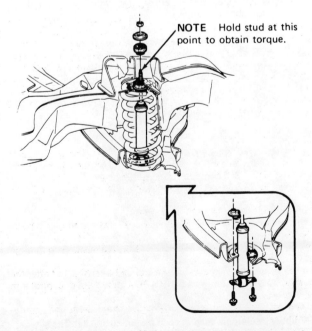

Fig. 11.3 Typical front shock absorber mounting (Sec 4)

Rear shock absorber

9   Raise the rear end of the vehicle, and support the rear axle.
10 Remove the lower shock absorber retaining nut, retainer and rubber grommet (photo).
11 Remove the two upper attaching bolts and then remove the shock absorber (photo).
12 When installing, push the lower retainer and rubber grommet into position. Extend the shock absorber to the proper length.
13 Place the shock absorber into position and install the two upper attaching bolts.
14 Push the remaining retainer and grommet into position and install the lower attaching nut.
15 Torque all fasteners and lower the vehicle.

5   Stabilizer bar – removal and installation

Front stabilizer bar

1   Raise the front end of the vehicle then disconnect the stabilizer bar from the lower control arms (photo).
2   Remove the stabilizer bar brackets from the frame then lift away the stabilizer bar (photo).
3   Remove the link bolts, spacers and rubber grommets from the lower control arms or stabilizer bar.
4   Inspect all the parts for damage, wear and deterioration. Fit new parts as necessary.
5   If new frame bushings are required, slide them into position along the stabilizer bar. The slit should be facing the front of the car (photo).
6   When installing, fit the brackets over the bushings and connect them (loosely) to the frame.
7   Ensure that the stabilizer bar is centralized then torque-tighten all the bolts.
8   Lower the vehicle to the ground.

Rear stabilizer bar

9   Raise the rear end of the vehicle and support the rear axle.
10 Remove the stabilizer bar to spring retainer bracket attachment.
11 Remove the stabilizer bar to body bracket bolt and remove the assembly.
12 Fit the bushings onto the stabilizer bar then place the bar in position.
13 Fit the upper retaining bolts and the stabilizer bar to spring attachment. Install bolts loosely at this point.
14 Ensure that the weight of the vehicle is being carried by the rear axle only, then torque-tighten the bolts.
15 Lower the vehicle to the ground.

6   Front coil spring – removal and installation

NOTE: *As the coil spring is under pressure during part of the removal and installation process, proper tools should be used and caution exercised. For added safety, a chain should be used to secure the coil spring to the lower control arm.*

1   Raise the front end of the vehicle and support firmly with jack stands on the frame. The suspension arms should hang free.
2   Remove the shock absorber (Section 4).
3   Remove the wheel.
4   Disconnect the stabilizer bar from the lower control arm. It can remain intact by the frame brackets.
5   Position a floor jack under the lower control arm. GM dealers have a special adapter for use with floor jacks which cradle the inner bushings.
6   Slowly raise the jack to relieve the tension on the lower control arm pivot bolts. At this point the spring is under pressure. Install a chain around the spring and through the control arm as a safety measure. Check that the floor jack is firmly supporting the control arm and will not slip.
7   With tension off the pivot bolts, remove the rear pivot bolt nut. Remove the forward pivot bolt and nut. It may be necessary to follow the bolts through the control arm with a hammer and drift (photo).
8   Slowly and carefully lower the floor jack. The control arm should lower with it (photo).
9   Before removing the spring, note the position of the spring in

4.2 Removing the lower bolts for the front shock absorbers

4.10 Removing the rear shock absorber lower securing nut

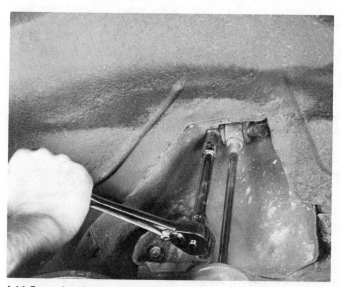

4.11 Removing the two upper screws for the rear shock absorber

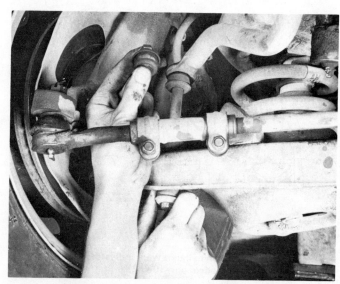

5.1 The ends of the stabilizer bar are secured with a lock nut and cushioned with rubber grommets

5.2 Removing the stabilizer bar mounting brackets from the frame rails

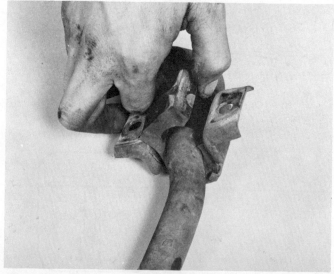

5.5 A rubber insulator is used at each mounting bracket. The slit should go towards the front of the vehicle

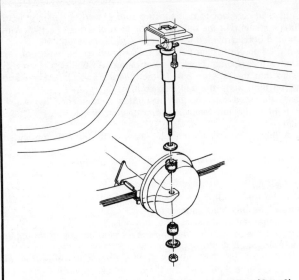

Fig. 11.4 Typical rear shock absorber mounting (Sec 4)

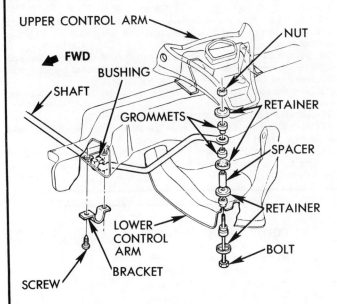

Fig. 11.5 Stabilizer bar attaching components (Sec 5)

NOTE Spring to be installed with tape at lowest position. Bottom of spring is coiled helical, and the top is coiled flat with a gripper notch near end of wire.

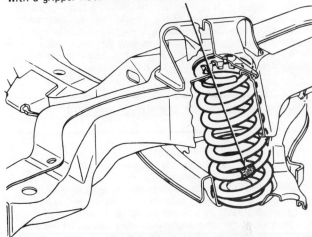

NOTE After assembly, end of spring coil must cover all or part of one inspection drain hole. The other hole must be partly exposed or completely uncovered.

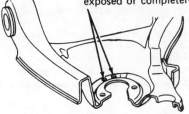

Fig. 11.6 Typical front coil spring mounting (Sec 6)

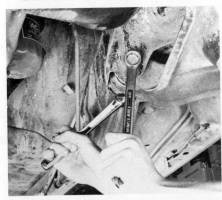

6.7 Using two wrenches to disconnect the lower control arm pivot bolt

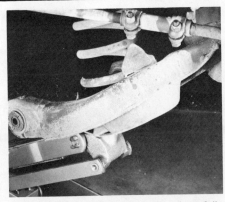

6.8 Lower the control arm slowly and carefully with the floor jack

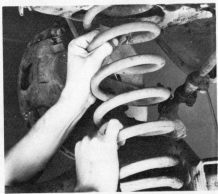

6.10 Lifting out the coil spring once all tension is relieved. Make sure spring is marked for top and bottom

relation to its bottom seat and the identifying tag attached to one of the coils.

10 When all the compression is removed from the spring, remove the safety chain and the spring (photo).

11 During installation, be sure that the coil is properly seated in the lower control arm. The end of the bottom coil should cover all or part of one of the small inspection/drain holes drilled in the control arm. The other hole should be partly or completely uncovered.

12 It is recommended that the safety chain be again used upon installation. With the control arm and spring raised into position, install the pivot bolts and nuts. It is necessary that the front bolt be installed with its head towards the front of the vehicle. The rear bolt can be installed in either direction. Torque-tighten these bolts to specifications before lowering the jack and removing the safety chain.

13 Install the remaining components in the reverse order of disassembly and tighten all fasteners to the proper torque.

7 Front suspension balljoints – removal, inspection and installation

Upper balljoint

1 Raise the front end of the vehicle and remove the wheel.

2 Remove the upper ball stud cotter pin.

3 Loosen the ball stud nut by one turn only (photo).

4 Using a proprietary balljoint separator, or GM tool no. J23742-1 press out the ball stud (If a tool is not available, insert a bolt and nut between the ends of the upper and lower balljoint studs. By unscrewing the nut on the bolt, its effective length will be increased and the balljoint will be pressed out). **Note:** While carrying out this operation the lower control arm must be supported so that the front spring does not force the arm down (photo).

5 Remove the upper balljoint stud and swing the steering knuckle out of the way.

6 Raise the upper arm and support it with a block of wood between it and the frame.

7 The balljoint is spring loaded in its socket to compensate for normal wear. If there is any lateral play or if the joint can be turned in its socket with the fingers, the joint should be replaced.

8 If replacement is necessary use a grinding wheel to remove the

rivets, but take care not to damage the control arm or balljoint seat.

9 When installing, fit the balljoint in the control arm and attach with the nuts and bolts provided (nuts at the top). Torque-tighten.

10 Turn the ball stud collar pin hole fore and aft to the length of car.

11 Remove the wooden block used at paragraph 6.

12 Ensure that the tapered hole in the steering knuckle is clean and undamaged then mate the ball stud to it.

13 Install the stud nut and torque-tighten to the specified value. Further tighten the nut to align the cotter pin holes then fit a new cotter pin.

14 Fit a lubrication nipple and lubricate with the recommended grease.

15 Fit the wheel and lower the vehicle to the ground.

Lower balljoint

16 Raise the front end of the vehicle.

17 Remove the ball stud cotter pin.

18 Loosen the ball stud nut by one turn only.

19 Press out the balljoint stud using the method described for upper balljoints (paragraph 4 of the previous sub-Section).

20 Remove the lower stud nut then pull outwards at the bottom of the tire. At the same time, push the tire and wheel upwards to free the knuckle from the ball stud.

21 Remove the wheel.

22 Raise the upper control arm and place a 2 x 4 inch block of wood between the frame and control arm. If found necessary, remove the tie-rod from the steering knuckle (Section 13).

23 Using a suitable vise and tubular spacers (GM tools J 9519-7 and J 9519-10 can be used if available) press the lower balljoint out of the control arm.

24 Using a suitable vise and tubular spacers (GM tools J 9519-9 and J 9519-10 can be used if available) fit the replacement balljoint with the bleed vent in the rubber boot facing inwards.

25 Turn the ball stud cotter pin hole fore-and-aft to the length of the car.

26 Remove the wooden block used at paragraph 22.

27 Ensure that the tapered hole in the steering knuckle is clean and undamaged then mate the ball stud to it.

28 Install the stud nut and torque-tighten to the specified value. Further tighten the nut to align the cotter pin holes then fit a new cotter pin.

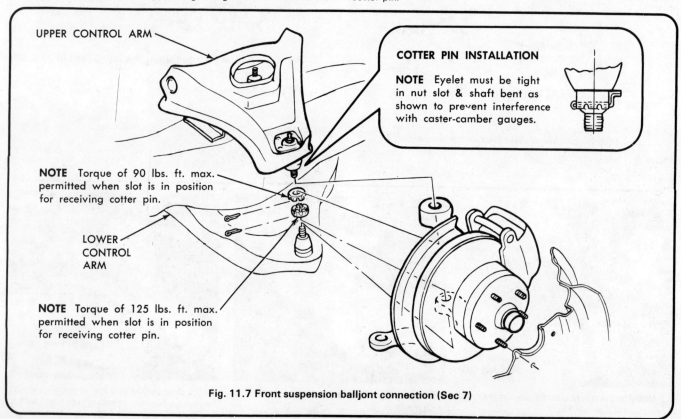

UPPER CONTROL ARM

COTTER PIN INSTALLATION

NOTE Eyelet must be tight in nut slot & shaft bent as shown to prevent interference with caster-camber gauges.

NOTE Torque of 90 lbs. ft. max. permitted when slot is in position for receiving cotter pin.

LOWER CONTROL ARM

NOTE Torque of 125 lbs. ft. max. permitted when slot is in position for receiving cotter pin.

Fig. 11.7 Front suspension balljoint connection (Sec 7)

29 Fit a lubrication nipple and lubricate with the recommended grease.
30 Fit the wheel (and tie-rod, if removed), then lower the car to the ground.

8 Upper suspension control arm – removal, servicing and installation

1 Raise the front end of the vehicle and lower the control arm onto a jack for support.
2 Remove the wheel.
3 Separate the upper control arm ball stud (Section 7).
4 Remove the 2 nuts securing the control arm shaft to the frame bracket. Tape together the shims and ensure that they are eventually installed in the same position.
5 In some cases it will be necessary to remove the upper control arm attaching bolts to provide clearance for removal of the upper control arm assembly. These bolts are splined, and may be removed as follows:

    a) Use a brass drift to tap the bolt gently downwards.
    b) Pry the bolt upwards using a suitable box wrench.
    c) Remove the nut, then use a suitable pry bar and block of wood to pry the bolts from the frame.

6 Remove the upper control arm.
7 If, on inspection, the control arm pivot bushings are worn, their

replacement is a job best left to your GM dealer, but if you are to carry out this work without the use of a press, employ a long bolt and suitable tubular spacers for both removal and installation of the bushings.
8 When installing, loosen the endshaft retainer bolts and/or nuts.
9 If removed, position the new control arm attaching bolts loosely in the frame and install the control arm cross-shaft on the attaching bolts.
10 Use a normal free-running nut (not a locknut) to tighten the serrated bolts onto their seats.
11 When the splined bolts are seated, remove the free-running nuts and fit the regular locknuts.
12 Install the shims in their original fitted positions then torque-tighten the nuts. Tighten the thinner shim pack nut first for improved clamping force and torque retention.
13 Install the ball stud through the knuckle, torque-tighten the nut, further tighten to align the cotter pin holes then fit a new cotter pin.
14 Fit the wheel and lower the vehicle to the floor.
15 Torque-tighten the shaft retainer bolts and/or nuts.

9 Lower suspension control arm – removal, servicing and installation

1 Remove the front coil spring (Section 6).
2 Remove the control arm ball stud (Section 7).
3 Remove the control arm from the vehicle.

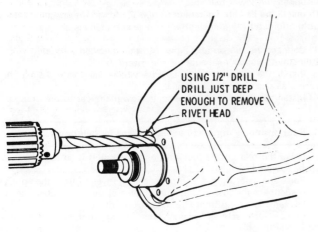

Fig. 11.8 Drilling upper balljoint rivet heads for removal (Sec 7)

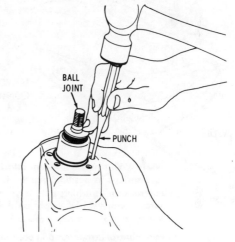

Fig. 11.9 Removing upper balljoint rivets with a punch (Sec 7)

7.3 Removing the upper ball joint nut at the top of the steering knuckle

7.4 A wedge-shaped ball joint splitter should be used to separate the joint

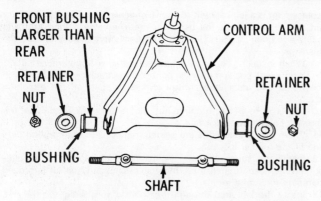

Fig. 11.10 Exploded view of upper control arm components (Sec 8)

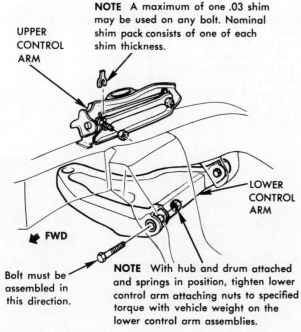

NOTE A maximum of one .03 shim may be used on any bolt. Nominal shim pack consists of one of each shim thickness.

UPPER CONTROL ARM

LOWER CONTROL ARM

FWD

Bolt must be assembled in this direction.

NOTE With hub and drum attached and springs in position, tighten lower control arm attaching nuts to specified torque with vehicle weight on the lower control arm assemblies.

Fig. 11.11 Upper and lower control arm mounting components (Sec 9)

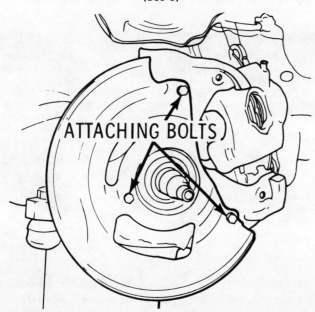

ATTACHING BOLTS

Fig. 11.12 Front rotor splash shield attachments (Sec 10)

4   If, on inspection, the control arm pivot bushings are worn, their replacement is best left to your GM dealer but if you are to carry out this work without the use of a press, employ a long bolt and suitable tubular spacers for both removal and installation. **Note:** It is not essential for the control arm to be removed for bushing replacement except for the front bushings on 1975 and later models.
5   Installation is the reverse of the removal procedure. Torque-tighten the nuts to the specified torque.

10 Steering knuckle – removal and installation

1   Raise the front end of the vehicle so that the weight is on the springs.
2   Remove the wheels.
3   Remove the disc brake caliper and rotor (Refer to Chapter 9, if necessary). When removing the caliper, use a block of wood to keep the disc pads separated.
4   Remove the splash shield.
5   Hang the caliper assembly from some convenient part of the suspension. Do not let the hydraulic line take the weight.
6   Remove the upper and lower ball joint stud cotter pins and disconnect the ball studs from the steering knuckle.
7   Disconnect the tie-rod end from the steering knuckle. This procedure can be found in Section 13.
8   Remove the steering knuckle.
9   When installing, place the steering knuckle into position and insert the upper and lower ball stud.
10 Install the ball stud nuts and torque-tighten to the specified value. Further tighten to align the cotter pin hole and then install a new cotter pin.
11 Connect the tie-rod and tighten to the specified torque.
12 Install the splash shield, hub and rotor.
13 Install the outer bearing, spindle washer and nut. Adjust the bearing as described in Chapter 1.
14 Install the caliper and the wheels. Lower the car to the ground.

11 Rear springs – removal, servicing and installation

1   Raise the rear end of the vehicle, and support it so that the axle can be lowered.
2   Raise the axle using a jack to relieve the weight from the spring.
3   Disconnect the lower attachment point of the shock absorber.
4   Loosen the spring front eye to bracket bolt.
5   Remove the screws securing the spring front bracket to the underbody (photo).
6   Lower the axle sufficiently to allow access to the spring front bracket; remove the bracket from the spring.
7   At this stage, the front bushing may be replaced, if no other work is to be carried out (see paragraph 11).
8   Pry the parking brake cable out of the retainer bracket on the spring mounting plate.
9   Remove the lower spring plate to axle bracket retaining nuts then the upper and lower spring pads and spring plate (photo).
10 Support the spring, then remove the lower bolt from the rear shackle. Separate the shackle and withdraw the spring (photos).
11 If the front spring bushings are worn, their replacement is a job best left for your dealer, but if you are to carry out this work without the use of a press, employ a long bolt and suitable tubular spacers for both removal and installation of the bushings.
12 When installing the spring, position the front mounting bracket to the front eyes. Install the attaching bolt with the bolt head towards the center of the vehicle.
13 Position the spring shackle upper bushings in the frame. Position the shackles to the bushings and loosely install the bolt and nut.
14 Install the bushing halves to the spring rear eye; place the spring to the shackles and loosely install the lower shackle bolt and nut. Ensure that the spring is positioned so that the parking brake cable is on the underside of the spring.
15 Raise the front end of the spring and position the bracket to the underbody. Guide the spring into position so that it will fit into the axle bracket and ensure that the tab on the spring bracket aligns with the slot in the underbody. It may be necessary to pry the spring forward.
16 Loosely install the spring bracket.
17 Position the spring upper cushion between the spring and the axle

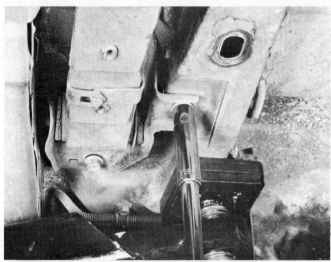
11.5 Removing the mounting bolt which secures the spring bracket on the rear leaf spring

11.9 Four nuts secure the leaf spring perch to the rear axle assembly. Note the center alignment pin

11.10A Removing the pivot bolt which runs through the rear of the leaf spring and the two shackles

11.10B Lowering the complete leaf spring assembly from the vehicle

bracket so that the ribs align with the locating ribs.

18 Fit the lower spring cushion and align with the upper cushion (where applicable).

19 Place the lower mounting plate over the locating dowel on the lower spring pad and loosely install the retaining nuts.

20 Where a new mounting plate is used, transfer the parking brake retaining bracket to the new plate.

21 Attach the shock absorber to the mounting plate.

22 Install the parking brake cable in the retaining bracket and securely clamp the bracket to retain the cable.

23 Torque-tighten all the nuts and bolts to the specified value with the weight on the rear springs.

24 Finally lower the vehicle to the ground.

12 Steering gear and linkage – inspection

1 See Chapter 1, Section 8 for the proper procedures involved in inspecting the steering system.

13 Steering linkage and balljoints – removal and installation

1 The balljoints on the two outer tie-rods and those on the central relay rod are all connected by means of a tapered ball stud located in a tapered hole and secured by a castellated nut and cotter pin.

2 The outer tie-rods are of tubular, internally threaded sleeve type and are secured to the tie-rod ends by clamps and bolts.

3 To remove the balljoint, first raise the front end of the car then remove the ball stud nut. On occasion the tapered studs have been known to simply pull out. More often they are well and truly wedged in position and a gear puller or slotted steel wedges may be driven between the ball unit and the arm to which it is attached. Another method is to place the head of a hammer (or other solid metal article) on one side of the hole in the arm into which the pin is fitted. Then hit it smartly with a hammer on the opposite side. This has the effect of squeezing the taper out and usually works, provided one can get a good swing at it. Always keep the stud nut at the top of the stud threads to protect the threads from damage (photos).

4 Measure the length of exposed thread on each of the tie-rod ends (as a guide to reassembly), release the pinch bolts from the clamps and unscrew the tie-rod end from the tie-rod sleeve (photo).

5 When installing the new tie-rod ends, screw them into the sleeves exactly the same amount as the original ones.

6 Arrange for your dealer to check the toe-in, or follow the procedure given in Section 33. Pay particular attention to the special instructions for the position of the clamps if you are carrying out this operation yourself.

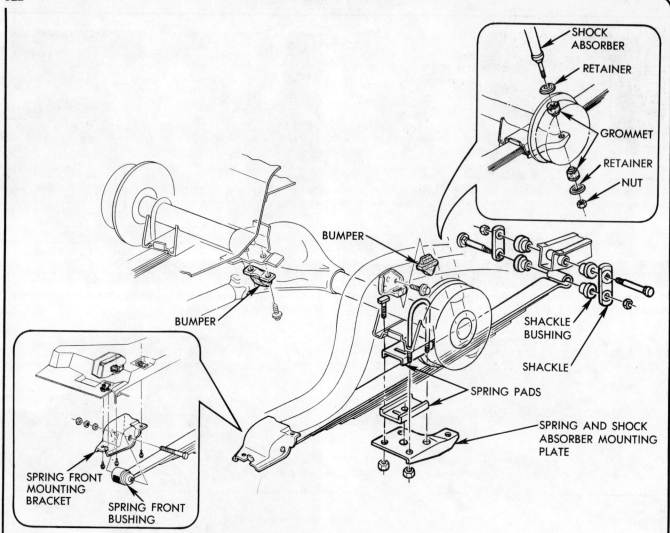

SHOCK ABSORBER

RETAINER

GROMMET

RETAINER

NUT

BUMPER

BUMPER

SHACKLE BUSHING

SHACKLE

SPRING PADS

SPRING AND SHOCK ABSORBER MOUNTING PLATE

SPRING FRONT MOUNTING BRACKET

SPRING FRONT BUSHING

Fig. 11.13 Rear suspension components (Sec 11)

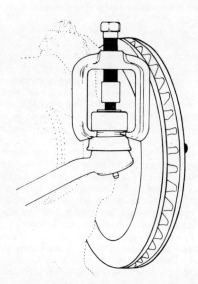

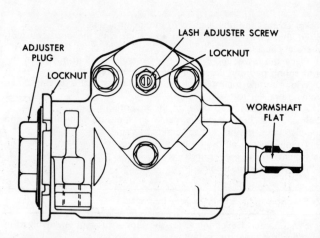

ADJUSTER PLUG

LOCKNUT

LASH ADJUSTER SCREW

LOCKNUT

WORMSHAFT FLAT

Fig. 11.14 Using a puller to loosen steering linkage connection (Sec 13)

Fig. 11.15 Typical steering gear adjustment points (Sec 14)

13.3A After removing the cotter pin, the lock nut is loosened to the end of the threaded stud

13.3B A puller is then installed in position and tightened against the threaded stud

13.3C With the puller tight, a sharp blow with a hammer will break the connection

13.4 When replacing tie-rods, count the number of exposed threads and mark the threaded shaft to enable the new tie-rod to be installed the same

13.8 Where a common puller cannot be used (as shown here with the idler arm), a wedge-shaped splitter should be used to break the joint connection

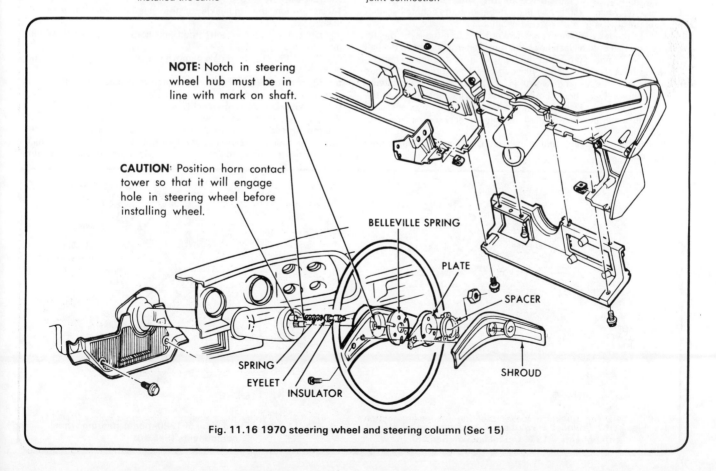

NOTE: Notch in steering wheel hub must be in line with mark on shaft.

CAUTION: Position horn contact tower so that it will engage hole in steering wheel before installing wheel.

BELLEVILLE SPRING

PLATE

SPACER

SPRING

EYELET

INSULATOR

SHROUD

Fig. 11.16 1970 steering wheel and steering column (Sec 15)

7   If the balljoints on the central relay rod are worn then the relay rod will have to be replaced as an assembly. Again, the toe-in will have to be checked afterwards (see previous paragraph).

8   If it is necessary to remove the idler arm this is first disconnected at the frame mounting (one nut, washer and bolt), then disconnected at the idler arm end by using the same procedure given for the other steering linkage joints (photo).

14 Manual steering gear – maintenance and adjustment (steering gear in place)

1   The steering gear is normally filled with lubricant for life and unless a severe leak occurs, necessitating a complete overhaul, refilling with lubricant will not be required.

2   In order to rectify conditions of lost motion, slackness and vibration which have been found to be directly attributable to the steering gear, carry out the following operations:

3   Disconnect the ground cable from the battery.

4   Remove the nut from the Pitman arm and then mark the relative position of the arm to the Pitman shaft.

5   Using a suitable extractor remove the Pitman arm.

6   Loosen the adjuster plug locknut on the steering gear and unscrew the adjuster plug one quarter-turn.

7   Remove the horn button or shroud from the steering wheel and then turn the steering wheel in one direction to full lock and then turn the wheel back through one half turn. Now apply a $\frac{3}{4}$ inch socket to the steering wheel center nut and either using a torque wrench or a spring balance check the bearing drag when the wheel is turned through a 90° arc of travel.

8   This drag is the thrust bearing preload and it should be within the specifications listed at the front of this chapter. Tighten or slacken the adjuster plug until the correct preload is obtained and then torque-tighten the adjuster plug locknut.

9   Any jerky or lumpy feeling as the steering wheel is turned will indicate worn or damaged bearings in the steering gear.

10   Now turn the steering wheel gently from one stop to the other counting the number of turns of the steering wheel from lock-to-lock. Now turn the wheel exactly half the number of turns counted so that the steering gear is in the centered position.

11   Loosen the lash adjuster screw locknut and turn the lash adjuster screw clockwise until all lash has been removed from between the ball nut and the Pitman shaft sector teeth. Torque-tighten the locknut.

12   Now check the 'over-center' preload by taking the highest torque reading obtainable as the wheel is moved through its centered position. The preload should be within the specifications listed at the front of this chapter, **in excess of** the torque stated at paragraph 8 above. Adjust the position of the lash adjuster screw if necessary to achieve this.

13   Install the Pitman arm and horn shroud, and connect the battery ground cable.

15 Steering wheel – removal and installation (1970 models)

1   Disconnect the negative battery cable.

2   Remove the two steering wheel shroud screws located at the underside of the shroud. Remove the shroud from the steering wheel.

3   Remove the spacer, plate and belleville spring. These components are held in place with three screws.

4   Mark the relation of the steering wheel to the steering column so that the wheel can be replaced in the same location.

5   Remove the steering wheel lock nut on the end of the shaft.

6   Use a steering wheel puller to remove the wheel from the column. The puller anchor screws should be installed in the threaded holes provided in the steering wheel and the center bolt turned clockwise until the wheel breaks free from the shaft. Do not strike the end of the shaft with a hammer as this may collapse certain components inside the column.

7   When installing, make sure the eyelet and insulator are correctly positioned in the horn contact tower.

8   Place the steering wheel onto the end of the steering shaft, aligning the marks made upon disassembly. When lowering the steering wheel into position, make sure the horn contact tower will engage with the hole in the steering wheel.

9   Install the steering wheel lock nut and torque to the proper specifications.

10   Install the belleville spring (concave side down), plate and spacer. Tighten the three screws.

11   Install the steering wheel shroud and tighten the two attaching screws.

12   Connect the negative battery cable and check the operation of the wheel and horn.

16 Steering wheel – removal and installation (1971 – 1980)

Standard production

1   Disconnect the negative battery cable.

2   Remove the two screws securing the steering wheel shroud. These are on the underside of the steering wheel towards the dashboard.

3   Lift the steering wheel shroud and horn contact lead assembly from the steering wheel.

4   On 1975 – 1980 models, remove the snap ring from the steering shaft.

5   Mark the steering wheel and column to enable installation of the wheel in the same position.

6   Remove the steering wheel lock nut from the shaft.

7   Using a steering wheel puller, remove the steering wheel from the column. Threaded holes are provided in the steering wheel to accept the puller anchor screws. Use the lock nut to protect the top threads of the threaded shaft. Do not strike the puller or the end of the column

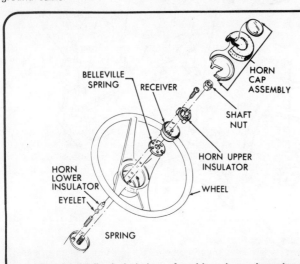

Fig. 11.17 Exploded view of cushioned steering wheel components – 1974 model shown (Sec 16)

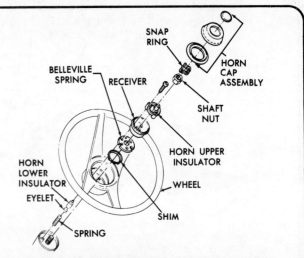

Fig. 11.18 Exploded view of 1980 model steering wheel components (Sec 16)

16.13A The steering wheel horn button assembly

16.13B The spring-loaded horn plunger

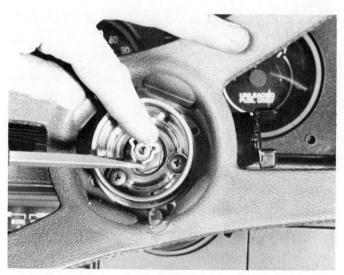

16.14 Some models may have a retaining clip over the main shaft nut

16.17 A steering wheel puller being used to draw the steering wheel from the column

as this may damage components of the collapsible steering column.
8   When installing, set the turn signal lever to the neutral position and set the wheel into position. Use the alignment marks made upon disassembly to correctly position the wheel.
9   Tighten the steering wheel lock nut to the proper specifications. Do not overtighten this nut as this may cause interference problems. Install the snap ring (1975 – 1980 models).
10   Place the shroud onto the wheel, guiding the horn contact lead into the directional signal canceling cam tower.
11   Install the shroud attaching screws and connect the negative battery cable. Check the operation of the horn.

Cushioned steering wheel
12   Disconnect the negative battery cable.
13   Carefully pry off the horn button cap with a screwdriver (photos).
14   On 1975 – 1980 models, remove the snap ring from the end of the shaft (photo).
15   Remove the steering wheel lock nut.
16   Remove the three screws securing the upper horn insulator and remove the insulator, receiver, belleville spring and shim (if used).
17   Use a steering wheel puller to remove the steering wheel from the column (photo). Threaded holes are provided in the steering wheel for the puller anchor screws. Use the lock nut to protect the top threads of the steering shaft. Do not strike the puller or the end of the

column with a hammer as this may damage internal components of the collapsible column.
18   To install, place the turn signal lever in the neutral position and set the wheel onto the steering shaft. Use the alignment marks made upon disassembly to correctly position the steering wheel. Secure with the lock nut, tightening the nut to the proper specifications. Do not overtighten this nut.
19   Install the snap ring (1975 – 1980 models).
20   Install the horn lower insulator, eyelet and spring in the horn contact tower.
21   Install the belleville spring, receiver and horn upper insulator and secure with the three screws.
22   Install the horn button cap and connect the negative battery cable. Check the operation of the horn.

17   Steering column couplings – removal and installation

Flexible coupling
1   Disconnect the battery ground cable (and coupling shield if applicable).
2   Remove the intermediate steering shaft flange to flexible coupling retaining bolts.

3   Remove the steering gear to frame bolts; lower the steering gear.
4   Push the intermediate shaft rearwards and rotate it out of the way.
5   Using a suitable 12-point socket wrench, remove the coupling clamp bolt. Remove the flexible coupling.
6   Install the flexible coupling to the steering gear wormshaft splined end, taking care to align the mating flats.
7   Install the coupling clamp bolt and torque tighten, after ensuring that the coupling reinforcement is bottomed on the wormshaft.
8   Install the intermediate shaft to the coupling and loosely install the flange to coupling bolts.
9   Install the steering gear to frame bolts and torque-tighten.
10   Align the flexible coupling pins centrally in the intermediate shaft flange slots then torque-tighten the coupling bolts.
11   Connect the battery ground lead (and the coupling shield, if applicable).

Pot joint coupling

1   Disconnect the battery ground cable (and the coupling shield, if applicable).
2   Remove the intermediate shaft flange to flexible coupling retaining bolts.
3   Remove the pot joint clamping bolt (at the steering shaft).
4   Remove the steering gear to frame bolts; lower the gear.
5   Push the intermediate steering shaft rearwards until it bottoms in the pot joint and clears the flexible coupling alignment pins.
6   Remove the intermediate shaft and pot joints as an assembly.
7   When installing, align the flats on the pot joint and steering shaft then mate them. Install the clamp and bolt, and torque-tighten.
8   Install the intermediate shaft to the flexible coupling and loosely install the coupling bolts.
9   Install the steering gear to the frame bolts and torque-tighten.
10   Align the flexible coupling pins centrally in the intermediate shaft flange slots then torque-tighten the coupling bolts.
11   Connect the battery ground cable (and the coupling shield, if applicable).

18 Pot joint coupling – dismantling and reassembly

1   To disassemble the pot joint, pry off the snap-ring and slide the coupling over the shaft. Remove the bearings and tension spring from the pivot pin. Clean the pin and the end of the shaft then scribe a location mark on the pin on the same side as the shaft chamber. Support the shaft securely then press out the pin taking care that it is not damaged, or bearing damage may occur. Remove the seal clamp then slide the seal off the end of the shaft.
2   To reassemble the pot joint, first ensure that all the parts are clean then slide the seal onto the shaft so that the lip of the seal is against the shoulder on the shaft. Install the clamp. Press the pin into the shaft, aligning the scribed location marks. Ensure that the pin is centered within 0.012 inch, or binding will result. Liberally grease the inside and outside of the bearings and the inside of the cover then install the tension spring and bearings on the pin. Install the seal into the end of the cover and secure with the snap-ring.

19 Manual steering gear – removal and installation

1   Remove the battery ground cable (and the coupling shield, if applicable).
2   Remove the nuts, lockwashers and bolts at the steering shaft to coupling flange.
3   Remove the Pitman arm lock nut and washer. Mark the position of the Pitman arm in relation to the shaft and remove the Pitman arm with a suitable puller.
4   Remove the screws securing the steering gear to the frame and remove it from the vehicle (photo).
5   When installing, place the gear into position so that the coupling mounts properly to the flanged end of the steering shaft. Secure the gear to the frame, fit the washers and bolts, then torque-tighten.
6   Secure the steering coupling to the flanged end of the column with the lockwashers and nuts. Torque-tighten the nuts.
7   Install the Pitman arm.
8   Connect the battery ground cable (and the coupling shield, if applicable).

20 Pitman shaft seal (manual steering) – replacement, steering gear in vehicle

1   Remove the Pitman arm.
2   Turn the steering from stop-to-stop and count the exact number of turns. Now rotate the wheel half the number of turns counted so that the steering gear is centered (wormshaft flat at 12 o'clock position).
3   Remove the side cover from the steering gear housing (three screws) and lift the Pitman shaft and side cover from the housing.
4   Pry the seal from the housing using a screwdriver and tap a new one into position using a suitable socket or piece of tube.
5   Remove the lash adjuster screw locknut and detach the side cover from the Pitman shaft by turning the adjuster screw clockwise.
6   Insert the Pitman shaft into the steering gear so that the center tooth of the shaft sector enters the center tooth of the ball nut.
7   Pack the specified grease into the housing and install a new side cover gasket. Install the side cover onto the lash adjuster screw. This is achieved by inserting a small screwdriver through the threaded adjuster hole in the side cover and turning the lash adjuster screw counterclockwise. When the screw bottoms, turn it back $\frac{1}{4}$ turn.
8   Tighten the side cover bolts to the specified torque.
9   Carry out the adjustments described previously and tighten the lash adjuster screw locknut.
10   Install the Pitman arm.

21 Turn signal switch – removal and installation

1   Disconnect the negative battery cable and remove the steering wheel as detailed in Sections 15 or 16.
2   Remove the steering column trim cover located at the base of the dashboard.
3   At the end of the steering column, late models have a plastic cover plate which should be pried out of the column using a screwdriver in the slots provided (photo).
4   The lock plate will now have to be removed from the steering column. This is held in place with a snap ring which fits into a groove in the steering shaft. The lock plate must be depressed to relieve pressure on the snap ring. A special U-shaped tool which fits on the shaft should be used to depress the lock plate as the snap ring is removed from its groove (photo).
5   Slide the cancelling cam, upper bearing preload spring and thrust washer off the end of the shaft (photo).
6   Remove the turn signal lever attaching screw and withdraw the turn signal lever from the side of the column.
7   Push in on the hazard warning knob and unscrew the knob from the threaded shaft.
8   Remove the three turn signal assembly mounting screws (photo).
9   Pull the switch wiring connector out of the bracket on the steering

19.4 The three bolts which run through the frame rail to secure the steering box

21.3 Removing the plastic cover with a screwdriver

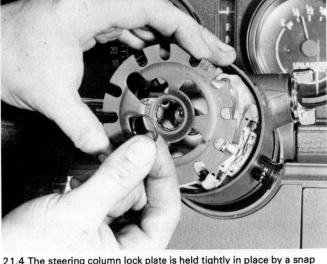

21.4 The steering column lock plate is held tightly in place by a snap ring on the center shaft. The plate must be depressed as the snap ring is pried off

21.5 The cancelling cam, pre-load spring and thrust washer being removed from the shaft

21.8 The turn signal mechanism is held in place with three screws and can be drawn off the column once the lever is removed

column jacket. Tape the connector terminals to prevent damage. Feed the wiring connector up through the column support bracket and pull the switch, wiring harness and connectors out the top of the steering column.

10 Installation is a reversal of removal, however, make sure the wiring harness is in the protector as it is pulled into position. Before installing the thrust washer, upper bearing preload spring and cancelling cam, make sure the switch is in the neutral position and the warning knob is pulled out. Always use a new snap ring on the shaft for the lock plate.

22 Ignition lock cylinder – removal and installation

1970 – 1978

1 The lock cylinder is located on the upper right-hand side of the steering column. On models built in 1970, the lock cylinder can be removed in any position from 'ACCESSORY' to 'ON' but removal in 'LOCK' position is recommended. From 1971 on, the lock cylinder should only be removed in the 'RUN' position, 'otherwise damage to the warning buzzer switch may occur.

2 Remove the steering wheel (Section 15 or 16) and directional

signal switch (Section 21). **Note:** *The directional signal switch need not be fully removed provided that it is pushed rearwards far enough for it to be slipped over the end of the shaft. Do not pull the harness out of the column.*

3 Insert a thin blade or driver into the slot in the turn signal switch housing. Break the housing flash loose and at the same time depress the spring latch at the lower end of the lock cylinder. Holding the latch depressed withdraw the lock cylinder from the housing.

4 The lock cylinder cannot be dismantled; a new one (coded to accept the original key) must be installed in the original cylinder sleeve after the assembly has been dismantled by releasing the cylinder to sleeve staking.

5 To assemble the new lock cylinder to the sleeve, insert the ignition key part way into the lock and then place the wave washer and anti-theft ring onto the lower end of the lock cylinder, making sure that the plastic keeper in the sleeve protrudes.

6 Now align the lock bolt on the cylinder and the tab of the anti-theft washer with the slot in the sleeve. Push the lock cylinder fully onto the sleeve and then insert the ignition key fully and rotate the cylinder clockwise.

7 Rotate the lock counterclockwise to 'LOCK'.

8 Secure the lock assembly in the jaws of a vise suitably protected with wood or cloth. Install the adaptor ring onto the lower end of the cylinder so that the finger of the adaptor is located at the step in the

sleeve and the serrated edge of the adaptor can be seen after assembly to the cylinder. The key must also be free to rotate at least 120°.

9   Tap the adaptor onto the cylinder until it is at the bottom of the cylinder flats and the cylinder projects about $\frac{1}{16}$ inch above the adaptor.

10   Using a small punch, stake the lock cylinder over the adaptor ring in four positions just outboard of the four dimples.

11   To install the new lock cylinder/sleeve assembly, hold the sleeve and rotate the lock clockwise against the stop.

12   Insert the cylinder/sleeve assembly into the housing so that the key on the cylinder sleeve is aligned with the housing key way.

13   Insert a 0.070 in diameter drill between the lock bezel and the housing and then rotate the cylinder counterclockwise, maintaining pressure on the cylinder until the drive section mates with the sector.

14   Press in the lock cylinder until the snap-ring engages in the grooves and secures the cylinder in the housing. Remove the drill and check the lock action.

15   Install the turn signal switch and the steering wheel.

1979 – 1980

16   The lock cylinder should be removed in the 'RUN' position only.

17   Remove the steering wheel (Section 15 or 16) and turn signal switch (Section 21). It is not necessary to completely remove the switch. Pull it up and over the end of the steering shaft. Do not pull the wiring harness out of the column.

18   Remove the ignition key warning switch (Section 23).

19   Using a magnetized screwdriver, remove the lock retaining screw. Do not allow this screw to drop down into the column as this will require a complete disassembly of the steering column to retrieve the screw.

20   Pull the lock cylinder out of the side of the steering column.

21   To install, rotate the lock cylinder set and align the cylinder key with the keyway in the steering column housing.

22   Push the lock all the way in and install the retaining screw.

23   Install the remaining components referring to the appropriate Sections.

23   Ignition key warning switch – removal and installation

1   The ignition key warning switch is located within the column housing. It can be removed with or without the ignition lock cylinder.

2   Remove the steering wheel (Section 15 or 16).

3   Follow the procedures outlined in Section 21 for removing the turn signal switch, however do not completely remove the switch. Pull the switch over the end of the column shaft. Do not pull the wiring harness out of the steering column.

4   If the ignition lock cylinder is still intact, set the key to the 'ON' position.

5   Use a piece of stiff wire (a paper clip will work fine) to remove the switch. Make a hook at the end of the wire and lip this hooked end into the loop of the clip at the top of the switch. Pull up on the wire and remove the clip and switch together from the steering column. Do not allow the clip to fall down into the column.

6   If the lock cylinder is still in the column, the buzzer switch actuating button (on the lock cylinder) must be depressed before the new warning switch can be installed.

7   Install the switch with the contacts towards the upper end of the steering column and with the formed end of the spring clip at the lower end of the switch. Reinstall the remaining components referring to the appropriate Sections.

24   Ignition switch – removal and installation

1   As a precaution against theft of the vehicle, the ignition switch is located inside the channel section of the brake pedal support and remotely controlled by a rod and rack assembly from the ignition lock cylinder.

1970 thru 1976

2   To remove the ignition switch, the steering column must either be removed or lowered and well supported. There is no need to remove the steering wheel.

3   Before removing the switch (two screws) set it to the 'LOCK'

position. If the lock cylinder and actuating rod have already been removed, the 'LOCK' position of the switch can be determined by inserting a screwdriver in the actuating rod slot and then moving the switch slide up until a definite stop is felt and then moving it down one detent.

4   Installation is a reversal of removal but again the switch must be in the 'LOCK' position and the original or identical type securing screws must be used. Longer or thicker screws could cause the collapsible design of the steering column to become inoperative.

5   When installing the steering column, refer to Section 25.

1977 on

6   On these models, the switch should be set to the 'OFF-UN-LOCKED' position before removal. If the lock cylinder has already been removed, the switch actuating rod should be pulled up until a definite stop is felt and then pushed down two detents.

7   Before installing the switch, set it to the 'OFF-UNLOCK' position and set the gearshift lever in neutral. Setting the switch should be carried out in the following way. Move the switch slider two positions to the right from 'ACCESSORY' to 'OFF/UNLOCK'. Fit the actuator rod into the slider hole and assemble to the steering column using two screws. These screws must be of the original type and only tighten the lower one to 35 lbf in torque.

25   Steering column – removal and installation

1   As described in previous Sections, many of the steering column components can be serviced without removal of the steering column. When the steering column is removed, extreme caution should be exercised because of the energy absorbing design of the column. Avoid hammering, jarring, dropping or leaning on any part of the steering column assembly. Also, it is important to use only the factory-installed fasteners or their exact equivalents. Screws and bolts other than those specified could prevent the column from compressing under impact.

2   Disconnect the negative battery cable.

3   Remove the steering wheel using an appropriate puller as described in Section 15 or 16.

4   Inside the engine compartment, disconnect the flanged end of the steering shaft at the flexible coupling. Separate the coupling from the lower end of the steering column.

5   Also at the lower end of the column, disconnect the shift control linkage (back drive linkage on floor shift models).

6   At the base of the steering column, inside the car, disconnect all electrical connectors. These include the main ignition connector and wiring for the neutral-start switch and back-up lamp switch. Pull the wiring free of any steering column clips.

7   Remove the screws which fasten the column plate to the floor pan.

8   The column must now be disconnected from its mounting on the dashboard. On models 1970 – 1978 this requires the ashtray, steering column trim plate and heater/air conditioner control to be lowered as an assembly. 1979 – 1980 models have the column bracket-to-dashboard nuts readily accessible.

9   Disconnect the shift position indicator where applicable.

10   Move the seat as far to the rear as possible for better clearance and carefully guide the column through the firewall opening. This is best done with an assistant helping under the hood.

11   To install the steering column, first position it inside the vehicle, again carefully guiding the lower end through the firewall opening.

12   Loosely install the dashboard attaching nuts to support the column.

13   Connect all electrical connections.

14   Connect the lower end of the column to the steering linkage and tighten the fasteners to the appropriate torque.

15   Connect the shift linkage and/or backdrive linkage at the lower end of the column.

16   Align the column plate seal with the column plate and secure the steering column to the floor pan.

17   Tighten the dashboard attaching nuts.

18   Connect the transmission shift indicator (if equipped).

19   Install the steering wheel referring to Section 15 or 16.

20   For 1970 – 1978 models, install the trim panel and ashtray.

21   Connect the battery cable. Raise the front end and check that the steering wheel is free to rotate from stop to stop without any lumpiness, sticking or binding. Check that the flexible coupling is not

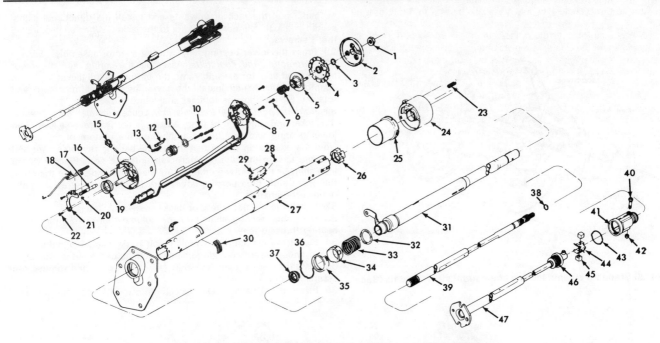

Fig. 11.19 Standard steering column components (Sec 26)

1 Shaft nut
2 Cover
3 Lock plate retaining ring
4 Lock plate
5 Cancelling cam
6 Bearing preload spring
7 Directional signal screws
8 Directional signal switch
9 Protector cover
10 Directional signal housing screws
11 Bearing thrust washer
12 Key warning switch

13 Switch clip
14 Directional signal housing
15 Ignition switch sector
16 Switch rack preload spring
17 Shaft lock bolt
18 Switch rod and rack assembly
19 Thrust cap
20 Shaft lock bolt washer
21 Shift lever detent plate
22 Detent plate screws
23 Shift lever spring

24 Gearshift lever housing
25 Shift shroud
26 Gearshift housing bearing
27 Mast jacket
28 Ignition switch screws
29 Ignition switch
30 Neutral safety or back-up switch retainers
31 Shift tube
32 Thrust spring washer
33 Shift tube thrust spring
34 Lower bearing adapter
35 Lower bearing reinforcement

36 Retainer
37 Lower bearing
38 Shaft stop ring
39 Steering shaft
40 Pot joint bolt
41 Nut
42 Pot joint cover
43 Seal retaining ring
44 Bearing spring
45 Bearing blocks
46 Pot joint seal
47 Intermediate shaft

distorted due to the pot joint bottoming in either direction.

26 Steering column (standard version) – dismantling and reassembly

1 Remove the four dash panel bracket to steering column screws and retain the bracket so that the mounting capsules will not be damaged.
2 Secure the column in a vise by gripping one set only of the weld nuts.
3 Remove the directional signal switch and lock cylinder, and the ignition key warning switch and the ignition switch as described previously.
4 On column shift models, drive out the upper shift lever pivot pin and remove the shift lever.
5 Remove the upper bearing and thrust washer.
6 Remove the 4 screws which attach the directional signal switch and ignition lock housing to the jacket; remove the housing assembly.
7 Take out the thrust cap from the lower side of the housing.
8 Lift the ignition switch actuating rod and rack assembly together with the shaft lock bolt and spring assembly from the housing.
9 Remove the shift gate.
10 Remove the ignition switch actuator sector through the lock cylinder hole by pushing on the block tooth sector with a rod or punch.
11 Remove the gearshift lever housing and shroud, or the transmission control lock tube housing and shroud, as applicable.
12 Remove the shift lever spring from the gearshift housing, or the lock tube spring, as applicable.
13 Pull the steering shaft from the lower end of the jacket assembly.
14 Remove the back-up switch or neutral safety switch (2 screws).

15 Remove the lower bearing retainer.
16 *Automatics and floorshifts:* Remove the lower bearing retainer, adaptor assembly, shift tube spring and washer. Press out the lower bearing by applying pressure to the outer race then slide out the shift tube assembly.
17 *Column shift (manual transmission):* Remove the lower bearing adaptor, bearing and first/reverse shift lever. Press out the lower bearing by applying pressure to the outer race. Remove 3 screws from the lower end bearing and slide out the shift tube assembly.
18 From the upper end of the mast jacket, remove the gearshift housing lower bearing.
19 Replace any worn components and commence reassembly by applying a thin coating of lithium soap grease to all friction surfaces, and then installing the sector into the turn signal housing. To do this, reach through the lock cylinder hole, place the sector onto the shaft using a blunt tool.
20 Install the shift gate onto the housing.
21 Insert the rack preload spring into the housing from the lower end so that both ends of the spring are attached to the housing.
22 Assemble the locking bolt to the crossover arm on the rack.
23 Insert the rack and lock bolt assembly into the housing (teeth upwards). Align the first tooth on the sector with the first tooth on the rack so that the block teeth will line up when the rack assembly is pushed right in.
24 Install the thrust cup into the housing.
25 Install the gearshift housing lower bearing, aligning the indentations with the projections in the jacket.
26 Install the shift lever spring into the housing.
27 Install the housing and shroud assemblies onto the mast jacket, rotating slightly to ensure proper seating in the bearing.
28 With the shift lever housing in position, and the gearshift housing

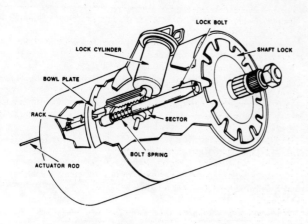

Fig. 11.20 Standard column locking and neutral start systems (Sec 26)

at 'park', pull the rack downwards and install the directional signal switch and lock cylinder housing onto the jacket. When seated, install the 4 screws.

29 Press the lower bearing fully into the adaptor assembly.

30 *Automatics and floorshifts:* Assemble the spring, and the lower bearing and adaptor assembly into the bottom of the jacket. Hold the adaptor in place then install the lower bearing reinforcement and retainer. Ensure that the retainer snaps into the slots.

31 *Column shift (manual transmission):* Loosely install the 3 screws in the jacket and shift tube bearing. Assemble the first/reverse lever, and lower bearing and adaptor assembly into the bottom of the jacket. Hold the adaptor in place then install the bearing reinforcement and retainer. Ensure that the retainer snaps into the slots. Place a 0.005 inch shim (feeler) between the first/reverse lever and spacer then turn the upper shift tube bearing down and tighten the 3 screws. Finally remove the shim.

32 Install the neutral safety or back-up switch.

33 Slide the steering shaft into the column then install the upper bearing thrust washer.

34 Install the ignition key warning switch, directional signal switch, lock cylinder assembly and ignition switch, as described previously.

35 Install the shift lever and shift lever pivot pin, then remove the assembly from the vise.

36 Install the 4 dash bracket to column screws and torque-tighten.

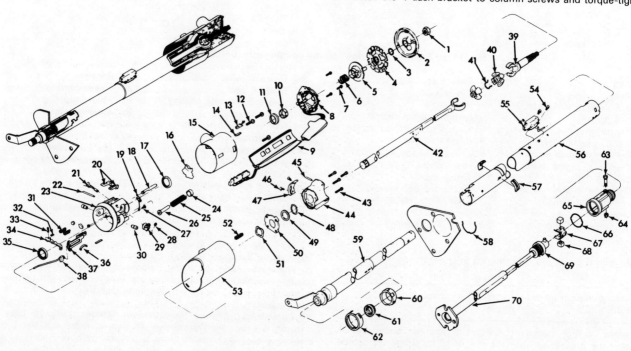

Fig. 11.21 Tilt steering column components (Sec 27)

1 Shaft nut	19 Lock bolt spring	37 Ignition switch rack	55 Ignition switch
2 Cover	20 Lock shoes	38 Ignition switch rod	56 Mast jacket
3 Lock plate retaining ring	21 Sector shaft	39 Upper steering shaft	57 Neutral-safety or back-up
4 Lock plate	22 Lock shoe pin	40 Centering spheres	switch retainers
5 Cancelling cam	23 Bearing housing	41 Centre sphere spring	58 Shift tube
6 Bearing preload spring	24 Tilt lever spring retainer	42 Lower steering shaft	59 Lower bearing adapter
7 Directional signal screws	25 Tilt lever spring	43 Screws	60 Lower bearing
8 Directional signal switch	26 Tilt lever spring guide	44 Bearing housing support	61 Lower bearing reinforcement
9 Protector cover	27 Lock bolt spring screw	45 Pin	62 Retainer
10 Upper bearing seat	28 Sector snap ring	46 Shift tube index plate screws	63 Pot joint bolt
11 Upper bearing race	29 Sector	47 Shift tube index plate	64 Nut
12 Turn signal housing screws	30 Bearing housing pivot pins	48 Support retaining ring	65 Pot joint cover
13 Key warning switch	31 Shoe release springs	49 Support thrust washer	66 Seal retaining ring
14 Switch clip	32 Spring	50 Support plate lock	67 Bearing spring
15 Directional signal housing	33 Shoe release lever pin	51 Support wave washer	68 Bearing blocks
16 Tilt lever opening shield	34 Shoe release lever	52 Gearshift lever spring	69 Pot joint seal
17 Upper bearing	35 Lower bearing	53 Gearshift lever housing	70 Intermediate shaft
18 Shaft lock bolt	36 Ignition switch rack spring	54 Ignition switch screws	

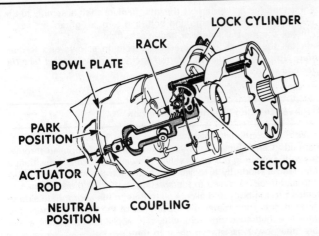

Fig. 11.22 Tilt column locking and neutral start systems (Sec 27)

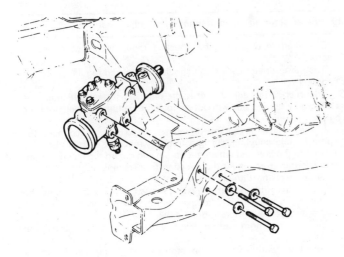

Fig. 11.23 Typical power steering gear mounting (Sec 30)

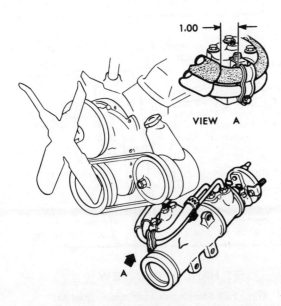

Fig. 11.24 Power steering hose routing (Sec 30)

27 Steering column (tilt version) – dismantling and reassembly

1   Initially follow the procedure given in paragraphs 1, 2 and 3 for dismantling of the standard version column.

2   Remove the tilt release lever then drive out the shift lever pivot pin and remove the shift lever from the housing.

3   Remove the directional signal housing (3 screws).

4   Install the tilt release lever and move the column to the highest position. Use a suitable screwdriver to remove the tilt lever spring retainer by pressing inwards approximately $\frac{3}{16}$ inch then turning $\frac{1}{8}$ turn (45°) counterclockwise until the ears align with the grooves in the housing.

5   Remove the pot joint to steering shaft clamp bolt then remove the intermediate shaft and pot joint assembly.

6   Push the upper shaft in sufficiently to remove the upper bearing inner race and seat. Pry off the lower bearing retainer and remove the bearing reinforcement, bearing and bearing adaptor assembly from the lower end of the mast jacket.

7   Withdraw the upper bearing housing pivot pins using a suitable nut and bolt (GM tool no J-21854-1 is recommended).

8   Install the tilt release lever and disengage the lock shoes then remove the bearing housing by pulling upwards to extend the rack fully down. Now move the housing to the left to disengage the ignition switch rack from the actuator rod.

9   Remove the steering shaft assembly from the upper end of the column, then the upper bearing seat and inner race.

10 Disassemble the shaft by removing the centering spheres and anti-lash spring.

11 Remove the transmission indicator wire, where applicable.

12 Remove the 4 screws retaining the shaft bearing housing support followed by the housing support. Remove the ignition switch actuator rod.

13 Using a suitable extractor, remove the shift tube (or transmission control lock tube – floorshift) from the lower end of the mast jacket.

14 Remove the bearing housing support lockplate by sliding out of the jacket notches and tipping it down towards the hub at the 12 o'clock position. Slide it under the jacket opening and remove the wave washer.

15 Remove the shift lever housing or lock tube housing from the mast jacket. Remove the shift lever spring by winding it up with pliers, then pulling it out. On floor change models the spring plunger has to be removed.

16 To disassemble the bearing housing, remove the tilt lever opening shield then take out the lock bolt spring by removing the retaining screw and moving the spring clockwise.

17 Remove the snap-ring from the sector driveshaft then use a small punch to lightly tap the driveshaft from the sector. Remove the driveshaft, sector, lockbolt, rack and rack spring.

18 Drive out the tilt release lever then remove the lever and spring. To relieve the load on the release lever, hold the shoes inwards and wedge a block between the top of the shoes (over the slots) and the bearing housing.

19 Drive out the lock shoe retaining pin then the lock shoe springs. **Note:** *With the tilt lever opening on the left and the shoes uppermost, the 4-slot shoe is on the left.*

20 If the bearings are to be replaced, remove the separator and balls. Carefully drive out the race from the housing, followed by the second race.

21 During the assembly procedure, all friction surfaces should be lightly smeared with lithium based grease.

22 Where dismantled, carefully press the bearing into the housing using a suitable sized socket.

23 Install the lockshoe springs, shoes and shoe pin, using a suitable rod (approx. 0.180 inch) for locating purposes.

24 Install the shoe release lever, spring and pin. To relieve the release lever load, hold the shoes inwards and wedge a block between the top of the shoes (over the slots) and bearing housing.

25 Install the sector driveshaft; lightly tap it on until the snap-ring can be installed.

26 Install the lockbolt and engage it with the sector cam surface then install the rack and spring. The block tooth on the rack must engage correctly in the sector. Install the tilt release lever.

27 Install the lockbolt spring. Torque-tighten the retaining screw.

28 Wind up the shift lever spring with pliers and install (push) it onto the housing. On floor shift models the plunger has to be installed.

29 Slide the gearshift lever housing onto the steering mast jacket.
30 Install the wave-washer for the bearing support lockplate.
31 Install the lockplate, working it into the notches in the jacket by tipping towards the housing hub at the 12 o'clock position and sliding it under the jacket opening. The lockplate can then be slid into the notches in the jacket.
32 Carefully install the shift tube into the lower end of the mast jacket, aligning the keyway in the tube with the key in the shift lever housing. The next part of the operation ideally requires the use of GM tool no J-23073 although by the judicious use of spacers, washers and a long bolt a suitable alternative can be made up. Install the tube as shown and pull the shift tube into the housing by rotating the outer nut. Do not exert any load on the end of the shift tube and ensure that the shift tube lever is aligned with the slotted opening at the lower end of the mast jacket.
33 Install the bearing support thrust washer and retaining ring by pulling the shift lever housing upwards to compress the wave washer.
34 Install the bearing support, aligning the 'V' in the support with the 'V' in the jacket. Insert the support to lockplate screws and torque-tighten.
35 Align the lower bearing adapter with the notches in the jacket then push the adapter into the lower end. Install the lower bearing, bearing reinforcement and retainer, ensuring that the slip is aligned with the slots in the reinforcement, jacket and adapter.
36 Install the centering spheres and anti-lash spring in the upper shaft then install the lower shaft from the same side of the spheres as the spring ends protrude.
37 Install the steering shaft assembly into the shift tube from the upper end, guiding the shaft carefully through the tube and bearing.
38 Install the ignition switch actuator rod through the shift lever housing and insert it in the bearing support slot. Extend the rack downwards from the housing.
39 Assemble the bearing housing over the steering shaft, engaging the rack over the end of the actuator rod.
40 Install the external release lever then hold the lock shoes in the disengaged position and assemble the bearing housing over the steering shaft until the pivot pin holes align. Now install the pivot pins.
41 Place the bearing housing in the fully up position then install the tilt lever spring guide, spring and spring retainer. Using a suitable screwdriver, push in the retainer and turn clockwise to engage in the housing.
42 Install the upper bearing inner race and seat.
43 Install the tilt lever opening shield.
44 Remove the tilt release lever, install the directional signal housing and torque-tighten the 3 retaining screws.
45 Install the tilt release lever and the shift lever, then drive in the shift lever pin.
46 Install the ignition key warning switch, lock cylinder, directional signal switch and ignition switch, as described previously.
47 Align the grooves across the upper end of the pot joint with the

steering shaft flat and assemble the intermediate shaft assembly to the upper shaft. Install the clamp and bolt, and torque-tighten.
48 Install the neutral safety or back-up switch.
49 Install the 4 dash panel bracket to column screws and torque-tighten. **Note**: *Ensure that the slotted openings in the bracket face the upper end of the column.*

28 Power steering – general description

1 With the optional power steering gear, hydraulic pressure is generated in an engine-driven vane type pump and supplied through hoses to the steering box spool valve. The valve is normally positioned in the neutral mode by a torsion bar but when the steering wheel is turned and force is applied to the steering shaft then the spool moves in relation to the body and allows oil to flow to the appropriate side of the piston nut. The greater the movement of the steering wheel, the greater the hydraulic pressure which is applied and therefore the greater the power assistance given to the drive.
2 Apart from the procedures given in the following sections, it is recommended that where any major fault develops, rectification is entrusted to a dealer or specialist in power steering systems.

29 Power steering – maintenance and adjustment

1 The fluid level should be checked regularly, as described in Chapter 1.
2 The pump drive belt tension should be checked regularly, refer to Chapter 1.
3 The over-center adjustment is the only adjustment which can be satisfactorily carried out without removing the steering gear from the vehicle.
4 If the vehicle is equipped with a tilt-column, disconnect the column flexible coupling. Using a torque wrench or a spring balance attached to the steering wheel nut obtain and record the steering shaft turning torque. Reconnect the coupling (if installed).
5 Disconnect the Pitman arm from the relay rod.
6 Loosen the Pitman shaft adjusting screw locknut and unscrew the adjuster screw out of the side cover as far as it will go.
7 Disconnect the battery ground cable.
8 Remove the horn button (already carried out on tilt column vehicles).
9 Turn the steering wheel from stop to stop through its full travel and then turn it to its center (wheels straight ahead) position.
10 Now check the combined ball/thrust bearing preload using a (pound/inch) torque wrench on the steering wheel nut and turning it a quarter turn through the center position in both directions. Take the highest reading. On vehicles equipped with a tilt column, subtract the

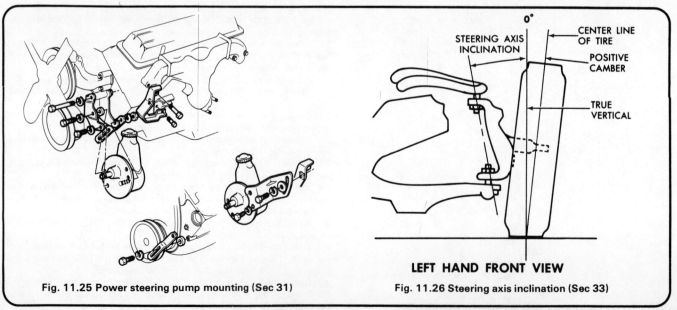

Fig. 11.25 Power steering pump mounting (Sec 31)

Fig. 11.26 Steering axis inclination (Sec 33)

turning torque recorded earlier when the coupling was disconnected.
11 Tighten the Pitman shaft adjusting screw in small increments rechecking the over-center preload between each adjustment until the total gear preload falls within that specified (see Specifications Section).
12 Tighten the adjuster screw locknut, install the Pitman arm, the horn button and reconnect the battery ground cable.

30 Power steering gear – removal and installation

1 The procedure is similar to that described previously for the manual type except that the hydraulic hoses must be disconnected from the steering gear housing.
2 Plug the ends of the hoses and the fluid inlet and outlet holes in the housing.
3 When installation is complete, bleed the system as described in Section 32.

31 Power steering pump – removal and installation

1 Disconnect the hydraulic hoses either from the pump or the steering gear and keep them in the raised position to prevent the fluid draining away until they can be plugged.
2 Remove the pump drive belt by loosening the pump mounts and pushing it in towards the engine.
3 Unscrew and remove the pump mounting bolts and braces and remove the pump.
4 To remove the pump pulley it will almost certainly require the use of a special extractor, the type depending upon the actual pulley fitted. Consult your dealer if the pulley is to be removed.
5 Installation is a reversal of removal but tighten the hose unions to the specified torque and then fill the fluid reservoir.
6 Prime the pump by turning the pulley in the reverse direction to that of normal rotation until air-bubbles cease to emerge from the fluid when observed through the reservoir filler cap.
7 Install the drive belt and tension it as described in Chapter 1.
8 Bleed the system as described in Section 32 of this Chapter.

32 Power steering hydraulic system – bleeding

1 This is not a routine operation and will normally only be required when the system has been dismantled and reassembled.
2 Fill the reservoir to its correct level with fluid of recommended type, and allow it to remain undisturbed for at least 2 minutes.
3 Start the engine and run it for two or three seconds only. Check the reservoir fluid level and top-up if necessary.
4 Repeat the operations described in the preceding paragraph until the fluid level remains constant.
5 Raise the front of the vehicle until the wheels are clear of the ground.
6 Start the engine and increase its speed to about 1500 rpm. Now turn the steering wheel gently from stop-to-stop. Check the reservoir fluid level adding some if necessary.
7 Lower the vehicle to the ground and with the engine still running move the vehicle forward sufficiently to obtain full right lock followed by full left lock. Re-check the fluid level. If the fluid in the reservoir is extremely foamy, allow the vehicle to stand for a few minutes with the engine switched off and then repeat the previous operations.
8 Air in the power steering system is often indicated by a noisy pump but a low fluid level can also cause this.

33 Front wheel alignment and steering angles

1 Accurate front wheel alignment is essential for good steering and slow tire wear. Before considering the steering angles; check that the tires are correctly inflated, that the front wheels are not buckled, the hub bearings are not worn or incorrectly adjusted and that the steering linkage is in good order, without slackness or wear at the joints.
2 Wheel alignment consists of four factors:
   Camber which is the angle at which the front wheels are set from the vertical when viewed from the front of the car. Positive camber is the amount (in degrees) that the wheels are tilted outwards at the top from the vertical.
   Caster is the angle between the steering axis and a vertical line when viewed from each side of the car. Positive caster is when the

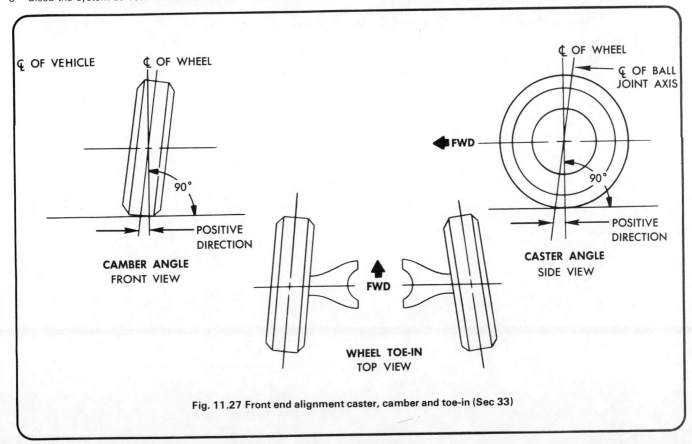

Fig. 11.27 Front end alignment caster, camber and toe-in (Sec 33)

steering axis is inclined rearward.

   Steering axis inclination is the angle, when viewed from the front of the car, between the vertical and an imaginary line drawn between the upper and lower suspension control arm balljoints.

   Toe-in is the amount by which the distance between the front inside edges of the wheels (measured at hub height) is less than the diametrically opposite distance measured between the rear inside edges of the front wheels.

3   On all other models, the caster and camber angles are set by means of shims inserted between the upper control arm shaft and the frame bracket.

4   Due to the need for special gauges and equipment, it is not advised that camber or caster angles should be adjusted at home.

5   To adjust the toe-in (which should only be done after establishing that caster and camber are correct), obtain or make a toe-in gauge. Once can be made up from a length of tubing, cranked to clear the oil pan and clutch or torque converter housing and having a screw and locknut at one end.

6   Use a gauge to measure the distance between the two inner wheel rims at hub height at the rear of the wheels.

7   Push the vehicle to rotate the wheel through 180° (half a turn) and then measure the distance between the inner wheel rims at hub height at the front of the wheels ('Y').

8   The distance between the two measurements is the toe-in (where the first measurement is larger than the second). Refer to the specifications for the correct value.

9   Toe-in or toe-out can be altered by increasing or decreasing the length of the tie-rods. For 1975 models, the tie-rods must be decreased in length to increase the toe-in; for other models the tie-rod length must be increased to increase the toe-in. Where any adjustment is made, the screwed sleeves should be turned by equal amounts at each side.

10 Where new tie-rods, tie-rod ends or steering components have been installed, always commence adjustment with the overall lengths of the tie-rods exactly equal. Take the measurements from the balljoint centers and have the wheels and steering wheel in the straight-ahead position.

34 Wheels and tires

1   The wheels are of pressed steel type and the tires may be conventional, radial or bias belted. Never mix tires of different construction on the same axle.

2   Check the tire pressures weekly, including the spare, preferably when the tires are cold, first thing in the morning.

3   The wheel nuts should be tightened to the specified torque, and it is an advantage if a smear of grease is applied to the wheel stud threads.

4   Every 7500 miles, the wheels should be moved round the vehicle in order to even out the tire tread wear. To do this, remove each wheel in turn, clean it thoroughly (both sides) and remove any stones which may be embedded in the tread. Check the tread wear pattern which will indicate any mechanical or adjustment faults in the suspension or steering components. Examine the wheel bolt holes for elongation or wear. If such conditions are found, replace the wheel.

5   Replacement of the tires should be carried out when the thickness of the tread pattern is worn to a minimum of $\frac{1}{16}$ inch or the wear indicators (if incorporated) are visible.

6   The method of moving the tires depends on whether the spare (5th) wheel is brought into the rotational pattern, and to the type off construction of the tire. With radial ply tires, move them front to rear on the same side only.

7   The type of tire and inflation pressures are recorded on a sticker located on the vehicle door and the specification varies according to the particular vehicle model and tires fitted. Always adjust the front and rear tire pressures after moving the wheels round as previously described.

8   Have all wheels balanced initially and again half way through the useful life of the tires.

Chapter 12 Bodywork

Contents

Specifications

Overall dimensions

1970

Overall length	188.0 in
Overall width	74.4 in
Height	50.1 in
Wheelbase	108.0 in

1971 – 1972
As 1970 models except:

Height	50.5 in

1973
As 1970 models except:

Overall length	188.5 in
Height	49.1 in

1974 – 1978
As 1970 models except:

Overall length	195.4 in
Height	49.1 in

1979 – 1980

Overall length	197.6 in
Overall width	74.5 in
Height	49.2 in
Wheelbase	108.0 in

Curb weights*

1970	3313 lbs
1971	3313 lbs
1972	3310 lbs
1973	3354 lbs
1974	3627 lbs
1975	3733 lbs
1976	3679 lbs
1977	3663 lbs
1978	3612 lbs
1979	3610 lbs
1980	3545 lbs

*With base V-8 engine and standard accessories.

1 General description

1 The Camaro has been available with many trim options, all variations of the basic 2-door body style. Cosmetic body packages such as the Type LT, Rally Sport or Berlinetta have slight body component modifications which are dealt with separately in this Chapter where appropriate.

2 Certain body panels which are particularly vulnerable to accident damage can be replaced by unbolting them and installing replacement items. These panels include the fenders, inner fender skirts, radiator support panel, grille, bumper and trunk.

2 Maintenance – bodywork and underframe

1 The condition of your vehicle's bodywork is of considerable importance as it is on this that the resale value will mainly depend. It is much more difficult to repair neglected bodywork than to replace mechanical assemblies. The hidden portions of the body, such as the wheel arches, fender skirts, the underframe and the engine compartment are equally important, although obviously not requiring such frequent attention as the immediately visible paint.

2 Once a year or every 12 000 miles it is a sound scheme to visit your local dealer and have the underside of the body steam cleaned. All traces of dirt and oil will be removed and the underside can then be inspected carefully for rust, damaged hydraulic pipes, frayed electrical wiring and similar trouble areas. The front suspension should be greased on completion of this job.

3 At the same time, clean the engine and the engine compartment either using a steam cleaner or a water-soluble cleaner.

4 The wheel arches and fender skirts should be given particular attention as undercoating can easily come away here and stones and dirt thrown up from the wheels can soon cause the paint to chip and flake, and so allow rust to set in. If rust is found, clean down to the bare metal and apply an anti-rust paint.

5 The bodywork should be washed once a week or when dirty. Thoroughly wet the vehicle to soften the dirt and then wash down with a soft sponge and plenty of clean water. If the surplus dirt is not washed off very gently, in time it will wear the paint down.

6 Spots of tar or bitumen coating thrown up from the road surfaces are best removed with a cloth soaked in a cleaner made especially for this purpose.

7 Once every six months, or more frequently depending on the weather conditions, give the bodywork and chrome trim a thoroughly good wax polish. If a chrome cleaner is used to remove rust on any of the vehicle's plated parts, remember that the cleaner can also remove part of the chrome, so use it sparingly.

3 Maintenance – upholstery and carpets

1 Remove the carpets or mats and thoroughly vacuum clean the interior of the vehicle every three months or more frequently if necessary.

2 Beat out the carpets and vacuum clean them if they are very dirty. If the upholstery is soiled apply an upholstery cleaner with a damp sponge and wipe off with a clean dry cloth.

3 Consult your local dealer or auto parts store for cleaners made especially for newer automotive upholstery fabrics. Always test the cleaner in an inconspicuous place.

4 Maintenance – roof covering

Under no circumstances try to clean any external vinyl roof covering with detergents, caustic soap or spirit cleaners. Plain soap and water is all that is required, with a soft brush to clean dirt that may be ingrained. Wash the covering as frequently as the rest of the vehicle.

5 Minor body damage – repair

See photo sequence on pages 342 and 343.

Repair of minor scratches in the vehicle's bodywork

If the scratch is very superficial, and does not penetrate to the metal of the bodywork, repair is very simple. Lightly rub the area of the scratch with a paintwork renovator, or a very fine cutting paste, to remove loose paint from the scratch and to clear the surrounding bodywork of wax polish. Rinse the area with clean water.

Apply touch-up paint to the scratch using a thin paint brush; continue to apply thin layers of paint until the surface of the paint in the scratch is level with the surrounding paintwork. Allow the new paint at least two weeks to harden; then blend it into the surrounding paintwork by rubbing the paintwork, in the scratch area, with a paintwork renovator or a very fine cutting paste. Finally, apply wax polish.

An alternative to painting over the scratch is to use a paint transfer. Use the same preparation for the affected area, then simply pick a patch of a suitable size to cover the scratch completely. Hold the patch against the scratch and burnish its backing paper; the paper will adhere to the paintwork, freeing itself from the backing paper at the same time. Polish the affected area to blend the patch into the surrounding paintwork.

Where the scratch has penetrated right through to the metal of the bodywork, causing the metal to rust, a different repair technique is required. Remove any loose rust from the bottom of the scratch with a penknife, then apply rust inhibiting paint to prevent the formation of rust in the future. Using a rubber or nylon applicator fill the scratch with bodystopper paste. If required, this paste can be mixed with cellulose thinners to provide a very thin paste which is ideal for filling narrow scratches. Before the stopper-paste in the scratch hardens, wrap a piece of smooth cotton rag around the top of a finger. Dip the finger in cellulose thinners and then quickly sweep it across the surface of the stopper-paste in the scratch; this will ensure that the surface of the stopper-paste is slightly hollowed. The scratch can now be painted over as described earlier in this Section.

Repair of dents in the vehicle's bodywork

When deep denting of the vehicle's bodywork has taken place, the first task is to pull the dent out, until the affected bodywork almost attains its original shape. There is little point in trying to restore the original shape completely, as the metal in the damaged area will have stretched on impact and cannot be reshaped fully to its original contour. It is better to bring the level of the dent up to a point which is about $\frac{1}{8}$ in (3 mm) below the level of the surrounding bodywork. In cases where the dent is very shallow anyway, it is not worth trying to pull it out at all.

If the underside of the dent is accessible, it can be hammered out gently from behind, using a mallet with a wooden or plastic head. Whilst doing this, hold a suitable block of wood firmly against the impact from the hammer blows and thus prevent a large area of the bodywork from being 'belled-out'.

Should the dent be in a section of the bodywork which has double skin or some other factor making it inaccessible from behind, a different technique is called for. Drill several small holes through the metal inside the area – particularly in the deeper section. Then screw long self-tapping screws into the holes just sufficiently for them to gain a good purchase in the metal. Now the dent can be pulled out by pulling on the protruding heads of the screws with a pair of pliers.

The next stage of the repair is the removal of the paint from the damaged area, and from an inch or so of the surrounding 'sound' bodywork. This is accomplished most easily by using a wire brush or abrasive pad on a power drill, although it can be done just as effectively by hand using sheets of sandpaper. To complete the preparation for filling, score the surface of the bare metal with a screwdriver or the tang of a file, or alternatively, drill small holes in the affected area. This will provide a really good 'key' for the filler paste.

To complete the repair see the Section on filling and re-spraying.

Repair of rust holes or gashes in the vehicle's bodywork

Remove all paint from the affected area and from an inch or so of the surrounding 'sound' bodywork, using an abrasive pad or a wire brush on a power drill. If these are not available a few sheets of sandpaper will do the job just as effectively. With the paint removed you will be able to gauge the severity of the corrosion and therefore decide whether to renew the whole panel (if this is possible) or to repair the affected area. New body panels are not as expensive as most people think and it is often quicker and more satisfactory to fit a new panel than to attempt to repair large areas of corrosion.

Remove all fittings from the affected area except those which will act as a guide to the original shape of the damaged bodywork (eg headlamp shells etc). Then, using tin snips or a hacksaw blade, remove all loose metal and any other metal badly affected by corrosion. Hammer the edges of the hole inwards in order to create a slight depression for the filler paste.

Wire brush the affected area to remove the powdery rust from the surface of the remaining metal. Paint the affected area with rust inhibiting paint; if the back of the rusted area is accessible treat this also.

Before filling can take place it will be necessary to block the hole in some way. This can be achieved by the use of Zinc gauze or Aluminum tape.

Zinc gauze is probably the best material to use for a large hole. Cut a piece to the approximate size and shape of the hole to be filled, then position it in the hole so that its edges are below the level of the surrounding bodywork. It can be retained in position by several blobs of filler paste around its periphery.

Aluminum tape should be used for small or very narrow holes. Pull a piece off the roll and trim it to the approximate size and shape required, then pull off the backing paper (if used) and stick the tape over the hole; it can be overlapped if the thickness of one piece is insufficient. Burnish down the edges of the tape with the handle of a screwdriver or similar, to ensure that the tape is securely attached to the metal underneath.

Having blocked off the hole the affected area must now be filled and sprayed – see Section on bodywork fitting and re-spraying.

Bodywork repairs – filling and re-spraying

Before using this Section, see the Sections on dent, deep scratch, rust holes and gash repairs.

Many types of bodyfiller are available, but generally speaking those proprietary kits which contain a tin of filler paste and a tube of resin hardener are best for this type of repair. A wide, flexible plastic or nylon applicator will be found invaluable for imparting a smooth and well contoured finish to the surface of the filler.

Mix up a little filler on a clean piece of card or board – measure the hardener carefully (follow the maker's instructions on the pack) otherwise the filler will set too rapidly or too slowly.

Using the applicator apply the filler paste to the prepared area; draw the applicator across the surface of the filler to achieve the correct contour and to level the filler surface. As soon as a contour that approximates the correct one is achieved, stop working the paste – if you carry on too long the paste will become sticky and begin to 'pick up' on the applicator. Continue to add thin layers of filler paste at twenty-minute intervals until the level of the filler is just proud of the surrounding bodywork.

Once the filler has hardened, excess can be removed using a metal plane or file. From then on, progressively finer grades of sandpaper should be used, starting with a 40 grade production paper and finishing with 400 grade wet-and-dry paper. Always wrap the sandpaper around a flat rubber, cork or wooden block – otherwise the surface of the filler will not be completely flat. During the smoothing of the filler surface the wet-and-dry paper should be periodically rinsed in water. This will ensure that a very smooth finish is imparted to the filler at the final stage.

At this stage the 'repair area' should be surrounded by a ring of bare metal, which in turn should be encircled by the finely 'feathered' edge of the good paintwork. Rinse the repair area with clean water, until all of the dust produced by the rubbing-down operation has gone.

Spray the whole repair area with a light coat of primer – this will show up any imperfections in the surface of the filler. Repair these imperfections with fresh filler paste or bodystopper, and once more smooth the surface with sandpaper. If bodystopper is used, it can be mixed with cellulose thinners to form a really thin paste which is ideal for filling small holes. Repeat this spray and repair procedure until you are satisfied that the surface of the filler, and the feathered edge of the paintwork are perfect. Clean the repair area with clean water and allow to dry fully.

The repair area is now ready for final spraying. Paint spraying must be carried out in warm, dry, windless and dust free atmosphere. This condition can be created artificially if you have access to a large indoor working area, but if you are forced to work in the open, you will have to pick your day very carefully. If you are working indoors, dousing the floor in the work area with water will help to settle the dust which would otherwise be in the atmosphere. If the repair area is confined to one body panel, mask off the surrounding panels; this will help to minimise the effects of a slight mis-match in paint colours. Bodywork fittings (eg chrome strips, door handles etc) will also need to be masked off. Use genuine masking tape and several thicknesses of newspaper for the masking operations.

Before commencing to spray, agitate the aerosol can thoroughly, then spray a test area (an old tin, or similar) until the technique is mastered. Cover the repair area with a thick coat of primer; the thickness should be built up using several thin layers of paint rather than one thick one. Using 400 grade wet-and-dry paper, rub down the surface of the primer until it is really smooth. While doing this, the work area should be thoroughly doused with water, and the wet-and-dry paper periodically rinsed in water. Allow to dry before spraying on more paint.

Spray on the top coat, again building up the thickness by using several thin layers of paint. Start spraying in the center of the repair area and then using a circular motion, work outwards until the whole repair area and about 2 inches of the surrounding original paintwork is covered. Remove all masking material 10 to 15 minutes after spraying on the final coat of paint. Allow the new paint at least two weeks to harden, then, using a paintwork renovator or a very fine cutting paste, blend the edges of the paint into the existing paintwork. Finally, apply wax polish.

---

6 Bodywork and frame repairs – major damage

1   Major damage must be repaired by competent mechanics with the necessary welding and hydraulic straightening equipment.
2   If the damage has been serious it is vital that the frame is checked for correct alignment as otherwise the handling of the vehicle will suffer and many other faults – such as excessive tire wear, and wear in the transmission and steering – may occur.
3   There is a special body jig which most body repair shops have and to ensure that all is correct it is important that this jig be used for all major repair work.

---

7 Hood – maintenance and adjustments

1   As a safety measure, a protruding adjustable screw and nut is located at each side of the cowl area, at the rear of the hood. This bolt must be adjusted to a height of exactly one inch. At this height the head of the bolt will fit into an opening provided in the inner hood reinforcement. The purpose of this bolt is to prevent the hood from riding into the windshield in the event of a front end collision (photo).
2   To prevent engine compartment fumes from being pulled into the car interior through the cowl vent it is important that the hood be properly adjusted and sealed at the cowl area. The alignment of the hood is controlled by the position of the hood hinges and the height of

7.1 Hood safety catch bolts are used at each side of the hood, near the base of the windshield. The bolts must extend 1-inch from the cowling

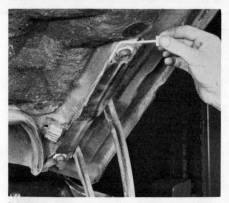

8.1 Use a scribe, felt pen or paint to mark the position of the hinge plate on the underside of the hood

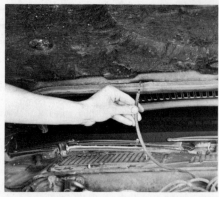

8.3 Disconnect the windshield washer tubes from the hood

8.4 Removing the hinge bolts going into the hood. An assistant should be supporting the hood at this time

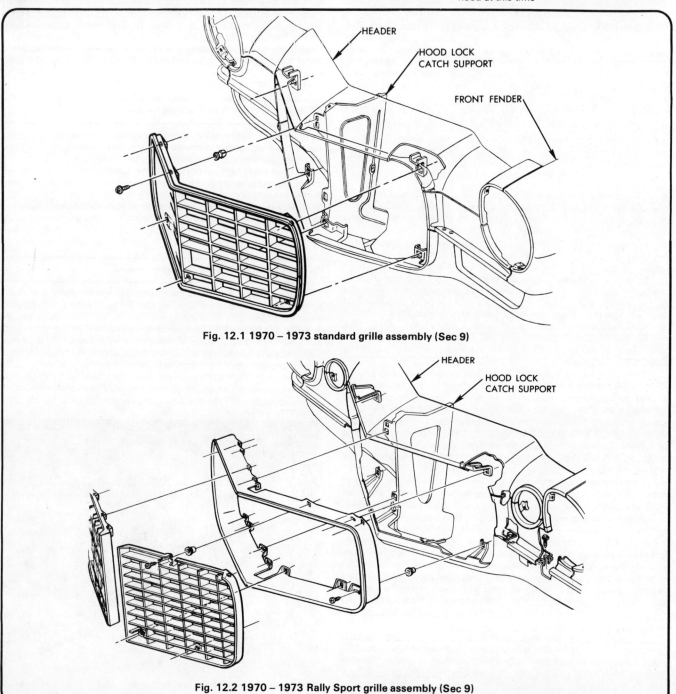

Fig. 12.1 1970 – 1973 standard grille assembly (Sec 9)

Fig. 12.2 1970 – 1973 Rally Sport grille assembly (Sec 9)

the two bumpers located at each side of the radiator support. The hood is adjusted as follows:

   a) *Scribe a line around the entire hinge plate to be repositioned. This will enable you to judge the amount of movement.*

   b) *Loosen the appropriate screws on the hood hinge to be adjusted and move the hood into the correct alignment. Move the hood only a little at a time. Tighten the hinge screws and carefully lower the hood to check the position.*

   c) *Adjust the hood bumpers on the radiator support so that the hood, when closed, is flush with the fender and grille top surfaces.*

   d) *The hood catch and lock assembly is adjustable to provide a positive closing of the hood. The hood catch assembly on the radiator support section has slotted mounting holes to allow the catch to be moved into alignment with the hood lock bolt. The lock bolt on the hood can be lengthened or shortened to engage with the catch. When closed properly the hood bumpers should be slightly compressed.*

3   The catch and lock assembly, as well as the hinges should be periodically lubricated to prevent sticking or jamming.

8   Hood – removal and installation

1   The hood assembly may be removed with or without the hinges. Whichever method is chosen, it is important to scribe a line around the hinge mounting on the hood or the body to replace the assembly in the same location (photo).
2   Use blankets or cloths to cover the cowl area of the body and the fenders. This will protect the body and paint as the hood is lifted free of the car.
3   Disconnect the windshield washer hoses from the hood (photo).
4   With the help of an assistant to take the weight of the hood, remove the appropriate screws (photo).
5   Carefully lift the hood off the car.
6   When installing the hood, again cover the bodywork and then lift the hood into position.
7   Install all of the mounting screws loosely and position the hood in its original position, using th scribe marks as a guide.
8   Tighten the screws and check the hood alignment. Connect windshield washer hoses.

9   Grille – removal and installation

1970 – 1973 standard
1   Remove the bumper face bar (see Section 10).
2   Remove the screws securing the grille to the body and remove the grille.
3   Installation is a reversal of removal.

1970 – 1973 Rally Sport
4   Remove the screws from either left or right grille assembly and remove the grille.
5   The cast filler panel surrounding the grille panels can be removed by unbolting it from the body.
6   Installation is a reversal of removal.

1974 – 1980
7   The upper (main) grille is removed by removing the screws attaching the grille to the header panel.
8   The smaller, lower grille is attached to the valance panel with five attaching screws.

10 Bumper (front) – removal and installation

1970 – 1972 Standard
1   The bumper or face bar on these models, is attached to brackets near the parking lights. Remove the nuts on the inside of the bumper where it meets the outer brackets.

2   Remove the nuts and bolts from the inner brackets.
3   Remove the bolts which mount the bumper guards to the body and lift the bumper away from the car. You must disengage one side from its outer bracket and then lower the other end of the bumper. Do not scratch the paint as this is done.
4   The outer brackets can be removed from inside the engine compartment and the inner bumper bracket bolts are accessible after the parking light assembly is removed from the vehicle.

1970 – 1972 Rally Sport
5   Remove the bolts from the chrome face bar and remove the face bar(s).
6   The urethane bumper/grille assembly can be removed as an assembly by removing the mounting bolts.
7   The outer brackets for the face bars can be removed by using a socket wrench from the inside of the engine compartment.
8   The inner bracket bolts are accessible by using a flex socket through the bracket body opening.

1973 Standard
9   Remove the bolts securing the bumper bracket assembly to the radiator support.
10 Remove the lower bolts connecting the bumper brace metal to the bumper face bar.
11 Remove the lower guard bolts which go into the body sheet metal valance. Remove the bumper assembly.

1973 Rally Sport
12 The outer face bars are secured to brackets with bolts in a similar manner to the earlier models described above.
13 To remove the center face bar the two-piece grille must first be removed. These grille panels are held in place with screws.
14 Remove the bolts securing the upper and lower face bars to the face guard braces. Then remove the bolts going into the side brackets and remove center face bar.

1974 – 1977
15 Remove the horn assemblies from the top of the grille cavity.
16 Remove the windshield washer reservoir.
17 Remove the two bolts (one at each side) which connects the bumper frame brace to the top of the support frame.
18 Remove the four bolts attaching the crossmember to the bumper brackets. Remove the crossmember.
19 Raise the vehicle for better access underneath and remove the screws attaching the sheet metal valance panel to the fender extensions, hoodlock support and radiator support. Remove the

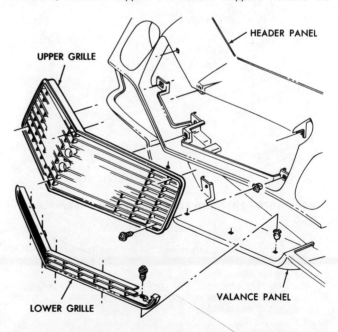

Fig. 12.3 1974 – 1980 grille assembly (Sec 9)

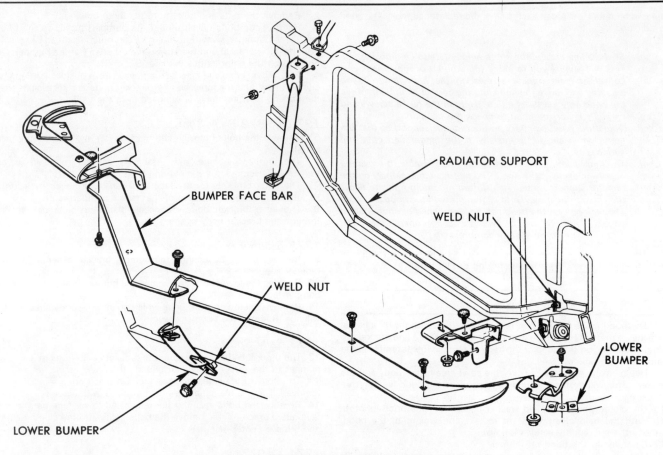

Fig. 12.4 1970 – 1972 standard front bumper assembly (Sec 10)

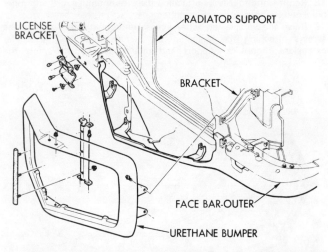

Fig. 12.5 1970 – 1972 Rally Sport front bumper assembly (Sec 10)

valance.

20 With the bumper supported, remove the four bumper bracket to frame bolts. There are two bolts on each side of the bumper. Remove the bumper assembly.

21 If the bumper assembly is to be disassembled, make alignment marks on bumper brackets and spring assemblies to properly align the components on reassembly.

1978 – 1980

22 Remove the headlamp bezels. Do not accidently turn the headlight adjusting screws to remove this decorative bezel.

23 Remove the parking light assemblies, disconnecting the wires to the parking lights and headlights.

24 Working through the headlight openings, remove the six bolts attaching the cover support to the fender extensions.

25 Remove the upper and lower grilles (Section 9).

26 Working through the grille opening, remove the three screws attaching the cover to the impact bar.

27 Remove the two bolts at the hood latch support which go into the bumper cover.

28 Remove the four bolts attaching the cover support brackets to the radiator support.

29 Raise the vehicle for better access underneath.

30 Remove the three screws attaching the cover to the impact bar.

31 Remove the six nuts attaching the cover to the fender extensions.

32 The cover can now be removed from the impact bars and brackets.

11 Bumper (rear) – removal and installation

1970 – 1973

1 Near the center of the vehicle, remove the bolts from beneath the bumper. Remove the bumper guards if equipped.

2 Remove the bolts from inside the trunk and remove the bumper.

1974 – 1977

3 From inside the trunk, remove the four bolts connecting the bumper bracket to the body rails.

4 Raise the vehicle for better access and support the bumper assembly.

5 Remove the four lower bolts attaching the bumper brackets to the body and remove the bumper assembly.

6 If the bumper brackets and spring assemblies are to be disas-

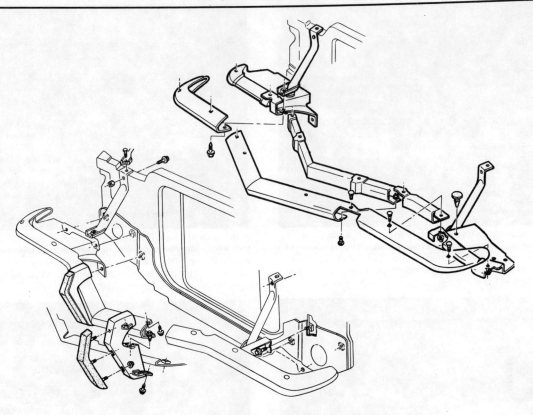

Fig. 12.6 1973 standard front bumper assembly (Sec 10)

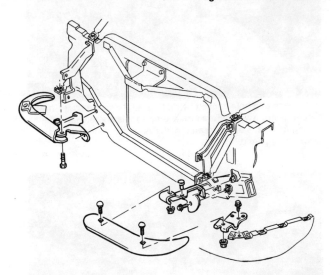

Fig. 12.7 Rally Sport front bumper outer face bars (Sec 10)

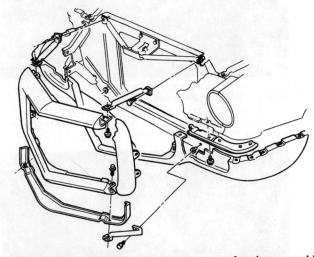

Fig. 12.8 1973 Rally Sport front bumper center face bar assembly (Sec 10)

sembled, scribe alignment marks to aid in proper alignment upon reassembly.

1978 – 1980

7   Remove the four nuts (inside the trunk) and two screws retaining the cover bar moldings to the rear quarter panel.

8   Disconnect the wires to the license plate light.

9   Raise the vehicle for better access and remove the four nuts attaching the bumper to the vehicle.

10 Lower the vehicle and remove the remaining four nuts attaching the bumper to the vehicle. These are located inside the trunk.

11 Remove the bumper.

12 If the cover is to be removed from the bumper assembly, it will be necessary to drill out the rivets which secure the cover to the impact bar.

12   Front fenders and skirt – removal, adjustment and installation

1   Disconnect the negative battery cable. If the right hand fender is being moved, disconnect both battery cables and remove the battery.

2   Raise the vehicle and remove the wheel.

3   To protect the paint on the adjoining body panels it is a good idea to apply tape at the edge of the door and outer surfaces of the front header panel. Make sure the tape itself does not cause the paint to peel or chip.

4   Remove the front bumper as detailed in Section 10.

5   Remove the hood with the hinges attached. If the inner fender panel is being replaced with a new one, alignment marks for the hood hinges will not be needed. See Section 8.

6   Disconnect all cables, wiring harness clips, windshield washer

This sequence of photographs deals with the repair of the dent and paintwork damage shown in this photo. The procedure will be similar for the repair of a hole. It should be noted that the procedures given here are simplified – more explicit instructions will be found in the text

In the case of a dent the first job – after removing surrounding trim – is to hammer out the dent where access is possible. This will minimise filling. Here, the large dent having been hammered out, the damaged area is being made slightly concave

Now all paint must be removed from the damaged area, by rubbing with coarse abrasive paper. Alternatively, a wire brush or abrasive pad can be used in a power drill. Where the repair area meets good paintwork, the edge of the paintwork should be 'feathered', using a finer grade of abrasive paper

In the case of a hole caused by rusting, all damaged sheet-metal should be cut away before proceeding to this stage. Here, the damaged area is being treated with rust remover and inhibitor before being filled

Mix the body filler according to its manufacturer's instructions. In the case of corrosion damage, it will be necessary to block off any large holes before filling – this can be done with aluminium or plastic mesh, or aluminium tape. Make sure the area is absolutely clean before ...

... applying the filler. Filler should be applied with a flexible applicator, as shown, for best results; the wooden spatula being used for confined areas. Apply thin layers of filler at 20-minute intervals, until the surface of the filler is slightly proud of the surrounding bodywork

Initial shaping can be done with a Surform plane or Dreadnought file. Then, using progressively finer grades of wet-and-dry paper, wrapped around a sanding block, and copious amounts of clean water, rub down the filler until really smooth and flat. Again, feather the edges of adjoining paintwork

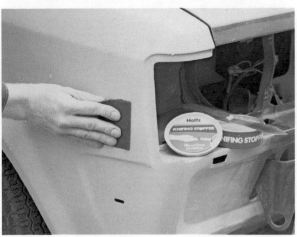

Again, using plenty of water, rub down the primer with a fine grade wet-and-dry paper (400 grade is probably best) until it is really smooth and well blended into the surrounding paintwork. Any remaining imperfections can now be filled by carefully applied knifing stopper paste

The top coat can now be applied. When working out of doors, pick a dry, warm and wind-free day. Ensure surrounding areas are protected from over-spray. Agitate the aerosol thoroughly, then spray the centre of the repair area, working outwards with a circular motion. Apply the paint as several thin coats

The whole repair area can now be sprayed or brush-painted with primer. If spraying, ensure adjoining areas are protected from over-spray. Note that at least one inch of the surrounding sound paintwork should be coated with primer. Primer has a 'thick' consistency, so will find small imperfections

When the stopper has hardened, rub down the repair area again before applying the final coat of primer. Before rubbing down this last coat of primer, ensure the repair area is blemish-free — use more stopper if necessary. To ensure that the surface of the primer is really smooth use some finishing compound

After a period of about two weeks, which the paint needs to harden fully, the surface of the repaired area can be 'cut' with a mild cutting compound prior to wax polishing. When carrying out bodywork repairs, remember that the quality of the finished job is proportional to the time and effort expended

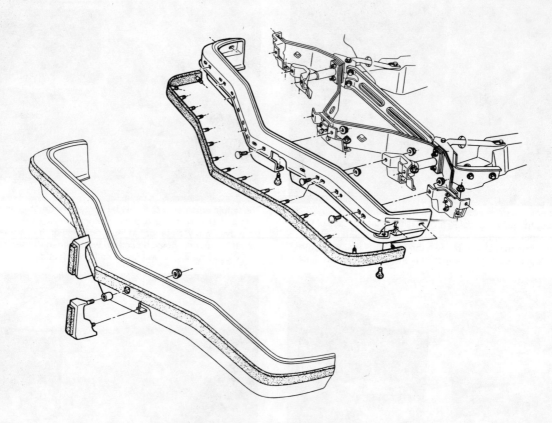

Fig. 12.9 1974 – 1977 front bumper assembly (Sec 10)

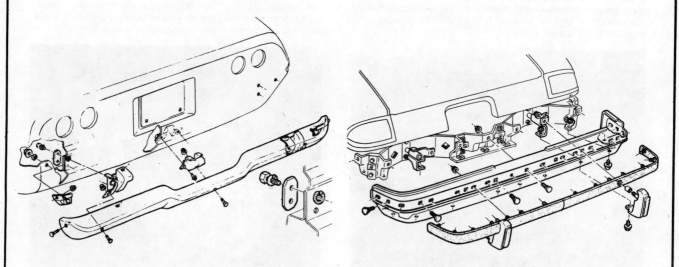

Fig. 12.10 1970 – 1973 rear bumper assembly (Sec 11)

Fig. 12.11 1974 – 1977 rear bumper assembly (Sec 11)

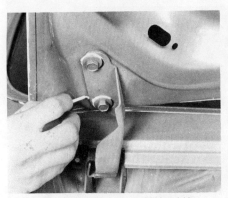

14.3 Like the hood, the trunk lid should be marked around the hinges for proper repositioning

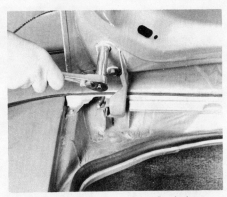

14.4A Removing the hinge securing bolts

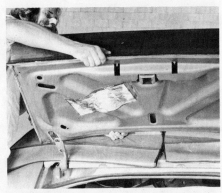

14.4B It may take two people to lift the trunk lid away from the body once the four bolts are removed

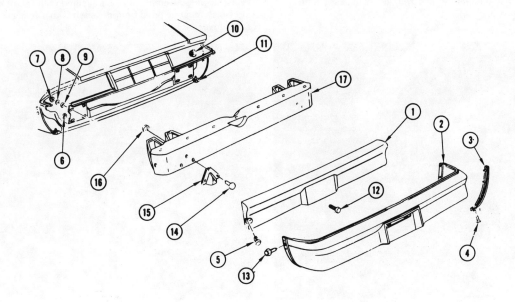

Fig. 12.12 1978 – 1980 rear bumper assembly (Sec 11)

1	Cushion	6	Washer	10	Nut	14	Bolt
2	Cover	7	Nut	11	Nut	15	Bracket
3	Molding ass	8	Nut	12	Bolt	16	Nut
4	Bolt	9	Washer	13	Screw	17	Bar ass.
5	Bolt						

reservoir, battery tray, etc. from the inner fender panels. Identify all wires and hoses to aid in reassembly.

7   Disconnect the header panel, filler panels (one on each side) and lower valance panel where they meet the front of each fender.

8   Remove the fender brace.

9   Remove the headlamp bezel, headlamp and two retainer support screws. See Chapter 10.

10   Remove the radio antenna if applicable.

11   Disconnect the wiring to the fender side marker light.

12   Begin removing the screws retaining the fender to the skirt, cowl, filler panel and rocker panel. Note any shims used to align the fender. Leave one or two forward and aft screws intact to support the assembly until the fender can be lifted free of the vehicle.

13   When installing the fender, guide it first into position at the bottom, adjacent to the door.

14   Install the original number of shims at the screw locations at the rocker panel and cowl. Install all the other attaching screws loosely and adjust the fender with the appropriate number of shims. Tighten the cowl and rocker panel screws, followed by the remaining screws.

15   Install the remaining components in reverse order of disassembly. The hood should be adjusted referring to Section 7.

13   Hood latch and lock assemblies – removal and installation

1   To maintain the proper alignment of the catch and lock, open the hood and scribe a line around the lock plate on the hood and the catch plate mechanism on the support brace.

16.2 The two retaining nuts for the lock cylinder are accessible from the inside of the trunk

18.1 The window crank handle is secured to the shaft with a retaining clip which must be pried from the shaft with a special tool or a screwdriver

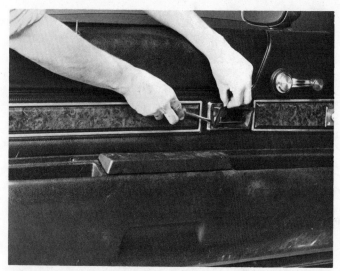

18.2 Before the latch lever can be removed, the decorative bezel must be pried from the trim panel

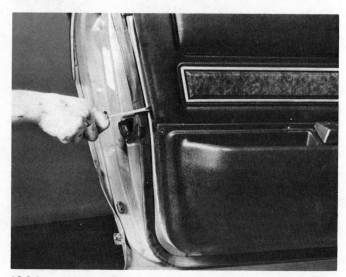

18.8 A screwdriver is used to gently pry the trim panel away from the door

2   Remove the catch plate assembly by removing the screws retaining the catch to the radiator support, center support and tie bar.
3   Remove the screws retaining the lock plate to the inside of the hood.
4   Upon reinstallation, line up the identifying scribe marks on both the catch plate and the lock plate and tighten the attaching screws. For further information on adjusting the hood see Section 7.

14 Trunk lid – removal and installation

1   Open the trunk and place blankets or some form of protective covering around the forward edge of the trunk opening to protect the window and body panel.
2   If a trunk light installed, disconnect the wiring to it.
3   Carefully scribe an outline of the hinge straps on the inner trunk lid. This will enable you to replace the trunk lid in the same location (photo).
4   With the aid of an assistant, remove the four attaching bolts and lift away the trunk lid (photos).
5   Installation is a reversal of the removal process, however make sure the trunk lid is installed in the same location and adjusted properly (see Section 15).

15 Trunk lid – adjustments

1   All adjustments for the trunk to be moved forward, rearward or sideways are done at the hinges. With the four retaining bolts slightly loosened, move the trunk lid to the desired position and tighten the bolts. Move the lid only a little at a time and check that the locking assembly remains in line (Section 17).
2   To adjust the trunk lid in an up or down fashion, and to align properly with the rear quarter panels, shims should be installed between the hinge strap and the trunk lid. Loosen the appropriate securing bolts enought to slide body shims into position and then tighten the bolt(s). Carefully close the trunk lid, checking the alignment of the lock assembly and lid in relation to the quarter panels.
3   Torque rods are incorporated to control the amount of effort needed to operate the trunk lid. The torque rod ends are located in cutout notches adjacent to the hinges. They are adjusted as follows:

a)   To increase the amount of effort required to raise the trunk lid (which will make the lid easier to close), move the torque rod(s) to a lower adjusting notch.
b)   To make the trunk lid rise easier (thus making the lid more difficult to close), reposition the torque rod end(s) to a higher notch.

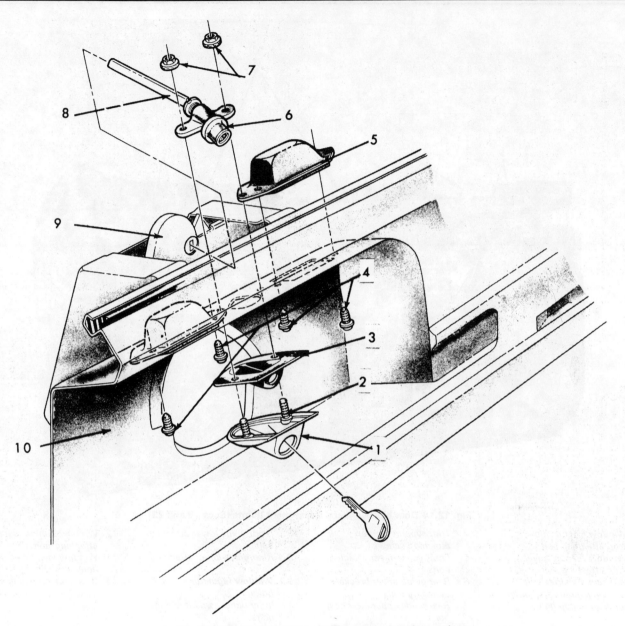

Fig. 12.13 Rear trunk lock cylinder components (Sec 17)

1 Lock cylinder housing	3 Lock cylinder housing
2 Lock cylinder housing	gasket
attaching bolts	4 Lamp assembly attaching
	bolts

5 Lamp assembly rear license	8 Lock cylinder shaft
6 Lock cylinder assembly	9 Rear compartment lock
7 Lock cylinder assembly	assembly
housing attaching nuts	10 Rear end panel

To grip the end of the torque rod for adjusting, use a $\frac{1}{4}$ inch pipe. Also, it is not necessary for each side to be adjusted to the same notch position.

16 Trunk lid lock cylinder – removal and installation

1 The lock cylinder is secured to the rear body panel by two lock nuts and washers.

2 Open the trunk lid and remove the two retaining nuts, washers and guards (photo).

3 For best access, lower the chrome bezel on the rear outside panel.

4 Remove the lock cylinder from the lock body.

5 When installing, make sure the lock cylinder shaft engages with the lock.

17 Trunk lid lock assembly – removal, adjusting and installation

1 To remove the lid lock assembly attached to the rear body panel, first remove the lock cylinder as prevously described.

2 Scribe identifying marks around each of the lock attaching bolts and then remove the bolts.

3 Remove the lock assembly from the lock body.

4 The lid lock striker is attached to the inside of the trunk lid, secured by screws. Before removing the screws, and the striker assembly, mark the vertical position of the striker to enable the assembly to be replaced in the same location.

5 Before attempting to adjust the lock striker or lock assembly, it is important that the trunk lid itself is correctly positioned.

6 To check the engagement of the striker to the lock, place a small amount of modeling clay at both sides of the lock bolt. Carefully close

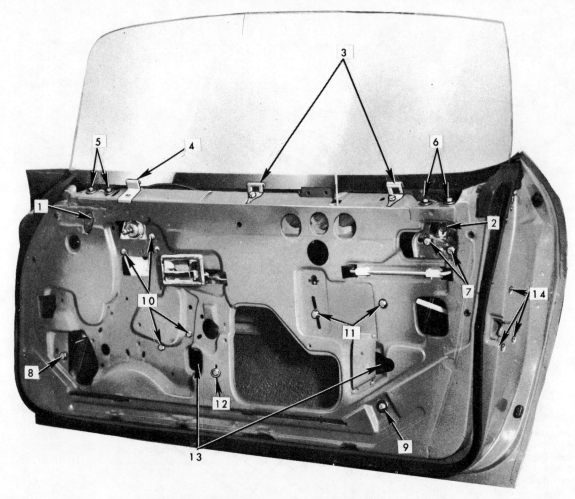

Fig. 12.14 Door hardware and adjustment points (Secs 19 and 23)

1	*Window front up-travel stop attaching bolt*	4	*Trim support hanger attaching screws*
2	*Window rear up-travel stop attaching bolt*	5	*Front guide upper attaching bolts*
3	*Window stabilizer strip and adjustable trim hanger plate attaching bolt*	6	*Rear guide upper bracket attaching bolts*
		7	*Rear guide upper attaching bolts*

8	*Front guide lower attaching bolt*	12	*Window bumper support attaching bolt*
9	*Rear guide lower attaching bolt*	13	*Window lower sash access holes*
10	*Window regulator attaching bolts*	14	*Door lock attaching screws*
11	*Inner panel cam attaching bolts*		

the trunk lid. Open the lid and check the impression left in the clay. The depression in the clay should be centered in the lock frame. Where required, the lock frame can be adjusted sideways or the striker up or down to obtain the proper engagement. These adjustments should be performed with the attaching bolts only slightly loosened, and the components should be moved only a little at a time.

18 Door trim panel – removal and installation

1   Remove the window crank handle. This is secured to the regulator shaft with a clip. The trim panel should be pushed away from the base of the handle to expose the crankshaft and clip. A special forked tool is available to push the clip out of the groove, or you can carefully use a screwdriver (photo).
2   The handle which operates the door latch mechanism is retained with screws. It is first necessary to remove the decorative cover plate (photo). With the screws removed, the remote control rod can be disconnected from the rear of the handle and the handle assembly removed from the door.
3   Remove the inside locking knob by unscrewing it from its shaft.
4   On models equipped with a remote control mirror, remove the control escutcheon from the trim panel and disengage the control cable.
5   On models with an armrest built into the trim panel, remove the

screws which are located in the recessed area meant to be used to pull the door shut.
6   If equipped with a separate armrest not intended to be a part of the trim panel, remove the screws which attach it to the trim panel and the inner door skin. The screws are sometimes hidden with decorative plugs which should be carefully pried out to reveal the screw.
7   Depending on the style and year of production, there may or may not be exposed screws securing a portion of the trim panel. If so, remove any exposed screws.
8   Where no screws can be readily seen, chances are that the panel is held in place with retaining clips. To disengage these clips, insert a flat, blunt tool (like a screwdriver blade wrapped with tape) between the metal door skin and the trim panel. Carefully pry the door panel away from the door, keeping the tool close to the clips to prevent damage to the panel. Start at the bottom and work around the door towards the top. The top section is secured at the window channel. Once the retaining clips are pried free, lift the trim panel upwards and away from the door (photo).
9   Before installing the trim panel, check that all the trim retainer clips are in good condition and the water shield is correctly applied to the metal door skin.
10 Engage the top of the trim panel first and then position the panel correctly on the door. The cutout for the window winder can be used as a rough guide.
11 Press the retaining clips into their respective cups or holes in the

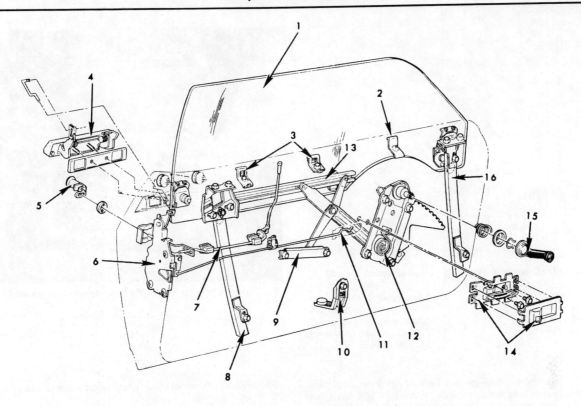

Fig. 12.15 Door hardware and components (Secs 19 and 23)

1 Window assembly	5 Lock cylinder
2 Trim pad hanger plates	6 Lock assembly
3 Trim pad hanger plate	7 Inside locking rod
and stabilizer strip	8 Rear guide
4 Door outside handle	9 Inner panel cam

10 Window down travel bumper	14 Remote control handle
support	assembly and escutcheon
11 Remote control to lock rod	15 Window regulator handle
12 Window regulator (manual)	16 Front guide
13 Lower sash channel cam	

metal door skin. Pressure can be used by the palm of your hand or a clean rubber mallet.

12 Follow the removal process in the reverse order to install the various components to the door.

13 To install the window crank handle, first install the retaining clip to the handle, then push the handle onto the shaft. Check that the clip is properly seated in the shaft groove.

19 Door lock cylinder – removal and installation

1   Remove the inside door trim as described in Section 18.

2   Raise the window to the full up position and pry the water shield away from the inner door skin to gain access to the rear of the lock cylinder.

3   To help prevent tools or inner door components from falling down to the bottom of the door cavity, place rags or newspapers inside the cavity.

4   With a screwdriver, slide the lock cylinder retaining clip (on the inboard side of the outer door skin) out of the lock cylinder. Be careful not to damage the outer door skin.

5   With the clip removed, the lock cylinder can be removed from the outside of the door.

6   Installation is a reversal of removal.

20 Door lock assembly – removal and installation

1   Remove the door trim panel as described in Section 18.

2   Pry back the water shield at the rear of the door to gain access to the inside locking assembly.

3   Temporarily install the window crank and roll the window to the full up position.

SEALING GASKET

LOCK CYLINDER (REMOVED)

RETAINER

LOCK EXTENSION

VIEW A

Fig. 12.16 Front door lock cylinder assembly (Sec 19)

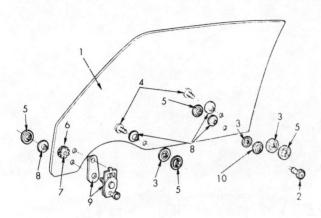

Fig. 12.17 Door window assembly and attachment (Sec 22)

1	Window assembly	6	Glass bearing fastener
2	Window roller	7	Glass bearing fastener cap
3	Washer (plastic)	8	Spacers
4	Bolt inner panel cam	9	Roller assembly (bell crank)
5	Nut	10	Washer (metal)

20.5 The attaching screws for the lock assembly are located at the rear door jamb

4   Working through the large access hole in the inner door skin, disconnect the connecting rod at the lock mechanism. This rod is held in place with a gripper clip which is released by rotating it off the rod.

5   Remove the three lock attaching screws located in the door jamb at the rear of the door. Remove the lock assembly through the access hole.

6   Installation is a reversal of removal.

21 Door exterior handle – removal and installation

1   Remove the inside door trim panel and pry back the water shield at the rear of the door.

2   Raise the window to the full up position.

3   From inside the door, remove the two attaching nuts to the exterior handle and remove the handle assembly from the outside of the door. On some later models it will be necessary to first remove the guide bracket for access to the handle nuts. This bracket is held in place with four screws on the door skin.

4   When installing, make sure the handle gasket is in good condition to prevent water leaks. The installation procedure is a reversal of removal.

22 Door window glass – removal and installation

Note: *If equipped with power windows, see Chapter 10 for important electrical information on this procedure.*

1   Remove the door trim panel (Section 18)

2   Remove the inner water shield

3   Remove the up-travel stops at the front and rear of the door.

4   Loosen the front and rear belt trim support retainers located at the top of the door in the window channel.

5   Position the window in the three-quarter-down position and remove the lower sash channel to glass attaching nuts through the small access holes in the inner door skin.

6   Lift the window straight up and out of the channel, aligning the rollers with the notches provided in the inner door skin.

7   Installation is a reversal of removal, however, install all attaching screws loosely and adjust the channels, guides and stops as necessary before finally tightening the fasteners.

23 Door window regulator – removal and installation

Note: *If equipped with power windows, see Chapter 10 for details on*

this operation. Personal injury could result if the sequence in Chapter 10 is not followed.

1   Remove the door inner trim panel and water shield (Section 18).

2   Mark the location and remove the door window and inner panel cam (Section 22).

3   Remove the regulator-to-inner door attaching fasteners. Early models use bolts, while later models have rivets which must be carefully drilled out with a $\frac{1}{4}$-inch drill bit. Remove the regulator through the large access hole.

4   When installing, if rivets were drilled out, U-nuts on the regulator body and $\frac{1}{4}$-20x$\frac{1}{2}$ inch attaching screws should be substituted. Tighten attaching screws or bolts and reverse the removal sequence.

24 Door – removal and installation

1   Disconnect the battery ground cable.

2   Open the door fully and support it on blocks and cloth pads placed under its lower edge.

3   If the vehicle is equipped with power-operated windows, remove the trim panel and disconnect the regulator wiring harness.

4   Prior to removal of doors, scribe round the fitted position of the hinge on the door.

5   Using a cranked wrench, and with an assistant supporting the weight of the door, remove the door hinge retaining bolts.

6   Having removed the door, it is now possible to remove the hinge from the hinge pillar, but again scribe round the fitted position first.

7   Refitting doors and hinges is the reverse of the removal procedure. If necessary the hinge positions may be altered slightly to ensure correct alignment.

Note: *When refitting the door, ensure that the lock striker fork-bolt engages with the striker. If necessary the position of the fork bolt can be adjusted by loosening with a wrench, repositioning, then retightening.*

25 Windshield and back window – removal and installation

1   These operations are best left to specialists as the glass is retained by quick setting adhesive/caulk material which leaves no room for error in application or positioning of the windshield.

2   The rear view mirror support is bonded to the windshield and can only be removed by extremely careful application of heat from an air gun (250° to 350°F) – another job for a specialist.

Chapter 13 Supplement:
Revisions and information on 1981 models

Contents

1 Introduction

This supplement contains specifications and changes that apply to Camaros produced in 1981. Also included is information related to previous models that was not available at the time of original publication of this manual.

Where no differences (or very minor differences) exist between 1981 models and 1980 models, no information is given. In those instances, the original material included in Chapters 1 through 12 pertaining to 1980 models should be used.

2 Specifications

Note: *The specifications listed here include only those items which differ from those listed in Chapters 1 through 12 pertaining to 1980 model vehicles. For information not specifically listed here, refer to the appropriate Chapter.*

Tune-up specifications

5.7 liter 350 cu in A/T

Emission label	AWM (Calif)
	AVA (Fed)
Carburetor part number	17081218 w/AC
	17081216 w/o AC
Curb idle	500 rpm (D)
Idle solenoid	600 rpm (D)
Fast idle	2200 rpm (P or N)
Spark plug type/gap	R45TS/0.045 in
Distributor part number	1103443
Initial timing.	6° BTDC @ 500 rpm (D)

5.0 liter 305 cu in A/T

Emission label	ALW (Calif)
	ALN (Fed)
Carburetor part number	17081204 w/AC
	17081202 w/o AC
Curb idle.	500 rpm (D)
Idle solenoid.	600 rpm (D)
Fast idle	2000 rpm (P or N)
Spark plug type/gap	R45TS/0.045 in
Distributor part number	1103443
Initial timing.	6° BTDC @ 500 rpm (D)

Tune-up specifications (continued)

5.0 liter 305 cu in M/T

Emission label	ALX (Calif)
	ALS (Fed)
Carburetor part number	17081207 w/AC
	17081203 w/o AC
Curb idle	700 rpm (N)
Idle solenoid	800 rpm (N)
Fast idle	2200 rpm (N)
Spark plug type/gap	R45TS/0.045 in
Distributor part number	1103443
Initial timing	6° BTDC @ 700 rpm (N)

4.4 liter 267 cu in A/T

Emission label	ALK (Fed)
Carburetor part number	17081140 w/AC
	17081138 w/o AC
Curb idle	500 rpm (D)
Idle solenoid	600 rpm (D)
Fast idle	2200 rpm (P or N)
Spark plug type/gap	R45TS/0.045 in
Distributor part number	1103443
Initial timing	6° BTDC @ 500 rpm (D)

Engine specifications — 1981 models

All dimensions in inches

Pistons and piston rings
Oil ring (all engines)

Clearance in groove	0.002 to 0.007
Ring end gap	0.015 to 0.055

Crankshaft
Main bearing oil clearance (all engines)

Journal 1	0.001 to 0.0015 max
Journal 2-3-4	0.001 to 0.0025 max
Journal 5	0.0025 to 0.0035 max
Rod bearing oil clearance	0.0035 max

Camshaft runout	0.004 to 0.012 in

Fuel and exhaust systems — 1981 models

Carburetor specifications — Rochester E2ME

Engine displacement	267 cu in
Float level	3/8 in
Pump rod location	inner
Choke rod	20°
Vacuum break (front)	25°
Choke unloader	40°

Carburetor specifications — Rochester E4ME

Engine displacement	305, 350 cu in
Float level	11/32 in
Choke rod	20°
Air valve rod	0.025 in
Vacuum break (front)	26°
Air valve windup	7/8 in
Unloader	38°
Idle mixture needle	3 1/3 turns

Throttle position sensor (TPS) — adjustment

Engine	**Volts**
267 cu in (4.4 liter)	0.51 volts at curb idle
305 cu in (5.0 liter)	0.56 volts at curb idle
350 cu in (5.7 liter)	0.56 volts at curb idle
Idle speed/CO mixture	See vehicle Emission Control Information Label in the engine compartment

Torque specifications	**Ft-lb**
Spark plugs	22

Automatic transmission

Fluid capacities	**US qts**
Turbo Hyda-Matic 200	
Routine fluid change*	1.5
Filling from dry (new or overhauled unit)	6

Turbo Hydra-Matic 250
    Routine fluid change* 2.5
    Filling from dry (new or overhauled unit) 10.0

* The small quantity required during routine fluid change is due to the fact that the torque converter is not drained.

Torque specifications (Turbo Hydra-Matic 200)	Ft-lb
Pump cover bolts	18
Pump-to-case bolts	18
Parking pawl bracket bolts.	18
Control valve body bolts	11
Oil screen retaining bolts	11
Oil pan bolts.	12
Torque converter-to-flexplate bolts.	35
Transmission-to-engine bolts.	25
Converter dust shield screws.	8
Speedometer driven gear bolts.	23
Fluid cooler line-to-transmission	25
Fluid cooler line-to-radiator	20
Linkage swivel clamp nut	30
Converter bracket-to-adapter	13
Transmission rear support bolts.	40
Rear mounting support nuts.	21
Support center nut	33
Adapter-to-transmission bolts	33

Brakes

All dimensions in inches

Disc size
Diameter 11.00
Width. 1.030
Minimum width (refinished). 0.980
Minimum width (discard) 0.965

Wheel cylinder piston diameter 0.9375

Master cylinder piston diameter
Power assisted. 1.125
Manual 0.9375

Torque specifications	In-lb
Brake line nuts-to-front brake and master cylinder	210
Brake shoe anchor pin	110
Flexible hose-to-caliper.	32

Steering and suspension

Torque specifications	Ft-lb
Steering knuckle-to-tie-rod end	40
Tie-rod clamp nuts	14
Tie-rod-to-intermediate rod	40
Pitman arm-to-intermediate rod.	40
Pitman arm-to-steering gear	180
Idler arm-to-intermediate rod	40
Idler arm-to-frame	60
Clamp-to-steering shaft nut	55
Rack-piston plug	75
Side cover bolts	30
Pitman shaft adjusting screw locknut.	25
Bearing pre-load adjuster locknut	85
Swivel joint upper ballstud nut	65
Swivel joint lower ballstud nut	90
Swivel joint securing bolts (replacement only)	8
Control arm pivot-to-frame (upper).	73
Control arm pivot-to-frame (lower).	90
Upper control arm pivot shaft nuts	85
Shock absorber upper mounting	85
Wheel nuts	
With aluminum wheels	80
Without aluminum wheels	90

Tune-up and routine maintenance

Routine maintenance intervals

Note: *The following maintenance intervals are recommended by the manufacturer. In the interset of vehicle longevity, we recommend shorter intervals between certain operations such as fluid and filter replacements. Section references refer to Chapter 1.*

Every 250 miles or weekly — whichever comes first

Check the engine oil level (Section 2).
Check the engine coolant level (Section 2).
Check the windshield washer fluid level (Section 2).
Check the battery water level (if equipped with removable vent caps) (Section 2).
Check the tires and tire pressures (Section 3).
Check the automatic transmission fluid level (Section 2).
Check the power steering fluid level (Section 2).

At the first 7500 miles or 6 months — whichever comes first

Check the carburetor choke and the fuel hoses (Section 20).
Adjust the idle speed (Section 16).
Check the EFE system (Section 17).
Torque the carburetor-to-manifold bolts (Section 28).
Rotate the wheels and tires (Section 14).

Every 7500 miles or 12 months — whichever comes first

Lubricate the chassis components (Section 5).
Change the engine oil (Section 4).
Rotate the tires (if they are bias ply) (Section 14).
Change the oil filter (Section 4).
Check the brake master cylinder fluid level (Section 2).
Check the power steering fluid level (Section 2).
Check the rear axle lubricant level (Section 2).
Check the manual transmission fluid level (Section 2).
Check the brake and power steering hoses and lines (Section 2).
Check the exhaust system (Section 7).
Check the tires, wheels and front brake discs (Section 26).
Check the suspension and the steering (Section 15).
Change the rear axle lubricant (if the vehicle is used to pull a trailer) (Section 22).

Every 15000 miles or 12 months — whichever comes first

Rotate the tires (Section 14).
Check the cooling system (Section 6).
Check and adjust (if necessary) the drivebelts (Section 9).
Check the drum brakes (Section 26).
Check the throttle linkage for interference, binding and damaged or missing parts.
Check the fuel cap, tank and lines (Section 10).
Change the transmission fluid and filter (Section 25).

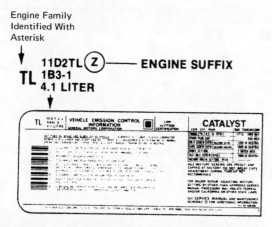

Fig. 13.1 The emissions control and tune-up decal is located under the hood. The engine code numbers are in the upper left-hand corner (Sec 3)

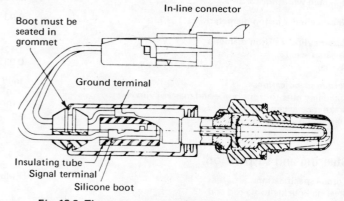

Fig. 13.2 The oxygen sensor and its integral electrical 'pig-tail' (Sec 3)

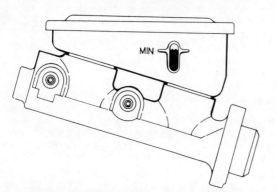

Fig. 13.3 To check the brake fluid level, merely observe the level through the window. The level should be above the minimum marking (Sec 3)

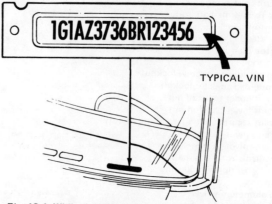

Fig. 13.4 While the VIN plate itself is in the same position, The engine code is the 8th digit instead of the 5th as in previous years (Sec 4)

Every 30 000 miles

Check and repack the front wheel bearings (perform this procedure whenever brakes are relined, regardless of maintenance interval) (Section 24).

Check the rear axle for leaks.

Check the manual transmission for leaks.

Lubricate the clutch cross shaft (if equipped).

Check the carburetor choke and fuel hoses (Section 20).

Check and adjust (if necessary) the idle speed (Section 16).

Check the EFE system (Section 17).

Torque the carburetor-to-manifold bolts (Section 27).

Check the thermostatically controlled air cleaner (Section 15).

Check the vacuum advance system and hoses.

Check the ignition wires (Section 28).

Replace the spark plugs (Section 23).

Replace the air cleaner and the PCV filter (Section 12).

Replace the PCV valve (Section 11).

Check the operation of the EGR valve (Section 21).

Check the ignition timing and adjust (if necessary) (Section 19).

Change the oxygen sensor (Chapter 13) on engines with code Z only (see Fig. 13.1).

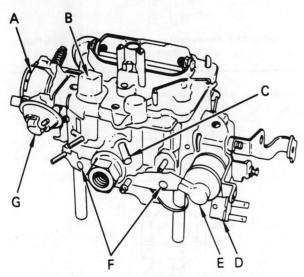

Fig. 13.5 Typical E2MC carburetor used on 1981 models (Sec 5)

A   *Electric Choke*
B   *Mixture controls solenoid connector (from ECM)*
C   *Vapor vent tube (to canister)*
D   *Wide open throttle switch*
E   *Idle speed solenoid*
F   *Plug (idle mixture needle)*
G   *Front vacuum break*

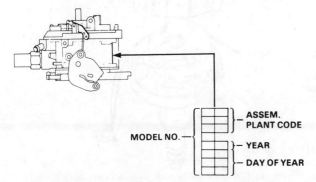

Fig. 13.6 Location of model number for E2MC/E2ME carburetors (Sec 5)

Oxygen sensor — replacement

Note: *Special care must be taken when handling the sensitive oxygen sensor:*

   a) Do not damage or disconnect the electrical connector from the sensor. Upon removal, disconnect the electrical wires only at the pull-apart connector.

   b) Grease, dirt or other contaminants should be kept away from the electrical connector and the louvered end of the sensor.

   c) Do not use cleaning solvents of any kind on the oxygen sensor.

   d) Do not drop or roughly handle the sensor.

   e) The silicone boot must be installed in the correct position to prevent the boot from being melted and the sensor to operate properly.

1 Since the oxygen sensor may be difficult to remove with the engine cold, begin by operating the engine until it has warmed to at least 120° F (48°C).

2 Disconnect the electrical connector to the oxygen sensor.

3 Note the position of the silicone boot and carefully back out the oxygen sensor from the exhaust manifold. Be advised that excessive force may damage the threads.

4 A special anti-seize compound must be used on the threads of the oxygen sensor to aid in future removal. New or service sensors will have this compound already applied, but if for any reason an oxygen sensor is removed and then reinstalled, the threads must be coated prior to reinstallation.

5 Install the sensor and tighten it to 30 ft-lb.

6 Connect the electrical connector.

Brake fluid level check

7 A new brake system master cylinder was introduced in 1981. The top of the master cylinder no longer needs to be removed to check the fluid level inside. A window is incorporated into the fluid body to view the fluid level. See Section 10 of this supplement for more information.

---

4 Engine

General description

1 Starting in 1981, the engine code of the Vehicle Identification Number (VIN) is the 8th character as opposed to being the 5th as in previous years.

Engine removal

2 In addition to all steps given in Chapter 2, carefully note the positions of all Computer Command Control (C-4) wiring and then disconnect.

Exhaust manifold — removal and installation

3 In addition to all steps given in Chapter 2:

   a) Disconnect the wiring to the oxygen sensor. Read through all of the information in Section 3 of this supplement concerning the oxygen sensor.

   b) Disconnect the air hose at the catalytic converter.

---

5 Fuel and exhaust systems

General description

1 All carburetors used on 1981 models are either 2-barrel (E2ME) or 4-barrel (E4ME).

2 The first letter of these carburetor codes, (E) designates that this carburetor is for use with the Computer Command Control emission system. The last letter indicates the type of choke system used — E for electric.

3 The carburetor model number is very important for obtaining replacement parts and for adjustment specifications. This number can be found stamped vertically on the left rear corner of the float bowl.

Adjustments

4 The curb idle speed on these carburetors is now controlled by the Electronic Control Module (ECM) of the Computer Command Control emission system. Electric signals are sent from the ECM to the Idle Speed Control (ISC) which is mounted on the carburetor. Due to this, curb idle speed is no longer a mechanical adjustment which can be carried out by the home mechanic. Refer to Section 7 of this sup-

plement for more information concerning this system.

5   The fuel/air mixture previously set with adjustable screws and/or a special propane method is now controlled by the ECM as in curb idle above. The ECM sends electrical signals to a mixture control solenoid built into the carburetor body. Due to this, no previously-used adjustment methods can be used and adjustment should be referred to a dealer or competent repair shop. More information on this system can be found in Section 7 of this supplement.

Electric choke heater checking procedure (E4ME carburetors only)

6   Allow the engine to cool so that when the throttle is opened slightly, the choke valve closes completely. This check must be performed with the engine off (at an ambient temperature of from 60° F to 80° F).

7   Start the engine and determine how long it takes for the choke valve to reach the fully open position (start the timer the moment the engine starts).

8   If the choke valve fails to open completely within 3 1/2 minutes, proceed with steps 9 through 11 below.

9   Check the voltage at the choke heater connection (the engine must be running). If it is approximately 12 to 15 volts, replace the electrical choke unit with a new one.

10 If the voltage is low or zero, check all wires and connections. No gasket is used between the choke cover and the choke housing because of grounding requirements. If any connections in the oil pressure switch circuit are faulty or if the oil pressure sending unit has failed (open), the oil warning light will be on with the engine running. Repair the wires or connections as required.

11 If all wiring and connections are good, replace the oil pressure sending unit with a new one.

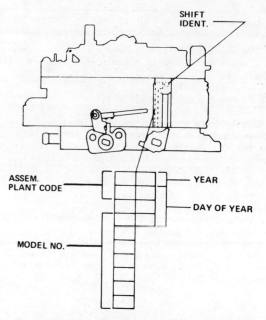

Fig. 13.7 Location of model number for E4MC/E4ME carburetors (Sec 5)

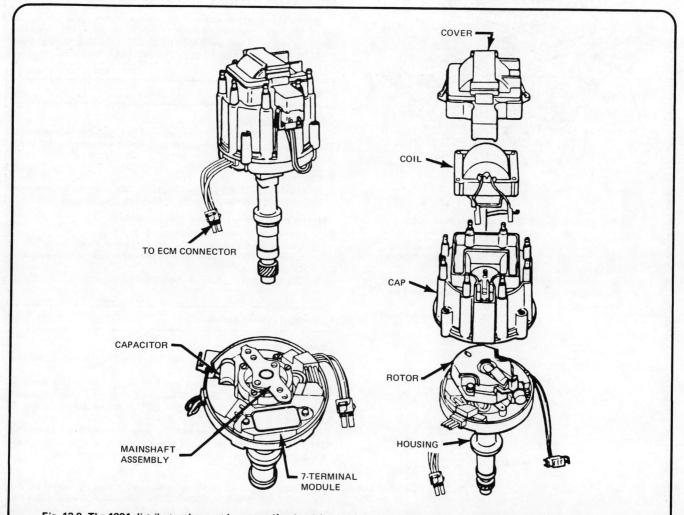

Fig. 13.8 The 1981 distributor does not have centrifugal weights inside or a vacuum canister outside to control spark advance (Sec 6)

Overhaul

12 Due to the very complex design of these carburetors, it is recommended that the home mechanic not attampt an overhaul. In addition, special equipment not ordinarily available to the home mechanic will be required for adjustment following the overhaul.

6 Ignition

Charging system – general description

1 The alternator used on 1981 models is designated a 15-SI. It is very similar to the 10-SI used on earlier models (and discussed in Chapter 5) except for the following:

a) The 15-SI is slightly larger in size.
b) It will produce approximately 70 amps at full speed and 40 amps when at idle speed.
c) Slightly different drive end and slip ring end bearings are used.
d) The stator incorporates delta windings, and thus cannot be checked for opens.

Ignition system – general description

2 The distributor, like the carburetor previously discussed, is now controlled by the ECM of the Computer Command Control emissions system. All timing changes in the distributor are done electrically by the ECM as opposed to vacuum and centrifugal advance mechanisms

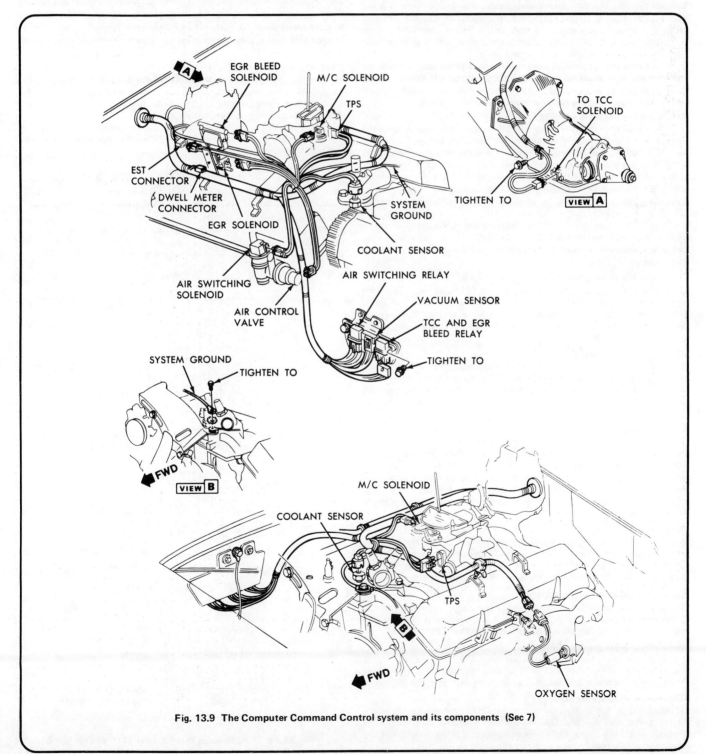

Fig. 13.9 The Computer Command Control system and its components (Sec 7)

used previously. If a fault in this system occurs, it will appear as a 'trouble code' through the ECM. See Section 7 of this supplement for more information.

Distributor — removal and installation

3   In addition to all steps given in Chapter 5, disconnect the electrical connector which leads from the distributor to the ECM.

7   Emissions systems

General description

1   All 1981 vehicles are equipped with the Computer Command Control system. The computer system controls exhaust emissions while retaining drivability by maintaining a continuous interaction between all of the emissions systems. Any malfunction in the computer system is signaled by a 'check engine' light on the dash which goes on and remains lit until the malfunction is corrected.

2   The Computer Command Control system requires special tools for maintenance and repair, so any work on it should be left to your dealer or a qualified technician. Although complicated, the system can be understood by examining each component and its function.

Electronic control module (ECM)

3   The electronic control module (ECM) is essentially a small onboard computer located under the dash which monitors up to 15 engine/vehicle functions and controls as many as 9 different operations. The ECM contains a programmable read only memory (PROM) calibration unit which tailors each ECM's performance to conform to the vehicle. The PROM is programmed with the vehicle's particular design, weight, axle ratio, etc. and cannot be used in another ECM in a car which differs in any way.

4   The ECM receives continuous information from the computer system and processes it in accordance with PROM instructions. It then sends out electronic signals to the system components, modifying their performance.

Oxygen sensor (OS)

5   The oxygen sensor (OS) is mounted in the exhaust pipe, upstream of the catalytic converter. It monitors the exhaust stream and sends information to the ECM on how much oxygen is present. The oxygen level is determined by how rich or lean the fuel mixture in the carburetor is.

Mixture control solenoid

6   This controls the fuel flow through the carburetor idle and main metering circuits. The solenoid cycles 10 times per second, constantly adjusting the fuel/air mixture. The ECM energizes the solenoid on information it receives from the oxygen sensor to keep emissions within limits.

Coolant sensor

7   This sensor in the coolant stream sends information to the ECM concerning engine temperature. The ECM can then vary the fuel/air ratio for conditions such as cold start. The ECM can also perform various switching functions on the EGR, EFE, and AIR management systems, according to engine temperature. This feedback from the coolant sensor to the ECM is used to vary spark advance and activate the hot temperature light.

Pressure sensors

8   The ECM uses the information from various pressure sensors to adjust engine performance. The sensors are: barometric pressure sensor (BARO), manifold absolute pressure (MAP) sensor and the throttle position sensor (TPS) as well as the above mentioned coolant sensor.

Barometric pressure sensor (BARO)

9   Located in the engine compartment, the barometric pressure sensor provides a voltage to the ECM indicating ambient air pressure which varies with altitude. Not all vehicles are equipped with this sensor.

Manifold absolute pressure (MAPS)

10   Also located in the engine compartment, the MAPS senses engine vacuum (manifold) pressure. The ECM uses this information to adjust fuel/air mixture and spark timing in accordance with driving conditions.

Throttle position sensor (TPS)

11   Mounted in the carburetor body, the TPS is moved by the accelerator pump and sends a low voltage signal to the ECM when the throttle is closed and a higher voltage when it is opened. The ECM uses this voltage feed to recognize throttle position.

Dual-bed convertor and air control/air switching valve

12   During cold warm ups, this system provides air to the exhaust ports. When the engine is warm, it routes the air through the convertor during decelleration.

Transmission converter clutch (TCC)

13   At a pre-determined speed, the ECM energizes a transmission mounted solenoid, which in turn, couples the engine with the transmission.

14   When the brake is depressed or when operating conditions require it, the solenoid is de-energized causing the transmission to operate as a normal fluid coupled transmission.

15   The system consists of a vehicle speed sensor (VSS) mounted behind the speedometer. A high gear switch mounted to the transmission which opens only when the transmission is in high gear. Also, a Park/Neutral (P/N) switch is used. The P/N switch is connected to the shift linkage and opens only when the transmission is shifted into a drive-gear.

Electronic spark timing (EST)

16   The high energy ignition (HEI) distributor used with this system has no provision for centrifugal or vacuum advance of spark timing. This is controlled electronically by the ECM (except under certain conditions such as cranking the engine).

17   The EGR, EFE and fuel evaporative systems explained elsewhere in this chapter are also controlled by the ECM in the computer controlled catalytic converter system.

Air injection reactor

18   When the engine is cold, the ECM energizes an air switching valve which allows air to flow to the exhaust ports to lower carbon monoxide (CO) and hydrocarbon (HC) levels in the exhaust.

Exhaust gas recirculator (EGR)

19   The ECM controls the ported vacuum to the EGR with a solenoid valve. When the engine is cold, the solenoid is energized to block vacuum to the EGR valve until the engine is warm.

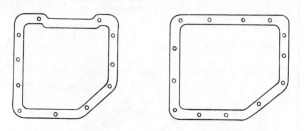

Fig. 13.10 At left is the oil pan of the Turbo Hydra-Matic 200 transmission and at right is the 250 series pan (Sec 8)

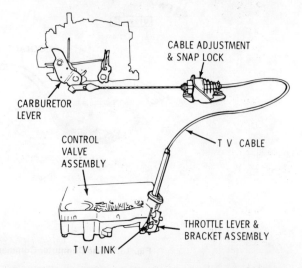

Fig. 13.11 The 200-series throttle valve (TV) system (Sec 8)

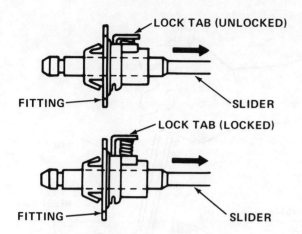

Fig. 13.12 The self-adjusting type of throttle valve cable
(Sec 8)

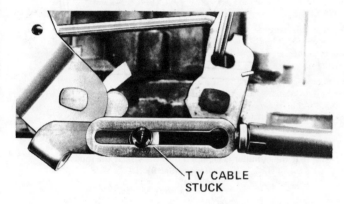

Fig. 13.13 A sticking TV cable at the carburetor lever (Sec 8)

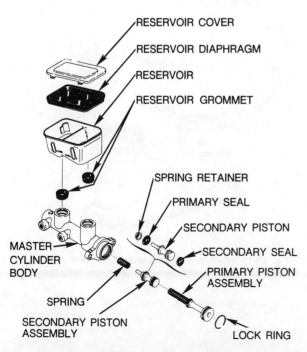

Fig. 13.14 The new brake master cylinder features an
aluminum body and plastic reservoir (Sec 9)

Evaporative emission system

20 When the engine is cold or idling, the ECM solenoid blocks vacuum to the valve at the top of the charcoal canister. When the engine is warm and at a specified rpm, the ECM de-energizes the valve, releasing the collected vapors into the intake manifold.

Early fuel evaporation (EFE)

21 The ECM controls a valve which shuts off the system until the engine is warm.

Computer Command Control system circuit check

22 With the proper equipment, the computer controlled system can be used to diagnose malfunctions within itself. The 'check engine'' light can flash trouble codes stored in the ECM 'trouble code memory'. As stated before, this diagnosis should be left to your dealer or a qualified technician because of the tools required and the fact that ECM programming varies from one model vehicle to another.

8 Automatic transmission

General description and identification

1 In addition to the Turbo Hydra-Matic 350 transmission, 1981 vehicles may be equipped with either a 200-series transmission or a 250-series transmission. Since all Turbo Hydra-Matic transmissions are nearly identical for the purposes covered in this manual most of the information in Chapter 7 Part B will be applicable.

2 The Turbo Hydra-Matic 200 transmission can be identified by having an oil pan with 11 bolts and one angled corner. The Turbo Hydra-Matic 250 has an oil pan with 13 bolts.

Turbo Hydra-Matic 200 — throttle valve (TV) cable adjustment
Manual type

3 Disengage the snap-lock and check that the cable is free to slide through the lock.

4 Move the carburetor throttle lever to the fully open position.

5 Push the snap-lock down until it is flush and then gently release the throttle lever.

Self-adjusting type

6 Depress the lock tab and move the slider back through the fitting (away from the pump lever) until it stops against the fitting.

7 Release the lock tab.

8 Open the carburetor lever to the 'wide open' position. This will automatically adjust the TV cable.

9 Release the tab and check the cable for binding or sticking.

Turbo Hydra-Matic 250 — downshift (detent) cable adjustment

10 The cable will normally only require adjustment if a new one has been installed.

11 Disengage the snap-lock button and depress the accelerator fully. The ball will slide into the cable sleeve and automatically pre-set the cable tension.

12 Engage the snap-lock.

Turbo Hydra-Matic 250 — intermediate band adjustment

13 This adjustment should be carried out every 60 000 miles or if the performance of the transmission indicates the need for it.

14 Raise the vehicle to gain access to the transmission.

15 Place the speed selector lever in Neutral.

16 On the right-hand side of the transmission case is located the adjusting screw and locknut for the intermediate band.

17 Loosen the locknut one quarter-turn using a wrench or special tool J24367. Hold the locknut in this position and tighten the adjusting screw to a torque of 30 in-lb. Now back off the screw *three complete turns exactly*.

18 Without moving the adjusting screw, tighten the locknut to 15 ft-lb.

9 Braking system

General description

1 A new master cylinder has been incorporated into the braking system of 1981 models. The master cylinder is made of aluminum, as opposed to cast iron in previous years. It also has a plastic reservoir with a window for viewing the fluid level.

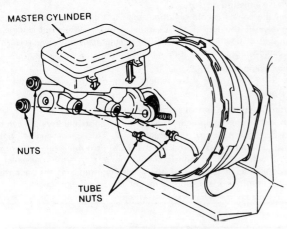

Fig. 13.15 The mounting of the new master cylinder is basically the same as in previous years. To add fluid, note the new cap features built-in tabs (Sec 9)

Master cylinder — overhaul

2   The removal, overhaul and installation of the new master cylinder is nearly the same as the previous model discussed in Chapter 9 with the following exceptions:

   a) To remove the plastic reservoir, clamp the body into a vise (using the mounting flange) and then pry the reservoir from the body.

   b) Be sure to use new rubber reservoir grommets during overhaul and lubricate them thoroughly with brake fluid.

   c) To install the reservoir, lay it on a flat, hard surface and press the body (and grommets) onto the reservoir by using a rocking motion until it is fully seated.

   d) Since the master cylinder body is made of aluminum, no abrasives can be used to remove inperfections in the bore. If the bore is visibly worn or shows any signs of damage, the master cylinder body must be replaced with a new one.

10 Electrical system

General information

1   The C-4 emission control system used on some vehicles (see Section 4) is monitored and controlled by a very complex and easily damaged electrical/electronic system. It is highly recommended that trouble-shooting, adjustments and component replacement or repair be left to a GM dealer service department.

Battery jump starting

Note: *Do not push or tow the vehicle to start it. Damage to the emission system and/or other parts of the vehicle may result.*

2   Both the booster battery and the discharged battery should be treated carefully when using jumper cables. Follow the procedure outlined here and be careful not to cause sparks. **Note:** *Departure from these conditions or the following procedure could result in serious personal injury (particularly to the eyes) or property damage from such causes as battery explosion, battery acid or electrical burns, and/or damage to electronic components of either vehicle.*

3   Set the parking brake and place the transmission in 'Park' (automatic) or 'Neutral' (manual). Turn off the lights, heater and other electrical accessories.

4   Check the battery's built-in hydrometer. If it is clear or light yellow, replace the battery. Do not attempt a jump start.

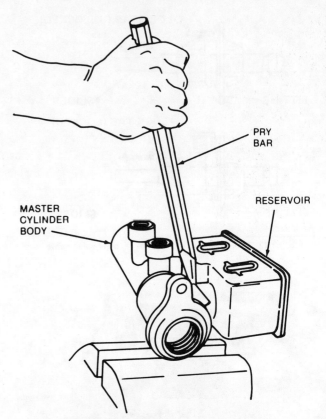

Fig. 13.16 Prying the plastic reservoir from the body. Note that the cylinder is clamped into the vise at the mounting flange (Sec 9)

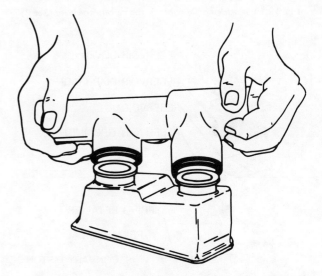

Fig. 13.17 When installing the body to the reservoir, use a rocking motion to seat the rubber grommets fully (Sec 9)

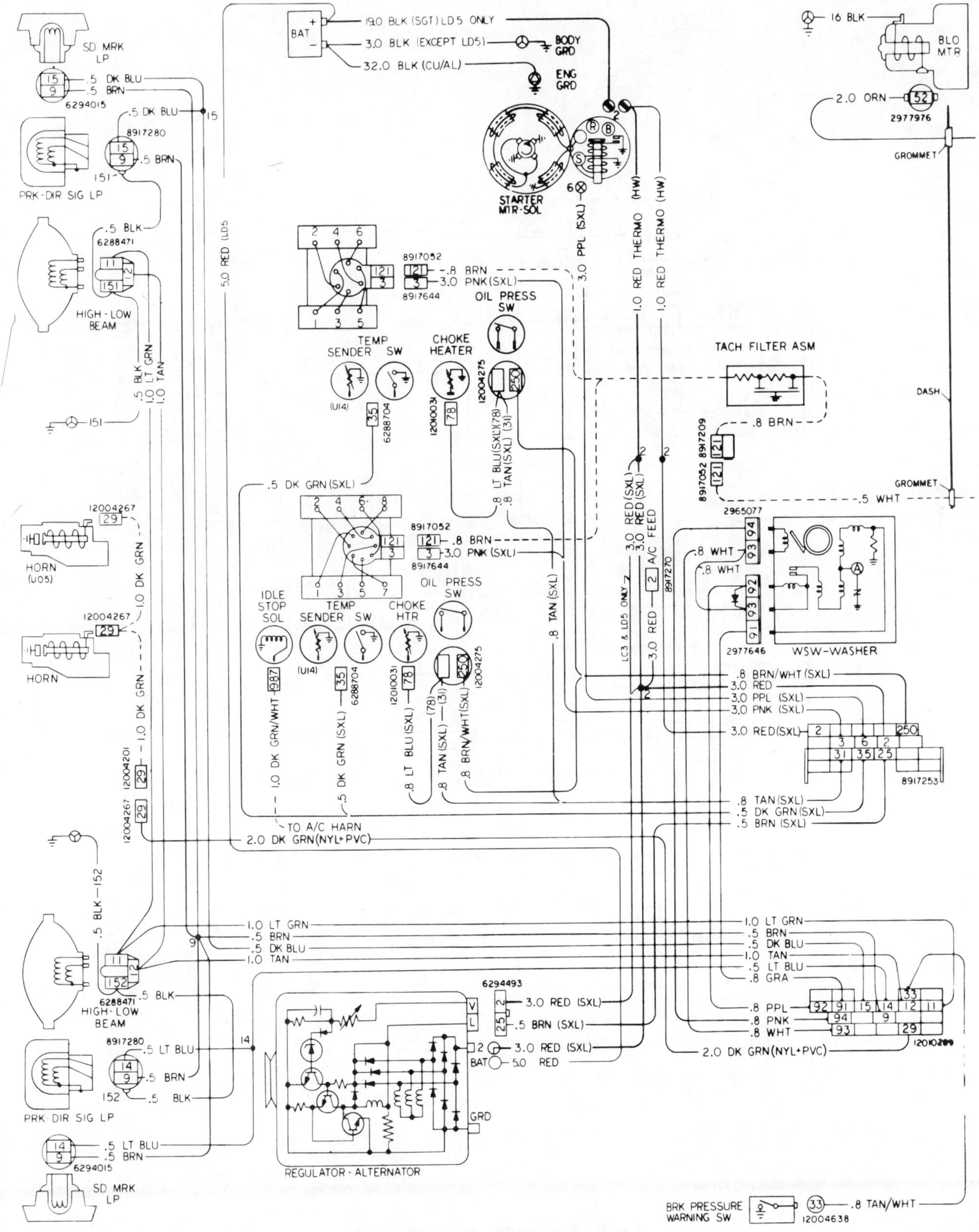

SD MRK LP

15
9

.5 DK BLU
.5 BRN

6294015

PRK·DIR SIG LP

8917280
15
9
.5 DK BLU
.5 BRN

151

151

.5 BLK

6288471

11
12

HIGH·LOW BEAM

151

.5 BLK
1.0 LT GRN
1.0 TAN

151

12004267
29

HORN (U05)

1.0 DK GRN

12004267
29

HORN

1.0 DK GRN
1.0 DK GRN

1.0 DK GRN/WHT

12004201

12004267
29

TO A/C HARN
2.0 DK GRN(NYL+PVC)

.5 BLK — 152

.5 BLK

152

11
2

HIGH·LOW BEAM

6288471

.5 BLK

8917280

14
9
.5 LT BLU
.5 BRN

152 .5 BLK

PRK DIR SIG LP

14
9
.5 LT BLU
.5 BRN

6294015

SD MRK LP

BAT
+
−

19.0 BLK (SGT) LD5 ONLY
3.0 BLK (EXCEPT LD5)
32.0 BLK (CU/AL)

BODY GRD
ENG GRD

5.0 RED (LD5)

5.0 RED

R
B
S
6

STARTER MTR·SOL

3.0 PPL (SXL)
1.0 RED THERMO (HW)
1.0 RED THERMO (HW)

2
4
6
1
3
5
2
1
3

8917052
8917644

12
3
.8 BRN
3.0 PNK (SXL)

TEMP SENDER SW
(U14)

35
6288704

CHOKE HEATER

78
1200003

OIL PRESS SW

12004275
250

.5 DK GRN (SXL)

.8 LT BLU (SXL)(78)
.8 TAN (SXL) (31)

2
4
6
1
3
5
2
1
3

8917052
8917644

12
3
.8 BRN
3.0 PNK (SXL)

IDLE STOP SOL

987

TEMP SENDER SW
(U14)

35
6288704

CHOKE HTR

78
1200003

OIL PRESS SW

12004275
250

.8 LT BLU (SXL) (78)
.8 TAN (SXL) (31)
.8 BRN/WHT(SXL)

.8 TAN (SXL)

1.0 RED (SXL)
1.0 RED (SXL)
A/C FEED

3.0 RED
3.0 RED
2

LC3 & LD5 ONLY

3.0 RED
2 A/C FEED
897270

TACH FILTER ASM

.8 BRN

8917052 8917209
121

GROMMET
.5 WHT

16 BLK

BLO MTR

2.0 ORN
52
2977976

GROMMET

DASH

2965077

93 94

.8 WHT

.8 WHT

91 93 92

91 92

WSW-WASHER

2977646

.8 BRN/WHT (SXL)
3.0 RED
3.0 PPL (SXL)
3.0 PNK (SXL)
3.0 RED(SXL)

2
3
1
6
2
250

31 35 25

8917253

.8 TAN (SXL)
.5 DK GRN (SXL)
.5 BRN (SXL)

1.0 LT GRN
.5 BRN
.5 DK BLU
1.0 TAN
.5 LT BLU
.8 GRA

.8 PPL
.8 PNK
.8 WHT

92 91 5 4
94 9
93

33
2 11
29

12010200

1.0 LT GRN
.5 BRN
.5 DK BLU
1.0 TAN

9

14

6294493

V
L

25 2 12

3.0 RED (SXL)
.5 BRN (SXL)

2 3.0 RED (SXL)

BAT 5.0 RED

GRD

REGULATOR - ALTERNATOR

2.0 DK GRN(NYL+PVC)

BRK PRESSURE WARNING SW
33
12004638
.8 TAN/WHT

Fig. 13.18 Wiring diagram — engine compartment (1981)

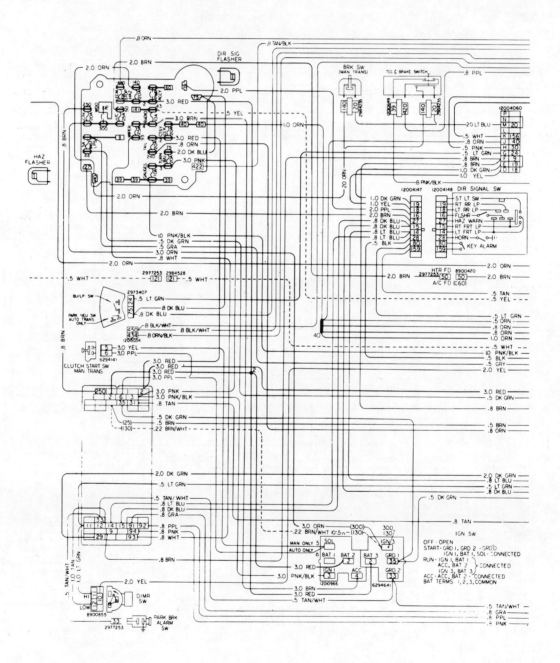

Fig. 13.19 Wiring diagram — dash (1981)

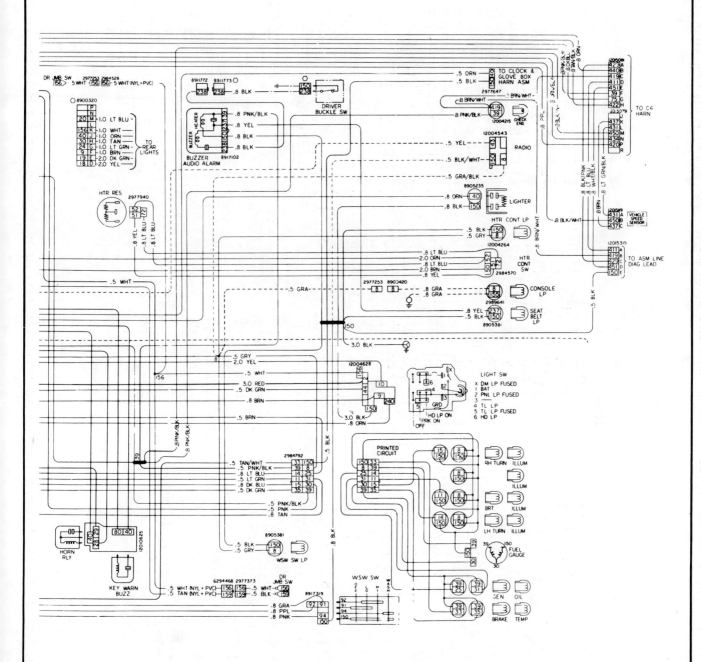

Fig. 13.20 Wiring diagram – dash and interior (1981)

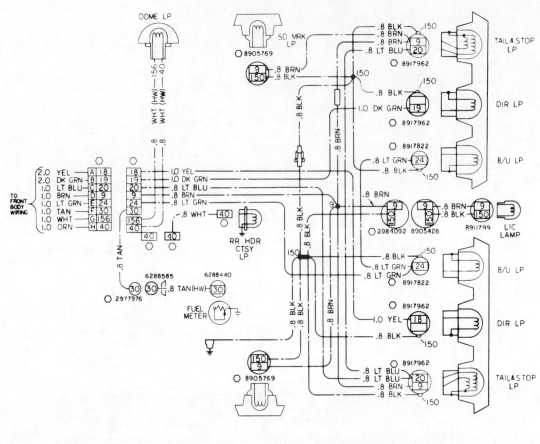

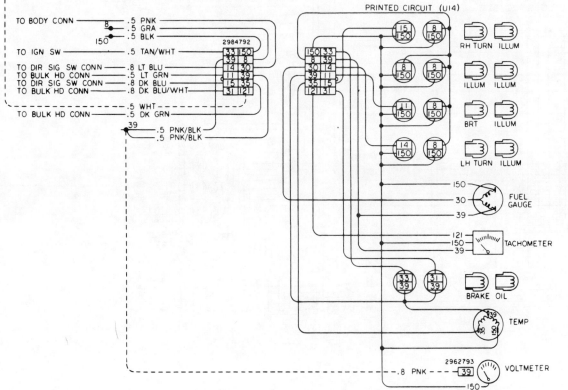

Fig. 13.21 Wiring diagram – instruments and taillights (1981)

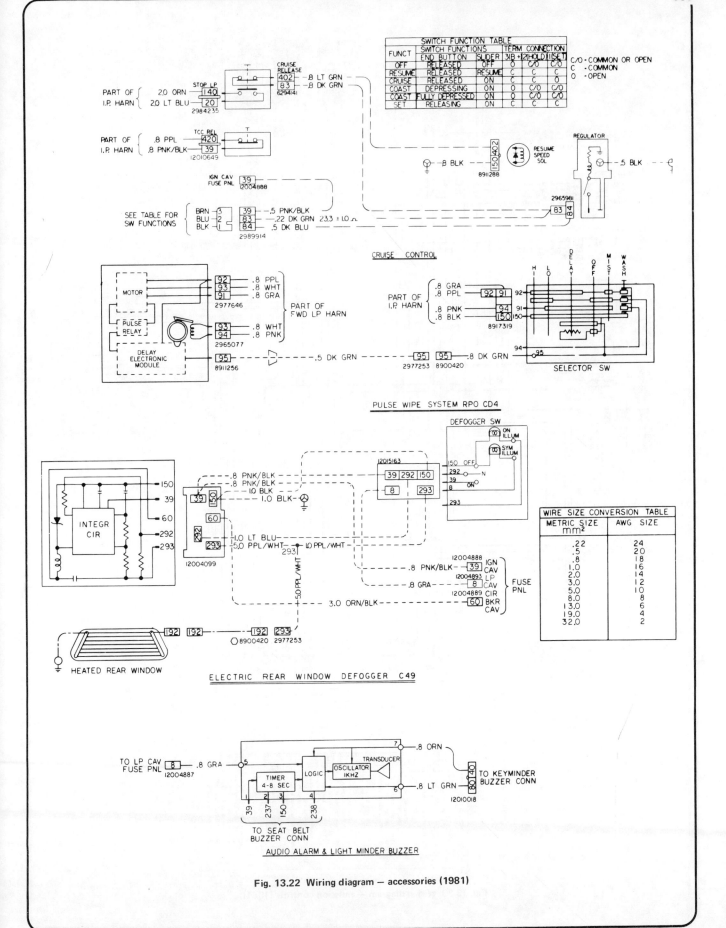

Fig. 13.22 Wiring diagram — accessories (1981)

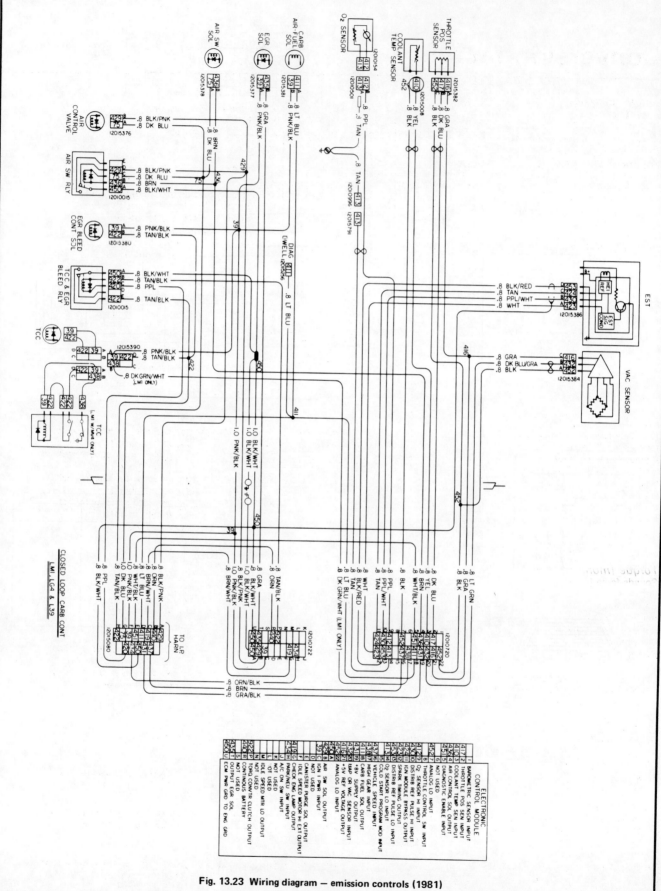

Fig. 13.23 Wiring diagram — emission controls (1981)

Conversion factors

Length (distance)
Inches (in)	X	25.4	= Millimetres (mm)	X	0.0394	= Inches (in)
Feet (ft)	X	0.305	= Metres (m)	X	3.281	= Feet (ft)
Miles	X	1.609	= Kilometres (km)	X	0.621	= Miles

Volume (capacity)
Cubic inches (cu in; in³)	X	16.387	= Cubic centimetres (cc; cm³)	X	0.061	= Cubic inches (cu in; in³)
Imperial pints (Imp pt)	X	0.568	= Litres (l)	X	1.76	= Imperial pints (Imp pt)
Imperial quarts (Imp qt)	X	1.137	= Litres (l)	X	0.88	= Imperial quarts (Imp qt)
Imperial quarts (Imp qt)	X	1.201	= US quarts (US qt)	X	0.833	= Imperial quarts (Imp qt)
US quarts (US qt)	X	0.946	= Litres (l)	X	1.057	= US quarts (US qt)
Imperial gallons (Imp gal)	X	4.546	= Litres (l)	X	0.22	= Imperial gallons (Imp gal)
Imperial gallons (Imp gal)	X	1.201	= US gallons (US gal)	X	0.833	= Imperial gallons (Imp gal)
US gallons (US gal)	X	3.785	= Litres (l)	X	0.264	= US gallons (US gal)

Mass (weight)
Ounces (oz)	X	28.35	= Grams (g)	X	0.035	= Ounces (oz)
Pounds (lb)	X	0.454	= Kilograms (kg)	X	2.205	= Pounds (lb)

Force
Ounces-force (ozf; oz)	X	0.278	= Newtons (N)	X	3.6	= Ounces-force (ozf; oz)
Pounds-force (lbf; lb)	X	4.448	= Newtons (N)	X	0.225	= Pounds-force (lbf; lb)
Newtons (N)	X	0.1	= Kilograms-force (kgf; kg)	X	9.81	= Newtons (N)

Pressure
Pounds-force per square inch (psi; lbf/in²; lb/in²)	X	0.070	= Kilograms-force per square centimetre (kgf/cm²; kg/cm²)	X	14.223	= Pounds-force per square inch (psi; lbf/in²; lb/in²)
Pounds-force per square inch (psi; lbf/in²; lb/in²)	X	0.068	= Atmospheres (atm)	X	14.696	= Pounds-force per square inch (psi; lbf/in²; lb/in²)
Pounds-force per square inch (psi; lbf/in²; lb/in²)	X	0.069	= Bars	X	14.5	= Pounds-force per square inch (psi; lbf/in²; lb/in²)
Pounds-force per square inch (psi; lbf/in²; lb/in²)	X	6.895	= Kilopascals (kPa)	X	0.145	= Pounds-force per square inch (psi; lbf/in²; lb/in²)
Kilopascals (kPa)	X	0.01	= Kilograms-force per square centimetre (kgf/cm²; kg/cm²)	X	98.1	= Kilopascals (kPa)

Torque (moment of force)
Pounds-force inches (lbf in; lb in)	X	1.152	= Kilograms-force centimetre (kgf cm; kg cm)	X	0.868	= Pounds-force inches (lbf in; lb in)
Pounds-force inches (lbf in; lb in)	X	0.113	= Newton metres (Nm)	X	8.85	= Pounds-force inches (lbf in; lb in)
Pounds-force inches (lbf in; lb in)	X	0.083	= Pounds-force feet (lbf ft; lb ft)	X	12	= Pounds-force inches (lbf in; lb in)
Pounds-force feet (lbf ft; lb ft)	X	0.138	= Kilograms-force metres (kgf m; kg m)	X	7.233	= Pounds-force feet (lbf ft; lb ft)
Pounds-force feet (lbf ft; lb ft)	X	1.356	= Newton metres (Nm)	X	0.738	= Pounds-force feet (lbf ft; lb ft)
Newton metres (Nm)	X	0.102	= Kilograms-force metres (kgf m; kg m)	X	9.804	= Newton metres (Nm)

Power
Horsepower (hp)	X	745.7	= Watts (W)	X	0.0013	= Horsepower (hp)

Velocity (speed)
Miles per hour (miles/hr; mph)	X	1.609	= Kilometres per hour (km/hr; kph)	X	0.621	= Miles per hour (miles/hr; mph)

Fuel consumption*
Miles per gallon, Imperial (mpg)	X	0.354	= Kilometres per litre (km/l)	X	2.825	= Miles per gallon, Imperial (mpg)
Miles per gallon, US (mpg)	X	0.425	= Kilometres per litre (km/l)	X	2.352	= Miles per gallon, US (mpg)

Temperature
Degrees Fahrenheit = (°C x 1.8) + 32   Degrees Celsius (Degrees Centigrade; °C) = (°F - 32) x 0.56

*It is common practice to convert from miles per gallon (mpg) to litres/100 kilometres (l/100km),
where mpg (Imperial) x l/100 km = 282 and mpg (US) x l/100 km = 235

Index

Printed by
Haynes Publishing Group
Sparkford Yeovil Somerset
England